MICROWAVE CUISINE

MICROWAVE CUISINE

THE COMPLETE BOOK OF MICROWAVE COOKING

Elisa Vergne

Macdonald
Orbis

A Macdonald Orbis Book

Based upon:
Gastronomie au four à micro-ondes
Micro-ondes cuisine des jours de fêtes
Micro-ondes cuisine de tous les jours
Toute la cuisine aux micro-ondes
© Compagnie Internationale du Livre (C.I.L.), Paris, 1986,
1988

This English-language edition
© Macdonald & Co (Publishers) Ltd 1989

First published in Great Britain in 1989
by Macdonald & Co (Publishers) Ltd
London & Sydney

A member of Maxwell Pergamon Publishing Corporation plc

British Library Cataloguing in Publication Data

Vergne, Elisa
    Microwave Cuisine.
    1. Food: French dishes: Dishes prepared using
    microwave ovens — Recipes
    I. Title
    641.5'882'0944

ISBN 0-356-17966-4

Text prepared by MANDER GOOCH CALLOW
in association with
SX Composing Ltd, Rayleigh, Essex

Printed and bound by G. Canale & Co, Turin

Gastronomie au four à Micro-ondes
Micro-ondes cuisine des jours de fêtes
Micro-ondes cuisine de tous les jours
Toute la cuisine aux micro-ondes

Editors: Françoise Bosquet, Filgrane
Photography: APRIFEL (Henri Yeru), BIAC
(Marie Sanner), CIL (Raymond Landin) L Bianquis,
F Botkine

Designers: Richard Médioni, Filgrane

MICROWAVE CUISINE
Compiled, adapted, edited and designed by
MANDER GOOCH CALLOW
7 Hanover Street, London W1

Macdonald & Co (Publishers) Ltd
66-73 Shoe Lane
Holborn
London EC4P 4AP

Contents

Symbols

The symbols will enable you to see at a glance how easy a recipe is, and the preparation and cooking times

easy

more difficult

for experienced cooks

preparation time

cooking time

When using the recipes in this book, remember the following points.

All quantities are for four people, unless otherwise stated.

Use only one set of measurements for the recipes, since American, imperial and metric measurements are not exact equivalents.

In the text of the recipes, American quantities and ingredients are listed first, with the British equivalents in brackets.

Introduction

Introduction

Although the microwave cooker has only been on the culinary scene for the past few years, it has revolutionized and become an integral part of the way we prepare our food.

Millions of people have already discovered that fast food need not be junk food. One look at this collection of superb original recipes will show that the microwave is more than a means to defrost and reheat. With this book, you can cook simple, nutritious dishes for everyday family meals and quick lunches and suppers. But that is not all, you can also create sumptuous banquets for special occasions – all in a fraction of the time it would take with a conventional cooker. Just choose from the 750 recipes to create perfect menus.

Now every cook can use this brilliant modern cooking aid to its full potential, but if you are new to microwave cooking or suffered unfortunate experiences with the early models, it is useful to understand how the microwave works.

It is not simply a faster, more efficient and cleaner version of a conventional cooker; in fact, microwave cooking bears little or no resemblance to traditional methods of preparing and cooking food.

It looks like a conventional oven and it is a container that needs to be tightly closed before anything can be cooked in it, but there the similarity ends. It remains cold while it cooks. It doesn't broil (grill), it doesn't roast, or fry and the food doesn't get brown. Nonetheless, the microwave oven does cook! Once you have grasped how it actually operates, it becomes easier to accept it.

How the Microwave Oven Works

Electrical energy provided by alternating current is converted into electro-magnetic waves or "hertz" (the same type as radio, television or radar waves), but shorter. The conversion takes place in a magnetron built into the oven itself. These microwaves, which generate no heat, are reflected off the metal sides of the oven and have nowhere to go but through the molecules of fat, sugar and water present in the food that is in the oven.

The changes of direction in alternating current, and therefore in the microwaves themselves, cause the molecules of food to vibrate about 2.45 million times per second. The friction between the molecules caused by this vibration generates sufficient heat to "cook" the food.

It is a relatively simple chemical reaction and, because the cooking is done internally, it is ideal for foods that are normally poached, boiled or steamed. Obviously, however, in the absence of any exterior heat, food will not become brown or crisp on the outside.

Component Parts of the Microwave Oven

All microwave ovens consist of a container that can be closed so that it becomes completely airtight, a magnetron, a stirrer fan and a power regulator.

The Stirrer Fan

This element guides the microwaves as regularly as it is possible to do. However, microwaves being capricious, the latest and most sophisticated ovens are also equipped with an antenna that ensures that the food is exposed to the microwaves evenly.

Older models not equipped with this antenna will generally have a turntable that physically turns the food and therefore fulfils the same role. Turntables that can be installed in the earliest forms of microwave oven that were not equipped with them are also available on the market.

Without an antenna or turntable, food will not cook as evenly, and to remedy this problem the dish has to be turned manually, one quarter-turn four times during the cooking time (always in the same direction). Long dishes need to be turned once, midway through the cooking time.

The Power Regulator

Variable power enables the user to choose different power levels to cook different foods. Variable power operates either in a continuous manner (HIGH, Full Power, or 100% Power), or by pulsations, the electrical energy being pulsated on and off according to the power level selected. Between each pulsation there is a period of stasis which slows down the vibration of the molecules.

The simplest models are equipped with only two power levels, HIGH (Full/100%) and MEDIUM (50%), but the latest microwave ovens offer levels ranging from 1 to 10. Use this table to establish equivalents.

Power Level	Type of Cooking	Power Mark
HIGH/FULL/100%	Cooking & reheating	10
MEDIUM-HIGH/75%	More delicate dishes	7-8
MEDIUM/50%	Very delicate foods	5
MEDIUM-LOW/25%	Defrosting	3
LOW/15%	Keeping warm	1-2

Microwave Power Output

The output of a microwave oven can vary considerably depending on the individual piece of equipment. The input power indicated by the manufacturer will never correspond exactly to the power that is actually given out, since some of the electricity is used up by the magnetron to convert into microwave energy.

The majority of ovens have an input of 1,000 – 1,500 watts. Energy output, however, will only be 500-700 watts, which means a notable variation in cooking times. The higher the input power, the faster the cooking and vice-versa. This factor should therefore be taken into account when you want to test the timings for recipes.

Accessory Features

Apart from the elements described above, certain ovens may come equipped with some or all of the following:

● A so-called "browner", designed to compensate for the lack of color that is characteristic of microwave cooking. It is generally used at the end of the actual microwave cooking period (depending on the manufacturer's instructions) but it does not fully replace a conventional broiler (grill).

● Temperature probes, or food sensors, connected to a socket inside the oven, which can be inserted into the food to test the internal temperature: once the desired temperature is reached, the oven automatically switches itself off or reduces power to keep-warm heat level.

● Programmed memory features can ensure various operations in the correct order: defrosting, cooking, movement from one power level to another, standing time, etc.

● Finally, there are combination ovens on the market which unite in one piece of equipment a microwave oven, a broiler (grill) and a traditional oven. These are certainly the most sophisticated, but naturally also the most expensive.

How to Make Good Use of Your Oven

Because different makes of oven produce different results, it is important to note that the oven used for testing all the recipes in this book was the Moulinex FM 465, 30 quarts (30 litres) in volume and with an input power of 1,300 watts (output power of 650 watts). It has 5 power levels and a turntable.

● If the volume of your oven is less than this, make sure in advance that the dishes and receptacles you plan to use will fit into the oven. If the quantities in a given recipe are too much, halve them or cook them in two batches, reducing the cooking times accordingly.

● If the power of your oven is more than 650 watts, decrease the cooking times indicated by about 30 seconds per minute for a power output of 750 watts.

● If the power is significantly lower, say 500 watts, increase the cooking time by 20 seconds per minute. It will be a question of trial and error, but after several attempts you will establish the correct timings.

● However, it should be noted that even if you are using exactly the same model of oven, cooking times will vary according to the weight, shape and freshness of the ingredients and also the type of cooking container used.

Geographical variations such as altitude can also affect cooking times so it is important to check the manufacturer's instructions and test average cooking times on an inexpensive recipe to establish some averages. It is not advisable to discover the variations in cooking times on your particular model, on the night the boss is coming to dinner! Even if you feel you know your oven well, always take care to check a recipe slightly before the end of the suggested cooking time. It is always easier to continue cooking a dish for a little longer than it is to undo an overcooked recipe!

Safety Precautions

All microwave ovens are submitted to stringent controls which guarantee airtightness, the strength of the oven and the safety of its electrical components. The controls are based on 100,000 door-openings at the rate of six per minute, equivalent to 30 years of daily use.

The microwaves themselves automatically cease immediately the oven door is opened. The myths that arose in the early days of the microwave oven about people cooking their fingers by mistake have caused much of the popular resistance to microwave cooking. On the other hand, it is essential to study the manufacturer's instructions on your particular model so that it is correctly installed and maintained.

Materials That Can Be Used

Microwave ovens do not require a special collection of cooking utensils and in most cases you can use the utensils to be found in your own kitchen.

However, this does not mean that you can use everything. Certain materials, for various reasons, are not suitable for microwave use and risk damaging the oven or being damaged themselves.

Penetration By Microwaves

The utensils used must allow the microwaves to pass through them without absorbing them. If the utensil absorbs the microwaves or reflects them back against the sides of the oven, it stands to reason that the food will not cook. Materials to be avoided at all costs are:

● Metal, which reflects the waves back against the magnetron and will therefore damage the oven. You must not use any utensil made of iron, steel or aluminum (aluminium), nor any utensil that has silver or gold decorations on it.

● For the same reasons, do not use aluminum (aluminium) foil, unless the manufacturer clearly stipulates that it can be used. Remember also to avoid metal spoons and forks and do not use metal skewers.

● Wood stands the risk of splitting or shattering under prolonged microwave bombardment, which suppresses all external moisture. It is possible, for recipes that require only a few minutes cooking time, to use wooden skewers if absolutely necessary.

● There are no specific reasons not to employ other materials, although plastic containers stand a chance of melting because of the heat transferred by the food. For obvious reasons, avoid

using valuable utensils made of fine porcelain or glass or unglazed pottery. Glass is best reserved only for heating foods in the oven for very short periods.

● All Pyrex containers, fire-proof porcelain and glazed china dishes can be used without any fear of problems, as can most earthenware dishes. As you go along you may wish to purchase dishes made of special substances designed for microwave use.

The Water Test

If you have any doubt at all about a given dish (pottery, for example), do the water test before trying to cook any food in it. Fill the receptacle with water and microwave it for 1 minute on HIGH. The water should become hot, but the utensil remain cold. If this is the case, you have proved that the substance of which the utensil is made allows microwaves to pass through it, and it is therefore suitable for use in microwave cooking. To test a plastic container, do the water test but microwave it for 15 seconds only. Don't forget, plastic stands more danger of being deformed or melted by the heat from the food than from microwave action.

Cooking Utensils

Shape and Size
The shape of containers used in microwave cooking is important. Round dishes and molds (moulds) provide the best results because their shape corresponds to the rays put out by the magnetron, which can penetrate all parts of the container at once. Sometimes it is necessary to use a long dish, but make sure that it has rounded corners (square corners attract microwave energy to the detriment of the food in the rest of the dish).

Naturally, the size of the containers should also correspond to the amount of food being cooked. You will therefore need a number of soufflé molds (moulds) of different sizes and at least 2 different sizes of savarin (ring) mold (mould).

A set of casseroles 1, 2 and 3 quarts (litres) in size will also be necessary and ideally each casserole should have its own lid.

You will also need a special microwave steamer with an outer container plus lid and an inner, perforated container into which you put the food to be steamed. Finally, do not forget that the size and shape of the receptacle will have an influence on the cooking time.

A jug with a handle is extremely useful for heating liquids; at the same time, any of your Pyrex bowls, pottery dishes or ceramic ramekin dishes can have multiple uses.

Broiling (Grilling)
If you want to broil (grill) meat and need a broiling (grilling) pan, buy a rectangular dish with a ribbed bottom so that the meat does not sit in its own juices. Take care when you buy it that you have taken the handles into account when measuring it for size; often the handles on such a dish can prevent the turntable from functioning properly.

Browning Dishes
Microwave ovens are not capable of browning food because microwaves give off no heat.

If your oven does not have an inbuilt browner or microwave broiler (grill), you can use a browning dish. These have an absorbent base and can be heated empty. When the food is put in, it acquires a light brownish coloration. The effect created is better than nothing but cannot be claimed to be ideal, particularly because these dishes are heavy and do not retain heat for very long.

You can, of course, brown meat in a conventional skillet (frying pan) before microwaving it, or alternatively brown it quickly under a conventional broiler (grill) after microwaving.

Roasting Bags

These can be purchased in 2 sizes, the smaller of which is large enough to cook a 4 lb (1.8 kg) chicken. They come provided with special plastic tags designed for microwave ovens and are useful in that they prevent the meat from drying out during cooking.

Container Lids

A lid of some kind is essential for virtually all microwave cooking, both to prevent the food from drying out and to stop it from splashing and making the interior of the oven dirty.

Casseroles normally have their own lids, as do terrine dishes (even if the lid itself has no hole in it, the fit will never be so tight that it seals the container hermetically and prevents steam from escaping).

In the case of soufflé molds (moulds) and other dishes which do not have lids, it is always possible to cover them with saran wrap (cling film) (pierce it in a couple of places with a fork, because it will otherwise act as a hermetic seal).

Cooking Thermometers

Cooking thermometers are extremely useful for testing the internal temperature of roast meat or poultry. Always insert it right into the center of the thickest part of the meat or bird, but take care that it does not touch the bone.

TABLE OF COOKING TIMES

FRESH VEGETABLES	Quantity	Liquid	Cooking time on HIGH
Artichokes	2	⅓ cup (4½ tbsp)	6-10 minutes
Asparagus	18 oz/500 g	⅓ cup (4½ tbsp)	12-15 minutes
Eggplant (aubergine), finely sliced	18 oz/500 g	¼ cup (3 tbsp)	10 minutes
Beetroot, finely sliced	18 oz/500 g	⅓ cup (4½ tbsp)	12-15 minutes
Broccoli florets	18 oz/500 g	⅓ cup (4½ tbsp)	8-10 minutes
Carrots, very finely sliced	18 oz/500 g	¼ cup (3 tbsp)	12-15 minutes
Celeriac strips	18 oz/500 g	¼ cup (3 tbsp)	9-10 minutes
White button mushrooms, sliced	9 oz /250 g	2 tbsp (1 tbsp) lemon juice	4 minutes
Brussels sprouts	18 oz/500 g	¼ cup (3 tbsp)	10-12 minutes
Cabbage, shredded	18 oz/500 g	¼ cup (3 tbsp)	12-15 minutes
Cauliflower florets	18 oz/500 g	¼ cup (3 tbsp)	9-10 minutes
Zucchini (courgettes), finely sliced	1¾ lb/750 g	¼ cup (3 tbsp)	8-10 minutes
Whole endive (chicory)	4 x 5 oz/150 g	¼ cup (3 tbsp)	7-8 minutes
Spinach	9 oz/250 g		5 minutes
Fennel strips	18 oz/500 g	¼ cup (3 tbsp)	10 minutes
White beans	18 oz/500 g	⅓ cup (4½ tbsp)	8-10 minutes
Green (haricot) beans, very thin	18 oz/500 g	⅓ cup (4½ tbsp)	10 minutes
Sweet corn on the cob	2	¼ cup (3 tbsp)	8-10 minutes
Turnips, sliced	18 oz/500 g	¼ cup (3 tbsp)	10 minutes
Onions, sliced	5 oz/150 g		4 minutes
Squash, sliced	18 oz/500 g	¼ cup (3 tbsp)	10 minutes
Tiny green peas	18 oz/500 g	¼ cup (3 tbsp)	8-10 minutes
Leeks, sliced	18 oz/500 g	¼ cup (3 tbsp)	10-12 minutes
Bell pepper strips	18 oz/500 g		10 minutes
Potatoes, sliced	18 oz/500 g	¼ cup (3 tbsp)	12 minutes
Jacket potatoes	2 x 7 oz/200 g		7-8 minutes
New potatoes	18 oz/500 g		10 minutes
Pumpkin, cubed	18 oz/500 g	3½ tbsp (2 tbsp)	8-10 minutes
Tomatoes, sliced	18 oz/500 g		3-4 minutes
Salsify	18 oz/500 g	¼ cup (3 tbsp)	12 minutes

FROZEN VEGETABLES	Quantity	Liquid	Cooking time on HIGH
Asparagus	7 oz/200 g 18 oz/500 g	3 tbsp (2 tbsp) ¼ cup (3 tbsp)	9-11 minutes 14-16 minutes
Broccoli	7 oz/200 g 18 oz/500 g	3 tbsp (2 tbsp) ¼ cup (3 tbsp)	7-9 minutes 12-14 minutes
Carrots, finely sliced	7 oz/200 g 18 oz/500 g	3 tbsp (2 tbsp) ¼ cup (3 tbsp)	5-6 minutes 12-14 minutes

TABLE OF COOKING TIMES

FROZEN VEGETABLES continued	Quantity	Liquid	Cooking time on HIGH
Cabbage, shredded	7 oz/200 g 18 oz/500 g	3 tbsp (2 tbsp) ⅓ cup (4½ tbsp)	7-9 minutes 10-12 minutes
Zucchini (Courgettes), sliced	7 oz/200 g 18 oz/500 g		5-7 minutes 10-12 minutes
Spinach, frozen blocks	7 oz/200 g		5 minutes
Leaf spinach	18 oz/500 g		10-12 minutes
White beans	7 oz/200 g 18 oz/500 g	3 tbsp (2 tbsp) ⅓ cup (4½ tbsp)	8-10 minutes 14-16 minutes
Green (haricot) beans, very thin	7 oz/200 g 18 oz/500 g	3 tbsp (2 tbsp) ⅓ cup (4½ tbsp)	7-9 minutes 12-15 minutes
Sweet corn on the cob	1	3 tbsp (2 tbsp)	5-7 minutes
Sweet corn off the cob	7 oz/200 g 18 oz/500 g	3 tbsp (2 tbsp) ⅓ cup (4½ tbsp)	4-5 minutes 8-10 minutes
Chestnuts	7 oz/200 g	⅓ cup (4½ tbsp)	10-12 minutes
Whole turnips	7 oz/200 g	3 tbsp (2 tbsp)	9-11 minutes
Petits pois	7 oz/200 g 18 oz/500 g	3 tbsp (2 tbsp) 4 tbsp (3 tbsp)	5-6 minutes 10-12 minutes
Salsify	7 oz/200 g 18 oz/500 g	3 tbsp (2 tbsp) ⅓ cup (4½ tbsp)	8-10 minutes 12-15 minutes

FRESH MEAT	Quantity	Cooking time on HIGH	Resting time
Boneless roast lamb	18 oz/500 g	7-8 minutes	5 minutes
Rolled, boneless lamb	2¼ lb/1 kg	12-14 minutes	10 minutes
Lamb cutlets	2	2 minutes	5 minutes
Boneless roast beef (rare)	2¼ lb/1 kg	8 minutes	15 minutes
Boneless roast beef (medium rare)	2¼ lb/1 kg	10 minutes	15 minutes
Boneless roast beef (well done)	2¼ lb/1 kg	12 minutes	15 minutes
Hamburgers	4 (½ inch/1.25 cm)	3 minutes	
Boneless roast pork	2¼ lb/1 kg	25-30 minutes	15 minutes
Pork loin (bone in)	2¼ lb/1 kg	20-22 minutes	15 minutes
Pork tenderloin	14 oz/400 g	10 minutes	5 minutes
Pork chops	6 (5 oz/150 g)	12 minutes	3 minutes
Boneless roast veal	2¼ lb/1 kg	22-25 minutes	15 minutes
Veal chops	4 (5 oz/150 g)	3-4 minutes	3 minutes
Poussin, pigeon	1 (18 oz/500 g)	12-15 minutes	5 minutes
Turkey scallops	4 (5 oz/150 g)	6 minutes	5 minutes
Chicken pieces, bone in	4	12-14 minutes	5 minutes
Lamb brains	2 (3 oz/75 g)	3 -4 minutes	
Strips of liver	18 oz/500 g	4 minutes	3 minutes
Lambs' kidneys	8	3 minutes	2 minutes
Sliced smoked streaky bacon	4 strips (rashers)	4 minutes	
Chipolata sausages	4	3 minutes	

Pros and Cons of Microwave Cooking

Any cooking method has its inherent advantages and disadvantages: you will find it difficult to fry steak in a steamer or bake custard in a 200°C oven. The microwave oven is no exception; sophisticated though it is technologically, it cannot be adapted to every kind of cooking.

The word "oven" in the widest sense means an enclosed container, but in the case of microwave cooking it is necessary to rid oneself of the association of the word "oven" with the concept of heat. It should also be borne in mind that although the microwave oven is a definite "plus" in today's culinary world it will never fully replace traditional methods of cooking in conventional ovens.

The Many Advantages of Microwave Cooking

On the other hand, the advantages are numerous: speed when defrosting food (the microwave oven is the ideal partner for your freezer); minimal use of electric power; no heat given off; no food smells during cooking; easy cleaning of cooking utensils; cleaning of the oven itself unnecessary or at worst extremely easy; possibility of cooking without fat; the preservation of nutrients and the true flavor of the food.

Choosing and Preparing Food

Shape

There is nothing revolutionary involved here: simply the obvious fact that the more regular in shape the pieces of food are, the more evenly they will cook. A compact and uniformly shaped roast will cook more evenly than one which is irregular in shape, the more so because in a microwave oven the extremities of a roast cook more quickly than the middle.

Along the same lines, food that is chopped into pieces of uniform size will cook more quickly than if left whole, but it is important to emphasize the need to cut the food evenly in order to achieve evenness of cooking. This is where the food processor comes into its own for slicing carrots, turnips, potatoes, zucchini (courgettes) etc. For vegetables that are softer and not so amenable to food processing, a board and a good sharp knife will do the necessary work.

Quantities

This is the fundamental basis of microwave cooking: the cooking time is in direct proportion to the quantity – the less food, the less time needed to cook it.

This is why the microwave oven is such a spectacular invention, because it allows food to be cooked in very small quantities and is therefore the friend and savior of people who live alone, couples and those who want to give dinner parties for up to four people. Technically this phenomenon can be explained by the fact that the energy put out remains constant: it either concentrates on a single portion or disperses through a larger quantity. Remember also that the microwaves themselves only penetrate to a depth of 1¼ inches (3 cm) and the rest of the cooking is actually done by conduction. It is therefore advisable in many cases to cook a given recipe in 2 batches; the overall cooking time will be shorter.

Density of the Food

Meat molecules are very tightly bonded together and will take longer to microwave than, say, a light gâteau with a fluffy texture. Fats and sugar absorb energy more quickly and require shorter cooking time. Vegetables that are very fresh and therefore still full of water will cook more rapidly than older vegetables that have already lost much of their water content.

Temperature

It stands to reason that the colder the food, the longer it will need to be microwaved. For example, 2¼ cups (500 ml/18 fl oz) milk at room temperature takes less time to reach the boil than a similar quantity straight out of the refrigerator. By the same token, if you are cooking frozen food without defrosting it beforehand, you will need to allow longer cooking time than for defrosted frozen food or fresh food.

Seasoning and Spices

Seasoning and spices become more pronounced in foods cooked in a microwave oven, simply because of the shorter cooking time, whereas with conventional methods, much of the flavor may be lost by the time the food is actually cooked. To counteract this, either add the seasonings (herbs, spices, alcohol, vinegar, lemon or citron, salt, pepper, etc.) toward the end of the cooking time or, if that is not possible, use them more sparingly than you would in normal cooking.

Positioning of Food

Given the fact that the microwaves emitted by the magnetron are directed in the form of a cone (of which the magnetron is the apex), they will reach the outside portions of food first. If you are cooking food of uneven shape (chops or chicken legs, for example), always put the thickest part toward the outside of the cooking dish, where the microwave action will be more intense; the thinnest portions, the bones (in chops or chicken) or sometimes nothing at all should be in the center of the dish.

Ideally, for food of irregular shape, you should turn it mid-way through cooking so that it is exposed to the microwaves in a regular way. For larger pieces (roasts, whole chicken) turn them upside down mid-way through cooking: the vibration of the molecules will continue in the part that was face upward, while the part that started out face down will benefit from the enhanced microwave action.

Stirring

Depending on the type of microwave oven you have, you will need to stir food at some point during cooking. Generally once will suffice, although if your oven is not equipped with an antenna or a turntable you may find that you have to stir 3 or 4 times. This is something you can only learn by experience with your own particular oven.

Covering Food

Virtually all food cooked in a microwave oven needs to be covered. This permits foods with a high water content to cook in their own juices. You should also always cover recipes where there is a danger of splashing or boiling over.

Never forget that even though the cooking container is cold when you remove it from the oven, the food itself may well be boiling; take great care when you remove the cover, whether it is an ordinary lid or (particularly) if it is saran wrap (cling film).

Pâtisserie recipes do not need to retain their moisture content and do not need to be covered. Equally, if you are attempting to reduce the water content of a given food (frozen spinach, for example), it is unnecessary to cover the dish.

Resting or Equalizing Time

Because food continues to cook by heat conduction even after the microwave bombardment has ceased, a period of resting time outside the oven has to be taken into account in the majority of recipes in order to avoid overcooking.

For soups, eggs, fish, and sliced vegetables, a few minutes resting time will suffice and it is not even worth mentioning this in the recipe because the time taken to serve the food will achieve the necessary objective.

When cooking roasts and whole chickens or other poultry, the resting time rule must be observed. To avoid loss of external heat, cover the food concerned with a double thickness of aluminum (aluminium) foil and leave it to stand for 15-20 minutes. If you have inserted a cooking ther-

mometer you will notice the internal temperature of the meat rising gradually.

For the same reason, remove a cake from the oven when the edges have shrunk away from the mold (mould) and when a toothpick (cocktail stick) inserted into the middle of the dough comes out clean.

Reheating

This is one of the most spectacular talents of the microwave oven: you can reheat all food without exception, including vegetables, dough, rice and potatoes; they reheat quickly and do not dry out. Simply take the precaution of covering the receptacle.

It is difficult to give specific timings for reheating because it all depends on the amount involved, the receptacle and original temperature of the food concerned. If you are unsure, try at first heating for 1-2 minutes on HIGH, then check the temperature; it will be easy to continue until the food is hot. Stir once or twice if the quantities are relatively large.

The ease with which it is possible to reheat food not only means that you can reheat leftovers with minimal fuss but also allows you to feed people at different times or to prepare certain dishes ahead of time and thus utilize your oven to its full potential.

Adapting Recipes

If you want to adapt a conventional recipe, experiment following these simple rules because the cooking time is proportional to the amounts involved: microwave cooking times range from ¼ to ⅓ of the time required for conventional recipes, and the quantities of liquid should be significantly cut because they will not have the time to reduce or absorb the flavorings.

Ingredients

The quality of the ingredients used in microwave cooking is of primary importance. Fish or chicken that is not fresh and fruit and vegetables that are either not ripe enough or over-ripe can not be camouflaged. Meat that is tough has no time to become tender through prolonged cooking.

On the positive side, however, the ingredients lose nothing of their freshness during cooking, the color of vegetables is retained and in many cases enhanced, and the basic flavors and vitamins are preserved to a far greater degree than in normal cooking methods.

Certain foods require special precautions:

Lamb: this is a meat that is naturally high in fat content and lends itself well to microwave cooking. Avoid pieces that are irregular in shape (leg or shoulder of lamb should be boned before being microwaved). Use a meat thermometer, particularly for leg of lamb if you want to serve it rare.

Sausages: prick the skins with a fork so that they do not explode during cooking.

Eggplant (Aubergines): if you want to cook them whole, make grooves in the skin and lay them side by side on a double thickness of kitchen paper.

Beef: do not count on the microwave oven to tenderize a tough piece of beef and do not imagine that a stew can be made in a matter of minutes; on the other hand it is perfectly possible to roast a good quality cut of meat very quickly. Do not forget the meat thermometer if you want to serve the joint rare, and try to slice it before bringing it to the table.

Black sausage: again, do not forget to prick the skin with a fork.

Broccoli: make cross-shaped incisions in the stalks so that they cook more quickly.

Squid: avoid microwave cooking because it toughens. In addition this is a rather tasteless seafood which requires longer cooking to absorb added seasonings.

Duck: breast fillets are preferable because they cook very quickly (remove the skin and any fat). A whole duck is generally difficult to carve and will not crisp in the microwave oven. If you do want to cook a whole duck, however, microwave it for ¾ of the cooking time and then complete the operation in a conventional oven set very hot.

Carrots: choose young baby carrots or remove the hard inner core of larger carrots. Always chop them very finely to avoid long cooking.

Cabbage: always shred it and then steam it. It is more digestible cooked this way and will not give off any smell.

Brains: prick them in 3 or 4 places with a toothpick (cocktail stick) so that they do not explode during cooking.

Heart: avoid microwave cooking, which only serves to toughen it.

Scallops: prick the corals in 2 or 3 places with a toothpick (cocktail stick) so that they do not explode during cooking.

Turkey: scaloppine (escalopes) pose no problem. Common sense will tell you that it is not wise to expose a bird whose flesh is dry in the first place to a form of cooking that tends to dehydrate food. It is also worth pondering the question of whether a turkey weighing more than 6½ lb (3 kg) would fit into the average microwave oven.

Spinach: always use frozen spinach, because fresh raw spinach reduces in volume so much that you would have to fill the microwave oven with it in order to obtain even a normal portion of cooked spinach.

Snails: never cook snails in a microwave oven because they will explode.

Cheese: Gruyère has a tendency to become rubbery. Add it only at the very end of cooking.

Tongue: microwaves very unsuccessfully because of its irregular shape and also because of its high water content.

Rabbit: marinate it or serve it with a highly-flavored sauce. It is often better reheated, because it has had the time to absorb the seasonings used during cooking.

Pulses: the cooking time required is very long and there is a risk of boiling over. It is better not to microwave them, but you can certainly use the microwave oven for soaking them: put the pulses into a large receptacle, cover completely with cold water and bring to the boil in the microwave oven. Leave to stand outside the oven for 1 hour before proceeding with conventional cooking in fresh water.

Eggs: never cook eggs in their shells because they will explode. Prick the yolks with a toothpick (cocktail stick) so that the membrane does not break. Egg ramekins can be cooked much more successfully in a microwave oven than in a bain-marie.

Pasta: not much time is gained and the risk of boiling over is considerable.

Pastry bases for flans and tarts: these can be cooked blind, but do not be surprised at their lack of color, which may well affect their presentation value. If cooked with their filling they will become soggy.

Cakes: the microwave oven is not ideal, but it can be used for ring molds (moulds). Traditional recipes can be adapted but the quantity of flour must be reduced and the texture needs to be much runnier than in normal cooking. This is why in most instances cane sugar syrup is recommended rather than dry sugar. Large containers should be used because cake doughs that contain yeast or egg whites rise considerably during cooking. Remember that the color will not change so do not use that as a test for doneness.

Fish: cooks perfectly in small portions, slices or fillets and is spectacularly suited to microwave cooking. It is possible to cook whole fish if they are not too large (mackerel, whiting, red mullet) but remove the head to facilitate cooking speed. Do not forget to make several grooves in the skin of the fish at the thickest point to avoid bursting. Fish cooks extremely quickly and needs constant attention.

Pork: there is no major problem but choose tender cuts (tenderloin and chops) and brush them with mustard or brown sugar to prevent them drying out. Alternatively, use a roasting bag.

Chicken: cooks perfectly but does not brown or become crisp, even if you use a browning dish or roasting bag, although it will take on a slight color if you do so. If you find the lack of color unattractive, brown the bird in a skillet (frying pan) before microwaving or utilize the resting time (essential for a whole bird) to slip it under a conventional broiler (grill) to brown.

Rice: there is little purpose in cooking plain boiled rice in a microwave because no time is gained. Rice pudding cooks successfully, however, and micro-

waving affords the added advantage of an easy-to-clean cooking container. Use more liquid (milk or water) than you would for conventional cooking.

Sugar: the microwave oven is perfectly suited to prepare caramel and it is the preferred method of making it. Do not forget, however, that the temperature reached is very high and this is one of the rare cases in microwave cooking where it is absolutely essential to protect yourself with oven gloves.

Tomatoes: prick whole tomatoes with a fork.

Veal: everything depends on the quality of the cut. If you are roasting veal, lard it with bacon to keep it moist or use a roasting bag.

What Cannot Be Done in a Microwave Oven

• Classic pastry demands radical adaptation and is never fully successful; some types of pastry such as choux pastry simply cannot be made by the microwave method.

• Soufflés and meringues (difficult enough to make successfully by conventional methods) cannot be cooked in a microwave oven.

• Baked dishes like gratins, where the brown topping is an essential part of the recipe.

• Broiled (grilled) meats and fish.

• Any fried food. The temperature of the frying oil cannot be controlled and it is therefore dangerous to deep-fat fry.

• Eggs in their shells (they will burst).

But in the final analysis, your kitchen already possesses the necessary appliances for successful preparation of the above, and the microwave oven is an adjunct to those.

Soups

Left to right: Apple and lettuce soup with almonds, Carrot soup, Cauliflower soup

Apple and Lettuce Soup with Almonds

00.10 Serves 4 **00.21**

American	Ingredients	Metric/Imperial
1	peeled cored apple	1
2	lettuces, cut into thin strips	2
¼ cup	blanched almonds	50 g/2 oz
4 tbsp	olive oil	3 tbsp
2 cups	milk	450 ml/¾ pint
¼ tsp	grated nutmeg	¼ tsp
	salt	
	pepper	
2 tbsp	butter	1 tbsp
2 tbsp	chopped parsley	2 tbsp

1. Cut the apple into rounds and put in a casserole dish with 3 (2) tablespoons of water. Cover and microwave on HIGH for 7 minutes or until the apple slices are soft.

2. Add the lettuce strips to the casserole with ½ cup (125 ml/ 4 fl oz) of water. Cover and microwave for a further 10 minutes.

3. Purée the almonds and olive oil in a food processor until smooth. Set aside.

4. Purée the apple and lettuce mixture in a food processor. Pass the purée through a strainer (sieve), if it is not smooth enough. Return the mixture to the casserole.

5. Add the puréed almonds and the milk. Stir well.

6. Season with nutmeg and add salt and pepper to taste. Microwave for 4 minutes on HIGH.

7. Add the butter and parsley to the soup and serve hot.

If your microwave oven is not equipped with a turntable, rotate the dish once during (1) above and once during (2).

Previous page: Cream of zucchini (courgette) soup

Carrot Soup I

```
00.15          00.23
Serves 4
```

American	Ingredients	Metric/Imperial
1	coarsely chopped onion	1
1	stick celery	1
1	chicken bouillon (stock) cube	1
1 lb	thinly sliced carrots	450 g/1 lb
1	medium size turnip, thinly sliced	1
1	bay leaf	1
1	sprig of thyme	1
	salt	
	pepper	
⅔ cup	milk	150 ml/¼ pint
2 tbsp	butter	1 tbsp
1 tbsp	chopped parsley	1 tbsp

1. Put the onion in a casserole and microwave on HIGH for 3 minutes.
2. Cut the celery stick into strips and chop the leaves.
3. Crumble the chicken bouillon (stock) cube over the onion and add the carrots, turnip, celery, bay leaf and thyme. Add salt and pepper to taste. Add 1¾ cups (400 ml/14 fl oz) of hot water. Cover the casserole and microwave on HIGH for 15 minutes.
4. Discard the thyme and bay leaf.
5. Set 2 tablespoons of the mixture aside and purée the rest in a food processor.
6. Return the mixture to the casserole. Add 1¾ cups (400 ml/14 fl oz) of hot water and the milk. Stir well and leave for 5 minutes in the microwave. Adjust seasoning.
7. Add the reserved mixture, the butter and parsley. Serve hot. If your microwave does not have a turntable, stir the contents of the casserole once halfway during (2) above.

Carrot Soup II

```
00.10          00.19
Serves 4-6
```

American	Ingredients	Metric/Imperial
1	large sliced onion	1
1 lb	cubed carrots	450 g/1 lb
½ cup	fresh orange juice	5 tbsp
1 cup	milk	250 ml/8 fl oz
2 tbsp	mustard	1 tbsp
1 tsp	soft brown sugar	1 tsp
	salt	
	pepper	
1 tbsp	butter	½ tbsp

1. Put the onion and carrots in a casserole and add 2¼ cups (500 ml/18 fl oz) of hot water. Cover and microwave on HIGH for 15 minutes.
2. Purée the mixture in a food processor.
3. Pour the carrot and onion purée back into the casserole.
4. Stir in the orange juice, milk, mustard and brown sugar.
5. Add salt and pepper to taste. Stir carefully with a hand whisk. Reheat in the oven on HIGH for 3-4 minutes.
6. Add the butter and serve hot.

Cauliflower Soup

```
00.10          00.20
Serves 4
```

American	Ingredients	Metric/Imperial
½	medium size cauliflower, cut into florets	½
1	finely sliced onion	1
1	grated carrot	1
3	coarsely chopped tomatoes	3
	salt	
	pepper	
¼ lb	ham	125 g/4 oz
⅓ cup	sour cream (crème fraîche)	4½ tbsp

1. Put the cauliflower florets in a casserole.
2. Add the onion, carrot and tomatoes and 1 cup (250 ml/8 fl oz) of water. Add salt and pepper to taste. Cover the casserole and microwave on HIGH for 15 minutes.
3. Set a few cauliflower florets aside and purée the rest in a food processor with the ham.
4. Return the mixture to the casserole. Add 1½ cups (350 ml/12 fl oz) of hot water. Taste and adjust seasoning. Microwave on HIGH for 5 minutes.
5. Stir in the sour cream (crème fraîche) and the reserved cauliflower florets and serve hot.
If your oven is not equipped with a turntable, stir the contents of the casserole once during (2) above.

Creamy Cauliflower Soup

00.15   **00.21**
Serves 4

American	Ingredients	Metric/Imperial
1	large cauliflower, divided into florets	1
1	small finely chopped onion	1
2 oz	butter	50 g/2 oz
2 tbsp	all-purpose (plain) flour	1 tbsp
2 cups	milk	450 ml/¾ pint
½ tsp	turmeric	½ tsp
½ tsp	dried mixed herbs	½ tsp
	salt	
	pepper	
¼ tsp	grated nutmeg	¼ tsp
1	egg yolk	1
¼ cup	light (single) cream	4 tbsp
	fresh dill	

1. Put the cauliflower florets and onion into a casserole with ¾ cup (200 ml/7 fl oz) water. Cover and cook on HIGH for 8 minutes. Drain and set aside the liquid.
2. Set half the cauliflower aside and purée the remainder.
3. In a large bowl, heat the butter on HIGH for ½-1 minute.
4. Stir in the flour and add the milk and reserved liquid from the vegetables, a little at a time.
5. Add the turmeric, herbs, salt, pepper and nutmeg. Heat on HIGH for 5 minutes, stirring twice.
6. Stir in the puréed cauliflower and reserved florets. Heat on HIGH for 3-5 minutes, stirring once. Taste and adjust seasoning; add extra liquid if the soup is too thick.
7. Mix the egg yolk and cream together lightly and add to the soup, stirring constantly. Reheat on HIGH for 2 minutes and then serve, garnished with chopped dill.

Chicory Soup

00.07   **00.20**
Serves 4

American	Ingredients	Metric/Imperial
4	heads of endive (chicory)	4
¼ cup	butter	3 tbsp
2 tbsp	all-purpose (plain) flour	1 tbsp
1 quart	hot chicken bouillon (stock)	1 litre/2 pints
2 tsp	sugar	2 tsp
	salt	
	pepper	
½ cup	dry vermouth	125 ml/4 fl oz
	hot croûtons to garnish	

1. Chop the endive (chicory) and put in a large bowl with the butter.
2. Cover and heat on HIGH for 6 minutes.
3. Stir in the flour.
4. Blend in the bouillon (stock), sugar, salt and pepper.
5. Heat on HIGH for 10-12 minutes.
6. Stir in the vermouth and cook for a further 1-2 minutes.
7. Serve garnished with freshly made hot croûtons.

Leek and Potato Soup

00.10   **00.17**
Serves 4

American	Ingredients	Metric/Imperial
1	vegetable bouillon (stock) cube	1
3	large leeks	3
1 lb	finely sliced potatoes	450 g/1 lb
¾ cup	milk	200 ml/7 fl oz
2 tbsp	butter	1 tbsp
	salt	
	pepper	
1 tbsp	chopped parsley	1 tbsp

1. Put 2¼ cups (500 ml/18 fl oz) of water into a bowl and microwave on HIGH for 3 minutes. Crumble the vegetable bouillon (stock) cube into the water and stir well.
2. Remove the base and outer skin of the leeks. Cut off the tough part of the green leaves. Slice the leeks lengthwise and then in fine slices across. Rinse thoroughly.
3. Put the leeks and potatoes into a casserole. Add the vegetable bouillon (stock) and microwave on HIGH for 12 minutes.
4. Purée the vegetable mixture in a food processor.
5. Pour the milk into a bowl and microwave on HIGH for 2 minutes.
6. Pour the vegetable purée into a soup tureen. Add the hot milk and the butter. Stir well. Add salt and pepper to taste.
7. Sprinkle with chopped parsley. Serve hot.

Microwave hint: When a soup or sauce contains a high proportion of milk, use a large container because the food will foam up and rise much more than if water or bouillon (stock) is the main liquid ingredient.

Cream of céleriac soup

Cream of Céleriac Soup

00.15 00.20

Serves 4

American	Ingredients	Metric/Imperial
1 lb	peeled, diced céleriac	450 g/1lb
1	finely sliced, large onion	1
1	medium size potato, finely sliced	1
1 cup	white wine	250 ml/8 fl oz
4 tbsp	milk	3 tbsp
2 tbsp	butter	1 tbsp
2	egg yolks	2
1 tsp	celery salt	1 tsp
¼ tsp	ground allspice	¼ tsp
	pepper	
	salt	

1. Put the céleriac, potato and onion in a casserole and add the white wine. Cover and microwave on HIGH for 15 minutes or until the vegetables are tender.

2. Pour the mixture into a food processor.

3. Pour the milk and ¾ cup (200 ml/7 fl oz) of water into a large dish and heat in the oven on HIGH for 4-5 minutes. Do not allow the mixture to boil over.

4. Stir the milk and water mixture into the vegetables in the food processor.

5. Add the butter, egg yolks, celery salt, allspice and pepper. Purée until smooth. Add salt to taste. Pour into a soup tureen and serve hot.

Cream of Scallop Soup

| | 00.10 | 00.17 | |
| | Serves 4 | | |

American	Ingredients	Metric/Imperial
4	scallops	4
¾ cup	dry white wine	200 ml/7 fl oz
	salt	
	pepper	
1 lb	fennel	450 g/1 lb
2	sliced shallots	2
½	chicken bouillon (stock) cube	½
1	egg yolk	1
2 tbsp	sour cream (crème fraîche)	1 tbsp

1. Rinse the scallops under plenty of cold running water and remove any impurities. Prick the coral in 3 or 4 places with a toothpick (cocktail stick).
2. Put the scallops in a small casserole with ¼ cup (4½ tablespoons) of the wine. Add salt and pepper. Cover and microwave on HIGH for 3 minutes.
3. Remove the stalks and tough base of the fennel and discard. Cut the fennel into strips.
4. Drain the scallops and pour the cooking liquid back into the casserole. Add the shallots, fennel and remaining white wine. Cover and microwave on HIGH for 10 minutes.
5. Bring 1¼ cups (300 ml/½ pint) of water to the boil on a conventional cooker and dissolve the ½ cube chicken bouillon (stock) in it.
6. Cut the scallop whites and corals into small pieces.
7. When the fennel is cooked, purée the mixture from the casserole in a food processor. Pour the purée back into the casserole and add the chicken bouillon (stock). Cover and microwave on HIGH for 3-4 minutes.
8. Put the egg yolk and sour cream (crème fraîche) into a soup tureen. Pour the contents of the casserole over gradually, whisking vigorously. Add the scallops and serve immediately.

Cauliflower soup with mussels

Cauliflower Soup with Mussels

| | 00.15 | 00.20 | |
| | Serves 4 | | |

American	Ingredients	Metric/Imperial
7 oz	potatoes, sliced into rounds	200 g/7 oz
½	medium size cauliflower, divided into florets	½
1 quart	mussels in their shells	1 litre/1¾ pints
4	finely chopped shallots	4
½ cup	dry white wine	5 tbsp
2¼ cups	milk	500 ml/18 fl oz
	salt	
	pepper	
½ tsp	grated nutmeg	½ tsp
1	egg yolk	1
2½ tbsp	butter	1½ tbsp
2 tbsp	chopped chervil	2 tbsp

1. Put the potatoes and cauliflower florets in a casserole with 1¼ cups (300 ml/½ pint) of water. Cover and microwave on HIGH for 12 minutes.
2. Scrub and rinse the mussels thoroughly under plenty of cold running water. Discard any with open or broken shells.
3. Put the shallots and white wine into a dish. Cover and microwave on HIGH for 2 minutes.
4. Add the mussels. Cover and microwave on HIGH for 3 minutes. Remove the mussels from their shells. Discard any that have not opened. Filter through a coffee filter and set aside the cooking liquid.
5. Set aside a few cauliflower florets and purée the rest. Return the purée to the casserole and add the milk and cooking liquid from the mussels. Stir well. Add salt and pepper to taste and the grated nutmeg. Cover and microwave on HIGH for 3 minutes.
6. Put the egg yolk into a soup tureen. Pour the soup gently over, stirring with a hand whisk. Add the mussels and butter. Put the cauliflower florets in the soup and sprinkle with chopped chervil. Serve hot.

Haddock Soup

00.10
Serves 4

00.18

American	Ingredients	Metric/Imperial
7 oz	diced potatoes	200 g/7 oz
1	thinly sliced onion	1
1	bayleaf	1
⅔ cup	white wine	150 ml/¼ pint
2½ cups	milk	600 ml/1 pint
10½ oz	skinned cubed haddock, thawed if frozen	300 g/10½ oz
1	egg	1
¼ cup	fresh lemon juice	4 tbsp
1	small bunch chervil	1
	pepper	

1. Put the potatoes and onion in a casserole. Slide the bayleaf underneath. Add the white wine and ⅔ cup (150 ml/¼ pint) of water. Cover and microwave on HIGH for 10 minutes.

2. Pour the milk into the casserole with the potatoes and onion and add the haddock. Cover and microwave on MEDIUM-HIGH for 8 minutes, taking care that the milk does not boil over.

3. Break the egg into a soup tureen, add the lemon juice and whisk vigorously.

4. Rinse the chervil, pat dry on kitchen paper and snip finely with kitchen scissors.

5. Pour the soup gradually on to the egg and lemon mixture, stirring carefully. Discard the bayleaf, add pepper, sprinkle with chervil and serve.

Haddock soup

Mussel Soup

00.25
Serves 4

00.19

American	Ingredients	Metric/Imperial
4	leeks, white part only	4
2	sticks celery	2
½ lb	finely grated potatoes	225 g/8 oz
½ lb	finely grated carrots	225 g/8 oz
1	quartered garlic clove	1
2 tbsp	butter	1 tbsp
⅓ cup	dry white wine	4½ tbsp
1	sprig thyme	1
1	bayleaf	1
2 quarts	mussels in their shells	2 litres/3½ pints
2	egg yolks	2
¾ cup	sour cream (crème fraîche)	200 ml/7 fl oz
3 tbsp	fresh lemon juice	2 tbsp
	salt	
	pepper	

1. Trim the leeks and remove the outer skin. Slice in quarters lengthwise and then in ½ inch (1.25 cm) slices across. Wash thoroughly.

2. Wash the celery and chop the stalks and leaves.

3. Put all the vegetables into a large casserole with the butter. Cover and microwave on HIGH for 5 minutes.

4. Stir the white wine and 1¼ cups (300 ml/¼ pint) of hot water into the vegetable mixture.

5. Add the thyme and bayleaf. Stir well. Cover and microwave on HIGH for 10 minutes.

6. Scrub the mussels and wash carefully in plenty of cold running water, discarding any that are already open or have broken shells.

7. Put the mussels into another casserole, cover and microwave on HIGH for 4 minutes, shaking gently every minute.

8. When the mussel shells have all opened, remove the mussels from the shells and filter the cooking liquid through fine muslin or a coffee filter. Discard any mussels that have not opened.

9. Discard the thyme and bayleaf from the vegetable casserole and purée the mixture in a food processor. Add the cooking liquid from the mussels.

10. Beat the egg yolks, sour cream (crème fraîche) and lemon juice together in a soup tureen.

11. Gradually pour the purée over, whisking with a hand whisk.

12. Stir in the mussels and salt and pepper to taste. Serve hot.

Cream of Fish Soup

00.10   00.16
Serves 4

American	Ingredients	Metric/Imperial
1	salmon head and tail	1
½ lb	sliced onions	225 g/8 oz
¼ lb	grated carrot	125 g/4 oz
3 oz	grated celeriac	75 g/3 oz
1 tbsp	butter	½ tbsp
2¼ cups	white wine	500 ml/18 fl oz
½ tsp	curry powder	½ tsp
½	chicken bouillon (stock) cube	½
¾ cup	milk	200 ml/7 fl oz
2 tsp	horseradish mustard	2 tsp
1	egg	1
	salt	
	pepper	

Left: Fish soup
Right: Mussel soup

1. Rinse the fish head and tail in plenty of cold running water and cut the head into 4 pieces.
2. Put the onions, carrots and celeriac in a casserole with the butter and half the white wine. Cover and microwave on HIGH for 6 minutes.
3. Add the fish head to the casserole, cover and microwave on HIGH for 4 minutes.
4. Stir in the remaining white wine, the curry powder and the fish tail. Crumble the ½ bouillon (stock) cube over the mixture. Cover and microwave on HIGH for a further 4 minutes.
5. Purée the mixture in a food processor until smooth.
6. Put the milk into a bowl and heat in the microwave oven for 2 minutes on HIGH.
7. Pour the milk into the soup.
8. Stir in the horseradish mustard and the egg. Add salt and pepper to taste.
9. Pour the soup into 4 small bowls and serve very hot.

Fish Soup

00.15   00.23
Serves 4

American	Ingredients	Metric/Imperial
1	leek, white part only	1
1	finely sliced small carrot	1
1	small zucchini (courgette), trimmed and sliced	1
1	coarsely chopped onion	1
1 cup	dry white wine	250 ml/8 fl oz
1	chicken bouillon (stock) cube	1
1	dried red bell pepper	1
1 lb	whiting fillets, thawed if frozen	450 g/1 lb
2	eggs	2
¾ cup	sour cream (crème fraîche)	200 ml/7 fl oz
	salt	
	pepper	
¼ tsp	curry powder	¼ tsp

1. Rinse the leek thoroughly and slice into 1 inch (2.5 cm) pieces.
2. Put the leek, carrot, zucchini (courgette) and onion into a casserole. Add the white wine, chicken bouillon (stock) cube and red bell pepper. Cover the casserole and microwave on HIGH for 13 minutes.
3. Cut the fish fillets into pieces and add to the casserole. Cover and microwave for a further 5 minutes on HIGH.
4. Discard the red bell pepper and purée the mixture in a food processor.
5. Mix together the eggs and the sour cream (crème fraîche) in the casserole. Add salt and pepper to taste.
6. Stir in the curry powder, 1 cup (250 ml/8 fl oz) of hot water and the purée. Stir well and microwave for a further 5 minutes on HIGH. Serve very hot.
If your oven does not have a turntable, rotate the casserole once during (2) above, after 8 minutes of cooking. You can also reserve a few pieces of fish (or alternatively some cooked crabmeat) to add during (5) above.

Provençale Cod Soup

00.10 **00.22**
Serves 4

American	Ingredients	Metric/Imperial
1¾ lb	finely diced potatoes	750 g/1¾ lb
1	large sliced onion	1
1	trimmed, finely chopped leek	1
1	large, skinned, chopped tomato	1
3 tbsp	oil	2 tbsp
2	peeled crushed garlic cloves	2
1½ quarts	hot water	1.4 litres/2½ pints
	bouquet garni	
	strip orange zest	
¼ tsp	saffron	¼ tsp
	salt	
	pepper	
1 lb	white fish (cod) fillet	450 g/1 lb
4	thick slices of bread	4
1 tbsp	chopped parsley	1 tbsp

1. Put the potatoes, onion, leek and tomato in a large casserole.
2. Add the oil and garlic and heat on HIGH for 10-12 minutes.
3. Add the water, bouquet garni, zest of orange, saffron and seasoning.
4. Chop the fish into pieces and stir into the liquid. Heat on HIGH for a further 8-10 minutes.
5. To serve, put a slice of bread into each serving bowl, sprinkle with chopped parsley and spoon over the soup.

American Fish Chowder

00.20 **00.35**
Serves 4

American	Ingredients	Metric/Imperial
2 lb	mixed white fish	900 g/2 lb
1	large finely chopped onion	1
4	medium size finely diced potatoes	4
4	finely diced carrots	4
4	finely chopped celery sticks	4
¼ lb	diced bacon	125 g/4 oz
1 tbsp	chopped parsley	1 tbsp
14 oz	can tomatoes	396 g/14 oz
1 quart	hot fish bouillon (stock)	1 litre/2 pints
3 tbsp	tomato ketchup	2 tbsp
3 tbsp	Worcestershire sauce	2 tbsp
¼ tsp	dried thyme	¼ tsp
	salt	
	pepper	

1. Rinse the fish under plenty of cold running water, skin and bone it. Cut into even, bite-size pieces.

2. Put the potatoes, carrots and celery in to a large casserole dish with the bacon and cook on HIGH for 10-12 minutes or until soft.
3. Stir in the parsley, tomatoes and their juice, bouillon (stock), tomato ketchup, Worcestershire sauce, thyme and salt and pepper.
4. Add the fish pieces and stir well.
5. Cover and cook on HIGH for 10 minutes, then LOW for 10 minutes.
6. If a thicker soup is preferred, stir in 3 teaspoons of cornstarch (cornflour) mixed to a paste with a little water. Heat on HIGH for 2-3 minutes to thicken.

Cream of Fennel Soup with Smoked Salmon

00.10 **00.15**
Serves 4

American	Ingredients	Metric/Imperial
1¾ lb	fennel	750 g/1¾ lb
¾ cup	dry white wine	200 ml/7 fl oz
¾ cup	sour cream (crème fraîche)	200 ml/7 fl oz
	salt	
	pepper	
½ tsp	grated nutmeg	½ tsp
3½ oz	smoked salmon	100 g/3½ oz

1. Remove the tough base and the stalks from the fennel. Set aside the soft green fronds. Slice the fennel bulbs into thin pieces and then into strips.
2. Put the fennel strips into a casserole with the white wine. Cover and microwave on HIGH for 14 minutes.
3. When the fennel is cooked, purée the mixture in a food processor.
4. Heat the sour cream (crème fraîche) on HIGH for 1 minute. Add to the purée with a pinch of salt, pepper and the grated nutmeg. Purée once more. If the mixture is not smooth enough, force it through a fine strainer (sieve), pressing it with the bowl of a spoon.
5. Pour the soup into 4 bowls. Chop the green fennel fronds and sprinkle over. If the fennel does not have enough green, substitute chopped fresh dill.
6. Slice the salmon into thin strips and arrange them decoratively on each portion. Serve.

Right: Cream of fennel soup with smoked salmon

Curried Chicken Soup

◣ 00.05   00.09 〰️
Serves 4

American	Ingredients	Metric/Imperial
½ lb	chicken or turkey breast	225 g/8 oz
3	sliced shallots	3
3 tbsp	butter	2 tbsp
5 tbsp	all-purpose (plain) flour	4 tbsp
1 tsp	curry powder	1 tsp
2¼ cups	milk	500 ml/18 fl oz
1	chicken bouillon (stock) cube	1
4 tbsp	sour cream (crème fraîche)	3 tbsp
3 tbsp	dry sherry	2 tbsp
	salt	
	pepper	

1. Cut the chicken or turkey breasts into pieces. Put the chicken or turkey and the shallots into a casserole with the butter. Cover and microwave on HIGH for 3 minutes.
2. Sieve the flour and curry powder together and stir into the casserole.
3. Add the milk and ¾ cup (200 ml/7 fl oz) of water. Crumble the bouillon (stock) cube into the mixture and stir well. Cover and microwave on HIGH for 6 minutes. Stir carefully mid-way through cooking.
4. Purée the mixture in a food processor.
5. Add the sour cream (crème fraîche) and sherry. Add salt and pepper to taste. Serve immediately.

Vegetable Soup with Chicken

◣ 00.15   00.45 〰️
Serves 4

American	Ingredients	Metric/Imperial
3	leeks	3
1	bayleaf	1
2	sprigs thyme	2
5 oz	cubed carrots	150 g/5 oz
5 oz	cubed baby turnips	150 g/5 oz
2 oz	cubed celeriac	50 g/2 oz
1	crushed garlic clove	1
1	chicken	1
	salt	
	pepper	
3	cloves	3
1 cup	white wine	250 ml/8 fl oz
2 tbsp	soup noodles	2 tbsp
1	bunch chives	1

1. Remove the green part of the leeks, wash thoroughly and tie it into a bunch with the bayleaf and thyme. Remove the base and the outer skin of the white part of the leeks, slice in half lengthwise and then in ½ inch (1.25 cm) slices across. Wash them thoroughly.

2. Put the carrots, turnips, celeriac, white leeks, garlic and the bunch of herbs into a large casserole. Add 2¼ cups (500 ml/18 fl oz) of hot water. Cover and microwave for 5 minutes on HIGH.

3. Cut the chicken into 8 pieces, removing as much fat as possible.

4. Add salt, pepper, cloves, the white wine and chicken pieces to the casserole. Cover and microwave for 15 minutes on HIGH.

5. Stir the casserole, cover and microwave for a further 20 minutes on MEDIUM-HIGH.

6. When the chicken is cooked, remove it from the casserole and set aside.

7. Discard the cloves and bunch of herbs.

8. Stir in the soup noodles and milk, cover and microwave for 5 minutes on HIGH.

9. Rinse the chives, pat dry on kitchen paper and snip with a pair of kitchen scissors.

10. Pour the mixture into a soup tureen, sprinkle the chives over and serve hot.

11. To serve the chicken, remove the bones and skin. Slice the meat and serve with Sauce Tartare or with a Vinaigrette of capers and fines herbes, accompanied by a green salad.

Below: Curried chicken soup, Vegetable soup with chicken

Lentil Soup

	00.15	00.50	
	Serves 4		

American	Ingredients	Metric/Imperial
1 cup	lentils	225 g/8 oz
1 quart	beef bouillon (stock)	1 litre/1¾ pints
	assorted peeled, roughly chopped pot vegetables including 1 onion	
¼ tsp	dried thyme	¼ tsp
1 tsp	cornstarch (cornflour)	1 tsp
1 tsp	water	1 tsp
	salt	
2-3	frankfurter sausages	2-3
	finely snipped chives	

1. Rinse the lentils and remove any black seeds. Put the lentils into a large bowl. Bring the bouillon (stock) to the boil and pour over the lentils to cover. Cook on HIGH for 15 minutes.

2. Leave the pot vegetables to stand in a bowl of cold water.

3. Sieve and purée the lentils in a food processor and return to the bowl with the vegetables, thyme and seasoning.

4. Stir the cornstarch (cornflour) with the water until it forms a paste and stir well into the soup. Return the bowl to the microwave and cook for 25 minutes on HIGH. Add a little boiling water if the mixture is too thick.

5. Taste and adjust the seasoning and check that the vegetables are cooked.

6. Slice the frankfurters and add to the soup. Return to the microwave and cook on HIGH for 10 minutes. Leave to stand for 5 minutes and serve sprinkled with snipped chives.

Provençale Style Soup

00.15   00.17

Serves 4

American	Ingredients	Metric/Imperial
5	red bell peppers	5
2	medium size sliced onions	2
3 tbsp	olive oil	2 tbsp
½ lb	zucchini (courgettes)	225 g/8 oz
1 lb	coarsely chopped tomatoes	450 g/1 lb
5	crushed garlic cloves	5
1	sprig thyme	1
2	bayleaves	2
4	basil leaves	4
3 tbsp	dry white wine	2 tbsp
	salt	
	pepper	
1 cup	grated Parmesan cheese	50 g/2 oz

1. Rinse the bell peppers, seed and remove the stalks and pith. Chop the flesh coarsely.
2. Put the onions and bell peppers into a large casserole and pour over the olive oil. Cover and microwave on HIGH for 5 minutes.
3. Rinse and trim the zucchini (courgettes) and slice into rounds.
4. Add the tomatoes, zucchini (courgettes) and garlic to the casserole, with 1¼ cups (300 ml/½ pint) of hot water, the thyme and bayleaves. Cover and microwave on HIGH for 12 minutes, stirring midway through cooking time.
5. Rinse the basil and pat dry on kitchen paper. Snip the leaves with kitchen scissors.
6. Discard the thyme and bayleaves.
7. Purée the mixture in a food processor.
8. Add the white wine and salt and pepper to taste.
9. Pour the soup into a tureen and sprinkle the basil on top. Serve hot with the grated Parmesan as a side dish.

Russian vegetable soup (Bortsch)

Provençale Vegetable Soup with Basil

| | 00.10 Serves 4 | 00.15 | 〰 |

American	Ingredients	Metric/Imperial
¼ lb	cubed potatoes	125 g/4 oz
2	sliced onions	2
2	red bell peppers, seeded and chopped	2
14 oz	coarsely chopped tomatoes	400 g/14 oz
7 oz	zucchini (courgettes), trimmed, sliced into rounds	200 g/7 oz
6	chopped garlic cloves	6
3 tbsp	olive oil	2 tbsp
1	sprig thyme	1
1	bayleaf	1
3 tbsp	white wine	2 tbsp
	salt	
	pepper	
2 tbsp	chopped fresh basil	2 tbsp
4	slices stale French bread	4
4	slices dry goat's cheese	4

1. Put 1¼ cups (300 ml/½ pint) of water in a bowl and heat in the microwave for 2 minutes on HIGH.
2. Put all the vegetables into a casserole and add the hot water, olive oil, thyme and bayleaf. Cover and microwave on HIGH for 12 minutes, stirring midway through the cooking time.
3. Discard the bayleaf and thyme.
4. Add the white wine and purée the mixture in a food processor. Add salt and pepper to taste.
5. Pour the soup into a tureen and sprinkle the chopped basil over.
6. Put the slices of French bread on a plate and place a slice of cheese on top of each. Microwave on HIGH for 1 minute and serve with the soup.

Russian Vegetable Soup (Bortsch)

| | 00.15 Serves 4 | 00.31 | 〰 |

American	Ingredients	Metric/Imperial
½ tbsp	dried mushrooms (cêpes)	½ tbsp
7 oz	cabbage	200 g/7 oz
1	stick celery	1
4	sprigs parsley	4
3½ oz	coarsely chopped onions	100 g/3½ oz
5 oz	finely diced carrots	150 g/5 oz
5 oz	finely diced potatoes	150 g/5 oz
3 tbsp	oil	2 tbsp
4 tbsp	tomato concentrate	3 tbsp
	salt	
	pepper	
7 oz	cooked beetroot, peeled and grated	200 g/7 oz
2 tbsp	wine vinegar	1 tbsp
⅓ cup	sour cream (crème fraîche)	4½ tbsp

1. Put the mushrooms in a bowl, with ¾ cup (200 ml/7 fl oz) of hot water to cover and microwave on HIGH for 3 minutes.
2. Cut the cabbage into thin strips and rinse.
3. Wash and roughly chop the celery.
4. Rinse the parsley and pat dry on kitchen paper.
5. Put the onions in a large casserole and pour over the oil. Cover and microwave on HIGH for 3 minutes.
6. Add the carrots and potatoes and 1¼ cups (300 ml/½ pint) of hot water. Cover and microwave for 10 minutes on HIGH.
7. Stir in the parsley, celery, cabbage and mushrooms in their soaking liquid.
8. Mix together the tomato concentrate and 2¼ cups (500 ml/18 fl oz) of hot water and stir into the casserole.
9. Add a dash of salt and pepper. Stir well. Cover and microwave on HIGH for 15 minutes.
10. Mix together the grated beetroot and the vinegar.
11. When the soup is ready, discard the parsley.
12. Stir in the beetroot and pour the soup into a tureen.
13. Pour the sour cream (crème fraîche) gently on top of the soup and serve.

Vegetable Soup with Mozzarella Cheese

00.10 **00.23**
Serves 4

American	Ingredients	Metric/Imperial
1	sprig thyme	1
1	bayleaf	1
	salt	
	pepper	
7 oz	diced carrots	200 g/7 oz
7 oz	finely diced potatoes	200 g/7 oz
3	diced leeks, white part only	3
1	stick of celery, diced	1
1¼ cups	milk	300 ml/½ pint
3½ oz	Mozzarella cheese	100 g/3½ oz
2 tbsp	chopped chervil	2 tbsp

1. Pour 2½ cups (600 ml/1 pint) of water into a casserole. Add the thyme and bayleaf, salt and pepper. Cover and microwave on HIGH for 5 minutes.
2. Put the vegetables into the boiling water. Cover and microwave on HIGH for 15 minutes.
3. When the vegetables are cooked, purée half and return the purée to the casserole. Add the milk. Cover and microwave on HIGH for 3 minutes.
4. Pour the mixture into a soup tureen.
5. Discard the thyme and bayleaf.
6. Cut the Mozzarella into cubes and add to the soup. Stir well, taste and adjust seasoning. Sprinkle with chopped chervil and serve at once.

Mushroom Soup

00.10 **00.20**
Serves 4

American	Ingredients	Metric/Imperial
3	chopped shallots	3
1	quartered garlic clove	1
2 tbsp	butter	1 tbsp
1 lb	white button mushrooms	450 g/1 lb
3 tbsp	all-purpose (plain) flour	2 tbsp
	salt	
	pepper	
3 tbsp	Madeira	2 tbsp
3 tbsp	fresh lemon juice	2 tbsp
1	egg yolk	1
2¼ cups	milk	500 ml/18 fl oz
1 tbsp	chopped parsley	1 tbsp

1. Put the shallots, garlic and butter in a casserole. Cover and microwave on HIGH for 3 minutes.
2. Wipe the mushrooms with a damp cloth or kitchen paper and slice them finely.
3. Sift the flour into the casserole. Add 1¼ cups (300 ml/½ pint) of water. Stir well. Microwave on HIGH for 3 minutes, stirring from time to time, with a hand whisk.

Vegetable soup with Mozzarella cheese

4. Stir in the mushrooms, salt and pepper. Cover and microwave on HIGH for 10 minutes.
5. When the mushrooms are cooked, remove 2 tablespoons of mushrooms from the casserole and put in a soup tureen.
6. Add the Madeira, lemon juice and egg yolk to the mushrooms in the tureen and stir well.
7. Purée the remaining mixture in a food processor.
8. Put the milk in a bowl and heat on HIGH for 4 minutes.
9. Add the milk to the mushroom purée and pour the mixture into the soup tureen over the mushrooms. Stir well, taste and adjust seasoning.
10. Sprinkle with chopped parsley and serve hot.

Zucchini (Courgette) Soup

00.10　　**00.14**
Serves 4

American	Ingredients	Metric/Imperial
2	finely sliced shallots	2
1	finely sliced garlic clove	1
2 tbsp	butter	1 tbsp
1 lb	zucchini (courgettes)	450 g/1 lb
3 tbsp	all-purpose (plain) flour	2 tbsp
1 tsp	curry powder	1 tsp
1	chicken bouillon (stock) cube	1
2	basil leaves	2
1¼ cups	milk	300 ml/½ pint
	salt	
	pepper	
2 tbsp	grated Parmesan cheese	2 tbsp

1. Put the shallots and garlic in a casserole with the butter. Cover and microwave on HIGH for 2 minutes.
2. Rinse and top-and-tail the zucchini (courgettes) and slice into ¼ inch (0.75 cm) rounds.
3. Sieve the flour and curry powder together over the shallots and garlic and stir well.
4. Crumble the bouillon (stock) cube over the mixture.
5. Add the zucchini (courgettes) and 1¼ cups (300 ml/½ pint) of water. Cover and microwave on HIGH for 10 minutes, stirring after 2 minutes and again after 4 minutes.
6. Rinse the basil and snip with kitchen scissors.
7. Purée the vegetable mixture in a food processor.
8. Heat the milk in a bowl on HIGH for 2 minutes. Add the purée and salt and pepper to taste.
9. Pour the soup into a tureen, add the Parmesan and snipped basil, stir and serve hot.

Cream of Zucchini (Courgette) Soup

00.10　　**00.14**
Serves 4

American	Ingredients	Metric/Imperial
1¼ lb	diced zucchini (courgettes)	550 g/1¼ lb
2 oz	thinly sliced shallots	50 g/2 oz
2 tbsp	butter	1 tbsp
2 tbsp	all-purpose (white) flour	1 tbsp
1¼ cups	milk	300 ml/½ pint
½	chicken bouillon (stock) cube	½
	salt	
	pepper	
30	basil leaves	30

1. Put the zucchini (courgettes) and shallots in a casserole with ⅔ cup (150 ml/¼ pint) of water. Cover and microwave on HIGH for 10 minutes.
2. When the zucchini (courgettes) are cooked, purée the zucchini (courgette) and onion mixture until smooth. Leave the purée in the bowl of the food processor.
3. To make the sauce, put the butter in a dish and melt in the microwave oven for 1 minute on HIGH.
4. Stir in the flour. Add the milk and stir well. Cover and microwave on HIGH for 3 minutes, whisking with a hand beater every minute.
5. Crumble the ½ cube of bouillon (stock) into the sauce. Pour the sauce into the food processor. Add salt and pepper to taste. Purée until smooth. Taste and adjust seasoning.
6. Rinse the basil leaves, pat dry on kitchen paper and snip with kitchen scissors.
7. Pour the soup into 4 plates, sprinkle the basil over and serve at once.

Zucchini (courgette) soup

Cream of tomato soup

Cream of Tomato Soup with Cucumber

▬▷	00.10	00.16	〰
	Serves 4		

American	Ingredients	Metric/Imperial
5 oz	finely sliced onions	150 g/5 oz
2 lb	thickly sliced tomatoes	1 kg/2 lb
1	finely grated cucumber	1
1	quartered garlic clove	1
1	stick of celery, cut into four	1
1	sprig thyme	1
1	bayleaf	1
1 cup	milk	250 ml/8 fl oz
1 tsp	sugar	1 tsp
	salt	
	pepper	
3 tbsp	sour cream (crème fraîche)	2 tbsp
2	egg yolks	2

1. Put the onions in a casserole with 3 (2) tablespoons of water. Cover and microwave on HIGH for 2 minutes.
2. Add the tomatoes, cucumber, garlic, celery, thyme and bayleaf to the onions in the casserole. Add 1 cup (250 ml/8 fl oz) of water. Cover and microwave on HIGH for 10 minutes.
3. Discard the thyme, bayleaf and celery and liquidize the mixture in a food processor. Return to the casserole.
4. Pour the milk into a bowl and heat in the microwave oven on HIGH for 2 minutes.
5. Stir the milk, sugar, salt and pepper into the casserole. Reheat for 2 minutes. Stir well.
6. Mix together the sour cream (crème fraîche) and egg yolks in a soup tureen. Pour the vegetable purée over them, stirring with a hand whisk, and serve.

Italian Style Tomato Soup

▬▷	00.10	00.12	〰
	Serves 4		

American	Ingredients	Metric/Imperial
2	finely chopped garlic cloves	2
2	finely chopped onions	2
4 tbsp	olive oil	3 tbsp
2 lb	firm, ripe sliced tomatoes	1 kg/2 lb
2	sprigs thyme	2
1 cup	white wine	250 ml/8 fl oz
	salt	
	pepper	
1 cup	Mozzarella cheese	100 g/3½ oz
4	basil leaves	4

1. Put the garlic and onion in a casserole. Pour the olive oil over, cover and microwave on HIGH for 2 minutes.
2. Add the tomatoes to the casserole.
3. Crumble the thyme into the mixture and add the white wine. Cover and microwave on HIGH for 10 minutes.
4. Purée the vegetable mixture in a food processor, then pass it through a fine strainer (sieve).
5. Add salt and pepper to taste. Pour into a soup tureen.
6. Cut the Mozzarella into small cubes and stir into the soup.
7. Rinse the basil leaves and snip them with kitchen scissors directly into the soup. Serve hot.

Cream of Tomato Soup

00.10   00.17
Serves 4

American	Ingredients	Metric/Imperial
3	sticks celery	3
5 oz	finely sliced onions	150 g/5 oz
2 lb	quartered tomatoes	1 kg/2 lb
2	quartered garlic cloves	2
1	sprig thyme	1
1	bayleaf	1
1	chicken bouillon (stock) cube	1
1¼ cups	milk	300 ml/½ pint
1 tsp	sugar	1 tsp
	salt	
	pepper	
4 tbsp	sour cream (crème fraîche)	3 tbsp
2	egg yolks	2

1. Remove the celery leaves from the stalks and set aside. Cut the stalks into matchstick (julienne) strips.
2. Put the onions and celery in a casserole with 3 (2) tablespoons of water. Cover and microwave on HIGH for 3 minutes.
3. Add the tomatoes, garlic, thyme and bayleaf to the casserole.
4. Crumble the chicken bouillon (stock) cube over the mixture, stir well, cover and microwave on HIGH for 10 minutes.
5. Discard the thyme and bayleaf.
6. Purée the mixture in a food processor, then pass through a fine strainer (sieve) and return the purée to the casserole.
7. Pour the milk into a bowl and heat on HIGH for 2 minutes. Stir the hot milk, sugar, salt and pepper into the casserole. Reheat for 2 minutes on HIGH. Stir well.
8. Chop the celery leaves finely.
9. Whisk the sour cream (crème fraîche) and egg yolks lightly in a soup tureen. Slowly add the contents of the casserole, stirring constantly with a hand whisk.
10. Sprinkle the chopped celery over and serve hot.

Microwave tip: to skin a tomato by microwave:
1. Prick the skin of the tomato with a fork.
2. Put tomato on to a plate and heat on HIGH for 30-40 seconds.
3. Leave to cool for a few minutes before peeling off the skin.

Italian style tomato soup

Pea and Ham soup

00.05   00.15
Serves 4

American	Ingredients	Metric/Imperial
3¼ cups	chicken bouillon (stock)	750 ml/1¼ pints
1 lb	frozen peas	450 g/1 lb
3 tbsp	light (single) cream	2 tbsp
¼ tsp	sugar	¼ tsp
	salt	
	pepper	
¼ lb	cooked ham	125 g/4 oz

1. Put the bouillon (stock) and the peas in a large bowl, cover and cook on HIGH for 10 minutes.
2. Set aside one-third of the peas and purée the remainder in a food processor or by passing through a fine mesh strainer (sieve).
3. Return all the peas to a bowl and stir in the cream, sugar, salt and pepper.
4. Dice the ham and add to the bowl.
5. Cook on HIGH for 5 minutes and serve hot.

Cold Apricot Soup

00.10   00.26
plus chilling time

American	Ingredients	Metric/Imperial
1 lb	ripe apricots	450 g/1 lb
½ cup	sugar	125 g/4 oz
½	stick cinnamon	½
2	lemon slices	2
5 tbsp	cornstarch (cornflour)	4 tbsp
	few drops vanilla extract (essence)	
	lemon juice	

1. Bring 1 quart (1 litre/1¾ pints) of water to the boil on a conventional cooker. Cover the apricots with the water. Remove the apricots, skin, halve and stone them. Set aside 4 apricot halves. Cut the remaining flesh into ½ inch (1.25 cm) strips.
2. Bring the water back to the boil and pour into a large Pyrex bowl.
3. Stir in the sugar, cinnamon and lemon slices. Microwave on HIGH for 6 minutes.
4. Add the apricot strips and microwave on HIGH for 10 minutes. Leave to cool slightly.
5. Purée the soup in a food processor.
6. Mix the cornstarch (cornflour) with a little cold water to form a paste. Stir in a little of the hot soup. Stir well until smooth. Whisk the cornstarch (cornflour) paste into the soup until smooth.
7. Add the vanilla extract (essence) and lemon juice to taste.
8. Return the soup to the microwave and cook on HIGH for 10 minutes. Whisk the soup, leave to cool and chill thoroughly before serving.

Above: Spinach soup with poached eggs
Below: Soup with petits pois

Soup with Petits Pois

00.10   00.15
Serves 4

American	Ingredients	Metric/Imperial
¼ lb	sliced onions	125 g/4 oz
1 lb	frozen petits pois	450 g/1 lb
1	bunch chervil	1
2 tbsp	sorrel	2 tbsp
¼ lb	ham	125 g/4 oz
2	egg yolks	2
4 tbsp	white port	3 tbsp
	salt	
	pepper	

1. Put the onion in a casserole with the petits pois, still frozen. Add 2¼ cups (500 ml/18 fl oz) of hot water. Cover and microwave on HIGH for 13 minutes.
2. Rinse the chervil and sorrel and chop separately.
3. Cut the ham into matchstick (julienne) strips.
4. Stir the sorrel into the casserole, and microwave on HIGH for a further 2 minutes.
5. When the petits pois are tender, purée the mixture in a food processor, then pass through a fine strainer (sieve).
6. Mix together the egg yolks and the port in a soup tureen. Pour the pea soup over, stirring constantly with a whisk. Add 1 cup (250 ml/8 fl oz) of hot water and salt and pepper.
7. Stir in the ham and the chervil. Serve at once.

Spinach Soup with Poached Eggs

00.10   00.15
Serves 4

American	Ingredients	Metric/Imperial
1 lb	frozen spinach in a block	450 g/1 lb
3 tbsp	butter	2 tbsp
5 tbsp	all-purpose (plain) flour	4 tbsp
2¼ cups	milk	500 ml/18 fl oz
¼ cup	sour cream (crème fraîche)	4½ tbsp
¼ tsp	ground nutmeg	¼ tsp
	salt	
	pepper	
4	eggs	4

1. Put the spinach in a small casserole. Cover and microwave on HIGH for 8 minutes, stir once after 4 minutes.
2. Put the butter in a bowl and melt in the microwave on HIGH for 1 minute. Stir in the flour.
3. Pour in the milk slowly and beat well with a hand whisk. Microwave on HIGH for 3 minutes, stir every minute.
4. Stir in the spinach and transfer to a soup tureen. Stir in the sour cream (crème fraîche), nutmeg, salt and pepper.
5. Break the eggs one at a time and place carefully on the surface of the soup. Prick each egg yolk in 2 or 3 places.
6. Put the soup tureen in the oven and microwave on HIGH for 3 minutes until the egg whites are cooked.

Sorrel Soup

	00.05	00.10	
	Serves 4		

American	Ingredients	Metric/Imperial
1	bunch sorrel	1
2 oz	very finely chopped, lean smoked bacon	50 g/2 oz
2 tbsp	butter	1 tbsp
3 tbsp	all-purpose (plain) flour	2 tbsp
1 tsp	sugar	1 tsp
	salt	
	pepper	
2¼ cups	milk	500 ml/18 fl oz
¼ cup	sour cream (crème fraîche)	4½ tbsp

1. Remove the tough stems from the sorrel, rinse the leaves and chop coarsely.
2. Put the sorrel, bacon and butter into a casserole. Cover and microwave on HIGH for 3 minutes.
3. Sift the flour into the casserole and stir well.
4. Add 2¼ cups (500 ml/18 fl oz) of hot water and the sugar.
5. Season to taste with salt and pepper. Cover and microwave on HIGH for 3 minutes, stirring every minute with a hand whisk.
6. Stir in the milk, cover and microwave for a further 4 minutes on HIGH.
7. Pour the soup into a tureen and add the sour cream (crème fraîche). Adjust seasoning. Serve hot.

Sorrel Soup with Shrimp (Prawns)

	00.05	00.10	
	Serves 4		

American	Ingredients	Metric/Imperial
2 oz	lean smoked bacon, very finely chopped	50 g/2 oz
1	bunch sorrel, trimmed and coarsely chopped	1
¼ cup	all-purpose (plain) flour	1 tbsp
1 tsp	sugar	1 tsp
	salt	
	pepper	
2¼ cups	milk	500 ml/18 fl oz
5 tbsp	couscous or semolina	4 tbsp
3½ oz	shelled frozen shrimp (prawns)	100 g/3½ oz
2	egg yolks	2
2 tbsp	butter	1 tbsp

1. Put the bacon and sorrel in a casserole with 5 tablespoons of water. Cover and microwave on HIGH for 3 minutes.
2. Sprinkle the flour over the mixture and stir well. Add 2¼ cups (500 ml/18 fl oz) of water, the sugar and salt and pepper to taste. Cover and microwave on HIGH for 3 minutes.
3. Add the milk, couscous or semolina and the shrimp (prawns), still frozen. Cover and cook on HIGH for a further 4 minutes.
4. Put the egg yolks in a saucepan. Stir in 2-3 tablespoons of the soup, stirring well. Gradually add the rest of the soup, stirring constantly. Add the butter. Taste and adjust seasoning. Serve hot.

Delicious fresh vegetables for sorrel, cabbage and pumpkin soups

Pumpkin Soup

	0.20	01.20	
	Serves 4		

American	Ingredients	Metric/Imperial
2¼ lb	beef bones	1 kg/2¼ lb
1½ quarts	water	1.5 litres/2½ pints
	salt	
	pepper	
	assorted peeled and roughly chopped pot vegetables	
2	bayleaves	2
1 tsp	white peppercorns	1 tsp
1	medium size chopped onion	1
¼ cup	butter or margarine	50 g/2 oz
6 cups	cubed pumpkin flesh	1 kg/2 lb
½ cup	pine nuts (kernels)	50 g/2 oz
3 tbsp	chopped dill weed	2 tbsp
½ cup	whipping cream	125 ml/4 fl oz

1. Bring the water to the boil and pour in a large bowl with the beef bones, bayleaves and peppercorns. Cover and cook on HIGH for 5 minutes.
2. Add the pot vegetables, cover and cook on MEDIUM for 45 minutes. Strain and measure 1 quart (1 litre/1¾ pints) of the bouillon (stock).
3. Put three-quarters of the butter and the onion in a large bowl. Cover and cook on HIGH for 4 minutes.
4. Stir in the pumpkin cubes and cook on HIGH for 2 minutes.
5. Add the stock and season lightly with salt and pepper. Cook on HIGH for 10 minutes. Reduce power to MEDIUM and cook for a further 10 minutes.
6. Set aside a few pumpkin cubes for the garnish and purée the soup in a food processor. Return to the bowl.
7. Heat the remaining butter in a small bowl on HIGH for 1 minute.
8. Add the pine nuts (kernels), cover and cook on HIGH for 2 minutes.
9. Stir in the dill, cream and reserved pumpkin pieces.
10. Cover and reheat on MEDIUM for 1 minute. Serve sprinkled with the pine nuts (kernels).
Variation: Use slivered almonds instead of pine nuts (kernels).

Pumpkin Soup with Shrimp (Prawns)

	00.10	00.14	
	Serves 4		

American	Ingredients	Metric/Imperial
1¾ lb	pumpkin	750 g/1¾ lb
2	sticks celery	2
3	coarsely chopped shallots	3
¼ lb	shelled shrimp (prawns)	125 g/4 oz
1 tsp	fresh lemon juice	1 tsp
2¼ cups	milk	500 ml/18 fl oz
	salt	
	pepper	
2 tbsp	butter	1 tbsp

1. Skin and seed the pumpkin and remove the pith, Cut the flesh into ½ inch (1.25 cm) slices and then into small cubes.
2. Wash the celery. Remove the leaves and set aside. Chop the stalks finely.
3. Put the shallots, pumpkin, celery stalks and leaves into a casserole. Add ½ cup (5 tablespoons) of water. Cover and microwave on HIGH for 10 minutes.
4. Set 1 oz (25 g) of the shrimp (prawns) aside. Purée the remaining shrimp (prawns) in a food processor. Add lemon juice.
5. When the pumpkin is cooked, discard the celery leaves and pour the mixture into the food processor with the shrimp (prawn) purée. Purée the mixture until smooth.
6. Put the milk into a bowl and microwave on HIGH for 4 minutes. Pour over the pumpkin purée and purée again.
7. Add salt and pepper to taste.
8. Pour the soup into a tureen and add the butter and the reserved shrimp (prawns).

Cabbage Soup

	00.10	00.23	
	Serves 4		

American	Ingredients	Metric/Imperial
1 lb	Savoy cabbage	450 g/1 lb
½ lb	finely diced potatoes	225 g/8 oz
1	finely chopped garlic clove	1
1	finely chopped onion	1
2	beef bouillon (stock) cubes	2
½ lb	cooked ham	225 g/8 oz
¼ cup	sour cream (crème fraîche)	4½ tbsp
3 tbsp	fresh lemon juice	2 tbsp
	salt	
	pepper	

1. Put 1 cup (250 ml/8 fl oz) of water into the lower compartment of a microwave steamer. Cover and microwave on HIGH for 3 minutes.
2. Remove the outer leaves of the cabbage and chop into slices with a large knife. Rinse and drain the leaves and place in the upper section of the steamer, cover and microwave on HIGH for 5 minutes.
3. Put the cabbage into a large casserole. Add the potatoes, garlic and onion and pour on 1 quart (1 litre/1¾ pints) of hot water to cover.
4. Crumble the bouillon (stock) cubes into the mixture and stir well. Cover and microwave on HIGH for 12 minutes.
5. Cut the ham into cubes and stir into the casserole and microwave for a further 3 minutes on HIGH.
6. Stir in the sour cream (crème fraîche) and the lemon juice.
7. Add salt and pepper to taste. Pour into 4 soup plates, add a little more cream to each and serve hot.

Watercress Soup

	00.15	00.18	〰
	Serves 4		

American	Ingredients	Metric/Imperial
1 lb	sliced potatoes	450 g/1 lb
1	finely sliced onion	1
1	bunch watercress	1
1¾ cups	milk	400 ml/14 fl oz
2 tbsp	butter	1 tbsp
	salt	
	pepper	

1. Put the potatoes and onion in a large casserole with 2¼ cups (500 ml/18 fl oz) water. Cover and microwave on HIGH for 12 minutes.

2. Remove the tough stalks from the watercress, rinse thoroughly, drain and purée until smooth in a food processor.

3. Stir the watercress purée into the casserole, cover and microwave for a further 3 minutes.

4. Heat the milk in a bowl for 3 minutes on HIGH.

5. Pour the vegetable mixture into a food processor and purée once more, then pour the soup into a tureen.

6. Stir in the butter and hot milk. Season with salt and pepper. Stir well. Serve hot.

Cream of Cauliflower Soup

	00.10	00.16	〰
	Serves 4		

American	Ingredients	Metric/Imperial
½ lb	finely sliced potatoes	225 g/8 oz
1 lb	cauliflower florets	450 g/1 lb
2¼ cups	milk	500 ml/18 fl oz
¼ cup	sour cream (crème fraîche)	4½ tbsp
	salt	
	pepper	
¼ tsp	grated nutmeg	¼ tsp
2 tbsp	butter	1½ tbsp
3 tbsp	chopped chervil	3 tbsp
3 tbsp	chopped parsley	3 tbsp

1. Put the potato slices and cauliflower florets in a casserole with 1¼ cups (300 ml/½ pint) of hot water. Cover and microwave on HIGH for 12 minutes.
2. Purée the vegetable mixture in a food processor until smooth. Return the purée to the casserole.
3. Stir in the milk and sour cream (crème fraîche).
4. Add salt and pepper to taste and the grated nutmeg. Cover and microwave on HIGH for a further 4 minutes.
5. Pour the soup into a tureen.
6. Add the butter, chervil and parsley. Serve hot.

Broccoli Soup

| | 00.10 Serves 4 | 00.23 | |

American	Ingredients	Metric/Imperial
1	quartered garlic clove	1
¼ cup	rice	50 g/2 oz
1½ lb	broccoli	700 g/1½ lb
¼ cup	dry white wine	4½ tbsp
	salt	
	pepper	
¼ tsp	ground cumin seed	¼ tsp
¾ cup	milk	200 ml/7 fl oz
2	egg yolks	2

1. Put the garlic and rice into a large casserole. Add 1¼ cups (300 ml/½ pint) of hot water. Cover and microwave for 3 minutes on HIGH, then a further 3 minutes on MEDIUM.
2. Remove the leaves of the broccoli and divide it into florets. Chop the stalks into small cubes.
3. Add the broccoli florets and stalks and white wine to the casserole. Cover and microwave on HIGH for 15 minutes.
4. Purée the mixture in a food processor. Add salt and pepper to taste and the ground cumin.
5. Pour the milk into a bowl and microwave on HIGH for 2 minutes. Stir the milk into the broccoli purée.
6. Put the egg yolks in a soup tureen. Carefully pour broccoli purée over, stirring gently with a hand whisk. Serve hot.

Cream of cauliflower soup

Turnip Soup

00.10 Serves 4   **00.17**

American	Ingredients	Metric/Imperial
½ lb	finely diced baby turnips	225 g/8 oz
½ lb	finely diced potatoes	225 g/8 oz
2 tbsp	butter	1 tbsp
2	chicken bouillon (stock) cubes	2
1 tsp	sugar	1 tsp
1	bunch chives	1
¾ cup	milk	200 ml/7 fl oz
3 tbsp	sour cream (crème fraîche)	2 tbsp
	salt	
	pepper	

1. Put the turnips and potatoes in a large casserole with the butter and ¼ cup (5 tablespoons) of water. Cover and microwave on HIGH for 5 minutes.
2. Crumble the chicken bouillon (stock) cubes over the vegetables.
3. Sprinkle the sugar over and stir well. Add 3¼ cups (750 ml/1¼ pints) of hot water. Cover and microwave on HIGH for 10 minutes.
4. Rinse the chives, pat dry on kitchen paper, and snip finely with kitchen scissors.
5. Pour the milk into a bowl and heat on HIGH for 2 minutes.
6. Add the milk to the vegetables.
7. Stir in the chives and sour cream (crème fraîche). Stir well, add salt and pepper to taste. Serve very hot.

Minestrone

00.20 Serves 4   **00.39**

American	Ingredients	Metric/Imperial
1	large finely chopped onion	1
1	small trimmed chopped leek	1
2 tbsp	olive oil	1 tbsp
1	peeled crushed garlic clove	1
1 tbsp	chopped parsley	1 tbsp
2	leaves sage	2
2	finely diced carrots	2
2	finely diced potatoes	2
2	sliced celery sticks	2
1	sliced zucchini (courgette)	1
½ lb	finely shredded savoy cabbage	225 g/8 oz
¼ lb	chopped bacon	125 g/4 oz
3	leaves chopped basil	3
2 tbsp	tomato purée	1 tbsp
14 oz	can tomatoes	396 g/14 oz
	salt	
	pepper	
1 quart	hot beef bouillon (stock)	1 litre/1¾ pints
14 oz	can cannellini beans	396 g/14 oz
¼ cup	short-cut macaroni	55 g/2 oz
	grated Parmesan cheese	

Minestrone soup

1. Put the onion and leek into in a large casserole dish with the olive oil, garlic, parsley and sage. Cover and cook on HIGH for 5 minutes.
2. Add the carrots, potatoes, celery and zucchini (courgette), cabbage, bacon and basil to the casserole. Re-cover and cook, stirring twice, for a further 10-12 minutes on HIGH.
3. Stir in the tomato purée, tomatoes, salt, pepper and bouillon (stock).
4. Drain the cannellini beans and add with the macaroni. Re-cover and cook for 10-12 minutes. Leave to stand for 10 minutes before serving.
5. Serve sprinkled with Parmesan cheese.

Minestrone Soup

00.15   00.18

Serves 4

American	Ingredients	Metric/Imperial
2	sticks celery	2
7 oz	zucchini (courgettes)	200 g/7 oz
2	leeks	2
¼ lb	fatty pork or bacon	125 g/4 oz
5 oz	finely diced carrots	150 g/5 oz
2	skinned tomatoes, coarsely chopped	2
1	vegetable bouillon (stock) cube	1
4	basil leaves	4
3	crushed garlic cloves	3
2 oz	grated Parmesan cheese	50 g/2 oz
4 tbsp	olive oil	3 tbsp
¼ lb	white haricot beans	125 g/4 oz
	salt	
	pepper	

1. Wash the celery and cut into matchstick (julienne) strips.
2. Rinse and top-and-tail the zucchini (courgettes). Cut in 4 lengthwise and then into dice.
3. Remove the green part of the leeks, the base and the outer skin. Slice in 4 lengthwise, rinse and dice.
4. Cut the fatty pork or bacon into small strips.
5. Put the fatty pork or bacon and the carrots into a large casserole with 3¼ cups (750 ml/1¼ pints) of hot water. Cover and microwave on HIGH for 5 minutes.
6. Add the celery, zucchini (courgettes), leeks and tomatoes to the casserole and crumble the bouillon (stock) cube over. Cover and microwave on HIGH for 10 minutes.
7. Rinse the basil leaves, pat dry on kitchen paper and chop.
8. Pound the garlic and basil together in a pestle and mortar or purée in a food processor. Add the Parmesan and olive oil and liquidize to a fine purée. Pour this into a soup tureen.
9. Stir the haricot beans into the casserole, cover and microwave on HIGH for a further 3 minutes.
10. Pour a little of this mixture over the Parmesan and basil purée and stir until blended. Add the remainder of the soup slowly, stirring constantly.
11. Add salt and pepper to taste. Serve very hot.

French Onion Soup

00.10   00.14
Serves 4

American	Ingredients	Metric/Imperial
7 oz	finely sliced onion	200 g/7 oz
2 tbsp	butter	1½ tbsp
1¼ cups	white wine	300 ml/½ pint
3 tbsp	all-purpose (plain) flour	2 tbsp
1	can beef consommé	1
4	slices crusty French bread	4
1 cup	grated Gruyere cheese	100 g/3½ oz
¼ cup	port	4 tbsp
	salt	
	pepper	

1. Put the onions in a casserole with the butter and the white wine. Cover and microwave on HIGH for 6 minutes.
2. Sprinkle the flour over the onions and stir well. Add 1¼ cups (300 ml/½ pint) of water and microwave on HIGH for 4 minutes, stirring with a hand whisk after each minute.
3. Stir in the consommé, cover and microwave on HIGH for 3-4 minutes, just to boiling point. Stir after 2 minutes of the cooking time.
4. Toast the bread and put on a plate. Put the cheese in a dish.

5. When the soup is ready, stir in the port. Add salt and pepper to taste.
6. Place a slice of toasted bread in each of 4 soup plates and spoon grated cheese on top. Pour the soup into each soup plate and serve very hot.

Onion Soup with Roquefort Cheese

00.10   00.15
Serves 4

American	Ingredients	Metric/Imperial
7 oz	finely chopped onions	200 g/7 oz
3 tbsp	butter	1½ tbsp
1 quart	milk	1 litre/1¾ pints
¼ tsp	curry powder	¼ tsp
1 cup	Roquefort cheese	75 g/2½ oz
1	egg	1
	salt	
	pepper	

1. Put the onions in a large casserole with the butter, cover and microwave on HIGH for 5 minutes.
2. Pour the milk over the onions and stir in the curry powder, cover and microwave for a further 8-10 minutes on HIGH until the milk reaches the boil. Take care that it does not boil over.
3. Mix together the Roquefort and the egg in a soup tureen.
4. Stir in ¼ cup (3-4 tablespoons) of the milk and onion mixture, stir well, then add the remaining mixture, stirring constantly.
5. Add salt and pepper to taste. Serve immediately.

Cream of Onion Soup

	00.15	00.13	
	Serves 4		

American	Ingredients	Metric/Imperial
½ lb	thinly sliced onions	225 g/8 oz
3 tbsp	butter	1½ tbsp
1 tsp	sugar	1 tsp
3 tbsp	all purpose (plain) flour	2 tbsp
1	bayleaf	1
2	chicken bouillon (stock) cubes	2
	salt	
	pepper	
¼ tsp	grated nutmeg	¼ tsp
2	egg yolks	2
¼ cup	sour cream (crème fraîche)	4½ tbsp

1. Put the onions in a large casserole with the butter and sugar. Cover and microwave on HIGH for 5 minutes.
2. Sprinkle the flour over the onions and stir well. Add 1¼ cups (300 ml/½ pint) of hot water. Stir thoroughly.
3. Add the bayleaf. Microwave on HIGH for 3 minutes, stirring after every minute with a hand whisk.
4. Crumble the bouillon (stock) cubes into the casserole. Stir in a further 1¼ cups (300 ml/½ pint) of hot water, cover and microwave on HIGH for 5 minutes.
5. Discard the bayleaf. Purée the contents of the casserole in a food processor. Taste before seasoning with salt and pepper.
6. Add the grated nutmeg.
7. Mix together the egg yolks and cream carefully, in a soup tureen. Gradually add the purée, stirring constantly with a hand whisk. Serve hot.

French onion soup

Iced Cucumber Soup

	00.10 plus chilling time	00.13

American	Ingredients	Metric/Imperial
2	sliced shallots	2
2 tbsp	butter	1 tbsp
1	large, peeled diced cucumber	1
1	chicken bouillon (stock) cube	1
¼ tsp	sugar	¼ tsp
3 tbsp	fresh lemon juice	2 tbsp
	salt	
	pepper	
1	small bunch mint	1
2	pots natural flavor yogurt	2

Iced cucumber soup,
Cream of avocado soup with salmon caviar

1. Put the shallots in a casserole with the butter. Cover and microwave on HIGH for 3 minutes.
2. Add the cucumber to the shallots.
3. Crumble the bouillon (stock) cube over the mixture.
4. Add the sugar and 1 cup (250 ml/8 fl oz) of water. Stir well, cover and microwave on HIGH for 10 minutes.
5. Purée the mixture in a food processor.
6. Stir in ¼ cup (4½ tablespoons) of water, the lemon juice and salt and pepper to taste. Leave to cool, then chill in the refrigerator for at least 2 hours.
7. Just before serving, rinse the mint and chop finely. Stir the yogurts into the soup, sprinkle the mint over and serve.

Cream of Avocado Soup with Salmon Caviar

	00.05 Serves 4	00.05

American	Ingredients	Metric/Imperial
2	avocado pears	2
4 tbsp	fresh lemon juice	3 tbsp
2	chicken bouillon (stock) cubes	2
¼ cup	sour cream (crème fraîche)	4½ tbsp
	salt	
	pepper	
1	small jar salmon caviar	1

1. Pour 2¼ cups (500 ml/18 fl oz) of water into a bowl and microwave on HIGH for 5 minutes.
2. Halve, stone and peel the avocado pears and slice into strips. Add the lemon juice and purée until smooth in a food processor.
3. When the water is very hot, crumble the bouillon (stock) cubes into it. Pour this liquid into the food processor and stir in the sour cream (crème fraîche). Purée once more. Add salt and pepper to taste (the soup should not be too salty).
4. Pour the soup into 4 bowls. Spoon 1 teaspoon of salmon caviar on each and serve.

Avocado Soup

00.05 00.07

Serves 4

American	Ingredients	Metric/Imperial
2	large avocado pears	2
¼ cup	fresh lime juice	3 tbsp
1	chicken bouillon (stock) cube	1
¼ cup	milk	4½ tbsp
2 tbsp	chopped fresh dill	2 tbsp
	salt	
	pepper	

1. Pour 2¼ cups (500 ml/18 fl oz) of water into a bowl and microwave on HIGH for 5 minutes.
2. Halve the avocados and remove the stones. Peel the half avocados, cut into small pieces and put into a food processor. Pour the lime juice over and purée.
3. When the water is very hot, crumble the chicken bouillon (stock) cube into it. Stir until dissolved. Pour the bouillon (stock) into the food processor. Add the milk.
4. Return the mixture to the bowl. Add the chopped dill. Add salt and pepper to taste. Reheat on HIGH for 2 minutes.
5. Pour into a heated soup tureen and serve at once.

Avocado soup

Hors D'Oeuvres

Mushroom vol-au-vents

Mushroom Vol-au-Vents

00.05 Serves 4 | 00.12

American	Ingredients	Metric/Imperial
1	very finely chopped shallot	1
¼ cup	butter	3 tbsp
12 oz	tiny white button mushrooms	350 g/12 oz
3 tbsp	fresh lemon juice	2 tbsp
	salt	
	pepper	
2 tbsp	all-purpose (plain) flour	1 tbsp
¼ cup	sour cream (crème fraîche)	4½ tbsp
4	cooked vol-au-vent cases	4
3 oz	cooked ham	75 g/3 oz
1	egg yolk	1
3 tbsp	cognac	2 tbsp

1. Put the shallot in a casserole with 1 tablespoon of butter, cover and microwave on HIGH for 2 minutes.
2. Wipe the mushrooms with a damp cloth or kitchen paper and cut into thin slices. Pour the lemon juice over.
3. Add the mushrooms and 3 (2) tablespoons of water to the casserole, stir well and add salt and pepper to taste. Cover and microwave on HIGH for 5 minutes.
4. When the mushrooms are cooked, drain and set aside the liquid.
5. Put the remaining butter into a bowl and melt on HIGH for 1 minute. Stir in the flour until smooth. Add the reserved liquid from the mushrooms. Microwave on HIGH for 1 minute, stir and microwave for a further 1 minute on HIGH.
6. Add the sour cream (crème fraîche) and microwave a further 1 minute on HIGH. Taste and adjust seasoning.
7. Line the base of the microwave oven with kitchen paper. Put the 4 vol-au-vent cases on it and heat them on HIGH for 1½ minutes.
8. Cut the ham into cubes and add to the sauce.
9. Mix the egg yolk with the cognac and pour over the mushrooms. Stir in the sauce. Fill the vol-au-vent cases with the mixture and serve at once.

Mushrooms à la grecque

00.10 plus chilling time | 00.10

American	Ingredients	Metric/Imperial
1 lb	white button mushrooms	450 g/1 lb
3 tbsp	lemon juice	2 tbsp
3 tbsp	tomato concentrate	2 tbsp
¾ cup	dry white wine	200 ml/7 fl oz
3 tbsp	olive oil	2 tbsp
½ tsp	sugar	½ tsp
1	bayleaf	1
1	sprig thyme	1
½ tsp	coriander seeds	½ tsp
1	dried red chili	1
	salt	
	pepper	
1 tbsp	chopped parsley	1 tbsp

1. Wipe the mushrooms with a damp cloth or kitchen paper. Cut the larger mushrooms into quarters. Pour over the lemon juice.
2. Mix the tomato concentrate and white wine together. Add the olive oil, sugar, bayleaf, thyme, coriander and chili. Add salt and pepper to taste.
3. Put the mushrooms into a casserole. Pour the marinade over, cover and microwave on HIGH for 8-10 minutes, depending on the size of the mushrooms. They should be crisp to the bite.
4. Leave to cool at room temperature. Remove the thyme and bayleaf and chill in a refrigerator for 24 hours.
5. Sprinkle the mushrooms with chopped parsley before serving.

Previous page: Chicken salad with lamb's lettuce

Spinach and Chervil Ring Mold (Mould)

00.15 plus chilling time | 00.15

American	Ingredients	Metric/Imperial
1	*can frozen chervil soup*	*1*
7 oz	*frozen chopped spinach*	*200 g/7 oz*
1	*grated zucchini (courgette)*	*1*
½ cup	*fresh lemon juice*	*6 tbsp*
2 tbsp	*gelatin (gelatine)*	*2 tbsp*
3	*natural flavor yogurts*	*3*
2 tbsp	*mustard*	*1 tbsp*
	pepper	
	lemon slices	
	tomatoes	
	fresh watercress	

1. Put the frozen chervil soup and the frozen spinach into a dish with 3 (2) tablespoons of water. Cover and microwave on HIGH for 5 minutes.
2. Stir the contents of the dish to break them up. Cover and microwave on HIGH for a further 2 minutes. Leave to stand for 5 minutes. Stir carefully.
3. Put the zucchini (courgette) in a small dish, cover and microwave on HIGH for 2 minutes.
4. Put ¼ cup (4 tablespoons) of lemon juice into a bowl and add the gelatin (gelatine). Leave to swell for 2 minutes. Put the bowl in the microwave oven and dissolve for 1 minute on LOW.
5. Add the gelatin (gelatine) mixture to the hot chervil and spinach.
6. Add the grated zucchini (courgette). Stir carefully. Leave to cool.
7. Add two of the yogurts to the cooled mixture. Pour into a ring mold (mould) and chill in the refrigerator for at least 6 hours.
8. Just before serving, prepare the sauce: mix together the mustard, lemon juice, pepper and the remaining yogurt. Pour the sauce into a sauceboat.
9. Plunge the mold (mould) into hot water for a few seconds and turn out on to a serving dish. Serve with lemon slices, tomato quarters and fresh watercress.

Spinach and chervil ring mold (mould)

Apple and Onion Ring Mold (Mould)

□▷ 00.15 00.25
plus chilling time

American	Ingredients	Metric/Imperial
1¼ lb	very finely sliced onions	500 g/1¼ lb
1 lb	apples	450 g /1 lb
5	eggs	5
4 tbsp	sour cream (crème fraîche)	3 tbsp
1 tsp	curry powder	1 tsp
½ tsp	garlic powder	½ tsp
	salt	
	pepper	
1 tsp	butter	1 tsp
1 tsp	Dijon mustard	1 tsp
3 tbsp	sherry vinegar	2 tbsp
3 tbsp	walnut oil	2 tbsp
3 tbsp	peanut oil	2 tbsp
1	frisée lettuce	1
1-2	hearts of radicchio	1-2
7 oz	pressed goose	200 g/7 oz

1. Put the onions in a dish with 1 tablespoon of water, cover and microwave on HIGH for 7 minutes.
2. Peel, core and seed the apples and cut into quarters, then into thin strips.
3. Put the onions in a strainer (sieve). Place the apples in the dish, cover and microwave on HIGH for 4 minutes.
4. Purée the onions and apples in a food processor and leave to cool.
5. Break the eggs into a bowl and whisk with a hand-beater.
6. Add the apple and onion purée, sour cream (crème fraîche), curry powder, garlic powder, salt and pepper. Stir carefully.
7. Butter the base and sides of a Pyrex ring mold (mould) 10 inches (22 cm) in diameter. Pour the mixture into it. Cover with saran wrap (cling film) and make several holes in the film with a fork. Microwave on HIGH for 14 minutes. Check whether the mixture is cooked by gently moving the ring mold (mould) from left to right: you should not be able to hear any liquid moving inside the container.
8. Leave to cool completely at room temperature, then chill in the refrigerator for at least 2 hours.
9. Just before serving, mix together the mustard, vinegar, walnut oil, peanut oil and salt and pepper to taste.
10. Rinse the salads thoroughly and cut the leaves into small pieces. Put into a salad bowl and toss with the vinaigrette.
11. Trim any fat from the pressed goose. Cut the meat into very fine strips.
12. Pass a knife blade round the edges of the mold (mould) and turn out on to a serving dish.
13. Put some of the salad in the center of the ring. Arrange the strips of goose decoratively on the mousse. Serve with the salad.

Green Bean Salad with Chicken Livers

□▷ 00.10 00.11
Serves 4

American	Ingredients	Metric/Imperial
14 oz	very young green beans	400 g/14 oz
½ tsp	garlic powder	½ tsp
	salt	
	pepper	
4	chicken livers	4
5 oz	smoked streaky bacon, rind removed, cut into strips	150 g/5 oz
½	lemon	½
3 tbsp	sour cream (crème fraîche)	2 tbsp
2 tbsp	mustard	1 tbsp
1 tbsp	chopped parsley	1 tbsp

1. Top-and-tail the green beans and cut into 1 inch (2.5 cm) lengths. Rinse and put on a dish with ¼ cup (3 tablespoons) of water. Sprinkle with garlic powder, salt and pepper. Cover and microwave on HIGH for 6 minutes. Take care not to overcook, the beans should be crisp.
2. Rinse the chicken livers and chop into pieces.
3. Put the bacon on a plate and microwave, uncovered, for 1 minute on HIGH.
4. Add the chicken livers, salt and pepper. Cover and microwave on HIGH for 2 minutes.
5. Squeeze the lemon. Mix together the sour cream (crème fraîche), mustard and lemon juice in a bowl. Add salt and pepper to taste. Heat for 2 minutes in the microwave oven on MEDIUM.
6. Arrange the green beans in a serving dish. Add the chicken livers and bacon. Pour the sauce over. Sprinkle with chopped parsley and serve.

Salad of Baby Onions

□▷ 00.20 00.22
plus chilling time

American	Ingredients	Metric/Imperial
1 lb	firm ripe tomatoes	450 g/1 lb
1	stick celery, cut into matchstick (julienne) strips	1
2	crushed garlic cloves	2
1	sprig thyme	1
1	bayleaf	1
¼ cup	white wine	4½ tbsp
3 tbsp	vinegar	2 tbsp
2 tbsp	sugar	1 tbsp
¼ tsp	Cayenne pepper	¼ tsp
	salt	
	pepper	
1 lb	peeled new baby onions	450 g/1 lb
¼ cup	washed golden raisins (sultanas)	50 g/2 oz
4 tbsp	olive oil	3 tbsp

Salad of baby onions

1. Rinse the tomatoes and remove the stalks. Make several incisions in the skin with a sharp knife. Put in the microwave oven on a double layer of kitchen paper. Cover and microwave on HIGH for 2 minutes.

2. Skin the tomatoes, chop coarsely and put in the bowl of a food processor.

3. Add the celery and garlic and purée until smooth.

4. Pour the purée into a small casserole. Add the thyme, bayleaf, white wine, vinegar, sugar, Cayenne pepper and salt and pepper to taste. Stir well. Put in the microwave oven, uncovered, and cook on HIGH for 10 minutes, stirring midway through the cooking time.

5. Add the onions and golden raisins (sultanas) and pour over the olive oil. Cover and microwave on HIGH for 10 minutes. Prick the onions with a toothpick (cocktail stick) to test whether they are tender. Actual cooking time will vary according to the size of the onions.

6. Leave to cool. Discard the thyme and bayleaf and chill in the refrigerator for 2 hours. Serve very cold.

Warm Beetroot Salad with Bacon

◤	00.10 Serves 4	00.23	〰

American	Ingredients	Metric/Imperial
10½ oz	uncooked beetroot, peeled and grated	300 g/10½ oz
2	finely chopped shallots	2
¼ lb	lean smoked bacon, rind removed, chopped into thin strips	100 g/4 oz
1 tsp	mustard	1 tsp
2 tbsp	vinegar	1 tbsp
4 tbsp	oil	3 tbsp
	salt	
	pepper	

1. Put the beetroot in a small casserole with ¼ cup (4½ tablespoons) of water. Cover and microwave on HIGH for 15 minutes. Leave to stand for 5 minutes.

2. Put the shallots and the bacon in a small dish and microwave, uncovered, on HIGH for 3 minutes.

3. Mix together the mustard, vinegar, oil, salt and pepper. Whisk thoroughly with a hand whisk until the sauce emulsifies. Pour over the shallots and bacon and stir well.

4. Put the beetroot in a bowl, add the shallot and bacon mixture, stir well.

5. Serve at once.

Squash Melon Mousse

	00.09	00.21	
	plus chilling time		

American	Ingredients	Metric/Imperial
1¼ lb	squash melon	500 g/1¼ lb
1	can cream of chicken soup (frozen)	1
¼ cup	cognac	4 tbsp
2 tbsp	gelatin (gelatine)	2 tbsp
¼ lb	pâté de foie gras	125 g/4 oz

1. Cut the squash melon into 1 inch (2.5 cm) slices and peel. Cube the slices, removing the pith and seeds in the center. Put the cubed flesh into a casserole with ¼ cup (3 tablespoons) of water. Cover and microwave on HIGH for 10 minutes.

2. When the squash is tender, drain in a strainer (sieve).

3. Put the cream of chicken soup into the casserole, cover and leave to defrost for 5 minutes on HIGH. Turn the casserole round and defrost it covered for a further 5 minutes on HIGH.

4. Dissolve the gelatin (gelatine) in a cup with the cognac. Leave to swell.

5. Purée the squash in a food processor and leave the purée in the food processor bowl.

6. Put the cognac and gelatin (gelatine) in the microwave oven for 1 minute on LOW . Stir and pour into the squash purée.

7. Add the defrosted cream of chicken soup and purée, gradually adding the pâté de foie gras.

8. Pass the purée through a fine strainer (sieve). Pour the mixture into a 2½ cup (600 ml/1 pint) mold (mould) and chill in the refrigerator for at least 8 hours.

9. Just before serving, plunge the mold (mould) into hot water for a few seconds. Slide the blade of a knife between the mousse and the sides of the mold (mould) and turn out on to a serving dish.

10. Serve this delicate mousse with toast and butter, or garnish with cherry tomatoes and serve with a green salad. This dish is also delicious made with Jerusalem artichokes.

Squash melon mousse

Olive and Walnut Loaf

00.10 plus cooling time — 00.23

American	Ingredients	Metric/Imperial
2 cups	wholewheat (wholemeal) flour	225 g/8 oz
1 tsp	salt	1 tsp
1 pkt	yeast	1 pkt
4	beaten eggs	4
⅔ cup	oil	150 ml/¼ pint
¾ cup	dry white wine	200 ml/7 fl oz
2	natural flavor yogurts	2
½ cup	coarsely chopped walnuts	50 g/2 oz
5 oz	pimento-stuffed green olives	150 g/5 oz

1. Sieve the flour, salt and yeast into a bowl.
2. Stir the eggs into the flour.
3. Add the oil, white wine and yogurt. Stir carefully.
4. Add the walnuts to the mixture and stir well.
5. Put the mixture in a Pyrex cake mold (mould). Sprinkle the olives on top. Do not cover.
6. Microwave for 20 minutes on HIGH.
7. Turn out the loaf on to a rack. If not fully cooked underneath, return to the oven, upside down, and microwave for a further 3 minutes, then leave to cool.
This bread slices perfectly. Serve it as a starter with a selection of raw vegetables (crudités) or broil (grill) it and serve it hot with cheese.

Charlotte of Pumpkin Squash

00.30 plus chilling time — 00.23

American	Ingredients	Metric/Imperial
1¾ lb	pumpkin squash	750 g/1¾ lb
12 oz	can frozen chicken soup	350 g/12 oz
1 tsp	mild curry powder	1 tsp
2 tsp	dried tarragon	2 tsp
½ cup	dry sherry	5 tbsp
2½ tbsp	gelatin (gelatine)	2½ tbsp
⅔ cup	whipping cream	150 ml/¼ pint
1 tsp	lemon juice	1 tsp

1. Cut the squash into quarters and remove the seeds and pith. Peel each quarter and slice thinly. Put the sliced squash into a dish with 2 tablespoons of water. Cover and microwave on HIGH for 12 minutes. Leave to cool for 5 minutes.
2. Put the frozen chicken soup in another dish. Cover and microwave on HIGH for 5 minutes to defrost.
3. Add the curry powder and dried tarragon to the block of chicken soup, turn upside down and leave to defrost for a further 5 minutes on HIGH.
4. Put the squash into a strainer (sieve) to drain, then purée in a food processor.
5. Pour the sherry into a cup. Sprinkle the gelatin (gelatine) over, leave to swell for 2 minutes, then put the cup in the microwave oven and dissolve the gelatin (gelatine) for 1 minute on LOW.

Charlotte of pumpkin squash

6. Stir the chicken soup vigorously and add the sherry and gelatin (gelatine) mixture. Add the puréed squash. Leave to cool.
7. Whip the cream and add to the cooked mixture.
8. Add the lemon juice. Pour into a charlotte mold (mould) or bowl. Chill in the refrigerator for at least 8 hours.
9. Just before serving, plunge the mold (mould) into hot water for several seconds and turn out the mousse on to a serving dish. Serve cold.

Leeks with Chopped Egg

00.10 Serves 4 — 00.25

American	Ingredients	Metric/Imperial
1	egg	1
8	young leeks, white part only	8
	salt	
	pepper	
¼ cup	white wine	4 tbsp
1 tsp	mustard	1 tsp
2 tbsp	wine vinegar	1 tbsp
4 tbsp	oil	3 tbsp
1 tbsp	chopped parsley	1 tbsp
1 tbsp	chopped chives	1 tbsp

1. Put the egg into a small pan filled with water and boil for 15 minutes on a conventional cooker.
2. Remove the base and the outer leaves of the leeks and cut them almost in half lengthwise. Rinse carefully and leave to drain.
3. Sprinkle salt and pepper in the base of a rectangular dish. Put the leeks in it, head-to-tail, pour the white wine over, cover and microwave on HIGH for 10 minutes.
4. Plunge the egg into cold water and shell it. Remove the yolk and set aside. Chop the white finely.
5. Mix together the mustard, vinegar, oil, egg white, parsley, chives, salt and pepper.
6. Drain the leeks over a bowl, reserving the liquid and put them in a serving dish.
7. Add the cooking liquid to the sauce and pour over the leeks. Press the egg yolk through a sieve over the leeks. Serve warm.

Leek salad

Leek Salad

	00.10	00.16	
	Serves 4		

American	Ingredients	Metric/Imperial
1 lb	leeks, white part only	450 g/1 lb
2	tomatoes	2
	salt	
	pepper	
4 tbsp	white wine	2 tbsp
½ tsp	thyme	½ tsp
½ tsp	sugar	½ tsp
2 tbsp	olive oil	1 tbsp

1. Remove the base and the outer skin of the leeks. Cut in half lengthwise, wash thoroughly and leave to drain.
2. Make an incision in the form of a cross in the top of each tomato. Put in the microwave oven for 1 minute on HIGH. Skin and chop coarsely.
3. Sprinkle salt and pepper in the base of a dish and arrange the leeks on it. Pour the white wine over. Cover with the chopped tomatoes. Sprinkle with thyme and sugar. Add more salt and pepper and sprinkle with olive oil.
4. Cover and microwave on HIGH for 15 minutes.
5. Serve this dish warm or cold.

Vegetable Terrine with Tomato Sauce

	00.20	00.44	
	plus chilling time		

American	Ingredients	Metric/Imperial
5 oz	finely sliced onions	150 g/5 oz
1¼ lb	eggplant (aubergines), sliced into rounds	600 g/1¼ lb
½ tsp	garlic powder	½ tsp
½ tsp	mixed herbs	½ tsp
3 tbsp	white wine	2 tbsp
½ cup	olive oil	5 tbsp
1	large green bell pepper	1
2	large red bell peppers	2
1 lb	small zucchini (courgettes)	450 g/1 lb
¼ cup	sour cream (crème fraîche)	4½ tbsp
4	eggs	4
¼ tsp	curry powder	¼ tsp
	salt	
	pepper	
1 tsp	butter	1 tsp
3	canned tomatoes	3
1½ tsp	basil preserved in oil	1½ tsp
2 tbsp	vinegar	1 tbsp
¼ tsp	sugar	¼ tsp
3	black olives	3

1. Put the onions in a casserole and microwave on HIGH for 2 minutes.

2. Add the eggplant (aubergines), garlic powder, mixed herbs, white wine and half the olive oil. Cover and microwave on HIGH for 12 minutes.

3. Rinse and seed the bell peppers and remove the pith. Set aside one of the red bell peppers. Cut the second red bell pepper and the green bell pepper into strips and dice finely.

4. Rinse and trim the zucchini (courgettes), cut in four lengthwise and then into small dice.

5. Put the bell peppers into a small casserole, cover and microwave on HIGH for 5 minutes.

6. Add the zucchini (courgettes) and 3 (2) tablespoons of water. Cover and microwave on HIGH for 5 minutes.

7. Drain the eggplant (aubergines) and onions and purée in a food processor. Add the sour cream (crème fraîche), eggs, curry powder, salt and pepper. Purée once more. Pour the mixture into a bowl.

8. Drain the bell peppers and the zucchini (courgettes) carefully. Stir into the eggplant (aubergine) and onion mixture.

9. Butter the base of a 1½ quart (1.5 litre/2¾ pint) Pyrex cake mold (mould). Pour the vegetable mixture into it. Microwave on HIGH for 18 minutes. When the terrine is cooked, leave to cool at room temperature then chill in the refrigerator for at least 12 hours.

10. Just before serving, prepare the sauce. Put the canned tomatoes into a food processor.

11. Put the reserved red bell pepper on a double layer of kitchen paper and microwave on HIGH for 2 minutes.

12. Plunge the red bell pepper into cold water. Cut into four and remove the skin as you would fillet a fish: place it skin side down on a board and slide a sharp knife between the skin and the flesh.

13. Add the red bell pepper to the tomatoes in the food processor and purée.

14. Add the remaining ingredients and the remaining olive oil and purée again. Pour into a sauceboat.

15. Turn out the terrine on to a long serving dish. Pour a little of the tomato and pepper sauce along the top.

16. Garnish with the black olives and serve.

If the center of the terrine appears a little soft to the touch after cooking, it will firm up during the refrigeration period.

Vegetable terrine with tomato sauce

Vegetable Mousse, Provençale Style

	00.25	00.28
	plus chilling time	

American	Ingredients	Metric/Imperial
2	red bell peppers	2
1 lb	zucchini (courgettes)	450 g/1 lb
½ lb	sliced onions	225 g/8 oz
4	sliced garlic cloves	4
1½ lb	eggplant (aubergines)	600 g/1½ lb
3 tbsp	concentrated tomato juice	2 tbsp
½ tsp	curry powder	½ tsp
½ tsp	sugar	½ tsp
	salt	
	pepper	
½ cup	tarragon vinegar	6 tbsp
3 tbsp	gelatin (gelatine)	3 tbsp
2	pots natural yogurt	2
1	egg white	1

1. Rinse and seed the bell peppers and remove the pith. Cut into quarters lengthwise and lay side by side on a dish. Microwave on HIGH for 7 minutes.

2. Peel and top-and-tail the zucchini (courgettes). Cut in half lengthwise and dice. Put into a dish, cover and microwave on HIGH for 5 minutes.

3. Put the onions and garlic in a dish with 1 tablespoon of water. Cover and microwave on HIGH for 5 minutes.

4. Remove the stalks and peel the eggplant (aubergines) and cut into ½ inch (1.75 cm) slices. Put the slices in a dish with ¼ cup (3 tablespoons) of water. Cover and microwave on HIGH for 10 minutes.

5. Drain the bell peppers, zucchini (courgettes) and onions in a colander. Put into a food processor. Add the tomato juice, curry powder, sugar, salt and pepper. Purée until smooth. Pour the mixture into a large bowl.

6. Pour the vinegar into a bowl. Sprinkle the gelatin (gelatine) over and leave to swell.

7. Put the eggplant (aubergines) into a colander.

8. Put the bowl containing the vinegar and gelatin (gelatine) into the microwave oven and leave to dissolve for 1 minute on LOW. Add the gelatin (gelatine) and vinegar mixture to the bowl and mix thoroughly.

9. Purée the eggplant (aubergines) in the food processor.

10. Add the eggplant (aubergine) purée to the bowl.

11. Stir in the yogurt. Taste and adjust seasoning: this dish should be highly seasoned. Leave to cool.

12. When the mixture is cool, add a pinch of salt to the egg white and whisk until it forms firm peaks. Fold gently into the eggplant (aubergine) mixture. Pour the mixture into a rectangular Pyrex terrine dish and chill in the refrigerator for 12 hours.

13. Just before serving, slide the blade of a knife between the mixture and the terrine dish. Plunge the dish into hot water for several seconds, then turn out on to a serving dish.

Cabbage Terrine with Chestnut Purée

	00.20	00.25
	plus chilling time	

American	Ingredients	Metric/Imperial
1	green cabbage	1
7	shallots	7
5 oz	smoked streaky bacon or pork, rind removed and chopped into small pieces	150 g/5 oz
½ lb	coarsely chopped cooked ham	225 g/8 oz
½	can chestnut purée	½
1	egg	1
4 tbsp	sour cream (crème fraîche)	3 tbsp
¼ tsp	cinnamon	¼ tsp
½ tsp	allspice	½ tsp
½ tsp	ground cumin	½ tsp
	salt	
	pepper	
¼ cup	white port	4 tbsp
1 lb	cooking apples (Bramleys), peeled, cored and finely sliced	450 g/1 lb

1. Put 1 cup (250 ml/8 fl oz) of water in the lower compartment of a microwave steamer. Cover and microwave on HIGH for 3 minutes.

2. Remove 5 large, whole leaves from the cabbage and set aside. Remove the hard stalk and shred the remaining cabbage with a kitchen cleaver. Put the whole leaves into the perforated compartment of the steamer and put into the steamer. Cover and microwave on HIGH for 3 minutes.

3. Remove the cooked cabbage leaves and arrange on a clean dish cloth. Put the shredded cabbage in the perforated compartment of the steamer. Cover and microwave on HIGH for 5 minutes.

4. Peel the shallots and set three aside. Chop the remaining four.

5. Put the bacon or pork and the chopped shallots on a small dish. Do not cover. Microwave on HIGH for 2 minutes.

6. Put the cooked shredded cabbage into a colander and leave to drain.

7. Purée the ham, bacon or pork and chopped shallots in a food processor, adding the chestnut purée in small spoonfuls, the egg, sour cream (crème fraîche), cinnamon, allspice and cumin. Add salt and pepper. Pour the mixture into a large bowl, add the shredded cabbage and stir thoroughly.

8. Line a 2 quart (2 litre/3½ pint) oval terrine dish with four of the whole cabbage leaves, making sure they overlap each other. Pour the mixture into the terrine and fold the edges of the cabbage leaves over. Cover with the remaining cabbage leaf. Press with the palm of your hand. Cover and microwave on HIGH for 5 minutes.

9. When the terrine is cooked, remove the cover and leave to cool at room temperature. Chill in the refrigerator for 1 hour.

10. To prepare the sauce: chop the remaining 3 shallots finely and put in a small bowl with the port. Cover and microwave on HIGH for 2 minutes.

11. Add the apples to the shallot and port mixture. Cover and microwave on HIGH for 5 minutes.

12. Purée the mixture in a food processor. Add salt and pepper and purée until smooth. Leave to cool.

13. Just before serving, turn out the terrine on to a serving dish and serve with the apple sauce.

Vegetable mousse, Provençale style

Three-Vegetable Ham Loaf

	00.20 plus chilling time	00.15	

American	Ingredients	Metric/Imperial
10½ oz	zucchini (courgettes)	300 g/10½ oz
	salt	
	pepper	
¼ lb	baby carrots	125 g/4 oz
¼ cup	wine vinegar	4 tbsp
1 tbsp	gelatin (gelatine)	1 tbsp
¼	can petits pois	¼
1 lb	cooked ham	450 g/1 lb
2	egg whites	2
½ cup	oil	6 tbsp
2	chopped shallots	2
1	stick celery, (leaves whole) cut into matchstick (Julienne) strips	1
1 lb	coarsely chopped tomatoes	450 g/1 lb
¼ tsp	dried thyme	¼ tsp
½ tsp	sugar	½ tsp
4 tbsp	dry white wine	3 tbsp
2 tbsp	olive oil	1 tbsp

1. Rinse and top-and-tail the zucchini (courgettes) and cut into long strips. Put these in a dish with 3 (2) tablespoons of water. Add salt and pepper. Cover and microwave on HIGH for 3 minutes.

2. Scrape the carrots and cut into matchstick (julienne) strips. Put the strips in a dish with 3 (2) tablespoons of water. Cover and microwave on HIGH for 6 minutes.

3. Put the vinegar in a cup and sprinkle the gelatin (gelatine) over. Leave to swell for 2 minutes, then dissolve in the microwave oven for 1 minute on LOW.

4. Drain the petits pois.

5. Remove the rind and fat from the ham and cut it into small pieces. Purée in a food processor.

6. Add the egg whites one at a time, the oil, vinegar and gelatin (gelatine) mixture, liquidizing as you do so. Taste and adjust seasonings.

7. Line the base of a cake mold (mould) with non-stick parchment (greaseproof paper) and oil lightly. Spread a layer of ham mousse in the base of the mold (mould), followed by a layer of zucchini (courgettes), and a layer of ham mousse. Spread a layer of carrots, followed by another layer of ham mousse and a layer of petits pois. Finish with a covering layer of ham mousse. Press well down. Cover and chill in the refrigerator for 8 hours.

8. To make the sauce, put the shallots, celery strips, celery leaves and chopped tomatoes into a bowl. Add the thyme, sugar, white wine, olive oil and salt and pepper to taste. Cover and microwave on HIGH for 5 minutes.

9. Discard the celery leaves and purée the vegetables in a food processor. Taste and adjust seasoning. Keep the sauce in the refrigerator until just before serving.

10. Turn out the ham loaf on to a serving dish. Pour the sauce into a sauceboat and serve cold.

Mediterranean carrot salad

4. Add the remaining oil in a thin trickle, beating constantly to obtain a thick mayonnaise. Add the remaining lemon juice. Taste and adjust seasoning.

5. Add the chopped parsley and the olives to the carrots. Pour the mayonnaise into a sauceboat and serve cold.

Artichokes with Lemon Sauce

	00.10	00.21	
	Serves 4		

American	Ingredients	Metric/Imperial
4	young globe artichokes	4
	salt	
½ cup	butter	115 g/4 oz
4 tbsp	fresh lemon juice	3 tbsp
3	egg yolks	3
	pepper	

1. Remove the stalks of the artichokes and take off the outer leaves. Rinse the artichokes in cold water. Stand side by side in a large casserole with ¼ cup (4 tablespoons) of water. Add salt. Cover and microwave on HIGH for 16-18 minutes, depending on the size of the vegetables. A leaf will pull out easily when cooked.

2. Leave the artichokes to stand for 5 minutes then turn upside-down in a strainer (sieve) to drain.

3. To prepare the sauce, cut the butter into tiny pieces and put into a bowl. Melt in the microwave oven on MEDIUM for 2 minutes.

4. Add the lemon juice and egg yolks and beat with a hand whisk. Microwave on MEDIUM for 1 minute. Whisk again. Add salt and pepper to taste. Pour the sauce into a sauceboat.

5. Put the artichokes on to a serving dish covered with a folded white table napkin.

6. Serve at once, with the sauce on the side.

Mediterranean Carrot Salad

	00.10	00.12	
	plus chilling time		

American	Ingredients	Metric/Imperial
1 lb	new young carrots	450 g/1 lb
4	crushed garlic cloves	4
2 tsp	sugar	2 tsp
	salt	
	pepper	
½ cup	oil	125 ml/4 fl oz
½ cup	fresh lemon juice	6 tbsp
1	egg yolk	1
1 tsp	mustard	1 tsp
1 tbsp	chopped parsley	1 tbsp
12	seedless black olives	12

1. Scrape the carrots, quarter lengthwise and then cut into ½ inch (1.25 cm) strips.

2. Put the carrots and garlic in a dish. Add the sugar and salt and pepper to taste. Sprinkle with 1½ tablespoons of oil and half the lemon juice. Cover and microwave on HIGH for 12 minutes. Leave to cool completely, then chill in the refrigerator.

3. Just before serving, mix together the egg yolk, mustard and salt and pepper to taste. Stir well.

Warm Carrot Salad

	00.10	00.12	
	Serves 4		

American	Ingredients	Metric/Imperial
1 lb	baby carrots, cut into thin rounds	450 g/1 lb
3 tbsp	white wine	2 tbsp
½ tsp	sugar	½ tsp
1	small crushed garlic clove	1
3 tbsp	wine vinegar	2 tbsp
4 tbsp	olive oil	3 tbsp
	salt	
	pepper	
8	seedless black olives	8
2 tbsp	mixed chopped fresh herbs	2 tbsp

1. Put the carrots into a casserole with the white wine and sugar. Cover and microwave on HIGH for 12 minutes.
2. Mix together the garlic, vinegar and olive oil. Add salt and pepper to taste.
3. When the carrots are cooked, put into a bowl and add the sauce. Stir well. Leave to cool for 5 minutes.
4. Add the olives and mixed herbs. Stir carefully and serve.

Stuffed Artichokes

	00.10	00.11
	Serves 4	

American	Ingredients	Metric/Imperial
4	frozen artichoke hearts	4
3 tbsp	fresh lemon juice	2 tbsp
1	finely diced small carrot	1
1	finely diced baby turnip	1
	salt	
	pepper	
3½ oz	cooked ham	100 g/3½ oz
3 tbsp	petits pois	2 tbsp
1 tbsp	chopped chervil	1 tbsp
3 tbsp	mayonnaise	2 tbsp
4	large lettuce leaves	4
4	black olives	4

1. Put the artichoke hearts, still frozen, into a casserole or on a plate, pour the lemon juice over, cover and microwave on HIGH for 5 minutes. Leave to cool in the casserole.
2. Put the carrot and turnip in a bowl with 3 (2) tablespoons of water. Add salt and pepper. Cover and microwave on HIGH for 6 minutes.
3. When the vegetables are cooked, drain under cold running water.
4. Cut the ham into dice the same size as the vegetables. Put it into a bowl with the carrot, turnip, petits pois and chopped chervil. Add the mayonnaise and stir carefully.
5. Rinse the lettuce leaves and pat dry on kitchen paper. Arrange on a serving platter. Drain the artichoke hearts and place one on each lettuce leaf. Carefully fill each one with the ham and vegetable mixture. Decorate with black olives and serve cold.

Stuffed artichokes

Artichokes with Crabmeat Salad

American	Ingredients	Metric/Imperial
1	egg	1
6	frozen artichoke hearts	6
¼ cup	fresh lemon juice	4 tbsp
	salt	
	pepper	
7 oz	frozen carrots and peas	200 g/7 oz
¼ lb	crabmeat	125 g/4 oz
1	egg yolk	1
1 tsp	mustard	1 tsp
¼ cup	oil	4½ tbsp
¼ cup	whipping cream	4½ tbsp
3 tsp	salmon caviar	3 tsp
3 tbsp	chopped fresh mixed herbs	3 tbsp

00.25 plus chilling time   00.12

1. Put the whole egg into a small saucepan of boiling water and boil on a conventional cooker for 10 minutes.
2. Put the frozen artichokes side by side, on a plate and sprinkle with three-quarters of the lemon juice. Add salt and pepper. Cover and microwave on HIGH for 6 minutes. The artichokes should still be quite firm. Leave to cool on the plate.
3. Put the frozen vegetables on another plate. Add salt and pepper and 3 tablespoons of water. Cover and microwave on HIGH for 6 minutes, stirring midway through the cooking time. Leave to cool on the plate.
4. Drain the crabmeat and break up with a fork.
5. Mix together the egg yolk and mustard in a bowl. Add salt and pepper to taste. Stir well. Gradually add the oil in a thin trickle to obtain a thick mayonnaise, beating constantly. Add the remaining lemon juice and beat again.
6. Whip the cream and fold gently into the mayonnaise.
7. Add the crabmeat. Taste and adjust seasoning.
8. Drain the cold vegetables. Add ¾ of the crabmeat mayonnaise and spoon over the artichokes generously.
9. Plunge the hard-boiled egg into cold water and peel it. Cut off both ends and slice carefully into 6 rounds. Put one round on each artichoke. Decorate with a little whirl of cream and a teaspoon of salmon caviar.
10. Sprinkle the whole with chopped mixed herbs and serve cold.

Artichokes with crabmeat salad

Artichoke Mousse with Pâté de Foie Gras

	00.15 plus chilling time	00.13

American	Ingredients	Metric/Imperial
1 lb	frozen artichoke hearts	450 g/1 lb
¼ cup	dry sherry	4½ tbsp
2 tbsp	gelatin (gelatine)	2 tbsp
¼ cup	fresh lemon juice	4 tbsp
5 oz	pâté de foie gras	150 g/5 oz
	dash of Tabasco sauce	
	salt	
	pepper	
1	egg white	1
	lamb's lettuce or radicchio	
6	chopped walnuts	6
1 tbsp	chopped chives	1 tbsp

1. Put the artichokes into a casserole with ¼ cup (3 tablespoons) of water. Cover and microwave on HIGH for 12 minutes.

2. Pour half the sherry into a cup. Sprinkle the gelatin (gelatine) over and leave to swell.

3. When the artichokes are cooked, drain and purée in a food processor, gradually adding the lemon juice.

4. Put the gelatin (gelatine) and sherry into the microwave and leave to dissolve for 1 minute on LOW. Stir well and add to the purée in the food processor. Purée again gradually adding the foie gras in little pieces and the remaining sherry.

5. Force the mixture through a fine strainer (sieve), pressing firmly with the back of a wooden spoon. Add a dash of Tabasco sauce and salt and pepper to taste: this dish should be highly seasoned. Leave to cool at room temperature.

6. Add a pinch of salt to the egg white and whisk to firm peaks. Fold gently into the artichoke purée. Pour the mixture into a 1 quart (1 litre/1¾ pint) mold (mould). Smooth the surface, cover with saran wrap (cling film) and chill in the refrigerator for at least 8 hours.

7. Just before serving, plunge the mold (mould) into hot water for several seconds and run the blade of a knife gently between the mousse and the sides of the container. Turn out on to a serving dish.

8. Sprinkle with chopped walnuts and chopped chives and serve with a salad.

Microwave hint: To cook vegetables in a cook bag by microwave, secure the ends of the bag loosely with an elastic band so that steam does not build up inside the bag and make it burst.

Artichokes with Prosciutto

Artichoke with Prosciutto

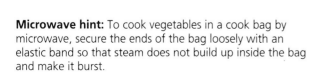

	00.05 Serves 6	00.09

American	Ingredients	Metric/Imperial
6	frozen artichoke hearts	6
3 tbsp	fresh lemon juice	2 tbsp
	salt	
	pepper	
15	slices Prosciutto	15
4	sticks young celery	4
2	finely chopped shallots	2
2 tsp	butter	2 tsp
3½ oz	coarsely chopped walnuts	100 g/3½ oz
2 tbsp	vinegar	1 tbsp
2 tbsp	mild mustard	1 tbsp
4 tbsp	oil	3 tbsp
3 tbsp	chopped parsley	3 tbsp

1. Put the frozen artichoke hearts side by side, in a dish and sprinkle the lemon juice over. Add salt and pepper. Microwave on HIGH for 6 minutes.

2. Cut 3 slices of the Prosciutto into thin strips.

3. Rinse the celery and cut into matchstick (julienne) strips.

4. Put the shallots and celery into a bowl with the butter and microwave on HIGH for 2 minutes. Add the strips of Prosciutto and chopped walnuts. Stir well. Heat for 1 minute on HIGH.

5. Mix together the vinegar, mustard, oil and parsley. Add pepper.

6. Put 1 artichoke heart on each plate and fill with the Prosciutto and nut mixture. Pour the vinaigrette sauce over. Arrange 2 slices of Prosciutto on each plate and serve warm.

Breton-style artichoke and potato salad

1. Put the artichokes into a small casserole. Sprinkle with lemon juice and season with salt and pepper. Cover and microwave on HIGH for 5 minutes.
2. Scrub the potatoes under cold running water and pat dry on kitchen paper. Prick the skin with a fork. Put in a circle on a double thickness of kitchen paper in the microwave oven and cook on HIGH for 5 minutes. Turn them over and microwave for a further 5 minutes.
3. Mix together the mustard, vinegar, sour cream (crème fraîche), salt and pepper. Add the oil in a thin trickle.
4. Slice the artichoke hearts.
5. Cover the potatoes with a cloth and leave to stand for 5 minutes.
6. Put the shallots in a bowl with the white wine. Microwave on HIGH for 3 minutes.
7. Peel the potatoes and slice into rounds.
8. Season the white wine and shallot mixture with salt and pepper and pour over the potatoes.
9. Arrange the lettuce, potatoes, artichokes, shrimp (prawns) and the pickled cucumbers in a bowl and pour the sauce over. Sprinkle with chives and serve.

Breton-style Artichoke & Potato Salad

00.12   00.18
Serves 4

American	Ingredients	Metric/Imperial
4	frozen artichoke hearts	4
3 tbsp	fresh lemon juice	2 tbsp
	salt	
	pepper	
4	large firm potatoes	4
2 tbsp	mustard	1 tbsp
2 tbsp	vinegar	1 tbsp
4 tbsp	sour cream (crème fraîche)	3 tbsp
3 tbsp	oil	2 tbsp
2	chopped shallots	2
¼ cup	white wine	4½ tbsp
1	small, rinsed Batavia lettuce	1
7 oz	shelled shrimp (prawns)	200 g/7 oz
2	sweet pickled cucumbers, cut into thin strips	2
2 tbsp	chopped chives	2 tbsp

Asparagus with Foie Gras Mousse

00.10   00.16
Serves 4

American	Ingredients	Metric/Imperial
1¾ lb	fresh asparagus	800 g/1¾ lb
1	very finely chopped shallot	1
¼ cup	sherry vinegar	4 tbsp
	salt	
	pepper	
3 tbsp	peanut oil	2 tbsp
3 tbsp	walnut oil	2 tbsp
1 tbsp	chopped chervil	1 tbsp
1	can pâté de foie gras	1

1. Peel the asparagus with a paring knife, starting from the tips. Remove the fibrous part of the stalks. Put 1 cup (250 ml/8 fl oz) of hot water into the lower compartment of a microwave steamer. Arrange the asparagus carefully in the perforated section of the steamer, put it into the steamer and cover. Microwave on HIGH for 12-14 minutes according to the size of the asparagus (prick with a fork to test for tenderness).
2. When the asparagus is cooked, set the perforated compartment to drain over a bowl of hot water to keep warm.
3. Put the shallot into a bowl with the vinegar. Heat in the microwave oven on MEDIUM for 1 minute.
4. Whisk together the salt, pepper, peanut oil, walnut oil and chopped chervil.
5. Cut the pâté de foie gras into 4 equal slices. Put on a plate and microwave on MEDIUM for 1 minute.
6. Put the hot asparagus on a serving dish. Lay the slices of foie gras in the center.
7. Pour the vinaigrette over and serve immediately.

Zucchini (Courgette) Loaf with Pink Sauce

00.15 *plus chilling time* 00.35

American	Ingredients	Metric/Imperial
¾ lb	frozen chicken soup	350 g/12 oz
⅔ cup	milk	150 ml/¼ pint
¾ lb	grated zucchini (courgettes)	350 g/12 oz
7 oz	grated eggplant (aubergines)	200 g/7 oz
1	crushed garlic clove	1
½ tsp	dried thyme	½ tsp
1 tsp	curry powder	1 tsp
	salt	
	pepper	
2	large beaten eggs	2
1 tsp	oil	1 tsp
10½ oz	red bell peppers, seeded and coarsely chopped	300 g/10½ oz
2 tbsp	concentrated tomato juice	1 tbsp
1 tsp	superfine (caster) sugar	1 tsp
3 tbsp	olive oil	2 tbsp
2 tbsp	wine vinegar	1 tbsp
	salad in season	
1 tbsp	chopped chives	1 tbsp
1 tbsp	chopped chervil	1 tbsp

1. Put the frozen chicken soup and the milk into a small casserole. Cover and defrost for 5 minutes in the microwave oven on HIGH. Remove from the oven, stir well, cover and microwave for a further 5 minutes on HIGH.
2. Mix together the zucchini (courgettes), eggplant (aubergines), garlic, ¼ teaspoon of thyme and the curry powder in a dish. Add salt and pepper to taste. Add 2 tablespoons of water. Microwave on HIGH for 4 minutes.
3. Beat the chicken soup with a hand whisk.
4. Drain the vegetables. Stir them into the beaten eggs.
5. Add the chicken soup and stir well. Taste and adjust seasoning.
6. Oil the base of a Pyrex cake mold (mould), cover the base with a piece of non-stick parchment (greaseproof paper) and oil that also. Pour the mixture into the mold (mould). Cover and microwave on HIGH for 10 minutes. Remove the cover and cook for a further 5 minutes. Leave to cool at room temperature, then chill in the refrigerator for 2 hours.
7. To prepare the sauce, put the red bell peppers in a small casserole with 1 tablespoon of water. Cover and microwave on HIGH for 6 minutes.
8. Drain the peppers and purée in the food processor, adding the concentrated tomato juice, ¼ teaspoon thyme, sugar, olive oil, vinegar and salt and pepper to taste.
9. Force the purée through a fine strainer (sieve), pressing it with the back of a wooden spoon. Chill in the refrigerator for 2 hours.
10. To serve, turn out the loaf on to a serving dish and garnish with chopped chives and chopped chervil. Serve with the sauce and a green side salad.

Zucchini (Courgette) Salad with Mint

00.10 *plus chilling time* 00.17

American	Ingredients	Metric/Imperial
1	thinly sliced onion	1
1½ lb	zucchini (courgettes)	600 g/1½ lb
3 tbsp	olive oil	2 tbsp
	salt	
	pepper	
1	lemon	1
1	sprig mint	1

1. Put the onion on a dish and microwave for 2 minutes on HIGH.
2. Rinse and top-and-tail the zucchini (courgettes). Quarter lengthwise, then chop into ½ inch (1.25 cm) cubes.
3. Add the zucchini (courgettes) to the onion and sprinkle the olive oil over. Add salt and pepper to taste. Cover and microwave on HIGH for 10 minutes. Leave to stand for 5 minutes.
4. Squeeze the lemon and sprinkle the juice over the vegetables, stirring well. Transfer the mixture to a bowl and chill in the refrigerator for 1 hour.
5. Rinse the mint and chop it finely. Sprinkle on top of the salad. Serve cold.

Zucchini (courgette) salad with mint

Stuffed Red Bell Peppers

00.10   **00.22**

Serves 4

American	Ingredients	Metric/Imperial
4	medium size red bell peppers	4
1	chopped onion	1
10	strips (rashers) streaky bacon, de-rinded	10
½ lb	ground (minced) beef and pork (combined)	225 g/8 oz
1	egg	1
5 tbsp	rolled oats	4 tbsp
	salt	
	pepper	

1. Cut the tops off the bell peppers to form lids. Scoop out the insides and discard the seeds. Put the peppers on a plate with ¼ cup (3 tablespoons) of cold water. Cook on HIGH for 5 minutes and drain.
2. Mix together the onion, one-third of the bacon, the ground (minced) meats, egg, oats, salt and pepper. Stuff the bell peppers with the mixture.
3. Stand the bell peppers upright in a deep dish with ½ cup (125 ml/4 fl oz) of water and microwave on HIGH for 5 minutes. Leave to stand for 3 minutes.
4. Put the remaining bacon evenly on top and cook on HIGH for 3 minutes. Put the lids on top and cook on HIGH for a further 3 minutes.

Zucchini (courgettes) with salmon filling

Zucchini (Courgettes) with Salmon Filling

00.15   **00.09**

Serves 4

American	Ingredients	Metric/Imperial
4	zucchini (courgettes)	4
5 oz	salmon steak	150 g/5 oz
	salt	
1	egg yolk	1
1 tsp	horseradish mustard	1 tsp
	pepper	
¼ cup	oil	4½ tbsp
3 tbsp	fresh lemon juice	2 tbsp
1 tbsp	chopped dill	1 tbsp
4	unshelled shrimp (prawns)	4

1. Rinse and top-and-tail the zucchini (courgettes). Peel a strip of skin lengthwise from each about ½ inch (1.25 cm) wide. Put the zucchini (courgettes) on a dish with 2 tablespoons of water. Cover and microwave on HIGH for 7 minutes.
2. Remove the zucchini (courgettes) carefully with a spatula and leave to cool.
3. Put the salmon on a small dish. Cover and microwave on HIGH for 2 minutes, then leave to cool.
4. With a teaspoon, carefully remove the pulp from the zucchini (courgettes) on the peeled side. Leave a thin layer of pulp in the vegetable. Salt the zucchini (courgette) shells and replace on the dish.
5. Remove the bones and skin from the salmon steaks. Purée the flesh with the pulp from the zucchini (courgettes).
6. Mix together the egg yolk and the mustard. Add salt and pepper.
7. Gradually add the oil in a thin trickle, whisking constantly until a thick mayonnaise is obtained.
8. Add the lemon juice and continue to whisk until it is incorporated.
9. Stir the mayonnaise into the salmon and zucchini (courgette) purée and add the chopped dill. Taste and adjust seasoning.
10. Fill the zucchini (courgette) cases with this mixture. Arrange on a serving dish and decorate with whole unshelled shrimp (prawns). Serve cold.

Parsleyed Zucchini (Courgette) & Onion Flan

	00.10	00.23	
	Serves 4		

American	Ingredients	Metric/Imperial
1	large green bell pepper	1
7 oz	onions, cut into very thin strips	200 g/7 oz
1 lb	grated zucchini (courgettes)	450 g/1 lb
	salt	
	pepper	
1	small bunch chives	1
8	eggs	8
4 tbsp	sour cream (crème fraîche)	3 tbsp
¼ tsp	grated nutmeg	¼ tsp
1 tsp	butter	1 tsp
1	red bell pepper	1
1	chopped shallot	1
1	pinch dried thyme	1
2 tbsp	concentrated tomato juice	1 tbsp
½ tsp	sugar	½ tsp
2 tbsp	wine vinegar	1 tbsp

1. Rinse and seed the green bell pepper and remove the pith. Cut into thin strips and then dice.
2. Put the onions and the pepper into a casserole, cover and microwave on HIGH for 6 minutes.
3. Add the zucchini (courgettes) to the casserole with 3 (2) tablespoons of water. Add salt and pepper. Stir well. Cover and microwave on HIGH for 4 minutes.
4. Rinse the chives, pat dry on kitchen paper and snip with kitchen scissors.
5. Break the eggs into a large bowl and whisk with a fork.
6. Drain the vegetables, pressing with a saucer to extract as much liquid as possible.
7. Stir the sour cream (crème fraîche) salt, pepper, nutmeg, chives and vegetables into the beaten eggs.
8. Butter the base of a mold (mould) 10 inches (22 cm) in diameter. Pour in the mixture and microwave on MEDIUM-HIGH for 5 minutes. Stir the edges toward the center, then microwave on HIGH for a further 3 minutes.
9. To prepare the sauce, rinse and seed the red bell pepper and remove the pith. Chop coarsely and put into a small casserole with the shallot. Add the thyme and cover.
10. When the flan is cooked, remove the dish from the oven and put the casserole in its place. Microwave on HIGH for 5 minutes.
11. Blend the mixture in a food processor with the tomato juice, sugar and vinegar.
12. Add salt and pepper to taste.
13. Pour into a sauceboat. Serve immediately with the flan.

Parsleyed zucchini (courgette) and onion flan

Zucchini (Courgette) Ramekins

00.10 Serves 4   **00.11**

American	Ingredients	Metric/Imperial
3	finely sliced shallots	3
2 tbsp	butter	1 tbsp
½ lb	finely grated zucchini (courgettes)	225 g/8 oz
2	lightly beaten eggs	2
4 tbsp	concentrated tomato juice	3 tbsp
4 tbsp	sour cream (crème fraîche)	3 tbsp
4 tbsp	grated Parmesan cheese	3 tbsp
	salt	
	pepper	

1. Put the shallots into a casserole with the butter, cover and microwave on HIGH for 2 minutes.
2. Add the zucchini (courgettes) to the casserole, cover and microwave on HIGH for 4 minutes.
3. Mix together the beaten eggs, tomato juice, sour cream (crème fraîche) and Parmesan. Add salt and pepper to taste.
4. Stir the mixture into the zucchini (courgettes), stir well, and divide between 4 ramekin dishes.
5. Put the dishes in a circle in the microwave oven and cook on HIGH for 5 minutes: the center should remain slightly soft.
6. Leave to stand for a few minutes, then serve in the ramekin dishes.

Zucchini (courgette) ramekins

Zucchini (Courgette) Mold (Mould)

00.15 plus chilling time   **00.25**

American	Ingredients	Metric/Imperial
1¾ lb	grated zucchini (courgettes)	750 g/1¾ lb
1	chopped onion	1
2	crushed garlic cloves	2
2 tbsp	butter	1 tbsp
4	eggs	4
1¼ cups	cream cheese	300 g/10½ oz
2 tbsp	chopped mixed herbs	2 tbsp
3 tbsp	strong Dijon mustard	2 tbsp
½ tsp	Cayenne pepper	½ tsp
	salt	
	pepper	

1. Put the zucchini (courgettes) in a dish with ¼ cup (4½ tablespoons) of water. Cover and microwave on HIGH for 10 minutes.
2. Put the onion, garlic and butter in a small dish. Microwave on HIGH for 3 minutes.
3. Put the zucchini (courgettes) in a strainer (sieve) and leave to drain.

4. Break the eggs into a bowl and beat with a hand whisk.
5. Stir in the cream cheese, herbs, mustard, Cayenne pepper and the onion and garlic mixture. Add salt and pepper to taste. Stir carefully.
6. Gently press down on the zucchini (courgettes) to extract as much liquid as possible, then add to the bowl and stir well.
7. Butter the base of a Pyrex cake mold (mould) 10 inches (22 cm) in diameter. Pour in the mixture. Cover and microwave on HIGH for 12 minutes.
8. Remove the cover and chill in the refrigerator for 2 hours. Serve cold.

Microwave hint: Small packs of frozen vegetables can be cooked in the microwave from frozen in a freezer bag. Pierce the bag in two places. Line the microwave with a layer of kitchen paper and put the bag on the paper, so that the water from the bag will be absorbed.

Potato Terrine

American	Ingredients	Metric/Imperial
00.20 plus cooling time		00.44
10½ oz	sliced onions	300 g/10½oz
2 tbsp	butter	1 tbsp
1¾ lb	potatoes	750 g/1¾ lb
¼ lb	thin green runner beans	125 g/4 oz
½ lb	ham in one slice	225 g/8 oz
¾ cup	sour cream (crème fraîche)	200 ml/8 fl oz
3	eggs	3
	salt	
	pepper	
¼ tsp	grated nutmeg	¼ tsp

1. Put the onions in a dish with the butter and 2 tablespoons of water. Cover and microwave on HIGH for 8 minutes.
2. Scrub the potatoes and prick them with a fork.
3. Top-and-tail the green beans and rinse.
4. Slice the ham into ½ inch (1.25 cm) strips.
5. When the onions are cooked, put the potatoes in the microwave oven on a double thickness of kitchen paper and microwave on HIGH for 10-12 minutes according to size. Turn over midway through the cooking time. Set aside for 5 minutes.
6. Put the green beans in a dish with 2 tablespoons of water. Cover and microwave on HIGH for 4 minutes.
7. Purée the onions in a food processor and leave in the processor bowl. Peel and dice the potatoes and add to the onions. Purée again, adding the sour cream (crème fraîche), eggs, grated nutmeg and a generous pinch of salt and pepper. Purée until the mixture is smooth.
8. Line the base of a Pyrex cake mold (mould) with buttered non-stick parchment (greaseproof paper).
9. Drain the green beans.
10. Pour a layer of purée into the mold (mould), followed by a layer of green beans, another layer of purée, the ham strips, the remaining green beans and a final layer of purée. Smooth the surface.
11. Place uncovered in the oven and microwave on HIGH for 20 minutes. Leave to cool for 2 hours then turn out on to a long dish.

Potato and Cheese Bake

American	Ingredients	Metric/Imperial
00.10 Serves 4		00.31
2¼ lb	medium size sliced potatoes	1 kg/2¼ lb
	salt	
	pepper	
½ cup	fresh breadcrumbs	25 g/1 oz
¼ cup	butter	50 g/2 oz
¾ cup	grated Cheddar cheese	40g/1½ oz

1. Put the potatoes in a dish with 2 cups (450 ml/¾ pint) of water. Microwave on HIGH for 6 minutes. Leave to stand for 5 minutes and drain.
2. Butter a shallow dish and sprinkle with half the breadcrumbs, salt and pepper. Arrange the potato slices overlapping in layers, sprinkling each layer with half the cheese and salt and pepper.
3. Mix together the remaining breadcrumbs and cheese and spoon evenly over the potatoes. Dot the butter on the top. Cook on HIGH for 10 minutes, leave to stand for 5 minutes. Test with a skewer and if the potaoes seem too firm, cook for a further 5 minutes. Brown under a hot broiler or grill for a few minutes before serving. Serve hot.

Potato terrine

Festive potato salad

Cold Pâté of Potatoes with Sausage Meat

	00.25	00.40
	Serves 6	

American	Ingredients	Metric/Imperial
7 oz	finely sliced onions	200 g/7 oz
1½ lb	potatoes, sliced in ¼ inch (.85 cm) rounds	600 g/1½ lb
⅔ cup	sour cream (crème fraîche)	150 ml/¼ pint
2	whole eggs	2
1	egg yolk	1
¼ tsp	grated nutmeg	¼ tsp
1 tsp	curry powder	1 tsp
	salt	
	pepper	
1 tsp	butter	1 tsp
7 oz	sausage meat	200 g/7 oz
2 tbsp	shelled pistachio nuts	2 tbsp

1. Put the onions in a casserole and microwave on HIGH for 6 minutes.
2. Add the potatoes to the casserole with ¼ cup (3 tablespoons) of water. Cover and microwave on HIGH for 14 minutes.
3. Drain the vegetables and purée in a food processor, gradually adding the sour cream (crème fraîche), the whole eggs, egg yolk, grated nutmeg, curry powder, salt and pepper. Purée until smooth.
4. Butter the base of a 1½ quart (1.5 litre/2¾ pint) Pyrex cake mold (mould). Spoon in half the potato mixture.
5. Form the sausage meat into a roll the same length as the terrine, stick the pistachio nuts into it at regular intervals and put it in the terrine. Cover with the remaining potato mixture.
6. Do not cover the mold (mould). Put in the oven and microwave on HIGH for 20 minutes.
7. Leave the pâté to cool, then turn out on to a platter. Serve cold with a green salad.

Microwave hint: To cook three large peeled potatoes by microwave, stir together ½ cup (5 tablespoons) of water and a pinch of salt in a bowl. Quarter each potato, put into the bowl, cover and microwave on HIGH for 8 minutes. Test for tenderness. If too firm, cook for another 2 minutes. Leave to stand for 3 minutes before serving.

Festive Potato Salad

⊏⊐⊐.1⊐   ⊐⊐.15

Serves 4

American	Ingredients	Metric/Imperial
7 oz	turkey breasts	200 g/7 oz
4	large firm potatoes	4
1	small celery heart	1
14 oz	white button mushrooms	400 g/14 oz
2 tbsp	lemon juice	1 tbsp
	few lettuce leaves	
1	egg yolk	1
1 tsp	mustard	1 tsp
	salt	
	pepper	
½ cup	peanut oil	4½ tbsp
¼ cup	olive oil	4 tbsp
3 tbsp	vinegar	2 tbsp
2 tbsp	light (single) cream	1 tbsp
½ cup	white wine	6 tbsp
12	coarsely chopped walnuts	12

1. Put the turkey breasts on to a small plate, cover and microwave on HIGH for 3 minutes.

2. Rinse the potatoes under cold running water, prick with a fork and place in the microwave oven on a double layer of kitchen paper. Microwave on HIGH for 10 minutes until tender.

3. Drain the turkey breasts over a bowl and reserve the liquid. Slice the turkey breasts into fine strips.

4. Rinse the celery, divide into stalks and slice into fine strips.

5. Wipe the mushrooms over with a damp cloth or kitchen paper and cut into thin slices. Pour the lemon juice over.

6. Rinse the lettuce leaves, pat dry on kitchen paper and line a serving dish with them.

7. Mix together the egg yolk, mustard, salt and pepper. Add the peanut oil and olive oil drop by drop, whisking constantly with an electric egg-beater until a thick mayonnaise is obtained.

8. Beat in the vinegar and cream.

9. When the potatoes are cooked, peel and slice into rounds.

10. Add the white wine to the bowl containing the turkey cooking liquid. Add salt and pepper to taste. Microwave on HIGH for 2 minutes. Pour over the potatoes.

11. Mix together the potatoes, celery, turkey breast slices, mushrooms, walnuts and mayonnaise. Spoon carefully on top of the lettuce leaves in the serving dish. Serve warm.

Cold pâté of potatoes with sausage meat

Eggplant (Aubergine) and Lime Mousse

◤▱▷   00.10   00.12   〰
         plus chilling time

American	Ingredients	Metric/Imperial
1½ lb	eggplant (aubergines), peeled and cut into 1.25 cm (½ inch) dice	700 g/1½ lb
1	crushed garlic clove	1
4 tbsp	olive oil	3 tbsp
3 tbsp	fresh lime juice	2 tbsp
	Tabasco sauce	
	salt	
	pepper	

1. Put the eggplant (aubergine) into a casserole with ¼ cup (3 tablespoons) of water. Cover and microwave on HIGH for 12 minutes, stirring midway through the cooking time.
2. Drain the eggplant (aubergines) in a colander and leave to cool. Purée in a food processor.
3. Add the garlic, olive oil, lime juice, a dash of Tabasco sauce and salt and pepper to taste, and purée once more.
4. Transfer the purée to a bowl and chill in the refrigerator until just before serving. The mousse should be chilled for at least 2 hours.
5. Serve either with toast and butter or with a selection of other hors d'oeuvres.

Eggplant (Aubergine) Mousse

◤▱▷   00.15   00.23   〰
         Serves 6

American	Ingredients	Metric/Imperial
1¾ lb	eggplant (aubergines), peeled, sliced into rounds	750 g/1¾ lb
2	peeled garlic cloves	2
3	slices white bread	3
¼ cup	sour cream (crème fraîche)	4½ tbsp
½ tsp	ground cumin	½ tsp
3 tbsp	olive oil	2 tbsp
3 tbsp	vinegar	2 tbsp
2	eggs	2
	salt	
	pepper	
1 tsp	butter	1 tsp
	handful lamb's lettuce	
3	seedless black olives	3
¾ cup	whipping cream	200 ml/7 fl oz
3 tbsp	fresh lemon juice	2 tbsp

1. Put the eggplant (aubergine) on a large dish with ¼ cup (3 tablespoons) of water.
2. Add the garlic to the eggplant (aubergines). Cover and microwave on HIGH for 10 minutes.

3. Remove the crusts from the white bread. Add the sour cream (crème fraîche) and knead with your hands to form a paste.
4. Drain the eggplant (aubergines) in a colander. Purée the eggplant (aubergines) in a food processor, gradually adding the bread and sour cream (crème fraîche) paste, ground cumin, olive oil, vinegar, eggs, salt and pepper. Purée until smooth.
5. Lightly butter the base of a soufflé mold (mould) 6 inches (14 cm) in diameter and pour the mixture into it. Cover with saran wrap (cling film) and pierce in 2 or 3 places with a fork. Microwave on HIGH for 13 minutes. Leave the mousse to cool in its container.
6. Just before serving, wash the lamb's lettuce. Slice the olives into slivers.
7. Whip the cream, add salt and pepper and the lemon juice very gradually. Pour it into a sauceboat.
8. Turn out the mousse on to a serving dish. Arrange the lamb's lettuce around and garnish the top with slices of olive. Serve accompanied by the sauce.

Eggplant (Aubergine) Salad

◤▱▷   00.05   00.15   〰
         plus chilling time

American	Ingredients	Metric/Imperial
¼ lb	chopped onions	125 g/4 oz
1	large red bell pepper	1
1	large eggplant (aubergine), peeled and cubed	1
2 tbsp	fresh lemon juice	1 tbsp
4 tbsp	concentrated tomato juice	3 tbsp
1 tsp	sugar	1 tsp
4 tbsp	lime juice	2 tbsp
3 tbsp	Madeira	1½ tbsp
4 tbsp	olive oil	3 tbsp
	Tabasco sauce	
	salt	
	pepper	

1. Put the onions in a casserole. Cover and microwave on HIGH for 2 minutes.
2. Rinse and seed the red bell pepper and remove the pith. Cut the flesh into long strips and then into dice. Add the strips to the onions. Cover and microwave on HIGH for 5 minutes.
3. Stir the eggplant (aubergine), lemon juice, tomato juice and sugar into the casserole. Cover and microwave on HIGH for 8 minutes.
4. To make the sauce, mix together the lime juice, madeira and olive oil. Add several dashes of Tabasco sauce and salt and pepper to taste.
5. When the vegetables are cooked, Pour the sauce over and stir carefully. Leave to cool at room temperature, then chill in the refrigerator for at least 1 hour. Serve very cold.

Vegetable Omelette

◼▷ 00.15   00.19   〰

Serves 4

American	Ingredients	Metric/Imperial
¼ lb	onions	125 g/4 oz
4 tbsp	olive oil	3 tbsp
1	red bell pepper, cored, seeded, cut into thin strips	1
1	green bell pepper, cored, seeded cut into thin strips	1
2	skinned, coarsely chopped tomatoes	2
1	small green chili, seeded and chopped	1
1	crushed garlic clove	1
	salt	
	pepper	
6	eggs	6
2 tbsp	sour cream (crème fraîche)	1 tbsp

1. Peel and slice the onions into rings, separate the rings and put on a round plate with half the olive oil. Microwave for 3 minutes on HIGH.

2. Add all the vegetables to the onions. Add salt and pepper. Sprinkle the remaining olive oil over the mixture, cover and microwave on HIGH for 10 minutes.

3. Break the eggs into a bowl, add the sour cream (crème fraîche) and beat thoroughly with a whisk.

4. Pour the egg and cream mixture over the vegetables. Microwave on MEDIUM for 4 minutes, then on HIGH for 2 minutes.

5. Slide the omelette on to a dish and serve.

If your oven is not equipped with a turntable, stir the vegetables once during (2) above and rotate the plate after 2 minutes of cooking on MEDIUM during (4) above.

Microwave tip: Increase the length of cooking time if a firmer center to the omelette is liked. Do not forget, however, that the eggs will continue to cook after being removed from the microwave, and that the vegetables will need slightly longer if they are particularly juicy.

Vegetable omelette

Crab Quiche

00.25 *plus resting time*   00.20

American	Ingredients	Metric/Imperial
1¾ cups	all-purpose (plain) flour	200 g/7 oz
½ tsp	salt	½ tsp
½ cup	butter	115 g/4 oz
2 oz	coarsely chopped shallots	50 g/2 oz
3 tbsp	cognac	2 tbsp
7 oz	crabmeat, thawed if frozen	200 g/7 oz
3	large eggs	3
½ cup	sour cream (crème fraîche)	5 tbsp
	pepper	
	Tabasco sauce	
2 tbsp	chopped chives	2 tbsp
2 tbsp	chopped parsley	2 tbsp

1. To make the pastry: sieve the flour into a bowl with the salt. Add half the butter, cut into small cubes. Work the mixture rapidly with the fingers until it resembles coarse breadcrumbs. Add 2 or 3 tablespoons iced water and mix carefully until the mixture forms a ball. Leave to stand in the refrigerator for at least 30 minutes. Roll the pastry out on to a floured board.
2. Butter a Pyrex flan case 10 inches (24 cm) in diameter. Line the flan case with the pastry and prick all over with a fork. Chill in the refrigerator for a further 15 minutes. Microwave the pastry on HIGH for 5 minutes, then leave to cool.
3. To make the filling, put the shallots into a bowl with the cognac and 2 (1) tablespoon of butter. Microwave on HIGH for 3 minutes.
4. Pick over and break up the crabmeat with a fork.
5. Break the eggs into a bowl and whisk with a fork. Add the sour cream (crème fraîche), salt and pepper to taste and a few dashes of Tabasco sauce. Beat thoroughly.
6. Add the crabmeat, chopped chives, chopped parsley and shallots.
7. Pour the mixture into the cooled pastry case. Microwave the quiche on MEDIUM-HIGH for 2 minutes until the center of the filling is firm. Serve hot in the flan case.

Soufflé Omelette

00.05 *Serves 4*   00.05

American	Ingredients	Metric/Imperial
4	eggs	4
¾ cup	milk	200 ml/7 fl oz
	salt	
	pepper	
¼ cup	butter	50 g/2 oz

1. Separate the eggs, beat the whites until stiff but not dry.
2. Blend the egg yolks with the milk for each yolk, add salt and pepper to taste and gradually fold in the whites.
3. Melt the butter in a shallow dish in the microwave on HIGH for 30 seconds. Pour in the egg mixture and cook on MEDIUM for 5 minutes, lifting the edges of the omelette with a spatula, midway through the cooking time.
4. Fold carefully in half with the spatula and slide on to a serving dish.

Gourmet Quiche

00.20 *plus standing time*   00.22

American	Ingredients	Metric/Imperial
1 cup	wholewheat (wholemeal) flour	115 g/4oz
½ cup	all-purpose (plain) flour	50 g/2 oz
	salt	
4	eggs	4
¼ cup	butter, cut into small pieces	75 g/3 oz
10½ oz	chicken breast	300 g/10½ oz
	pepper	
7 oz	white button mushrooms	200 g/7 oz
2 tbsp	fresh lemon juice	1 tbsp
¼ tsp	thyme	¼ tsp
1	chopped sprig tarragon	1
¼ cup	sour cream (crème fraîche)	4½ tbsp
¼ cup	Gruyère cheese	50 g/2 oz
¼ tsp	grated nutmeg	¼ tsp

1. To make the pastry, sift the flours together, into a bowl. Add the salt, 1 beaten egg and the butter. Work the dough rapidly with your fingers until you have a smooth paste. Form a ball and leave to stand for 1 hour.
2. Butter the base of a Pyrex flan case 10-12 inches (22-24 cm) in diameter. Roll out the pastry on a floured board and line the flan case with it. Prick the base of the flan with a fork and microwave on HIGH for 6 minutes. The pastry is ready when it is firm to the touch. Leave to cool completely.
3. Put the chicken breast in a small dish, season with salt and pepper and add 2 (1) tablespoon of water. Cover and microwave on HIGH for 3 minutes.
4. Wipe the mushrooms with a damp cloth or kitchen paper and slice thinly. Put the slices in a dish with the lemon juice, salt, pepper and thyme. Cover and microwave on HIGH for 5 minutes. Drain the mushrooms.
5. Break the remaining 3 eggs into a bowl and whisk.
6. Slice the chicken into thin slivers.
7. Add the chopped tarragon, chicken, mushrooms, sour cream (crème fraîche), cheese and nutmeg to the beaten eggs. Add salt and pepper to taste. Mix thoroughly.
8. Pour the mixture into the pastry case. Microwave on HIGH for 8 minutes until the quiche is firm in the center. Leave to stand for 2-3 minutes and serve.

Crab quiche

Basque-style Piperade

	00.10	00.16
	Serves 4	

American	Ingredients	Metric/Imperial
1	red bell pepper	1
1	green bell pepper	1
1 lb	tomatoes	450 g/1 lb
4 tbsp	olive oil	3 tbsp
8	eggs	8
	salt	
	pepper	
¼ lb	thinly sliced smoked ham	125 g/4 oz

1. Rinse and seed the bell peppers and remove the pith. Slice the flesh into thin strips and then dice. Put the bell pepper strips into a soufflé mold (mould) 18 inches (45 cm) in diameter, cover and microwave on HIGH for 5 minutes.
2. Remove the stalks from the tomatoes, skin and halve and remove the seeds and juice. Chop the flesh coarsely with a kitchen knife.
3. Add the tomatoes to the mold (mould), pour the olive oil over, cover and microwave on HIGH for 5 minutes.
4. Beat the eggs with a fork. Add salt and pepper.
5. Dice the ham.
6. Pour the eggs over the vegetables. Add the ham, stir carefully and microwave on MEDIUM-HIGH for 6 minutes, stirring every two minutes. Serve very hot.

Baked Eggs with Tomato Sauce

	00.05	00.05
	Serves 4	

American	Ingredients	Metric/Imperial
¼ cup	concentrated tomato juice	4 tbsp
¼ cup	sour cream (crème fraîche)	4 tbsp
3 tbsp	grated Parmesan cheese	2 tbsp
	salt	
	pepper	
4	large eggs	4

1. Mix together the tomato juice, sour cream (crème fraîche) and Parmesan cheese. Taste and add salt and pepper. Divide the mixture between 4 ramekin dishes. Put the dishes in a circle in the microwave oven and cook on HIGH for 2 minutes.
2. Break 1 egg into each ramekin dish. Prick the yolk of the egg in 2 or 3 places with a toothpick (cocktail stick) so that it does not burst. Replace the ramekins in the oven in a circle, leaving the center of the oven empty. Microwave on HIGH for 3 minutes.
3. Leave to stand for 1 minute before serving.

Baked Eggs with Lobster Bisque

	00.05	00.07
	Serves 4	

American	Ingredients	Metric/Imperial
2	crushed shallots	2
2 tsp	butter	2 tsp
½ cup	lobster bisque	5 tbsp
3 tbsp	sour cream (crème fraîche)	2 tbsp
2 tbsp	cognac	1 tbsp
2 oz	shelled shrimp (prawns)	50 g/2 oz
4	large eggs	4

1. Put the shallots in a bowl with the butter and microwave on HIGH for 2 minutes.
2. Mix together the lobster bisque, sour cream (crème fraîche) and cognac in a bowl. Microwave on HIGH for 2 minutes.
3. Stir in the shrimp (prawns) and the shallots. Divide the mixture between 4 ramekin dishes. Break 1 egg into each dish. Gently prick each yolk with a toothpick (cocktail stick) in 2 or 3 places so that it does not burst.
4. Arrange the ramekins in a circle in the microwave oven, leaving the center of the oven empty. Microwave on HIGH for 3 minutes. Leave to stand for 1 minute before serving.

Microwave hint: When preparing baked eggs in individual ramekins, first make a bed of chopped spinach or cooked chopped potato in the dishes. Break the eggs on top, prick the yolks carefully with a toothpick (cocktail stick) to prevent them bursting during cooking. Sprinkle with salt, pepper and grated cheese. Cook the ramekins, 2 at a time, for 1½ minutes on HIGH. Remove and leave to stand for 1 minute to let the eggs finish cooking.

Baked eggs with tomato sauce

Baked eggs with pâté de foie gras

Baked Eggs with Pâté de Foie Gras

American	Ingredients	Metric/Imperial
	00.05 Serves 4	00.05
3 oz	pâté de foie gras with truffles	75 g/3 oz
4	eggs	4
4 tbsp	sour cream (crème fraîche)	3 tbsp
2 tbsp	white port	1 tbsp
	salt	
	pepper	

1. Line the base of 4 ramekin dishes with the pâté.
2. Break an egg into each ramekin. Pierce the yolk of each egg in 3 or 4 places with a toothpick (cocktail stick) so that it does not burst during cooking.
3. Mix together the sour cream (crème fraîche) and the port. Add salt and pepper. Pour this mixture into the 4 ramekin dishes.
4. Place the ramekins in a circle in the oven, leaving the center of the oven empty. Microwave on MEDIUM for 5 minutes. Serve as quickly as possible.

Microwave hint: To make an omelette, to cut in strips to use as a garnish, put 1 tablespoon of butter in a small round dish and melt on HIGH for 30 seconds.
Swirl the butter over the base and sides of the dish. Beat 2 eggs with 1 teaspoon of soy sauce and add salt and pepper to taste. Pour into a dish, cover with saran wrap (cling film). Pierce the wrap in several places with a fork, and cook on HIGH 1 minute.
Remove the dish and turn to distribute the mixture evenly. Cook, covered, on HIGH for a further 1 minute. If not fully set, cook uncovered for a further 30 seconds. Leave to cool then cut into narrow strips.

Baked Eggs with Asparagus

American	Ingredients	Metric/Imperial
	00.05 Serves 4	00.06
½ cup	canned cream of asparagus soup	5 tbsp
3 tbsp	sour cream (crème fraîche)	2 tbsp
2 tbsp	dry sherry	1 tbsp
4	eggs	4

1. Mix together the cream of asparagus soup, sour cream (crème fraîche) and the sherry in a bowl. Heat on HIGH in the microwave oven for 2 minutes.
2. Divide the mixture between 4 ramekin dishes. Break 1 egg into each dish. Carefully prick the yolk of each egg with a toothpick (cocktail stick) in 2 or 3 places so that it does not burst.
3. Place the ramekin dishes in a circle in the microwave oven. Leave the center empty. Microwave on HIGH for 3 minutes. Leave to stand for 1 minute, then serve.

Baked Eggs Spanish Style

American	Ingredients	Metric/Imperial
	00.10 Serves 4	00.09
7 oz	sliced onions	200 g/7 oz
7 oz	red bell peppers	200 g/7 oz
1	crushed garlic clove	1
2 tbsp	concentrated tomato juice	1 tbsp
¼ tsp	Cayenne pepper	¼ tsp
½ tsp	sugar	½ tsp
¼ tsp	dried thyme	¼ tsp
2 tbsp	olive oil	1 tbsp
	salt	
	pepper	
4	eggs	4

1. Put the onions in a small casserole. Cover and microwave on HIGH for 3 minutes.
2. Rinse and seed the bell peppers and remove the pith. Chop the flesh coarsely.
3. Add the bell peppers and garlic to the onions in the casserole. Cover and microwave on HIGH for 3 minutes.
4. Purée the mixture in a food processor, gradually adding the concentrated tomato juice, Cayenne pepper, sugar, thyme and olive oil. Add salt if needed. Purée until the mixture is smooth.
5. Pour the purée into a serving dish. Make 4 hollows in it with the back of a spoon. Break the eggs carefully one by one and put one in each of the hollows. Prick the yolk of each egg with a toothpick (cocktail stick) so that it does not burst while cooking. Microwave on HIGH for 3 minutes and serve immediately.

Egg and mussel ramekins

Egg and Mussel Ramekins

00.15		00.13
Serves 4		

American	Ingredients	Metric/Imperial
1 quart	mussels, in their shells	1 litre/1¼ pints
2	sliced shallots	2
2 tsp	butter	2 tsp
4 tsp	sour cream (crème fraîche)	4 tsp
4	eggs	4
	pepper	

1. Scrub the mussels and rinse under plenty of cold running water. Discard any with shells that are broken or already open. Spread on a dish, and add 2 tablespoons of water. Cover and microwave on HIGH for 3 minutes. Shake the dish midway through the cooking time.
2. Divide the shallots and butter between four ramekin dishes. Microwave for 2 minutes on HIGH.
3. Remove the mussels from their shells.
4. Add 1 teaspoon of sour cream (crème fraîche) to each of the ramekins.
5. Put the mussels on top of the cream and carefully break one egg into each. Prick the yolks in 2 or 3 places with a toothpick (cocktail stick) so that they do not burst during cooking.
6. Cover the ramekins and arrange in a circle in the microwave oven, leaving the center empty. Cook on MEDIUM for 5 minutes. Leave to stand for 3 minutes, add pepper and serve.

Ham, Cheese and Egg Ramekins

00.05		00.06
Serves 4		

American	Ingredients	Metric/Imperial
2 oz	diced, cooked ham	50 g/2 oz
⅓ cup	grated Cheddar cheese	40 g/1½ oz
4	eggs	4
	lettuce leaves	

1. Mix together the ham and the cheese.
2. Butter four ramekins and break one egg into each dish. Pierce the yolks carefully with a toothpick (cocktail stick) to prevent them bursting during cooking.
3. Divide the ham and cheese mixture between the four ramekins, topping each egg with the mixture. Put the ramekins in the microwave, covered with a piece of kitchen paper. Cook on HIGH for 4 minutes. Leave to stand for 2 minutes.
4. Line a serving dish with the lettuce leaves. Turn the ramekins out on to the lettuce. Serve immediately.

Microwave hint: To cook scrambled eggs by microwave: whisk the egg whites in a bowl. Add salt and pepper to taste. Stir in 2 (1) tablespoon of cream for every 2 eggs and cook, uncovered, on HIGH for 1 minute. Stir the cooked egg from the edges into the middle. Cook for a further minute but do not leave to set fully. Stir again and leave to stand for 1 minute, by which time the eggs should be fully set.

Eggs in Tomato Cases

◼▷ 00.15   00.16   〰️
Serves 4

American	Ingredients	Metric/Imperial
4	large firm tomatoes	4
	salt	
2 oz	diced smoked streaky bacon	50 g/2 oz
1	large coarsely chopped onion	1
1	red bell pepper, seeded and coarsely chopped	1
1	crushed garlic clove	1
5 oz	coarsely chopped eggplant (aubergines)	150 g/5 oz
2 tbsp	olive oil	1 tbsp
	pepper	
¼ tsp	Cayenne pepper	¼ tsp
4	eggs	4
¼ cup	sour cream (crème fraîche)	4 tbsp

1. Cut a circle in the top of each tomato with a sharp knife and scoop out the flesh with a small spoon, leaving a layer of pulp inside each. Salt the tomato shells and put upside-down on a plate to drain.
2. Chop the tomato pulp and put into a colander.
3. Put the bacon, onion, red bell pepper and garlic into a small casserole. Cover and microwave on HIGH for 3 minutes.
4. Add the tomato pulp, eggplant (aubergines) and olive oil. Add salt and pepper and stir well. Cover and microwave on HIGH for 5 minutes.
5. Place the tomatoes in a circle on a plate. Cook on HIGH for 2 minutes, then drain.
6. Add the Cayenne pepper to the casserole and stir well with a fork. Put three-quarters of the mixture into the middle of the plate with the tomatoes.
7. Break the eggs one by one, into a cup and pour 1 egg carefully into each tomato shell. Prick the yolk of each egg in 2 or 3 places with a toothpick (cocktail stick) so that it does not burst during cooking. Cover the eggs with the remaining mixture. Cover and microwave on HIGH for 3 minutes.
8. Leave the tomatoes to stand for 3 minutes. Heat the sour cream (crème fraîche) in a cup in the microwave oven on HIGH for 1 minute. Pour into a sauceboat. Serve with the stuffed tomatoes.

Goat's Cheese with Cabbage

◼▷ 00.10   00.10   〰️
plus chilling time

American	Ingredients	Metric/Imperial
½ lb	shredded cabbage	225 g/8 oz
1 tsp	Dijon mustard	1 tsp
½ tsp	sugar	½ tsp
3 tbsp	vinegar	2 tbsp
	salt	
	pepper	
2 tbsp	walnut oil	1 tbsp
2 tbsp	olive oil	1 tbsp
2 tbsp	peanut oil	1 tbsp
10	shelled walnuts	10
1	goat's cheese (chèvre)	1
¼ tsp	dried thyme	¼ tsp

1. Pour 1 cup (250 ml/8 fl oz) of water into the lower compartment of a microwave steamer. Put in the microwave oven and heat on HIGH for 3 minutes.
2. Put the cabbage in the perforated upper section of the steamer. Cover and microwave on HIGH for 6 minutes.
3. Mix together the mustard, sugar and vinegar. Add salt and pepper to taste. Gradually add the walnut oil, olive oil and peanut oil, beating constantly with a fork. Set two whole walnuts aside and chop the rest with a large knife.
4. When the cabbage is ready, put in a bowl, add the chopped walnuts and pour the vinaigrette sauce over. Stir carefully. Leave to cool, then chill in the refrigerator for 30 minutes.
5. About 2 minutes before serving, cut the goat's cheese (chèvre) into two equal slices and place them on a dish. Add pepper and sprinkle with thyme. Melt in the microwave oven on HIGH for 1 minute or slightly longer, depending upon the size of the cheese.
6. Divide the cabbage salad between two plates. Put a half cheese in the middle of each. Garnish with a walnut and serve.

Microwave hint: Never cook eggs in their shells in the microwave as they tend to explode. Even eggs broken into a dish for poaching will explode unless the yolks are pricked with a toothpick (cocktail stick) in several places.

Chicken Liver Pâté 1

00.10   00.07

plus marinating and chilling time

American	Ingredients	Metric/Imperial
7 oz	chicken livers	200 g/7 oz
2	crumbled sage leaves	2
1	sprig thyme, crumbled	1
⅓ cup	Madeira	4½ tbsp
3½ oz	very finely sliced onions	100 g/3½ oz
¼ cup	butter	50 g/2 oz
2 tbsp	tomato ketchup	1 tbsp
	salt	
	pepper	

1. Rinse the chicken livers and pat dry on kitchen paper. Cut each one into 2 or 3 pieces. Put in a bowl with the crumbled sage and thyme. Pour the Madeira over and leave to marinate for 1 hour (optional).
2. Cover the bowl with saran wrap (cling film), prick in several places with a fork and microwave on HIGH for 3 minutes.
3. Remove the chicken livers from their cooking liquid with a slotted spoon and put into a food processor.
4. Put the onions into the bowl containing the cooking liquid, cover and microwave on HIGH for 4 minutes.
5. Purée the chicken livers, gradually adding the onions in the cooking liquid until smooth.
6. Add the butter in small pieces, then the tomato ketchup. Add salt and pepper to taste.
7. Pass the mixture through a fine strainer (sieve) to obtain an extremely smooth cream. Pour this into a small bowl, cover with saran wrap (cling film) and chill in the refrigerator for at least 4 hours.

Chicken Liver Pâté 11

00.15   00.08

plus chilling time

American	Ingredients	Metric/Imperial
7 oz	sliced onions	200 g/7 oz
½ cup	port	5 tbsp
10½ oz	chicken livers	300 g/10½ oz
¼ tsp	dried thyme	¼ tsp
¼ tsp	garlic salt	¼ tsp
¼ cup	butter	75 g/3 oz
¼ tsp	grated nutmeg	¼ tsp
	salt	
	pepper	

1. Put the onions in a small casserole with half the port. Cover and microwave on HIGH for 5 minutes.
2. Rinse the chicken livers and pat dry on kitchen paper. Cut each one into 2 or 3 pieces.
3. Add the chicken liver, thyme and garlic salt to the onions. Cover and microwave on HIGH for 3 minutes.
4. Transfer the mixture to a food processor. Add the butter, grated nutmeg, salt, pepper and remaining port. Liquidize to a smooth purée, then pass through a fine strainer (sieve) to remove any lumps.
5. Pour the mixture into a bowl. Leave to cool at room temperature, then cover with saran wrap (cling film) and chill in the refrigerator for at least 4 hours. Serve with toast and butter.

Chicken Liver Pâté 111

00.10   00.14

plus chilling time

American	Ingredients	Metric/Imperial
3½oz	smoked fatty bacon, rind removed, cut into strips	100 g/3½ oz
¼ lb	sliced onions	125 g/4 oz
2 tbsp	butter	1 tbsp
¾ lb	chicken livers	350 g/12 oz
½ tsp	dried thyme	½ tsp
2	sage leaves	2
2	egg yolks	2
¼ cup	milk	4½ tbsp
	salt	
	pepper	

Chicken liver gâteau

1. Put the bacon on a small plate and microwave on HIGH for 2 minutes, uncovered.

2. Put the onions in a small casserole with the butter. Cover and microwave on HIGH for 3 minutes.

3. Rinse the chicken livers and pat dry on kitchen paper. Chop coarsely. Add to the onions and microwave for a further 2 minutes on HIGH.

4. Purée the onions, chicken livers and bacon in a food processor gradually adding the thyme, sage, egg yolks and milk. Add salt and pepper to taste. Pour the mixture into a small terrine. Cover and microwave on HIGH for 7 minutes.

5. Leave the pâté to cool at room temperature, then chill in the refrigerator for at least 12 hours.

Chicken Liver Gâteau

00.30   **00.31**

Serves 8

American	Ingredients	Metric/Imperial
¼ cup	butter	75 g/3 oz
3 tbsp	all-purpose (plain) flour	1½ tbsp
2¼ cups	milk	500 ml/18 fl oz
1 lb	chicken livers	450 g/1 lb
2 tbsp	chopped parsley	2 tbsp
2	coarsely chopped garlic cloves	2
½ cup	cognac	4 tbsp
5	whole eggs	5
5	egg yolks	5
2 cups	sour cream (crème fraîche)	450 ml/¾ pint
½ tsp	grated nutmeg	½ tsp
	dash of Tabasco sauce	
	salt	
	pepper	
2 oz	shallots, cut into strips	50 g/2 oz
⅔ cup	white wine	150 ml/¼ pint
1	can frozen tomato juice	1
½ tsp	celery salt	½ tsp
½ tsp	sugar	½ tsp

1. Put half the butter into a bowl and microwave for 1 minute on HIGH. Sift the flour into it and stir well.

2. Add the milk, stirring constantly with a hand whisk, and microwave on HIGH for 2 minutes, then for a further 3 minutes, beating vigorously after each minute. Leave to cool.

3. Rinse the chicken livers and pat dry on kitchen paper. Purée the livers in a food processor.

4. Rinse the parsley and chop coarsely with kitchen scissors. Add the parsley, garlic, cognac, whole eggs and egg yolks to the chicken liver purée. Purée once again.

5. Add 1 cup (200 ml/7 fl oz) sour cream (crème fraîche) and ¼ teaspoon of grated nutmeg to the sauce in the bowl, with a dash of Tabasco sauce and the salt and pepper. Stir well. Add the chicken liver purée.

6. Butter a 2¼ quart (3 litre/5 pint) soufflé mold (mould), 10 inches (22 cm) in diameter and pour the mixture into it. Microwave on HIGH for 18 minutes.

7. To prepare the sauce, put the shallots in a bowl with 3 (2) tablespoons of butter and the white wine. Microwave for 3 minutes on HIGH.

8. Defrost the frozen tomato juice, uncovered, on HIGH for 1 minute.

9. Blend the mixture from the bowl in a food processor. Add the tomato juice, 1 cup (200 ml/7 fl oz) sour cream (crème fraîche), celery salt, sugar, ¼ teaspoon grated nutmeg, salt and pepper. Taste and adjust seasoning. Pour into a bowl and microwave on HIGH for 3 minutes.

10. Turn out the gâteau on to a serving dish. Serve at once with the sauce.

Chicken Liver Pâté with Madeira

00.05   **00.08**

plus chilling time

American	Ingredients	Metric/Imperial
7 oz	sliced onions	200 g/7 oz
4 tbsp	Madeira	3 tbsp
2	finely chopped chicken livers	2
¼ cup	butter	50 g/2 oz
2 tbsp	wine vinegar	1 tbsp
3 tbsp	sour cream (crème fraîche)	2 tbsp
¼ tsp	grated nutmeg	¼ tsp
	salt	
	pepper	

1. Put the onions in a small casserole with the Madeira. Cover and microwave on HIGH for 5 minutes.

2. Add the chicken livers, butter and vinegar. Cover and microwave on HIGH for 3 minutes.

3. Purée the mixture in a food processor, gradually adding the sour cream (crème fraîche), grated nutmeg and salt and pepper to taste. Purée until smooth.

4. Transfer the purée to a bowl. Leave to cool at room temperature, then cover with saran wrap (cling film) and chill in the refrigerator for at least 2 hours.

Chicken Liver Pâté with Juniper Berries

�▶ 00.10   00.08   〰
Serves 4

American	Ingredients	Metric/Imperial
¼ cup	butter	50 g/2 oz
2 oz	sliced shallots	50 g/2 oz
1	sliced garlic clove	1
10½ oz	chicken livers	300 g/10½ oz
4	crushed juniper berries	4
¼ tsp	thyme	¼ tsp
2	eggs	2
3 tbsp	prune brandy or cognac	2 tbsp
	salt	
	pepper	
	Cayenne pepper	

1. Put the butter in a bowl and melt on HIGH for 30 seconds.
2. Add the shallots and garlic, stir and cook, uncovered, on HIGH for 3 minutes.
3. Rinse the chicken livers and pat dry on kitchen paper.
4. Purée the chicken livers, juniper berries, shallots, garlic and thyme in a food processor.
5. Add the eggs, prune brandy or cognac, salt and pepper and a good pinch of Cayenne. Purée again.
6. Pour the mixture into a bowl and make a small hollow in the center with the back of a spoon. Cover and microwave on HIGH for 5 minutes.
7. Leave the pâté to cool in the bowl, chill in the refrigerator until just before serving.

Chicken Salad with Lamb's Lettuce

▶ 00.10   00.06   〰
Serves 4

American	Ingredients	Metric/Imperial
3½ oz	peeled, cubed céleriac	100 g/3½ oz
10½ oz	chicken breasts	300 g/10½ oz
1 tsp	Dijon mustard	1 tsp
3 tbsp	honey vinegar	2 tbsp
3 tbsp	olive oil	2 tbsp
⅓ tsp	curry powder	⅓ tsp
2	pots natural flavor yogurt	2
	salt	
	pepper	
2	shallots	2
3½ oz	lamb's lettuce	100 g/3½ oz
12	black olives	12
12	coarsely chopped walnuts	12

1. Put the céleriac on a small dish with 2 tablespoons of water, cover and microwave on HIGH for 3 minutes.
2. Put the chicken breasts on to a dish, cover and microwave on HIGH for 3 minutes.
3. Mix together the mustard, vinegar, olive oil, curry powder and yogurt. Add salt and pepper.
4. Peel the shallots and crush through a garlic press into the yogurt sauce.
5. Cut the céleriac into matchstick (julienne) strips and stir into the sauce.
6. Slice the chicken into thin strips, stir into the sauce and leave to cool.
7. Rinse the lamb's lettuce and pat dry on kitchen paper. Garnish 4 plates with it.
8. Remove the olive pits (stones).
9. Spoon a portion of the chicken mixture on to each plate, sprinkle with chopped walnuts and garnish with black olives. This dish can be served warm or chilled.

Turkey Mousse with Asparagus

▶ 00.10   00.17   〰
plus chilling time

American	Ingredients	Metric/Imperial
2	sliced shallots	2
½ lb	sliced turkey breast	225 g/8 oz
⅔	can asparagus soup	⅔
¼ cup	white port	4 tbsp
	salt	
	pepper	
⅔ cup	whipping cream	150 ml/¼ pint
1 tsp	fresh lemon juice	1 tsp
1¾ lb	fresh young asparagus	750 g/1¾ lb

1. Put the shallots and turkey breasts in a casserole. Cover and microwave on HIGH for 4 minutes. Leave to cool.
2. Purée the turkey, shallots, asparagus soup and port in a food processor. Add salt and pepper to taste.
3. Whip the cream until it is firm. Fold it carefully into the turkey purée. Add lemon juice to taste. Pour the mixture into a terrine dish, smooth the surface and chill in the refrigerator until ready to serve.
4. Peel the asparagus with a paring knife, moving from the tips to the base. Remove any part of the stalk that is tough. Rinse the asparagus carefully.
5. Pour 1¾ cups (300 ml/½ pint) of water into the lower compartment of a microwave steamer. Cover and microwave on HIGH for 3 minutes.
6. Arrange the asparagus in the perforated section of the steamer and put it into the steamer. Cover and microwave on HIGH for 10 minutes.
7. Set the perforated compartment on the bias to leave the asparagus to drain.
8. Place a folded table napkin on a serving dish and carefully arrange the asparagus on it. Serve either warm or cold with the cold turkey mousse.

Turkey liver pâté

Turkey Liver Pâté

00.15 plus cooling and chilling time **00.08**

American	Ingredients	Metric/Imperial
10½ oz	turkey livers	300 g/10½ oz
½ lb	fresh streaky pork or bacon	225 g/8 oz
2 oz	sliced shallots	50 g/2 oz
2	eggs	2
1	crushed garlic clove	1
3 tbsp	Madeira	2 tbsp
½ tsp	ground allspice	½ tsp
½ tsp	dried thyme	½ tsp
	salt	
	pepper	

1. Rinse the turkey livers and pat dry on kitchen paper. Remove the central tendons.
2. De-rind the streaky pork or bacon and cut into strips.
3. Purée the shallots in a food processor. Gradually add the turkey livers, pork or bacon, and the eggs. Stir in the garlic, Madeira, allspice, thyme, salt and pepper.
4. When the purée is smooth transfer to a 1 quart (1 litre/1¾ pint) oval terrine dish. Cover and microwave on HIGH for 8 minutes. To check whether it is cooked, push a skewer into the center of the terrine, count 10 seconds, pull it out and touch your lips with it. It should be warm to the touch. Leave the terrine uncovered for 15 minutes, then put a plate with a heavy weight on top and leave to cool at room temperature. When cool, chill in the refrigerator for at least 12 hours.
5. The terrine can be served either in the terrine, in its own dish or on a serving plate.

Turkey and Avocado Mousse

◣▷ 00.45   00.12   〰
plus chilling time

American	Ingredients	Metric/Imperial
1½ lb	turkey breast	600 g/1½ lb
	salt	
	pepper	
2 tbsp	gelatin (gelatine)	2 tbsp
	dash of Tabasco sauce	
2	avocado pears	2
¼ cup	fresh lemon juice	4½ tbsp
½ cup	prune brandy or cognac	5 tbsp
1	sprig tarragon	1

1. Cut the turkey breast into small pieces. Put the pieces in a casserole with ¼ cup (3 tablespoons) of water. Add salt and pepper to taste. Cover and microwave on HIGH for 5 minutes. Leave to stand for 5 minutes.

2. Filter the mixture through a strainer (sieve) held over a terrine dish, then pour the liquid obtained into a measuring cup and add the gelatin (gelatine). Stir and microwave on MEDIUM for 2 minutes. Stir again and add enough water to make up to 1 cup (250 ml/8 fl oz) of liquid. Add a dash of Tabasco sauce.

3. Pour half the gelatin (gelatine) mixture into a 1½ quart (1.5 litre/2¾ pint) terrine and chill in the refrigerator for 20 minutes until firm.

4. Peel, halve and stone the avocado pears.

5. Purée the turkey breast in a food processor with the avocadoes, lemon juice, prune brandy or cognac and the remaining aspic jelly. Taste and adjust seasoning: the terrine should be highly seasoned.

6. Rinse the sprig of tarragon and pat dry on kitchen paper. Carefully remove the leaves.

7. When the aspic in the base of the terrine is firm, arrange the tarragon leaves on top in a decorative pattern.

8. Spoon the turkey mousse carefully on top, smoothing from time to time to eliminate air bubbles. Cover with saran wrap (cling film) and chill in the refrigerator for 12 hours.

9. Just before serving, plunge the terrine dish into hot water for several seconds. Pass a knife blade around the edges to loosen it, then turn out on to a serving dish.

Turkey and avocado mousse

Terrine of Pheasant

◣▷ 00.30   00.26   〰
plus marinating and chilling time

American	Ingredients	Metric/Imperial
1	large pheasant	1
½ tsp	allspice	½ tsp
½ tsp	dried thyme	½ tsp
2	bayleaves	2
1 tsp	ground black pepper	1 tsp
¼ cup	cognac	4½ tbsp
3 tbsp	finely chopped shallots	2 tbsp
1 tbsp	butter	½ tbsp
2 tbsp	dried mushrooms (cêpes)	1½ tbsp
¼ cup	white port	4½ tbsp
7 oz	unsmoked bacon	200 g/7 oz
1	egg	1
7 oz	pâté de foie gras	200 g/7 oz
	salt	
	pepper	

1. Remove the bones and skin from the pheasant. Leave the breasts whole, cut the rest into pieces, removing any tendons.

2. Put the pheasant breasts and pieces into a bowl. Add the allspice, thyme, bayleaves and ground black pepper. Pour the cognac over. Cover and marinate in the refrigerator for 24 hours.

3. Put the shallots in a bowl with half the butter. Microwave on HIGH for 3 minutes.

4. Put the dried mushrooms into a bowl with warm water to cover. Cover the bowl and microwave on HIGH for 3 minutes. Drain the mushrooms and chop coarsely with kitchen scissors. Rinse very carefully and put into a small casserole with the remaining butter and the white port. Cover and microwave on HIGH for 5 minutes.

5. Remove the rind from the bacon. Cut into small pieces and put into the food processor.

6. Drain the pheasant over a bowl, setting aside the cooking liquid. Discard the bayleaves.

7. Add the pheasant pieces to the food processor. Set aside the breast fillets.

8. Purée the pheasant pieces and the bacon.

9. Add the shallots, egg, pâté de foie gras and the marinade, and process until a smooth purée is obtained. Season well with salt and pepper.

10. Place the purée in a bowl, taste and adjust seasoning (this dish should be highly seasoned). Add the mushrooms.

11. Cut the pheasant breasts into thin strips. Pour one-third of the purée mixture into a 1 quart (1.25 litre/2¼ pint) terrine dish.

12. Arrange half the pheasant breast strips on top, cover with half the remaining purée, then the other half of the pheasant and finish with the remaining purée. Press the mixture well down.

13. Cover the terrine and microwave on MEDIUM-HIGH for 15 minutes.

14. When the terrine is cooked, remove the lid and leave to stand for 15 minutes, then place a small plate with a heavy weight on top and leave to cool at room temperature.

15. When the terrine is cool, chill in the refrigerator for at least 24 hours. Serve in the terrine dish or turned out on to a serving dish.

Duck terrine with prunes

Duck Terrine with Prunes

00.30   **00.36**
plus marinating and chilling time

American	Ingredients	Metric/Imperial
2	finely chopped garlic cloves	2
1	finely chopped carrot	1
2	finely chopped sticks celery	2
2	finely chopped onions	2
3	bayleaves	3
2	dried chilis	2
3	cloves	3
1 tsp	black peppercorns	1 tsp
2¼ cups	vin rosé d'Anjou	500 ml/18 fl oz
1¼ lb	skinned duck breasts, cut into small pieces	500 g/1¼ lb
½ lb	prunes	225 g/8 oz
1¼ lb	rindless smoked bacon, cut into small pieces	500 g/1¼ lb
10	juniper berries	10
¼ cup	prune brandy	4 tbsp
1	egg	1
1½ tsp	salt	1½ tsp
1 tsp	ground black pepper	1 tsp
½ tsp	allspice	½ tsp

1. Put the garlic, carrot, celery and onions in a bowl with the bayleaves, chilis, cloves and peppercorns.

2. Stir in the wine. Put the duck breasts into the bowl, stir well and leave to marinate in the refrigerator for 24 hours.

3. Remove the duck from the marinade and set aside. Filter the marinade through a fine strainer (sieve) and pour the liquid into a bowl.

4. Remove the pits (stones) from the prunes. Put the prunes into the marinade and microwave on HIGH for 6 minutes.

5. Purée the bacon and duck breasts in the food processor, gradually adding the juniper berries, prune brandy, egg, salt, ground black pepper and allspice.

6. Drain the prunes. Set aside the three largest.

7. Spoon one-third of the duck mixture into a 1 quart (1.25 litre/2¼ pint) rectangular terrine. Push one half of the prunes down into the pâté. Cover with half the remaining duck mixture and decorate as before with the remaining prunes. Finally cover with the last third of the duck mixture. Gently press the three reserved prunes into the surface of the terrine as a decorative garnish.

8. Cover the terrine and microwave on MEDIUM-HIGH for 30 minutes. Test the temperature of the pâté with a kitchen thermometer: it should reach 70°C.

9. When the terrine is cooked, cover with a double layer of aluminum (aluminium) foil so that it reaches another 5°C, then put a small plate on top with a heavy weight and leave to cool at room temperature.

10. When cool, chill the terrine in the refrigerator for at least 24 hours.

Fennel Salad with Mussels

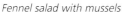

| | 00.10 | 00.10 | |
| | plus cooling and marinating time | | |

American	Ingredients	Metric/Imperial
2 quarts	mussels in their shells	2 litres /3½ pints
1½ lb	fennel	600 g/1½ lb
2 tbsp	honey vinegar	1 tbsp
4 tbsp	orange juice	3 tbsp
	pepper	
2	finely chopped shallots	2
4 tbsp	mayonnaise	3 tbsp
8	coarsely chopped walnuts	8

1. Scrub the mussels thoroughly in plenty of cold running water. Discard any with open or broken shells. Place half in a casserole. Cover and microwave on HIGH for 3 minutes, shaking the casserole midway through cooking. Set aside in their cooking liquid and repeat with the remaining mussels.

2. Remove the stalks and tough base of the fennel. Set aside the green fronds. Rinse the fennel and slice, lengthwise, then into strips across. Put the fennel into a casserole with 3 (2) tablespoons of water. Cover and microwave on HIGH for 7 minutes.

3. Drain the mussels, discarding any that have not opened. Set aside 1 tablespoon of the cooking liquid. Remove the shells.

4. Put the shelled mussels in a bowl and pour the vinegar and orange juice over. Add pepper.

5. Mix the shallots into the mussels. Stir well. Leave to marinate.

6. Leave the fennel to cool, drain and put into a bowl.

7. Drain the mussels through a colander over a bowl, to reserve the marinade, and add to the fennel.

8. Stir the mayonnaise and walnuts into the mussel marinade. Add the mussel cooking liquid that was set aside and stir well.

9. Chop the green fronds of the fennel and add to the mixture.

10. Pour the mixture over the fennel and mussels.
Stir carefully.

11. Serve with a fresh green salad or garnish the dish with black olives and cherry tomatoes.

Fennel salad with mussels

Salmon Loaf with Watercress

	00.15	00.23	
	plus chilling time		

American	Ingredients	Metric/Imperial
4	frozen salmon steaks	4
10½ oz	white button mushrooms	300 g/10½ oz
3½ oz	chopped shallots	100 g/3½ oz
4 tbsp	oil	2½ tbsp
1	bunch watercress	1
3	sprigs tarragon	3
1	bunch chives	1
2	eggs	2
¾ cup	sour cream (crème fraîche)	200 ml/7 fl oz
2 tbsp	breadcrumbs	1 tbsp
	salt	
	pepper	
2 tsp	superfine (caster) sugar	2 tsp
⅓ cup	oil	4½ tbsp
3 tbsp	mild mustard	2 tbsp
2	natural flavor yogurts	2
1	bunch chervil	1
	cherry tomatoes	
	black olives	
1 tsp	chopped chives	1 tsp

1. Line a dish with a double thickness of kitchen paper. Arrange the frozen salmon steaks on it and defrost in the microwave oven on HIGH for 1½ minutes.
2. Wipe the button mushrooms with a damp cloth or kitchen paper and roughly chop them.
3. Purée the shallots and the mushrooms in a food processor. Pour the purée into a small casserole and add the oil. Microwave on HIGH for 7 minutes until the vegetable liquid has evaporated.
4. Discard the stalks of the watercress and rinse carefully. Put on kitchen paper to drain.
5. Rinse the tarragon and chives.
6. Put the watercress into the food processor, and add the tarragon leaves. Snip the chives with kitchen scissors and add them. Purée and leave to stand in the food processor bowl.
7. Remove the bones and skin from the salmon steaks. Add the fish to the food processor and purée again, adding the eggs and sour cream (crème fraîche).
8. Add the mushroom purée, breadcrumbs and salt and pepper to taste.
9. Oil the base of a 1½ quart (1.5 litre /2¾ pint) Pyrex mold (mould). Pour in the mixture, cover and microwave on HIGH for 15 minutes.
10. Leave the salmon loaf to cool at room temperature, then chill in the refrigerator for at least 12 hours until firm.
11. Just before serving, make the sauce: Mix the sugar and mustard together in a bowl. Add the oil in a thin trickle, beating constantly with a fork. Gradually add the yogurt. Add pepper. Rinse the chervil, pat dry on kitchen paper, chop and add to the sauce. Pour the sauce into a sauceboat.
12. Pass a knife blade around the edge of the salmon loaf, gently lifting the loaf in places to aerate it. Turn out on to a long dish. Garnish with cherry tomatoes, black olives and fresh herbs. Serve the sauce on the side.

Salmon Pâté with Button Mushrooms

	00.10	00.26	
	plus cooling time		

American	Ingredients	Metric/Imperial
2	frozen salmon tails	2
½ lb	white button mushrooms	225 g/8 oz
2 oz	thinly sliced shallots	50 g/2 oz
2 tbsp	butter	1 tbsp
2 tbsp	fresh lemon juice	1 tbsp
	salt	
	pepper	
2	slices white bread	2
½ cup	milk	5 tbsp
4	eggs	4
⅔ cup	sour cream (crème fraîche)	150 ml/¼ pint
1	can shrimp (prawn) bisque	1
3 tbsp	cognac	2 tbsp
¼ tsp	Cayenne pepper	¼ tsp
1	lamb's lettuce	1
1	radicchio	1
3 tbsp	oil	2 tbsp
2 tbsp	honey vinegar	1 tbsp

Salmon pâté with button mushrooms

1. Defrost the salmon tails in the microwave oven for about 10 minutes on HIGH.

2. Wipe the mushrooms with a damp cloth or kitchen paper and chop coarsely.

3. Put the shallots into a small casserole with the butter, cover and microwave on HIGH for 2 minutes.

4. Stir in the mushrooms, lemon juice, salt and pepper to taste. Cover and microwave on HIGH for 4 minutes.

5. Remove the crusts from the bread, crumble coarsely and soak in the milk.

6. Remove the bones and skin from the fish, pat dry on kitchen paper and cut into pieces.

7. Purée the fish in a food processor, gradually stirring in the eggs, sour cream, (crème fraîche) shrimp (prawn) bisque, cognac, bread and milk. When the purée is smooth, pour into a bowl.

8. Add salt and pepper generously: the pâté should be highly seasoned. Add the Cayenne pepper.

9. Stir in the shallot and mushroom mixture carefully.

10. Butter the base of a 1½ quart (1.5 litre/2½ pint) Pyrex cake mold (mould). Pour in the mixture. Cover and microwave on HIGH for 7 minutes. Remove the lid and microwave for a further 3 minutes.

11. Leave to cool at room temperature for at least 3 hours.

12. Just before serving rinse the two salads. Mix the oil and vinegar and season with salt and pepper. Toss the salads in the vinaigrette separately.

13. Turn out the pâté on to a serving dish and arrrange the salads around it in alternate colors.

Terrine of fresh and smoked salmon

Terrine of Fresh and Smoked Salmon

	00.10	00.04	
	plus chilling time		

American	Ingredients	Metric/Imperial
14 oz	fresh salmon	400 g/14 oz
3 tbsp	dry white wine	2 tbsp
2 tbsp	cognac	1 tbsp
¼ cup	butter	50 g/2 oz
½ lb	smoked salmon	225 g/8 oz
20	sprigs fresh dill	20
1 tsp	drained green peppercorns	1 tsp

1. Rinse the fresh salmon under plenty of cold running water. Pat dry on kitchen paper. Put in a small bowl with the white wine. Cover and microwave on HIGH for 3 minutes.

2. Remove the skin and bones from the fish. Break the fish up with a fork and pour the cognac over.

3. Put the butter in a cup and microwave on HIGH for 30 seconds, until it has just melted.

4. Purée the smoked salmon with the melted butter in a food processor.

5. Rinse the dill and snip coarsely with kitchen scissors.

6. Add the dill and the green peppercorns to the smoked salmon purée. Purée until smooth.

7. Add this mixture to the fresh salmon, mixing well with a fork. Pour into a small terrine.

Cover and chill in the refrigerator for at least 3 hours.

Salmon soufflé

Salmon Soufflé

	00.10	00.12
	Serves 6	

American	Ingredients	Metric/Imperial
1 lb	raw salmon	450 g/1 lb
1	egg	1
3	egg whites	3
2¼ cups	sour cream (crème fraîche)	500 ml/18 fl oz
	salt	
	pepper	
	Cayenne pepper	
1	can lobster bisque	1
3½ oz	shelled shrimp (prawns)	100 g/3½ oz

1. Remove the bones and skin from the salmon and cut into pieces.
2. Purée the fish in a food processor, gradually adding the whole egg, 1 egg white and the sour cream (crème fraîche). Add salt and pepper and a pinch of Cayenne pepper. Put the mixture in the refrigerator.
3. Whisk the 2 remaining egg whites to firm peaks. Take the salmon mixture out of the refrigerator and carefully fold in the beaten egg whites. Pour the mixture into a 7 inch (17 cm) soufflé mold (mould). Put the mold (mould) in the microwave oven and cook on HIGH for 10 minutes.
4. Put the lobster bisque into a bowl with the shelled shrimp (prawns). Heat in the oven for 2 minutes on HIGH.
5. Turn out the salmon mold (mould) on to a serving dish. Pour the lobster and shrimp (prawn) sauce over and serve at once.

Terrine of Trout with Petits Pois

◀▷ 00.10
plus chilling time
00.13

American	Ingredients	Metric/Imperial
3	large cleaned trout, heads and tails removed	3
3	slices white bread	3
¾ cup	sour cream (crème fraîche)	200 ml/7 fl oz
2 tbsp	dry vermouth	1 tbsp
2	large eggs	2
½ tsp	grated nutmeg	½ tsp
	salt	
	pepper	
3½ oz	shelled shrimp (prawns)	100 g/3½ oz
¼ cup	canned petits pois	4 tbsp
1 tsp	butter	1 tsp
12	sorrel leaves	12
1 tsp	sugar	1 tsp
2 tbsp	strong Dijon mustard	1 tbsp
4 tbsp	oil	3 tbsp
2	natural flavor yogurts	2
1 tbsp	chopped chervil	1 tbsp
1 tbsp	chopped dill	1 tbsp

1. Rinse the fish under plenty of cold running water. Pat dry on kitchen paper and arrange on an oval dish. Cover and microwave on HIGH for 4 minutes. Leave to cool.
2. Remove the crusts from the bread and cut into cubes. Put the bread into a bowl and pour over the sour cream (crème fraîche). Heat in the microwave oven for 1 minute on HIGH.
3. Stir in the vermouth. Stir again with a fork.
4. Remove the bones and skin from the trout. Purée the fish in a food processor, gradually adding the bread and sour cream (crème fraîche), 2 eggs and the nutmeg. Season generously with salt and pepper. Purée until the mixture is smooth.
5. Pour the mousse into a bowl. Carefully add the shrimp (prawns) and the petits pois.
6. Butter the base of a 1 quart (1.25 litre/2¼ pint) terrine dish. Pour in the mixture and smooth the surface. Cover and microwave on HIGH for 8 minutes until the mixture shrinks slightly away from the sides of the dish.
7. Remove the lid from the terrine dish and leave to cool completely at room temperature. Chill in the refrigerator for at least 4 hours.
8. Just before serving, prepare the sauce. Bring a small pan of water to the boil on a conventional cooker and plunge the sorrel leaves into it for 1 minute. Drain.
9. Mix together the sugar and mustard in a bowl and add the oil in a thin trickle, beating constantly with a fork.
10. Add the yogurt a little at a time. Add pepper. Chop the sorrel and add. Add the chervil.
11. Serve the terrine either in its dish or turned out on to a platter. Sprinkle some chopped dill over and serve with the sauce.

Terrine of trout with petits pois

Trout and Avocado Mousse

00.10 plus chilling time   **00.05**

American	Ingredients	Metric/Imperial
2	cleaned trout, heads and tails removed	2
1	ripe avocado pear, peeled and stoned and cut into small pieces	1
4 tbsp	fresh lemon juice	3 tbsp
3 tbsp	almond liqueur	2 tbsp
	Tabasco sauce	
	salt	
	pepper	

1. Put the fish on a long dish with 3 (2) tablespoons of water. Cover and microwave on HIGH for 5 minutes. Leave to cool.
2. Remove the bones and skin from the fish. Put the flesh in a food processor and purée for several seconds.
3. Gradually add the avocado and purée until smooth.
4. Add the lemon juice, almond liqueur, several dashes of Tabasco sauce and salt and pepper to taste. Purée once more. Put the mousse into the refrigerator for at least 1 hour.
5. To serve, divide the mousse into four individual servings.

Trout and avocado mousse

Pâté of Trout with Mushrooms

00.15 plus chilling time   **00.20**

American	Ingredients	Metric/Imperial
2 tbsp	dried mushrooms (cèpes)	1 tbsp
2 oz	finely chopped shallots	50 g/2 oz
2 tbsp	butter	1 tbsp
¼ cup	port	4 tbsp
2	slices white bread	2
½ cup	milk	5 tbsp
2 lb	salmon trout	1 kg/2 lb
4	large eggs	4
⅔ cup	sour cream (crème fraîche)	150 ml/¼ pint
1	can lobster bisque	1
3 tbsp	cognac	2 tbsp
	salt	
	pepper	
¼ tsp	Cayenne pepper	¼ tsp
1	egg yolk	1
2 tbsp	strong mustard	1 tbsp
⅔ cup	olive oil	150 ml/¼ pint
1	can mushroom soup	1
3 tbsp	fresh lemon juice	2 tbsp
¼ lb	lamb's lettuce	125 g/4 oz

1. Put the mushrooms into a bowl with 1¾ cups (400 ml/14 fl oz) of water and microwave on HIGH for 3 minutes.
2. Put the shallots into a small casserole with the butter. Cover and microwave on HIGH for 2 minutes.
3. Drain the mushrooms. Chop coarsely, rinse carefully in warm water. Stir the mushrooms into the shallots. Add the port. Cover and microwave on HIGH for 5 minutes.
4. Remove the crusts from the bread, cut into pieces and soak in the milk.
5. Rinse the fish under plenty of cold running water and pat dry on kitchen paper. Cut into large pieces and purée in the food processor.
6. Gradually add the eggs, sour cream (crème fraîche), lobster bisque, cognac, bread and milk.
7. When the mixture is smooth, pour into a bowl. Season generously with salt and pepper and add the Cayenne pepper: this dish should be highly seasoned. Add the shallot, mushroom and port mixture and stir well.
8. Butter the base and sides of a rectangular 1½ quart (1.5 litre/2¾ pint) terrine dish. Pour in the mixture. Cover and microwave on HIGH for 7 minutes. Remove the lid and cook for a further 3 minutes on HIGH.
9. Leave to cool at room temperature for at least 3 hours.
10. For the sauce, mix together the egg yolk and mustard in a bowl. Add the oil gradually in a thin trickle, beating as for a mayonnaise. Add the mushroom soup and lemon juice. Add pepper if needed. Chill in the refrigerator.
11. Rinse the lamb's lettuce carefully. Pat dry on kitchen paper. Turn out the pâté on to a large serving plate. Put several leaves of lamb's lettuce around it. Serve with the sauce.

Pâté of trout with mushrooms

Gâteau of Sea Trout

00.15   **00.23**
Serves 4

American	Ingredients	Metric/Imperial
1	large sea trout, cleaned, head removed	1
¼ cup	butter	50 g/2 oz
3	large eggs	3
¾ cup	milk	200 ml/7 fl oz
	salt	
	pepper	
¾ cup	sour cream (crème fraîche)	200 ml/7 fl oz
2 tbsp	cognac	1 tbsp
3 tbsp	concentrated tomato juice	2 tbsp
1	sprig tarragon	1
4	unshelled shrimp (prawns)	4

1. Cut the fish into pieces and arrange on a round dish. Cover and microwave on HIGH for for 5 minutes. Remove lid and leave to cool.
2. Put the butter in a bowl and soften in the microwave oven for 30 seconds on HIGH.
3. When the fish is cooked, remove the bones and skin and purée the flesh in a food processor.
4. Break 1 egg and separate the white from the yolk.
5. Add the melted butter, milk, egg yolk and 2 whole eggs to the fish purée, purée once more. Add salt and pepper to taste. Pour the mixture into a bowl.
6. Add a pinch of salt to the remaining egg white and whisk to form soft peaks. Fold gently into the fish mixture. Pour the mixture into a soufflé dish, 7 inches (18 cm) in diameter.
7. Put the soufflé dish into the microwave oven and microwave on HIGH for 10 minutes. Leave to stand for 5 minutes.
8. To prepare the sauce, mix together the sour cream (crème fraîche), cognac and tomato juice in a bowl. Heat in the microwave oven on HIGH for 2 minutes. Taste and adjust seasoning.
9. Rinse the tarragon and pat dry on kitchen paper. Remove the leaves, chop and add to the sauce.
10. Turn out the gâteau on to a serving dish. Garnish with the shrimp (prawns). Pour the sauce into a sauceboat and serve alongside.
This dish can also be prepared with cooked sea trout. Allow for 1¼ lb (500 g) of fish including the bones and skin.

Ring Mold (Mould) of Sea Trout

00.15   **00.14**
plus chilling time

American	Ingredients	Metric/Imperial
1	sea trout, cleaned, head and tail removed	1
3	eggs	3
3 tbsp	butter	2½ tbsp
¾ cup	milk	200 ml/7 fl oz
	salt	
	pepper	
1 tsp	horseradish sauce	1 tsp
¼ tsp	sugar	¼ tsp
3 tbsp	oil	2 tbsp
2	pots natural flavor yogurt	2
2 tbsp	chopped parsley	2 tbsp

1. Rinse the fish under plenty of cold running water. Pat dry on kitchen paper. Cut the fish into ½ inch (1.25 cm) slices. Arrange on a round platter, cover and microwave on HIGH for 4 minutes.
2. Leave the fish to cool for a few minutes before removing the bones and skin.
3. Separate the white and yolk of one of the eggs.
4. Put the fish into a food processor and purée for several seconds, then add the butter in small pieces, the 2 remaining eggs, the egg yolk, milk, salt and pepper. Purée until smooth.
5. Add a pinch of salt to the egg white and whisk until firm peaks are formed. Fold gently into the purée.
6. Pour the mixture into a ring mold (mould) and smooth the surface. Put the mold (mould) uncovered in the oven and microwave on HIGH for 10 minutes.
7. When it is cooked, turn the mold (mould) out on to a serving dish and leave to cool before placing in the refrigerator. Chill for at least 3 hours.
8. Just before serving, put the horseradish sauce into a bowl and add the sugar and pepper. Add the oil very slowly in a thin trickle, beating constantly with a fork. Gradually add the yogurt and parsley. Serve with the fish.

Mousse of Sea Trout with Avocado Slices

00.15   **00.21**
plus chilling time

American	Ingredients	Metric/Imperial
1½ lb	thinly sliced potatoes	600 g/1½ lb
1	sea trout, cleaned, head removed	1
¼ cup	butter	4½ tbsp
1	avocado pear	1
½ cup	fresh lemon juice	5 tbsp
	Cayenne pepper	
	salt	
	pepper	
1	small jar black lumpfish caviar	1

1. Pour 1 cup (250 ml/8 fl oz) of water into the lower compartment of a microwave steamer. Put the potatoes into the upper compartment, cover and microwave on HIGH for 9 minutes.

2. Cut the fish into pieces and put in a dish with 3 (2) tablespoons of water. Cover.

3. When the potatoes are cooked, take out of the steamer and leave to stand for 5 minutes.

4. Put the trout into the oven and microwave on HIGH for 6 minutes. Leave to cool.

5. Put the butter into a bowl and soften in the oven for 30 seconds on HIGH.

6. Quarter the avocado, remove the stone, and peel 3 of the quarters. Wrap the fourth quarter in saran wrap (cling film) and set aside.

7. Drain the fish and remove the bones and skin. Purée the fish in a food processor.

8. Add the potatoes, the three peeled avocado quarters, butter and three-quarters of the lemon juice. Liquidize once more.

9. Add a pinch of Cayenne pepper and generous pinches of salt and pepper. The mousse should be highly seasoned.

10. Divide the mixture between six glass serving bowls. Smooth the surface and chill in the refrigerator for at least 4 hours.

11. Just before serving, peel and slice the remaining avocado quarter. Sprinkle the remaining lemon juice over. Arrange the slices on top of the fish mousse in each serving dish and place a spoonful of lumpfish caviar in the center of each. Serve.

Mousse of sea trout with avocado slices

Whiting and asparagus ring mold (mould)

Whiting and Asparagus Ring Mold (Mould)

American	Ingredients	Metric/Imperial
1 lb	whiting fillets	450 g/1 lb
	salt	
	pepper	
¼ cup	fresh lemon juice	4 tbsp
2 tbsp	dry sherry	1 tbsp
1 tbsp	gelatin (gelatine)	1 tbsp
⅔	can cream of asparagus soup	⅔
3 tbsp	sour cream (crème fraîche)	2 tbsp
2 tbsp	chopped chervil	2 tbsp
¼ lb	shelled shrimp (prawns)	125 g/4 oz
10½ oz	zucchini (courgettes)	300 g/10½ oz
¼ lb	salmon caviar	125 g/4 oz

1. Rinse the whiting fillets and put on a dish. Add salt and pepper and half the lemon juice. Cover and microwave on HIGH for 4 minutes.

2. Pour the remaining lemon juice and the sherry into a bowl. Sprinkle the gelatin (gelatine) over and leave to swell.

3. When the fish is cooked, leave to stand for 5 minutes.

4. Put the bowl containing the gelatin (gelatine) mixture into the oven and microwave for 1 minute on LOW. Stir well.

5. Pour the cream of asparagus soup into a terrine dish, add the sour cream (crème fraîche), chopped chervil, shrimp (prawns), gelatin (gelatine) mixture and the cooking liquid from the fish. Stir carefully.

6. Break up the fish with a fork, removing any bones. Stir into the above mixture, then pour the whole into a ring mold (mould), cover with aluminum (aluminium) foil and chill in the refrigerator for at least 4 hours.

7. Peel the zucchini (courgettes), cut in half lengthwise and then into cubes. Put in a dish, cover and microwave on HIGH for 4 minutes.

8. Drain the zucchini (courgettes) and put in a food processor with half the salmon caviar. Purée until smooth. Pour the mixture into a sauceboat.

9. Just before serving, turn out the ring mold (mould) on to a serving dish and garnish with the remaining salmon caviar. Serve with the zucchini (courgette) sauce.

Terrine of Fresh Anchovies

00.12   00.08
plus chilling time

American	Ingredients	Metric/Imperial
½ lb	coarsely chopped tomatoes	225 g/8 oz
1	finely sliced onion	1
1	chopped garlic clove	1
3 tbsp	wine vinegar	2 tbsp
4 tbsp	olive oil	3 tbsp
1	bayleaf	1
1	sprig thyme	1
1 tsp	sugar	1 tsp
	salt	
	pepper	
1 lb	fresh anchovies	450 g/1 lb
3 tbsp	Madeira	2 tbsp

1. Put the tomatoes, onion and garlic in a small casserole.
2. Add the vinegar, olive oil, bayleaf, thyme, salt and pepper. Cover and microwave on HIGH for 5 minutes.
3. Clean the anchovies: remove the heads and backbones and cut off the tails. Rinse the fish well under cold running water and pat dry on kitchen paper.
4. Discard the thyme and bayleaf. Purée the sauce in a food processor, adding the Madeira. Taste and adjust seasoning.
5. Pour half the sauce into a small terrine dish. Arrange the anchovies on top and pour over the remaining sauce to cover. Cover and microwave on HIGH for 3 minutes.
6. Leave to cool in the terrine dish at room temperature. Chill in the refrigerator for at least 12 hours.

Terrine of Fish Florentine

00.20   00.28
plus chilling time

American	Ingredients	Metric/Imperial
4	large firm potatoes	4
¼ lb	frozen chopped spinach	125 g/4 oz
1 lb	cod fillets, thawed if frozen	450 g/1 lb
2 tbsp	chopped tarragon	2 tbsp
2 tbsp	chopped parsley	2 tbsp
2 tbsp	chopped chives	2 tbsp
3	eggs	3
4 tbsp	sour cream (crème fraîche)	3 tbsp
	salt	
	pepper	
1 tsp	Dijon mustard	1 tsp
⅔ cup	oil	150 ml/¼ pint
2 tbsp	vinegar	1 tbsp
2 tsp	cream of horseradish	2 tsp
	salad in season	

1. Rinse the potatoes and prick the skin in several places with a fork. Line the microwave with a double thickness of kitchen paper. Arrange the potatoes in a circle, leaving the middle of the oven empty. Microwave on HIGH for 10 minutes. Peel the potatoes and cut into rounds.
2. Put the frozen spinach in a small dish and defrost in the microwave oven for 3 minutes on HIGH.
3. Rinse the fish under plenty of cold running water and pat dry on kitchen paper. Cut into small pieces and purée in a food processor.
4. Add the potatoes, spinach, tarragon, parsley and chives to the fish purée. Purée again, adding 2 of the eggs, the sour cream (crème fraîche), salt and pepper.
5. Pour the mixture into a mold (mould) 9 inches (22 cm) in diameter. Cover with saran wrap (cling film) and pierce in several places. Microwave on HIGH for 15 minutes. Leave to cool in the container. Chill in the refrigerator for at least 3 hours.
6. Just before serving, make the sauce, separate the yolk and white of the remaining egg and mix the Dijon mustard with the yolk. Add the oil in a thin trickle, beating constantly with an electric beater until a thick mayonnaise is obtained. Add the vinegar and horseradish and salt and pepper to taste. Beat well.
7. Add a pinch of salt to the egg white and whisk until it forms firm peaks. Fold gently into the mayonnaise.
8. Turn out the fish terrine on to a serving dish.
9. Serve with the mayonnaise sauce and a green salad.

Soused Mackerel with Fennel

00.10   00.16
plus chilling time

American	Ingredients	Metric/Imperial
1	can concentrated tomato juice	1
½	finely chopped fennel bulb	½
¾ cup	white wine	200 ml/7 fl oz
2	sprigs thyme	2
1	bayleaf	1
3	mackerel, cleaned. heads and tails removed	3
	salt	
	pepper	

1. Put the tomato juice in a small casserole.
2. Stir in the fennel, white wine, thyme and bayleaf. Cover and microwave on HIGH for 10 minutes.
3. Rinse the mackerel thoroughly under cold running water and pat dry on kitchen paper. Sprinkle salt and pepper in the base of a rectangular dish. Arrange the fish on top.
4. If the tomato juice is too thick, stir in 2-3 tablespoons of water. Pour the tomato juice over the fish. Cover and microwave on HIGH for 6 minutes.
5. Leave to cool at room temperature, then chill in the refrigerator for at least 12 hours.

Two-fish Terrine with Spinach

◥◢ 00.30   00.16 ▨
Serves 8

American	Ingredients	Metric/Imperial
½ lb	spinach	225 g/8 oz
1	carrot	1
10½ oz	boned skinned salmon	300 g/10½ oz
4	eggs	4
½ cup	sour cream (crème fraîche)	6 tbsp
½ cup	canned petits pois	5 tbsp
½ lb	whiting fillets, thawed if frozen	225 g/8 oz
	salt	
	pepper	
1 tsp	butter	1 tsp
1	egg yolk	1
2 tbsp	horseradish mustard	1 tbsp
½ cup	oil	125 ml/4 fl oz
3 tbsp	white wine vinegar	2 tbsp
½ cup	sour cream (crème fraîche)	6 tbsp
1	bunch dill	1

1. Bring a large pot of water to the boil. Rinse the spinach and discard any tough leaves or stalks. Cook the spinach in the boiling water for 1 minute, drain in a colander under cold running water. Set aside to cool.
2. Cut the carrot into matchstick (julienne) strips and put in a bowl with ¼ cup (3 tablespoons) of water, cover and microwave for 5 minutes on HIGH.

3. Cut the salmon into pieces and purée in a food processor, gradually adding 2 whole eggs, half the sour cream (crème fraîche), salt and pepper. Pour the mixture into a bowl and rinse the food processor.
4. Rinse the whiting fillets and pat dry on kitchen paper. Cut into pieces and purée with the 2 remaining eggs, the remaining sour cream (crème fraîche), salt and pepper. Pour the mixture into another bowl.
5. Drain the carrots under cold running water and stir into the whiting mixture.
6. Drain the petits pois and stir into the salmon mixture.
7. Pat the spinach leaves dry carefully, on kitchen paper.
8. Butter the base and sides of a 1½ quart (1.5 litre/2¾ pint) Pyrex cake mold (mould). Line with a layer of spinach leaves, which will stick easily to the butter.
9. Pour the salmon mixture into the mold (mould). Smooth the surface. Place another layer of spinach leaves on top of the salmon. Pour the whiting mixture on top. Cover with the remaining spinach. Press the mixture down gently with the palm of your hand. Cover and microwave on HIGH for 10 minutes.
10. Leave the terrine to cool in the mold (mould) at room temperature. If planning to eat it that same day, do not chill.
11. Just before serving, prepare the sauce. Mix together the egg yolk and horseradish mustard in a bowl with some salt and pepper. Add the oil gradually in a thin trickle, beating with an electric or hand beater. When all the oil is absorbed, add the vinegar, beating constantly. Whip the sour cream (crème fraîche) into soft peaks and fold gently into the mayonnaise.
12. Rinse the dill and pat dry on kitchen paper. Chop finely and add to the sauce. Taste and adjust seasoning.
13. Turn out the terrine on to a long dish. Pour the sauce into a sauceboat and serve.

Two-fish terrine with spinach

Pâté of pike with shrimp (prawns) and mussels

Pâté of Pike with Shrimp (Prawns) and Mussels

00.20 plus chilling time   **00.09**

American	Ingredients	Metric/Imperial
4	slices white bread	4
½ cup	milk	5 tbsp
1¾ lb	pike, with its caviar	700 g/1¾ lb
¾ cup	sour cream (crème frâiche)	200 ml/7 fl oz
2	eggs	2
½ tsp	grated nutmeg	½ tsp
	salt	
	pepper	
3½ oz	shelled shrimp (prawns)	100 g/3½ oz
3½ oz	cooked mussels	100 g/3½ oz
1 tsp	butter	1 tsp
¼ cup	oil	4½ tbsp
1	pot natural flavor yogurt	1
4 tbsp	fresh lemon juice	3 tbsp
2 tbsp	chopped dill	2 tbsp

1. Remove the crusts from 3 of the slices of bread and crumble into a bowl. Add the milk and mix well.
2. Rinse the fish under plenty of cold running water and pat dry on kitchen paper. Cut into pieces and purée in a food processor.
3. Squeeze the bread with your fingers and add to the purée with the sour cream (crème fraîche), eggs and grated nutmeg. Season generously with salt and pepper. Purée again until smooth.
4. Pour the mixture into a bowl. Carefully stir in the shrimp (prawns) and mussels.
5. Butter the base of a 1 quart (1 litre/1¾ pint) terrine and pour in the mixture. Smooth the surface. Cover and microwave on HIGH for 9 minutes.
6. When the terrine is cooked (the edges should have shrunk slightly away from the sides of the dish), remove the cover and set aside for 15 minutes. Put a plate and a heavy weight on to the terrine and chill in the refrigerator for 4 hours.
7. To make the sauce, put the pike caviar in the food processor. Remove the crusts from the remaining slice of bread and soak in 3 (2) tablespoons of water. Squeeze the excess water and add to the pike caviar. Purée, adding the oil gradually in a thin trickle.
8. Stir in the yogurt, lemon juice and chopped dill. Add salt and pepper to taste. Purée once more. Pour the sauce into a bowl and chill in the refrigerator. It will thicken slightly.
9. Just before serving, turn out the pâté on to a dish, garnish with herbs or lettuce leaves.
Serve with the sauce alongside.

Crab and Zucchini (Courgette) Terrine

◼▷ 00.20	00.25	〰
plus chilling time		

American	Ingredients	Metric/Imperial
1 lb	finely grated zucchini (courgettes)	450 g/1 lb
3 tbsp	butter	2 tbsp
3 tbsp	all-purpose (plain) flour	2 tbsp
2¼ cups	milk	500 ml/18 fl oz
1	chicken bouillon (stock) cube	1
2 tbsp	curry powder	1 tbsp
	salt	
½ lb	crabmeat, thawed if frozen	225 g/8 oz
1	bunch chives	1
3	eggs	3
2 tbsp	Dijon mustard	1 tbsp
	pepper	
1 cup	oil	250 ml/8 fl oz
2 tbsp	tomato concentrate	1 tbsp
	salad in season	

1. Put the zucchini (courgettes) in a casserole with ¼ cup (3 tablespoons) of water, cover and microwave on HIGH for 5 minutes.
2. Pour the zucchini (courgettes) into a colander and leave to drain.
3. Put the butter into a bowl and melt in the microwave oven for 1 minute on HIGH.
4. Stir in the flour and the milk and microwave on HIGH for 3 minutes, stirring constantly, with a hand whisk. If by the end of 3 minutes the mixture has not come to the boil, microwave for 1 minute more. Whisk gently with a fork.
5. Crumble the chicken bouillon (stock) cube over the mixture.
6. Add the curry powder and salt to taste. Stir well and leave to cool.
7. Break up the crabmeat with a fork.
8. Rinse the chives and snip with kitchen scissors.
9. Beat 2 of the eggs with a fork.
10. Butter the base of a 1 quart (1.25 litre/1¾ pint) oval-shaped terrine.
11. Press the zucchini (courgettes) gently with a saucer to extract as much liquid as possible.
12. Stir the beaten eggs, zucchini (courgettes), crabmeat and chives into the curry sauce.
13. Cover the terrine and microwave on HIGH for 10 minutes, microwave for a further 5 minutes, uncovered. Leave to cool at room temperature, then chill in the refrigerator for at least 3 hours.
14. For the sauce, separate the white and yolk of the third egg. Mix the yolk with the mustard and add salt and pepper to taste. Beat the oil into the mixture drop by drop to obtain a thick mayonnaise. Add the tomato concentrate.
15. Slide the blade of a knife round the edge of the terrine to separate it from the sides of the dish, then turn out on to a plate and garnish with lamb's tails or other salad in season.
16. Whisk the egg white until it forms soft peaks and fold gently into the sauce. Pour into a sauceboat and serve with the terrine.

Red Mullet Salad with Zucchini (Courgettes)

◼▷ 00.15	00.12	〰
Serves 4		

American	Ingredients	Metric/Imperial
½ lb	young zucchini (courgettes)	225 g/8 oz
2	red mullet, cleaned, heads removed	2
5 oz	red bell peppers	150 g/5 oz
12	black olives	12
2 tbsp	Dijon mustard	1 tbsp
1 tbsp	sugar	½ tbsp
4 tbsp	olive oil	3 tbsp
1	pot natural flavor yogurt	1
12	basil leaves	12
	salt	
	pepper	

1. Rinse and trim the zucchini (courgettes). Slice extremely thinly in a food processor and put in a small casserole with 2 (1) tablespoons of water. Cover and microwave on HIGH for 4 minutes.
2. Put the fish in a long dish. Cover and microwave on HIGH for 4 minutes.
3. Rinse and seed the red bell peppers and remove the pith. Cut the flesh into pieces and put in a small casserole. Cover and microwave on HIGH for 4 minutes.
4. Drain the zucchini (courgettes) under cold running water and pat dry on kitchen paper.
5. Skin and fillet the fish. Arrange the zucchini (courgettes) on a warmed serving dish with the fish on top. Garnish with black olives.
6. Purée the bell peppers in a food processor.
7. Mix together the mustard and sugar in a bowl. Add the oil in a thin trickle, beating constantly with a fork. Gradually add the yogurt. Stir in the bell pepper purée. Chop the basil leaves and add to the sauce. Taste and adjust seasoning.
8. Pour a little of the sauce over each fish fillet.
9. Serve the remaining sauce in a sauceboat accompanying the fish.

Crab and zucchini (courgette) terrine

Whiting Mousse with Lime Juice

	00.15	00.13	
	plus chilling time		

American	Ingredients	Metric/Imperial
2	whiting fillets	2
½ lb	finely sliced zucchini (courgettes)	225 g/8 oz
2 tbsp	butter	1 tbsp
2 tbsp	all-purpose (plain) flour	1 tbsp
1 cup	milk	250 ml/8 fl oz
4 tbsp	fresh lime juice	3 tbsp
4 tbsp	gelatin (gelatine)	4 tbsp
	salt	
	pepper	
1	bunch chervil	1
1	bunch chives	1
1	egg white	1
	mayonnaise	
	green salad in season	

Whiting mousse with lime juice

1. Rinse the whitings under plenty of cold running water. Pat dry on kitchen paper and put on a long dish. Cover and microwave on HIGH for 4 minutes. Leave to cool.
2. Put the zucchini (courgettes) in a casserole with ¼ cup (3 tablespoons) of water. Cover and microwave on HIGH for 4 minutes.
3. Put the butter in a bowl and melt in the microwave oven for 1 minute on HIGH.
4. Stir in the flour and gradually add the milk, stirring constantly. Microwave on HIGH for 3 minutes, stirring every minute with a hand whisk.
5. Put the lime juice into a cup and sprinkle the gelatin (gelatine) over. Leave the gelatin (gelatine) to swell for 2 minutes, then put the cup in the oven and microwave for 1 minute on LOW. Stir the gelatin (gelatine) into the sauce, which should be still hot, stir well.
6. Remove the bones and skin from the fish and purée in a food processor.
7. Drain the zucchini (courgettes) and add to the food processor. Stir in the sauce. Purée the mixture until smooth. Add salt and pepper to taste. Pass the purée through a fine strainer (sieve) to make sure that all the small bones are removed. Leave to cool.
8. Rinse the chives and chervil and pat dry on kitchen paper. Chop the herbs and stir into the mixture.
9. Beat the egg white into stiff peaks and fold gently into the mixture.
10. Transfer the mixture to a 1 quart (1 litre/1¾ pint) terrine mold (mould) and chill in the refrigerator for at least 6 hours.
11. Just before serving, plunge the terrine mold (mould) into hot water for a few seconds, slide a knife blade round the edge of the mousse and turn out on to a serving dish. Garnish with salad and serve along with the mayonnaise.

Lobster Bavarian Cream

00.20 plus chilling time **00.11**

American	Ingredients	Metric/Imperial
¾ lb	frozen lobster bisque	350 g/12 oz
¼ cup	cognac	4 tbsp
2 tbsp	gelatin (gelatine)	2 tbsp
1¼ cups	whipping cream	300 ml/½ pint
½ tsp	fresh lemon juice	½ tsp
6	large shrimp (prawns)	6
	salad in season	

1. Put the lobster bisque in a bowl with 3 (2) tablespoons of water. Cover and defrost in the microwave oven for 5 minutes on HIGH. Stir the bisque, cover and leave for 5 minutes until completely defrosted.
2. Put the cognac in a cup and sprinkle the gelatin (gelatine) over. Do not stir, leave the gelatin (gelatine) to dissolve in the cognac for 2 minutes, then put the cup into the microwave oven for 1 minute on LOW.
3. Fold the cognac and gelatin (gelatine) mixture carefully into the lobster bisque. Chill in the refrigerator.
4. When the soup is completely cold, whip the cream until just firm. Gently fold into the soup.
5. Add the lemon juice. Pour the mixture into a fluted mold (mould) and chill in the refrigerator for 12 hours.
6. Just before serving, plunge the mold (mould) into hot water for a few seconds, then turn out on to a serving dish. Garnish with the shrimp (prawns).
7. Serve with a green salad.

Ring Mold (Mould) of Crab with Cucumber

00.35 plus chilling time **00.06**

American	Ingredients	Metric/Imperial
2	large cucumbers, peeled and grated	2
4 tbsp	fresh orange juice	3 tbsp
½ cup	fresh lemon juice	5 tbsp
3 tbsp	cognac	2 tbsp
1½ tbsp	gelatin (gelatine)	1½ tbsp
1	chicken bouillon (stock) cube	1
	dash of Tabasco sauce	
7 oz	frozen crabmeat	200 g/7 oz
3	shallots	3
2 tbsp	chopped tarragon	2 tbsp
2 tbsp	chopped chives	2 tbsp
5 oz	shelled shrimp (prawns)	150 g/5 oz
1½ tsp	horseradish mustard	1½ tsp
1	pot natural flavor yogurt	1
3 tbsp	sour cream (crème fraîche)	2 tbsp
2 tbsp	chopped fresh dill	2 tbsp
	salt	
	pepper	
6	shrimp (prawns) in shells	6

1. Put the grated cucumber into a strainer (sieve) and leave to drain.
2. Put the orange juice, half the lemon juice, and the cognac into a small bowl. Sprinkle the gelatin (gelatine) over and leave to swell.
3. Pour 1¼ cups (300 ml/½ pint) of water into a bowl and microwave on HIGH for 3 minutes. Crumble the bouillon (stock) cube into the water and stir. Add a dash of Tabasco sauce.
4. Put the small bowl containing the gelatin (gelatine) into the oven and microwave on MEDIUM-LOW for 1 minute. Stir and then pour into the bowl containing the bouillon (stock), stirring constantly. Leave to cool.
5. Put the crabmeat, still frozen, on to a plate. Defrost in the microwave oven for 2 minutes on HIGH. Leave to stand at room temperature for a further 10 minutes until completely defrosted.
6. Peel the shallots, cut into pieces and crush in a garlic press. Put the shallots in a bowl with the tarragon and chives.
7. Squeeze the cucumber to extract as much liquid as possible and stir into the mixture.
8. Break up the crabmeat with a fork and stir into the mixture. Stir well and gradually add the cold bouillon (stock).
9. Pour the mixture into a ring mold (mould) and chill in a refrigerator for 12 hours.
10. Just before serving, prepare the sauce. Purée the shelled shrimp (prawns) and mix with the mustard, the remaining lemon juice, yogurt, sour cream (crème fraîche), dill, salt and pepper. Purée once more.
11. Plunge the ring mold (mould) into hot water for a few seconds, then turn out on to a dish. Pour half the sauce into the center and arrange the unshelled shrimp (prawns) decoratively round it. Serve very cold with the rest of the sauce on the side.

Monkfish terrine with parsley

Monkfish Terrine with Parsley

	00.20	00.21	
	plus chilling time		

American	Ingredients	Metric/Imperial
1¾ lb	monkfish	750 g/1¾ lb
1¾ lb	whiting fillets	750 g/1¾ lb
3-4	slices white bread	3-4
3 tbsp	coarsely chopped parsley	3 tbsp
1 tbsp	coarsely chopped chervil	1 tbsp
1	bunch chives	1
3	large eggs	3
1½ cups	sour cream (crème fraîche)	400 ml/14 fl oz
	salt	
	pepper	
4-5	sprigs basil	4-5
1	can concentrated tomato juice	1
2 tbsp	cognac	1 tbsp
¾ cup	heavy (double) cream	200 ml/7 fl oz
	lettuce leaves to garnish	

1. Remove the large central cartilage from the monkfish. Put the two fillets on a long dish. Cover and microwave on HIGH for 6 minutes.

2. Rinse the whiting fillets, pat dry on kitchen paper and cut into small pieces.

3. Remove the crusts from the white bread and cut each slice in four.

4. Rinse the parsley, chervil and chives. Coarsely chop the parsley and chervil. Snip the chives with kitchen scissors.

5. Purée the whiting fillets in a food processor.

6. Gradually add the white bread, herbs, eggs, sour cream (crème fraîche), salt and pepper. Purée until smooth.

7. Carefully drain the monkfish, gently pat dry with kitchen paper and cut each fillet into three long strips.

8. Put one-third of the whiting and herb mixture into the base of a 2 quart (2 litre/3½ pint) oval terrine. Lay three strips of monkfish on top. Cover with another layer of the mixture. Lay the remaining three strips of monkfish on top. Finish with the remaining mixture and press down well. Cover the terrine and microwave on HIGH for 15 minutes.

9. When the terrine is cooked, remove the cover and leave to cool at room temperature. Chill in a refrigerator for at least 4 hours. Remove the terrine from the refrigerator at least 1 hour before serving, so that it is not too cold.

10. To prepare the sauce, rinse and dry the basil and snip the leaves with kitchen scissors. Mix together the concentrated tomato juice, 2 (1) tablespoons of water, the cognac and heavy (double) cream. Add the snipped basil. Pour into a sauceboat.

11. Rinse the lettuce leaves, dry on kitchen paper and cut into strips. Turn out the terrine on to a long dish. Arrange the lettuce leaves around it and serve with the sauce.

Shrimp (Prawn) Cocktail

00.15 plus chilling time   **00.08**

American	Ingredients	Metric/Imperial
1	cucumber, peeled and diced	1
	salt	
2	red bell peppers	2
3½ oz	sliced onions	100 g/3½ oz
½	crushed garlic clove	½
2 tbsp	concentrated tomato juice	1 tbsp
2 tbsp	olive oil	1 tbsp
2 tsp	sherry vinegar	2 tsp
1 tsp	sugar	1 tsp
½ tsp	dried thyme	½ tsp
2 tbsp	mayonnaise	1 tbsp
	pepper	
7 oz	shelled shrimp (prawns)	200 g/7 oz
	lettuce leaves	
4	unshelled shrimp (prawns)	4

1. Put the cucumber in a colander with a pinch of salt and drain.
2. Rinse and seed the red bell peppers, pat dry on kitchen paper and remove pith. Cut the flesh into cubes.
3. Put the onions into a small casserole. Cover and microwave on HIGH for 3 minutes. Add the bell peppers. Cover and microwave on HIGH for 5 minutes.
4. Drain the onions and peppers. Purée the garlic.
5. Rinse the cucumber well and pat dry on kitchen paper.
6. Add the tomato juice and cucumber to the food processor and purée, gradually adding the oil, vinegar, sugar and thyme.
7. Pour the mixture into a bowl and stir in the mayonnaise. Add salt and pepper to taste.
8. Stir in the shelled shrimp (prawns) carefully and chill in the refrigerator for at least 2 hours.
9. Just before serving, rinse the lettuce and line 4 individual serving dishes with it. Arrange the shrimp (prawn) mixture on top. Garnish with an unshelled shrimp (prawn).

Hawaiian Fish Salad

00.10 Serves 4   **00.02**

American	Ingredients	Metric/Imperial
2	white fish fillets	2
¼ lb	lamb's lettuce	125 g/4 oz
1	pawpaw (papaya)	1
12	peeled fresh lychees	12
3 tbsp	sherry vinegar	2 tbsp
3 tbsp	peanut oil	2 tbsp
2 tbsp	olive oil	1 tbsp
½ tsp	curry powder	½ tsp
	salt	
	pepper	
1	bunch chives	1
1 oz	crabmeat	25 g/1 oz

1. Rinse the fish fillets under plenty of cold running water. Pat dry on kitchen paper and slice into thin strips on the bias. Arrange on a dish. Cover and microwave on HIGH for 2 minutes. Leave to cool.
2. Rinse the lamb's lettuce thoroughly under cold running water and pat dry on kitchen paper.
3. Cut the pawpaw (papaya) in half and remove the seeds with a small spoon. Peel the fruit and cut into slices.
4. Line a serving dish with the lamb's lettuce. Arrange the strips of fish, pawpaw (papaya) slices and lychees on top.
5. Mix together the vinegar, peanut oil, olive oil, curry powder, salt and pepper.
6. Rinse the chives, pat dry on kitchen paper and snip with kitchen scissors into the sauce.
7. Break up and pick over the crabmeat with a fork and add to the sauce.
8. Beat the sauce with a fork until it emulsifies, pour over the fish and fruit, and serve.

Left to right: Shrimp (prawn) cocktail, Hawaiian fish salad

Pork Liver Pâté

◼▷   00.15   00.10   〰
plus chilling time

American	Ingredients	Metric/Imperial
2	finely chopped shallots	2
2	finely chopped garlic cloves	2
¾ lb	pork liver, cut into small pieces	350 g/12 oz
½ lb	unsmoked, rindless back bacon, cut into pieces	225 g/8 oz
2	eggs	2
¼ tsp	allspice	¼ tsp
3 tbsp	port	2 tbsp
2 tbsp	cognac	1 tbsp
½ tsp	mixed herbs	½ tsp
1½ tsp	salt	1½ tsp
	pepper	
8	strips (rashers) streaky bacon	8

1. Purée the shallots, garlic, pork liver and back bacon in a food processor.
2. Gradually add the eggs, allspice, port, cognac, mixed herbs and salt and pepper. Purée until smooth.
3. Line a 1 quart (1.25 litre/2¼ pint) oval terrine with the streaky bacon, leaving enough to fold over the top of the pâté. Spoon the purée into the terrine. Press down well, then fold the rashers of bacon over to cover the surface. Cover and microwave on MEDIUM-HIGH for 10 minutes.
4. Leave the terrine to cool at room temperature for 15 minutes, then put a small plate with a heavy weight on top and chill in the refrigerator for at least 24 hours.

Pork Terrine with Herbs

◼▷   00.15   00.35   〰
plus chilling time

American	Ingredients	Metric/Imperial
1 lb	frozen spinach	450 g/1 lb
1	bunch watercress	1
1	small bunch tarragon	1
1	bunch parsley	1
1¾ lb	boneless chine of pork	750 g/1¾ lb
1 lb	unsmoked bacon	450 g/1 lb
5	sliced scallions (spring onions)	5
3	crushed garlic cloves	3
2	eggs	2
½ tsp	grated nutmeg	½ tsp
¼ tsp	Cayenne pepper	¼ tsp
	salt	
	pepper	
1	strip (rasher) streaky bacon	1
	mayonnaise	

1. Put the frozen spinach in a dish and defrost, uncovered, for 6 minutes in the microwave oven on HIGH. Pour the spinach into a colander.
2. Remove the tough stalks from the watercress, rinse carefully and spread out on a plate. Cover. Microwave the watercress for 4 minutes on HIGH. Drain in a colander.
3. Rinse the tarragon and parsley, pat dry on kitchen paper and remove the leaves from the stalks. Discard the stalks.
4. Slice the pork and bacon into pieces.
5. Put the pork and bacon into a food processor and grind (mince).
6. Add the tarragon, parsley and scallions (spring onions).
7. Squeeze the spinach and watercress to extract as much liquid as possible. Add to the food processor.
8. Add the garlic and purée again, gradually adding the eggs, nutmeg, Cayenne pepper and salt and pepper to taste: this terrine should be highly seasoned.
9. Pour the mixture into a 2 quart (2 litre/3½ pint) terrine dish. Press down well with the palm of your hand. Put the bacon strip (rasher) on top. Cover the terrine and microwave for 25 minutes on MEDIUM-HIGH.
10. When the terrine is cooked, remove the cover, set a small plate with a heavy weight on top and leave to cool at room temperature. Chill in the refrigerator for 24 hours.
11. To serve, remove the bacon and serve the terrine either in its dish or turned out on to a serving dish, accompanied by a light mayonnaise.

Snails in Herb Sauce

◼▷   00.07   00.04   〰
Serves 4

American	Ingredients	Metric/Imperial
12	snipped sorrel leaves	12
¾ cup	sour cream (crème fraîche)	200 ml/7 fl oz
1	egg	1
2 tbsp	chopped chervil	2 tbsp
½ tsp	garlic powder	½ tsp
2 tbsp	kirsch brandy	1 tbsp
	salt	
	pepper	
48	canned snails	48

1. Put the sorrel into a bowl, cover and microwave on HIGH for 1 minute.
2. Drain the sorrel and return to the bowl.
3. Add the sour cream (crème fraîche), egg, chopped chervil, garlic powder, kirsch brandy, salt and pepper. Stir thoroughly, microwave on HIGH for 1 minute.
4. Drain the snails, rinse under cold running water, then drain again. Divide between 4 ramekins.
5. Taste the sauce and adjust seasoning. Pour over the snails. Put the ramekin dishes in the microwave oven in a circle, leaving the center empty. Heat on HIGH for 1½ minutes. Serve at once.
If the snails are to be served in their shells, they will need to be reheated once placed in the shells.

Cream Cheese Canapés

00.03   **00.02**
Serves 4

American	Ingredients	Metric/Imperial
1 tbsp	butter	½ tbsp
4	slices of spice bread	4
2	Chavignol cream cheeses	2
½ tsp	dried thyme	½ tsp
	pepper	

1. Lightly butter the slices of spice bread. Put in a circle on a plate, leaving the center of the plate empty.
2. Cut each of the cheeses into 2 slices. Put one half cheese on each slice of spice bread. Sprinkle with thyme and pepper.
3. Cover and microwave on HIGH for 2 minutes until the cheese begins to melt. Serve at once.

Veal Terrine with Orange

00.30   **00.20**
plus marinading and chilling time

American	Ingredients	Metric/Imperial
1 lb	veal leg or rump	450 g/1 lb
10½ oz	boneless pork chine	300 g/10½ oz
2	oranges	2
1	finely sliced onion	1
1	finely chopped garlic clove	1
1	carrot, sliced into thin rounds	1
1	dried chili	1
2	bayleaves	2
½ cup	cognac	4 tbsp
3 tbsp	oil	2 tbsp
½ tsp	mixed herbs	½ tsp
½ tsp	ground ginger	½ tsp
½ lb	fresh pork fat	225 g/8 oz
2	eggs	2
1½ tsp	salt	1½ tsp
	pepper	
6	strips (rashers) streaky bacon	6

1. Slice half the veal into long strips ½ inch (1.25 cm) wide. Cut the other half into small pieces, including the fat. Cut the pork chine into small pieces.
2. Rinse the oranges, dry and peel them, removing as much of the pith as possible. Halve and squeeze in a liquidizer to obtain at least ¾ cup (200 ml/7 fl oz) of juice.
3. Put the onion, garlic, carrot and orange juice in a bowl.
4. Cut the chili in two and add to the vegetable mixture.
5. Crumble one bayleaf into the mixture.
6. Stir in the cognac, oil, ground ginger and half the mixed herbs. Stir well.
7. Add the veal and pork, stir again, and marinade in the refrigerator for 24 hours. Remove the veal and pork and set aside.
8. De-rind the pork fat and cut into small pieces. Put the pieces into a food processor. Add the pork and pieces of veal (but not the long strips) and grind (mince) finely.
9. Add the eggs, marinade, remaining mixed herbs, and salt and pepper.
10. Carefully line the base and sides of a 1¼ quart (1.25 litre/2¼ pint) oval terrine with the strips (rashers) of bacon. Put half a bayleaf at each end.
11. Spoon one-third of the ground (minced) meat into the terrine. Lay the veal strips on top. Add the remaining ground (minced) meat. Press down well. Cover with strips (rashers) of bacon. Cover the terrine and microwave on MEDIUM-HIGH for 20 minutes.
12. When the terrine is cooked, remove the cover. Place a dish with a heavy weight on top directly on the mixture and leave to cool at room temperature. Chill in the refrigerator for at least 24 hours.

Veal terrine with orange

Fish

Whiting on a Bed of Vegetables

	00.10	00.17
	Serves 4	

American	Ingredients	Metric/Imperial
1	chopped shallot	1
¼ lb	fennel, cut into strips	125 g/4 oz
14 oz	sliced tomatoes	400 g/14 oz
1	sprig thyme	1
1	crushed garlic clove	1
1 tbsp	chopped parsley	1 tbsp
3 tbsp	port	2 tbsp
2 tbsp	wine vinegar	1 tbsp
2 tbsp	olive oil	1 tbsp
	salt	
	pepper	
4	cleaned whiting or silver hake	4

1. Arrange the shallot and fennel in a rectangular dish, large enough to contain the fish. Cover and microwave on HIGH for 5 minutes.
2. Arrange the tomatoes over the fennel and shallot mixture. Crumble the thyme over. Add the garlic and parsley. Pour the port, vinegar and olive oil over all. Add salt and pepper to taste. Cover and microwave on HIGH for 3 minutes.
3. Rinse the fish under cold running water and pat dry on kitchen paper. Salt and pepper the inside of the fish. Make 2 or 3 deep incisions in the fleshiest part of the fish. Arrange the fish, head-to-tail on the vegetables. Cover and microwave on HIGH for 7 minutes. Leave to stand for 1 minute. Serve in the cooking dish.

Whiting Fillets with Anchovy Cream

	00.08	00.08
	Serves 4	

American	Ingredients	Metric/Imperial
⅓ cup	dry white wine	100 ml/3 fl oz
2 tbsp	fish bouillon (stock) powder	1 tbsp
8	anchovy fillets in oil	8
2 tbsp	softened butter	1 tbsp
4	silver hake or whiting fillets	4
1 tsp	cornstarch (cornflour)	1 tsp
3 tbsp	sour cream (crème fraîche)	2 tbsp
2 tbsp	tomato ketchup	1 tbsp
	salt	
	pepper	

1. Mix the white wine and fish bouillon (stock) powder together in a bowl. Cover and microwave on HIGH for 1 minute.
2. Purée the anchovy fillets and the butter in a food processor. Rinse the whiting fillets and pat dry on kitchen paper. Spread one side of each fillet with the anchovy paste and fold in two. Put the folded fillets side by side in a dish and pour the white wine and fish bouillon (stock) over. Cover and microwave on HIGH for 5 minutes.

3. Transfer the fish fillets to a serving dish with a slotted spoon. Cover with aluminum (aluminium) foil to keep warm.
4. Put the cornstarch (cornflour) into a bowl, add the sour cream (crème fraîche) and mix to a smooth paste. Add the cooking liquid from the fish and the tomato ketchup. Cook on HIGH for 1 minute. Beat with a hand whisk and cook for 1 further minute on HIGH.
5. Taste the sauce and adjust seasoning. Pour over the fish and serve hot.

Whiting with Shallot Sauce

	00.10	00.15
	Serves 4	

American	Ingredients	Metric/Imperial
2 oz	finely chopped shallots	50 g/2 oz
⅔ cup	dry white wine	150 ml/¼ pint
4	cleaned silver hake or whiting	4
	salt	
	pepper	
3 tbsp	fresh lemon juice	2 tbsp
2 tsp	butter	2 tsp
3 tbsp	sour cream (crème fraîche)	2 tbsp
2 tbsp	chopped parsley	2 tbsp

1. Put the shallots in a bowl. Pour the white wine over the shallots and cook in the microwave oven for 6 minutes on HIGH.
2. Rinse the fish under cold running water and pat dry on kitchen paper. Season the insides of the fish with salt and pepper. Make 2 or 3 deep incisions in the fleshiest part of the fish. Sprinkle the base of a rectangular or oval dish with salt and pepper and arrange the fish on it, side by side and head-to-tail. Pour the lemon juice over. Dot with butter, cover and microwave on HIGH for 7 minutes.
3. Using two large spatulas, carefully transfer the fish to a serving dish.
4. Pour the cooking liquid into the bowl with the shallots and white wine. Stir in the sour cream (crème fraîche) and reheat in the microwave oven on HIGH for 2 minutes.
5. Add the parsley and stir well. Taste and adjust seasoning. Pour the sauce over the fish and serve hot.

Microwave hint: Yogurt makes a good base for a sauce to serve with white fish. Purée cooked zucchini (courgette) or spinach in a blender with yogurt, lemon juice, salt and pepper. Transfer to a suitable dish and cook on MEDIUM for 3 minutes. Pour over the cooked fish and serve.

Previous page: Sea trout with field mushrooms, Sea bream in red sauce

Whiting roulades with zucchini (courgette) sauce

Whiting Roulades with Zucchini (Courgette) Sauce

	00.10	00.12	
	Serves 4		

American	Ingredients	Metric/Imperial
7 oz	zucchini (courgettes), very thinly sliced	200 g/7 oz
3 tbsp	butter	1½ tbsp
1¾ lb	whiting or silver hake fillets	700 g/1¾ lb
¼ cup	Roquefort cheese	75 g/3 oz
	pepper	
1 tbsp	chopped parsley	1 tbsp
2 tsp	cornstarch (cornflour)	2 tsp
4 tbsp	fresh lemon juice	3 tbsp
3 tbsp	sour cream (crème fraîche)	2 tbsp

1. Put the zucchini (courgettes) in a small casserole. Cover and microwave on HIGH for 5 minutes.
2. Use 1 teaspoon of the butter to grease the base of a round dish.
3. Rinse the whiting fillets under cold running water and pat dry on kitchen paper. Cut into 4 equal pieces.
4. Mix together the remaining butter with the Roquefort. Add pepper and the chopped parsley and stir well. Spread the whiting fillets with this mixture, and roll up, with the spread side inside.
5. Put the roulades in a circle on the buttered dish, leaving the center of the dish empty. Cover and microwave on HIGH for 6 minutes.
6. Drain the zucchini (courgettes) and purée in a food processor. Pour the purée into a bowl.
7. Stir in the cornstarch (cornflour) and mix well. Heat in the microwave oven for 1 minute on HIGH. Stir, cook for 1 further minute on HIGH and stir again.

8. Transfer the roulades to a serving dish with a slotted spatula. Pour the cooking liquid into the bowl containing the zucchini (courgette) mixture and stir in the lemon juice and sour cream (crème fraîche). Taste and adjust seasoning. Stir well. Reheat on HIGH for 1 minute.
9. Coat the roulades with the sauce and serve at once.

Fennel Sauce for Fish

	00.03	00.07	
	Serves 4		

American	Ingredients	Metric/Imperial
1	fennel bulb, trimmed and thinly sliced	1
2 tbsp	olive oil	1 tbsp
½ tsp	green peppercorns	½ tsp
3 tbsp	sour cream (crème fraîche)	2 tbsp
4 tbsp	fresh lemon juice	3 tbsp
	salt	

1. Put the fennel in a dish with 3 (2) tablespoons of water. Cover and microwave on HIGH for 7 minutes.
2. Purée the contents of the dish in a food processor, adding the oil, green peppercorns, sour cream (crème fraîche) and lemon juice. Season lightly with salt. Purée once more until smooth.
This sauce is perfect with any grilled or poached fish.

Whiting Fillets with Avocado

	00.10	00.09
	Serves 4	

American	Ingredients	Metric/Imperial
1	crushed garlic clove	1
1 tbsp	butter	½ tbsp
2½ lb	whiting or cod fillets, thawed if frozen	1.5 kg/2½ lb
	salt	
	pepper	
1	bunch chives	1
1	sweet pimento in brine	1
2	ripe avocado pears	2
⅓ cup	lime juice	4½ tbsp
4 tbsp	sour cream (crème fraîche)	3 tbsp

1. Put the crushed garlic in a bowl with the butter. Cover and microwave on HIGH for 1 minute.
2. Rinse the fish fillets and pat dry on kitchen paper. Season with salt and pepper. Arrange the fish on a rectangular dish, cover and microwave on HIGH for 5 minutes.
3. Rinse the chives and snip with kitchen scissors.
4. Chop the sweet pimento.
5. Peel the two avocados and remove the stones. Cut one of the avocados into long strips and put on a dish. Pour half the lime juice over and lay the pimento on top.

6. Purée the second avocado in a food processor, adding the garlic, sour cream (crème fraîche) and remaining lime juice.
7. Stir in the chives and the cooking liquid from the fish. Add salt and pepper to taste. Cook in the microwave oven for 2 minutes on HIGH.
8. Warm the sliced avocado and pimento in the oven for 1 minute on HIGH. Cut the fish fillets in half and put in the center of the dish. Pour the sauce into a sauceboat and serve on the side.

Whiting in Chili Sauce

	00.10	00.09
	plus marinating time	

American	Ingredients	Metric/Imperial
1¾ lb	silver hake or whiting fillets	700 g/1¾ lb
3	limes	3
	salt	
	pepper	
1	finely chopped onion	1
1	fresh green chili, trimmed, seeded and very finely chopped	1
1 tbsp	butter	½ tbsp
4 tbsp	sour cream (crème fraîche)	3 tbsp
1 tbsp	chopped parsley	1 tbsp

Whiting fillets with avocado

Whiting in chili sauce

1. Rinse the silver hake or whiting fillets and pat dry on kitchen paper. Cut the fillets into pieces.
2. Squeeze two of the limes to obtain about ½ cup (100 ml/4 fl oz) of juice.
3. Sprinkle salt and pepper over the base of a hollow dish. Arrange half the fish fillets in the dish in one layer. Season with salt and pepper, then arrange the other half on top. Season again. Pour the lime juice over. Cover and leave to marinate in the refrigerator for at least 2 hours.
4. Put the onion and chili in a small dish and add the butter. Cover and microwave on HIGH for 3 minutes.
5. Spread this mixture over the fish, then coat it with sour cream (crème fraîche). Cover and microwave on HIGH for 4 minutes.
6. Leave to stand for 2 minutes. Rinse the third lime very carefully and pat dry on kitchen paper. Slice it into rounds. Add the parsley to the fish. Garnish with slices of lime and serve hot.

Microwave hint: To make a thickened sauce to serve with fish, blend 1-2 teaspoons cornstarch (cornflour) with a little water. Stir into the cooking liquid, from the fish, whisking well. Cook, uncovered, on HIGH for 2 minutes. Whisk again, bringing the sauce to the boil. If the sauce has not boiled, return to the microwave for a further minute. Spoon over the fish and serve.

Merlan à la sauce au concombre

Whiting with Cucumber Sauce

American	Ingredients	Metric/Imperial
00.06	Serves 4	00.09

American	Ingredients	Metric/Imperial
1	peeled, diced cucumber	1
4	whiting or silver hake fillets	4
	salt	
	pepper	
2	egg yolks	2
1½ tsp	mild mustard	1½ tsp
1 tbsp	chopped chives	1 tbsp
2 tbsp	butter	1 tbsp

1. Put the cucumber in a small casserole. Cover and microwave on HIGH for 3 minutes.
2. Rinse the whiting fillets and pat dry on kitchen paper. Season with salt and pepper and fold each fillet in half. Arrange the fish, side by side on a dish. Cover and microwave on HIGH for 4 minutes.
3. Purée the cucumber in a food processor and put it into a bowl. Stir in the egg yolks and mustard carefully.
4. When the fish is cooked, lift it on to a serving dish with a slotted spatula. Sprinkle with chopped chives.
5. Put the bowl containing the cucumber mixture into the microwave oven and cook for 2 minutes on HIGH, beating well midway through the cooking time. Stir once more and add the butter in tiny pieces. Taste and adjust seasoning. Pour into a sauceboat and serve with the fish.

Turban de merlan aux brocolis

Ring Mold (Mould) of Whiting with Broccoli

00.15	Serves 4	00.21

American	Ingredients	Metric/Imperial
1	bunch watercress	1
10½ oz	frozen creamed broccoli	300 g/10½ oz
14 oz	silver hake or whiting fillets	400 g/14 oz
	salt	
	pepper	
3	eggs	3
⅔ cup	sour cream (crème fraîche)	150 ml/¼ pint
1 tsp	butter	1 tsp
3½ oz	shelled shrimp (prawns)	100 g/3½ oz

1. Remove the tough stalks from the watercress, Rinse it under plenty of cold running water and put it in a casserole. Cover and microwave on HIGH for 2 minutes. Drain the watercress in a strainer (sieve).
2. Put the frozen creamed broccoli in a dish and microwave, uncovered, for 4 minutes on HIGH.
3. Rinse the whiting fillets under plenty of cold running water and pat dry on kitchen paper. Purée in a food processor for 1 minute. Add the watercress, salt and pepper. Purée again.

4. Beat two of the eggs with a fork. Add ¼ cup (3 tablespoons) of sour cream (crème fraîche), beating constantly. Season with salt and pepper. Add the whiting and watercress purée and the broccoli. Taste and adjust seasoning.
5. Butter the base and sides of a small Pyrex ring mold (mould) and pour in the mixture. Cover and microwave on HIGH for 10 minutes.
6. Put a serving dish upside down on the ring mold (mould) and turn it over. Leave the mixture in the mold (mould) to stand for 3 minutes.
7. To make the sauce, mix together 1 egg, the remaining sour cream (crème fraîche) and the shrimp (prawns) in a bowl. Season with salt and pepper. Heat in the microwave oven for 1 minute on HIGH.
8. Remove the Pyrex ring mold (mould) and drain off any liquid from the dish. Put half the sauce in the middle of the whiting mousse and pour the rest into a sauceboat. Serve at once.

Colinot à l'estragon

Hake with Tarragon

00.08	Serves 4	00.14

American	Ingredients	Metric/Imperial
1	hake (about 2 lb/1 kg), cleaned	1
2	finely chopped shallots	2
2 tbsp	chopped tarragon	1 tbsp
½ tsp	sugar	½ tsp
2 tbsp	tarragon vinegar	1 tbsp
½ cup	dry white wine	125 ml/4 fl oz
2	egg yolks	2
	salt	
	pepper	
¼ cup	butter	50 g/2 oz

1. Rinse the fish under plenty of cold running water and pat dry on kitchen paper. Curl round in a dish or ring mold (mould). Cover and microwave on HIGH for 9 minutes.
2. Put the shallots in a bowl with the tarragon, sugar and tarragon vinegar.
3. When the fish is cooked, leave to stand for 2 minutes. Put the bowl containing the shallot mixture into the oven and cook on HIGH for 2 minutes.
4. Add the white wine and the egg yolks one at a time, beating constantly with a hand whisk. Add salt and pepper to taste. Return the bowl to the oven and microwave on HIGH for 30 seconds. Whisk vigorously once more and microwave for a further 30 seconds.
5. Cut the butter into tiny pieces and add to the sauce, a few at a time, beating constantly.
6. Remove the skin from the top side of the fish. Put the fish upside down on a serving dish. Remove the rest of the skin.
7. Return the sauce to the oven and reheat for a further 30 seconds. Whisk again, coat the fish with half the sauce and put the rest in a sauceboat. Serve at once.

Hake with tarragon sauce

Colin, sauce Choron

Hake with Tarragon Sauce

00.10   00.12
Serves 4

American	Ingredients	Metric/Imperial
1	chopped shallot	1
1	sprig tarragon	1
½ tsp	coarsely ground black pepper	½ tsp
¼ cup	vinegar	4 tbsp
4	hake fillets, thawed if frozen	4
	salt	
	pepper	
½ cup	butter	125 g/4 oz
3	egg yolks	3
1 tsp	tomato concentrate (purée)	1 tsp

1. Put the shallot in a bowl. Rinse the tarragon and chop 5 leaves. Add the 5 tarragon leaves, black pepper and vinegar to the shallot. Microwave for 3 minutes on HIGH until the liquid is reduced to 2 (1) tablespoon. Filter and return to the bowl. Set aside.

2. Rinse the fish and pat dry on kitchen paper. Season with salt and pepper on both sides. Put the fillets in a round dish, skin side outward. Cover and microwave on HIGH for 5-6 minutes according to the thickness of the fillets.

3. Remove the skin and place the fish on a serving dish. Cover with aluminum (aluminium) foil to keep it warm.

4. Cut the butter into tiny pieces and put in a large bowl. Melt in the microwave oven for 1 minute on HIGH. Beat with a hand beater.

5. Mix the egg yolks and the reduced vinegar liquid together, whisking constantly. Gradually pour over the butter, stirring gently. Microwave on MEDIUM for 1 minute. Whisk again. If the sauce is smooth and creamy, add the tomato concentrate; if not, microwave for a further 30 seconds on MEDIUM. Add the tomato concentrate (purée).

6. Chop the remaining tarragon. Add to the sauce, pour into a sauceboat and serve with the fish.

Colin à la crème safranée
Hake in Saffron Sauce

	00.10	00.15	
	Serves 4		

American	Ingredients	Metric/Imperial
1	finely chopped shallot	1
2	small carrots, cut into matchstick (Julienne) strips	2
⅔ cup	dry white wine	150 ml/¼ pint
2 tbsp	butter	1 tbsp
1	fish bouillon (stock) cube	1
4	hake fillets, thawed if frozen	4
¼ tsp	saffron	¼ tsp
¼ cup	sour cream (crème fraîche)	4 tbsp
	salt	
	pepper	

1. Put the shallot and carrots in a round dish with the white wine, butter and fish bouillon (stock). Cover and microwave on HIGH for 6 minutes.
2. Rinse the fish under plenty of cold running water. Pat dry on kitchen paper and put in the dish, skin side outward. Cover and microwave on HIGH for 5-6 minutes according to the thickness of the fillets.
3. Remove the fish with a slotted spatula and transfer to a serving dish. Cover with aluminum (aluminium) foil to keep warm.
4. Stir the saffron and sour cream (crème fraîche) into the fish cooking liquid. Stir well and cook, uncovered, for 3 minutes on HIGH.
5. Remove the skin from the fish. Taste the sauce and adjust seasoning. Pour over the fish and serve.

Colin aux endives
Hake with Belgian Chicory (Endives)

	00.15	00.19	
	Serves 4		

American	Ingredients	Metric/Imperial
14 oz	Belgian chicory (endives)	400 g/14 oz
1 tbsp	butter	½ tbsp
½ cup	white port	125 ml/4 fl oz
	salt	
	pepper	
4	hake slices	4
3 tbsp	fresh lemon juice	2 tbsp
2 oz	shelled shrimp (prawns)	50 g/2 oz
2	eggs	2

1. Remove the outer leaf and bitter heart of the Belgian chicory (endives) and cut into rounds. Put the chicory (endive) in a casserole with the butter, white port and salt and pepper to taste. Stir well. Cover and microwave on HIGH for 8 minutes.
2. Rinse the fish. Sprinkle salt and pepper into the base of a small dish and add the fish. Season with salt and pepper and pour the lemon juice over. Cover and microwave on HIGH for 5-6 minutes depending on the thickness of the fish steaks. Add the shrimp (prawns) 1 minute before the end of cooking to heat them through.

3. Beat the eggs in a bowl with a fork. Add 1-2 tablespoons of water and beat again.
4. Drain the fish and the chicory (endives) and set aside. Pour the cooking liquid from both into a small bowl and heat on HIGH for 1 minute.
5. Pour the hot liquid into the eggs in a thin trickle, whisking constantly. Put the sauce in the oven and microwave on MEDIUM for 2½ minutes.
6. Arrange the fish and chicory (endives) on a serving dish. Whisk the sauce (which will have separated slightly) and pour over. Serve at once.

Savarin de colinot
Hake Mousse with Shrimp (Prawns) and Mushrooms

	00.10	00.18	
	Serves 4		

American	Ingredients	Metric/Imperial
4	hake fillets	4
4 tbsp	lobster bisque	3 tbsp
1 cup	sour cream (crème fraîche)	250 ml/8 fl oz
2 tbsp	cognac	1 tbsp
3	eggs	3
	salt	
	pepper	
¼ lb	white button mushrooms, finely sliced	125 g/4 oz
1	egg yolk	1
2 tbsp	fresh lemon juice	1 tbsp
3	sprigs fresh dill, chopped	3
2 oz	shelled shrimp (prawns)	50 g/2 oz

1. Rinse the fish fillets and pat dry on kitchen paper. Purée in a food processor, adding the lobster bisque, ⅓ cup (100 ml/3 fl oz) of sour cream (crème fraîche), the cognac and 1 whole egg. Separate the remaining two eggs. Add the yolks to the fish mixture and purée once more, adding salt and pepper to taste. Pour the mixture into a bowl.
2. Add a pinch of salt to the 2 egg whites and whisk to firm peaks. Fold carefully into the mixture and pour into a Pyrex ring mold (mould) 10 inches (22 cm) in diameter. Cover and microwave on HIGH for 8 minutes. Leave to stand for 5 minutes.
3. To make the sauce, put the mushrooms in a small casserole. Cover and microwave on HIGH for 3 minutes. Whisk the remaining sour cream (crème fraîche) with the single egg yolk and the lemon juice. Season with salt and pepper. Add the dill and the shelled shrimp (prawns). Pour over the mushrooms and stir well. Cover and microwave on MEDIUM for 2 minutes. Stir once more.
4. Turn the mousse out on to a serving dish, pour the sauce over and serve.

Couronne aux deux poissons

Festive Two-Fish Ring Mold (Mould)

	00.12	00.14	
	Serves 4-6		

American	Ingredients	Metric/Imperial
1 tsp	butter	1 tsp
8	flounder fillets	8
¾ lb	hake, boned and skinned	350 g/12 oz
¾ cup	sour cream (crème fraîche)	200 ml/7 fl oz
1	large egg	1
1½ tbsp	chopped tarragon	1½ tbsp
	salt	
	pepper	
2 lb	clams in their shells	1 kg/2 lb
1½ tsp	cornstarch (cornflour)	1½ tsp
4 tbsp	white wine	3 tbsp
2 tbsp	dry Vermouth	1 tbsp
½ cup	finely grated Cheddar cheese	25 g/1 oz
3½ oz	shelled shrimp (prawns)	100 g/3½ oz

Hake mousse with shrimp (prawns) and mushrooms

1. Butter a small Pyrex ring mold (mould) 10 inches (22 cm) in diameter.
2. Rinse the flounder fillets under plenty of cold running water and pat dry on kitchen paper. Flatten the fish as much as possible with a pastry roller (rolling-pin). Line the ring mold (mould) with the fillets, overlapping on the bias if necessary.
3. Cut the hake into small pieces and purée until smooth in a food processor, adding ⅔ cup (150 ml/¼ pint) of sour cream (crème fraîche), the egg, half the tarragon, salt and pepper. Fill the mold (mould) with the purée, folding the ends of the flounder over to cover the mixture. Cover and microwave on HIGH for 8 minutes.
4. To make the sauce, rinse the clams carefully under plenty of cold running water to remove any grit. Put in a large dish. When the fish mousse is cooked, take it out of the oven and leave to stand. Put the clams in the oven and heat for 1-1½ minutes until the shells open. Remove the clams from their shells and filter the cooking liquid.
5. Put the cornstarch (cornflour) in a bowl and gradually stir in the white wine and Vermouth until a smooth paste is obtained. Add the remaining sour cream (crème fraîche) and the clam liquid. Cook for 1 minute on HIGH. Stir well, then cook for 1 more minute on HIGH.
6. If there is any liquid on the surface of the mousse, add to the sauce. Add the grated cheese and remaining tarragon. Stir carefully until the cheese has melted. Taste and adjust seasoning. Add the clams. Reheat for 1 minute if necessary.
7. Turn the mousse out on to a serving dish. Pour the sauce into the center, garnish with the shrimp (prawns) and serve.

Rascasse à la sétoise
White Fish with Garlic Mayonnaise

▰▷ 00.10   00.11   〽
Serves 4

American	Ingredients	Metric/Imperial
2	sticks celery	2
2	small finely chopped carrots	2
⅓ cup	white wine	4½ tbsp
3 lb	cod or whiting fillets	1.5 kg/3 lb
	salt	
	pepper	
¾ cup	olive oil	200 ml/7 fl oz
1	egg yolk	1
1 tsp	mustard	1 tsp
½ tsp	Cayenne pepper	½ tsp
1 tsp	cognac	1 tsp
2	garlic cloves	2

1. Set the celery leaves aside and cut the stalks into matchstick (julienne) strips.
2. Put the celery and carrot into a bowl with the white wine. Cover and microwave on HIGH for 6 minutes.
3. Rinse the fish and cut each fillet in quarters. Season with salt and pepper.
4. Season the carrots and celery and put into a rectangular dish, large enough to contain the fish. Put the fish on top and cover with the celery leaves. Pour ¼ cup (50 ml/2 fl oz) olive oil over. Cover and microwave on HIGH for 5 minutes.
5. Mix together the egg yolk and mustard. Add the remaining olive oil in a thin trickle, whisking with an electric beater. Add the Cayenne pepper and cognac.
6. Lift the fish out of the dish with a slotted spoon and put it in a serving dish. Discard the celery leaves.
7. Peel and crush the garlic over the cooking liquid. Stir well and pour the liquid carefully into the mayonnaise sauce. Stir gently.
8. Cover the fish with the sauce and serve.

Cabillaud à la cressonnette
Cod in Watercress Sauce

▰▷ 00.08   00.10   〽
Serves 4

American	Ingredients	Metric/Imperial
2 tbsp	butter	1 tbsp
2 tbsp	all-purpose (plain) flour	1 tbsp
1 cup	milk	250 ml/8 fl oz
3 tbsp	sour cream (crème fraîche)	2 tbsp
	salt	
	pepper	
4	thick cod steaks	4
1	bunch watercress	1

1. To make the sauce, put the butter in a large bowl and melt in the microwave oven for 1 minute on HIGH. Sprinkle the flour over and stir well. Add the milk, stirring constantly. Cook on HIGH for 3 minutes, stirring with a hand whisk every minute. Add the sour cream (crème fraîche). Add salt and pepper to taste and stir thoroughly.

2. Rinse the fish steaks. Sprinkle with salt and pepper on both sides. Arrange the fish skin side outward in a round dish, leaving the center of the dish empty. Cover and microwave on HIGH for 4-5 minutes, depending on the thickness of the steaks.
3. Remove the tough stalks of the watercress, rinse thoroughly, drain and purée. Add the purée to the sauce and stir well.
4. Put the fish on a serving dish and remove the skin. Reheat the sauce for 1 minute on HIGH. Coat the fish with the sauce and serve.

Simple Poached Cod

▰▷ 00.20   00.40   〽
Serves 4

American	Ingredients	Metric/Imperial
3¼ lb	tail piece of cod	1.5 kg/3¼ lb
3 tbsp	lemon juice	2 tbsp
1	onion, sliced into rings	1
2	sliced carrots	2
1	sliced leek	1
1	small céleriac, peeled and diced	1
3 oz	mixed herbs	75 g/3 oz
1	bay leaf	1
10	black peppercorns	10
5	white peppercorns	5
3	whole cloves	3
¼ tsp	mustard seeds	¼ tsp
1	sliced lemon	1
2 tbsp	vinegar	1 tbsp
1 tsp	salt	1 tsp

1. Sprinkle the fish with the lemon juice and leave to stand for 15 minutes.
2. Put the fish in a dish with 1 cup (250 ml/8 fl oz) water. Arrange the vegetables around the fish and stir in the remaining ingredients. Cover and microwave on HIGH for 10 minutes. Turn the fish carefully and baste with the cooking liquid. Cook for a further 10 minutes on HIGH. Leave to stand for 5 minutes.
3. Divide the fish between four plates and serve with a spoonful of vegetables and a little melted butter poured over each portion.

Cabillaud au concombre

Cod in Cucumber Sauce

00.10 **00.15**
Serves 4

American	Ingredients	Metric/Imperial
4	finely chopped shallots	4
1	cucumber, peeled and diced	1
½ tsp	garlic powder	½ tsp
½ tsp	dried thyme	½ tsp
1 tsp	superfine (caster) sugar	1 tsp
	salt	
	pepper	
4 tbsp	white wine	3 tbsp
1½ lb	cod fillets	600 g/1½ lb
4 tbsp	fresh lemon juice	3 tbsp
1	natural flavor yogurt	1
1	egg yolk	1
1 tbsp	chopped parsley	1 tbsp

1. Put the shallots in a small casserole, cover and microwave on HIGH for 2 minutes.
2. Add the diced cucumber, half the garlic powder, half the thyme, sugar, salt and pepper to taste, and the white wine. Stir well. Cover and microwave on HIGH for 6 minutes.
3. Rinse the fish and pat dry on kitchen paper. Cut the fish into pieces. Sprinkle salt and pepper in the base of a dish and put in the fish. Sprinkle with salt and pepper, the remaining garlic powder and thyme, and add the lemon juice. Cover and microwave on HIGH for 6 minutes.
4. Mix together the yogurt and the egg yolk, whisking vigorously, and add the cooking liquid from the fish. Pour the sauce over the cucumber, stir well and microwave on HIGH for 1 minute.
5. Put the vegetables and the fish on a serving dish. Sprinkle with chopped parsley and serve.

Morue aux poireaux

Salt Cod with Leeks

00.15 **00.19**
plus soaking time

American	Ingredients	Metric/Imperial
1 lb	salt cod	450 g/1 lb
	pepper	
⅓ cup	milk	100 ml/3 fl oz
2 tbsp	butter	1 tbsp
1½ lb	leeks	600 g/1½ lb
	salt	
4 tbsp	white wine	3 tbsp
3 tbsp	golden raisins (sultanas)	3 tbsp
3 tbsp	sour cream (crème fraîche)	2 tbsp
1 cup	grated Gruyère cheese	50 g/2 oz

1. Put the salt cod in cold water to soak for 24 hours, changing the water frequently.
2. Drain the salt cod and cut into pieces. Put the fish in a dish and add the pepper, milk and butter. Cover and microwave on HIGH for 5 minutes.
3. Remove the tough green part of the leeks, the roots and the outer leaves. Cut in half and then into ½ inch (1.25 cm) pieces. Rinse thoroughly.
4. Put the leeks in a dish, season with salt and pepper and add the white wine. Cover and microwave on HIGH for 12 minutes.
5. Rinse the golden raisins (sultanas).
6. Using two spatulas, remove the salt cod from the dish and flake with a fork.
7. Pour the cooking liquid from the leeks into the dish in which the cod was cooked. Add the sour cream (crème fraîche) and golden raisins (sultanas) and reheat for 2 minutes on HIGH.
8. Arrange the cod on top of the leeks.
9. Add the grated Gruyère to the sauce, stir until just melted and coat the cod and leeks with it. Serve at once.

Cod in watercress sauce

Sweet-and-sour fish

Rascasse à la fondue d'oignon

Fish with Onion Purée

◄▷ 00.07   00.08   〰
         Serves 2

American	Ingredients	Metric/Imperial
10½ oz	onions, sliced in rings	300 g/10½ oz
1½ lb	fillets of any white fish	600 g/1½ lb
	salt	
	pepper	
3 tbsp	dry sherry	2 tbsp
¼ tsp	curry powder	¼ tsp
2 tbsp	sour cream (crème fraîche)	1 tbsp

1. Put the onions in a dish with 1-2 tablespoons of water. Cover and microwave on HIGH for 5 minutes.
2. Rinse the fish fillets under plenty of cold running water and pat dry on kitchen paper. Arrange the fish, side by side in a long dish and season with salt and pepper. Add the sherry. Cover and microwave on HIGH for 2½ minutes.
3. Drain the onions in a strainer (sieve) and purée until smooth in a food processor. Add the curry powder, sour cream (crème fraîche) and salt and pepper to taste. Leave the purée in the bowl of the food processor.
4. Transfer the fish to two plates with a slotted spoon. Add the cooking liquid to the onion purée. Purée once more.
5. Put half the purée on each plate beside the fish and serve at once.

Roussette à l'aigre-douce

Sweet-and-Sour Fish

◄▷ 00.10   00.23   〰
         Serves 4

American	Ingredients	Metric/Imperial
1½ lb	any firm white fish	650 g/1½ lb
2 tbsp	all-purpose (plain) flour	1 tbsp
2 tbsp	oil	1 tbsp
7 oz	finely chopped onion	200 g/7 oz
3	finely chopped garlic cloves	3
3 tbsp	vinegar	2 tbsp
1 oz	golden raisins (sultanas)	25 g/1 oz
2 tbsp	nuoc-nam (Vietnamese Fish Sauce)	1 tbsp
½ tsp	curry powder	½ tsp
	salt	
	pepper	
1	slice spice-bread	1

1. Heat a browning-dish in the microwave oven on HIGH for 6-8 minutes according to the manufacturer's instructions.
2. Rinse the fish under cold running water and pat dry on kitchen paper. Cut into 4 equal pieces. Toss the pieces in the flour.
3. When the browning-dish is hot, pour in the oil and tilt the dish in all directions to distribute the oil over its surface. Put the pieces of fish in the browning-dish, skin-side downward, and leave to cook until they stop sizzling. Remove the fish and set aside on a plate.
4. Put the onions and garlic on the browning-dish and microwave on HIGH for 6 minutes.
5. Add the vinegar, golden raisins (sultanas), nuoc-nam, curry powder and 1 cup (250 ml/8 fl oz) of water. Add salt and pepper to taste.
6. Crumble the spice-bread into the sauce and microwave on HIGH for 4 minutes.
7. Stir the dish carefully. Add the fish and stir gently to coat with the sauce. Cover and microwave on HIGH for 5 minutes. Serve very hot.

Roussette au curry

Fish in Curry Sauce

◄▭▭◄ 00.10   00.13   〰
Serves 4

American	Ingredients	Metric/Imperial
¼ lb	chopped onions	125 g/4 oz
2	chopped garlic cloves	2
2 tbsp	oil	1 tbsp
¾ cup	concentrated tomato juice	175 ml/6 fl oz
1 tbsp	curry powder	1 tbsp
2 tbsp	brandy	1 tbsp
¼ cup	coconut milk	4 tbsp
	salt	
	pepper	
1¾ lb	any firm white fish	750 g/1¾ lb
1	small banana, not too ripe	1

1. Purée the onions and garlic coarsely, in a food processor. Put the purée in a small casserole. Pour the oil over. Cover and microwave on HIGH for 3 minutes.
2. In a bowl, mix together the tomato juice, curry powder, brandy and coconut milk. Stir well. Pour over the onion mixture and stir thoroughly. Taste and adjust seasoning. Cover and microwave on HIGH for 5 minutes.
3. Rinse the fish under plenty of cold running water. Pat dry on kitchen paper. Cut the fish into 8 equal pieces and season with salt and pepper. Add the fish pieces to the casserole and stir carefully. Cover and microwave on HIGH for 4 minutes.
4. Peel the banana and slice into rounds. Add to the fish mixture and cook for 1 further minute. Serve very hot.

Rascasse à la méridionale

Mediterranean Style Fish

◄▭▭◄ 00.15   00.21   〰
Serves 4

American	Ingredients	Metric/Imperial
5 oz	sliced onions	150 g/5 oz
2	large garlic cloves, peeled and halved	2
5 oz	red bell pepper, seeded and chopped	150 g/5 oz
5 oz	diced zucchini (courgettes)	150 g/5 oz
1 lb	eggplant (aubergines), peeled and finely diced	450 g/1 lb
¼ tsp	dried thyme	¼ tsp
2 tbsp	olive oil	1 tbsp
	salt	
	pepper	
2½ lb	fillets of any white fish	1.5 kg/2½ lb
4 tbsp	fresh lemon juice	3 tbsp
2 tbsp	sour cream (crème fraîche)	1 tbsp
1 tbsp	chopped parsley	1 tbsp

1. Put the onions and garlic in a casserole with 1-2 tablespoons of water and microwave for 3 minutes on HIGH.
2. Remove the onions and garlic from the casserole and put in the red bell pepper. Cover and microwave on HIGH for 3 minutes.
3. Add the zucchini (courgettes) and 4 (2) tablespoons of water. Cover and microwave on HIGH for a further 3 minutes. Drain all the vegetables in a colander.
4. Put the eggplant (aubergines) in a dish with ¼ cup (3 tablespoons) of water. Cover and microwave on HIGH for 7 minutes. Drain.
5. Put all the vegetables in a food processor. Add the thyme, oil and salt and pepper to taste and purée.
6. Sprinkle salt and pepper in the base of an oval dish. Arrange the fish fillets in the dish and pour the lemon juice over. Sprinkle with salt and pepper. Cover and microwave on HIGH for 4 minutes.
7. Stir the sour cream (crème fraîche) into the vegetable purée and reheat on HIGH for 1 minute.
8. Spread the purée in a serving dish with the fish fillets on top. Sprinkle each fillet with chopped parsley and serve at once.

Microwave hint: To cook thin fillets of fish evenly by microwave, arrange them in a dish, tucking the thinnest part underneath the remainder of the fillet.

Fish in curry sauce

Haddock à la ciboulette
Haddock with Chive Sauce

◢▽ 00.10   00.06 〰
Serves 4

American	Ingredients	Metric/Imperial
2	haddock fillets, thawed if frozen	2
1/3 cup	fresh lemon juice	4½ tbsp
2	natural flavor yogurts	2
1	bunch chives	1
1 tsp	cornstarch (cornflour)	1 tsp
2 tbsp	white wine vinegar	1 tbsp
1	egg yolk	1
	salt	
	pepper	

1. Remove the skin from the haddock by inserting a sharp knife between the skin and the flesh and pushing gently in a downward direction, away from the tail. Cut each skinned fillet in half.
2. Put the 4 pieces of fish in a dish and pour over the lemon juice. Coat with the yogurt. Cover and microwave on HIGH for 4 minutes.
3. Rinse the chives and pat dry on kitchen paper. Snip them with kitchen scissors.
4. When the fish is cooked, lift out carefully with a slotted spatula and transfer to a serving dish.
5. Put the cornstarch (cornflour) in a bowl and gradually stir in the vinegar until smooth. Add the cooking liquid from the fish, stir well and microwave on HIGH for 1 minute.
6. Add the egg yolk, beating constantly with a hand whisk. Microwave for 1 minute on MEDIUM. Whisk again. Add the chives, whisking constantly. Taste and adjust seasoning.
7. Coat the fish with the sauce and serve any remaining sauce in a sauceboat on the side.

Haddock à la florentine
Haddock Florentine

◢▽ 00.05   00.10 〰
plus soaking time

American	Ingredients	Metric/Imperial
1½ lb	haddock, skinned	600 g/1½ lb
1 cup	milk	250 ml/8 fl oz
1 lb	frozen spinach	450 g/1 lb
2 tbsp	sour cream (crème fraîche)	1 tbsp
1	egg yolk	1
	pepper	
5 oz	streaky bacon	150 g/5 oz

1. Cut the haddock into four equal pieces. Put the fish pieces in a dish and pour the milk over. If not completely covered, add a little water. Leave to soak for 1 hour.
2. Put the spinach in a dish 10 minutes before serving. Cover and microwave on HIGH for 6 minutes.
3. Mix together the sour cream (crème fraîche) and the egg yolk. Season with pepper. Stir into the cooked spinach.
4. Cut the bacon into 4 slices and flatten as much as possible with the blade of a knife. Drain the haddock. Stir the spinach well. Arrange the haddock on the spinach and place a piece of bacon on top of each piece of fish. Cover and microwave on HIGH for 4 minutes. Serve at once.

Left: Haddock with chive sauce
Below: Haddock Florentine

Haddock aux poireaux

Haddock in Leek Cream Sauce

00.10 00.15

Serves 4

American	Ingredients	Metric/Imperial
14 oz	diced leeks, white part only	400 g/14 oz
2	haddock fillets	2
¼ cup	fresh lemon juice	4 tbsp
2	natural flavor yogurts	2
1 tsp	red peppercorns (baies roses)	1 tsp
1	egg yolk	1

1. Pour ¾ cup (200 ml/7 fl oz) of water into the lower compartment of a microwave steamer and heat in the oven for 2 minutes on HIGH.
2. Put the leeks in the perforated section and then into the steamer. Cover and microwave on HIGH for 9 minutes.
3. To skin the haddock, put each fillet, skin side down, on a board with the tail towards you. Make a small incision through the flesh at the tail end. Dip the fingers of one hand in salt and hold the tail firmly, while with the other hand, ease a sharp, flexible knife between flesh and skin, pushing the flesh away from the skin. Cut each fillet in half.
4. Put the 4 pieces of haddock in a dish. Pour the lemon juice and yogurt over. Add the red peppercorns (baies roses). Cover and microwave on HIGH for 4 minutes.
5. When the fish is cooked, transfer to a serving dish. Beat the cooking liquid and egg yolk together with a hand whisk.
6. Coat the fish with the sauce, arrange the leeks around it and serve.

Haddock in leek cream sauce

Rôti de poisson en cocotte

Provençale Fish Casserole

00.15 00.37

Serves 4-5

American	Ingredients	Metric/Imperial
5 oz	thinly sliced onions	150 g/5 oz
2	crushed garlic cloves	2
2 tbsp	white wine	1 tbsp
1	red bell pepper, rinsed seeded, cut into thin strips	1
14 oz	diced eggplant (aubergines)	400 g/14 oz
½ lb	diced zucchini (courgettes)	225 g/8 oz
3	coarsely chopped tomatoes	3
2 tbsp	olive oil	1 tbsp
	salt	
	pepper	
2	sprigs thyme	2
12	black olives	12
2 lb	haddock or salmon, rolled	1 kg/2 lb
3 tbsp	fresh lemon juice	2 tbsp
3 tbsp	sour cream (crème fraîche)	2 tbsp

1. Put the onions and garlic into a large casserole with the white wine. Cover and microwave on HIGH for 3 minutes.
2. Add the bell pepper to the casserole. Cover and microwave on HIGH for 3 minutes.
3. Add the eggplant (aubergines), zucchini (courgettes) and tomatoes to the casserole and pour the oil over.
4. Add salt and pepper to taste and stir well. Put the 2 sprigs of thyme between the vegetables. Cover and microwave on HIGH for 12 minutes, stirring mid-way through the cooking time.
5. Add the olives to the vegetable mixture.
6. Make a hollow in the center of the mixture. Put the rolled fish (it should resemble a boned roast of pork or beef) into this hollow and pour half the lemon juice over. Add salt and pepper. Cover and microwave on HIGH for 7 minutes.
7. Turn the fish over and pour the remaining lemon juice over.
8. Add more salt and pepper and pour in the sour cream (crème fraîche). Cover and microwave on HIGH for 7 minutes.
9. Leave the fish to stand for 5 minutes. Discard the thyme sprigs. Put the vegetables into a serving dish and place the fish in the center. Serve hot.

Lotte au fenouil

Monkfish with Fennel

00.08 00.11

Serves 4

American	Ingredients	Metric/Imperial
1¾ lb	monkfish	700 g/1¾ lb
	salt	
	pepper	
5 oz	very thinly sliced fennel	150 g/5 oz
1	chopped tomato	1
4 tbsp	sour cream (crème fraîche)	3 tbsp
2 tbsp	dry Vermouth	1 tbsp
2 tbsp	chopped dill	2 tbsp

Monkfish with fennel

1. Remove the central cartilage and rinse the fish under plenty of cold running water. Pat dry on kitchen paper. Cut into thick pieces and season with salt and pepper. Cover and microwave on HIGH for 5 minutes.

2. Drain the fish with a slotted spatula and transfer to a serving dish. Cover with aluminum (aluminium) foil.

3. Put the fennel and tomato in the dish in which the fish was cooked. Cover and microwave on HIGH for 5 minutes. Add the sour cream (crème fraîche) and the Vermouth and cook for 1 minute on HIGH.

4. Purée the mixture in a food processor. Taste and adjust seasoning and add the chopped dill.

5. Pour the sauce over the fish and serve hot, with the fennel fronds as a garnish.

Lotte à la crème d'ail

Monkfish in Garlic Sauce

	00.15	00.22	
	Serves 4		

American	Ingredients	Metric/Imperial
4	leeks, white part only	4
3 tbsp	white wine	2 tbsp
2 lb	monkfish fillets	1 kg/2 lb
30	young garlic cloves	30
	salt	
	pepper	
2 tbsp	butter	1 tbsp
4 tbsp	sour cream (crème fraîche)	3 tbsp

1. Remove the base and the outer leaves of the leeks. Cut in half lengthwise and then into dice. Rinse thoroughly and leave to drain. Put into a bowl with the white wine. Cover and microwave on HIGH for 6 minutes.
2. Rinse the monkfish fillets under plenty of cold running water. Pat dry on kitchen paper and cut into thick slices.
3. Peel and halve the young garlic cloves and remove the central green stem.
4. Arrange the slices of monkfish on top of the leeks. Season with salt and pepper. Cover and microwave on HIGH for 5 minutes.
5. Put the garlic cloves in a bowl with the butter. Spoon the cooking liquid from the monkfish over. Cover and microwave on HIGH for 10 minutes.
6. Blend the contents of the bowl with the sour cream (crème fraîche), salt and pepper. Pour the sauce back into the bowl. Reheat in the microwave oven on HIGH for 1 minutes.
7. Transfer the monkfish and leeks to a serving dish. Pour the sauce over them and serve very hot.

Lotte aux pleurotes

Monkfish with Mushrooms

	00.12	00.19	
	Serves 4		

American	Ingredients	Metric/Imperial
1½ lb	field mushrooms	600 g/1½ lb
3 oz	smoked streaky bacon, de-rinded and cut into thin strips	75 g/3 oz
1	finely chopped shallot	1
1	finely chopped garlic clove	1
	salt	
	pepper	
2 lb	monkfish	1 kg/2 lb
2 tbsp	fresh lemon juice	1 tbsp
2 tbsp	cognac	1 tbsp
2 tsp	cornstarch (cornflour)	2 tsp
¼ cup	sour cream (crème fraîche)	3 tbsp

1. Wipe the mushrooms with a damp cloth or kitchen paper, making sure all the earth is removed, and slice.
2. Put the bacon, shallot and garlic in a casserole. Microwave for 2 minutes on HIGH. Add the mushrooms. Season with salt and pepper. Cover and microwave on HIGH for 6 minutes, stirring midway through the cooking time.
3. Rinse the monkfish under plenty of cold running water and pat dry on kitchen paper. Cut the fish into thick slices, and arrange the slices, side by side on a dish. Add salt and pepper to taste. Cover and microwave on HIGH for 6 minutes. Discard the cooking liquid.
4. Drain the mushrooms into a small bowl, setting aside the cooking liquid.
5. Mix together the mushroom cooking liquid, lemon juice and cognac. Stir in the cornstarch (cornflour) carefully. Microwave for 1 minute on HIGH.
6. Stir in the sour cream (crème fraîche) and mix the sauce with the mushrooms.
7. Pour the mushroom sauce over the slices of fish. Cover and microwave on HIGH for 4 minutes. Serve at once in the casserole.

Braised Monkfish Tails

	00.05	00.06	
	Serves 4		

American	Ingredients	Metric/Imperial
1 lb	monkfish tail fillets	450 g/1 lb
2 tbsp	cornstarch (cornflour)	1 tbsp
4	lightly beaten egg whites	4
3 tbsp	vegetable oil	2 tbsp
3 tbsp	bouillon (stock)	2 tbsp
1 tsp	salt	1 tsp
1 tsp	finely chopped scallions (spring onions)	1 tsp
2 tbsp	dry sherry	1 tbsp
2 tsp	vinegar	2 tsp
2	egg yolks	2
	few drops sesame seed oil	

1. Skin and bone the fish and cut into thin shreds.
2. Coat the fish with the cornstarch (cornflour) then mix well with egg whites.
3. Heat the oil on HIGH for 1 minute. Stir in the fish shreds and cook on HIGH for 3 minutes, stirring very gently two or three times.
4. Stir in the stock, salt, scallions (spring onions), sherry and vinegar. Cook for 2 minutes on HIGH, stirring gently once or twice.
5. Transfer the fish to a serving dish with the egg yolks on top. Sprinkle with the sesame seed oil and bring the dish to the table. Break the yolks and stir into the dish just before serving.

Gigot de lotte à la moutarde

Whole Monkfish with Mustard

	00.10	00.19	
	Serves 4		

American	Ingredients	Metric/Imperial
1	small green bell pepper, rinsed, seeded and diced	1
5 oz	thinly sliced onions	150 g/5 oz
2 oz	smoked back bacon, cut into tiny pieces	50 g/2 oz
5 oz	thinly sliced zucchini (courgettes)	150 g/5 oz
5 oz	thinly sliced eggplant (aubergines)	150 g/5 oz
2	crushed garlic cloves	2
3 tbsp	dry white wine	2 tbsp
1	sprig thyme	1
1	bayleaf	1
1	whole monkfish (1¾ lb/750 g)	1
2 tbsp	horseradish mustard	1 tbsp
1 tsp	ground black pepper	1 tsp
2	large tomatoes	2
	salt	
	pepper	
2 tbsp	sour cream (crème fraîche)	1 tbsp

1. Put the bell pepper, onions and bacon into a small casserole. Cover and microwave on HIGH for 3 minutes.
2. Add the zucchini (courgettes), eggplant (aubergines), garlic, white wine, thyme and bayleaf to the casserole. Cover and microwave on HIGH for 7 minutes.
3. Rinse the fish under plenty of cold running water. Pat dry on kitchen paper and remove the central cartilage. Spread one of the fillets with half the mustard, then sandwich the other fillet on top. Bind the two fillets together with kitchen string.
4. Sprinkle the base of an oval dish with half the ground black pepper and put the fish on top. Spread the top of the fish with the remaining mustard and sprinkle the remaining black pepper over.
5. Skin and quarter the tomatoes and cut the quarters in two. Arrange the tomato around the fish. Season only the tomatoes with salt and pepper. Cover and microwave on HIGH for 6 minutes. Leave to stand for 3 minutes.
6. Transfer the fish to a serving dish with a slotted spoon. Remove the kitchen string.
7. Add the sour cream (crème fraîche) to the dish in which the fish was cooked and stir well. Discard the thyme and bayleaf from the casserole. Stir the vegetables into the cooking liquid from the fish. Season lightly with salt and pepper. Pour the vegetable mixture around the fish and serve hot.

Whole monkfish with mustard

Lotte au curry
Monkfish in Curry Sauce

▬◣ 00.15   **00.19**   〰
Serves 6-7

American	Ingredients	Metric/Imperial
4 lb	monkfish	2 kg/4 lb
	salt	
	pepper	
7 oz	chopped onions	200 g/7 oz
2	chopped garlic cloves	2
5 oz	grated carrots	150 g/5 oz
1	small green chili, seeded and very finely chopped	1
2 tbsp	oil	1 tbsp
2 tbsp	cognac	1 tbsp
⅓ cup	white wine	100 ml/3 fl oz
¾ cup	concentrated tomato juice	175 ml/6 fl oz
2 tsp	curry powder	2 tsp
½ tsp	sugar	½ tsp
¾ cup	sour cream (crème fraîche)	200 ml/7 fl oz

1. Remove the central cartilage from the monkfish. Rinse under plenty of cold running water and pat dry on kitchen paper. Put the two fillets in a long dish. Season with salt and pepper. Cover and microwave on HIGH for 5 minutes.
2. Purée the onions and garlic in a food processor.
3. Put the garlic and onion purée in a small casserole. Cook for 2 minutes on HIGH. Add the carrots, chili, oil, cognac and white wine. Stir well. Cover and microwave on HIGH for 5 minutes.
4. Add the curry powder, sugar and sour cream (crème fraîche) to the concentrated tomato juice and stir well. Pour the mixture into the casserole. Stir thoroughly, taste and adjust seasoning.
5. Drain the monkfish and cut it into ½ inch (1.25 cm) cubes. Put into a dish and pour the sauce over. Stir well. Cover and microwave on HIGH for 5 minutes. Serve very hot.
In season, you can add 3 or 4 fresh lychees per person. Remove the skin and heat them in a small bowl for 1 ½ minutes on HIGH.

Médaillons de lotte aux figues fraîches
Medallions of Monkfish with Fresh Figs

▬◣ 00.08   **00.11**   〰
Serves 4

American	Ingredients	Metric/Imperial
2 lb	monkfish	1 kg/2 lb
3 oz	lean smoked streaky bacon, chopped into thin strips	75 g/3 oz
2	chopped shallots	2
2 tbsp	butter	1 tbsp
12	fresh figs	12
	salt	
	pepper	
3 tbsp	sherry vinegar	2 tbsp

1. Rinse the monkfish under plenty of cold running water. Pat dry on kitchen paper and remove the central cartilage. Cut the flesh into ½ inch (1.25 cm) cubes and arrange the pieces side by side in a dish. Cover and microwave on HIGH for 5 minutes.
2. Put the bacon and shallots in a dish. Add the butter and cook, uncovered, in the microwave oven for 2½ minutes on HIGH.
3. Rinse the figs and remove the stalks. Cut into four without quite separating the quarters.
4. Put the figs in the dish with the bacon and shallots. Add salt and pepper and the vinegar. Microwave for 3 minutes on HIGH.
5. Drain the monkfish. Arrange the figs around the edges of a serving platter. Put the monkfish into the dish with the bacon, shallots and cooking liquid from the figs. Season with salt and pepper and stir well.
6. Transfer the mixture to the center of the serving dish with the figs and serve at once.

Lotte à l'italienne
Monkfish Italian Style

▬◣ 00.10   **00.14**   〰
Serves 4

American	Ingredients	Metric/Imperial
3½ oz	carrots, cut into matchstick (julienne) strips	100 g/3½ oz
3½ oz	baby turnips, cut into matchstick (julienne) strips	100 g/3½ oz
3½ oz	potatoes, cut into matchstick (julienne) strips	100 g/3½ oz
2	coarsely chopped sticks celery	2
4	diced leeks, white part only	4
1	twist orange zest (peel)	1
1	sprig thyme	1
1	bayleaf	1
¼ tsp	saffron powder	¼ tsp
⅔ cup	white wine	150 ml/¼ pint
4 tbsp	olive oil	3 tbsp
	salt	
	pepper	
2 lb	monkfish	1 kg/2 lb
1	skinned, chopped tomato	1
4	crushed garlic cloves	4
15-20	basil leaves	15-20
2 tbsp	butter	25 g/1 oz
1 cup	grated Parmesan cheese	50 g/2 oz

1. Put the carrots, turnips, potato, celery, leeks, twist of orange zest (peel), thyme and bayleaf into a casserole.
2. Add the saffron, white wine and 3 (2) tablespoons of olive oil. Season with salt and pepper. Stir well. Cover and microwave on HIGH for 8 minutes.
3. Rinse the fish under plenty of cold running water. Pat dry on kitchen paper. Remove the central cartilage, cut each fillet into thick slices and season with salt and pepper.
4. Stir the contents of the casserole and add the fish. Cover and microwave on HIGH for 6 minutes.

5. To make the sauce: purée the tomato, garlic and basil leaves in a food processor, adding the butter in tiny pieces, the Parmesan cheese and the remaining olive oil. Purée until smooth.

6. Transfer the fish to a dish. Discard the thyme, bayleaf and orange zest (peel).

7. Add the cooking liquid from the fish to the sauce and stir well. Add the sauce to the vegetable mixture. Stir well again, pour over the fish and serve hot.

Médaillons de lotte flambés
Monkfish Flamed in Cognac

	00.10	00.18	
	Serves 4		

American	Ingredients	Metric/Imperial
14 oz	coarsely chopped tomatoes	400 g/14 oz
2	crushed garlic cloves	2
4	finely chopped shallots	4
2 tbsp	vinegar	1 tbsp
2 tbsp	tomato concentrate (purée)	1 tbsp
½ cup	white wine	5 tbsp
	salt	
	pepper	
¼ tsp	Cayenne pepper	¼ tsp
2 lb	monkfish	1 kg/2 lb
1 tsp	curry powder	1 tsp
¼ cup	cognac	3 tbsp
3 tbsp	butter	1½ tbsp
1 tbsp	chopped parsley	1 tbsp

1. Put the tomatoes, garlic, shallots, vinegar and tomato concentrate (purée) in a casserole. Pour the white wine over. Add salt, pepper and Cayenne pepper. Cover and microwave on HIGH for 10 minutes.

Monkfish flamed in cognac

2. Remove the central cartilage of the monkfish, rinse under plenty of cold running water and pat dry on kitchen paper. Cut the flesh into ½ inch (1.25 cm) cubes.

3. Purée the vegetable mixture in a food processor.

4. Sprinkle salt and pepper into a dish and add the curry powder. Roll the monkfish cubes in the mixture until well coated. Cover and microwave on HIGH for 5 minutes.

5. Discard the cooking liquid from the fish. Put the cognac in a cup and heat in the microwave oven for 30 seconds. Pour over the fish and flambé.

6. Coat the fish with the tomato sauce. Stir well. Cover and microwave on HIGH for a further 2 minutes.

7. Transfer the fish to a serving dish with a slotted spoon. Cut the butter into tiny pieces and beat into the sauce.

8. Coat the fish with the sauce. Sprinkle with chopped parsley and serve at once.

Gâteau de lotte
Monkfish Gâteau

	00.20	00.32	
	plus standing time		

American	Ingredients	Metric/Imperial
1¾ lb	monkfish, bone removed	750 g/1¾ lb
	salt	
	pepper	
⅔ cup	concentrated tomato juice	150 ml/¼ pint
12	eggs	12
2 tbsp	chopped parsley	2 tbsp
2 tbsp	butter	1 tbsp
7 oz	white button mushrooms	200 g/7 oz
1	can mushroom soup	1
3 tbsp	dry sherry	2 tbsp
7-8	unshelled shrimp (prawns)	7-8

1. Rinse the monkfish under plenty of cold running water and pat dry on kitchen paper. Cut into ½ inch (1.25 cm) pieces. Put in a dish and season with salt and pepper. Cover and microwave on HIGH for 4 minutes. Leave to cool.

2. Put the concentrated tomato juice into a bowl.

3. Break the eggs into a large bowl and beat them with a fork. Add the tomato juice, chopped parsley and salt and pepper to taste. Mix thoroughly.

4. Use 1 teaspoon of the butter to grease a 2 quart (1.75 litre/3 pint) ring mold (mould). Drain the monkfish and break up in the dish. Pour the egg mixture over. Stir well and pour into the ring mold (mould). Cover and microwave on MEDIUM for 10 minutes, then on HIGH for 6 minutes.

5. Wipe the button mushrooms with a damp cloth or kitchen paper and discard the stalks. Slice the caps thinly. Pour the cream of mushroom soup into a small bowl.

6. Take the ring mold (mould) out of the oven to rest for 1 hour.

7. Just before serving, heat a browning dish in the microwave oven for 6 minutes on HIGH. Put the remaining butter into the hot browning dish, add the mushrooms and stir with a spatula until they stop sizzling. Season with salt and pepper. Cover and microwave on HIGH for 4 minutes.

8. Remove from the oven. Heat the soup for 2 minutes on HIGH.

9. Turn the ring mold (mould) out on to a serving dish.

10. Add the sherry and mushrooms to the mushroom soup and pour the mixture into the center of the mold (mould). Garnish with the shrimp (prawns). Serve hot.

Red mullet in caper sauce

Rougets à la sauce aux câpres

Red Mullet in Caper Sauce

 00.05   00.09
Serves 4

American	Ingredients	Metric/Imperial
4	red mullet	4
	salt	
	pepper	
4 tbsp	white wine	3 tbsp
½ cup	butter	75 g/3 oz
1 tsp	cornstarch (cornflour)	1 tsp
⅓ cup	milk	100 ml/3 fl oz
2	egg yolks	2
3 tbsp	capers	2 tbsp
2	slices lemon	2
4	sprigs flat parsley	4

1. Rinse the red mullet under plenty of cold running water and pat dry on kitchen paper. Season the insides with salt and pepper. Put on a dish and add the white wine. Dot the fish with ⅓ of the butter. Cover and microwave on HIGH for 5 minutes. Leave to stand for 2 minutes. Put the red mullet on a serving dish.
2. Put the cornstarch (cornflour) in a bowl and add the milk, stirring constantly until smooth. Stir in the cooking liquid from the fish and the egg yolks. Stir well. Cook for 2 minutes on HIGH.

3. Whisk the sauce and add the remaining butter in tiny pieces, whisking the whole time. Taste and adjust seasoning. Add the capers and pour into a sauceboat.
4. Garnish the red mullet with the lemon slices and chopped parsley. Serve hot.

Grondins aux poireaux

Red Mullet with Leek Sauce

00.12   00.19
Serves 4

American	Ingredients	Metric/Imperial
3	leeks, white part only	3
1	chopped onion	1
2 tbsp	butter	1 tbsp
¾ cup	dry white wine	200 ml/7 fl oz
4	red mullet, thawed if frozen, cleaned, heads and fins removed	4
	salt	
	pepper	
2 tbsp	fish bouillon (stock) powder	1 tbsp
1	bunch chives	1
2 tsp	cornstarch (cornflour)	2 tsp
¼ cup	sour cream (crème fraîche)	3 tbsp

1. Remove the base and the outer layer of the leeks. Cut in half lengthwise, then into dice. Rinse thoroughly.

2. Put the onion and leeks into an oval dish, large enough to contain the fish. Add the butter and wine. Cover and microwave on HIGH for 10 minutes.

3. Rinse the fish under plenty of cold running water and pat dry on kitchen paper. Season the insides of the fish with salt and pepper. Make 2 or 3 incisions in the fleshiest part of the fish.

4. Stir the fish bouillon (stock) powder into the leek and onion. Arrange the fish side by side on the dish. Cover and microwave on HIGH for 7 minutes.

5. Rinse the chives, pat dry on kitchen paper and snip with kitchen scissors.

6. When the fish are cooked, lift out with two spatulas. Remove the skin, take out the fillets and arrange on a serving dish.

7. Put the cornstarch (cornflour) into a bowl and carefully stir in the sour cream (crème fraîche). Add the contents of the cooking dish and stir well. Microwave for 1 minute on HIGH, stir again and cook for a further 1 minute. Stir, taste and adjust seasoning, pour over the fish fillets, sprinkle with chopped chives and serve.

Mulet à la provençale

Grey Mullet, Provençale Style

American	Ingredients	Metric/Imperial
	00.10 Serves 4	00.13
3½ lb	grey mullet	1.5 kg/3½ lb
2	onions, sliced into thin rings	2
3 tbsp	white wine	2 tbsp
4	tomatoes	4
	salt	
	pepper	
2	sprigs thyme	2
12	seedless black olives	12
3 tbsp	olive oil	2 tbsp

1. Clean and scale the fish carefully. Rinse under plenty of cold running water and pat dry on kitchen paper. Cut the fish into ½ inch (1.25 cm) slices. Discard the head and tail.

2. Line the base of a large round dish with the onions. Add the white wine and microwave for 2 minutes on HIGH.

3. Rinse the tomatoes, remove the stalks and cut them in half and remove the seeds and juice. Cut each half into thick slices.

4. Put the tomatoes on top of the onions in a single layer. Season with salt and pepper. Crumble 1 sprig of thyme over and return the dish to the oven and microwave on HIGH for 3 minutes.

5. Arrange the fish slices on top of the tomatoes, skin side outward. Pour the olive oil over and crumble the second thyme sprig on top. Season with salt and pepper. Put the olives on top of the tomatoes. Cover and microwave on HIGH for 6 minutes.

6. Leave to stand for 2 minutes, then serve.

Rascasse à la crème d'aubergine

Red Snapper in Eggplant (Aubergine) Sauce

American	Ingredients	Metric/Imperial
	00.10 Serves 4	00.22
1	eggplant (aubergine), peeled and sliced into thin rounds	1
1	quartered garlic clove	1
4 tbsp	fresh lemon juice	3 tbsp
4 tbsp	sour cream (crème fraîche)	3 tbsp
1	egg	1
	salt	
	pepper	
4	red snapper fillets	4

1. Put the garlic and eggplant (aubergine) in a casserole. Cover and microwave on HIGH for 12 minutes. Leave to stand for 5 minutes.

2. Drain the eggplant (aubergine) slices. Purée in a food processor, gradually adding 2 (1) tablespoons of lemon juice, 3 (2) tablespoons of sour cream (crème fraîche), the egg and salt and pepper to taste.

3. When the eggplant (aubergine) purée is smooth and creamy, spread over the base of a serving dish.

4. Rinse the fish fillets under plenty of cold running water and pat dry on kitchen paper. Cut each fillet in half. Arrange on the eggplant (aubergine) cream and add salt and pepper. Cover and microwave on HIGH for 4 minutes.

5. Mix the remaining sour cream (crème fraîche) with the remaining lemon juice and pour over the fish. Cover and microwave on HIGH for 30 seconds. Serve immediately.

Microwave hint: To defrost and cook frozen fish fillets in the microwave: Put 1 lb (450g) of frozen fillets in a dish and defrost on LOW for 3-4 minutes. Drain the liquid produced and use as a base for a sauce. Stir in an equal quantity of milk, 1 teaspoon of cornstarch (cornflour) and a few drops of anchovy essence (extract). Cook the defrosted fish on HIGH for a further 2 minutes and test that the flesh flakes with a fork. Add any further excess liquid to the sauce and reheat on MEDIUM for 3 minutes. Stir well and pour over the fish.

Roussette à la paysanne
Dogfish Peasant-Style

00.15 **00.13** Serves 4

American	Ingredients	Metric/Imperial
3½ oz	smoked streaky bacon, diced	100 g/3½ oz
3½ oz	diced carrots	100 g/3½ oz
2	chopped onions	2
2	leeks, white part only, finely sliced	2
2	skinned tomatoes, coarsely chopped	2
2	crushed garlic cloves	2
3 oz	button mushrooms, sliced	75 g/3 oz
⅓ cup	dry white wine	100 ml/3 fl oz
1¾ lb	dogfish	750 g/1¾ lb
3 tbsp	cognac	1 tbsp
¼ tsp	saffron powder	¼ tsp
	salt	
	pepper	
3 tbsp	butter	1½ tbsp
1 tbsp	chopped chives	1 tbsp

1. Put the bacon, carrots and onions in a casserole with 2 tablespoons of water. Cover and microwave on HIGH for 4 minutes.
2. Add the leeks, tomatoes, garlic, mushrooms and white wine. Cover and microwave on HIGH for 3 minutes.
3. Rinse the fish under plenty of cold running water. Pat dry on kitchen paper and cut into 4 equal pieces. Add the cognac and saffron, salt and pepper to the casserole.
4. Season the fish with salt and pepper. Arrange the fish on top of the vegetable mixture. Cover and microwave on HIGH for 3 minutes. Turn fish over and cook for a further 3 minutes.
5. Remove the fish from the casserole with a slotted spatula.
6. Cut the butter into tiny pieces and stir into the vegetables. Put the vegetables on a serving dish and arrange the fish on top. Sprinkle with chopped chives and serve.

Roussette à la ratatouille de fenouil
Dogfish with Fennel Ratatouille

00.15 **00.18** Serves 4

American	Ingredients	Metric/Imperial
7 oz	finely chopped onions	200 g/7 oz
3½ oz	lean bacon, cut into thin strips	100 g/3½ oz
2 tbsp	oil	1 tbsp
1¾ lb	finely grated fennel	750 g/1¾ lb
14 oz	puréed tomatoes	400 g/14 oz
2	crushed garlic cloves	2
½ tsp	thyme	½ tsp
	salt	
	pepper	
3 tbsp	white wine	2 tbsp
1¾ lb	dogfish	750 g/1¾ lb
3 tbsp	sour cream (crème fraîche)	2 tbsp

1. Put the onion, bacon and oil into a dish and microwave, uncovered, on HIGH for 3 minutes.
2. Mix together the fennel, tomatoes, garlic, thyme, salt and pepper. Pour into the dish on top of the onions. Add the white wine. Cover and microwave on HIGH for 5 minutes.
3. Rinse the fish under plenty of cold running water and pat dry on kitchen paper. Cut the fish into 4 equal pieces.
4. Stir the sour cream (crème fraîche) into the vegetable mixture. Stir well. Put the fish on top of the vegetables. Cover and microwave on HIGH for 3 minutes.
5. Turn the fish over. Cover and microwave on HIGH for a further 3-4 minutes, depending on the thickness of the slices.
6. Leave to stand for 3 minutes. Serve hot.

Roussette à la vendangeuse
Dogfish with Green Grapes

00.10 **00.10** Serves 4

American	Ingredients	Metric/Imperial
4	finely chopped shallots	4
1	finely chopped garlic clove	1
3 tbsp	butter	2 tbsp
1¾ lb	dogfish	750 g/1¾ lb
2 tbsp	all-purpose (plain) flour	1 tbsp
2 tbsp	curry powder	1 tbsp
¼ tsp	turmeric	¼ tsp
	salt	
	pepper	
3 tbsp	fresh lemon juice	2 tbsp
2 tbsp	white port	1 tbsp
1 tsp	Scotch whisky	1 tsp
10½ oz	seedless green grapes	300 g/10½ oz
1	egg yolk	1
¼ cup	sour cream (crème fraîche)	100 ml/3 fl oz
¼ tsp	Cayenne pepper	¼ tsp

1. Put the shallots and garlic in a dish with the butter. Cover and microwave on HIGH for 3 minutes.
2. Cut the fish into 3 inch (7.5 cm) pieces. Rinse under plenty of cold running water and pat dry on kitchen paper.
3. Mix together the flour, curry powder and turmeric. Add salt and pepper. Roll the pieces of fish in the mixture until coated.
4. Add the lemon juice, port and Scotch whisky to the shallots. Arrange the fish side by side on top. Cover and microwave on HIGH for 5 minutes.
5. Rinse and peel the grapes. Mix together the egg yolk, sour cream (crème fraîche) and Cayenne pepper. Coat the fish with the mixture. Add the grapes. Cover and microwave on HIGH for 2 minutes.
6. Put the fish on a serving dish. Mix together the cooking liquids and pour over. Serve at once.

Dogfish with green grapes

Daurade au fenouil
Sea Bream with Fennel

	00.15	00.24	
	Serves 2		

American	Ingredients	Metric/Imperial
2	chopped shallots	2
2 tsp	butter	2 tsp
14 oz	fennel	400 g/14 oz
1	red bell pepper, seeded and coarsely chopped	1
6	anchovy fillets in oil	6
½ tsp	mixed herbs	½ tsp
¼ cup	white wine	4 tbsp
4 tbsp	sour cream (crème fraîche)	3 tbsp
	salt	
	pepper	
1	dorade or sea bream, cleaned and scaled	1
1 tbsp	chopped parsley	1 tbsp

1. Put the shallots in a bowl with the butter and microwave on HIGH for 2 minutes.
2. Remove the tough stalks of the fennel and cut the bulb into thin strips. Put in a large oval dish with ¼ cup (4 tablespoons) of water. Cover and microwave on HIGH for 10 minutes.
3. Put the red bell pepper, anchovy fillets, shallots, mixed herbs, white wine and sour cream (crème fraîche) into a food processor. Add salt and pepper and purée.
4. Rinse the fish under plenty of cold running water. Pat dry on kitchen paper. Make sure that all scales have been removed. Make 2 or 3 deep incisions in the fleshiest part of the fish close to the head, on each side. Season the inside of the fish with salt and pepper.
5. When the fennel is tender, stir into the sauce. Return the sauce to the dish in which the fennel was cooked and put the fish on top. Cover and microwave on HIGH for 6 minutes.
6. Turn the fish over and cook for a further 6 minutes.
7. Sprinkle the fish and fennel with parsley and serve hot.

Daurade au chou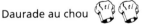
Sea Bream with Savoy Cabbage

	00.05	00.18	
	Serves 4		

American	Ingredients	Metric/Imperial
14 oz	shredded crinkly (Savoy) cabbage	400 g/14 oz
1½ lb	dorade or sea bream fillets	600 g/1½ lb
	salt	
1 tsp	thyme	1 tsp
1 tsp	honey vinegar	1 tsp
3 tbsp	cognac	2 tbsp
	pepper	
3 tbsp	butter	2 tbsp
3 tbsp	lime juice	2 tbsp

1. Put 1 cup (250 ml/8 fl oz) water in the lower compartment of a microwave steamer. Cover and microwave on HIGH for 3 minutes.
2. Rinse and drain the cabbage and put into the perforated compartment of the steamer and place above the boiling water. Cover and microwave on HIGH for 10 minutes.
3. Rinse the fish under plenty of cold running water and pat dry on kitchen paper. Cut the fillets in half lengthwise. Salt both sides. Crumble half the thyme over.
4. Mix together the vinegar, cognac and remaining thyme.
5. Sprinkle salt and pepper over the base of a square shallow casserole.
6. Spread the shredded cabbage over the base of the casserole.
7. Pour the vinegar and cognac mixture over and add salt and pepper to taste. Using half the butter, dot tiny pieces on top. Arrange the fish fillets on top. Dot with the remaining butter. Cover and microwave on HIGH for 5 minutes.
8. When the fish is cooked, adjust seasoning and pour the lime juice over. Serve at once.

Daurade au parmesan
Sea Bream with Parmesan Cheese

	00.05	00.08	
	Serves 2		

American	Ingredients	Metric/Imperial
2	sea bream fillets	2
	salt	
	pepper	
3 tbsp	grated Parmesan cheese	2 tbsp
4	large tomatoes	4
3 tbsp	sour cream (crème fraîche)	2 tbsp

1. Rinse the fish fillets and pat dry on kitchen paper. Sprinkle salt and pepper into the base of a long dish. Put the fish in and season again with salt and pepper. Sprinkle the Parmesan over.
2. Rinse and slice the tomatoes and arrange on top of the fish to cover. Coat the tomatoes with the sour cream (crème fraîche). Season lightly with salt and pepper. Cover and microwave on HIGH for 7 minutes.
3. Leave to stand for 1 minute. Serve hot.

Daurade douce
Sea Bream in Mild Curry Sauce

	00.05	00.08	
	plus marinating time		

American	Ingredients	Metric/Imperial
1	sea bream, cleaned and scaled	1
	salt	
	pepper	
⅓ cup	wine vinegar	100 ml/3 fl oz
2	finely sliced onions	2
½ tbsp	mild curry powder	½ tbsp
4 tbsp	concentrated tomato juice	3 tbsp
3 tbsp	sour cream (crème fraîche)	2 tbsp

1. Rinse the fish under plenty of cold running water and pat dry on kitchen paper. Cut into ½ inch (1.25 cm) slices. Discard the head and tail. Sprinkle salt and pepper into the base of a dish. Add the slices of fish. Pour the vinegar over and season with salt and pepper. Leave to marinate for at least 1 hour.

2. Put the onions into a dish large enough to hold the fish. Cook, uncovered, for 3 minutes on HIGH.

3. Add the curry powder, concentrated tomato juice, sour cream (crème fraîche) and 1-2 tablespoons of the fish marinade to the onions and stir well.

4. Drain the slices of fish and arrange on top of the onion mixture. Cover and microwave on HIGH for 5 minutes. Serve hot in the same dish.

Daurade corail

Sea Bream in Red Sauce

	00.10	00.15	
	Serves 4		

American	Ingredients	Metric/Imperial
1 lb	red bell peppers, seeded and coarsely chopped	450 g/1 lb
7 oz	tomatoes	200 g/7 oz
4	sea bream fillets	4
2 tbsp	olive oil	1 tbsp
	salt	
½ tsp	coarsely ground black pepper	½ tsp
2 tbsp	wine vinegar	1 tbsp
½ tsp	sugar	½ tsp
3 tbsp	sour cream (crème fraîche)	2 tbsp
	pepper	
12	basil leaves	12

1. Put the bell peppers in a casserole. Cover and microwave on HIGH for 8 minutes.

2. Rinse and quarter the tomato and remove the seeds and juice.

3. Rinse the fish fillets under plenty of cold running water and pat dry on kitchen paper. Cut each fillet in two. Put the fish pieces side by side in a dish. Pour the olive oil over, add salt and sprinkle them with the coarsely ground black pepper.

4. Drain the bell peppers in a colander.

5. Put the fish in the oven. Cover and microwave on HIGH for 5 minutes.

6. Purée the bell peppers and tomato in a food processor, adding the vinegar, sugar and sour cream (crème fraîche). Season lightly with salt and pepper. Force the mixture through a strainer (sieve) over a bowl.

7. Rinse and chop the basil leaves.

8. Reheat the bell pepper sauce for 1 minute in the oven on HIGH and pour into a serving dish. Arrange the fish fillets carefully on top, sprinkle with chopped basil and serve.

Filets de daurade à la sauce au raifort

Sea Bream with Horseradish Sauce

	00.07	00.08	
	Serves 4		

American	Ingredients	Metric/Imperial
4	porgy (sea bream) fillets	4
	salt	
	pepper	
2 tbsp	fresh lemon juice	1 tbsp
⅓ cup	butter	75 g/3 oz
3	egg yolks	3
4 tbsp	wine vinegar	3 tbsp
½ tsp	sugar	½ tsp
3 tsp	prepared horseradish	3 tsp

1. Rinse the fish under plenty of cold running water. Pat dry on kitchen paper and season with salt and pepper on both sides. Arrange the fillets side by side in a rectangular dish and pour the lemon juice over. Cover and microwave on HIGH for 5 minutes.

2. Put the butter into a large bowl and melt in the oven for 1½ minutes on HIGH.

3. Put the egg yolks, vinegar and sugar into another bowl and whisk together. Whisk into the butter. Cook on HIGH for 30 seconds, whisk again, then cook a further 30 seconds. Whisk once more, then add the horseradish, still whisking vigorously.

4. Drain the fish and divide each fillet in two. Put one piece of fish on each plate, coat them with the horseradish sauce and serve at once.

If liked, garnish each plate with a sprig of parsley, tarragon or chervil.

Sea bream in red sauce

Sea bream, Provençale style

Poisson à la provençale

Sea Bream, Provençale Style

◀▭▷ 00.10 Serves 3-4   **00.31**

American	Ingredients	Metric/Imperial
3½ oz	sliced onions	100 g/3½ oz
1	red bell pepper, seeded and thinly sliced	1
1	zucchini (courgette), cut into rounds	1
1	eggplant (aubergine), cut into rounds	1
1	tomato, skinned and chopped	1
3 tbsp	vinegar	2 tbsp
4 tbsp	olive oil	3 tbsp
½ tsp	dried thyme	½ tsp
½ tsp	garlic powder	½ tsp
	salt	
	pepper	
1	sea bream, cleaned and scaled	1
1	lemon	1

1. Put the onion and pepper into an oval dish large enough to contain the fish. Cover and microwave on HIGH for 5 minutes.
2. Add the zucchini (courgette), eggplant (aubergine) and tomato to the dish. Pour the vinegar and ⅓ cup (2 tablespoons) of olive oil over. Sprinkle with thyme and garlic powder and season with salt and pepper. Cover and microwave on HIGH for 10 minutes.
3. Rinse the fish under plenty of cold running water and pat dry on kitchen paper, inside and out. Stir the vegetables and put the fish on top. Pour the rest of the oil over the mixture. Cover and microwave on HIGH for 8 minutes.
4. Turn the fish over. Slice the lemon and garnish the top of the fish with lemon slices. Cover and microwave on HIGH for 8 minutes. Serve hot.

Microwave hint: Whole fish such as trout can be cooked from frozen. Defrost a trout of about 1 lb (450 g) on LOW for 6 minutes, then cook on HIGH for 4 minutes, turning mid-way through the cooking time.

Harengs, sauce Soubise

Herrings in Soubise Sauce

	00.12	00.17	
	Serves 4		

American	Ingredients	Metric/Imperial
5 oz	chopped onions	150 g/5 oz
1	small, finely diced carrot	1
1	bayleaf	1
1	sprig thyme	1
⅔ cup	white wine	150 ml/¼ pint
4	herrings, heads removed	4
	salt	
	pepper	
2 tbsp	butter	1 tbsp
2 tbsp	all-purpose (plain) flour	1 tbsp
1¼ cups	milk	300 ml/½ pint

1. Put the onions and carrot into a bowl with the bayleaf, thyme and white wine. Cover and microwave on HIGH for 6 minutes.

2. Clean the herrings and rinse under plenty of cold running water. Pat dry on kitchen paper. Set aside the roes. Make 2 or 3 deep incisions in the fleshiest part of the fish.

3. Pour the onion and carrot mixture into a rectangular dish. Arrange the herrings on top and add salt and pepper. Cover and microwave on HIGH for 6 minutes.

4. Put the butter into a bowl and melt in the microwave oven for 1 minute on HIGH. Sprinkle over the flour and stir well. Add the milk and stir again. Microwave on HIGH for 3 minutes, whisking with a hand beater after every minute.

5. Transfer the fish to a serving dish with a slotted spatula. Cover to keep warm.

6. Discard the thyme and bayleaf and add the fish cooking liquid to the sauce in the bowl. Add the herring roes. Cook on HIGH for 1 minute. Taste and adjust seasoning. Force the sauce through a fine strainer (sieve) by pressing it with the back of a wooden spoon. Pour the sauce over the herrings and serve at once.

Herrings in soubise sauce

Harengs à la crème d'oeufs

Herrings in Herring Roe Sauce

▬▷ 00.05   00.07 〰
Serves 4

American	Ingredients	Metric/Imperial
4	herrings, heads removed	4
3½ oz	fresh herring roe	100 g/3½ oz
2 tsp	horseradish mustard	2 tsp
4 tbsp	fresh lemon juice	3 tbsp
4 tbsp	sour cream (crème fraîche)	3 tbsp
½ tsp	sugar	½ tsp
	salt	
	pepper	

1. Clean the fish and rinse under plenty of cold running water. Pat dry on kitchen paper. Make 2 or 3 incisions in the fleshiest part of the fish. Arrange the fish, side by side in a rectangular dish, with the cut sides downward. Cover and microwave on HIGH for 6 minutes.
2. Purée the herring roe in a food processor.
3. Pour the purée into a bowl and stir in the horseradish mustard, lemon juice, sour cream (crème fraîche), sugar, and salt and pepper. Stir well.
4. Put the bowl in the microwave oven and cook for 1 minute on HIGH. Stir again.
5. Transfer the fish to a serving dish and serve with the sauce on the side.

Flan vert aux sardines

Sardine Flan Florentine

▬▷ 00.30   00.14 〰
plus marinating time

American	Ingredients	Metric/Imperial
1½ lb	large fresh sardines	600 g/1½ lb
⅓ cup	vinegar	100 ml/4 fl oz
½ lb	frozen chopped spinach	225 g/8 oz
2	eggs	2
2	crushed garlic cloves	2
1	bunch parsley, finely chopped	1
½ tsp	grated nutmeg	½ tsp
	salt	
	pepper	

1. Butterfly the sardines: cut the head almost through from the backbone and pull. As the head comes off, the gut will come with it. Slit the fish along the belly and lift out the backbone, cutting the tail off with kitchen scissors. Rub off scales with kitchen paper or scrape off with a knife.
2. Rinse the filleted sardines under plenty of cold running water and pat dry on kitchen paper. Put the fish in a flan dish, sprinkle with vinegar and leave to marinate for 10-15 minutes.
3. Put the frozen spinach in a dish and defrost, uncovered, in the microwave oven for 3 minutes.
4. Break the eggs into a bowl and beat with a fork. Add the garlic, chopped parsley, spinach and grated nutmeg. Add salt and pepper to taste and stir well.

5. Drain the sardines and arrange them in two layers in a small soufflé case 6 inches (14 cm) in diameter. Microwave on HIGH for 5 minutes.
6. Holding the sardines with a spatula, pour out the cooking liquid from the soufflé case. Cover the sardines with the spinach mixture. Microwave, uncovered, on HIGH for 6 minutes.
7. Turn out the flan on to a serving dish and serve hot.

Maquereaux au vert

Mackerels Florentine

▬▷ 00.10   00.19 〰
Serves 4

American	Ingredients	Metric/Imperial
2	large chopped shallots	2
2 tbsp	butter	1 tbsp
1	crisp pear, peeled and sliced into strips	1
2 tbsp	fresh lemon juice	1 tbsp
1 lb	chopped frozen spinach	450 g/1 lb
2 tbsp	mild mustard	1 tbsp
	salt	
	pepper	
4	mackerel	4

1. Put the shallots in a bowl with the butter. Cover and microwave on HIGH for 3 minutes.
2. Add the pear to the bowl and pour the lemon juice over. Cover and microwave on HIGH for 2 minutes.
3. Put the frozen spinach in a rectangular dish large enough to hold the fish and microwave, uncovered, for 7 minutes on HIGH.
4. Purée the shallot and pear mixture in a food processor. Add the purée to the defrosted spinach.
5. Add the mustard and salt and pepper to taste.
6. Rinse the fish under plenty of cold running water and pat dry on kitchen paper. Make 2 or 3 incisions in the fleshiest part of the fish. Arrange the mackerel, side by side on the spinach mixture. Cover and microwave on HIGH for 7 minutes. Serve hot.

Mackerel with potato salad

Mackerel with Tarragon

Maquereaux à l'estragon

	00.05	00.08	
	Serves 4		

American	Ingredients	Metric/Imperial
2	large mackerel	2
3 tbsp	butter	1½ tbsp
	salt	
	pepper	
1½ tbsp	tarragon	1½ tbsp
1	lemon	1
1 tsp	tomato purée	1 tsp
1	natural flavor yogurt	1
1 tbsp	capers	1 tbsp

1. Clean the mackerel and remove the heads. Rinse well under cold running water and pat dry on kitchen paper. Put the fish side by side in a long dish.
2. Dot the fish with the butter. Season with salt and pepper and sprinkle with 1-2 tablespoons of tarragon.

3. Cut the lemon in two and squeeze half over the fish. Cover and microwave on HIGH for 3 minutes, turn the fish over and cook for a further 3 minutes.
4. To make the sauce: squeeze the other half-lemon and put the juice into a bowl. Add the tomato purée and yogurt, beating constantly. Add salt and pepper to taste, the remaining tarragon, the capers and the cooking liquid from the fish.
5. Put the bowl in the microwave oven and heat the sauce for 2 minutes on MEDIUM. Stir well.
6. Fillet the mackerel and put the fillets on a serving dish. Coat the fish with half the sauce and serve the rest of the sauce on the side.

Mackerel with Potato Salad

Maquereaux à la salade de pommes de terre

	00.15	00.30	
	plus standing time		

American	Ingredients	Metric/Imperial
1½ lb	sliced potatoes	600 g/1½ lb
	salt	
	pepper	
½ cup	white wine	125 ml/4 fl oz
⅓ cup	oil	100 ml/3 fl oz
3	chopped scallions (spring onions)	3
1	small carrot, cut into matchstick (julienne) strips	1
1	baby leek, very finely sliced	1
½ tsp	sugar	½ tsp
5	coriander seeds	5
6	black peppercorns	6
4	mackerels, cleaned	4
2 tsp	mustard	2 tsp
2 tbsp	chopped fresh herbs	2 tbsp

1. Put the potatoes in a dish with ½ cup (5 tablespoons) of water. Add salt and pepper. Cover and microwave on HIGH for 12 minutes. Leave to stand for 5 minutes.
2. Mix 3 (1½) tablespoons of the white wine with the oil. Season with salt and pepper.
3. Add the scallions (spring onions) to the white wine and oil and pour over the potatoes. Stir carefully and cover.
4. Put the carrot and leek into a dish large enough to hold the fish. Add the remaining white wine, the sugar, coriander and black peppercorns. Cover and microwave on HIGH for 5 minutes.
5. Rinse the mackerel under plenty of cold running water and pat dry on kitchen paper. Arrange the fish, side by side on the bed of vegetables. Season with salt and pepper. Cover and microwave on HIGH for 6 minutes. Leave to stand for 2 minutes.
6. Transfer the mackerel to a serving dish, add the mustard to the vegetables and pour over the fish.
7. Add the chopped mixed herbs to the potatoes and serve with the fish.

Soles au raisin
Sole with Grapes

⊣▷ 00.10   00.10 🔲
Serves 4

American	Ingredients	Metric/Imperial
4	sole fillets, thawed if frozen	4
	salt	
	pepper	
2 tbsp	fish bouillon (stock) powder	1 tbsp
¾ cup	dry white wine	200 ml/7 fl oz
¼ cup	butter	50 g/2 oz
4 tbsp	all-purpose (plain) flour	3 tbsp
¾ cup	sour cream (crème fraîche)	200 ml/7 fl oz
2	egg yolks	2
3 tbsp	white port	2 tbsp
½ lb	large white seedless grapes, peeled	225 g/8 oz

1. Rinse the sole fillets under plenty of cold running water and pat dry on kitchen paper. Season with salt and pepper, and roll each fillet up, skin side outward, starting with the thick end and finishing with the tail.
2. Stir the fish bouillon (stock) powder into the white wine.
3. Butter a large round Pyrex dish with ½-1 tablespoon of the butter. Put the fish rolls in the dish and pour over the white wine and bouillon (stock) mixture. Cover and microwave on HIGH for 6 minutes. After 4 minutes of cooking, move the fish from the center to the outside of the dish and vice versa.
4. When the fish is ready, remove from the dish with two spatulas and put in a serving dish. Cover with aluminum (aluminium) foil to keep warm.
5. Put the remaining butter in a bowl to melt in the microwave oven for 1 minute on HIGH.
6. Stir in the flour, gradually add the cooking liquid from the fish and the sour cream (crème fraîche). Microwave on HIGH for 3 minutes, beating with a hand whisk after every minute.
7. Mix the egg yolks and port together and add to the sauce, stirring vigorously.

8. Add the peeled grapes. Microwave for 1 minute on HIGH. Stir carefully. Taste and adjust seasoning. Pour the sauce over the sole fillets and serve at once.

Panaché de poissons aux poireaux
Savory Fish with Leeks

⊣▷ 00.15   00.22 🔲
Serves 4

American	Ingredients	Metric/Imperial
1 lb	leeks, white part only	450 g/1 lb
1	diced carrot	1
3 tbsp	butter	1½ tbsp
2 tbsp	fish bouillon (stock) powder	1 tbsp
¾ cup	dry white wine	200 ml/7 fl oz
⅓ cup	cognac	4½ tbsp
1½ lb	sole fillets	600 g/1½ lb
	salt	
	pepper	
½ lb	haddock fillets	225 g/8 oz
⅓ cup	sour cream (crème fraîche)	4½ tbsp
3½ oz	shelled baby shrimp (prawns)	100 g/3½ oz
2	egg yolks	2
2 tbsp	chopped chervil	2 tbsp

1. Remove the base and the outer leaves of the leeks. Cut the leeks in quarters lengthwise and then into dice. Rinse thoroughly and leave to drain.
2. Put the leeks and carrot into a large bowl with the butter.
3. Mix together the fish bouillon (stock) powder, white wine and cognac. Pour over the vegetables. Cover and microwave on HIGH for 15 minutes. Stir mid-way through the cooking time.

4. Rinse the sole fillets under plenty of cold running water. Pat dry on kitchen paper and season with salt and pepper. Cut in half lengthwise and roll up each half. Remove the skin from the haddock with the aid of a small sharp knife and cut into diagonal strips.

5. Add the sour cream (crème fraîche) and the shrimp (prawns) to the vegetable dish and stir well. Put the rolled fillets of sole and the strips of haddock on top of the vegetable mixture. Cover and microwave on HIGH for 6 minutes.

6. When the fish is cooked, remove carefully from the dish with a slotted spoon and put into a serving dish.

7. Add the egg yolks to the vegetable mixture and stir vigorously. Taste and adjust seasoning. Cook for 1 minute on HIGH. Stir again.

8. Arrange the vegetables around the fish, sprinkle with chopped chervil and serve at once.

Paupiettes de sole au velouté d'asperges

Roulades of Sole with Asparagus Cream Sauce

00.10 **00.13**
Serves 8

American	Ingredients	Metric/Imperial
8	sea scallops with their corals	8
2	large sole fillets	2
	salt	
	pepper	
4	slices smoked salmon	4
3 tbsp	white wine	2 tbsp
½	can cream of asparagus soup	½
4 tbsp	sour cream (crème fraîche)	3 tbsp

1. Separate the whites of the scallops from the corals. Rinse the corals under plenty of cold running water, removing any impurities. Purée the corals in a food processor. Remove any impurities from the whites. Rinse under plenty of cold running water and cut them in half across. Put them in a small dish. Cover and microwave on HIGH for 1½ minutes.

2. Rinse the sole fillets and pat dry on kitchen paper. Put the fish on a board, skin side down. Season with salt and pepper. Cut the slices of smoked salmon to fit the sole fillets, place a slice on top of each fillet and roll up from the wide end.

3. Put the rolled fillets, side by side in a round dish, leaving the center empty. Add the white wine. Cover and microwave on HIGH for 5 minutes. Leave to stand for 3 minutes, or until ready to serve.

4. Transfer the roulades to a serving dish, carefully with a slotted spoon. Put the scallop whites in the center of the dish.

5. Purée the corals in a food processor with the cooking liquid from the fish and scallops. Add the cream of asparagus soup, sour cream (crème fraîche) and pepper to taste. Do not add salt. Purée until smooth. Coat the rolled fish fillets and scallop whites with the sauce. Cover and reheat in the microwave oven for 3 minutes on HIGH. Serve at once.

If possible, use Norwegian smoked salmon as it is slightly less salty than the other kinds. If you feel the dish can stand a little more salt, season only the outside of the sole fillets.

Poisson au pistou

Fish in Basil Sauce

00.05 **00.05**
Serves 4

American	Ingredients	Metric/Imperial
2	sole fillets	2
	salt	
	pepper	
50	large basil leaves	50
2	whiting fillets	2
1	egg	1
4 tbsp	dry white wine	3 tbsp
1 tbsp	butter	½ tbsp
2 tbsp	ground almonds	1 tbsp
3 tbsp	oil	2 tbsp
2 tbsp	sour cream (crème fraîche)	1 tbsp

1. Rinse the fish and pat dry on kitchen paper. Put the sole fillets in a dish, skin side down. Season with salt and pepper.

2. Rinse the basil leaves and pat dry on kitchen paper.

3. Cut the whiting fillets into pieces and purée in a food processor, adding 10 leaves basil, the egg and salt and pepper to taste. Spread the sole fillets with this mixture and fold into three.

4. Pour the white wine into a round dish. Put the stuffed fish fillets in and dot each fillet with butter. Cover and microwave on HIGH for 3 minutes.

5. Purée the remaining basil leaves, adding the ground almonds, oil and sour cream (crème fraîche). Add salt and pepper and continue to purée until the mixture is smooth and creamy. Pour into a bowl.

6. Transfer the fish to a serving dish with a slotted spoon. Pour the cooking liquid into the food processor bowl with the basil mixture. Stir well. Heat in the microwave oven for 1½ minutes on HIGH.

7. Pour a little of the sauce over the fish. Pour the rest into a sauceboat and serve at once.

Roulades of sole with asparagus cream sauce

Paupiettes à la mousse d'avocat

Fillets of Sole with Avocado Cream

00.05   00.06

Serves 4

American	Ingredients	Metric/Imperial
4	large fillets sole or flounder	4
	salt	
	pepper	
1	large ripe avocado pear	1
⅓ cup	sour cream (crème fraîche)	4½ tbsp
4 tbsp	fresh lemon juice	3 tbsp
	Tabasco sauce	
2 tbsp	chopped fresh dill	2 tbsp
1	jar red lumpfish roe	1

1. Rinse the fish under plenty of cold running water and pat dry on kitchen paper. Season with salt and pepper. Roll up each fillet starting at the wide end, skin side outward. Put the rolls in a circle in a dish, leaving the center empty. Cover and microwave on HIGH for 4 minutes.
2. Peel, halve and stone the avocado and chop the flesh coarsely. Purée in a food processor, adding the sour cream (crème fraîche), lemon juice, several dashes of Tabasco sauce, and salt and pepper to taste. Purée until smooth.

Fillets of sole with avocado cream

3. Pour the purée into a bowl, add the chopped dill and stir well. Heat in the microwave oven on HIGH for 2 minutes.
4. Spread the base of a serving dish with half the avocado cream and arrange the fish rolls on top. Spoon a little avocado cream on top of each roll,
5. Garnish each roll with 1 teaspoon of lumpfish roe and Serve with the rest of the avocado sauce.

Sole in Wine and Caper Sauce

00.10   00.20

plus standing time

American	Ingredients	Metric/Imperial
1¾ lb	sole fillets	700 g/1¾ lb
4 tbsp	lemon juice	3 tbsp
1 tsp	salt	1 tsp
2 tbsp	butter	1 tbsp
¼ cup	all-purpose (plain) flour	25 g/1 oz
2 cups	chicken bouillon (stock)	450 ml/¾ pint
¼ cup	dry white wine	4 tbsp
1 tbsp	drained capers	1 tbsp
½ tsp	celery salt	½ tsp
½ tsp	paprika	½ tsp
2	egg yolks	2
3 tbsp	ice water	2 tbsp
	lemon wedges	
	tomato wedges	
	chopped parsley	

1. Sprinkle the fish fillets with the lemon juice and leave to stand for 30 minutes. Pat dry on kitchen paper and sprinkle with salt. Cut into bite-size pieces.
2. To make the sauce, put the butter in a dish and melt in the microwave for 30 seconds on HIGH. Remove from the oven and stir in the flour. Return to the oven and microwave for a further 30 seconds. Stir well.
3. Mix 2 (1) tablespoons of the stock and the white wine together and stir into the flour mixture. Beat well. Pour the remaining stock into a bowl and heat in the microwave on HIGH for 2 minutes.
4. Add half the warmed stock a little at a time to the sauce and stir well. Heat in the microwave on HIGH for 2 minutes. Remove and stir in the remaining stock gradually. Beat thoroughly.
5. Stir in the fish, capers, lemon juice, celery salt and paprika and stir gently. Cover and microwave on HIGH for 5 minutes, remove and stir well. Return to the microwave and cook on HIGH for a further 5 minutes and leave to stand for 3 minutes. Stir again.
6. Beat the egg yolks together with the ice water and stir a little into the hot sauce. Gradually stir in the remaining egg yolk and cook on HIGH for 2 minutes. Taste and adjust seasoning.
7. Garnish with the lemon and tomato wedges and sprinkle chopped parsley over. Serve with plain boiled rice.

Sole in champagne sauce

Soles au champagne

Sole in Champagne Sauce

00.10   00.22

Serves 4

American	Ingredients	Metric/Imperial
½ lb	baby white button mushrooms	225 g/8 oz
3 tbsp	fresh lemon juice	2 tbsp
	salt	
	pepper	
¼ cup	butter	50 g/2 oz
8	sole or flounder fillets	8
1½ tbsp	fish bouillon (stock) powder	1 tbsp
¾ cup	dry champagne	200 ml/7 fl oz
4 tbsp	all-purpose (plain) flour	3 tbsp
¾ cup	sour cream (crème fraîche)	200 ml/7 fl oz
½ tsp	saffron	½ tsp
2	egg yolks	2
8	tiny preserved mushrooms	8

1. Wipe the mushrooms with a damp cloth or kitchen paper. Slice thinly. Put the slices in a small casserole and add half the fresh lemon juice, salt and pepper to taste and 1 teaspoon of butter. Cover and microwave on HIGH for 6 minutes.

2. Rinse the fish under plenty of cold running water and pat dry on kitchen paper. Season each fillet with salt and pepper, then roll up and secure with a toothpick (cocktail stick).

3. Mix the fish bouillon (stock) with the champagne and pour it into a large Pyrex dish. Put the fish rolls in the dish side by side. Cover and microwave on HIGH for 6 minutes, moving the fish from the outside to the center of the dish and vice versa after 4 minutes of cooking time.

4. When the fish is cooked, remove with a slotted spatula and put on a serving dish. Cover with aluminum (aluminium) foil to keep warm. Filter the cooking liquid.

5. Put the remaining butter in a bowl to melt in the microwave oven for 1 minute on HIGH.

6. Stir in the flour and add the cooking liquid from the fish and the sour cream (crème fraîche), stirring constantly. Microwave on HIGH for 3 minutes, beating with a hand whisk after every minute.

7. Add the saffron and the mushrooms in their cooking liquid. Whisk the egg yolks with the remaining lemon juice. Add to the sauce and whisk vigorously. Microwave for 1 minute. Stir. Taste and adjust seasoning. Pour over the sole fillets.

8. Heat the tiny preserved mushrooms in the microwave oven for 1 minute and put one on each fish fillet. Serve at once.

If champagne proves too expensive for this dish, substitute a good dry white wine.

Rolled Sole with Tomato Sauce

	00.10 plus standing time	00.24

American	Ingredients	Metric/Imperial
1¾ lb	sole	700 g/1¾ lb
4 tbsp	lemon juice	3 tbsp
	salt	
	celery salt	
	sweet paprika pepper	
2 tbsp	mild mustard	1 tbsp
½ cup	dry white wine	125 ml/4 fl oz
3 tbsp	butter	2 tbsp
1	chopped small onion	1
¾ lb	finely chopped tomatoes	350 g/12 oz
¼ cup	all-purpose (plain) flour	25 g/1 oz
4 tbsp	tomato concentrate	3 tbsp
	few drops Tabasco sauce	

1. Sprinkle the fish with the lemon juice reserving 1-2 tablespoons. Leave to stand for 30 minutes. Drain and sprinkle with the salt, celery salt and paprika. Cut the fillets into long strips 2 inches (5 cm) wide. Spread one side of each fillet with mustard and roll up. Secure with wooden toothpicks (cocktail sticks).
2. Arrange the fish in a dish and pour over the wine. Cover and microwave on HIGH for 5 minutes. Leave to stand for 3 minutes.
3. To make the sauce, melt the butter in a dish in the microwave for 1 minute on HIGH.
4. Stir in the onion and tomato and cook on HIGH for 2 minutes.
5. Remove the dish from the oven and stir in the flour, stir well. Gradually add ¾ cup (175 ml/6 fl oz) of water, tomato concentrate, the remaining lemon juice and a dash of Tabasco. Cook on HIGH for 5 minutes, stir and cook for a further 3 minutes on HIGH.
6. Remove the sticks from the fish. Pour the cooking liquid into the sauce and strain the sauce over the fish. Reheat on HIGH for 5 minutes.

Paupiettes au beurre de poivron

Lemon Sole with Red Bell Pepper Butter

	00.10 Serves 4	00.11

American	Ingredients	Metric/Imperial
1	red bell pepper, seeded and coarsely chopped	1
4	lemon sole fillets	4
	salt	
	pepper	
2 oz	shelled shrimp (prawns)	50 g/2 oz
3 tbsp	chopped chives	2 tbsp
1 tsp	vinegar	1 tsp
½ tsp	sugar	½ tsp
¼ cup	butter	50 g/2 oz

1. Put the red bell pepper in a small casserole. Cover and microwave on HIGH for 4 minutes.
2. Rinse the fish fillets and pat dry on kitchen paper. Season with salt and pepper on both sides. Place on a board, white side up.
3. Purée the shrimp (prawns) and chives in a food processor and add salt and pepper.
4. Spread the fillets on one side with the purée, and roll up, starting with the thick end and ending with the tail.
5. Drain the red bell pepper and purée.
6. Put the fish rolls on a round dish. Cover and microwave on HIGH for 6 minutes.
7. Pour the red pepper purée into a bowl and add the vinegar, sugar and salt to taste. Stir well. Heat for 1 minute on HIGH.
8. Cut the butter into tiny pieces and beat vigorously into the red pepper purée.
9. Transfer the fish rolls to a serving dish, coat with the pepper butter and serve at once.

Limandes-soles à la crème l'oseille

Lemon Sole in Cream of Sorrel Sauce

	00.08 Serves 4	00.08

American	Ingredients	Metric/Imperial
2	lemon sole fillets	2
	salt	
	pepper	
3½ oz	frozen sorrel	100 g/3½ oz
1 tbsp	butter	½ tbsp
¾ cup	sour cream (crème fraîche)	200 ml/7 fl oz
½ tsp	sugar	½ tsp
1	egg yolk	1

1. Rinse the lemon sole fillets and pat dry on kitchen paper. Season on both sides with salt and pepper and fold in two. Arrange the fish in a circle in a dish. Put the frozen sorrel in the center. Cover and microwave on HIGH for 5 minutes.
2. When the fish is cooked, transfer to a serving dish with a slotted spoon. Cover with aluminum (aluminium) foil to keep warm.
3. Add the butter in tiny pieces to the sorrel.
4. Stir in the sour cream (crème fraîche) and sugar. Stir well. Microwave on HIGH for 2 minutes.
5. Put the egg yolk in a bowl. Add 3 (2) tablespoons of cold water and beat with a hand whisk. Gradually pour in the sorrel mixture, beating constantly. Taste and adjust seasoning. Cook for 30 seconds on HIGH and whisk again.
6. Pour the sauce over the fish fillets and serve at once.

Limande-sole aux champignons

Lemon Sole with Mushrooms

▬▷ 00.06   00.14 🔲
Serves 4

American	Ingredients	Metric/Imperial
2	chopped shallots	2
3 tsp	butter	3 tsp
10½ oz	mushrooms	300 g/10½ oz
⅓ cup	cream of mushroom soup	5 tbsp
¼ cup	sour cream (crème fraîche)	3 tbsp
2 lb	lemon sole fillets	1 kg/2 lb
	salt	
	pepper	
3 tbsp	fresh lemon juice	2 tbsp

1. Put the shallots in a bowl with 1 teaspoon of the butter and microwave on HIGH for 3 minutes.

2. Wipe the mushrooms with a damp cloth or kitchen paper and add to the shallots. Cover and microwave on HIGH for 5 minutes. Cut the largest mushrooms in smaller pieces.

3. Mix together the mushroom soup and sour cream (crème fraîche) and pour over the mushroom mixture. Cover and microwave on HIGH for 2 minutes.

4. Rinse the fish fillets and pat dry on kitchen paper. Season lightly with salt and pepper. Fold each fillet into three. Using the remaining butter, butter a round dish. Arrange the fish in the dish, leaving the center empty. Add the lemon juice, cover and microwave on HIGH for 4 minutes. Lift the fish out and arrange in a serving dish.

5. Add the cooking liquid to the mushroom mixture. Stir well. Taste and adjust seasoning. Pour over the fish and serve hot.

Paupiettes de limande-sole à la crème d'amande

Lemon Sole with Almond Filling

▬▷ 00.10   00.14 🔲
Serves 4

American	Ingredients	Metric/Imperial
½ lb	peeled, diced cucumber	225 g/8 oz
4	lemon sole fillets	4
7 oz	whiting fillets	200 g/7 oz
¾ cup	ground almonds	75 g/3 oz
1	large egg	1
¼ cup	sour cream (crème fraîche)	4 tbsp
½ cup	fresh lemon juice	6 tbsp
	salt	
	pepper	
1½ tbsp	butter	25 g/1 oz
1	bunch chives	1
2 tbsp	all-purpose (plain) flour	1 tbsp
1¼ cups	milk	300 ml/½ pint
½ tsp	grated nutmeg	½ tsp

1. Put the cucumber in a casserole. Cover and microwave on HIGH for 5 minutes.

2. Rinse the fish fillets under plenty of cold running water and pat dry on kitchen paper. Cut the whiting fillets into small pieces and purée in a food processor, adding the ground almonds, egg, half the sour cream (crème fraîche) and half the lemon juice, salt and pepper.

3. Butter the base of a small cake mold (mould) 10 inches (22 cm) in diameter. Using two spoons, form the almond and whiting purée into 4 servings around the edge of the dish, leaving the center empty. Wrap a fillet of sole round each mound of almond mixture. Cover and microwave on HIGH for 4 minutes.

4. Rinse the chives and pat dry on kitchen paper. Snip with kitchen scissors.

5. Put the butter into a large bowl to melt in the microwave oven on HIGH for 1 minute.

6. Stir in the flour and add the milk, stirring constantly. Cook in the microwave oven for 3 minutes on HIGH, stirring with a whisk after every minute.

7. Remove from the oven and add the remaining lemon juice, sour cream (crème fraîche), grated nutmeg and chopped chives.

8. Arrange the fish rolls on a serving dish. Pour the cooking liquid from the fish into the sauce. Taste and adjust seasoning. Heat on HIGH for 1 minute.

9. Drain the cucumber and transfer to the center of the serving dish with the fish rolls. Coat with the sauce and serve at once.

Lemon sole with almond filling

Paupiettes de limande au curry

Lemon Sole in Curry Sauce

	00.10	00.18	
	Serves 4		

American	Ingredients	Metric/Imperial
¼ lb	onions	125 g/4 oz
1	crushed garlic clove	1
2 tbsp	butter	1 tbsp
3 tbsp	concentrated tomato juice	2 tbsp
⅔ cup	milk	150 ml/¼ pint
1 tbsp	mild curry powder	1 tbsp
4 tbsp	desiccated coconut	3 tbsp
1 tsp	sugar	1 tsp
	salt	
	pepper	
4	Jumbo shrimp (prawns)	4
4	lemon sole fillets	4
3½ oz	shelled shrimp (prawns)	100 g/3½ oz

1. Peel the onions and purée them in a food processor. Put the onions and garlic in a dish with the butter. Cover and microwave on HIGH for 3 minutes.
2. Mix together the concentrated tomato juice, milk, curry powder, desiccated coconut, sugar, salt and pepper. Add the mixture to the onions. Cover and microwave on HIGH for 5 minutes.
3. Shell the Jumbo shrimp (prawns). Put the fish fillets on a board, skin side downward. Season with salt and pepper, then put 1 Jumbo shrimp (prawn) on each fish fillet at the wide end and roll up, ending with the tail.
4. Put the fish rolls in a dish in a circle, leaving the center of the dish empty. Cover and microwave on HIGH for 5 minutes.
5. Turn the rolls round and microwave for a further 3 minutes on HIGH. Leave to stand for 2 minutes.
6. Add the shelled shrimp (prawns) to the sauce and serve with the fish rolls.

Limande-sole surprise au coulis vert

Lemon Sole in Green Sauce

	00.10	00.12	
	Serves 4		

American	Ingredients	Metric/Imperial
7 oz	zucchini (courgettes), peeled and grated	200 g/7 oz
1 tsp	butter	1 tsp
7 oz	haddock fillets	200 g/7 oz
4	lemon sole fillets	4
5	sprigs parsley	5
2 tsp	cornstarch (cornflour)	2 tsp
½ cup	fresh lemon juice	6 tbsp
¼ cup	sour cream (crème fraîche)	3 tbsp
	salt	
	pepper	

1. Put the zucchini (courgettes) in a small casserole. Cover and microwave on HIGH for 5 minutes.
2. Butter the base of a round dish. Remove the skin from the haddock: place it skin side down on a board with the tail toward you. Make a small cut through the flesh at the tail end. Dip the fingers of one hand in salt and hold the tail firmly, with the other hand, ease a sharp, flexible knife between flesh and skin, pushing the flesh off the skin. Cut the haddock into 4 equal pieces.
3. Rinse the lemon sole under plenty of cold running water and pat dry on kitchen paper. Put one piece of haddock on each lemon sole fillet and roll the sole fillets, starting with the wide end.
4. Put the fish rolls in a circle on the buttered dish with the widest part facing outward. Dot with the remaining butter. Cover and microwave on HIGH for 4 minutes.
5. Rinse the parsley and discard the stalks. Put the parsley into a food processor with the zucchini (courgettes) and purée. Pour into a bowl and gradually add the cornstarch (cornflour), stirring constantly. Heat in the oven for 1 minute on HIGH. Stir well, then microwave for 1 further minute.
6. Lift the fish rolls out of the dish with a slotted spoon and put them on a serving platter. Pour the cooking liquid into the bowl with the zucchini (courgettes) and add the fresh lemon juice and sour cream (crème fraîche). Add salt and pepper to taste. Stir and reheat for 1 minute on HIGH.
7. Coat each fish roll with a little sauce and pour the rest into a sauceboat and serve alongside.

Barbue au cidre

Brill in Cider Sauce

	00.09	00.11	
	Serves 4		

American	Ingredients	Metric/Imperial
4	chopped shallots	4
½ lb	white button mushrooms, thinly sliced	225 g/8 oz
2 tbsp	butter	1 tbsp
2lb 14 oz	brill fillets	1 kg 400 g/ 2 lb 14 oz
	salt	
	pepper	
⅓ cup	dry cider	4½ tbsp
1	sprig chopped tarragon	1
3 tbsp	sour cream (crème fraîche)	2 tbsp
1	egg yolk	1
2	crabmeat sticks, cut into tiny pieces	2

1. Put the shallots and mushrooms in a round dish and dot with the butter. Cover and microwave on HIGH for 5 minutes.
2. Rinse the fish under plenty of cold running water and pat dry on kitchen paper. Season with salt and pepper and fold each fillet into three.
3. Sprinkle the mushrooms with salt and pepper and toss lightly. Arrange the fish on top of the mushrooms and pour the cider over the mixture. Cover and microwave on HIGH for 5 minutes.
4. Mix together the tarragon, sour cream (crème fraîche), egg yolk and chopped crabmeat sticks.

5. When the fish is cooked, lift out carefully with a slotted spatula and put in a serving dish. Cover the dish with aluminum (aluminium) foil to keep warm.

6. Pour the sour cream (crème fraîche) and egg mixture into the dish in which the fish was cooked, stirring with a wooden spoon. Return the dish to the microwave oven for 1 minute on HIGH. Stir well. Taste and adjust seasoning.

7. Pour the sauce over the fish and serve at once.

Paupiettes de barbue farcies

Stuffed Brill Roulades

▬▷ 00.10   00.13
Serves 4

American	Ingredients	Metric/Imperial
¼ lb	frozen celeriac purée	125 g/4 oz
2½ lb	brill fillets	1.25 kg/2½ lb
	salt	
	pepper	
3½ oz	shelled shrimp (prawns)	100 g/3½ oz
½ cup	ground almonds	50 g/2 oz
1	small egg	1
4 tbsp	sour cream (crème fraîche)	3 tbsp
4 tbsp	fresh lemon juice	3 tbsp
1 oz	butter	25 g/1 oz
2 tbsp	all-purpose (plain) flour	1 tbsp
1¼ cups	milk	300 ml/½ pint

1. Put the frozen celeriac into a bowl and defrost it in the microwave oven for 3 minutes on HIGH.

2. Rinse the fish fillets under plenty of cold running water and pat dry on kitchen paper. Season with salt and pepper.

3. Purée the shrimp (prawns) in a food processor, gradually adding the ground almonds, egg, 2 (1) tablespoons of sour cream (crème fraîche) and 1 tablespoon of lemon juice. Season with salt and pepper.

4. Spread the fish fillets with this mixture and roll up.

5. Use 1 teaspoon of the butter, to butter the base of a dish 10 inches (22 cm) in diameter. Arrange the fish rolls in a circle, leaving the center of the dish empty. Cover and microwave on HIGH for 5 minutes.

6. Lift the fish rolls out with two spatulas and put in a serving dish.

7. Put the remaining butter in a large bowl to melt in the microwave oven for 1 minute on HIGH.

8. Stir in the flour and gradually add the milk, stirring constantly. Microwave for 3 minutes, stirring with a hand whisk after every minute.

9. Add the remaining lemon juice and sour cream (crème fraîche), the cooking liquid from the fish and the céleriac purée to the sauce. Taste and adjust seasoning. Stir and heat on HIGH for 1 minute.

10. Coat the fish roulades with the sauce and serve at once.

Barbue aux litchis frais

Brill with Fresh Lychees

▬▷ 00.06   00.11
Serves 4

American	Ingredients	Metric/Imperial
4	brill fillets	4
	salt	
	pepper	
4 tbsp	white wine	3 tbsp
1	large grated carrot	1
¼ tsp	dried saffron	¼ tsp
20	fresh lychees, peeled and pitted (stoned)	20
3 tbsp	sour cream (crème fraîche)	2 tbsp

1. Rinse the fish fillets under plenty of cold running water and pat dry on kitchen paper. Put 2 fillets side by side in an oval dish. Season with salt and pepper. Add the white wine. Cover and microwave on HIGH for 3 minutes.

2. Remove the cooked fish fillets with a slotted spatula and replace with the uncooked ones, seasoning again with salt and pepper. Cover and microwave on HIGH for 3 minutes.

3. Remove the fish fillets and add to the first. Cover with aluminum (aluminium) foil to keep warm.

4. Pour the cooking liquid from the fish into a bowl. Add the grated carrot and saffron. Season lightly with salt and pepper. Cover and microwave on HIGH for 4 minutes.

5. Add the lychees to the carrot mixture and stir in the sour cream (crème fraîche). Stir well, cover and microwave on HIGH for 1 minute.

6. Pour over the fish and serve at once.

Brill with fresh lychees

Raie à la normande

Skate Wings in Cider Sauce

	00.05	00.09	
	Serves 4		

American	Ingredients	Metric/Imperial
1¾ lb	skate wings	750 g/1¾ lb
	salt	
	pepper	
¾ cup	dry cider	200 ml/7 fl oz
3 tbsp	sour cream (crème fraîche)	2 tbsp
2 tbsp	mild mustard	1 tbsp
1 tbsp	chopped parsley	1 tbsp

1. Rinse the skate wings under plenty of cold running water, pat dry on kitchen paper and divide into 4 equal portions. Sprinkle the base of a rectangular dish with salt and pepper and put the skate wings in it. Pour the cider over, cover and microwave on HIGH for 8 minutes.

2. Carefully lift the fish out and remove the skin. Put the fish portions in a serving dish. Filter the cooking liquid through a strainer (sieve).

3. Mix together the sour cream (crème fraîche) and mustard in a bowl. Add the cooking liquid and stir well. Microwave on HIGH for 1 minute.

4. Taste the sauce and adjust seasoning. Pour the sauce over the fish. Sprinkle with chopped parsley and serve hot.

Skate wings in cider sauce

Joues de raie en sauce
Skate Wings in Sauce

00.05 Serves 4   **00.10**

American	Ingredients	Metric/Imperial
1¼ lb	skate wings	500 g/1¼ lb
½	can mushroom soup	½
2 tbsp	concentrated tomato juice	1 tbsp
2 tbsp	cognac	1 tbsp
3 tbsp	sour cream (crème fraîche)	2 tbsp

1. Rinse the skate wings under plenty of cold running water and dry carefully. Prick with a fork and arrange, side by side in a dish. Cover and microwave on HIGH for 5 minutes.
2. Mix together the cream of mushroom soup, concentrated tomato juice, cognac and ¼ cup (3 tablespoons) of water in a bowl. Heat for 3 minutes on HIGH.
3. Drain the skate wings and return to the dish.
4. Add the sour cream (crème fraîche) to the mushroom sauce, coat the skate wings and reheat for 2 minutes on MEDIUM. Serve at once.

Joues de raie aux pleurotes
Skate Wings with Field Mushrooms

00.10 Serves 2   **00.11**

American	Ingredients	Metric/Imperial
2	chopped shallots	2
1	crushed garlic clove	1
10½ oz	field mushrooms, cut into thick slices	300 g/10½ oz
	salt	
	pepper	
3 tbsp	white wine	2 tbsp
14 oz	skate wings	400 g/14 oz
1	egg	1
2 tbsp	cognac	1 tbsp
1 tbsp	chopped parsley	1 tbsp
1 tsp	capers	1 tsp

1. Put the shallots, garlic and mushrooms in a small casserole and season with salt and pepper. Add the white wine. Cover and microwave on HIGH for 5 minutes.
2. Rinse the skate wings under plenty of cold running water and pat dry on kitchen paper. Arrange in a single layer in a casserole dish and season with salt and pepper. Cover and microwave on HIGH for 4 minutes.
3. Break the egg into a bowl and beat with a fork. Pour in the cooking liquid from the skate wings and beat until incorporated. Pour the sauce over the mushrooms and microwave on HIGH for 1 minute.
4. Heat the cognac in a cup, for 30 seconds on HIGH, set alight and pour over the skate wings. Add the chopped parsley, capers and mushrooms in their sauce. Stir well. Serve at once.

Skate wing with capers

Raie aux câpres
Skate Wing with Capers

00.05 Serves 4   **00.10**

American	Ingredients	Metric/Imperial
1¾ lb	skate wings	750 g/1¾ lb
4 tbsp	fresh lemon juice	3 tbsp
	salt	
	pepper	
1½ tbsp	butter	1 tbsp
3 tbsp	capers	2 tbsp
1 tbsp	chopped parsley	1 tbsp
	small new potatoes	

1. Rinse the skate wings under cold running water and dry very carefully. Put on a dish, dark skin side upward. Add the lemon juice. Cover and microwave on HIGH for 6 minutes.
2. Remove the dark skin from the fish. Season the cooking liquid with salt and pepper and return the skate wings to the dish, white skin side upward. Cover and microwave on HIGH for 3 minutes.
3. Remove the white skin from the fish. Dot the butter on top of the fish, season with salt and pepper, add the capers and cook for 1 minute on HIGH.
4. Sprinkle the fish with chopped parsley and serve with small boiled new potatoes.

Turbot farci

Stuffed Turbot

00.10	00.19	
Serves 4		

American	Ingredients	Metric/Imperial
2 tbsp	*butter*	*1 tbsp*
11 oz	*white button mushrooms, sliced*	*300 g/11 oz*
	salt	
	pepper	
2 tbsp	*fresh lemon juice*	*1 tbsp*
1	*egg*	*1*
3 oz	*fresh salmon*	*100 g/3 oz*
3 tbsp	*sour cream (crème fraîche)*	*2 tbsp*
4	*turbot fillets (about 2 lb/ 1 kg)*	*4*

1. Heat a browning dish in the microwave oven for 6 minutes on HIGH.
2. When the browning dish is hot, melt half the butter and add the mushrooms. Stir with a spatula, until they stop sizzling. Season with salt and pepper.
3. Add the lemon juice and stir well. Cover and microwave on HIGH for 3 minutes.
4. Separate the egg.
5. Skin and bone the salmon and purée in a food processor, gradually adding the egg white and then the sour cream (crème fraîche). Add salt and pepper to taste and purée once more.
6. Spread the remaining butter over the base of a serving dish. Sprinkle with salt and pepper.
7. Rinse the turbot fillets under plenty of cold running water and pat dry on kitchen paper. Put two fillets in the dish side by side. Season lightly with salt and pepper. Cover with the salmon purée, then with the remaining turbot fillets. Sprinkle salt and pepper over.
8. Arrange the mushrooms round the fish. Cover and microwave on HIGH for 5 minutes.
9. Whisk the egg yolk together with the cooking liquid from the mushrooms. Coat the fish and mushrooms with this sauce. Put the serving dish in the oven and cook for a further 2 minutes on HIGH. Leave to stand for 3 minutes before serving.

Turbot à la sauce au crabe

Turbot in Crab Sauce

00.10	00.08	
Serves 4		

American	Ingredients	Metric/Imperial
¼ lb	*crabmeat*	*125 g/4 oz*
4	*large turbot fillets*	*4*
3 tsp	*fish bouillon (stock) powder*	*3 tsp*
¼ cup	*sour cream (crème fraîche)*	*4 tbsp*
4 tbsp	*fresh lemon juice*	*3 tbsp*
2 tbsp	*cognac*	*1 tbsp*
	salt	
	pepper	
2 tsp	*butter*	*2 tsp*
1 tbsp	*chopped dill*	*1 tbsp*

1. Flake the crabmeat with a fork. Rinse the turbot under plenty of cold running water and pat dry on kitchen paper. Arrange the fish fillets side by side on a dish. Sprinkle with the fish bouillon (stock) powder.
2. Mix together the sour cream (crème fraîche), lemon juice and cognac. Season lightly with salt and pepper. Pour over the fish.
3. Spread the crabmeat in a layer over the fish and dot with butter. Cover and microwave on HIGH for 8 minutes.
4. Sprinkle with chopped dill and serve at once.

Saint-Pierre au vermouth

John Dory with Vermouth

00.10	00.15	
Serves 2		

American	Ingredients	Metric/Imperial
1	*finely chopped shallot*	*1*
2 tbsp	*butter*	*1 tbsp*
2	*John Dory, skinned and cleaned*	*2*
¼ cup	*dry Vermouth*	*4 tbsp*
	salt	
	pepper	
1	*red bell pepper*	*1*
2 oz	*frozen shrimp (prawns)*	*50 g/2 oz*
5 oz	*fresh tagliatelle*	*150 g/5 oz*
2 tbsp	*all-purpose (plain) flour*	*1 tbsp*
¼ cup	*milk*	*100 ml/3 fl oz*
1	*egg yolk*	*1*
3½ oz	*Cheddar or Gruyère cheese*	*100 g/3½ oz*

1. Put the shallot in a round dish with half the butter. Microwave on HIGH for 2 minutes.
2. Put the fish on top of the chopped shallot and add the Vermouth. Season with salt and pepper. Cover and microwave on HIGH for 5 minutes.
3. Rinse the red bell pepper, seed and remove the pith. Cut the flesh into thin strips and then into dice. Put the bell pepper and frozen shrimp (prawns) in a small casserole. Cover and microwave on HIGH for 4 minutes.
4. Bring a pan of salted water to the boil on a conventional cooker. Add the tagliatelle. Bring back to the boil and cook for 2 minutes. Drain in a colander.
5. Put the fish on two plates. Cover with aluminum (aluminium) foil to keep hot.
6. To make the sauce: put the remaining butter in a bowl and melt in the microwave oven for 1 minute on HIGH. Add the flour, stirring constantly. Add the cooking liquid from the fish and the milk, whisking with a hand beater. Add the egg yolk, beating vigorously. Put into the oven and cook for 1 minute on HIGH.
7. Whisk the sauce again. Grate the cheese into it and whisk once more. Taste and adjust seasoning.
8. Pour the tagliatelle into a serving bowl. Add the red bell pepper and shrimp (prawns) and stir well.
9. Put a serving of the mixture on each plate with the fish. Serve very hot with the sauce on the side.

Microwave hint: When cooking a whole fish in its skin, ie trout or salmon, make a few small slits in the skin to let the steam escape during cooking.

Halibut with citrus fruits

Assiette de poisson aux agrumes

Halibut with Citrus Fruits

00.10   00.06

Serves 4

American	Ingredients	Metric/Imperial
1	orange	1
1	lime	1
½ tsp	cornstarch (cornflour)	½ tsp
⅓ cup	sour cream (crème fraîche)	4½ tbsp
	salt	
	pepper	
1½ lb	halibut, filleted	600 g/1½ lb

1. Rinse the orange and lime very carefully under plenty of cold running water and pat dry on kitchen paper. Remove the zest (peel) with a small sharp knife or potato peeler, taking care not to bring any of the pith with it. Cut each of the fruit in half and squeeze the juice into two separate bowls.

2. Put the zest (peel) from both fruit into a cup of hot water. Microwave on HIGH for 1 minute. Drain the zest (peel) and plunge into cold water.

3. Put the cornstarch (cornflour) in a bowl and gradually stir in ¼ cup (3 tablespoons) of lime juice and ¼ cup (4 tablespoons) of orange juice until a smooth mixture is obtained. Stir in the sour cream (crème fraîche) and salt and pepper to taste. Microwave for 1 minute on HIGH. Stir. Microwave 1 further minute on HIGH. Stir well and cook for 1 final minute. Stir again.

4. Rinse the halibut under plenty of cold running water and pat dry on kitchen paper. Cut in half lengthwise, then cut each half-fillet diagonally into strips about 3 inches (7.5 cm) long.

5. Sprinkle salt and pepper on to 4 dinner plates. Arrange the strips of fish equally between them in a star shape.

6. Microwave each plateful on HIGH for 1½ minutes. Coat the fish with the citrus sauce. Sprinkle with the zest (peel) and serve at once.

Truites à l'estragon

Trout with Tarragon

00.05 **00.07** Serves 4

American	Ingredients	Metric/Imperial
4	trout, cleaned	4
2	sprigs tarragon	2
1 tbsp	butter	½ tbsp
¼ cup	dry white wine	4 tbsp
	salt	
	pepper	
¼ cup	sour cream (crème fraîche)	3 tbsp

1. Rinse the trout under plenty of cold running water and pat dry on kitchen paper. Put two tarragon leaves inside each trout. Make 2 deep incisions in the fleshiest part of the fish, close to the head.
2. Butter the base of a rectangular dish with one-third of the butter. Pour the white wine into the dish and season with salt and pepper. Place the trout in the dish. Cover and microwave on HIGH for 6 minutes, turning the fish midway through the cooking time.
3. When the fish are cooked, lift out with a slotted spoon, remove the skin and transfer to a serving dish.
4. Remove and chop the leaves from the remaining tarragon. Put into a bowl with the sour cream (crème fraîche).
5. Add the cooking liquid from the trout, stir well, and microwave on HIGH for 1 minute. Add the remaining butter. Taste and adjust seasoning. Pour over the trout and serve at once.

Truites aux endives

Trout with Belgian Chicory (Endive)

00.10 **00.12** Serves 2

American	Ingredients	Metric/Imperial
11 oz	Belgian chicory (endive)	300 g/11 oz
5 oz	smoked streaky bacon, cut into small pieces	150 g/5 oz
	salt	
	pepper	
3 tbsp	sour cream (crème fraîche)	2 tbsp
2	trout	2
2 tbsp	fresh lemon juice	1 tbsp

1. Remove the outer leaves and bitter heart of the Belgian chicory (endive). Rinse and slice in half lengthwise, then into ½ inch (1.25 cm) pieces.
2. Put the bacon in a dish and microwave, uncovered, for 30 seconds on HIGH.
3. Add the Belgian chicory (endive) to the dish with 3 (2) tablespoons of water and salt and pepper to taste. Cover and microwave on HIGH for 5 minutes.
4. Coat the Belgian chicory (endive) with sour cream (crème fraîche), stir well and microwave, covered, for 1 minute. Set aside.
5. Rinse the trout under plenty of cold running water, pat dry with kitchen paper and season with salt and pepper. Put the fish, side by side in a long dish. Add 3 (2) tablespoons of water. Cover and microwave on HIGH for 5 minutes.
6. Remove the skin from the fish. Transfer to a serving dish and pour the lemon juice over. Arrange the Belgian chicory (endive) round the fish and serve at once.

Trout with tarragon

Truites à l'orange
Trout with Oranges

American	Ingredients	Metric/Imperial
2	oranges	2
1	chopped shallot	1
	salt	
	pepper	
¼ tsp	dried thyme	¼ tsp
½ tsp	ground black pepper	½ tsp
2 tbsp	butter	1 tbsp
4	trout (14 oz/400 g each)	4
1 tsp	cornstarch (cornflour)	1 tsp
1 tsp	vinegar	1 tsp
⅓ cup	sour cream (crème fraîche)	4½ tbsp
1	egg yolk	1

1. Scrub one orange very carefully in plenty of soapy water. Rinse under cold running water until all traces of soap are removed. Using a vegetable peeler or sharp knife, remove the orange zest (peel), taking care not to peel any of the white pith.
2. Sprinkle salt and pepper into the base of an oval dish. Put the chopped shallot into the dish.
3. Sprinkle with the orange zest (peel) and ground black pepper.
4. Add the butter and cook in the microwave oven for 2 minutes on HIGH.
5. Rinse the trout under plenty of cold running water and pat dry on kitchen paper. Season inside with salt and pepper. Arrange the trout in the dish on top of the shallot mixture. Cover and microwave on HIGH for 6 minutes.
6. Rinse the second orange and pat dry on kitchen paper. Cut 4 slices in the middle of the fruit where it is thickest. Squeeze the first orange to obtain the juice.
7. When the trout are cooked, drain, remove the skin and transfer to a serving dish. Cover with aluminum (aluminium) foil to keep warm. Pour the cooking liquid into a bowl.
8. Mix the cornstarch (cornflour) with 1 teaspoon of orange juice, stirring until smooth. Add the remaining orange juice and the vinegar. Pour into a bowl and whisk. Cook for 1 minute on HIGH. Whisk again.
9. Stir in the sour cream (crème fraîche) and the egg yolk, stir well and return to the oven for 1 minute. Whisk again.
10. Pour the sauce over the trout. Garnish with the orange slices and serve.

Trout with Almonds

American	Ingredients	Metric/Imperial
¼ cup	butter	50 g/2 oz
2 oz	almonds	50 g/2 oz
2	cleaned trout	2
3 tbsp	lemon juice	2 tbsp
2	lemon slices	2
2 tbsp	chopped parsley	2 tbsp

1. Put the butter and almonds in a casserole and microwave on HIGH for 5 minutes, stirring once. If the almonds are not golden brown, return to the oven for a further minute.
2. Arrange the trout, head-to-tail and cut sides to center, in a shallow, oblong dish. Season the insides with a little salt and pepper and sprinkle with lemon juice. Cover the dish with saran wrap (cling film) and pierce in two places. Cook on HIGH for 7 minutes.
3. Remove the saran wrap (cling film), drain the fish and sprinkle the almonds over. Garnish with lemon slices and chopped parsley. Serve with boiled potatoes and mixed salad.

Truite de mer à la crème d'artichaut
Sea Trout with Artichoke Cream

American	Ingredients	Metric/Imperial
1	crushed shallot	1
3 tbsp	white wine	2 tbsp
2 tbsp	butter	1 tbsp
7 oz	frozen artichoke purée	200 g/7 oz
⅓ cup	sour cream (crème fraîche)	4½ tbsp
	salt	
	pepper	
2 lb	sea trout fillets	1 kg/2 lb
1	sprig basil	1
3 tbsp	fresh lemon juice	2 tbsp

1. Put the shallot in a large bowl with the white wine and 2 (1) tablespoons of butter. Microwave for 2 minutes on HIGH.
2. Add the artichoke purée to the bowl and microwave on HIGH for 3 minutes.
3. Stir in the sour cream (crème fraîche). Add salt and pepper to taste and stir well.
4. Rinse the fish under cold running water and pat dry on kitchen paper. Cut each fillet in half. Sprinkle salt and pepper over the base of an oval dish and put the fish fillets in the dish. Sprinkle with salt and pepper and dot with the remaining butter. Cover and microwave on HIGH for 5 minutes.
5. When the fish is cooked, lift out on to a serving dish. Rinse the basil, remove the leaves and snip them with kitchen scissors, over the fish. Pour the lemon juice over.
6. Add the cooking liquid from the fish to the artichoke sauce and stir well. Reheat for 1 minute on HIGH, then coat the fish with the sauce and serve at once.

Sea trout with field mushrooms

Truite de mer aux champignons des bois

Sea Trout with Field Mushrooms

◼▷   00.08   00.19   〰
Serves 5-6

American	Ingredients	Metric/Imperial
1¾ lb	field mushrooms	750 g/1¾ lb
2 oz	smoked streaky bacon, diced	50 g/2 oz
1	chopped shallot	1
	salt	
	pepper	
6	sea trout fillets	6
2 tbsp	fresh lemon juice	1 tbsp
2 tbsp	Madeira	1 tbsp
1½ tsp	cornstarch (cornflour)	1½ tsp
3 tbsp	sour cream (crème fraîche)	2 tbsp

1. Wipe the field mushrooms with a damp cloth or kitchen paper, peel if necessary and chop coarsely.
2. Put the bacon and shallot in a casserole. Microwave, uncovered, on HIGH for 2 minutes. Add the field mushrooms. Cover and microwave on HIGH for 4 minutes. Add salt and pepper and stir well. Cover and microwave on HIGH for a further 3 minutes.
3. Rinse the trout fillets under plenty of cold running water and pat dry on kitchen paper. Arrange the fish, side by side in an oval dish. Season with salt and pepper. Cover and microwave on HIGH for 5 minutes.
4. Drain the mushrooms over a bowl. Set aside the cooking liquid. Add the lemon juice and Madeira, and stir into the cornstarch (cornflour) gradually until smooth. Microwave for 1 minute on HIGH.
5. Add the sour cream (crème fraîche) and stir in the field mushrooms. Pour the whole over the fish, making sure it is completely covered with the sauce. Cover and microwave on HIGH for 4 minutes.
6. Serve immediately in the same dish.

Truite de mer au raisin

Sea Trout with Grapes

◼▷   00.10   00.09   〰
Serves 4

American	Ingredients	Metric/Imperial
1	sea trout about 2 lb (1 kg/2lb)	1
⅓ cup	white port	4½ tbsp
½ lb	seedless white grapes, peeled	225 g/8 oz
1 tsp	cornstarch (cornflour)	1 tsp
4 tbsp	sour cream (crème fraîche)	3 tbsp
1½ tsp	mild mustard	1½ tsp
	salt	
	pepper	

1. Clean the trout and remove the head. Rinse the fish under plenty of cold running water and pat dry on kitchen paper. Put the fish in a long dish and add the port. Cover and microwave on HIGH for 6 minutes.
2. Put the cornstarch (cornflour) in a bowl. Gradually stir in the sour cream (crème fraîche) until you have a smooth mixture. Add the mustard and the cooking liquid from the fish. Cook for 1 minute on HIGH. Stir and cook for 1 further minute. Add the grapes and heat for 30 seconds. Taste and adjust seasoning.
3. Remove the skin from the trout. Put the fish in a serving dish. Pour the sauce and grapes over and serve at once.

Microwave hint: Earthenware dishes and plates can be safely used in the microwave cooker on MEDIUM and LOW if they are indicated as suitable for the conventional oven up to temperatures of 400°F (200°C/Gas Mark 6). However, avoid using them to cook mixtures containing a high proportion of sugar as these get very hot.

Sea trout with grapes

Saumon à l'oseille

Salmon Steaks with Sorrel

■━▷ 00.10   00.08   〽️
          Serves 2

American	Ingredients	Metric/Imperial
	salt	
	pepper	
¼ cup	dry white wine	4 tbsp
3 tbsp	dry Vermouth	2 tbsp
2	salmon steaks, thawed if frozen	2
3 oz	frozen sorrel	75 g/3 oz
4 tbsp	sour cream (crème fraîche)	3 tbsp
1	egg yolk	1
2 oz	shelled shrimp (prawns)	50 g/2 oz

1. Sprinkle salt and pepper over the base of a dish and pour the white wine and Vermouth into it.
2. Rinse the salmon steaks under cold running water. Pat dry on kitchen paper and arrange in the dish, side by side. Season with salt and pepper. Cover and microwave on HIGH for 3 minutes.
3. Using two spatulas, carefully lift the fish out and put them on two dinner plates. Cover with aluminum (aluminium) foil.
4. Put the frozen sorrel into the dish with the cooking liquid from the fish and cook, uncovered, for 3 minutes on HIGH.
5. Stir in the sour cream (crème fraîche) and egg yolk. Taste and adjust seasoning.
6. Add the shelled shrimp (prawns). Stir and microwave for 2 minutes on HIGH.
7. Remove the skin from the fish and pour the sauce over. Serve at once.

Left to right: Salmon steaks with sorrel, Salmon with anchovy butter

Salmon au beurre d'anchois

Salmon with Anchovy Butter

00.06 Serves 4 **00.08**

American	Ingredients	Metric/Imperial
¼ cup	butter	50 g/2 oz
2 tbsp	all-purpose (plain) flour	1 tbsp
¾ cup	milk	200 ml/7 fl oz
4 tbsp	sour cream (crème fraîche)	3 tbsp
4	salmon steaks	4
	pepper	
3	anchovy fillets in oil	3
2	egg yolks	2
2 tbsp	fresh lemon juice	1 tbsp
	salt	
4 tsp	salmon caviar	4 tsp

1. Melt 1-2 tablespoons of the butter in a bowl in the microwave oven for 1 minute on HIGH.

2. Stir the flour in well. Add the milk and microwave for 2 minutes on HIGH, stirring mid-way through the cooking time.

3. Stir in the sour cream (crème fraîche).

4. Rinse the salmon steaks under cold running water and pat dry on kitchen paper. Season with pepper on both sides. Using ½-1 tablespoon of butter, grease the base of a round dish. Arrange the fish on the dish, skin side outward. Cover and microwave on HIGH for 4 minutes.

5. Purée the remaining butter and the anchovy fillets in a food processor.

6. Mix together the egg yolks and lemon juice.

7. Remove the skin from the salmon steaks and arrange them on a serving dish. Spread with the anchovy butter.

8. Pour the cooking liquid from the salmon into the sauce. Add the egg yolk and lemon juice mixture and stir well. Heat in the microwave oven for 1 minute on MEDIUM-HIGH. Taste and adjust seasoning.

9. Pour the sauce over the salmon and garnish each steak with a small teaspoon of salmon caviar. Serve.

Saumon aux coquilles Saint-Jacques

Salmon with Sea Scallops

00.10	00.14	
Serves 5		

American	Ingredients	Metric/Imperial
2 tbsp	butter	1 tbsp
1 tbsp	all-purpose (plain) flour	½ tbsp
⅔ cup	milk	200 ml/7 fl oz
½ tsp	saffron	½ tsp
5	salmon steaks	5
5	large sea scallops	5
1 oz	shallots	25 g/1 oz
⅓ cup	white wine	4½ tbsp
	salt	
	pepper	
1	egg yolk	1
1 tbsp	chopped dill	1 tbsp

1. Put 1 teaspoon of butter in a large bowl and melt in the microwave oven for 1 minute on HIGH.

2. Stir in the flour and add the milk, stirring constantly. Microwave on HIGH for 3 minutes, beating with a hand whisk after every minute. Whisk thoroughly, add the saffron, whisk again and set aside.

3. Rinse the salmon under plenty of cold running water and pat dry on kitchen paper. Remove any remaining bones. Separate the scallop corals from the whites, removing any impurities. Rinse under plenty of cold running water.

4. Put the shallots in a large round dish with the remaining butter. Microwave on HIGH for 2 minutes.

5. Add the white wine and heat on HIGH for 1 minute.

6. Season the white wine and shallot mixture with salt and pepper and add the salmon steaks, skin side facing outward. Microwave on HIGH for 1 minute.

7. Put the scallop whites in the dish with the salmon steaks. Cover and microwave on HIGH for 3 minutes.

8. Prick each scallop coral in 2 or 3 places with a toothpick (cocktail stick) and place them in the center of the dish. Cover and microwave on HIGH for 1 minute.

9. Transfer the salmon steaks to a serving dish. Place one scallop white inside each steak and one coral on top of each. Cover with aluminum (aluminium) foil to keep warm.

10. Add the egg yolk to the sauce that was set on one side. Whisk, adding the cooking liquid from the fish. Taste and adjust seasoning, then whisk thoroughly. Reheat on HIGH for 2 minutes.

11. Add the chopped dill to the sauce. Coat the fish with half the sauce and pour the other half into a sauceboat. Serve at once.

Microwave hint: When cooking a whole fish in the microwave, wrap a thin piece of foil around the tail, and remove mid-way through the cooking time. This prevents the tail from becoming very dry and fragile and breaking off when the fish is moved.

Saumon aux deux moutardes

Salmon with Two Mustards

00.10	00.12	
Serves 4		

American	Ingredients	Metric/Imperial
½ lb	leeks, white part only, cut into ½ inch(1.25 cm) pieces	225 g/8 oz
½ lb	grated carrots	225 g/8 oz
3 tbsp	white wine	2 tbsp
4	fresh salmon steaks	4
	salt	
	pepper	
3 tbsp	mild mustard	2 tbsp
2 tbsp	Dijon or Meaux mustard	1 tbsp
¾ cup	sour cream (crème fraîche)	200 ml/7 fl oz
3 tbsp	butter	2 tbsp
1 tbsp	chopped parsley	1 tbsp

1. Rinse and drain the leeks. Put the leeks and carrots in a dish with the white wine. Cover and microwave on HIGH for 8 minutes.

2. Rinse the salmon steaks under plenty of cold running water and pat dry on kitchen paper. Sprinkle salt and pepper over the base of a round dish and put the salmon into it in a circle, skin side outward. Season with salt and pepper and cover.

3. Remove the vegetables from the microwave oven and leave to stand.

4. Put the salmon in the oven and microwave on HIGH for 3 minutes.

5. Mix together the two mustards and the sour cream (crème fraîche) in a bowl. Add the butter.

6. Remove the fish from the oven and take off the skin.

7. Put the mustard and sour cream (crème fraîche) mixture into the oven and microwave on HIGH for 1 minute. Remove the bowl from the oven and whisk vigorously.

8. Pour three-quarters of the sauce over the vegetables and stir carefully. Put the vegetables in a serving dish and arrange the salmon steaks on top, using a slotted spatula. Coat the fish with the remaining sauce, sprinkle with chopped parsley and serve.

Salmon with sea scallops

Saumon Malcom

Salmon on a Bed of Vegetables

⏲ 00.10   00.13   〰️
Serves 4

American	Ingredients	Metric/Imperial
2 oz	chopped shallots	50 g/2 oz
2 tsp	butter	2 tsp
1	large grated carrot	1
1	large red bell pepper, seeded, cut into thin strips	1
⅓ cup	white wine	4½ tbsp
	salt	
	pepper	
4	salmon steaks	4
3 tbsp	sour cream (crème fraîche)	2 tbsp

1. Put the shallots in a round dish with the butter. Microwave, uncovered, on HIGH for 3 minutes.
2. Add the carrot and pepper to the shallots. Pour the white wine over, add salt and pepper to taste and stir well. Cover and microwave on HIGH for 6 minutes.
3. Rinse the fish under plenty of cold running water and pat dry on kitchen paper. Season with salt and pepper. Arrange the fish on top of the vegetables in a circle, skin side outward. Cover and microwave on HIGH for 4 minutes.
4. Remove the fish steaks and set aside.
5. Stir the sour cream (crème fraîche) into the vegetable mixture. Pour on to a serving dish. Put the salmon steaks on top and serve.

Saumon à la sauce au fenouil

Salmon in Fennel Sauce

⏲ 00.15   00.09   〰️
Serves 4

American	Ingredients	Metric/Imperial
4	salmon steaks	4
	salt	
	pepper	
3 tbsp	white wine	2 tbsp
5 oz	very finely sliced fennel	150 g/5 oz
1	egg yolk	1
⅓ cup	oil	4½ tbsp
4 tbsp	sour cream (crème fraîche)	3 tbsp
2 tbsp	dry Vermouth	1 tbsp
2 tbsp	fresh lemon juice	1 tbsp
2 tbsp	chopped chives	1 tbsp

1. Rinse the salmon steaks, pat dry on kitchen paper and put in a small casserole. Season with salt and pepper. Add the white wine. Cover and microwave on HIGH for 3-4 minutes, depending on the thickness of the steaks.
2. Remove the fish from the casserole with a slotted spatula, take off the skin and put the fish on a serving dish. Cover with aluminum (aluminium) foil, to keep warm.
3. Put the fennel in the casserole with the fish cooking liquid. Cover and microwave on HIGH for 5 minutes.
4. Put the egg yolk into a bowl and add the oil drop by drop, beating constantly until it thickens.
5. Add the sour cream (crème fraîche) little by little.
6. Add the Vermouth, lemon juice and chopped chives.
7. Drain and purée the fennel and stir into the sauce. Add salt and pepper to taste. Pour into a sauceboat and serve with the fish.

Pot-au-feu de poisson à la vapeur

Steamed Seafood and Vegetable Stew

◼▷ 00.15   00.28
Serves 4

American	Ingredients	Metric/Imperial
16	clams	16
1	red bell pepper, seeded and coarsely chopped	1
⅓ cup	white wine	4½ tbsp
2	sticks celery	2
1	sliced onion	1
1	sprig thyme	1
1	bayleaf	1
	salt	
	pepper	
4	leeks, white part only	4
7 oz	grated carrots	200 g/7 oz
11 oz	grated fennel	300 g/11 oz
4	sole fillets	4
2	large sea scallops	2
3	crushed garlic cloves	3
1	egg yolk	1
1 tsp	Dijon mustard	1 tsp
½ cup	olive oil	125 ml/4 fl oz
½ cup	peanut oil	125 ml/4 fl oz
½ tsp	Cayenne pepper	½ tsp
2 tbsp	cognac	1 tbsp
1	lemon	1
3 tbsp	sour cream (crème fraîche)	2 tbsp
2 tbsp	chopped parsley	2 tbsp

1. Rinse the clams thoroughly under plenty of cold running water. Put in a single layer in a dish. Cover and microwave on HIGH for 3 minutes.
2. Put the bell pepper in a small casserole with 2-3 tablespoons of water. Cover and microwave on HIGH for 4 minutes.
3. Remove the clams from their shells. Strain the cooking liquid and pour the clams into the lower compartment of a microwave steamer. Add the white wine and an equivalent amount of water.
4. Remove the leaves from the celery. Add the onion, celery leaves, thyme and bayleaf to the liquid in the steamer. Add salt and pepper to taste. Cover and microwave on HIGH for 6 minutes.
5. Remove the roots and outer leaves of the leeks. Rinse the leeks and the celery and slice finely.
6. Put all the vegetables in the upper compartment of the steamer and put it on top of the lower compartment and into the oven. Cover and microwave on HIGH for 8 minutes.
7. Season the fish fillets with salt and pepper and roll up, skin side out.
8. Remove any impurities from the scallop whites and rinse under plenty of cold running water. Separate the corals from the whites. Prick the corals with a toothpick (cocktail stick). Cut the whites in half.
9. Put the fish fillets on top of the vegetables. Cover and microwave on HIGH for 5 minutes. Add the scallop whites, clams and scallop corals. Cook for a further 2 minutes.

10. Drain the red bell pepper and purée with the garlic. Force the purée through a strainer (sieve), pressing it with the back of a wooden spoon.
11. Mix together the egg yolk and the mustard. Gradually add the olive oil and peanut oil, whisking constantly. When the mayonnaise thickens, add a pinch of Cayenne pepper, the cognac and the red pepper purée. Taste and adjust seasoning. Pour into a sauceboat.
12. When the vegetables and fish are cooked, transfer to a large soup tureen and cover with aluminum (aluminium) foil to keep warm. Set the corals to one side. Strain the cooking liquid from the steamer.
13. Squeeze the lemon. Put the juice into a food processor with the sour cream (crème fraîche) and the scallop corals. Purée, gradually adding the strained cooking liquid. Taste and adjust seasoning.
14. Pour half the sauce over the fish and vegetables and sprinkle with chopped parsley. Pour the rest into a second sauceboat. Serve with the two sauces on the side.

Poisson au curry

Seafood Curry

◼▷ 00.10   00.16
Serves 4

American	Ingredients	Metric/Imperial
2	chopped onions	2
1	large garlic clove	1
2 tbsp	oil	1 tbsp
1	small finely grated carrot	1
½	finely grated cooking apple	½
1 tsp	curry paste	1 tsp
¾ cup	sour cream (crème fraîche)	200 ml/7 fl oz
½ tsp	thyme	½ tsp
1	bayleaf	1
2 tbsp	tomato concentrate	1 tbsp
½ tsp	sugar	½ tsp
10 oz	silver hake or whiting fillet	300 g/10 oz
¾ lb	cod fillets	350 g/12 oz
3½ oz	shelled shrimp (prawns)	100 g/3½ oz
5 oz	cooked shelled mussels	150 g/5 oz

1. Purée the onions and garlic in a food processor. Put the purée in a casserole with the oil. Cover and microwave on HIGH for 4 minutes.
2. Add the carrot, apple, curry paste, sour cream (crème fraîche), crumbled thyme, bayleaf, tomato concentrate and sugar to the casserole. Stir well. Cover and microwave on HIGH for 7 minutes.
3. Rinse the fish under cold running water and pat dry on kitchen paper. Cut the fish into cubes.
4. Add the fish to the sauce and stir well. Cover and microwave on HIGH for 3-4 minutes, according to the size of the fish pieces.
5. Discard the bayleaf. Add the shrimp (prawns) and mussels to the casserole, stir and reheat on HIGH for 1 minute. Serve very hot.

Turban de semoule aux fruits de mer

Couscous Ring Mold (Mould) with Seafood

◀━▷ 00.15   **00.21** 🔲

Serves 4

American	Ingredients	Metric/Imperial
2 quarts	mussels in their shells	2 litres/3½ pints
4 tbsp	dry white wine	3 tbsp
7 oz	frozen shrimp (prawns)	200 g/7 oz
7 oz	white button mushrooms	200 g/7 oz
	salt	
	pepper	
2 tbsp	fresh lemon juice	1 tbsp
1 oz	butter	25 g/1 oz
¾ cup	couscous semolina	125 g/4 oz
1	chicken bouillon (stock) cube	1
1	large egg	1
½ tsp	allspice	½ tsp
4 tbsp	grated Parmesan cheese	3 tbsp
3 tbsp	golden raisins (sultanas)	2 tbsp
½ cup	pine nut kernels	50 g/2 oz
2 tbsp	sour cream (crème fraîche)	1 tbsp

1. Scrub and rinse the mussels, discarding any with open or broken shells. Put half the mussels into a dish with the white wine and microwave for 3 minutes on HIGH.
2. Lift the mussels out of the cooking liquid with a slotted spoon and set aside. Discard any that have not opened. Return the remaining mussels to the dish and microwave on HIGH for 3 minutes.

3. Put the frozen shrimp (prawns) in a small dish and defrost in the microwave oven for 1 minute on HIGH.
4. Wipe the mushrooms with a damp cloth or kitchen paper and slice finely.
5. Put the mushrooms in a small casserole, add salt and pepper and pour the lemon juice over. Cover and microwave on HIGH for 3 minutes.
6. Remove the mussels from their shells and filter the cooking liquid.
7. Put three-quarters of the butter in a bowl and melt in the microwave oven for 1 minute on HIGH. Add the couscous semolina, stir well, return to the oven and microwave for a further 2 minutes on HIGH.
8. Heat 1¾ cups (400 ml/14 fl oz) of water in the microwave oven for 2 minutes.
9. Crumble the chicken bouillon (stock) cube over the couscous. Pour the hot water over, stir well and microwave on HIGH for 3 minutes.
10. Whisk the egg with a fork. Stir into the couscous and season with salt and pepper. Add the allspice, grated Parmesan, raisins (sultanas) and pine kernels. Lightly butter the base of a Pyrex ring mold (mould). Pour the mixture into it and cook on HIGH for 2 minutes.
11. Mix together the shrimp (prawns), mussels, mushrooms, cooking liquid from the mussels and the sour cream (crème fraîche). Reheat in the microwave oven on HIGH for 1 minute.
12. Turn out the ring mold (mould) on to a round serving dish. Carefully spoon the seafood and mushroom mixture into the center of the mold (mould) and serve.

Seafood curry

Mousseline de poisson aux langoustines

Fish Mousse with Crawfish (Crayfish) in Sauce

00.06 Serves 4　　**00.14**

American	Ingredients	Metric/Imperial
10½ oz	pike or hake fillets, thawed if frozen	300 g/10½ oz
2	egg whites	2
¾ cup	whipping cream	200 ml/7 fl oz
1 tsp	fresh lemon juice	1 tsp
	salt	
	pepper	
1 tsp	butter	1 tsp
4	crawfish (crayfish)	4
⅓ cup	shrimp (prawn) bisque	5 tbsp
⅓ cup	sour cream (crème fraîche)	4½ tbsp
2 tbsp	white port	1 tbsp

1. Rinse the fish and pat dry on kitchen paper. Cut the fish into small pieces and purée in a food processor, gradually adding the egg whites one at a time and the whipping cream. Add the lemon juice. Add salt and pepper to taste.
2. Butter 4 ramekin dishes and divide the fish purée between them. Place them in a circle in the microwave oven, leaving the center empty, and cook for 6 minutes on MEDIUM-HIGH.
3. Bring a pan of salted water to the boil on a conventional cooker and boil the crawfish (crayfish) for 6 minutes.
4. Pour the shrimp (prawn) bisque into a bowl. Add the sour cream (crème fraîche) and the port. Stir well and microwave on HIGH for 2 minutes.
5. Drain the crawfish (crayfish).
6. Turn out each mousse on to a plate. Coat each with sauce and decorate with one crawfish (crayfish). Serve at once.
If crawfish (crayfish) are unavailable, large scampi, shrimp or Dublin Bay prawns make a good substitute.

Fish mousse with crawfish (crayfish) in sauce

Mussels in curry sauce

Moules au curry

Mussels in Curry Sauce

00.15   00.16

Serves 2-4

American	Ingredients	Metric/Imperial
2 quarts	mussels in their shells	2 litres/3½ pints
3 tbsp	white wine	2 tbsp
14 oz	leeks, white part only	400 g/14 oz
1 tsp	mild curry powder	1 tsp
1	egg	1
2 tbsp	sour cream (crème fraîche)	1 tbsp
1 tbsp	chopped parsley	1 tbsp

1. Scrub the mussels and rinse under cold running water. Discard any with open or broken shells. Put half the mussels in a dish, add the white wine and microwave on HIGH for 3 minutes.

2. Remove the cooked mussels with a slotted spoon and set over a bowl to drain. Put the remaining mussels into the dish and microwave on HIGH for 3 minutes. Drain.

3. Remove the mussels from their shells, discarding any that have not opened. Filter the cooking liquid and the liquid that has drained from the mussels.

4. Remove the roots and the outer leaves of the leeks. Cut them in half or in quarters if large, and then cut into ½ inch (1.25 cm) sections. Rinse thoroughly, drain and put into the dish in which the mussels were cooked. Stir the curry powder into the mussel liquid and pour over the leeks. Cover and microwave on HIGH for 9 minutes.

5. Mix together the egg and the sour cream (crème fraîche) with a fork. Stir into the leeks. Add the mussels, stir carefully and cook for 1 minute on HIGH. Sprinkle with chopped parsley and serve at once.

Coquilles Saint-Jacques à la mousse de poireaux

Scallops on a Bed of Leeks

	00.10	00.12	
	Serves 2-4		

American	Ingredients	Metric/Imperial
8	scallops with their corals	8
2 oz	chopped shallots	50 g/2 oz
	salt	
	pepper	
½ tsp	mild curry powder	½ tsp
3 tbsp	prune brandy	2 tbsp
11 oz	leeks, white part only	300 g/11 oz
1	egg	1
2 tbsp	sour cream (crème fraîche)	1 tbsp

1. Separate the white of the scallops from the corals, removing any impurites. Rinse scallops under plenty of cold running water and cut the whites in half.

2. Put the shallots in the base of a dish and season with salt and pepper. Put the scallop whites in a single layer on the bed of shallots, with the corals in the center of the dish.

3. Mix together the curry powder and the prune brandy (or cognac if prune brandy is not available) and pour into the dish. Season the scallops with salt and pepper. Cover and microwave on HIGH for 2 minutes.

4. Remove the roots and outer leaves of the leeks. Cut into quarters and then into ½ inch (1.25 cm) pieces. Rinse thoroughly and leave to drain.

5. Remove the scallops from the dish and set aside. Put the leeks into the dish on top of the shallots. Cover and microwave on HIGH for 8 minutes.

6. Purée the contents of the dish in a food processor. Add the egg and purée again. Add the sour cream (crème fraîche) and purée once more. Taste and adjust seasoning.

7. Pour the leek mousse into an ovenproof serving dish. Arrange the scallops on top of the mousse. Cover and reheat on MEDIUM for 2 minutes. Serve at once.

Oysters Baked in the Shell

	00.05	00.05	
	Serves 4		

American	Ingredients	Metric/Imperial
24	oysters	24
1 tbsp	chopped parsley	1 tbsp
½ tsp	dried dillweed	½ tsp
½ tsp	French mustard	½ tsp
¼ tsp	garlic powder	¼ tsp
	salt	
	pepper	
1 tbsp	fresh breadcrumbs	1 tbsp
¼ cup	grated Gouda cheese	25 g/1 oz

1. To open the oyster shells, hold the deep shell in one hand and prise off the other shell with an oyster knife. Remove any beards and rinse the oysters thoroughly, but carefully under plenty of cold running water. Gently remove the fish from the shells and keep cool. Rinse the deep shells under plenty of cold running water and set aside.

2. Melt the butter in a small dish for 30 seconds on HIGH. Beat in the parsley, dill, mustard, garlic, salt and pepper.

3. Divide two-thirds of the mixture between the deep oyster shells and put the fish on top.

4. Mix the breadcrumbs and cheese, sprinkle over the fish.

5. Dot the remaining flavored butter on top of the oysters.

6. Arrange six oysters at a time in a circle in the microwave, leaving the center empty. Cook for 4 minutes on HIGH and flash under a hot broiler (grill) until golden.

7. Serve with lemon twists, parsley sprigs and French bread.

Coquilles Saint-Jacques aux deux légumes

Scallops with Carrots and Leeks

	00.20	00.15	
	Serves 4		

American	Ingredients	Metric/Imperial
2	finely chopped shallots	2
2 tbsp	butter	1 tbsp
5 oz	diced baby carrots	150 g/5 oz
7 oz	young leeks, white part only, diced	200 g/7 oz
1	stick celery, cut into thin strips	1
	salt	
	pepper	
8	scallops with their corals	8
2 tbsp	sour cream (crème fraîche)	1 tbsp
2	egg yolks	2
2 tbsp	fresh lemon juice	1 tbsp
½ tsp	cornstarch (cornflour)	½ tsp
2 tbsp	chopped fresh dill	2 tbsp

1. Put the shallots in a dish with the butter and microwave, uncovered, on HIGH for 2 minutes.

2. Add the carrots, leeks and celery to the shallots with 3 (2) tablespoons of water, salt and pepper. Cover and microwave on HIGH for 10 minutes.

3. Clean the scallops, cutting in half if very large. Prick each scallop in 2 or 3 places with a toothpick (cocktail stick) to avoid bursting during cooking.

4. Put the scallops on top of the vegetables with the corals toward the center of the dish. Add 2 or 3 tablespoons of water. Season, cover and heat on HIGH for 2 minutes.

5. Transfer the scallops and vegetables to a serving dish.

6. Mix together the sour cream (crème fraîche), egg yolks, lemon juice and cornstarch (cornflour) in a bowl, stirring constantly. Carefully add the cooking liquid from the scallops and vegetables, stirring constantly. Heat in the oven for 1 minute. Stir well, taste and adjust seasoning.

7. Pour the sauce over the scallops and vegetables, sprinkle with chopped dill and serve.

Scallops with carrots and leeks

Meat

Beef

Steak in tomato cream sauce

5. Transfer the meat to a heated serving dish. Season with salt and pepper and cover with aluminum (aluminium) foil to keep warm.

6. Pour the cognac into the browning dish and stir with a wooden spatula until the cooking liquid is dissolved. Add to the cream sauce and heat for 3 minutes on HIGH. Stir well. Taste and adjust the seasoning, pour over the steak, sprinkle with chopped parsley and serve at once.

Boeuf sauté aux poivrons

Sautéed Steak with Bell Peppers

◼▷   00.15   00.20   〰〰
Serves 4

American	Ingredients	Metric/Imperial
14 oz	porterhouse (sirloin) steak	400 g/14 oz
2 tbsp	dry sherry	1 tbsp
3 tbsp	dark soy sauce	2 tbsp
½ tsp	superfine (caster) sugar	½ tsp
2 tbsp	olive oil	1 tbsp
	black pepper	
7 oz	thinly sliced onions	200 g/7 oz
1	large green bell pepper, rinsed, seeded and cut into strips	1
1	large red bell pepper, rinsed, seeded and cut into strips	1
1 tsp	garlic powder	1 tsp
¼ tsp	dried thyme	¼ tsp
	salt	
	pepper	
2 tbsp	vinegar	1 tbsp
1 tbsp	chopped parsley	1 tbsp

1. Trim the fat from the steak. Rinse under plenty of cold running water and pat dry on kitchen paper. Slice into 2 inch (5 cm) strips (it is important that they are of equal size). Mix the sherry, soy sauce, sugar, 1 teaspoon of oil and several grinds of black pepper. Pour over the steak, stir and leave to stand.

2. Put the onions in a dish. Microwave, uncovered, for 3 minutes on HIGH.

3. Add the bell peppers to the onions and sprinkle with garlic powder and thyme. Season with salt and pepper. Pour over the vinegar and remaining oil. Cover and microwave on HIGH for 10 minutes.

4. Remove the dish from the oven and cover with aluminum (aluminium) foil.

5. Heat a browning dish in the oven for 6 minutes, following the manufacturer's instructions. Seal the steak strips and turn with a wooden spatula. Microwave for 1 minute on HIGH.

6. Add the steak strips to the vegetables. Pour the marinade into the browning dish, scraping the base of the dish with the spatula. Pour the marinade over the steak and vegetables. Sprinkle with chopped parsley and serve at once.

Boeuf sauté, sauce rose

Steak in Tomato Cream Sauce

◼▷   00.10   00.17   〰〰
Serves 4

American	Ingredients	Metric/Imperial
1	finely chopped large shallot	1
2 tbsp	butter	1 tbsp
1½ lb	boneless rib (sirloin) steak, cut into thin strips	600 g/1½ lb
¼ cup	sour cream (crème fraîche)	3 tbsp
2 tbsp	tomato paste (purée)	1 tbsp
½ tsp	sugar	½ tsp
1 tsp	mild mustard	1 tsp
	salt	
	pepper	
1 tsp	cognac	1 tsp
1 tbsp	chopped fresh parsley	1 tbsp

1. Put the shallot and butter in a bowl and microwave, uncovered, for 3 minutes on HIGH.

2. Heat a browning dish in the microwave oven for 6-8 minutes, following the manufacturer's instructions.

3. When the browning dish is hot, put in the strips of steak, leave for 30-40 seconds, then turn over with a spatula. Microwave, uncovered, for 2 minutes on HIGH.

4. Stir the shallots and add the sour cream (crème fraîche), tomato paste (purée), sugar and mustard. Mix well.

Faux-filet au vinaigre

Piquant Rib (Sirloin) Steak

⬛▷   00.05   00.10   〰
       plus marinating time

American	Ingredients	Metric/Imperial
1 tsp	green peppercorns	1 tsp
1 tsp	black peppercorns	1 tsp
1½ lb	rib (sirloin) steak	600 g/1½ lb
⅔ cup	tarragon vinegar	150 ml/¼ pint
1 tsp	cornstarch (cornflour)	1 tsp
3 tbsp	Madeira	2 tbsp
3 tbsp	sour cream (crème fraîche)	2 tbsp
3 tbsp	Dijon mustard	2 tbsp
	salt	

1. Crush the green and black peppercorns in a pestle and mortar or pepper grinder. Roll the piece of steak in the pepper and pour over the vinegar. Marinate for 30 minutes at room temperature. Turn the steak over and marinate for a further 30 minutes.
2. Drain the meat and put in a small dish. Cover and microwave on HIGH for 3 minutes. Leave to stand for 5 minutes.
3. Put ¼ cup (3 tablespoons) of the marinade into a small bowl and mix in the cornstarch (cornflour) gradually to form a smooth paste. Add the Madeira, sour cream (crème fraîche) and mustard. Microwave on HIGH for 1 minute. Stir vigorously. Add the cooking liquid and microwave on HIGH for 1 further minute. Stir well, taste and adjust the seasoning. Pour into a heated sauceboat.
4. Slice the meat, arrange on a serving dish and serve with the sauce on the side.

Rti de boeuf au poivre

Roast Beef au Poivre

⬛▷   00.05   00.20   〰
       Serves 5-6

American	Ingredients	Metric/Imperial
2 lb	rib eye (topside) beef roast	1 kg/2 lb
½ tbsp	oil	½ tbsp
¼ cup	mild mustard	3 tbsp
2 tsp	coarse ground black pepper	2 tsp
½ tbsp	butter	½ tbsp
2 tbsp	sour cream (crème fraîche)	1 tbsp
3 tbsp	sherry or cognac	2 tbsp
	salt	

1. Heat a browning dish in the microwave oven on HIGH for 6 minutes, following the manufacturer's instructions. Brush the meat all over with the oil.
2. Seal the meat on all sides in the browning dish. Spread the top with half of the mustard and sprinkle with the black pepper.
3. Cover and microwave on HIGH for 8 minutes. At this stage the meat should still be very rare (but not "blue") inside. Use a meat thermometer to test the temperature, which should be 35°C. Put the meat on a heated serving dish and cover with aluminum (aluminium) foil, matt side outward. Leave to stand for 5 minutes.
4. Pour the cooking liquid into a bowl and stir in the butter, sour cream (crème fraîche), sherry or cognac and the remaining mustard. Heat in the oven for 1 minute on HIGH.
5. Whisk the sauce and adjust the seasoning. Serve with the meat. If you prefer the meat medium rare, let it cook for 2 minutes longer.

Roast beef au poivre

Roast beef with stuffed prunes

Rosbif aux pruneaux farcis

Roast Beef with Stuffed Prunes

	00.05	00.28	
	Serves 5-6		

American	Ingredients	Metric/Imperial
2 lb	boneless sirloin roast	1 kg/2 lb
2 tbsp	oil	1 tbsp
2 tbsp	cognac	1 tbsp
	salt	
	pepper	
9 oz	pitted prunes	250 g/9 oz
3½ oz	duck liver pâté	100 g/3½ oz
5	tomatoes	5
3	crushed garlic cloves	3
2	fresh thyme sprigs	2
2 tbsp	butter	1 tbsp
1	can mushroom sauce	1
3 tbsp	sour cream (crème fraîche)	2 tbsp

1. Heat a browning dish in the microwave oven for 6-8 minutes, following the manufacturer's instructions. Rinse the meat under plenty of cold running water. Pat dry on kitchen paper. Brush all over with the oil. Put in the hot browning dish to seal on one side.
2. Remove the meat and reheat the browning dish for a further 2-3 minutes, then seal the other side of the meat. Cover and microwave on HIGH for 7 minutes.
3. Pour the cognac into a cup, heat on HIGH for 30 seconds, set alight and pour over the meat to flambé. Season the meat with salt and pepper, cover with a double thickness of aluminum (aluminium) foil and leave to stand.
4. Stuff each prune with a small spoonful of duck pâté. Set aside the remaining pâté.
5. Rinse the tomatoes under plenty of cold running water. Pat dry on kitchen paper. Remove the stalks and cut in half. Put in a large round dish, cut side upward. Season the tomatoes with salt and pepper, put a little garlic, thyme and butter on each half, cover and cook on HIGH for 5 minutes.
6. Add the stuffed prunes to the tomatoes. Cover and microwave on HIGH for 1 further minute.
7. Pour the mushroom sauce into a small bowl and heat on HIGH for 2 minutes.
8. Carve the meat and arrange the slices on a serving dish. Pour the meat cooking liquid into the dish with the prunes and tomatoes. Arrange the prunes and tomatoes around the beef.
9. Add the sour cream (crème fraîche) and the cooking liquid to the mushroom sauce. Mix well. Add the remaining duck pâté, whisking constantly. Reheat for 1 minute, whisk again, pour into a sauceboat and serve.
The cooking time for the beef will vary according to the shape and thickness of the roast. The meat temperature should be between 40 and 45°C for rare meat. Remember that the temperature will rise several degrees during the resting period.

Microwave hint: Pot-roasting joints, such as topside or silverside, is particularly successful if cooked slowly by microwave. Place the marinated meat in a roasting bag together with the marinade and a few sliced onions and carrots. Secure the roasting bag loosely with an elastic band, taking care that the liquid will not spill out. Cook on MEDIUM for at least 1 hour. Leave to stand for 10 minutes before carving.

Boeuf aux anchois

Beef with Anchovies

	00.20	00.63	
	Serves 4-5		

American	Ingredients	Metric/Imperial
9 oz	thinly sliced onions	250 g/9 oz
2	crushed large garlic cloves	2
¾ cup	dry white wine	200 ml/7 fl oz
4	chopped anchovy fillets in oil	4
1	coarsely chopped tomato	1
½ tsp	ground black pepper	½ tsp
¼ tsp	powdered cloves	¼ tsp
1	fresh thyme sprig	1
1	bay leaf	1
1¾ lb	top round (topside) of beef	750 g/1¾ lb
2 tsp	soft brown sugar	2 tsp
3 tbsp	wine vinegar	2 tbsp
3 tbsp	sour cream (crème fraîche)	2 tbsp

1. Put the onions and garlic into a casserole. Cover and microwave on HIGH for 5 minutes.
2. Pour the white wine over the onions. Add the anchovies, tomato, black pepper, powdered cloves, thyme and bay leaf. Mix well. Cover and microwave on HIGH for 3 minutes.
3. Add the beef, brown sugar and vinegar. Stir well. Cover and microwave on HIGH for a further 5 minutes. Reduce the power to MEDIUM-HIGH and cook for 35-40 minutes until the meat is tender. Stir after every 10 minutes of cooking time.
4. Test to see if the beef is cooked, then transfer the meat to a heated serving dish. Leave to stand for 10 minutes.
5. Discard the thyme and bay leaf, add the sour cream (crème fraîche), pour over the meat and serve very hot.

Beef and Horseradish Loaf

	00.10	00.23	
	Serves 4		

American	Ingredients	Metric/Imperial
⅔ cup	strong beef bouillon (stock)	150 ml/¼ pint
½ lb	soft breadcrumbs	225 g/8 oz
1	finely chopped large onion	1
1 lb	ground (minced) beef	450 g/1 lb
2 tbsp	grated horseradish	1 tbsp
3	eggs	3
3 tbsp	cream sherry	2 tbsp
	salt	
	pepper	

1. Put the bouillon (stock) and breadcrumbs in a bowl and heat on HIGH for 2 minutes. Add the onion, beef, horseradish, eggs and sherry to the breadcrumbs and season well. Stir with a wooden spoon until all the ingredients are blended.
2. Press the mixture into an oblong loaf or casserole dish. Cover and cook on HIGH for 15-16 minutes. Leave to stand for 5 minutes. Drain off the excess cooking liquid before serving.

Filet de bœuf au céleri

Beef Tenderloin (Fillet) with Celery

00.10 plus marinating time   **00.23**

American	Ingredients	Metric/Imperial
2	onions	2
12	celery sticks	12
1	sliced carrot	1
2	fresh thyme sprigs	2
1	bay leaf	1
½ tsp	black peppercorns	½ tsp
1¾ lb	beef tenderloin (fillet)	700 g/1¾ lb
1 cup	white wine	250 ml/8 fl oz
2 tbsp	oil	1 tbsp
½ tsp	curry powder	½ tsp
1½ tsp	cornstarch (cornflour)	1½ tsp
3 tbsp	dry sherry	2 tbsp
3 tbsp	heavy (double) cream	2 tbsp
	salt	
	pepper	

1. Peel and thinly slice one of the onions. Separate the leaves from the celery sticks.
2. Put half of the onion slices, celery leaves, carrot slices, thyme, bay leaf and peppercorns into a dish just large enough to hold the meat. Put the meat on the bed of vegetables. Cover with the remaining celery leaves, carrots, thyme, bay leaf and peppercorns. Pour over the white wine and oil. Cover and leave to marinate for 12 hours in the refrigerator. If the meat is not completely covered by the liquid, turn it once or twice during the marinating period.
3. Peel and chop the second onion. Slice the celery sticks thinly. Remove the meat and strain the marinade.
4. Mix the onion and celery in a dish. Add the curry powder and 1 cup (8 fl oz) of the marinade liquid. Cover and microwave on HIGH for 5 minutes.
5. Put the meat on top of the vegetables. Cover and microwave on HIGH for 6-7 minutes. Use a meat thermometer to check the internal temperature of the meat, which should read 35°C. Cover the meat with a double layer of aluminum (aluminium) foil, matt side outward, and leave to stand for 10 minutes. Carve into slices.
6. Remove the celery and onion with a slotted spoon and put in a serving dish. Arrange the slices of meat on top.
7. Mix the cornstarch (cornflour) and sherry to a smooth paste in a small bowl. Add the cooking liquid from the meat and vegetables. Heat in the oven for 1 minute on HIGH. Stir well. Add the heavy (double) cream and stir again. Taste and adjust the seasoning. Pour into a sauceboat and serve with the meat.

Beef tenderloin (fillet) with celery

Filet de boeuf aux marrons

Beef Tenderloin (Fillet) with Chestnuts

00.10   00.51   plus marinating time

American	Ingredients	Metric/Imperial
1	celery stick	1
1	sliced carrot	1
1	chopped large onion	1
1	crushed garlic clove	1
1	fresh thyme sprig	1
1	bay leaf	1
1 tsp	black peppercorns	1 tsp
2 lb	beef tenderloin (fillet)	1 kg/2 lb
¼ cup	cognac	3 tbsp
2¼ cups	red wine	500 ml/18 fl oz
2 tbsp	oil	1 tbsp
2 tbsp	butter	1 tbsp
2 tbsp	all-purpose (plain) flour	1 tbsp
2 tbsp	Madeira	1 tbsp
	salt	
	pepper	
1	can whole chestnuts	1
¼ cup	sour cream (crème fraîche)	3 tbsp

1. To make the marinade: wash the celery and chop coarsely. Put the celery, carrot, onions and garlic into a terrine dish just large enough to hold the meat. Add the thyme sprig, bay leaf and black peppercorns. Put the meat in the dish. Pour over the cognac, red wine and the oil. Cover and leave to marinate in the refrigerator for 24 hours.
2. About 1 hour before serving, drain the meat and put in a dish. Cover and microwave on HIGH for 7 minutes.
3. Cover the meat with a double thickness of aluminum (aluminium) foil, matt side outward, and leave to stand for 15-20 minutes.
4. Pour the marinade into a casserole. Cover and microwave on HIGH for 15 minutes.
5. Melt the butter in a bowl for 1 minute. Add the flour and mix well. Strain the marinade over the bowl, then put in the oven and cook for 2 minutes on HIGH. Mix well, adding the cooking liquid from the meat and the Madeira. Cook for a further 2 minutes on HIGH. Mix again. Taste and adjust the seasoning. Pour into a sauceboat.
6. Drain the chestnuts, put in a dish and coat with the sour cream (crème fraîche). Cover and microwave on HIGH for 4 minutes.
7. Carve the meat and arrange the slices on a serving platter. Put the chestnuts in the center and serve with the sauce.
If the meat has cooled down too much, reheat on the serving dish for 1 minute on HIGH.

Microwave hint: To test if pot-roasted or braised meat is done, use a microwave thermometer, which can be left inside the meat in a roasting bag. If your microwave has a probe, make a slit in the bag and insert the probe through the slit. If you have neither, remove the meat from the cooker and test with a conventional meat thermometer.

Tournedos à l'échalote

Beef Tenderloin (Fillet) with Shallots

00.05   00.17   Serves 3

American	Ingredients	Metric/Imperial
3	beef tenderloin (fillet) steaks	3
½ tsp	oil	½ tsp
2 oz	finely chopped shallots	50 g/2 oz
2 tbsp	butter	1 tbsp
¼ cup	white wine vinegar	4 tbsp
	ground black pepper	
1 tsp	dried tarragon	1 tsp
3 tbsp	sour cream (crème fraîche)	2 tbsp
1	egg yolk	1
	salt	

1. Heat a browning dish in the microwave oven for 6-8 minutes on HIGH, following the manufacturer's instructions. Rinse the steaks under plenty of cold running water. Pat dry on kitchen paper. Brush the steaks on both sides with oil.
2. When the browning dish is hot, seal the steaks on both sides, turning with a wooden spatula. Cover and microwave on HIGH for 2 minutes. Leave to stand.
3. Put the onions and butter in a bowl and microwave, uncovered, on HIGH for 3 minutes.
4. Stir in the vinegar, several grinds of black pepper and the tarragon. Cook for a further 2 minutes on HIGH.
5. Whisk the sour cream (crème fraîche) with the egg yolk, and add to the dish. Add salt to taste and leave to stand for 2 minutes.
6. Place the steaks in a heated serving dish and pour over the sauce. Serve at once.

Hamburgers

00.10   00.08   Serves 4

American	Ingredients	Metric/Imperial
1 lb	ground (minced) beef	450 g/1 lb
1	finely chopped onion	1
	salt	
	pepper	
4	hamburger rolls, halved	4
2 tbsp	Dijon mustard	1 tbsp

1. Put the beef in a mixing bowl. Add the onion and plenty of seasoning. Divide and shape the mixture into 4 patties and put on a micro-proof meat roasting rack. Cook on HIGH for 5-6 minutes, turning once.
2. Lightly toast the rolls under a conventional broiler (grill). Spread with mustard. Put a hamburger in each roll, top with onions and ketchup or cheese.

Goulash with Bell Peppers

⏺ 00.10   00.54 〰
Serves 2

American	Ingredients	Metric/Imperial
¼ cup	oil	3 tbsp
¾ lb	chuck steak, cut into cubes	350 g/12 oz
	salt	
	pepper	
	sweet paprika pepper	
½ cup	hot water	6 tbsp
½ cup	red wine	6 tbsp
2	red bell peppers, rinsed, seeded and cut into strips	2
2	green bell peppers, rinsed, seeded and cut into strips	2
2	thinly sliced large onions	2
3½ oz	drained canned mushrooms	100 g/3½ oz
	chopped parsley	

1. Heat a browning dish for 6-8 minutes, following the manufacturer's instructions. Pour in the oil, tilting the dish to make sure the base is evenly covered. Add the beef cubes and cook on HIGH for 2 minutes. Turn the meat and cook for a further 2 minutes. Season with salt, pepper and paprika.
2. Pour in the water and wine. Cook on HIGH for 10 minutes. Leave to stand for 5 minutes. Add the peppers and onions to the beef and stir well. Heat on HIGH for 15 minutes.
3. Add the mushrooms and more paprika, if necessary. Heat on HIGH for 7 minutes. Leave to stand for 5 minutes. Sprinkle with chopped parsley.

Boeuf haché pimenté

Spicy Ground (Minced) Beef

⏺ 00.10   00.27 〰
Serves 4

American	Ingredients	Metric/Imperial
2	finely chopped large onions	2
2	crushed garlic cloves	2
2	red bell peppers, rinsed, seeded and diced	2
2 tbsp	olive oil	1 tbsp
1¼ lb	diced potatoes	500 g/1¼ lb
	salt	
1½ lb	ground (minced) beef	600 g/1½ lb
7 oz	tomato sauce in a can	200 g/7 oz
3 tbsp	white wine	2 tbsp
2 tbsp	chili powder	1 tbsp
½ tsp	ground cumin	½ tsp
	Tabasco sauce	
2 oz	grated Gruyère cheese	50 g/2 oz
	several lettuce leaves	

1. Put the onions, garlic and bell peppers in a large casserole. Pour over the olive oil. Cover and microwave on HIGH for 5 minutes.

2. Add the potatoes to the casserole. Add salt and stir well. Cover and microwave on HIGH for 10 minutes.
3. Place the ground (minced) beef in the casserole. Cover and microwave on HIGH for 5 minutes, stirring carefully mid-way through the cooking time.
4. Mix together the tomato sauce, white wine, chili powder, cumin and several dashes of Tabasco sauce. Pour over the contents of the casserole and stir thoroughly. Cover and microwave on HIGH for 4 minutes.
5. Add the grated cheese, stir and leave to stand for 3 minutes. Serve on a bed of lettuce.

Microwave hint: Defrosting ground (minced) beef by microwave can be difficult because the outer layer begins to cook while the center is still frozen. To avoid this, defrost the pack for 3 minutes on LOW, then scrape off the defrosted outer layer. Continue defrosting and scraping off the outer layer every few minutes.

Puits de concombre à la viande

Stuffed Cucumber Rings

⏺ 00.15   00.13 〰
Serves 3-4

American	Ingredients	Metric/Imperial
1	large cucumber	1
2 tbsp	fresh lemon juice	1 tbsp
	pepper	
1	egg	1
2	finely chopped shallots	2
2	crushed garlic cloves	2
2 tbsp	chopped fresh parsley	1 tbsp
2 tbsp	chopped fresh mint	1 tbsp
3½ oz	ground (minced) beef	100 g/3½ oz
3½ oz	sausage meat	100 g/3½ oz
	salt	
3 tbsp	white wine	2 tbsp
3 tbsp	sour cream (crème fraîche)	2 tbsp

1. Peel the cucumber and cut into 20 slices, each 1 inch (2.5 cm) thick. Remove the seeds. Arrange the cucumber slices in a circle in a large round dish, leaving the center of the dish empty. Pour the lemon juice over and add pepper to taste. Cover and microwave on HIGH for 8 minutes.
2. Whisk the egg in a bowl with a fork. Add the shallots, garlic, parsley, mint, ground (minced) beef and sausage meat. Season with salt and pepper. Mash the mixture with a fork.
3. Spoon the mixture into the middle of each cucumber ring with a small spoon. Pour over the white wine. Cover and microwave on HIGH for 5 minutes.
4. Add the sour cream (crème fraîche) to the cooking liquid, stir and serve.
This dish is good served with fresh pasta and 3 or 4 strips (rashers) of lean streaky bacon cooked, uncovered, in the microwave oven for 2 minutes on HIGH.

Stuffed cucumber rings

Pain de boeuf aux poivrons
Meat Loaf with Red Bell Peppers

	00.15	00.26
	Serves 4-5	

American	Ingredients	Metric/Imperial
2	crushed garlic cloves	2
2	finely chopped onions	2
¼ lb	smoked streaky bacon, rind removed and diced	125 g/4 oz
2	red bell peppers, rinsed, seeded and diced	2
3	eggs	3
1¼ lb	ground (minced) beef	500 g/1¼ lb
5 tbsp	breadcrumbs	3 tbsp
¼ cup	concentrated tomato juice	3 tbsp
½ tsp	allspice	½ tsp
½ tsp	dried mixed herbs	½ tsp
3 tbsp	pine kernels	2 tbsp
2 oz	golden raisins (sultanas)	50 g/2 oz
½ tsp	sugar	50 g/2 oz
	salt	
	pepper	
¼ tsp	butter	¼ tsp

1. Purée the garlic, onions and bacon in a food processor. Put the purée into a casserole. Cover and microwave on HIGH for 2 minutes.
2. Add the peppers to the onions and bacon. Cover and microwave on HIGH for 6 minutes.
3. Break the eggs into a bowl and whisk thoroughly with a balloon whisk. Put the ground (minced) beef into a large bowl. Add the breadcrumbs, tomato juice, allspice, mixed herbs, pine kernels, raisins (sultanas) and sugar. Season with salt and pepper and mix well.
4. Add the beaten eggs and the vegetable purée to the meat mixture. Stir very thoroughly.

5. Butter the base of a 1½ quart (1.5 litre /2¾ pint) Pyrex cake mold (mould) and pour in the mixture. Press down with a spatula to eliminate air pockets. Cover and microwave on HIGH for 13 minutes.
6. Leave the meat loaf to stand for at least 5 minutes. Serve either hot in the container or cold, inverted on to a serving dish.

Beef Carbonnade

	00.15	00.90
	Serves 4	

American	Ingredients	Metric/Imperial
¼ lb	bacon strips (rashers), cut into 1 in (2.5 cm) pieces	125 g/4 oz
½ lb	chopped onions	225 g/8 oz
2	crushed garlic cloves	2
2 tbsp	butter	1 tbsp
1½ lb	braising steak, cut into cubes	600 g/1½ lb
2 tbsp	brown sugar	1 tbsp
2 tbsp	wine vinegar	1 tbsp
2 cups	beer	450 ml/¾ pint
2 cups	hot beef bouillon (stock)	450 ml/¾ pint
1	bouquet garni	1
	salt	
	pepper	
3 tbsp	cornstarch (cornflour)	2 tbsp

1. Put the bacon, onions and garlic in a large casserole dish with the butter. Heat on HIGH for 5 minutes. Add the beef, sugar, vinegar, beer, bouillon (stock) and bouquet garni and season well. Put a small plate over the meat to submerge in the liquid. Cover the casserole and cook on HIGH for 10 minutes, then on LOW for 70 minutes.
2. Discard the bouquet garni. Mix the cornstarch (cornflour) to a paste with a little water. Stir into the stew. Heat on HIGH for 5 minutes. Serve at once.

Meat loaf with red bell peppers

Texan Stew

■▭ 00.15 00.85 〰
Serves 4

American	Ingredients	Metric/Imperial
2	chopped onions	2
1	green bell pepper, rinsed, seeded and sliced	1
1	red bell pepper, rinsed, seeded and sliced	1
1 oz	butter	25 g/1 oz
1 lb	stewing beef, cut into 1 in (2.5 cm) cubes	450 g/1 lb
14 oz	can tomatoes	400 g/14 oz
1¼ cups	hot beef bouillon (stock)	300 ml/½ pint
	salt	
	pepper	
2 tsp	cornstarch (cornflour)	2 tsp
¾ lb	drained canned sweetcorn	350 g/12 oz
10½ oz	drained canned peas and carrots	300 g/10½ oz

1. Put the onions and peppers in a casserole dish with the butter and cook on HIGH for 5 minutes. Add the meat, chopped tomatoes and their juice, bouillon (stock) and seasoning. Cover and cook on HIGH for 10 minutes, then on LOW for 60 minutes, stirring once during the cooking time and topping up with stock if necessary.
2. Mix the cornstarch (cornflour) to a paste with a little cold water. Add this mixture, the sweetcorn and the peas and carrots to the stew and stir well. Cover and cook on HIGH for 7-10 minutes. Serve in warm bowls.

Beef and Bean Casserole

■▭ 00.05 00.85 〰
Serves 4-6

American	Ingredients	Metric/Imperial
2	chopped onions	2
2 tbsp	oil	1 tbsp
1 lb	stewing beef	450 g/1 lb
¼ tsp	chili powder	¼ tsp
1 tsp	curry powder	1 tsp
3 tbsp	all-purpose (plain) flour	2 tbsp
1¼ cups	beef bouillon (stock)	300 ml/½ pint
14 oz	can tomatoes	400 g/14 oz
3 tbsp	tomato paste (purée)	2 tbsp
2 tsp	sugar	2 tsp
1	chopped large cooking apple	1
2 oz	golden raisins (sultanas)	50 g/2 oz
14 oz	drained canned cannellini beans	400 g/14 oz

1. Put the onions and oil in a large casserole dish. Heat on HIGH for 5 minutes. Stir in the meat and remaining ingredients, except the apple, raisins (sultanas) and beans.
2. Put a small plate on top of the meat to submerge in the liquid and cover the casserole. Cook on HIGH for 10 minutes, then on LOW for 45 minutes.

3. Add the apple, raisins (sultanas) and beans to the casserole and top up with bouillon (stock) if necessary. Cover and cook on LOW for 15 minutes. Leave to stand for 10 minutes. Taste and adjust the seasoning. Serve at once.

Beef Paprika

■▭ 00.10 00.95 〰
Serves 6

American	Ingredients	Metric/Imperial
1½ lb	sliced onions	225 g/8 oz
1 oz	butter	25 g/1 oz
2 lb	stewing beef, cut into cubes	1 kg/2 lb
2	crushed garlic cloves	2
3¼ cups	beef bouillon (stock)	750 ml/1¼ pints
½ tsp	dried marjoram	½ tsp
½ tsp	caraway seeds	½ tsp
¼ tsp	brown sugar	¼ tsp
2 tsp	paprika	2 tsp
	salt	
	pepper	
3 tbsp	cornstarch (cornflour)	2 tbsp

1. Put the onions in a casserole dish with the butter. Heat on HIGH for 3-5 minutes. Add the beef, garlic, bouillon (stock), marjoram, caraway seeds, brown sugar, paprika and seasoning. Put a small plate on top of the meat to submerge in the liquid. Cover the casserole and cook on HIGH for 10 minutes, then on LOW for 75 minutes.
2. Mix the cornstarch (cornflour) to a paste with a little cold water and stir into the stew. Heat on HIGH for 5 minutes until thickened. Serve at once.

Foie de veau à la vénitienne

Calves' Liver, Venetian Style

■▭ 00.05 00.08 〰
Serves 2

American	Ingredients	Metric/Imperial
7 oz	thinly sliced onions	200 g/7 oz
2 tbsp	vinegar	1 tbsp
½ tsp	sugar	½ tsp
	salt	
	pepper	
9 oz	calves' liver, cut into ¼ in (5 mm) strips	250 g/9 oz

1. Put the onions in a dish and add 2 tablespoons (1 tablespoon) of water. Microwave, uncovered, for 5 minutes on HIGH.
2. When the onions are tender, add the vinegar, sugar and salt and pepper to taste. Mix well. Arrange the strips of liver on top of the onions. Cover and microwave on HIGH for 2 minutes.
3. Stir the mixture. Cover and leave to stand for 1 minute before serving.

Lamb

Spicy lamb meatballs with couscous

Boulettes moelleuses à l'agneau

Spicy Lamb Meatballs with Couscous

	00.25	00.28
	Serves 4	

American	Ingredients	Metric/Imperial
2	eggplant (aubergines), rinsed	2
1	bunch fresh parsley, rinsed and stalks removed	1
14 oz	boneless shoulder of lamb, cut into pieces	400 g/14 oz
1	crushed garlic clove	1
2	slices white bread	2
1	egg	1
¼ cup	olive oil	4 tbsp
1 tsp	cumin seed	1 tsp
	salt	
	pepper	
3 tbsp	all-purpose (plain) flour	2 tbsp
3 tbsp	mild curry powder	2 tbsp
1 oz	butter	25 g/1 oz
¼ lb	couscous semolina	125 g/4 oz

1. Set one eggplant (aubergine) aside. Remove the stalk from the other and cut into slices. Put in a dish with 2 tablespoons (1 tablespoon) of water. Cover and microwave on HIGH for 5 minutes.

2. Pat the parsley dry on kitchen paper.

3. Put the lamb pieces into a food processor. Drain the eggplant (aubergine) slices and add to the lamb, with the garlic, parsley, bread, egg, half of the oil, cumin, and salt and pepper to taste. Purée until the mixture is smooth.

4. Mix the flour and curry powder on a plate. Form the lamb mixture into balls the size of large walnuts. Roll the balls in the curry and flour mixture until well coated.

5. Heat a browning dish in the oven for 6 minutes, following the manufacturer's instructions. Pour the remaining oil into the dish and add the meatballs one by one, turning to seal on all sides. Cover and microwave on HIGH for 3 minutes.

6. Place the meatballs on a plate and cover with aluminum (aluminium) foil to keep warm. Reheat the browning dish for a few minutes.

7. Remove the stalk from the second eggplant (aubergine) and cut into thin slices.

8. Put the butter into the hot browning dish and add the eggplant (aubergine) slices. Turn over, and microwave on HIGH for 3 minutes until tender.

9. Remove the eggplant (aubergine) slices and set aside. Pour the couscous semolina into the browning dish, season with salt and pepper and add 1 cup (250 ml/8 fl oz) of water. Stir well. Cover and microwave on HIGH for 3 minutes. Leave to rest for 5 minutes.

10. Put the couscous into a serving dish and break up with a fork. Add the eggplant (aubergine) slices and lamb balls and serve at once.

Spicy Ground (Minced) Lamb

Mincé d'agneau aux épices

⏱ 00.15   00.55   Serves 4-5

American	Ingredients	Metric/Imperial
2 lb	boneless shoulder of lamb	1 kg/2 lb
5 oz	finely chopped onions	150 g/5 oz
2	crushed garlic cloves	2
½ tbsp	butter	½ tbsp
3 tbsp	all-purpose (plain) flour	1½ tbsp
1 tsp	allspice	1 tsp
½ tsp	ground cinnamon	½ tsp
3 tbsp	concentrated tomato juice	2 tbsp
1 cup	dry white wine	250 ml/8 fl oz
2 tbsp	honey	1 tbsp
2 tbsp	vinegar	1 tbsp
	salt	
	pepper	

1. Remove all fat from the lamb and slice into extremely fine strips (the thinner the strips, the shorter the cooking time required).
2. Put the onions, garlic and butter into a casserole. Cover and microwave on HIGH for 3 minutes.
3. Add the strips of lamb to the casserole and sprinkle with flour. Stir well. Cover and microwave on HIGH for 3 minutes. Add the allspice, cinnamon, tomato juice and white wine and mix well. Cover and microwave on HIGH for 3-4 minutes until the sauce reaches the boil.
4. Reduce the power to MEDIUM and cook for a further 20 minutes, stirring midway through the cooking time.
5. Add the honey and vinegar to the casserole and stir well. Season with salt and pepper. Cover and cook for a further 20 minutes on MEDIUM.
6. When the meat is tender, leave to stand for 5 minutes and serve at once.

Lamb Shoulder Stuffed with Sausage Meat

Épaule d'agneau farcie au boudin blanc

⏱ 00.20   00.37   Serves 6

American	Ingredients	Metric/Imperial
1 lb	frozen leaf spinach	450 g/1 lb
2 lb	boneless lamb shoulder	1 kg/2 lb
	salt	
	pepper	
½ tsp	dried thyme	½ tsp
7 oz	white sausage meat	200 g/7 oz
2 tbsp	cornstarch (cornflour)	1 tbsp
3 tbsp	dry sherry	2 tbsp
2 tbsp	mustard	1 tbsp

1. Place the frozen spinach in a casserole, cover and defrost in the microwave oven for 5 minutes on HIGH. Turn the block of spinach over, cover again and microwave for a further 5 minutes. Pour into a colander and leave to drain.
2. Remove as much fat from the lamb as possible. Flatten with a pastry roller (rolling pin) and put on a board with the interior facing upward. Season with salt and pepper and sprinkle with the thyme.
3. Press the spinach between your hands to remove as much liquid as possible, then spread over the surface of the lamb.
4. Mash the white sausage meat with a fork and spread carefully on top of the spinach.
5. Roll the lamb round the spinach and sausage, and tie in several places with kitchen string.
6. Put the stuffed shoulder into a long oval dish. Cover and microwave on HIGH for 15 minutes. Check the inside temperature with a meat thermometer: it should read 45°C. Cover with aluminum (aluminium) foil and leave to stand for at least 10 minutes.
7. To make the sauce: put the cornstarch (cornflour) in a large bowl and gradually add the sherry until smooth. Add the mustard and the cooking liquid from the meat and stir well. Cook in the microwave oven for 1 minute on HIGH, stir well, and cook for a further 30 seconds or until the sauce has boiled. Stir again and pour into a sauceboat.
8. Remove the string from the meat and carve. Arrange the slices on a serving dish and serve with the sauce.

Lamb with Fennel

Agneau au fenouil

⏱ 00.10   00.24   Serves 4

American	Ingredients	Metric/Imperial
1½ lb	fennel	600 g/1½ lb
2	thinly sliced onions	2
10	unpeeled garlic cloves	10
3 tbsp	liquid honey	2 tbsp
⅓ cup	red wine	4½ tbsp
	salt	
1 tsp	curry powder	1 tsp
1	fresh thyme sprig	1
1	bay leaf	1
2 lb	lamb shoulder, bone in	1 kg/2 lb
	pepper	

1. Discard the base and tough stalks of the fennel and set the green fronds aside. Cut into slices, wash and drain in a colander.
2. Put the fennel, onions and garlic into a casserole. Pour over the honey and red wine. Season with salt. Add the curry powder and mix well. Add the thyme sprig and bay leaf. Cover and microwave on HIGH for 12 minutes, stirring midway through the cooking time.
3. Remove as much fat as possible from the meat and cut into thick slices (if you prefer, get your butcher to do this for you). Season with salt and pepper. Arrange the meat on top of the vegetables. Cover and microwave on HIGH for 12 minutes.
4. When the meat is tender, discard the thyme and bay leaf. Remove the garlic cloves from the casserole and skin by squeezing one end between thumb and forefinger. Mash the garlic pulp with a fork and add to the casserole.
5. Pour the vegetables and cooking liquid into a heated serving dish. Arrange the meat on top. Snip the reserved green fennel fronds over the dish and serve very hot.

Greek lamb casserole

Agneau en moussaka

Greek Lamb Casserole

00.15 plus draining time   **00.21**

American	Ingredients	Metric/Imperial
1¼ lb	eggplant (aubergines)	500 g/1¼ lb
	salt	
1 oz	butter	25 g/1 oz
1 oz	all-purpose (plain) flour	25 g/1 oz
1¼ cups	milk	300 ml/½ pint
¼ lb	grated Gruyère cheese	125 g/4 oz
2	eggs	2
½ tsp	grated nutmeg	½ tsp
	pepper	
7 oz	finely chopped onions	200 g/7 oz
2	crushed garlic cloves	2
1¼ lb	boneless shoulder of lamb	500 g/1¼ lb
½ tsp	dried oregano	½ tsp
½ tsp	sugar	½ tsp
3 oz	tomato paste (purée)	75 g/3 oz
¼ cup	white wine	4 tbsp
3 tbsp	olive oil	2 tbsp

1. Rinse the eggplant (aubergines) under plenty of cold running water. Pat dry on kitchen paper. Remove the stalks and cut into slices. Put in a strainer, sprinkle with salt and leave to drain for 30 minutes.

2. Put the butter into a bowl and melt in the microwave oven for 1 minute on HIGH. Sprinkle over the flour, mix well and add the milk, stirring until the mixture is smooth. Cook for 3 minutes on HIGH, whisking after every minute. Add the Gruyère and mix thoroughly. Break the eggs into another bowl, whisk with a fork and add to the sauce. Add the grated nutmeg and salt and pepper to taste.

3. Put the onions and garlic in a large casserole. Cover and microwave on HIGH for 4 minutes.

4. Remove as much of the fat as possible from the lamb, cut into pieces and grind (mince) in a food processor. Season with salt and pepper. Add the oregano. Mix the sugar with the tomato paste (purée) and white wine.

5. Rinse the eggplant (aubergines) under plenty of cold running water and pat dry on kitchen paper. Add to the onions in the casserole, pour over the olive oil and mix well. Cover and microwave on HIGH for 6 minutes.

6. Add the meat and tomato paste (purée) to the eggplant (aubergines). Stir well. Cover and microwave on HIGH for 5 minutes.

7. Stir the contents of the casserole thoroughly, breaking up any clumps of meat with a fork. Taste and adjust the seasoning. Pour the mixture into a serving dish and smooth the surface. Pour over the cheese sauce. Microwave, uncovered, for 2 minutes on HIGH or, alternatively, slide the dish under a conventional broiler (grill) for 3-4 minutes. Serve at once.

Moussaka

	00.20 Serves 4	00.26

American	Ingredients	Metric/Imperial
4	large eggplant (aubergines)	4
	salt	
½ cup	oil	6 tbsp
1¼ lb	ground (minced) lamb	500 g/1¼ lb
2	chopped onions	2
2	crushed garlic cloves	2
3 tbsp	chopped parsley	2 tbsp
1 tsp	chopped oregano	1 tsp
1 tsp	chopped basil	1 tsp
1 tsp	chopped thyme	1 tsp
8	sliced tomatoes	8
1	egg	1
⅔ cup	plain (natural) yogurt	150 ml/¼ pint
2 oz	grated Cheddar cheese	50 g/2 oz

1. Cut the eggplant (aubergines) into ½ inch (1.25 cm) slices, sprinkle with salt and leave to stand on a tray to allow the excess bitter juices to drain. Pat dry on kitchen paper.
2. Heat the oil in a browning dish for 1 minute on HIGH. Cover the base of the dish with eggplant (aubergine) slices and cook for 2 minutes on HIGH. The next stage will have to be done in batches: transfer the eggplant (aubergines) to a baking sheet and put each batch under a hot broiler (grill) for 1½ minutes. Drain on kitchen paper.
3. Heat the oil remaining from the eggplant (aubergines) in the browning dish and stir the lamb into the hot oil. Cook on HIGH for 3 minutes. Break up the mixture with a fork until crumbly.
4. Add the onions and garlic to the lamb with half the parsley, oregano, basil and thyme. Mix well and cook on HIGH for 2 minutes.
5. Put half of the eggplant (aubergines) in the base of a casserole dish, sprinkle with some of the remaining herbs and top with half the tomato slices. Add the remaining herbs and spoon the meat on top. Level the mixture and press down with the back of a spoon. Cover with the remaining eggplant (aubergine) and tomato slices. Cook on HIGH for 8 minutes.
6. Beat the egg and yogurt together with a little seasoning. Spread the yogurt mixture on top of the moussaka. Sprinkle with cheese and cook on HIGH for 5 minutes. Flash under a hot broiler (grill) to brown the top. Serve at once.

Lamb curry

Lamb Curry I

Agneau au curry

	00.20 Serves 4	00.35

American	Ingredients	Metric/Imperial
2	crushed garlic cloves	2
3	finely chopped onions	3
3 tbsp	peanut oil	2 tbsp
1	coarsely chopped apple	1
2	coarsely chopped tomatoes	2
2 lb	boneless leg of lamb, cut into ½ in (1.25 cm) cubes	1 kg/2 lb
1	bay leaf	1
1	fresh thyme sprig	1
3 tbsp	curry powder	1½ tbsp
5 tbsp	all-purpose (plain) flour	3 tbsp
3 oz	coconut	75 g/3 oz
	salt	
	pepper	
2 oz	golden raisins (sultanas)	50 g/2 oz
2 tbsp	vinegar	1 tbsp

1. Purée the garlic and onions in a food processor. Put the purée in a casserole and add the oil. Microwave, uncovered, on HIGH for 4 minutes.
2. Purée the apple and tomatoes in a food processor.
3. Add the apple and tomato purée to the casserole. Stir. Cover and microwave on HIGH for 3 minutes.
4. Add the meat cubes, bay leaf and thyme to the casserole. Cover and microwave on HIGH for 3 minutes. Add the curry powder, flour and coconut. Season with salt and pepper and mix well. Cover and microwave on HIGH for 12 minutes.
5. Rinse the raisins (sultanas) under plenty of cold running water. Pat dry on kitchen paper. Add to the casserole along with the vinegar. Stir well. Cover and microwave on HIGH a further 3 minutes. Check whether the meat is tender.
6. Leave the curry to stand for 10 minutes, then taste and adjust the seasoning. Discard the bay leaf and thyme. Pour into a heated serving dish and serve.

Curry d'agneau
Lamb Curry II

⏲ 00.15 00.36
Serves 6

American	Ingredients	Metric/Imperial
10½ oz	thinly sliced onions	300 g/10½ oz
2	large red bell peppers, rinsed, seeded and diced	2
4	crushed garlic cloves	4
2 tbsp	oil	1 tbsp
3 tbsp	all-purpose (plain) flour	2 tbsp
4 tbsp	curry powder	2½ tbsp
½ tsp	powdered thyme	½ tsp
	salt	
	pepper	
2½ lb	boneless leg of lamb, cut into ½ in (1.25 cm) cubes	1.2 kg/2½ lb
1	chicken bouillon (stock) cube	1
2 tbsp	concentrated tomato juice	1 tbsp
¼ cup	fresh lime juice	3 tbsp
¼ cup	sour cream (crème fraîche)	3 tbsp

1. Put the onions, bell peppers and garlic into a large casserole and pour over the oil. Microwave, uncovered, on HIGH for 6 minutes.
2. Put the flour, curry powder, thyme, salt and pepper on a plate and mix well. Roll the cubes of lamb in this mixture a few at a time, making sure they are all well coated. Add to the casserole. Cover and microwave on HIGH for 3 minutes.
3. Crumble the bouillon (stock) cube over the meat. Add the concentrated tomato juice and the remaining curry-thyme-flour mixture. Pour in 1 cup (250 ml/8 fl oz) of hot water. Cover and microwave on HIGH for 10 minutes, stirring midway through the cooking time.
4. Stir well, reduce the power to MEDIUM and microwave for a further 15 minutes.
5. When the meat is tender, add the lime juice and sour cream (crème fraîche) and reheat for 1-2 minutes on MEDIUM.
6. Transfer the meat with a slotted spoon to a serving dish. Pour over a little of the sauce and serve the rest in a sauceboat, with a bowl of plain cooked rice as accompaniment.

Gigot Cléopâtre
Oriental Leg of Lamb

⏲ 00.10 00.33
Serves 6

American	Ingredients	Metric/Imperial
1½ tsp	five-spice powder	1½ tsp
½ tsp	powdered thyme	½ tsp
	pepper	
2 tbsp	peanut oil	1 tbsp
3 lb	boneless rolled leg of lamb	1.5 kg/3 lb
1 tsp	cornstarch (cornflour)	1 tsp
3 tsp	dark soy sauce	3 tsp
¼ cup	dry sherry	3 tbsp
½ tsp	superfine (caster) sugar	½ tsp
	Tabasco sauce	
1 tsp	wine vinegar	1 tsp
2 tsp	concentrated tomato juice	2 tsp
	salt	

1. Mix the five-spice powder, thyme, a little pepper and the peanut oil in an oval dish. Brush the lamb on all sides with this mixture and put in the dish. Cover and microwave on HIGH for 15-20 minutes, depending on how you prefer your meat.
2. Remove the lamb from the oven and cover with a double thickness of aluminum (aluminium) foil, matt side outward. Leave to stand for 10 minutes.
3. Carve the meat, pouring the carving liquid into the cooking dish.
4. Put the cornstarch (cornflour) and soy sauce into a bowl and mix to a smooth cream. Add the sherry, sugar, a few dashes of Tabasco sauce, vinegar, tomato juice and cooking liquid from the lamb. Stir and cook for 3 minutes on HIGH, whisking after every minute. Taste and adjust the seasoning.
5. Coat the lamb with a little of the sauce and pour the rest into a sauceboat. Serve very hot.
This dish is delicious eaten with sweet potatoes baked in brown sugar and butter.

Lamb curry

4. Put the cooked bell peppers in a strainer (sieve). Place the onions and garlic in a large casserole. Cover and microwave on HIGH for 4 minutes.
5. Rinse the eggplant (aubergines) under plenty of cold running water. Pat dry on kitchen paper and add to the onions. Pour over the olive oil. Mix well. Cover and microwave on HIGH for 5 minutes.
6. Add the meat and tomato juice to the eggplant (aubergines). Mix well. Cover and microwave on HIGH for 5 minutes.
7. Purée the bell peppers in a food processor. Add salt to taste. Add the sugar and vinegar. Purée again and add the Gruyère.
8. Stir the contents of the casserole thoroughly, breaking up any clumps of meat with a fork. Taste and adjust the seasoning. Pour half the mixture into a soufflé mold (mould) 7 inches (18 cm) in diameter. Spread half the pepper mixture over it. Add another layer of meat mixture and finish with the rest of the pepper and cheese mixture.
9. Put the soufflé mold (mould) into the oven and microwave for 10 minutes on HIGH. Garnish with the chopped parsley and serve very hot.

Lamb and vegetable hotpot

Charlotte d'agneau

Lamb and Vegetable Hotpot

	00.20	00.36	
	Serves 4		

American	Ingredients	Metric/Imperial
1¼ lb	eggplant (aubergines)	500 g/1¼ lb
	salt	
1¼ lb	red bell peppers, rinsed, seeded and diced	500 g/1¼ lb
1¼ lb	boneless leg of lamb	500 g/1¼ lb
3½ oz	smoked streaky bacon, rind removed and diced	100 g/3½ oz
	pepper	
½ tsp	dried thyme	½ tsp
¼ cup	concentrated tomato juice	4 tbsp
¼ cup	white wine	4 tbsp
7 oz	finely chopped onions	200 g/7 oz
1	crushed garlic clove	1
2 tbsp	olive oil	1 tbsp
1 tsp	superfine (caster) sugar	1 tsp
2 tbsp	wine vinegar	1 tbsp
¼ lb	grated Gruyère cheese	125 g/4 oz
1 tbsp	chopped fresh parsley	1 tbsp

1. Rinse the eggplant (aubergines) under plenty of cold running water. Pat dry on kitchen paper. Remove the stalks and cut into slices. Put in a colander, sprinkle with salt and leave to drain.
2. Put the bell peppers in a small casserole with ¼ cup (3 tablespoons) of water. Cover and microwave on HIGH for 12 minutes.
3. Remove as much fat from the lamb as possible, cut into pieces and grind in a food processor with the bacon. Season with salt and pepper and add the thyme. Mix the tomato juice with the white wine.

Gigot au madère

Leg of Lamb with Madeira

	00.05	00.34	
	Serves 8		

American	Ingredients	Metric/Imperial
½ tsp	garlic powder	½ tsp
½ tsp	dried thyme	½ tsp
	pepper	
2 tbsp	olive oil	1 tbsp
3 lb	boned leg of lamb	1.5 kg/3 lb
1 tsp	Dijon mustard	1 tsp
3 tbsp	Madeira	2 tbsp
	salt	

1. Mix together the garlic powder, thyme, pepper and olive oil. Brush the leg of lamb with this mixture and put in a long dish. Cover and microwave on HIGH for 17 minutes.
2. Insert a meat thermometer into the thickest part of the meat. The internal temperature should be between 60°C-65°C, depending on how rare you like your meat. Cover the dish with a double thickness of aluminum (aluminium) foil, matt side outward, and leave to stand for 15 minutes.
3. Carve the meat into slices and remove the string. Arrange the slices of meat on a heated serving dish. Add the carving liquid to the cooking dish along with the mustard and Madeira. Stir well, then heat in the oven for 2 minutes on HIGH.
4. Season the sauce with salt and pepper, pour into a sauceboat and serve with the meat.

Microwave hint: To keep meat tasty and moist during cooking, cook in a browning dish on HIGH for 2 minutes on each side. Meanwhile, peel and slice a mild onion widthwise. Put the onion rings on the meat, overlapping over the surface. Cover and reduce the power to MEDIUM. Cook for a further 10-20 minutes, according to thickness, turning once and replacing the onion slices on top.

Fricassée of baby lamb

Lamb's liver with scallions (spring onions)

Fricassée d'agneau

Fricassée of Baby Lamb

00.10 Serves 4   **00.30**

American	Ingredients	Metric/Imperial
3	fresh thyme sprigs, crumbled	3
2 tbsp	mild curry powder	1 tbsp
1 tsp	allspice	1 tsp
2 lb	spring lamb, cut into 8 equal portions	1 kg/2 lb
	salt	
	pepper	
3 tbsp	olive oil	2 tbsp
3	finely sliced large shallots	3
14 oz	small ripe tomatoes, rinsed, seeded and quartered	400 g/14 oz
2 tbsp	vinegar	1 tbsp
1	diced cucumber	1
3 tbsp	mild mustard	2 tbsp
1 tbsp	chopped fresh mint	1 tbsp

1. Heat a browning dish in the microwave oven for 6-8 minutes on HIGH, following the manufacturer's instructions.
2. Mix the crumbled thyme, curry powder and allspice on a plate and roll the lamb pieces in the mixture. Season with salt and pepper.
3. When the browning dish is hot, pour in the olive oil and add the shallots, stirring vigorously. Add the pieces of meat, leaving for 30 seconds on one side, then turning. Arrange the tomato quarters round the meat and pour over the vinegar. Cover and microwave on HIGH for 10 minutes.
4. Add the diced cucumber to the browning dish. Cover and microwave on HIGH for a further 6 minutes.
5. Leave to stand for 5 minutes. Put the lamb in a serving dish.
6. Stir the mustard into the vegetables and arrange around the meat. Sprinkle with fresh mint and serve at once.

Foie d'agneau aux oignons nouveaux

Lambs' Liver with Scallions (Spring Onions)

00.06 Serves 4   **00.09**

American	Ingredients	Metric/Imperial
1	bunch scallions (spring onions)	1
1¼ lb	lambs' liver, cut into ½ in (1.25 cm) strips	500 g/1¼ lb
	salt	
	pepper	
3 tbsp	vinegar	2 tbsp
1 tsp	sugar	1 tsp

1. Peel and thinly slice the scallions (spring onions). Set aside 3 or 4 of the green stalks and chop finely. Put the scallions (spring onions) in a dish with 3 tablespoons (2 tablespoons) water. Cover and microwave on HIGH for 5 minutes.
2. Season the strips of liver with salt and pepper.
3. When the scallions (spring onions) are tender, add the vinegar and sugar. Season with salt and pepper. Stir well. Arrange the strips of liver on top of the vegetables. Cover and microwave on HIGH for 4 minutes.
4. Stir the contents of the dish. Sprinkle the liver with the reserved chopped green stalks and serve at once.

Rognons d'agneau au chou-fleur

Lambs' Kidneys with Cauliflower

⏱ 00.10 Serves 4		00.20 〽

American	Ingredients	Metric/Imperial
½	cauliflower, divided into florets	½
	salt	
	pepper	
8	lambs' kidneys	8
2 tbsp	oil	1 tbsp
3 tbsp	Madeira	2 tbsp
½ tsp	cornstarch (cornflour)	½ tsp
2 tbsp	mild herbed mustard	1 tbsp
2 tbsp	butter	1 tbsp
1 tbsp	chopped chives	1 tbsp

1. Place the cauliflower florets in a dish with ⅓ cup (4½ tablespoons) of water and season with salt and pepper. Cover and microwave on HIGH for 10 minutes. The cauliflower should be crisp to the bite; if you prefer it softer, microwave for 1 minute longer. Leave to stand.
2. With a sharp pointed knife, remove the membrane surrounding the kidneys, cut in half and remove the tubes and the fatty core. Heat a browning dish in the oven for 6 minutes on HIGH, following the manufacturer's instructions.
3. Pour the oil into the hot browning dish and add the kidneys, turning to seal on all sides. Season with salt and pepper. Cover and microwave on HIGH for 3 minutes.
4. Put the cauliflower in a serving dish. Remove the kidneys from the browning dish with a slotted spoon and add to the cauliflower.
5. Pour the Madeira into the browning dish and stir well with a wooden spatula to dissolve the cooking liquid. Pour into a bowl. Mix the cornstarch (cornflour) with the mustard, stir and microwave on HIGH for 1 minute. Whisk vigorously. Add the butter in small pieces, whisking constantly.
6. Pour into a sauceboat, sprinkle with chopped chives and serve at once.

Lamb's kidneys with cauliflower

Kidneys with mushrooms

Rognons aux champignons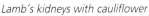

Kidneys with Mushrooms

⏱ 00.15 Serves 4		00.11 〽

American	Ingredients	Metric/Imperial
8	lambs' kidneys	8
10½ oz	white button mushrooms	300 g/10½ oz
2	finely sliced shallots	2
3 oz	butter	75 g/3 oz
3 tbsp	white wine	2 tbsp
	salt	
	pepper	
5 tbsp	chopped parsley	3 tbsp
8	cubes fried bread	8
¼ cup	sour cream (crème fraîche)	3 tbsp
3 tbsp	Dijon mustard	2 tbsp
	chopped parsley	

1. Halve the kidneys and cut out the core and white parts with a sharp knife or pair of scissors. Wipe the mushrooms with a damp cloth or kitchen paper and slice thinly.
2. Put the shallots in a dish with a third of the butter. Microwave on HIGH for 2 minutes. Add the mushrooms and white wine. Add salt and pepper to taste. Cover and microwave on HIGH for 3 minutes. Stir well.
3. Mix the remaining butter with 3 tablespoons (2 tablespoons) of chopped parsley. Spread the mixture on the flat side of the kidneys, and put the kidneys on top of the mushrooms. Cover and microwave on HIGH for 5 minutes.
4. Arrange the cubes of fried bread on a heated serving dish. Place a half kidney on each one. Season with salt and pepper. Mix the sour cream (crème fraîche) with the mustard and add to the mushrooms. Heat for 1 minute on HIGH, pour over the kidneys, sprinkle with parsley and serve hot.

Rognons d'agneau à la moutarde

Lambs' Kidneys in Mustard Sauce

■▷   00.10   00.12   ▥
Serves 3

American	Ingredients	Metric/Imperial
8	lambs' kidneys	8
2 oz	lean streaky bacon, diced	50 g/2 oz
	salt	
	pepper	
2 tbsp	mild mustard	1 tbsp
3 tbsp	sour cream (crème fraîche)	2 tbsp
¼ cup	port	3 tbsp
1 tbsp	chopped chervil	1 tbsp

1. Heat a browning dish in the microwave oven for 6-8 minutes, following the manufacturer's instructions.
2. Cut the kidneys in half lengthwise. Cut out the tubes and the fatty core with a sharp pointed knife and remove any white bits.
3. When the browning dish is hot, put in the half-kidneys and bacon. Turn the kidneys after 30 seconds. Season with salt and pepper. Cover and microwave on HIGH for 2 minutes.
4. Mix together the mustard, sour cream (crème fraîche) and port.
5. Pour over the kidneys. Stir with a wooden spatula to dissolve the cooking liquid. Cook for 1 further minute on HIGH.
6. Pour into a heated serving dish and sprinkle with the chopped chervil. Serve at once.

Rognons aux pommes

Lambs' Kidneys with Apples

■▷   00.15   00.08   ▥
Serves 2

American	Ingredients	Metric/Imperial
1	coarsely chopped large onion	1
1 tbsp	butter	½ tbsp
2	thinly sliced Golden Delicious apples	2
2 tsp	curry powder	2 tsp
6	lambs' kidneys	6
2 tbsp	all-purpose (plain) flour	1 tbsp
	salt	
	pepper	
1 tsp	vinegar	1 tsp
3 tbsp	sour cream (crème fraîche)	2 tbsp
2 tbsp	chopped parsley	2 tbsp

1. Purée the onion in a food processor. Put in a small casserole with the butter. Cover and microwave on HIGH for 2 minutes.
2. Add the apples to the onions with the curry powder. Mix well. Cover and microwave on HIGH for 3 minutes.
3. Remove the membrane surrounding the kidneys and cut in half. Remove the white tendons. Cut the half-kidneys in 3 pieces. Season the flour with salt and pepper, then roll the kidneys in the mixture.
4. Mash the apple mixture with a fork. Add salt to taste. Put the kidney pieces on top. Cover and microwave on HIGH for 2 minutes.
5. Add the vinegar and sour cream (crème fraîche) to the casserole. Mix well. Cover and microwave on HIGH for 1 minute. Sprinkle with chopped parsley and serve at once.

Cervelles à la crème d'oseille

Lambs' Brains with Sorrel

■▷   00.01   00.08   ▥
Serves 2

American	Ingredients	Metric/Imperial
7 oz	frozen chopped sorrel	200 g/7 oz
2	frozen lambs' brains	2
1	egg	1
2 tbsp	sour cream (crème fraîche)	1 tbsp
	salt	
	pepper	

1. Put the frozen sorrel in a bowl and microwave, uncovered, for 4 minutes on HIGH.
2. Put the frozen lambs' brains in a small casserole. Cover and microwave on HIGH for 3 minutes.
3. Add the egg and sour cream (crème fraîche) to the sorrel purée. Season with salt and pepper. Reheat on HIGH for 1 minute.
4. Pour the sauce over the brains and serve at once.

Lamb's kidneys with apples

Pork

Rôti de porc sauce aux pommes

Roast Pork with Apple Sauce

�▷ 00.20   00.55   〰
Serves 6

American	Ingredients	Metric/Imperial
1	boneless pork loin	1
1	garlic clove, cut into slivers	1
2 tbsp	soft brown sugar	1 tbsp
3 tbsp	mustard	2 tbsp
7 oz	thinly sliced onions	200 g/7 oz
1¾ lb	cooking apples (Bramleys), peeled, cored and thinly sliced	750 g/1¾ lb
2 tbsp	vinegar	1 tbsp
¼ cup	white wine	3 tbsp
1	slice toasted wholewheat (wholemeal) bread	1
½ tsp	cinnamon	½ tsp
½ tsp	grated nutmeg	½ tsp
	salt	
	pepper	
2 tbsp	butter	1 tbsp
3 tbsp	dry sherry	2 tbsp

1. With a small pointed knife, prick the meat here and there, sliding in a piece of garlic along the knife blade at each incision. Mix the brown sugar with the mustard and spread over the meat. Put the meat into a long dish. Cover and microwave on HIGH for 30 minutes.
2. When the meat is cooked (the cooking thermometer should register about 90°C), cover with a double thickness of aluminum (aluminium) foil, matt side outward, and leave to stand for 15 minutes.
3. Put the onions in a casserole. Cover and microwave on HIGH for 3 minutes.
4. Add the apples, vinegar and white wine. Cover and microwave on HIGH for 6 minutes.
5. Purée the mixture in a food processor. Crumble the toasted bread into the purée and add the cinnamon, grated nutmeg, salt, pepper and butter and liquidize once more.
6. Slice the meat and arrange on a serving dish. Add the sherry to the cooking liquid, stirring with a wooden spatula. Add salt and pepper to taste, pour into a bowl and reheat in the oven for 1 minute on HIGH. Pour into a sauceboat and serve with the apple sauce.

Rôti de porc à la cassonade

Chinese Roast Pork

▷ 00.05   00.36   〰
Serves 4-5

American	Ingredients	Metric/Imperial
4 tbsp	soft dark brown sugar	2 tbsp
4 tbsp	Dijon mustard	2½ tbsp
½ tsp	garlic powder	½ tsp
½ tsp	five-spice powder	½ tsp
2¼ lb	pork loin (center cut)	850 g/2¼ lb
1 tsp	cornstarch (cornflour)	1 tsp
1 tsp	dark soy sauce	1 tsp
3 tbsp	dry sherry	2 tbsp

1. Mix together the brown sugar, most of the mustard, the garlic powder and five-spice powder.
2. Place the pork in a casserole, with the fat side upward. Spread the top and sides with the mustard and brown sugar mixture.
3. Cover the casserole, making sure that the lid does not touch the meat. Microwave on HIGH for 20-25 minutes, depending on the thickness of the meat. Test with a meat thermometer: it should read 75°C. Remove the casserole from the oven and leave to stand for 5-10 minutes.
4. Mix the remaining mustard with the cornstarch (cornflour) and the soy sauce in a bowl to obtain a smooth paste. Slice the meat and arrange on a heated serving dish.
5. Pour the sherry into the casserole and stir well. Pour the cooking liquid into the bowl containing the cornstarch (cornflour) mixture and stir thoroughly. Put the bowl in the microwave oven and cook on HIGH for 1 minute. Whisk vigorously to make sure the sauce is well blended. Pour into a sauceboat and serve with the meat.

Pointe de porc aux abricots secs

Loin of Pork with Apricots

▷ 00.10   00.55   〰
Serves 4

American	Ingredients	Metric/Imperial
9 oz	dried apricots	250 g/9 oz
¾ cup	white wine	200 ml/7 fl oz
2	thinly sliced onions	2
1	crushed garlic clove	1
2	finely grated carrots	2
2 tbsp	olive oil	1 tbsp
2 lb	boneless loin of pork, cut into ½ in (1.25 cm) strips	1 kg/2 lb
2 tbsp	mango chutney	1 tbsp
1 tsp	coarse grind black pepper	1 tsp
2 tbsp	vinegar	1 tbsp
1	fresh thyme sprig	1
	salt	

1. Rinse the apricots under plenty of cold running water. Pat dry on kitchen paper and put in a bowl with the white wine and an equivalent amount of water. Microwave, uncovered, on HIGH for 5 minutes.
2. Place the onions, garlic and carrots in a casserole. Add the oil and mix well. Cover and microwave on HIGH for 5 minutes.
3. Drain the apricots and reserve the cooking liquid.
4. Add the meat to the casserole with the mango chutney, black pepper, vinegar and apricot cooking liquid. Crumble the thyme over and add salt to taste. Mix well. Cover and microwave on HIGH for 5 minutes.
5. Stir and cook, uncovered, for a further 20 minutes on MEDIUM.
6. Add the apricots to the casserole and stir well. Cover and cook on MEDIUM for a further 15-20 minutes until the meat is tender. Serve very hot.

Loin of pork in mustard sauce

Carré de porc à la moutarde

Loin of Pork in Mustard Sauce

00.10 Serves 5-6   **00.48**

American	Ingredients	Metric/Imperial
2 lb	loin of pork, bone in	1 kg/2 lb
2	garlic cloves, cut into slivers	2
½ tsp	mixed herbs	½ tsp
	salt	
	pepper	
1	finely chopped shallot	1
2 tbsp	butter	1 tbsp
3 tbsp	dry Vermouth	2 tbsp
2	leaves fresh sage	2
2 tbsp	mild mustard	1 tbsp
¼ cup	sour cream (crème fraîche)	3 tbsp
½ tsp	sugar	½ tsp

1. With a small pointed knife, prick the meat here and there, sliding in a piece of garlic along the knife blade at each incision. Sprinkle the meat with the mixed herbs and salt and pepper. Place the meat in a dish, cover, and microwave on MEDIUM-HIGH for 35 minutes.

2. Test the internal temperature of the meat with a meat thermometer, and when it reaches 80°C remove the dish from the oven and cover the meat with a double thickness of aluminum (aluminium) foil, matt side outward. Leave to stand for at least 10 minutes.

3. Put the shallot in a bowl with the butter and Vermouth and microwave, uncovered, for 2 minutes on HIGH.

4. Crumble the sage over the bowl. Add the mustard, sour cream (crème fraîche) and sugar. Mix well and cook for 1 further minute on HIGH.

5. Carve the meat into slices and arrange on a warmed serving dish. Pour the cooking liquid into the bowl containing the other ingredients and mix well. Taste and adjust the seasoning. Reheat for 1 minute, if necessary. Serve hot with the sauce on the side.

Filets mignons de porc à la mangue

Pork Tenderloin (Fillet) with Mango Sauce

	00.10	00.20	
	Serves 4-5		

American	Ingredients	Metric/Imperial
2	pork tenderloins (fillets)	2
	salt	
	pepper	
½ tbsp	softened butter	½ tbsp
3 tbsp	mild mustard	2 tbsp
½ tsp	garlic powder	½ tsp
½ tsp	five-spice powder	½ tsp
1	ripe mango	1
3 tbsp	mango chutney	2 tbsp
1 tsp	curry powder	1 tsp
3 tbsp	dry sherry	2 tbsp
½ tbsp	sherry vinegar	½ tbsp

1. Cut off the thin ends of the tenderloins (fillets) so that they are of an even thickness. Season with salt and pepper.
2. Mix together the butter, mustard, garlic powder and five-spice powder in an oval dish. Roll the tenderloins (fillets) in this mixture until well coated. Cover and microwave on HIGH for 13 minutes. Remove, cover with a double thickness of aluminum (aluminium) foil and leave to stand for at least 5 minutes.
3. To prepare the sauce, cut the mango in half around the middle and, with a small spoon, scoop out the flesh from the shell and around the stone. Put into a food processor and add the chutney, curry powder, sherry and vinegar. Purée until the mixture is smooth. Pour into a bowl and microwave for 2 minutes on HIGH.
4. Slice the meat. Pour the meat liquid into the mango sauce. Stir well. Pour into a sauceboat and serve with the meat.

Filet mignon à la banane

Pork Tenderloin (Fillet) in Banana Sauce

	00.15	00.29	
	Serves 4		

American	Ingredients	Metric/Imperial
3½ oz	finely sliced onions	100 g/3½ oz
1	halved garlic clove	1
2 oz	carrots, cut into thin strips	50 g/2 oz
3 tbsp	white wine	2 tbsp
14 oz	tomatoes	400 g/14 oz
	salt	
	pepper	
½ tsp	dried thyme	½ tsp
½ tsp	sugar	½ tsp
½ tsp	celery powder	½ tsp
3 tbsp	olive oil	2 tbsp
2 tbsp	grated Parmesan cheese	1 tbsp
1½ lb	pork tenderloin (fillet), cut into 4 slices	600 g/1½ lb
1	large banana or plantain, cut into ½ in/1.25 cm rounds	1

1. Put the onion, garlic and 2 tablespoons (1 tablespoon) of water in a dish. Microwave, uncovered, on HIGH for 2 minutes.
2. Add the carrot to the onion and pour over the white wine. Cover and microwave on HIGH for 3 minutes.
3. Prick the tomatoes with a fork. Put in a circle in the microwave oven on two layers of kitchen paper. Microwave for 1½ minutes on HIGH.
4. Skin and coarsely chop the tomatoes and add to the other vegetables. Season with salt and pepper. Stir in the thyme, sugar, celery powder and half of the olive oil. Cover and microwave on HIGH for 5 minutes.
5. Heat a browning dish in the microwave oven for 6-8 minutes, following the manufacturer's instructions.
6. Purée the vegetables in a food processor, adding the grated Parmesan.
7. Flatten the pork slices with a pastry roller (rolling pin). Brush with the remaining oil, and season with salt and pepper.
8. When the browning dish is hot, arrange the slices of meat in the base. Leave for 30 seconds then turn over. Arrange slices of banana or plantain around the meat slices and cover with the vegetable sauce. Cover and microwave on HIGH for 6 minutes. Leave to stand for 2 minutes.
9. Arrange the meat and sauce in a serving dish and serve at once.

Filet mignon aux myrtilles

Pork Tenderloin (Fillet) with Blueberries (Bilberries)

	00.05	00.16	
	Serves 4		

American	Ingredients	Metric/Imperial
1½ lb	pork tenderloin (fillet), cut into ½ in (1.25 cm) slices	600 g/1½ lb
½ tsp	coarse grind black pepper	½ tsp
	salt	
2 tbsp	oil	1 tbsp
¼ cup	cognac	3 tbsp
1 tsp	cornstarch (cornflour)	1 tsp
2 tbsp	port	1 tbsp
3 tbsp	sour cream (crème fraîche)	2 tbsp
3 tbsp	blueberry (bilberry) jam	2 tbsp

1. Heat a browning dish in the microwave oven for 6-8 minutes, following the manufacturer's instructions.
2. Flatten the slices of pork tenderloin (fillet) with a pastry roller (rolling pin), and brush on both sides with a mixture of the black pepper, salt and oil.
3. When the browning dish is hot, put in the slices of pork. Pour the cognac into a cup and heat in the oven for 1 minute on HIGH. Set alight and pour over the meat. When the flames go out, turn the slices of meat. Cover and microwave on HIGH for 5 minutes.
4. Place the meat on a heated serving dish and cover with aluminum (aluminium) foil.
5. Mix the cornstarch (cornflour) with the port until a smooth paste is formed. Add to the browning dish with the sour cream (crème fraîche) and jam. Heat for 2 minutes on HIGH. Stir well. Add more salt if needed, pour over the meat and serve hot.

Filet mignon à la périgourdine

Pork Tenderloin (Fillet) with Foie Gras

00.10 Serves 4   **00.26**

American	Ingredients	Metric/Imperial
14 oz	tiny white button mushrooms	400 g/14 oz
¼ cup	fresh lemon juice	3 tbsp
1¾ lb	pork tenderloin (fillet), fat removed and cut into ½ in (1.25 cm) slices	750 g/1¾ lb
2 tbsp	oil	1 tbsp
	salt	
	pepper	
1 oz	butter	25 g/1 oz
3 tbsp	all-purpose (plain) flour	2 tbsp
1	beef bouillon (stock) cube	1
¼ cup	Madeira	4 tbsp
5 oz	pâté de foie gras	150 g/5 oz
2 tbsp	sour cream (crème fraîche)	1 tbsp

1. Wipe the mushrooms with a damp cloth or kitchen paper. Slice finely. Put into a dish and pour over the lemon juice. Cover and microwave on HIGH for 5 minutes.

2. Flatten the pork slices with a pastry roller (rolling pin). Brush with oil and season with salt and pepper.

3. Heat a browning dish in the microwave oven for 6-8 minutes, following the manufacturer's instructions.

4. Arrange the slices of meat side by side in the browning dish, leave for a few seconds, then turn. When they have stopped sizzling, cover and microwave for 5 minutes on HIGH. Remove from the oven and cover with a double layer of aluminum (aluminium) foil to keep the meat hot.

5. Melt the butter in the oven for 1 minute on HIGH. Add the flour and mix well. Crumble over the beef bouillon (stock) cube and mix again. Pour over the cooking liquid from the mushrooms and the pork and mix thoroughly. Stir in the Madeira. Whisk. Microwave for 2 minutes on HIGH, whisk vigorously, then cook for a further 2 minutes.

6. Arrange the meat in a round serving dish, leaving the center free. Put a slice of foie gras on top of each piece of pork. Cover with aluminum (aluminium) foil.

7. Add the mushrooms and sour cream (crème fraîche) to the sauce and stir well. Reheat for 2 minutes on HIGH.

8. Put the serving dish containing the meat into the microwave oven for 1 minute on HIGH to heat the foie gras. Pour the mushroom sauce into the center of the dish and serve at once.

Pork tenderloin (fillet) with foie gras

Porc à l'ananas
Sweet-and-Sour Pork

00.15   00.27
Serves 4

American	Ingredients	Metric/Imperial
1	green bell pepper, rinsed, seeded and diced	1
1	red bell pepper, rinsed, seeded and diced	1
2	finely chopped onions	2
2 tbsp	oil	1 tbsp
4 tbsp	sugar	3 tbsp
2 tbsp	vinegar	1 tbsp
3 tbsp	nuoc-mam	2 tbsp
1½ lb	boneless shoulder of pork, cut into strips	600 g/1½ lb
	salt	
	pepper	
½ tsp	garlic powder	½ tsp
2 tbsp	tomato paste (purée)	1 tbsp
1 (1¾ lb)	pineapple, cut into cubes	1 (700 g/1¾ lb)

1. Put the bell peppers and onions into a casserole. Pour over the oil. Microwave, uncovered, on HIGH for 6 minutes.
2. Put the sugar in a bowl with 3 tablespoons (2 tablespoons) of water. Microwave on HIGH for 5 minutes, or until the liquid turns light brown. Carefully add the vinegar and nuoc-mam, avoiding splashing the inside of the oven. Microwave on HIGH for 1 minute.

3. Season the meat strips lightly with salt and pepper and add to the casserole. Add the garlic powder and tomato paste (purée) and pour over the caramel liquid. Stir thoroughly. Cover and microwave on MEDIUM-HIGH for 10 minutes, stirring midway through the cooking time.
4. Add the pineapple cubes to the casserole, stir well, cover and microwave for a further 5 minutes on MEDIUM-HIGH. Serve very hot.

Bouchées de porc à la chinoise
Chinese Pork

00.10   00.12
Serves 4

American	Ingredients	Metric/Imperial
3 tbsp	cornstarch (cornflour)	1½ tbsp
2 tbsp	nuoc-mam	1 tbsp
2 tbsp	honey vinegar	1 tbsp
1 tsp	sugar	1 tsp
½ tsp	garlic powder	½ tsp
½ tsp	five-spice powder	½ tsp
	Tabasco sauce	
	salt	
	pepper	
1½ lb	pork tenderloin (fillet), cut into cubes	600 g/1½ lb
2 tbsp	butter	1 tbsp
2 tbsp	oil	1 tbsp
2 tbsp	dry sherry	1 tbsp
2 tbsp	sour cream (crème fraîche)	1 tbsp
1 tbsp	chopped fresh chives	1 tbsp

Sweet-and-sour pork

1. Heat a browning dish in the microwave oven for 6-8 minutes, following the manufacturer's instructions.
2. Mix half of the cornstarch (cornflour) with the nuoc-mam and vinegar to a smooth paste. Add the sugar, garlic powder, five-spice powder, several dashes of Tabasco sauce and a little salt and pepper. Mix well. Add the meat and stir until all the cubes are well coated.
3. When the browning dish is hot, add the butter and oil, taking care to avoid spattering the inside of the oven. Tilt the dish so that the base is completely covered with fat. Put the meat cubes in the dish side by side. When they stop sizzling, turn to seal on all sides.
4. Microwave, uncovered, for 3 minutes on HIGH.
5. Mix the sherry and the remaining cornstarch (cornflour) in a cup.
6. Transfer the meat with a slotted spatula to a warmed serving dish.
7. Add the sour cream (crème fraîche) to the browning dish and stir with a wooden spoon until the cooking sediments are fully dissolved. Pour into the cup containing the sherry. Stir well and heat in the oven for 1 minute on HIGH. Stir, pour over the meat, sprinkle with chopped chives and serve at once.

Curried pork

Porc au curry

Curried Pork

◤▭	00.10	00.26	〰
	Serves 4-5		

American	Ingredients	Metric/Imperial
5 oz	finely sliced onions	150 g/5 oz
2	crushed garlic cloves	2
9 oz	coarsely chopped tomatoes	250 g/9 oz
¾ cup	white wine	200 ml/7 fl oz
3 oz	golden raisins (sultanas)	75 g/3 oz
3 tbsp	curry powder	2 tbsp
3 oz	desiccated coconut	75 g/3 oz
½ tsp	powdered thyme	½ tsp
2 tbsp	dark rum	1 tbsp
	salt	
	pepper	
1¾ lb	boneless pork shoulder, cut into ½ in (1.25 cm) cubes	750 g/1¾ lb
3 tbsp	sour cream (crème fraîche)	2 tbsp

1. Put the onions in a casserole. Cover and microwave on HIGH for 4 minutes.
2. Add the garlic, tomatoes and white wine to the casserole. Cover and microwave on HIGH for 3 minutes.
3. Rinse the raisins (sultanas) under plenty of cold running water. Pat dry on kitchen paper.
4. Add the raisins (sultanas), curry powder, desiccated coconut, powdered thyme and rum to the casserole. Season lightly with salt and pepper. Add the meat cubes, mixing thoroughly. Cover and microwave on HIGH for 6 minutes.
5. Stir the contents of the casserole, cover again and reduce the power to MEDIUM. Cook for 6-8 minutes, stirring once half-way through cooking time. When the meat is tender, remove the casserole from the oven and leave to stand for 5 minutes. Stir in the sour cream (crème fraîche), mix well and serve.

Pork with Bananas and Peanuts

◤▭	00.15	00.28	〰
	Serves 6		

American	Ingredients	Metric/Imperial
¾ lb	chopped onions	350 g/12 oz
2	crushed garlic cloves	2
2 tbsp	oil	1 tbsp
2 lb	boneless pork, cut into cubes	1 kg/2 lb
½ lb	long grain rice	225 g/8 oz
14 oz	can tomatoes	400 g/14 oz
1	chicken bouillon (stock) cube	1
¼ tsp	paprika	¼ tsp
¼ tsp	ground cinnamon	¼ tsp
	salt	
	pepper	
2	sliced bananas	2
¼ lb	salted peanuts	125 g/4 oz

1. Put the onions and garlic in a casserole dish with the oil and heat on HIGH for 2-3 minutes. Add the meat and the rice.
2. Pour the juice from the tomatoes into a measuring cup, crumble in the bouillon (stock) cube and add enough water to make up to 2 cups (450 ml/¾ pint). Add to the casserole. Chop the tomatoes and add with the paprika, cinnamon, salt and pepper. Cover and cook on MEDIUM for 20 minutes. Leave to stand for 5 minutes to allow the rice to absorb the last of the liquid.
3. Stir the banana slices and the peanuts into the stew. Fluff up the rice with a fork and serve at once.

Côtes de porc à la mozzarella

Pork Chops with Mozzarella

00.10 Serves 4   **00.28**

American	Ingredients	Metric/Imperial
3½ oz	thinly sliced onions	100 g/3½ oz
1	garlic clove, cut in half	1
1	finely grated carrot	1
2	celery sticks, cut into very thin strips	2
3 tbsp	tarragon vinegar	2 tbsp
1	can Italian tomatoes	1
	salt	
	pepper	
½ tsp	dried thyme	½ tsp
½ tsp	sugar	½ tsp
¼ tsp	chili powder	¼ tsp
3 tbsp	olive oil	2 tbsp
4	pork chops	4
4	slices Mozzarella cheese	4

1. Place the onions, garlic and 2 (1) tablespoons of water in a small casserole. Microwave, uncovered, on HIGH for 2 minutes.

2. Add the carrot, celery and vinegar to the casserole. Cover and microwave on HIGH for 3 minutes.

3. Add the tomatoes to the other vegetables. Season with salt and pepper and add the thyme, sugar, chili powder and half of the olive oil. Stir well. Cover and microwave on HIGH for 5 minutes.

4. Heat a browning dish in the microwave oven for 6-8 minutes, following the manufacturer's instructions.

5. Purée the contents of the casserole in a food processor. Make several grooves with a knife in each pork chop and brush on both sides with the remaining oil. Season with salt and pepper.

6. When the browning dish is hot, put in the pork chops, turning after 1 minute and placing the bone toward the center of the dish. Pour over the sauce. Cover and microwave on HIGH for 8 minutes. Put a slice of Mozzarella on each pork chop. Sprinkle pepper on the cheese. Leave to melt for 2 minutes at room temperature then serve.

Microwave hint: To cook chops or cutlets with a glaze by microwave, trim the fat neatly and arrange the chops in a shallow dish. Mix together ¼ cup (3 tablespoons) of bottled barbecue sauce and 2 tablespoons (1 tablespoon) of clear honey, then stir in 2 tablespoons (1 tablespoon) of Dijon or other French mustard. Brush half of the glaze over the chops. Leave to marinate for about 30 minutes, then brush with more glaze and arrange on a micro-proof roasting rack. Cook on HIGH for 3 minutes. Turn, brush with any remaining glaze and cook for a further 3 minutes. Leave to stand for 5 minutes before serving.

Pork chops with Mozzarella

Microwave hint: Lean pork chops can become rather dry when cooked in the microwave. To avoid this, coat in fine breadcrumbs, pressed well into the surface. Coat the inside of a preheated browning dish with oil and add the chops. Cook on HIGH for 2 minutes. Turn and cook for a further 2 minutes. Cover and cook on MEDIUM for a further 20 minutes, turning the chops once.

Russian Pork Chop Casserole

	00.10 Serves 4	00.30

American	Ingredients	Metric/Imperial
1 lb	diced potatoes	450 g/1 lb
1	chopped onion	1
¼ lb	sliced button mushrooms	125 g/4 oz
2 tbsp	butter	1 tbsp
1 tsp	garlic salt	1 tsp
4	pork loin chops	4
⅔ cup	sour cream (crème fraîche)	150 ml/¼ pint
	salt	
	pepper	
2 tbsp	chopped parsley	2 tbsp

1. Put the potatoes, onions and mushrooms in a bowl with the butter and cook on HIGH for 8 minutes, stirring twice. Season with the garlic salt.
2. Heat a browning dish for 6-8 minutes, following the manufacturer's instructions. Add the chops and cook on HIGH for 4 minutes. Turn and cook for a further 4 minutes.
3. Pour over the potato mixture and the cream. Cover and heat on HIGH for 5-6 minutes. Taste and adjust the seasoning. Sprinkle with the chopped parsley and serve.

Pork and Molasses (Treacle) Casserole

	00.10 Serves 6	00.30

American	Ingredients	Metric/Imperial
1 lb	lean boneless pork, cut into cubes	450 g/1 lb
1½ lb	thick bacon strips (rashers), cut into 1 in (2.5 cm) pieces	600 g/1½ lb
	salt	
	pepper	
2 tbsp	all-purpose (plain) flour	1 tbsp
3	chopped large onions	3
2	crushed garlic cloves	2
2 tbsp	oil	1 tbsp
¼ cup	molasses (black treacle)	3 tbsp
3 tbsp	tomato paste (purée)	2 tbsp
14 oz	can tomatoes	400 g/14 oz
2 cups	beef bouillon (stock)	450 ml/¾ pint

1. Toss the pork and bacon in seasoned flour. Put the onions, garlic and oil in a casserole and cook on HIGH for 3-5 minutes until soft.
2. Add the pork, bacon, black treacle (molasses), tomato paste (purée), tomatoes and their juice and bouillon (stock). Stir well. Cover and cook on MEDIUM for 20 minutes. Leave to stand for 5 minutes. Taste and adjust the seasoning. Serve immediately.

Couronne de foie aux épinards

Ring Mold (Mould) of Pork Liver with Spinach

	00.15 Serves 4	00.15

American	Ingredients	Metric/Imperial
2	finely chopped shallots	2
7 oz	frozen chopped spinach	200 g/7 oz
2 oz	frozen sorrel	50 g/2 oz
2 tbsp	frozen tarragon	1 tbsp
5 oz	chopped pork liver	150 g/5 oz
9 oz	sausage meat	250 g/9 oz
1	large egg	1
2 tbsp	chopped parsley	1 tbsp
¼ cup	mild mustard	3 tbsp
½ tsp	allspice	½ tsp
	salt	
	pepper	
2 tbsp	butter	1 tbsp
3 tbsp	all-purpose (plain) flour	2 tbsp
⅓ cup	dry white wine	4½ tbsp
⅔ cup	milk	150 ml/¼ pint
2 tbsp	chopped chervil	2 tbsp

1. Put the shallots, spinach, sorrel and tarragon in a small casserole. Microwave, uncovered, for 5 minutes on HIGH.
2. Purée the chopped liver in a food processor, adding the sausage meat, vegetables from the casserole, egg, parsley, half of the mustard and allspice. Purée until the mixture is smooth. Season lightly with salt and pepper, taking into account the seasoning in the sausage meat.
3. Pour the mixture into a small ring mold (mould) and smooth the surface. Cover and microwave on HIGH for 6 minutes.
4. When the mixture is cooked, make the sauce: melt the butter in a bowl for 1 minute on HIGH, add the flour and mix well. Pour in the white wine and milk. Whisk with a hand beater. Put the bowl in the oven and microwave on HIGH for a further 2 minutes. Add the remaining mustard, whisking constantly, and salt and pepper to taste. Microwave for 1 more minute. Whisk well and add the chopped chervil.
5. Invert the mold (mould) on to a plate and coat with the sauce.

Microwave hint: To make a garnish by microwave for joints of pork or ham, turn the contents of a large can of apricot halves or whole apricots into a suitable dish, with all the syrup. Add ½ teaspoon each of ground nutmeg, cinnamon and cloves and stir well. Cover and cook on HIGH for 7 minutes. Leave covered until completely cold. Lift out the fruit with a slotted spoon and use to garnish the meat.

Simmered Pork with Sherry Sauce

■▷ 00.05   00.45 Serves 2

American	Ingredients	Metric/Imperial
1 lb	boneless pork	450 g/1 lb
2 tbsp	oil	1 tbsp
	salt	
	pepper	
	dried rosemary	
1	chopped medium onion	1
5	skinned, seeded tomatoes	5
¼ cup	dry sherry	4 tbsp
2 tsp	all-purpose (plain) flour	2 tsp
4 tbsp	unsweetened evaporated milk	3 tbsp

1. Brush the pork on all sides with a little of the oil and sprinkle with salt, pepper and rosemary.
2. Heat a browning dish for 6-8 minutes, following the manufacturer's instructions. Add the remaining oil and tilt the dish to make sure the base is evenly covered. Put the pork in the dish and cook on HIGH for 3 minutes. Turn the meat and cook on HIGH for a further 3 minutes.
3. Add the onions and tomatoes to the meat and cook on HIGH for 3 minutes. Pour over the sherry and 1 cup (250 ml/8 fl oz) of hot water. Cover and cook on HIGH for 15 minutes. Turn the meat and cook for 5 minutes. Transfer to a plate.
4. Mix the flour with the evaporated milk. Purée the cooking liquid with the flour and milk in a food processor. Return to the dish and cook on HIGH for 3 minutes. Stir well.
5. Carve the meat into slices and add to the sauce. Heat on HIGH for 5 minutes.

Roulades de jambon aux abricots
Ham Rolls with Apricots

■▷ 00.05   00.15 Serves 4

American	Ingredients	Metric/Imperial
7 oz	rinsed dried apricots	200 g/7 oz
4	slices Virginia (honey roast) ham	4
½ tbsp	butter	½ tbsp
3 tbsp	dark Jamaica rum	2 tbsp
2 tbsp	mango chutney	1 tbsp

1. Cover the apricots with 2 cups (400 ml/14 fl oz) of hot water and microwave on HIGH for 10-12 minutes until swollen and soft.
2. Roll the ham slices and arrange in a dish. Dot with butter. Cover and microwave on HIGH for 2 minutes.
3. Pour the rum into a cup and heat on HIGH for 30 seconds. Set alight and flambé the ham.
4. Put the ham in a serving dish and arrange the apricots around the meat. Pour the cooking liquid from the ham and 4 tablespoons (2 tablespoons) of the apricot juice into a cup and stir in the chutney. Reheat on HIGH for 30 seconds. Pour over the ham and serve at once.

Ham rolls with apricots

Jambon à l'agenaise
Ham with Prune and Madeira Sauce

■▷ 00.05   00.13 Serves 2-4

American	Ingredients	Metric/Imperial
⅓ cup	Madeira	4½ tbsp
½ lb	pitted prunes	225 g/8 oz
2	coarsely chopped onions	2
¼ tsp	dried thyme	¼ tsp
⅓ cup	white wine	4½ tbsp
1 tsp	tomato paste (purée)	1 tsp
½ tsp	sugar	½ tsp
4	slices cooked ham	4
2 tbsp	butter	1 tbsp
3 tbsp	all-purpose (plain) flour	2 tbsp
¼ cup	sour cream (crème fraîche)	3 tbsp
	salt	
	pepper	

1. Pour the Madeira and ⅓ cup (4½ tablespoons) of water into a bowl. Add the prunes. Heat in the microwave oven for 3 minutes on HIGH.
2. Purée the onions in a food processor. Put the purée in a bowl with the thyme, white wine, tomato paste (purée) and sugar. Cover and microwave on HIGH for 5 minutes.
3. Roll the ham slices and put in a dish. Drain the prunes with a slotted spoon and arrange around the ham.
4. Put the butter into a bowl and melt for 1 minute on HIGH. Stir in the flour and add the cooking liquid from the prunes, whisking constantly. Cook on HIGH for 1½ minutes.
5. Whisk the sauce again, adding the sour cream (crème fraîche), onions and wine sauce. Force the mixture through a strainer by pushing with the back of a wooden spoon. Season with salt and pepper and stir well. Pour this sauce over the ham and prunes. Cover and microwave on HIGH for 2 minutes. Serve at once.

Ham with prune and Madeira sauce

Veal

Grenadins de veau au poivre vert

Veal Steaks in Green Peppercorn Sauce

◖▷ 00.10   00.05   〰️
Serves 4

American	Ingredients	Metric/Imperial
4	slices veal tenderloin (fillet)	4
½ tsp	dried thyme	½ tsp
	salt	
2 tbsp	soft green peppercorns	1 tbsp
1	egg yolk	1
2 tbsp	fresh lime juice	1 tbsp
2 tbsp	sour cream (crème fraîche)	1 tbsp

1. Flatten the veal steaks with a pastry roller (rolling pin). Mix the thyme with an equal amount of salt and sprinkle on both sides of the steaks. Put into a dish. Cover and microwave on HIGH for 3 minutes.
2. Pound the green peppercorns to a smooth paste in a pestle and mortar. Gradually mix the egg yolk with the lime juice and sour cream (crème fraîche). Add a little salt and the green peppercorn paste and mix well.
3. Turn the steaks, coat with the peppercorn sauce and microwave for a further 2 minutes on HIGH. Serve at once.

Médaillons de veau au miel

Veal Steaks with Honey

◖▷ 00.10   00.20   〰️
Serves 4

American	Ingredients	Metric/Imperial
4	slices veal tenderloin (fillet)	4
	salt	
	pepper	
½ tsp	powdered thyme	½ tsp
1 tbsp	oil	½ tbsp
¼ cup	white wine	3 tbsp
2	celery sticks, washed and cut into very thin strips	2
1	very finely sliced onion	1
2	carrots, cut into very thin strips	2
2 tbsp	honey	1 tbsp
2 tbsp	wine vinegar	1 tbsp
2 tbsp	butter	1 tbsp

1. Heat a browning dish in the microwave oven for 6-8 minutes, following the manufacturer's instructions.
2. Sprinkle each side of the veal steaks with salt and pepper and a little of the thyme.
3. Pour the oil into the hot browning dish and shake the dish from side to side so that the base is covered. Place the veal steaks in the dish for 40 seconds, then turn. When they stop sizzling, transfer to a plate and set aside.

Veal steaks with honey

4. Pour the white wine into the browning dish and scrape up the meat sediments from the base until dissolved. Add the vegetables and sprinkle with the remaining thyme. Cover and microwave on HIGH for 6 minutes.

5. Season the vegetables with salt and pepper. Make space for the steaks in the center of the browning dish. Pour the honey over the steaks. Cover and microwave on HIGH for 5 minutes.

6. Transfer the meat to a heated serving dish. Add the vinegar and butter to the vegetables and mix until the butter is melted. Pour over the steaks and serve hot.

Grenadins de veau à l'avocat

Veal Steaks with Avocado

◢▱ 00.10   00.14 〰
Serves 4

American	Ingredients	Metric/Imperial
2 tbsp	curry powder	1 tbsp
	salt	
	pepper	
4	veal tenderloin (fillet) steaks	4
2 tbsp	oil	1 tbsp
2 tbsp	dry sherry	1 tbsp
1	large ripe avocado, skinned, halved and stoned	1

1. Heat a browning dish in the microwave oven on HIGH for 6-8 minutes, following the manufacturer's instructions.

2. Mix the curry powder on a plate with salt and pepper and lightly coat the veal steaks. Pour over the oil.

3. When the browning dish is hot, heat the steaks for 30 seconds on HIGH, then turn over. Add the sherry. Cover and microwave on HIGH for 4 minutes.

4. Mash the avocado flesh with a fork. Season with salt and pepper.

5. Remove the browning dish from the oven, turn the steaks again and cover with the avocado purée. Return the dish to the oven and cook for 1 further minute on HIGH. Serve at once.

Petite blanquette de veau

Veal in a White Sauce

◢▱ 00.20   00.35 〰
Serves 4

American	Ingredients	Metric/Imperial
2 tbsp	butter	1 tbsp
5 oz	finely chopped onions	150 g/5 oz
1¾ lb	boneless breast of veal, cut into ½ in (1.25 cm) strips	700 g/1¾ lb
½	chicken bouillon (stock) cube	½
	salt	
	pepper	
⅔ cup	white wine	150 ml/¼ pint
1¼ lb	white button mushrooms	500 g/1¼ lb
1	egg	1
¼ cup	fresh lemon juice	3 tbsp
3 tbsp	sour cream (crème fraîche)	2 tbsp
½ tsp	masala or mild curry powder	½ tsp
1 tbsp	chopped parsley	1 tbsp

1. Put the butter into a casserole and add the onions. Cover and microwave on HIGH for 3 minutes.

2. Add the veal to the onions. Crumble the bouillon (stock) cube over and add salt and pepper to taste. Pour over the white wine. Cover and microwave on HIGH for 8 minutes.

3. Wipe the mushrooms with a damp cloth or kitchen paper and cut into thick slices.

4. Stir the meat and add the mushrooms. Cover and microwave on HIGH for 12 minutes. Leave to stand for 10 minutes.

5. To make the sauce: mix the egg, lemon juice, sour cream (crème fraîche), masala or curry powder and parsley together and pour into the casserole. Stir well. Cook on MEDIUM-HIGH for 2 minutes. Taste and adjust the seasoning. Serve hot.

Tendrons de veau à la basquaise

Basque Style Veal Breast

◢▱ 00.10   00.32 〰
Serves 4

American	Ingredients	Metric/Imperial
3½ oz	lean streaky bacon, rind removed and diced	100 g/3½ oz
2	thinly sliced onions	2
3	large red bell peppers, rinsed, seeded and cut into strips	3
3 tbsp	concentrated tomato juice	2 tbsp
3 tbsp	vinegar	2 tbsp
1 tsp	soft brown sugar	1 tsp
2 lb	boneless breast of veal, cut into 4 equal slices	1 kg/2 lb
	salt	
	pepper	
½ tsp	dried mixed herbs	½ tsp
1	crushed garlic clove	1
5 oz	zucchini (courgettes), cut into strips	150 g/5 oz

1. Put the bacon and onions in a casserole large enough to hold the meat. Microwave, uncovered, on HIGH for 2 minutes.

2. Add the bell peppers to the casserole. Cover and microwave on HIGH for 5 minutes.

3. Mix the tomato juice with the vinegar and brown sugar. Sprinkle the slices of veal breast with salt and pepper and mixed herbs on each side.

4. Add the garlic and the zucchini (courgettes) strips to the casserole and pour over the tomato juice and vinegar mixture. Season with salt and pepper and mix well. Arrange the slices of veal breast on top. Cover and microwave on HIGH for 10 minutes.

5. Turn the veal and move the pieces in the center to the outside of the casserole and vice versa. Cover once more and cook on MEDIUM-HIGH for a further 10 minutes.

6. When the meat is tender, leave to stand, covered, for 5 minutes. Serve hot.

Grenadins de veau aux girolles

Veal Tenderloin (Fillet) with Field Mushrooms

■▷ 00.10   00.12 〰
Serves 4

American	Ingredients	Metric/Imperial
1¼ lb	wild or field mushrooms (as much dark flesh as possible)	500 g/1¼ lb
4	veal tenderloin (fillet) steaks	4
½ tsp	dried thyme	½ tsp
	salt	
	pepper	
¼ cup	sour cream (crème fraîche)	3 tbsp
1	egg yolk	1
2 tbsp	cognac	1 tbsp
1 tbsp	chopped fresh parsley	1 tbsp

1. Wipe the mushrooms with a damp cloth or kitchen paper. Cut in half if very large. Put into a casserole. Cover and microwave on HIGH for 6 minutes.
2. Flatten the veal steaks with a pastry roller (rolling pin). Sprinkle with thyme on each side and season with salt and pepper. Arrange in a circle on a round dish, leaving the center of the dish empty. Cover and microwave on HIGH for 3 minutes.
3. Stir the mushrooms and add the sour cream (crème fraîche), egg yolk and cognac. Season with salt and pepper.
4. Turn the veal steaks. Pour over the mushroom mixture. Cover and microwave on HIGH for a further 3 minutes. Sprinkle with chopped parsley and serve at once.

Quasi de veau à la clémentine

Veal Loin with Clementines

■▷ 00.15   00.44 〰
Serves 4

American	Ingredients	Metric/Imperial
2	finely chopped shallots	2
1 tbsp	butter	½ tbsp
2 tbsp	oil	1 tbsp
1¾ lb	boneless veal loin	750 g/1¾ lb
	salt	
	pepper	
½ tsp	dried mixed herbs	½ tsp
3 tbsp	port	2 tbsp
1	orange	1
2	clementines or satsumas	2
1 tsp	cornstarch (cornflour)	1 tsp
2 tbsp	vinegar	1 tbsp
1 tsp	sugar	1 tsp

1. Put the shallots and butter in a dish. Microwave, uncovered, on HIGH for 2 minutes.
2. Brush the veal with oil, season with salt and pepper and sprinkle with the mixed herbs. Add the veal and port to the shallots. Cover and microwave on MEDIUM for 15 minutes.
3. Turn the meat, cover once more and cook for a further 12-15 minutes on MEDIUM until tender. Cover with a double thickness of aluminum (aluminium) foil and leave to stand for 10 minutes.

Veal loin with clementines

4. Wash the orange very carefully under plenty of cold running water. Pat dry on kitchen paper. Remove the zest (peel) with a potato peeler or small sharp knife, taking care not to include any of the bitter white flesh. Cut the orange in half and squeeze the juice, to obtain about ⅓ cup (4½ tablespoons). Peel the clementines or satsumas and separate the segments, removing any white pith or membrane.

5. Put the cornstarch (cornflour) into a bowl and gradually add the vinegar and orange juice. Add the sugar and orange rind (zest). Microwave on HIGH for 1 minute. Stir well. Add the clémentine segments and the cooking juices from the meat. Reheat for 1 minute on HIGH.

6. Slice the veal. Pour the sauce into a sauceboat and serve at once.

Rôti de veau aux tagliatelles de légumes

Roast Loin of Veal with Vegetables

◢▷ 00.15 00.58 **〰**
Serves 6

American	Ingredients	Metric/Imperial
2½ lb	boneless loin of veal	1.2 kg/2½ lb
5	strips (rashers) streaky bacon	5
	salt	
	pepper	
3 tbsp	Madeira	2 tbsp
10½ oz	carrots, cut into long, thin strips	300 g/10½ oz
10½ oz	zucchini (courgettes), cut into long, thin strips	300 g/10½ oz
2 tbsp	sugar	1 tbsp
½ tsp	grated nutmeg	½ tsp
2	finely chopped shallots	2
3½ oz	frozen artichoke hearts	100 g/3½ oz
3 tbsp	fresh lemon juice	2 tbsp
3 tbsp	white wine	2 tbsp
⅓ cup	sour cream (crème fraîche)	4½ tbsp
2 tbsp	concentrated tomato juice	1 tbsp

1. Wrap the veal in the strips (rashers) of bacon and secure with kitchen string. Sprinkle salt and pepper in the base of a cooking dish and add the Madeira. Put the meat in the dish. Cover and microwave on HIGH for 20 minutes. Check the internal temperature with a meat thermometer: it should read 60°C. Cook for a little longer if necessary. Remove the dish from the microwave oven, cover with a double layer of aluminum (aluminium) foil, matt side outward, and leave to stand for 15 minutes.

2. Put the vegetable strips into a dish. Add the sugar, grated nutmeg and ¼ cup (3 tablespoons) of water. Season with salt and pepper. Mix well and cover the dish.

3. Put the shallots in a small dish with the artichoke hearts. Pour over the lemon juice and white wine and cover.

4. Cook the carrots and zucchini (courgettes) on HIGH for 8 minutes.

5. Cook the shallots and artichoke hearts on HIGH for 14 minutes. Purée in a food processor with the sour cream (crème fraîche), tomato juice and cooking liquid from the meat. Taste and adjust the seasoning. Reheat the sauce for 1 minute on HIGH.

6. Carve the meat and arrange the slices in a warmed serving dish. Put the carrots and zucchini (courgettes) in the middle of the dish. Pour the sauce into a sauceboat and serve.

Rôti de veau à la crème d'oignons

Roast Veal in Onion Sauce

◢▷ 00.10 00.56 **〰**
Serves 5

American	Ingredients	Metric/Imperial
9 oz	thinly sliced onions	250 g/9 oz
1½ oz	butter	40 g/1½ oz
3 tbsp	all-purpose (plain) flour	2 tbsp
¾ cup	milk	200 ml/7 fl oz
	salt	
	pepper	
½ tsp	grated nutmeg	½ tsp
2 oz	grated Gruyère cheese	50 g/2 oz
2 lb	veal round (topside) roast	1 kg/2 lb
1¼ lb	oyster mushrooms	500 g/1¼ lb
3	finely chopped shallots	3

1. Put the onions into a small casserole. Cover and microwave on HIGH for 7 minutes.

2. Put half of the butter into a bowl and melt in the oven for 1 minute on HIGH. Add the flour and mix well. Pour in the milk and whisk until the mixture is smooth. Microwave for 3 minutes on HIGH, whisking after every minute. Season with salt and pepper. Stir in the grated nutmeg and Gruyère cheese and set aside.

3. Put the veal roast in a long oval casserole. Cover and microwave on HIGH for 10 minutes. Turn the meat and cook on HIGH for a further 8 minutes. Use a meat thermometer to check the internal temperature of the meat, which should be 60°C. Cover the meat with a double thickness of aluminum (aluminium) foil, matt side outward, and leave to stand for 10-15 minutes.

4. Wipe the mushrooms with a damp cloth or kitchen paper and cut into strips.

5. Put the shallots in a small casserole and microwave for 2 minutes on HIGH. Add the mushrooms and the remaining butter. Cover and microwave on HIGH for 5 minutes. Season with salt and pepper, mix well and cook, uncovered, for a further 3 minutes on HIGH.

6. Drain the shallots and purée in a food processor. Add the purée to the sauce. Taste and adjust the seasoning.

7. Reheat the onion and cheese sauce in the microwave oven for 2 minutes on HIGH. Stir well and pour into a large sauceboat.

8. Carve the meat into thin slices and arrange on a serving dish. Add the carving liquid to the mushrooms and spoon on top of the meat. Serve hot, with the onion sauce on the side. If oyster mushrooms are not available, field mushrooms, as wide open as possible, should be substituted.

Veau en blanquette

Veal with Mushrooms and Celery

◼▢▽	00.15	00.53	〰
	Serves 4		

American	Ingredients	Metric/Imperial
5 oz	thinly sliced onions	150 g/5 oz
3	celery sticks, washed and cut into very thin strips	3
2 tbsp	butter	1 tbsp
1¼ lb	white button mushrooms	500 g/1¼ lb
2 tbsp	fresh lemon juice	1 tbsp
1	chicken bouillon (stock) cube	1
1 cup	dry white wine	250 ml/8 fl oz
2 tbsp	all-purpose (plain) flour	1 tbsp
2 lb	boneless veal loin, cut into equal-size cubes	1 kg/2 lb
½ tsp	dried mixed herbs	½ tsp
	salt	
	pepper	
2	egg yolks	2
⅓ cup	sour cream (crème fraîche)	4½ tbsp

1. Put the onions, celery and butter into a 3 quart (3 litre/5¼ pint) casserole. Cover and microwave on HIGH for 3 minutes.
2. Wipe the mushrooms with a damp cloth or kitchen paper. Cut in quarters and pour over the lemon juice. Add to the casserole and crumble the chicken bouillon (stock) cube over. Pour in the white wine and mix well. Cover and microwave on HIGH for 5 minutes.
3. Sift the flour into the casserole and stir. Add the meat cubes, mixed herbs and salt and pepper to taste. Stir thoroughly. Cover and microwave on HIGH for 5 minutes.
4. Reduce the power to MEDIUM and cook for a further 30 minutes, stirring once or twice during the cooking time.
5. When the veal is tender, transfer to a heated serving dish, cover with a double thickness of aluminum (aluminium) foil and leave to stand for 10 minutes. Mix the egg yolks with the sour cream (crème fraîche) and add to the casserole, whisking vigorously. Taste and adjust the seasoning. Pour over the veal and serve at once.

Paupiettes à la mousse de foie gras

Veal Olives with Foie Gras

◼▢▽	00.10	00.30	〰
	Serves 4		

American	Ingredients	Metric/Imperial
8	large prunes	8
7 oz	very finely sliced onions	200 g/7 oz
14 oz	grated carrots	400 g/14 oz
⅔ cup	white port	150 ml/¼ pint
	salt	
	pepper	
4	veal scaloppine (escalopes)	4
¼ lb	pâté de foie gras	125 g/4 oz
⅓ cup	sour cream (crème fraîche)	4½ tbsp
1 tbsp	chopped fresh parsley	1 tbsp

1. Put the prunes into a bowl and cover with water. Heat in the microwave oven for 5 minutes on HIGH.
2. Put the onions in a round dish and microwave, uncovered, on HIGH for 3 minutes.
3. Add the carrots to the onions and mix well. Stir in ¼ cup (4 tablespoons) of port and season with salt and pepper. Cover and microwave on HIGH for 7 minutes.
4. While the vegetables are cooking, flatten the veal scaloppine (escalopes) with a pastry roller (rolling pin) as thin as possible. Spread with three-quarters of the foie gras, then roll up.
5. Drain the prunes.
6. Push the vegetables into the center of the dish and arrange the veal olives around the edge. Cover and microwave on HIGH for 5 minutes.
7. Add the remaining port, the remaining foie gras and the sour cream (crème fraîche) to the vegetables. Add the prunes. Turn the veal. Cover and microwave on HIGH for a further 10 minutes.
8. When the meat is tender, transfer the contents of the dish to a serving platter, sprinkle with parsley and serve hot.

Veal olives with foie gras

Veal birds

Paupiettes de veau forestières

Veal Birds

00.15 Serves 4 — 00.26

American	Ingredients	Metric/Imperial
2	carrots	2
3½ oz	smoked streaky bacon, rind removed and diced	100 g/3½ oz
2	finely chopped shallots	2
3 tbsp	white wine	2 tbsp
1¼ lb	white button mushrooms	500 g/1¼ lb
9 oz	tomatoes	250 g/9 oz
2	crushed garlic cloves	2
1	fresh thyme sprig	1
	salt	
	pepper	
2 tbsp	oil	1 tbsp
1	bay leaf	1
4	veal rolls, tied with string (from butcher)	4
3 tbsp	Madeira	2 tbsp
¼ cup	sour cream (crème fraîche)	3 tbsp

1. Peel and rinse the carrots under plenty of cold running water. Pat dry on kitchen paper. Grate into very fine rounds in a food processor.

2. Put the bacon, carrots, shallots and white wine into a casserole. Cover and microwave on HIGH for 6 minutes.

3. Wipe the mushrooms with a damp cloth or kitchen paper and slice thinly. Rinse the tomatoes under plenty of cold running water. Pat dry on kitchen paper and purée in a food processor.

4. Add the mushrooms, garlic and purée of tomatoes to the casserole. Crumble the thyme into the mixture and season with salt and pepper. Pour over the oil. Add the bay leaf to the vegetables and stir well. Cover and microwave on HIGH for 5 minutes. Stir the contents of the casserole.

5. Put the veal rolls into the casserole on top of the vegetables. Cover and microwave for 5 minutes on MEDIUM-HIGH.

6. Turn the rolls and pour over the Madeira and sour cream (crème fraîche). Cover and cook for a further 5 minutes on MEDIUM-HIGH.

7. Leave the meat to stand for 5 minutes. Transfer the veal birds to a heated serving dish. Remove the string. Arrange the vegetables around the veal rolls, discard the bay leaf and serve hot.

Côtes de veau aux carottes
Veal Chops with Carrots

▬▷	00.05	00.15	〰
	Serves 2		

American	Ingredients	Metric/Imperial
10½ oz	grated carrots	300 g/10½ oz
2	celery sticks, washed and cut into thin strips	2
2 tsp	oil	2 tsp
2	veal loin chops	2
	salt	
	pepper	
3 tbsp	concentrated tomato juice	2 tbsp
2 tbsp	butter	1 tbsp
3 tbsp	white wine	2 tbsp
½ tsp	dried thyme	½ tsp
1 tbsp	chopped fresh parsley	1 tbsp

1. Put the carrots and celery in a bowl with ¼ cup (4 tablespoons) of water. Cover and microwave on HIGH for 5 minutes.
2. Heat a browning dish in the oven for 6 minutes on HIGH, following the manufacturer's instructions. Brush the veal chops with the oil. Put in the hot browning dish, leave for 10 seconds, turn over and leave for another 10 seconds. Remove.
3. Season the carrots and celery with salt and pepper and add the tomato juice and the butter cut into tiny pieces. Arrange the veal chops on top, head-to-tail. Pour the white wine into the browning dish, stirring well with a wooden spoon to dissolve the cooking liquid. Pour over the veal and add the thyme. Season with salt and pepper. Cover and microwave on HIGH for 2 minutes.
4. Turn the chops. Cover and microwave on HIGH for a further 2 minutes. Sprinkle with the chopped parsley and serve hot.

Veal chops with carrots

2. Wipe the mushrooms with a damp cloth or kitchen paper. Slice thinly.
3. Put the mushrooms in a small casserole and pour over the lemon juice. Add the grated nutmeg and salt and pepper to taste. Mix well. Cover and microwave on HIGH for 4 minutes.
4. Turn the veal chops. Sprinkle with the Gruyère cheese. Add the sour cream (crème fraîche) to the mushrooms, mix well and pour over the meat. Cover and microwave on HIGH for 4 minutes. Serve very hot.

Côtes de veau aux champignons
Veal Chops with Mushrooms

▬▷	00.10	00.11	〰
	Serves 2		

American	Ingredients	Metric/Imperial
2	veal chops	2
	salt	
	pepper	
½ tsp	dried thyme	½ tsp
2 tbsp	Kirsch or cognac	1 tbsp
¾ lb	white button mushrooms	350 g/12 oz
2 tbsp	fresh lemon juice	1 tbsp
¼ tsp	grated nutmeg	¼ tsp
1 oz	grated Gruyère cheese	25 g/1 oz
2 tbsp	sour cream (crème fraîche)	1 tbsp

1. Season the veal chops with salt and pepper and sprinkle with the thyme. Put in a dish, bones toward the center. Add the Kirsch or cognac. Cover and microwave on HIGH for 3 minutes.

Couronne de veau forestière
Ring Mold (Mould) of Veal with Vegetables

▬▷	00.20	00.26	〰
	Serves 4		

American	Ingredients	Metric/Imperial
7 oz	finely sliced onions	200 g/7 oz
10½ oz	eggplant (aubergines)	300 g/10½ oz
½ tsp	dried thyme	½ tsp
5 oz	smoked streaky bacon, rind removed and cut into small pieces	150 g/5 oz
1¼ lb	veal, cut into pieces	500 g/1¼ lb
2	eggs	2
½ cup	sour cream (crème fraîche)	5 tbsp
2 tbsp	chopped fresh parsley	1 tbsp
	salt	
	pepper	
1	can cream of mushroom soup	1
3 tbsp	dry sherry	2 tbsp

1. Put the onions in a dish and microwave, uncovered, for 3 minutes on HIGH.
2. Rinse the eggplant (aubergines) under plenty of cold running water. Pat dry on kitchen paper and slice in rounds. Add the eggplant (aubergine) slices, the thyme and 3 tablespoons (2 tablespoons) of water to the onions. Cover and microwave on HIGH for 8 minutes.
3. Purée the bacon and veal pieces in a food processor until smooth. Leave in the food processor bowl.
4. Drain the onions and eggplant (aubergines) and add to the meat. Purée again, adding the eggs, half of the sour cream (crème fraîche) and the chopped parsley. Season with salt and pepper.
5. Pour the mixture into a ring mold (mould) 9 inches (23 cm) in diameter. Cover and microwave on HIGH for 12 minutes.
6. Cover the mold (mould) with a double layer of aluminum (aluminium) foil to keep warm.
7. Stir together the cream of mushroom soup, the sherry and the remaining sour cream (crème fraîche). Tip the ring mold (mould) gently towards you to obtain any liquid that may have formed and stir into the cream mixture. Reheat the sauce for 3 minutes on HIGH.
8. Invert the mold (mould) on to a dish, coat with a little sauce and pour the rest into a sauceboat. Serve with the sauce on the side.

Jarret de veau au pineau

Veal Shanks (Knuckle) in Brandy

◄ ▷   00.15   00.46   ▥
Serves 4

American	Ingredients	Metric/Imperial
2 tbsp	olive oil	1 tbsp
4	pieces veal shank (knuckle)	4
	salt	
	pepper	
3½ oz	finely chopped shallots	100 g/3½ oz
2	crushed garlic cloves	2
1	coarsely chopped tomato	1
1	grated small carrot	1
2	red bell peppers, rinsed, seeded and diced	2
1	green bell pepper, rinsed, seeded and diced	1
3 tbsp	brandy	2 tbsp
3 tbsp	wine vinegar	2 tbsp
½ tsp	crumbled fresh thyme	½ tsp
2 tbsp	fresh lemon juice	1 tbsp
1 tbsp	chopped fresh parsley	1 tbsp

1. Heat a browning dish in the microwave oven for 6-8 minutes, following the manufacturer's instructions.
2. When the browning dish is hot, pour in the oil and add the slices of veal. Leave to sizzle for 30 seconds, then turn. Season with salt and pepper. Add all the vegetables to the browning dish and stir. Add the brandy, vinegar and thyme. Cover and microwave on HIGH for 7 minutes.
3. Turn the veal shanks (knuckles), add more salt and pepper to taste, stir well and cover. Microwave on MEDIUM-HIGH for 20-25 minutes until the meat is tender.
4. When the meat is cooked, leave to stand for 5 minutes. Add the lemon juice, sprinkle with the chopped parsley and serve.

Rognon de veau au porto

Veal Kidney in Port

◄ ▷   00.10   00.12   ▥
Serves 2

American	Ingredients	Metric/Imperial
1	veal kidney, halved lengthwise	1
1 oz	diced, lean streaky bacon	25 g/1 oz
1 tbsp	fresh chopped tarragon	½ tbsp
	salt	
	pepper	
¼ cup	white port	3 tbsp
1	egg yolk	1
3 tbsp	sour cream (crème fraîche)	2 tbsp

1. Heat a browning dish in the microwave oven for 6-8 minutes on HIGH, following the manufacturer's instructions.
2. Cut out the tubes and the white fatty core from the kidney with a sharp pointed knife.
3. When the browning dish is hot, put in the bacon and the half-kidneys. After a few seconds, turn the kidneys and sprinkle with the tarragon and salt and pepper. Stir in half of the white port. Cover and microwave on HIGH for 3 minutes.
4. Mix together the egg yolk, sour cream (crème fraîche) and the remaining port.
5. Put each half-kidney on a dinner plate. Pour the egg and cream mixture into the browning dish, stirring well with a wooden spatula. Microwave for 1 further minute on HIGH.
6. Stir the contents of the dish vigorously, adding salt and pepper to taste. Pour over the kidneys and serve at once.

Veal shanks (knuckle) in brandy

Poultry and Game

Poulet rôti
Roast Chicken

American	Ingredients	Metric/Imperial
1 (2 lb)	ready-to-cook chicken	1 (1 kg/2 lb)
	salt	
	pepper	
1 tsp	dried tarragon	1 tsp
1 tsp	all-purpose (plain) flour	1 tsp
2 tbsp	sour cream (crème fraîche)	1 tbsp
2 tbsp	mustard	1 tbsp
3 tbsp	cognac	2 tbsp

1. Wipe the inside of the chicken with a damp cloth or kitchen paper. Season with salt and pepper and half of the dried tarragon. Truss the chicken.
2. Pour the flour into a medium size roasting bag (10 x 15 inches/25 x 38 cm) and shake the bag to distribute the flour evenly. Put the chicken in the bag, neck end first. Close the bag (not too tightly) with the special tag provided and put the chicken in a hollow dish, breast side down. Cut one of the top corners of the bag with kitchen scissors to allow the steam to escape.
3. Microwave, uncovered, on HIGH for 10 minutes.
4. Remove the bag from the oven and pour the cooking liquid into a bowl through the cut corner. Return the bag to the oven, with the chicken breast upward. Microwave, uncovered, on HIGH for a further 10 minutes.
5. Empty the bag again in the same manner, then remove the chicken, cover with a layer of aluminum (aluminium) foil and leave to stand for 10 minutes.
6. Skim the cooking liquid. Crumble over the remaining tarragon and add the sour cream (crème fraîche), mustard and cognac. Stir well and microwave for 1½ minutes on HIGH.
If desired, slide the chicken (breast side upward) under a conventional broiler (grill) for 5 minutes to crisp the skin.

Poulet aux crevettes
Chicken with Shrimp (Prawns)

American	Ingredients	Metric/Imperial
1	chicken, skin removed and cut into 8 pieces	1
1	can shrimp (prawn) bisque	1
3	tarragon sprigs	3
3½ oz	shelled shrimp (prawns)	100 g/3½ oz
2 tbsp	cognac	1 tbsp
4 tbsp	sour cream (crème fraîche)	2 tbsp
4	unshelled shrimp (prawns)	4

1. Put the chicken pieces in a casserole, with the smallest pieces in the center. Cover and microwave on HIGH for 5 minutes.
2. Mix the shrimp (prawn) bisque with ⅓ cup (4½ tablespoons) of water and pour over the chicken. Cover and microwave on HIGH for 10 minutes.

Chicken with shrimp (prawns)

3. Rinse the tarragon sprigs under plenty of cold running water. Pat dry on kitchen paper. Detach the leaves and chop finely.
4. Add the chopped tarragon, the shelled shrimp (prawns), cognac and sour cream (crème fraîche) to the casserole. Mix well. Cover and microwave on HIGH for 2 minutes.
5. Place the chicken on a serving dish. Stir the sauce well and pour over the chicken pieces. Garnish with the whole shrimp (prawns) and serve.

Sauce pour grillades
Wine Sauce for Broiled (Grilled) Meat

American	Ingredients	Metric/Imperial
¼ lb	finely chopped shallots	125 g/4 oz
⅔ cup	good quality red wine	150 ml/¼ pint
1 tsp	coarse grind black pepper	1 tsp
1 tsp	sugar	1 tsp
½ tsp	dried thyme	½ tsp
	salt	
3½ oz	butter	100 g/3½ oz

1. Put the onions in a bowl and microwave, uncovered, for 6 minutes on HIGH.
2. Pour the red wine over the shallots and add the black pepper, sugar, thyme and salt to taste. Microwave, uncovered, for a further 8 minutes on HIGH.
3. Cut the butter into tiny pieces and add gradually to the sauce, whisking continuously. Pour into a sauceboat and serve with any broiled (grilled) meat.

Poulet au citron et aux épices

Spicy Lemon Chicken

00.20   **00.21**
plus marinating time

American	Ingredients	Metric/Imperial
1	large chicken	1
½ cup	fresh lemon juice	6 tbsp
¼ cup	olive oil	3 tbsp
¼ tsp	Tabasco sauce	¼ tsp
¼ tsp	saffron threads	¼ tsp
½ tsp	ground cumin	½ tsp
1 tsp	cinnamon	1 tsp
2 tbsp	liquid honey	1 tbsp
1 tsp	dried mint	1 tsp
	salt	
	pepper	
10½ oz	onions	300 g/10½ oz
2 tbsp	butter	1 tbsp
1 oz	finely chopped preserved lemon zest (peel)	25 g/1 oz
2 tbsp	golden raisins (sultanas), rinsed	1 tbsp
⅓ cup	sour cream (crème fraîche)	4½ tbsp

Spicy lemon chicken

1. Cut the chicken into 8 pieces. Discard the wings and carcass. Remove the skin. Make a groove along each drumstick. Mix together the lemon juice, oil, Tabasco sauce, saffron, cumin, cinnamon, honey and mint. Add salt and pepper to taste. Put the chicken in this mixture, and turn until well coated. Cover and refrigerate for at least 6 hours.
2. Purée the onions in a food processor. Put the purée in a large dish and dot with butter. Cover and microwave on HIGH for 6 minutes.
3. Arrange the chicken pieces on top of the onion purée, with the small end of the drumsticks in the center. Pour over the marinade. Cover and microwave on HIGH for 7 minutes.
4. Turn the chicken pieces, cover and microwave for a further 7 minutes.
5. Add the lemon rind and raisins (sultanas) to the chicken. Coat with sour cream (crème fraîche) and reheat for 1 minute.
6. Arrange the chicken pieces in a heated serving dish, stir the sauce well and pour over. Serve at once.

Poulet au cerfeuil

Chicken with Chervil

00.10   **00.27**
Serves 4

American	Ingredients	Metric/Imperial
1 (2 lb)	chicken	1 (1 kg/2 lb)
2	finely chopped shallots	2
1 cup	dry white wine	250 ml/8 fl oz
1	small dried chili	1
1	chicken bouillon (stock) cube	1
	salt	
	pepper	
1	large bunch fresh chervil	1
½ tbsp	butter	½ tbsp
2 tbsp	all-purpose (plain) flour	1 tbsp
⅓ cup	sour cream (crème fraîche)	4½ tbsp
1	egg yolk	1

1. Cut the chicken into 4 pieces. Discard the skin, wings and backbone.
2. Put the shallots in a casserole. Cover and microwave on HIGH for 2 minutes. Add the white wine and chili. Crumble over the bouillon (stock) cube. Cover and microwave on HIGH for 2 minutes.
3. Add the chicken pieces to the casserole and season with salt and pepper. Cover and microwave on HIGH for 20 minutes, turning the meat midway through the cooking time.
4. Rinse the chervil under plenty of cold running water. Pat dry on kitchen paper. Chop finely.
5. When the chicken is tender, transfer to a heated serving dish with a slotted spoon.
6. Put the butter in a bowl and melt in the oven for 1 minute on HIGH. Add the flour and mix until smooth.
7. Remove the chili from the casserole and discard. Pour the cooking liquid over the butter and flour mixture, stir well and cook for 1 minute on HIGH. Whisk with a hand beater. Cook 1 further minute on HIGH and whisk again. Add the sour cream (crème fraîche) and egg yolk. Taste and adjust the seasoning.
8. Add the chopped chervil to the sauce. Coat the chicken with the sauce and serve at once.

Previous page: Stir-fried turkey breast with vegetables

Poulet à la flamande
Flemish Chicken

| | 00.20 | 00.32 | |
| Serves 4 | | | |

American	Ingredients	Metric/Imperial
10	fresh parsley sprigs	10
9 oz	coarsely chopped carrots	250 g/9 oz
5	leeks, white part only	5
1 (3¼ lb)	chicken	1 (1.5 kg/3¼ lb)
1	chicken bouillon (stock) cube	1
2	eggs	2
¼ cup	fresh lemon juice	3 tbsp
	salt	
	pepper	

1. For this dish, it is important to find flat, or Italian, parsley. Set the parsley leaves aside, cut off the base of the stalks and tie in a bunch.

2. Put the carrots and parsley stalks in a large casserole with 2 cups (450 ml/¾ pint) of water. Cover and microwave on HIGH for 6 minutes.

3. Remove the roots and outer leaves of the leeks and cut into quarters. Wash thoroughly under cold running water, then cut into strips widthwise. Add to the carrots and parsley. Cover and microwave on HIGH for 6 minutes.

4. Divide the chicken into 4 pieces: the two thighs plus the drumsticks and the breasts attached to the wings. Set the backbone and wing tips aside. Remove the skin.

5. Crumble the bouillon (stock) cube over the vegetables and mix well. Remove half of the vegetables with a slotted spatula, put the chicken pieces in the casserole, then replace the removed vegetables. Cover and microwave on HIGH for 20 minutes.

6. Break the eggs into a bowl and whisk with a fork. Add the lemon juice. Chop the parsley leaves.

7. When the chicken is ready, remove the parsley stalks from the casserole and pour in the egg and lemon mixture. Stir well and add the chopped parsley and salt and pepper to taste. Serve very hot.

Flemish chicken

Poulet de Birmanie

Burmese Chicken

	00.15	00.46	
	Serves 8		

American	Ingredients	Metric/Imperial
5 oz	desiccated coconut	150 g/5 oz
2 (2 lb)	chickens	2 (1 kg/2 lb)
6 tbsp	curry powder	4 tbsp
1 tsp	turmeric	1 tsp
2 tbsp	all-purpose (plain) flour	1 tbsp
	salt	
	pepper	
3	crushed garlic cloves	3
10½ oz	finely chopped onions	300 g/10½ oz
1 oz	butter	25 g/1 oz
½ cup	sour cream (crème fraîche)	5 tbsp

1. Put the desiccated coconut into a bowl with 2¼ cups (500 ml/18 fl oz) of water. Cover and microwave on HIGH for 10 minutes.

2. Remove the backbones of the 2 chickens with a kitchen cleaver or poultry scissors and cut each bird into 8 pieces.

3. Put the curry powder, turmeric and flour on a plate. Add salt and pepper and mix together. Roll each of the chicken portions in this mixture.

4. Put the garlic, onions and butter in a large casserole. Cover and microwave on HIGH for 5 minutes.

5. Force the desiccated coconut through muslin or a fine strainer (sieve) to extract as much milk as possible.

6. Put the chicken portions in the casserole and pour over the coconut milk. Add salt and pepper. Cover and microwave on HIGH for 20 minutes, stirring twice during the cooking period.

7. Add the sour cream (crème fraîche) to the casserole and stir thoroughly. Cover and microwave on HIGH for a further 10 minutes until the meat is tender.

8. Transfer the pieces of chicken with a slotted spoon to a heated serving platter. Pour the sauce into a deep bowl and leave to stand for 1 minute. Skim as much of the fat as possible from the surface. Coat the chicken portions with a little of the sauce and pour the rest into a sauceboat. Serve very hot.

Poulet Marengo

Chicken Marengo

	00.10	00.31	
	Serves 4		

American	Ingredients	Metric/Imperial
1 (2½ lb)	chicken	1 (1.2 kg/2½ lb)
3	large crushed garlic cloves	3
2	crumbled fresh thyme sprigs	2
	salt	
	pepper	
¼ cup	concentrated tomato juice	3 tbsp
¼ cup	white wine	3 tbsp
1¼ lb	white button mushrooms	500 g/1¼ lb
3 tbsp	fresh lemon juice	2 tbsp
½ tbsp	butter	½ tbsp
3 tbsp	sour cream (crème fraîche)	2 tbsp
1 tbsp	chopped fresh parsley	1 tbsp

1. Heat a browning dish in the microwave oven for 6-8 minutes, following the manufacturer's instructions.

2. Cut the chicken into 4 pieces, discarding the backbone, neck and wing tips.

3. Put the chicken pieces skin side down in the hot browning dish, with the thinnest pieces in the center of the dish. Sprinkle with garlic and crumbled thyme. Season with salt and pepper. Cover and microwave on HIGH for 6 minutes.

4. Mix the tomato juice with the white wine.

5. Turn the chicken pieces and pour over the tomato juice and white wine. Cover and microwave on HIGH for 6 further minutes. Remove from the oven and leave to stand.

6. Wipe the mushrooms with a damp cloth or kitchen paper. Slice thinly. Put in a casserole, add the lemon juice and butter and season with salt and pepper. Cover and cook on HIGH for 6 minutes.

7. Pour the mushrooms into the center of the browning dish and add the sour cream (crème fraîche). Cover and microwave on HIGH for 5 minutes.

8. Transfer the chicken and mushrooms to a heated serving dish, pour over the cooking liquid, sprinkle with chopped parsley and serve at once.

Poulet aux noix à la chinoise

Chinese Chicken with Walnuts

	00.05	00.10	
	Serves 2		

American	Ingredients	Metric/Imperial
1 tsp	cornstarch (cornflour)	1 tsp
2 tbsp	Chinese dark soy sauce	1 tbsp
1 tsp	superfine (caster) sugar	1 tsp
2 tbsp	fresh lemon juice	1 tbsp
⅓ tsp	five-spice powder	⅓ tsp
	pepper	
10½ oz	cooked chicken, cut into thin strips	300 g/10½ oz
2 tbsp	oil	1 tbsp
2 tbsp	white port	1 tbsp
8	coarsely chopped walnuts	8
1 tbsp	chopped chives	1 tbsp

1. Heat a browning dish in the oven for 6-8 minutes on HIGH, following the manufacturer's instructions.

2. Put the cornstarch (cornflour) in a dish and mix gradually with the soy sauce. Add the sugar, lemon juice, five-spice powder and pepper and mix well.

3. Add the chicken strips to the sauce and mix until the chicken is well coated.

4. Pour the oil into the hot browning dish and add the contents of the bowl carefully to avoid spattering the inside of the oven. Stir with a wooden fork until the mixture stops sizzling. Cover and microwave on HIGH for 2 minutes.

5. Divide the contents of the browning dish between two dinner plates. Pour the port into the browning dish and mix well with a spatula. Pour over the chicken. Sprinkle with chopped walnuts and chopped chives and serve at once.

Poulet aux fruits et au miel
Chicken with Fruit and Honey

	00.10	00.26	
	Serves 4		

American	Ingredients	Metric/Imperial
1	orange	1
2 oz	golden raisins (sultanas)	50 g/2 oz
2 tbsp	cognac	1 tbsp
1	finely chopped shallot	1
1	thinly sliced small apple	1
2 tbsp	butter	1 tbsp
1 (2 lb)	chicken	1 (1 kg/2 lb)
	salt	
	pepper	
3 tbsp	honey	2 tbsp
2 tbsp	fresh lemon juice	1 tbsp
½ tsp	cinnamon	½ tsp
½ tsp	ground cloves	½ tsp
2 oz	pine kernels	50 g/2 oz

1. Wash the orange very thoroughly under plenty of cold running water. Pat dry on kitchen paper. Remove the zest (peel) with a small sharp knife or vegetable peeler, taking care not to bring away any of the bitter white pith. Set the zest (peel) aside, cut the orange in half and squeeze. Rinse the raisins (sultanas) under plenty of cold running water. Pat dry on kitchen paper and put in a bowl, adding the orange juice and cognac. Cover and microwave on HIGH for 3 minutes.
2. Put the shallot and apple into a casserole with the butter. Cover and microwave on HIGH for 3 minutes.
3. Cut the chicken into 4 pieces, discarding the backbone and wing tips. Remove the skin. Season with salt and pepper.
4. Add the honey and lemon juice to the raisins (sultanas) and mix well. Put the chicken pieces in the casserole and sprinkle with the cinnamon and cloves. Add the orange zest (peel) and the honey mixture to the casserole. Cover and microwave on HIGH for 10 minutes.
5. Add the pine kernels. Stir well. Cover and microwave on HIGH for a further 10 minutes. Serve very hot.

Poulet à l'ail
Chicken with Garlic

	00.10	00.31	
	Serves 4		

American	Ingredients	Metric/Imperial
1 (2½ lb)	chicken plus its liver	1 (1.2 kg/2½ lb)
	salt	
	pepper	
½ tsp	mixed herbs	½ tsp
12	large garlic cloves	12
1 tsp	all-purpose (plain) flour	1 tsp
2 tbsp	wine vinegar	1 tbsp
3 tbsp	Malaga or dry sherry	2 tbsp

1. Wipe the inside of the chicken and season with salt and pepper and the mixed herbs. Remove the tough bases of the garlic but do not peel.

2. Put the flour in a medium size roasting bag (10 x 16 inches/25 x 38 cm) and shake the bag to distribute the flour evenly. Put the garlic cloves and the chicken in the roasting bag. Close the bag (not too tightly) with the tag provided. Snip one of the top corners of the bag to allow the steam to escape and put in a Pyrex dish, with the chicken breast-side down. Microwave, uncovered, on HIGH for 10 minutes.
3. Empty the roasting bag into a bowl through the snipped corner. Turn the chicken and microwave on HIGH for a further 10 minutes.
4. When the chicken is cooked, pour the liquid into a bowl. Remove the chicken from the bag and put under a conventional broiler (grill) for 5 minutes on each side to brown and crisp the skin. Skim the fat from the cooking liquid.
5. Remove the skins from the garlic cloves by pressing with finger and thumb at one end. Put in a food processor with the raw chicken liver and vinegar. Purée finely and pour into the bowl containing the cooking liquid. Add 3 tablespoons (2 tablespoons) of water and the Malaga or sherry. Stir well and heat in the microwave oven for 1 minute on HIGH. Stir again. Taste and adjust the seasoning. Pour into a sauceboat.
6. Put the chicken into a heated serving dish and serve very hot with the sauce on the side.

Poulet aux moules
Chicken with Mussels

	00.15	00.28	
	Serves 4		

American	Ingredients	Metric/Imperial
1	leek, white part only	1
2	finely chopped shallots	2
½ tbsp	butter	½ tbsp
⅓ cup	dry white wine	4½ tbsp
1 quart	mussels in their shells	1 litre /1¾ pints
1 (2 lb)	chicken	1 (1 kg/2 lb)
1	crushed garlic clove	1
	salt	
	pepper	
3 tbsp	dry Vermouth	2 tbsp
⅓ cup	sour cream (crème fraîche)	4½ tbsp
1 tbsp	chopped fresh parsley	1 tbsp

1. Remove the root and outer leaf of the leek and quarter lengthwise. Wash thoroughly, then cut into slices.
2. Put the shallots and leek in a casserole. Add the butter and white wine. Cover and microwave on HIGH for 5 minutes.
3. Scrub the mussels under plenty of cold running water, discarding any with broken shells. Put them in a dish with 3 tablespoons (2 tablespoons) of water. Cover and microwave on HIGH for 3 minutes, shaking the dish once or twice.
4. When all the mussels have opened, remove from their shells and set aside. Strain the cooking liquid.
5. Cut the chicken in 4 pieces, discarding the backbone. Remove the skin. Add the chicken to the shallots and leek. Add the garlic. Pour over the mussel cooking liquid and season lightly with salt and pepper. Cover and microwave on HIGH for 10 minutes.
6. Turn the chicken pieces. Add the Vermouth and sour cream (crème fraîche). Cook for a further 10 minutes on HIGH.
7. When the chicken is tender, transfer to a heated serving dish. Add the mussels and chopped parsley to the sauce, pour over the chicken and serve at once.

Chicken with garlic

Smoked chicken with shrimp (prawns)

Poulet fumé aux crevettes

Smoked Chicken with Shrimp (Prawns)

00.15   00.13

Serves 4

American	Ingredients	Metric/Imperial
9 oz	white button mushrooms	250 g/9 oz
1	celery stick, cut into thin strips	1
2 tbsp	fresh lemon juice	1 tbsp
¼ cup	canned lobster bisque	4 tbsp
⅓ cup	sour cream (crème fraîche)	4½ tbsp
¼ cup	dry sherry	3 tbsp
1 (2 lb)	smoked chicken	1 (1 kg/2 lb)
3½ oz	shelled shrimp (prawns)	100 g/3½ oz
	salt	
	pepper	
2	fresh tarragon sprigs	2
4	large unshelled shrimp (prawns)	4

1. Wipe the mushrooms with a damp cloth or kitchen paper. Slice thinly.
2. Put the celery and mushrooms in a casserole and add the lemon juice. Cover and microwave on HIGH for 5 minutes.
3. Mix the lobster bisque with ⅓ cup (4½ tablespoons) of water, the sour cream (crème fraîche) and sherry. Cut the chicken into pieces, remove the skin and discard the backbone and wing tips.
4. Pour the lobster and cream mixture into the casserole and mix well. Add the chicken pieces, placing the smallest in the center of the casserole. Cover and microwave on HIGH for 6 minutes.
5. Add the shelled shrimp (prawns) and mix again. Taste and adjust the seasoning. Cover and microwave on HIGH for 2 minutes.
6. Rinse the tarragon under plenty of cold running water. Pat dry on kitchen paper. Remove the leaves and chop finely. Sprinkle the contents of the casserole with chopped tarragon, garnish with whole shrimp (prawns) and serve.

Poulet fumé aux pêches
Smoked Chicken with Peaches

◢	00.15	00.10	〰
	Serves 4		

American	Ingredients	Metric/Imperial
1	smoked chicken	1
4	large fresh peaches	4
1 tsp	coarse grind black pepper	1 tsp
3 tbsp	cognac	2 tbsp
1 tsp	cornstarch (cornflour)	1 tsp
2 tbsp	wine vinegar	1 tbsp
2 tbsp	butter	1 tbsp
	salt	
	pepper	

1. Cut the smoked chicken into four, discarding the wings, carcass, skin and as much fat as possible. Put the pieces in a dish with the smallest in the center. Cover and microwave on HIGH for 6 minutes.
2. Blanch the peaches, cut in half, remove the pits (stones) and peel.
3. Transfer the chicken to a serving dish and cover with aluminum (aluminium) foil to keep warm.
4. Put the peaches in the dish with the chicken liquid and sprinkle with black pepper. Add the cognac and cook on HIGH for 3 minutes.
5. Arrange the peaches in the dish around the chicken. Mix the cornstarch (cornflour) and vinegar to a smooth paste in a bowl. Add the cooking liquid from the chicken and peaches and heat for 1 minute on HIGH. Stir well. Add the butter. Taste and adjust the seasoning. Coat the chicken and peaches with the sauce and serve at once.
If fresh peaches are not available, simply use canned peaches in light syrup.
Heat for 1 minute on HIGH and add 1 or 2 tablespoons of the syrup to the chicken liquid.

Poulet au vinaigre
Chicken in Tarragon Vinegar

◢	00.10	00.24	〰
	Serves 4		

American	Ingredients	Metric/Imperial
4	chicken legs, skin removed	4
	salt	
	pepper	
2 tbsp	all-purpose (plain) flour	1 tbsp
2	crushed garlic cloves	2
2 tbsp	tarragon vinegar	1 tbsp
⅓ cup	sour cream (crème fraîche)	4½ tbsp
1 tsp	chopped fresh tarragon	1 tsp

1. Heat a browning dish in the microwave oven for 6-8 minutes, following the manufacturer's instructions.
2. Season the chicken legs with salt and pepper and sprinkle with flour.

3. Put the chicken pieces in the hot browning dish. Leave to sizzle for 30 seconds then turn and place the thin end of the drumsticks toward the center of the dish. Add the garlic and vinegar. Cover and microwave on HIGH for 10 minutes.
4. Add the sour cream (crème fraîche) and chopped tarragon. Mix well. Turn the pieces of chicken. Cover and microwave on HIGH for 5 further minutes. Serve very hot.

Blanquette de poulet au roquefort
Chicken in Roquefort Sauce

◢	00.10	00.22	〰
	Serves 5		

American	Ingredients	Metric/Imperial
1¾ lb	chicken scaloppine (escalopes), cut into thin strips	700 g/1¾ lb
	salt	
	pepper	
¼ cup	fresh lemon juice	3 tbsp
3	finely chopped shallots	3
2 oz	butter	50 g/2 oz
1½ oz	all-purpose (plain) flour	40 g/1½ oz
2¼ cups	milk	500 ml/18 fl oz
14 oz	small white button mushrooms	400 g/14 oz
1	bunch fresh chives	1
2 oz	Roquefort cheese	50 g/2 oz
3 tbsp	white port	2 tbsp
3 tbsp	sour cream (crème fraîche)	2 tbsp
½ tsp	grated nutmeg	½ tsp

1. Put the chicken strips in a bowl. Add salt and pepper and the lemon juice and mix well.
2. Put the shallots into a casserole 7 inch (18 cm) in diameter and microwave, uncovered, on HIGH for 2 minutes. Add the butter and melt for 1 minute on HIGH. Sprinkle over the flour and stir well. Add the milk and stir until smooth. Microwave for 2 minutes on HIGH. Stir. Microwave for a further 5 minutes on HIGH, stirring after every minute.
3. Add the chicken pieces and lemon juice to the casserole. Stir to ensure the meat is well coated with the sauce. Cover and microwave on HIGH for 10 minutes.
4. Wipe the mushrooms with a damp cloth or kitchen paper. Rinse the chives under plenty of cold running water. Pat dry on kitchen paper and snip with kitchen scissors. Crumble the Roquefort and mix with the port.
5. When the chicken is cooked, add the Roquefort, sour cream (crème fraîche), mushrooms and grated nutmeg. Mix thoroughly. Return to the oven and microwave, uncovered, for 2 minutes on HIGH.
6. Sprinkle with the chives, taste and adjust the seasoning. Serve very hot in the same dish.

Microwave hint: All poultry benefits from being glazed before cooking by microwave. The simplest glaze is 1 teaspoon Worcestershire sauce mixed with 1 oz (25 g) of melted butter. Brush all over the bird before cooking.

Poulet à la châtelaine
Chicken in Port Wine

00.10   **00.07**
Serves 4

American	Ingredients	Metric/Imperial
1¾ lb	chicken breast meat, cut into ½ in (1.25 cm) strips	700 g/1¾ lb
	salt	
	pepper	
¼ cup	white port	3 tbsp
3½ oz	frozen artichoke purée	100 g/3½ oz
¼ cup	sour cream (crème fraîche)	3 tbsp
1	egg yolk	1
1 tbsp	chopped fresh parsley	1 tbsp

1. Season the chicken strips with salt and pepper. Put in a small casserole with the port. Cover and microwave on HIGH for 4 minutes.
2. Transfer the chicken with a slotted spatula to a plate and set aside. Keep hot.
3. Put the artichoke purée in the casserole with the cooking liquid from the chicken. Cover and microwave on HIGH for 2 minutes.
4. Mix the sour cream (crème fraîche) with the egg yolk and stir into the artichoke purée. Add with salt and pepper to taste. Return the chicken to the casserole and reheat for 1 minute on HIGH. Sprinkle with chopped parsley and serve hot.

Fricassée d'endives aux foies de volaille
Fricassée of Belgian Endive (Chicory) and Chicken Livers

00.10   **00.17**
Serves 4

American	Ingredients	Metric/Imperial
1¾ lb	Belgian endive (chicory)	700 g/1¾ lb
3½ oz	smoked streaky bacon, rind removed and cut into thin strips	100 g/3½ oz
	salt	
	pepper	
14 oz	chicken livers	400 g/14 oz
2 tbsp	butter	1 tbsp
3 tbsp	white port	2 tbsp
2 tbsp	sour cream (crème fraîche)	1 tbsp
3 tsp	Dijon mustard	3 tsp
1 tbsp	chopped fresh parsley	1 tbsp

1. Cut off the base of the Belgian endive (chicory) and remove the outer leaves. Cut first in half and then into ½ inch (1.25 cm) strips.
2. Put the bacon strips into a casserole and microwave, uncovered, for 3 minutes on HIGH. Add the Belgian endive (chicory) and season with salt and pepper. Cover and microwave on HIGH for 10 minutes, stirring midway through the cooking time.

3. Rinse the chicken livers under plenty of cold running water. Pat dry on kitchen paper. Cut each liver into 2 or 3 pieces and put in a small casserole with the butter. Cover and microwave on HIGH for 4 minutes. Season with salt and pepper and transfer to the center of a warmed serving dish.
4. Add the port, sour cream (crème fraîche) and mustard to the Belgian endive (chicory). Mix well. Arrange the vegetables around the chicken livers and sprinkle with chopped parsley. Serve at once.

Stewed Chicken with Basil

00.10   **00.35**
Serves 4

American	Ingredients	Metric/Imperial
¼ cup	oil	4 tbsp
1¾ lb	boneless, skinless chicken breasts, cut into 1 in (2.5 cm) cubes	750 g/1¾ lb
	salt	
	pepper	
2	chopped onions	2
½ cup	dry white wine	6 tbsp
2 tsp	lime or lemon juice	2 tsp
1	chicken bouillon (stock) cube	1
2 tsp	cornstarch (cornflour)	2 tsp
2	egg yolks	2
1 cup	whipping cream	250 ml/8 fl oz
4 tbsp	chopped basil	3 tbsp
1 tsp	Worcestershire sauce	1 tsp

1. Heat a browning dish for 6-8 minutes, following the manufacturer's instructions. Pour in the oil and tilt the dish to make sure the base is evenly covered. Add the chicken cubes and a little salt and pepper. Heat on HIGH for 2 minutes. Turn the chicken and cook for another 2 minutes.
2. Put the onions on top of the chicken and cook for 3 minutes.
3. Heat the wine and fruit juice for 1 minute on HIGH and crumble in the bouillon (stock) cube. Mix well to dissolve. Pour over the chicken, cover the dish and cook for 6 minutes on HIGH. Leave to stand for 3 minutes.
4. Mix the cornstarch (cornflour) to a paste with a little cold water. Spoon a little juice from the chicken into the cornflour (cornstarch) and mix well. Gradually add the egg yolks, cream, basil, Worcestershire sauce, salt and pepper and mix well.
5. Stir this mixture into the chicken and mix until evenly distributed. Microwave on MEDIUM for 10 minutes. Serve hot.

Poulet aux oignons
Chicken with Onions

	00.15	00.31	
	Serves 4		

American	Ingredients	Metric/Imperial
1½ oz	butter	40 g/1½ oz
14 oz	finely sliced onions	400 g/14 oz
4	chicken thighs, halved	4
	salt	
	pepper	
4 tbsp	apricot preserve	3 tbsp
2 tbsp	vinegar	1 tbsp
1	crushed garlic clove	1
1 tsp	cinnamon	1 tsp
¼ tsp	saffron threads	¼ tsp

1. Put half of the butter in a dish and add the onions. Cover and microwave on HIGH for 5 minutes.

2. Heat a browning dish in the oven for 6 minutes, following the manufacturer's instructions. Put in the remaining butter and add the chicken pieces, skin side down. Season with salt and pepper. Microwave for 3 minutes on HIGH. Turn the pieces of chicken, making sure the thickest parts are at the outside of the dish.

3. Mix the apricot preserve with the vinegar. Add the garlic, cinnamon and saffron. Season with salt and pepper. Mix with the onions and spread the mixture over the chicken pieces. Add 3 tablespoons (2 tablespoons) of water. Cover and microwave on HIGH for 12 minutes.

4. Leave to stand for 5 minutes and serve at once.

Roast Ginger Chicken

	00.15	00.45	
	Serves 4		

American	Ingredients	Metric/Imperial
1	tart apple	1
1	piece ginger root (1 in/2.5 cm)	1
5 oz	cooked long grain rice	150 g/5 oz
⅔ cup	natural yogurt	150 ml/¼ pint
1½ oz	softened butter	40 g/1½ oz
	salt	
	pepper	
3 lb	chicken	1.5 kg/3 lb
	chicken seasoning	

1. Peel, core and grate the apple. Peel and finely chop or grate the ginger. Add to the apple with the rice, yogurt, half of the butter and salt and pepper. Mix well and use to stuff the chicken.

2. Put the chicken on a meat roasting rack. Spread with the remaining butter and sprinkle with chicken seasoning. Cook on MEDIUM for 30 minutes.

3. Wrap in aluminum (aluminium) foil, shiny side inward. Leave to stand for 15 minutes before serving.

Chicken with onions

Turkey scaloppine (escalopes) with vegetables

Escalopes de dinde printanières

Turkey Scaloppine (Escalopes) with Vegetables

00.15   **00.25**

Serves 2

American	Ingredients	Metric/Imperial
2	frozen artichoke hearts	2
3 tbsp	fresh lemon juice	2 tbsp
2	leeks, white part only, halved lengthwise	2
2	carrots, cut into strips	2
2 tbsp	butter	1 tbsp
	salt	
	pepper	
2	turkey scaloppine (escalopes)	2
3 tbsp	sour cream (crème fraîche)	2 tbsp
1 tsp	chopped parsley	1 tsp

1. Put the frozen artichoke hearts into a small dish and pour over the lemon juice. Cover and microwave on HIGH for 6 minutes.
2. Wash the leeks thoroughly and cut into strips. Put the carrots and leeks into a dish with half of the butter and 3 (2) tablespoons of water. Season with salt and pepper. Cover and microwave on HIGH for 10 minutes.
3. Heat a browning dish in the oven for 6 minutes, following the manufacturer's instructions. Put the remaining butter in the dish and add the scaloppine (escalopes). Turn after several seconds, season with salt and pepper, cover and microwave for 2 minutes on HIGH.
4. Purée the artichoke hearts in a food processor and put in a bowl. Stir in the sour cream (crème fraîche), parsley and salt and pepper to taste. Heat for 1 minute on HIGH.
5. Put the scaloppine (escalopes) in a heated serving dish. Arrange the vegetables around the meat, coat with the artichoke sauce and serve at once.

Escalopes de dinde normandes

Normandy Style Turkey Scaloppine (Escalopes)

00.05   **00.11**

Serves 4

American	Ingredients	Metric/Imperial
1	thinly sliced large onion	1
4	turkey scaloppine (escalopes)	4
	salt	
	pepper	
2	Granny Smith apples, peeled, cored and quartered	2
⅓ cup	dry cider	4½ tbsp
1 tsp	coarse grind green pepper	1 tsp
3 tbsp	Calvados (apple brandy)	2 tbsp
¼ cup	sour cream (crème fraîche)	3 tbsp

1. Put the onion in a dish and microwave, uncovered, for 3 minutes on HIGH.
2. Season both sides of the turkey scaloppine (escalopes) with salt and pepper. Put on top of the onion and surround with the apple quarters. Add more salt and pepper if needed. Pour the cider into the dish and sprinkle over the ground green pepper. Cover and microwave on HIGH for 4-5 minutes, depending on the thickness of the meat.
3. Transfer the apples and turkey to a heat-proof serving dish. Put the Calvados (apple brandy) in a cup and heat in the microwave oven for 1 minute on HIGH. Set alight and pour over the meat.
4. Add the sour cream (crème fraîche) to the cooking liquid from the turkey. Stir well and cook on HIGH for 2 minutes. Taste and adjust the seasoning. Pour over the turkey and apples and serve very hot.

Normandy style turkey scaloppine (escalopes)

Émincé de dinde aux marrons

Oriental Sliced Turkey with Chestnuts

00.10 — Serves 4   **00.15**

American	Ingredients	Metric/Imperial
2 tbsp	cornstarch (cornflour)	1 tbsp
3 tbsp	dark soy sauce	2 tbsp
2 tbsp	sugar	1 tbsp
2 tbsp	vinegar	1 tbsp
3 tbsp	dry sherry	2 tbsp
½ tsp	five-spice powder	½ tsp
	pepper	
1½ lb	turkey scaloppine (escalopes), cut into very thin strips	600 g/1½ lb
3 tbsp	oil	2 tbsp
2	celery sticks, washed and cut into very thin strips	2
1	can chestnuts in brine	1
2	finely chopped scallions (spring onions)	2

1. Heat a browning dish in the microwave oven for 6-8 minutes, following the manufacturer's instructions.
2. Mix the cornstarch (cornflour) with the soy sauce in a small bowl. Add the sugar, vinegar, sherry, five-spice powder and pepper. Mix well.
3. Add the turkey strips, stirring carefully to make sure they are well coated.

4. Pour the oil into the hot browning dish, add the celery strips and then the turkey mixture, taking care to avoid splashing. Stir with a wooden fork until the mixture stops sizzling. Cover and microwave on HIGH for 4 minutes.
5. Drain and rinse the chestnuts and add to the browning dish. Mix well. Cover and microwave on HIGH for 3 minutes.
6. Add the chopped scallions (spring onions) to the dish, mix and serve at once.

Dinde à l'effilochée de navets

Turkey with Baby Turnips

00.10 — Serves 4   **00.14**

American	Ingredients	Metric/Imperial
1¾ lb	baby turnips	750 g/1¾ lb
	salt	
	pepper	
2 tbsp	superfine (caster) sugar	1 tbsp
3 tbsp	white wine	2 tbsp
1½ lb	turkey scaloppine (escalopes), cut into thin strips	600 g/1½ lb
½ tsp	grated nutmeg	½ tsp
½ tsp	dried thyme	½ tsp
½ tbsp	butter	½ tbsp
2 tsp	mild mustard	2 tsp
3 tbsp	sour cream (crème fraîche)	2 tbsp
1 tsp	cornstarch (cornflour)	1 tsp
3 tbsp	white port	2 tbsp

Oriental sliced turkey with chestnuts

1. Peel the baby turnips and rinse under plenty of cold running water. Pat dry on kitchen paper. Grate in a food processor. Put in a large dish, add salt and pepper and the sugar and mix well. Add the white wine. Cover and microwave on HIGH for 7 minutes.

2. Season the turkey strips with salt and pepper, add the grated nutmeg and dried thyme and mix well.

3. When the turnips are cooked, put the butter into a dish just large enough to contain the meat. Melt the butter in the oven for 1 minute on HIGH. Roll the strips of meat in the butter, then arrange side by side close together in the dish. Cover and microwave on HIGH for 4 minutes.

4. Mix the mustard with the sour cream (crème fraîche) in a bowl. Remove the turnips with a slotted spoon and put in a serving dish. Add the cooking liquid from the turnips to the mustard and sour cream (crème fraîche) mixture. Heat for 1 minute on HIGH.

5. Mix the cornstarch (cornflour) with the port. Using a slotted spoon, put the meat strips on top of the turnips and add the cooking liquid to the sauce with the cornstarch (cornflour) and port. Mix well. Reheat for 1 minute on HIGH. Mix, taste and adjust the seasoning. Pour over the turkey and turnips and serve at once.

Volaille sautée à la chinoise

Stir-Fried Turkey Breast with Vegetables

00.15   00.25
Serves 4

American	Ingredients	Metric/Imperial
1	crushed garlic clove	1
½ tsp	five-spice powder	½ tsp
3 tbsp	dark soy sauce	2 tbsp
1 tsp	sugar	1 tsp
1 tsp	vinegar	1 tsp
1½ lb	turkey breast, cut into 8 equal pieces	600 g/1½ lb
¼ lb	white button mushrooms	125 g/4 oz
2	red bell peppers, rinsed, seeded and diced	2
1	finely chopped large onion	1
¼ cup	oil	3 tbsp
2	celery sticks, cut into thin strips	2
3 tbsp	sherry	2 tbsp
	salt	
	pepper	
	chopped parsley	

1. Mix together the garlic, five-spice powder, soy sauce, sugar and vinegar. Pour over the turkey pieces and leave to marinate.

2. Wipe the mushrooms with a damp cloth or kitchen paper and slice thinly.

3. Put the peppers and onions in a dish and pour over half the oil. Cover and microwave on HIGH for 10 minutes. Add the celery, mushrooms and sherry. Stir well and season with salt and pepper. Cover and microwave on HIGH for 5 minutes.

4. Remove the turkey breast from the marinade and pat dry on kitchen paper. Heat a browning dish in the oven for 6 minutes, following the manufacturer's instructions. Pour in the remaining oil and add the turkey breast, turning after a few seconds. Cover and microwave on HIGH for 4 minutes.

5. Add the vegetables and turkey marinade to the browning dish and stir well. Pour into a serving dish and sprinkle with chopped parsley. Serve at once.

Cuisse de dinde à la bière

Turkey Legs with Beer

00.10   00.29
Serves 4

American	Ingredients	Metric/Imperial
2	celery sticks	2
3½ oz	smoked streaky bacon, rind removed and diced	100 g/3½ oz
1	coarsely chopped carrot	1
1	thinly sliced large onion	1
⅔ cup	lager	150 ml/¼ pint
3 tbsp	soft dark brown sugar	2 tbsp
2	crushed garlic cloves	2
1	fresh thyme sprig	1
1	bay leaf	1
1 (2 lb)	turkey leg, cut in half	1 (1 kg/2 lb)
½ tsp	five-spice powder	½ tsp
	salt	
	pepper	
2 tbsp	all-purpose (plain) flour	1 tbsp

1. Wash the celery, remove the leaves and set aside. Chop the stalks.

2. Put the bacon, carrot, onion and celery into a deep casserole and add 3 tablespoons (2 tablespoons) of water. Cover and microwave on HIGH for 6 minutes.

3. Pour the lager into the casserole and add the brown sugar, garlic, thyme and bay leaf. Cover and microwave on HIGH for 3 minutes.

4. Season the turkey pieces with five-spice powder and salt and pepper.

5. Sprinkle the flour over the contents of the casserole, mix and add salt and pepper to taste. Add the turkey pieces to the casserole and arrange the celery leaves on top. Cover and microwave on HIGH for 10 minutes.

6. Turn the turkey pieces. Cover and microwave on HIGH for a further 10 minutes.

7. When the meat is tender, discard the thyme, bay leaf and celery leaves and serve at once.

Magrets de canard aux griottes

Duck Breasts
with Cherries

	00.05	00.17	
	Serves 4		

American	Ingredients	Metric/Imperial
1	can pitted (stoned) cherries	1
3 tbsp	fresh orange juice	2 tbsp
2 tbsp	wine vinegar	1 tbsp
½ tsp	cinnamon	½ tsp
½ tsp	ground cloves	½ tsp
	salt	
	pepper	
2	duck breasts	2
2	finely chopped shallots	2
1 tsp	cornstarch (cornflour)	1 tsp
3 tbsp	port	2 tbsp

1. Heat a browning dish in the microwave oven for 6-8 minutes, following the manufacturer's instructions.
2. Mix together the cherries, orange juice, vinegar, cinnamon, cloves and salt and pepper.
3. When the browning dish is hot, put in the duck breasts, skin side down. Add the shallots. Microwave, uncovered, on HIGH for 2 minutes. Turn the duck breasts and cook for a further 2-3 minutes, according to your preference.
4. Transfer the duck breasts to a board ready for slicing. Pour the cherry mixture into the browning dish, stir well and heat for 1½ minutes on HIGH. Mix the cornstarch (cornflour) and the port to a smooth paste and add to the browning dish. Stir and heat for 2 minutes on HIGH. Stir again.
5. Slice the duck breasts thinly and arrange in a heated serving dish. Season with salt and pepper. Add the carving liquid to the cherries and stir. Pour into the dish containing the duck breast slices and serve.

Canard aux figues sèches

Duck with Dried Figs

	00.10	00.18	
	Serves 4		

American	Ingredients	Metric/Imperial
1	large orange	1
⅓ cup	port	4½ tbsp
9 oz	dried figs	250 g/9 oz
2	duck breasts, skin and fat removed	2
1 tsp	coarse grind black pepper	1 tsp
	salt	
3 tbsp	sour cream (crème fraîche)	2 tbsp
2 tbsp	mild mustard	1 tbsp

1. Wash the orange thoroughly under plenty of cold running water. Pat dry on kitchen paper. Remove the zest (peel) with a sharp knife or vegetable peeler, taking care not to bring away any of the bitter white flesh. Cut the zest (peel) into julienne (matchstick) strips. Cut the orange in half and squeeze to obtain about ⅓ cup (4½ tablespoons) of juice. Pour the juice into a bowl and add the zest (peel), port and figs. Cover and microwave on HIGH for 7 minutes.

2. Sprinkle both sides of each duck breast with black pepper and arrange side by side in an oval dish.
3. Drain the figs and pour their cooking liquid over the duck. Cover and microwave on HIGH for 9 minutes, turning the breast fillets midway through the cooking time.
4. Season the duck with salt and slice thinly. Put the slices in a dish and surround with the figs. Mix the sour cream (crème fraîche) and mustard in a bowl and add the cooking liquid from the duck. Mix well and microwave for 2 minutes on HIGH.
5. Coat the duck and figs with a little of the sauce, pour the rest into a sauceboat and serve immediately.

Magret de canard aux abricots

Duck Breast Slices
with Apricots

	00.10	00.12	
	Serves 2		

American	Ingredients	Metric/Imperial
¾ lb	breast of duck in one piece	350 g/12 oz
	salt	
	pepper	
2 tbsp	mango chutney	1 tbsp
½	can apricot halves, drained	½
2 tbsp	vinegar	1 tbsp
1 tbsp	butter	½ tbsp
2 tbsp	white port	1 tbsp

1. Heat a browning dish in the microwave oven for 6-8 minutes on HIGH, following the manufacturer's instructions.
2. Put the duck breast into the hot dish, skin side down. Season the top side of the meat with salt and pepper and spread it with half of the chutney.
3. When the duck has stopped sizzling, discard the fat, return to the browning dish, skin side up, and spread this side with the remaining chutney. Put the browning dish into the oven and cook on HIGH for 3 minutes.
4. Add the apricots and the vinegar to the dish. Season with salt and pepper. Return to the oven and cook for 1 further minute on HIGH.
5. Transfer the duck breast to a dish and carve into thick slices. Pour the carving liquid into the browning dish and add the butter and port. Stir well.
6. Arrange the apricots around the meat, pour over the cooking liquid and serve at once.

Duck breast slices with apricots

Canard, sauce barbecue

Duck in Barbecue Sauce

	00.05	00.14	
	Serves 4		

American	Ingredients	Metric/Imperial
1	crushed garlic clove	1
1	finely chopped shallot	1
2 tbsp	oil	1 tbsp
½ cup	tomato ketchup	6 tbsp
2 tbsp	vinegar	1 tbsp
2 tbsp	sugar	1 tbsp
2 tbsp	Worcester sauce	1 tbsp
2 tbsp	mild mustard	1 tbsp
1 tsp	cornstarch (cornflour)	1 tsp
2 tbsp	cognac	1 tbsp
	salt	
	pepper	
2	duck breasts, skin and fat removed	2

1. Put the garlic and shallots in a casserole with the oil and microwave, uncovered, for 1 minute on HIGH.
2. Add the tomato ketchup, vinegar, sugar, Worcester sauce, mustard and ¼ cup (4 tablespoons) of water. Mix well. Microwave, uncovered, on HIGH for 4 minutes.
3. Mix the cornstarch (cornflour) with the cognac to a smooth paste. Add to the sauce, mix and cook on HIGH for 1 further minute. Mix again and leave to cool.
4. Sprinkle the base of an oval dish with salt and pepper and put in the duck breasts, with the thinnest part of the meat toward the center of the dish. Pour over the sauce. Cover and microwave on HIGH for 8 minutes.
5. Cut each duck breast into 4 or 5 slices and serve very hot.

Duck with Oranges

	00.10	00.47	
	Serves 4		

American	Ingredients	Metric/Imperial
4 lb	duck	1.75 kg/4 lb
1 oz	butter	25 g/1 oz
	sweet paprika	
2 tbsp	redcurrant jelly	1 tbsp
1¼ cups	chicken bouillon (stock)	300 ml/½ pint
4	oranges	4
2 tsp	cornstarch (cornflour)	2 tsp
⅔ cup	red wine	150 ml/¼ pint

1. Prick the duck all over with a fork. Brush with butter and sprinkle with paprika. Put on a micro-proof meat roasting rack and cook on MEDIUM for 28 minutes. Wrap in aluminum (aluminium) foil, matt side outward, and leave to stand for 15 minutes.
2. To make the sauce, mix 2 tablespoons (1 tablespoon) of the duck cooking liquid with the redcurrant jelly and bouillon (stock). Heat on HIGH for 2 minutes.

3. Grate the zest (peel) and squeeze the juice from 2 oranges and add to the sauce. Mix the cornstarch (cornflour) with the wine to a smooth paste and stir into the sauce. Heat on HIGH for 1½-2 minutes, stirring once. The sauce should have thickened slightly; if not, heat for a further ½-1 minute.
4. Carve the duck into portions and arrange on a warm serving plate. Spoon a little of the sauce over the duck. Peel and segment the remaining oranges and use to garnish the duck. Serve the remaining sauce separately in a sauceboat.

Pintade aux groseilles

Guinea Fowl with Redcurrants

	00.15	00.30	
	Serves 4		

American	Ingredients	Metric/Imperial
2 oz	finely chopped shallots	50 g/2 oz
1 tbsp	butter	½ tbsp
1 (2 lb)	guinea fowl	1 (1 kg/2 lb)
½ tsp	powdered thyme	½ tsp
¼ tsp	five-spice powder	¼ tsp
	salt	
	pepper	
2 tbsp	oil	1 tbsp
7 oz	frozen redcurrants	200 g/7 oz
3 tbsp	Kirsch brandy	2 tbsp
3 tbsp	sour cream (crème fraîche)	2 tbsp
1 tsp	sugar	1 tsp

1. Put the shallots in a bowl with the butter. Microwave, uncovered, on HIGH for 3 minutes.
2. Heat a browning dish in the microwave oven for 6-8 minutes, following the manufacturer's instructions.
3. Cut the guinea fowl in half and remove the backbone and wing tips. Cut each half into two pieces. Brush the meat with thyme and five-spice powder and season with salt and pepper.
4. Pour the oil into the hot browning dish and tilt the dish (protecting yourself with an oven glove) until the oil is evenly distributed. Add the pieces of guinea fowl, skin side down, and the shallots. Cover and microwave on HIGH for 15 minutes.
5. Put the frozen redcurrants into a bowl with the Kirsch brandy, sour cream (crème fraîche), sugar and a little salt and pepper. Defrost at room temperature.
6. Pour the redcurrant mixture into the browning dish and cook for a further 4 minutes on HIGH.
7. Arrange the pieces of guinea fowl on a heated serving dish, skin side up. Mix the sauce thoroughly, pour over the meat and serve.

Microwave hint: Make up a thickened glaze for poultry with dry flesh, such as poussins and guinea fowl. Try mixing equal quantities of soy sauce and white wine with a little vegetable oil. For each ⅔ cup (150 ml/¼ pint) of sauce, stir in 1 teaspoon of cornstarch (cornflour) until blended. Cook on HIGH for 1½ minutes. Stir again before brushing the poultry with the glaze before cooking.

Pintade farcie
Stuffed Guinea Fowl

00.15 Serves 4 **00.28**

American	Ingredients	Metric/Imperial
2	chopped shallots	2
2 oz	finely diced smoked streaky bacon	50 g/2 oz
1 tbsp	butter	½ tbsp
¼ lb	frozen chestnut purée	125 g/4 oz
1	egg, separated	1
2 tbsp	breadcrumbs	1 tbsp
½ tsp	mixed herbs	½ tsp
¼ cup	white port	3 tbsp
	salt	
	pepper	
1 (2 lb)	guinea fowl	1 (1 kg/2 lb)
1 tsp	all-purpose (plain) flour	1 tsp
3 tbsp	sour cream (crème fraîche)	2 tbsp

1. Put the shallots and bacon in a bowl with the butter and microwave, uncovered, on HIGH for 3 minutes.
2. Put the chestnut purée in a bowl and defrost in the microwave oven on HIGH for 3 minutes.
3. Add the shallots, bacon, egg white, breadcrumbs, half the mixed herbs, half the port and salt and pepper to the chestnut purée. Mix thoroughly.
4. Stuff the guinea fowl with this mixture. Truss.
5. Put the flour in a medium size roasting bag (10 x 15 inches/25 x 38 cm). Shake the bag to distribute the flour evenly and put in the guinea fowl. Close the bag with the tag provided and put in a deep dish with the bird breast side down. Snip a corner of the roasting bag to allow the steam to escape. Microwave for 8 minutes on HIGH.
6. Pour the cooking liquid out of the bag into a bowl through the snipped corner and return the bag to the oven with the bird breast side up. Cook for a further 8 minutes on HIGH.
7. Pour the cooking liquid into the bowl. Remove the guinea fowl from the bag and put in a dish. Slide under a conventional broiler (grill) and brown for 5 minutes.
8. Add the remaining port and mixed herbs, the sour cream (crème fraîche), egg yolk and salt and pepper to the cooking liquid in the bowl. Microwave, uncovered, on HIGH for 1 minute. Stir well and pour into a sauceboat.
9. Carve the guinea fowl and the stuffing. Arrange on a warmed dish and serve with the sauce on the side.

Stuffed guinea fowl

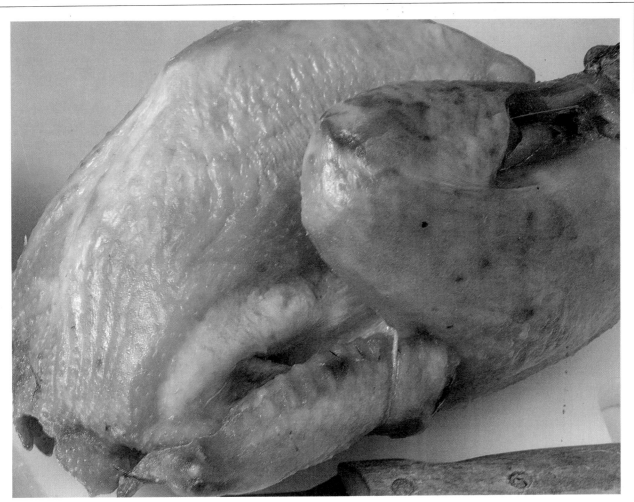

Pintade aux champignons séchés

Guinea Fowl with Dried Mushrooms

00.10 **00.20**
Serves 4

American	Ingredients	Metric/Imperial
1½ oz	dried mushrooms (cèpes)	40 g/1½ oz
3½ oz	finely chopped shallots	100 g/3½ oz
2 tbsp	butter	1 tbsp
1	guinea fowl with its liver	1
3 tbsp	all-purpose (plain) flour	1½ tbsp
½ tsp	dried thyme	½ tsp
	salt	
	pepper	
½ cup	Madeira	5 tbsp
1 tbsp	vinegar	½ tbsp

1. Put the mushrooms in a bowl with 1¼ cups (300 ml/½ pint) of warm water. Microwave, uncovered, on HIGH for 6 minutes.
2. Put the shallots in a large casserole with the butter. Remove the neck and backbone of the guinea fowl and cut into 8 pieces, separating the thighs from the drumsticks.
3. Cover the casserole containing the shallots and cook for 3 minutes on HIGH.
4. Sprinkle the flour over the shallots and mix well. Add the mushrooms with their cooking liquid. Stir well. Add the thyme, salt and pepper and most of the Madeira. Put the pieces of guinea fowl in the casserole, with the smaller pieces in the center. Season with salt and pepper. Cover and microwave on HIGH for 8 minutes.

5. Purée the guinea fowl liver in a food processor. Add the vinegar and the remaining Madeira and mix well.
6. Prick the pieces of guinea fowl with a fork to test which are cooked. If the liquid runs clear, remove from the casserole (the breast pieces will be ready first). Cook for a further 3 minutes on HIGH until all are cooked.
7. Put the guinea fowl into a serving dish. Pour the liver purée into the casserole and mix well. Taste and adjust the seasoning. Pour over the bird and serve.

Pintade à l'orange

Guinea Fowl in Orange Caramel Sauce

00.15 **00.23**
Serves 4

American	Ingredients	Metric/Imperial
1 (2 lb)	guinea fowl	1 (1 kg/2 lb)
	salt	
	pepper	
2 oz	finely chopped shallots	50 g/2 oz
1 oz	butter	25 g/1 oz
1	large orange	1
3 tbsp	all-purpose (plain) flour	2 tbsp
¼ cup	cognac	4 tbsp
½ tsp	ground cloves	½ tsp
½ tsp	garlic powder	½ tsp
3 oz	sugar	75 g/3 oz
2 tbsp	sherry vinegar	1 tbsp

Guinea fowl with dried mushrooms

Guinea fowl in orange caramel sauce

1. Remove the backbone of the guinea fowl with a kitchen cleaver or poultry scissors, then cut the bird into 4 pieces. Season with salt and pepper.

2. Put the shallots in a casserole with the butter. Cover and microwave on HIGH for 3 minutes.

3. Wash the orange thoroughly under plenty of cold running water. Pat dry on kitchen paper. Remove the zest (peel) with a small sharp knife or vegetable peeler, taking care not to bring away any of the bitter white pith. Slice the zest (peel) into julienne (matchstick) strips. Cut the orange in half and squeeze to obtain about ⅓ cup (4½ tablespoons) of juice.

4. Sprinkle the shallots with flour and mix well. Add the orange juice and zest (peel), cognac, cloves, garlic powder and salt and pepper to taste. Mix well.

5. Arrange the pieces of guinea fowl close together in the sauce, skin side down. Cover and microwave on HIGH for 8 minutes.

6. Turn the pieces of meat. Cover and microwave on HIGH for another 7 minutes until tender.

7. When the bird is cooked, put the sugar in a bowl with ¼ cup (3 tablespoons) of water. Microwave on HIGH for 5 minutes to obtain a clear caramel liquid. Add the vinegar, using an oven glove to protect your hand against splashing. Leave for several seconds, then mix well.

8. Pour the caramel over the guinea fowl. Arrange the pieces of meat in a heated serving dish, stir the sauce, pour into a sauceboat and serve with the meat.

If you wish, you can garnish the meat with orange slices or skinned and seeded orange quarters: heat in the microwave oven for 1 minute.

Salmis de pintade

Salmis of Guinea Fowl

00.20   00.28

Serves 4

American	Ingredients	Metric/Imperial
2 oz	diced smoked streaky bacon	50 g/2 oz
3	coarsely chopped carrots	3
3	finely chopped shallots	3
2 tbsp	butter	1 tbsp
1 cup	white wine	250 ml/8 fl oz
½ tsp	sugar	½ tsp
9 oz	white button mushrooms	250 g/9 oz
½ tsp	garlic powder	½ tsp
	salt	
	pepper	
1 (2 lb)	guinea fowl, cut into 8 pieces	1 (1 kg/2 lb)
2	chicken livers	2
1 tsp	vinegar	1 tsp
3 tbsp	cognac	2 tbsp
2 tbsp	sour cream (crème fraîche)	1 tbsp

1. Put the bacon, carrots, shallots and butter in a casserole and add the white wine and sugar. Cover and microwave on HIGH for 5 minutes.

2. Wipe the mushrooms with a damp cloth or kitchen paper. Slice finely.

3. Add the mushrooms to the casserole. Sprinkle with the garlic powder and season with salt and pepper. Arrange the pieces of guinea fowl on top and season. Cover and microwave on HIGH for 10 minutes.

4. Stir the contents of the casserole. Cover and microwave on HIGH for a further 10 minutes.

5. Add the chicken livers and vinegar. Cover and microwave on HIGH for 2 minutes.

6. Transfer the pieces of guinea fowl to a heat-proof serving dish. Pour the cognac into a cup and heat in the microwave oven for 30 seconds on HIGH, then set alight and pour over the guinea fowl.

7. Mash the chicken livers in the sauce with a fork. Stir in the sour cream (crème fraîche). Taste and adjust the seasoning. Coat the guinea fowl with some of the sauce, pour the rest into a sauceboat and serve very hot.

Salmis of guinea fowl

Quails with cherries

Cailles aux cerises

Quails with Cherries

00.10 Serves 4   **00.15**

American	Ingredients	Metric/Imperial
1½ oz	finely chopped shallots	40 g/1½ oz
½ tsp	grated nutmeg	½ tsp
	salt	
	pepper	
2 tbsp	butter	1 tbsp
4	quails, trussed	4
¼ cup	fresh orange juice	3 tbsp
2 tbsp	wine vinegar	1 tbsp
¼ tsp	ground cloves	¼ tsp
1 (12 oz)	can pitted (stoned) cherries	1 (350 g/12 oz)
1 tsp	cornstarch (cornflour)·	1 tsp
3 tbsp	port wine	2 tbsp

1. Put the shallots in a casserole. Cover and microwave on HIGH for 3 minutes.
2. Add the grated nutmeg and salt and pepper to the butter and mix well. Place ¼ of the butter inside each quail.
3. Mix together the orange juice, vinegar, ground cloves and a little salt and pepper.
4. Add the quails to the casserole and pour over the orange juice mixture. Cover and microwave on HIGH for 7 minutes.
5. Drain the cherries.
6. Add the cherries to the casserole. Cover and microwave on HIGH for 3 minutes.
7. Mix the cornstarch (cornflour) and port in a bowl to a smooth paste.
8. Remove the quails and cherries with a slotted spatula and transfer to a heated dish. Pour the cooking liquid into the bowl containing the cornstarch (cornflour) mixture and mix well. Microwave, uncovered, on HIGH for 1½ minutes, stirring midway through.
9. Remove the trussing strings from the quails, coat with the sauce and serve.

Cailles aux morilles

Quails with Wild Mushrooms

00.10 Serves 4   **00.21**

American	Ingredients	Metric/Imperial
1 oz	dried wild mushrooms	25 g/1 oz
1	coarsely chopped small carrot	1
3½ oz	chopped shallots	100 g/3½ oz
2 tbsp	butter	1 tbsp
4	large quails	4
	salt	
	pepper	
¼ tsp	powdered thyme	¼ tsp
2 tbsp	all-purpose (plain) flour	1 tbsp
½ cup	port wine	5 tbsp
⅓ cup	sour cream (crème fraîche)	4½ tbsp
1	egg yolk	1

1. Put the dried mushrooms in a bowl with 1½ cups (375 ml/13 fl oz) of warm water. Microwave, uncovered, on HIGH for 4 minutes.
2. Put the carrot and shallots in a casserole with the butter. Rub the insides of the quails with salt and pepper and the thyme.
3. Cover the casserole containing the shallots and carrots and microwave on HIGH for 5 minutes.
4. Drain the mushrooms and strain the cooking liquid through a piece of muslin or a very fine strainer (sieve). Chop the mushrooms coarsely with kitchen scissors.
5. Sprinkle the shallots with the flour and mix well. Add the mushrooms and their cooking liquid and mix again. Add most of the port and season with salt and pepper. Put the quails in the casserole and sprinkle with salt and pepper. Cover and microwave on HIGH for 10 minutes.
6. Coat the quails with sour cream (crème fraîche). Cover and cook for a further 2 minutes on HIGH.
7. Transfer the quails to a heated dish. Whisk the egg yolk with the remaining port and add to the sauce, still whisking. Taste and adjust the seasoning.
Pour over the quails and serve at once.

Breaded quails with raisin (sultana) sauce

Cailles panées en crapaudine

Breaded Quails with Raisin (Sultana) Sauce

00.10
Serves 2

00.15

American	Ingredients	Metric/Imperial
3 tbsp	golden raisins (sultanas)	2 tbsp
2	large quails	2
1	small egg	1
¼ cup	breadcrumbs	4 tbsp
2 tbsp	curry powder	1 tbsp
	salt	
3 tbsp	oil	1½ tbsp
3 tbsp	sour cream (crème fraîche)	2 tbsp
2 tbsp	mild mustard	1 tbsp
	pepper	
¼ cup	port wine	3 tbsp

1. Rinse the raisins (sultanas) under plenty of cold running water. Put in a bowl and cover with hot water.

2. Heat a browning dish in the microwave oven for 6-8 minutes, following the manufacturer's instructions.

3. Cut the quails in half and flatten with a pastry roller (rolling pin). Break the egg into a bowl and whisk with a fork. On a plate, mix the breadcrumbs, curry powder and a little salt.

4. Dip the quails first in the beaten egg then in the breadcrumb mixture, making sure they are well coated on all sides.

5. Pour half of the oil into the hot browning dish, tilting the dish to distribute the oil evenly over the base (use an oven glove to protect your hand). Put in the quails skin side upward, leave for 30 seconds, then turn skin side down. Pour over the remaining oil.

6. Cover and microwave on HIGH for 5 minutes.

7. Drain the raisins (sultanas) and put in a bowl. Add the sour cream (crème fraîche) and mustard and a little pepper.

8. Transfer the quails to a warmed dish. Pour the port into the browning dish and dissolve the cooking sediments with a wooden spatula. Pour the cooking liquid into the bowl containing the raisins (sultanas) and mix well. Microwave, uncovered, on HIGH for 1 minute. Stir, pour over the quails and serve immediately.

Faisan à la crème

Pheasant in Cream Sauce

00.15   00.30

Serves 4

American	Ingredients	Metric/Imperial
1	pheasant with its liver	1
10	juniper berries	10
1	medium carrot, cut into very thin strips	1
1	celery stick, cut into very thin strips	1
2	chopped shallots	2
1½ oz	diced smoked streaky bacon	40 g/1½ oz
1 tbsp	butter	½ tbsp
3½ oz	small white button mushrooms	100 g/3½ oz
	salt	
	pepper	
⅔ cup	white wine	150 ml/¼ pint
⅓ cup	sour cream (crème fraîche)	4½ tbsp
3 tbsp	juniper brandy	2 tbsp
2 tbsp	honey vinegar	1 tbsp
1	egg yolk	1

1. Remove the backbone of the pheasant with a kitchen cleaver or scissors. Set the liver aside. Cut the bird into 4 pieces.
2. Crush the juniper berries in a pestle and mortar. Put the carrot, celery, shallots, bacon, juniper berries and butter in a casserole. Cover and microwave on HIGH for 5 minutes.
3. Wipe the mushrooms with a damp cloth or kitchen paper. Slice thinly.
4. Add the mushrooms to the casserole. Season with salt and pepper and add the white wine. Season the pheasant quarters with salt and pepper and arrange on top of the vegetables. Cover and microwave on HIGH for 10 minutes.
5. Turn the pheasant pieces, cover and cook for a further 5 minutes. Test to see if the drumsticks are cooked: if they are overcooked they will become tough. Remove from the casserole as soon as they are tender.
6. Add the sour cream (crème fraîche) and juniper brandy. Cover and microwave on HIGH for 5-10 minutes.
7. Purée the pheasant liver in a food processor and add the vinegar and egg yolk. Mix well.
8. Transfer the pheasant to a heated serving dish. Add the liver and egg yolk mixture to the casserole, whisking rapidly. Pour over the pheasant and serve immediately.

Pheasant in cream sauce

Lapin aux poivrons

Rabbit with Red Bell Peppers and Garlic

00.20 Serves 5   00.37

American	Ingredients	Metric/Imperial
2 tsp	garlic powder	2 tsp
1 tsp	mixed herbs	1 tsp
	salt	
	pepper	
2¼ lb	rabbit, cut into 8 pieces	1 kg/2¼ lb
2 tbsp	olive oil	1 tbsp
3½ oz	smoked streaky bacon	100 g/3½ oz
7 oz	scallions (spring onions)	200 g/7 oz
8	garlic cloves	8
3	red bell peppers, rinsed, seeded and chopped	3
1	small fresh green chili, seeded	1
⅓ cup	white wine	4½ tbsp
2 tbsp	vinegar	1 tbsp
¼ cup	grated Parmesan cheese	3 tbsp

1. Heat a browning dish in the microwave oven for 6-8 minutes, following the manufacturer's instructions.
2. Mix the garlic powder, mixed herbs and salt and pepper on a plate. Roll the rabbit pieces in the mixture until well coated.
3. Pour the oil into the hot browning dish. Add the rabbit pieces, leave to sizzle for 1 minute, then turn. Cut the bacon into strips and add. Cover and microwave on HIGH for 5 minutes.
4. Peel and thinly slice the white parts of the scallions (spring onions). Discard the green stalks.
5. Add the garlic cloves, unpeeled, to the casserole. Cover the rabbit pieces with the scallions (spring onions), bell peppers and chili. Pour over the white wine and vinegar. Season with salt and pepper. Cover and microwave on HIGH for 10 minutes. Stir the vegetables, reduce the power to MEDIUM-HIGH and cook for a further 12 minutes.
6. When the meat is tender, transfer to a warmed serving dish. Cover with aluminum (aluminium) foil.
7. Remove the garlic cloves from the casserole and squeeze out the pulp by pressing one end between finger and thumb. Purée in a food processor with the other vegetables and cooking liquid. Pour the purée into a bowl and reheat on HIGH for 1 minute. Sprinkle over the grated Parmesan. Taste and adjust the seasoning. Pour over the rabbit and serve hot.

Rabbit with red bell peppers and garlic

Lapin à l'indienne
Rabbit in Curry Sauce

▬▷ 00.15 00.18 ⌇
plus marinating time

American	Ingredients	Metric/Imperial
2 tbsp	curry powder	1 tbsp
½ tsp	chili paste	½ tsp
¼ cup	fresh lemon juice	3 tbsp
2 tbsp	peanut oil	1 tbsp
1	pot natural flavor yogurt	1
	salt	
1	plump rabbit, boned and cut into portions	1
3 tbsp	sour cream (crème fraîche)	2 tbsp

1. Mix the curry powder, chili paste, lemon juice, peanut oil and yogurt in a bowl. Add salt to taste. Put the rabbit portions in the mixture, turn until well coated and marinate for at least 2 hours.

2. Put the rabbit and marinade in a dish. Cover and microwave on HIGH for 12 minutes, stirring midway through the cooking time.

3. Leave the rabbit to stand for 5 minutes. Pour the cooking juices into a bowl. Whisk in the sour cream (crème fraîche) and reheat in the oven for 1 minute on MEDIUM.

4. Pour the sauce over the rabbit and serve hot.

Lapin aux pruneaux
Rabbit with Prunes

▬▷ 00.20 00.63 ⌇
Serves 4-5

American	Ingredients	Metric/Imperial
9 oz	prunes	250 g/9 oz
1	stick cinnamon	1
1½ cups	red wine	375 ml/13 fl oz
3	finely grated carrots	3
5 oz	chopped shallots	150 g/5 oz
3½ oz	smoked streaky bacon, rind removed and cut into strips	100 g/3½ oz
2 tbsp	oil	1 tbsp
2½ lb	rabbit, cut in 8 pieces	1.2 kg/2½ lb
	salt	
	pepper	
2	crumbled fresh thyme sprigs	2
3 tbsp	all-purpose (plain) flour	2 tbsp
10	sugar cubes	10
3 tbsp	vinegar	2 tbsp

1. Remove the pits (stones) from the prunes with a small pointed knife. Break the cinnamon stick in half and put in a bowl with the prunes. Pour over the red wine and cook, uncovered, on HIGH for 8 minutes.

2. Put the carrots, shallots and bacon in a large casserole and pour over the oil. Cover and microwave on HIGH for 8 minutes.

3. Drain the prunes, reserving the cooking liquid. Discard the cinnamon. Season the rabbit pieces with salt and pepper. Sprinkle the rabbit with the crumbled thyme..

4. Sprinkle the contents of the casserole with flour and mix well. Add the prune cooking liquid. Season with salt and pepper and stir. Add the rabbit to the casserole. Cover and microwave on HIGH for 10 minutes.

5. Put the sugar lumps in a bowl with 4 (3) tablespoons of water. Microwave on HIGH for 5-6 minutes to obtain a clear caramel liquid. Add the vinegar, taking care to avoid splashing. Return to the oven for 1 minute on HIGH.

6. Mix the contents of the casserole thoroughly. Pour over the caramel liquid. Cover and microwave for 10 minutes on MEDIUM-HIGH.

7. Mix well and add the prunes. Cover and cook for a further 10 minutes on MEDIUM-HIGH. Leave to stand for 5-10 minutes, then serve at once.

Lapin au lait
Rabbit in Milk and Rum

▬▷ 00.10 00.33 ⌇
plus marinating time

American	Ingredients	Metric/Imperial
2	crushed garlic cloves	2
2	bay leaves, crumbled	2
2 tbsp	mixed herbs	1 tbsp
1 tsp	ground black pepper	1 tsp
	salt	
3 tbsp	dark rum	2 tbsp
2 tbsp	olive oil	1 tbsp
½	rabbit, cut in pieces	½
1¼ cups	milk	300 ml/½ pint
2 tbsp	butter	1 tbsp
2 tbsp	all-purpose (plain) flour	1 tbsp
1 tsp	mustard	1 tsp

1. Put the garlic, bay leaf, mixed herbs, black pepper and salt into a dish. Pour over the rum and olive oil and stir well. Add the rabbit pieces to this mixture and marinate for at least 12 hours.

2. Transfer the rabbit to a deep casserole and pour over the milk. Cover and microwave on HIGH for 10 minutes.

3. Turn the rabbit pieces. Cover and microwave on HIGH for a further 10 minutes. Leave to stand for 10 minutes.

4. Drain the rabbit and strain the cooking liquid, reserving 1¼ cups (300 ml/½ pint). Melt the butter in a bowl for 30 seconds on HIGH, and stir in the flour. Pour over the cooking liquid and stir well. Microwave for 2 minutes on HIGH.

5. Beat the sauce thoroughly with a hand whisk, and add the mustard, whisking constantly. Pour over the rabbit and serve hot.

This dish is delicious accompanied by a céleriac purée.

Vegetables

Pommes de terre en robe de chambre

Jacket Potatoes

	00.03	00.24	
	Serves 4 as side dish		

American	Ingredients	Metric/Imperial
4	large baking potatoes	4

1. Brush the potatoes under cold running water but do not peel. Prick with a fork to avoid bursting during cooking.
2. Place a sheet of kitchen paper in the base of the microwave oven. Put the potatoes on the paper in a circle, leaving the center of the oven empty. Cook for 8 minutes on HIGH.
3. Turn the potatoes over and cook for a further 6 minutes.
4. Remove the potatoes from the oven, cover with a clean kitchen towel and leave to stand for 10 minutes.
Depending on the dish the potatoes are accompanying, they can be served plain or with butter, sour cream (crème fraîche), Roquefort, etc.

Pommes de terre farcies

Stuffed Jacket Potatoes

	00.10	00.17	
	Serves 4 as side dish		

American	Ingredients	Metric/Imperial
4	large baking potatoes	4
3½ oz	tiny white button mushrooms, finely sliced	100 g/3½ oz
2 tbsp	fresh lemon juice	1 tbsp
1½ tbsp	butter	1 tbsp
3½ oz	cooked ham, finely diced	100 g/3½ oz
	salt	
	pepper	

1. Rinse the potatoes under running water. Do not peel. Prick each with a fork in several places to avoid bursting during cooking.
2. Put kitchen paper towel in the base of the microwave oven and arrange the potatoes in a circle, leaving the center empty. Microwave on HIGH for 8 minutes.
3. Turn the potatoes and cook for a further 6 minutes.
4. Cover the potatoes with a cloth and leave to stand.
5. Put the mushrooms in a bowl with the lemon juice and butter. Cover and microwave on HIGH for 3 minutes.
6. Add the ham to the mushrooms.
7. Cut the potatoes carefully in half and remove half of the flesh from each half, with a small spoon. Add to the mushrooms and ham and mix well. Season with salt and pepper.
8. Fill the potato halves with the mushroom and ham mixture and serve.

Pommes de terre à la crème

Creamed Potatoes

	00.10	00.18	
	Serves 4-5 as side dish		

American	Ingredients	Metric/Imperial
2 lb	firm, waxy potatoes, very finely sliced	1 kg/2 lb
2	finely sliced large onions	2
2	crushed garlic cloves	2
½ tsp	crumbled fresh thyme	½ tsp
	salt	
	pepper	
¼ cup	white wine	3 tbsp
¾ cup	sour cream (crème fraîche)	200 ml/7 fl oz
2	egg yolks	2
1 tbsp	chopped fresh chervil	1 tbsp
1 tbsp	chopped fresh chives	1 tbsp

Swiss-style potatoes (rosti)

Creamed potatoes

1. Mix together the potatoes, onions, garlic, thyme, salt and pepper. Put the vegetables in a small dish 9 inches (22 cm) in diameter. Add the white wine. Cover and microwave on HIGH for 14 minutes.

2. After 14 minutes, whisk the sour cream (crème fraîche) and egg yolks together with a fork and pour over the potatoes. Stir carefully. Cover and microwave on HIGH for 4 further minutes.

3. Sprinkle the potatoes with the chervil and chives and serve hot.

Paillasson de pommes de terre

Swiss Style Potatoes (Rosti)

◄▷	00.10	00.20	〰〰〰
	Serves 4 as side dish		

American	Ingredients	Metric/Imperial
1¾ lb	very finely sliced potatoes	700 g/1¾ lb
2 tbsp	all-purpose (plain) flour	1 tbsp
½ tsp	garlic powder	½ tsp
	salt	
	pepper	
2 tbsp	butter	1 tbsp
2 tbsp	oil	1 tbsp

1. Pat the potato slices dry on kitchen paper.

2. Heat a 9 inch (22 cm) browning dish in the microwave oven for 6-8 minutes on HIGH, following the manufacturer's instructions.

3. Sprinkle the potatoes with flour and garlic powder. Add salt and pepper to taste and stir well.

4. When the browning dish is hot, put in the butter and oil and tilt the dish in all directions to coat the base. Use an oven cloth to protect your hands. Put the potatoes into the browning dish in even layers. Microwave, uncovered, on HIGH for 6 minutes.

5. Using a spatula, make sure the potatoes have not stuck to the base of the browning dish. Put a plate on top and invert the browning dish on to it, then return the potatoes to the browning dish and microwave for a further 6 minutes.

6. Slide the potatoes on to a round platter and serve very hot.

Caramelized potatoes

Pommes de terre au caramel

Caramelized Potatoes

	00.10	00.23	
	Serves 4 as side dish		

American	Ingredients	Metric/Imperial
2 lb	firm, waxy potatoes, cut into thick slices	1 kg/2 lb
	salt	
	pepper	
¼ cup	sugar	4 tbsp
2 tbsp	vinegar	1 tbsp
1 oz	butter	25 g/1 oz

1. Pour 1 cup (250 ml/8 fl oz) of hot water into the lower compartment of a microwave steamer and put the potatoes in the upper compartment. Cover and microwave on HIGH for 15 minutes.
2. When the potatoes are cooked, season with salt and pepper and leave to stand, covered.
3. Put the sugar in a Pyrex bowl with ¼ cup (3 tablespoons) of water. Microwave for 6½ minutes on HIGH.
4. Add 2-3 tablespoons of hot water and then the vinegar, taking care to avoid splashing. When the mixture has stopped bubbling, return the bowl to the oven and microwave for 1 further minute on HIGH.
5. Add the butter and let it melt, tilting the bowl gently.
6. Put the potatoes in a heated serving dish and pour the caramel over them.

Pommes de terre au citron

Potatoes with Lemon Butter

■▷ 00.10   00.23
Serves 4 as side dish

American	Ingredients	Metric/Imperial
3 tbsp	butter	1½ tbsp
1¾ lb	sliced, waxy potatoes	700 g/1¾ lb
	salt	
	pepper	
½ cup	fresh lemon juice	5 tbsp
2 tbsp	chopped fresh dill	2 tbsp

1. Melt the butter in a bowl in the microwave oven for 1 minute on HIGH.
2. Put the potatoes on a dish and season with salt and pepper. Pour the melted butter and lemon juice over. Cover and microwave on HIGH for 17 minutes.
3. Leave to stand for 5 minutes, sprinkle with chopped dill and serve.

Rapée aux herbes

Baked Potato Cake with Herbs

■▷ 00.10   00.14
Serves 6 as side dish

American	Ingredients	Metric/Imperial
2½ lb	waxy potatoes	1.25 kg/2½ lb
1	chicken bouillon (stock) cube	1
	salt	
	pepper	
½ tsp	grated nutmeg	½ tsp
1	bunch fresh chervil	1
1	bunch fresh parsley	1
1	small bunch fresh chives	1
2	beaten eggs	2

1. Peel the potatoes and rinse under plenty of cold running water. Pat dry on kitchen paper and grate in a food processor. Place in a strainer to drain.
2. Put ¾ cup (200 ml/7 fl oz) of water in a bowl and heat in the microwave oven for 2 minutes on HIGH. Crumble the bouillon (stock) cube into the hot water and mix until dissolved.
3. Sprinkle a generous amount of salt and pepper on the base of a Pyrex dish. Add the grated nutmeg to half of the potatoes and stir well. Put in the dish. Cover with the remaining potatoes. Season again with salt and pepper. Add a little more grated nutmeg if liked and stir again with your hands.
4. Pour the bouillon (stock) over the potatoes. Cover and microwave on HIGH for 9 minutes. Leave to stand for 3 minutes.
5. Rinse the herbs under plenty of cold running water. Pat dry on kitchen paper. Chop finely. Break the eggs into a bowl and whisk with a fork.
6. Add the beaten eggs to the potatoes and mix with a fork. Add the chopped herbs, stir thoroughly and serve.

Pommes de terre au curry

Curried Potatoes

■▷ 00.15   00.20
Serves 6 as side dish

American	Ingredients	Metric/Imperial
2 lb	waxy potatoes	1 kg/2 lb
3½ oz	finely chopped shallots	100 g/3½ oz
3½ oz	diced smoked streaky bacon	100 g/3½ oz
	salt	
	pepper	
⅔ cup	milk	150 ml/¼ pint
1½ tsp	curry powder	1½ tsp
3 oz	grated Parmesan cheese	75 g/3 oz

1. Peel the potatoes and rinse under plenty of cold running water. Pat dry on kitchen paper. Grate in a food processor.
2. Put the shallots and bacon in an oval Pyrex dish. Microwave, uncovered, on HIGH for 3 minutes.
3. Sprinkle the mixture with salt and pepper and add the potatoes. Stir well and pour over the milk. Cover and microwave on HIGH for 12 minutes. Leave to stand for 3 minutes.
4. Mix together the curry powder and Parmesan cheese and sprinkle over the potato mixture. Microwave, uncovered, on HIGH for 2 minutes. Serve in the same dish.

Pommes de terre au cantal

Potatoes with Grated Cheese

■▷ 00.10   00.15
Serves 4-6 as side dish

American	Ingredients	Metric/Imperial
2 tbsp	butter	1 tbsp
	salt	
	pepper	
1¾ lb	grated potatoes	750 g/1¾ lb
1½ cups	grated Cantal or Gruyère cheese	100 g/3½ oz
¾ cup	sour cream (crème fraîche)	200 ml/7 fl oz

1. Put the butter in a small dish, 9 inches (22 cm) in diameter and melt in the microwave on HIGH for 1 minute. Make sure the butter covers the base of the dish.
2. Sprinkle with salt and pepper. Add the potatoes and season with salt and pepper. Pour 1¼ cups (300 ml/½ pint) of water over. Cover and microwave on HIGH for 8 minutes.
3. Add the cheese and sour cream (crème fraîche) to the potatoes. Stir carefully with a fork, making sure that no cheese is left on the surface. Cover and microwave on HIGH for 6 minutes. Serve very hot in the same dish.

Microwave hint: It is important to cook certain dishes uncovered in the microwave for re-heating purposes, such as those that have been pre-fried, like fried or croquette potatoes. If cooked covered, the coating tends to become soft and lose its crispness.

Pommes de terre au cheddar

Potatoes with Cheddar Cheese

00.10	00.18	
Serves 4-6 as side dish		

American	Ingredients	Metric/Imperial
2 tbsp	butter	1 tbsp
	salt	
	pepper	
2 lb	grated potatoes	1 kg/2 lb
1¼ cups	white wine	300 ml/½ pint
1	red sweet pimento in brine	1
2 cups	grated Cheddar cheese	100 g/3½ oz

1. Melt the butter in a bowl in the microwave oven for 1 minute on HIGH. Season generously with salt and pepper.
2. Sprinkle salt and pepper in the base of a round dish 9 inches (22 cm) in diameter. Add the potatoes and pour the white wine over. Cover and microwave on HIGH for 14 minutes.
3. Dice the sweet pimento very finely. Mix the Cheddar cheese with the diced pimento. Sprinkle on top of the potatoes and pour the melted butter over. Let the cheese melt for 2-3 minutes, then serve.

Microwave hint: When preparing chips or roast potatoes, place the prepared potatoes in a bowl, cover and microwave on HIGH for 3-5 minutes, depending on the quantity, until they are really warmed through. This will reduce the cooking time, whether frying or roasting.

Pommes de terre au crabe

Potatoes with Crabmeat

00.10	00.20	
Serves 4		

American	Ingredients	Metric/Imperial
1¾ lb	firm waxy potatoes, thickly sliced	750 g/1¾ lb
	salt	
¼ lb	crabmeat	125 g/4 oz
¼ cup	fresh lemon juice	3 tbsp
	pepper	
⅓ cup	sour cream (crème fraîche)	4½ tbsp
2 tbsp	chopped fresh dill	2 tbsp

1. Pour 1 cup (250 ml/8 fl oz) of water into the lower compartment of a microwave steamer and heat on HIGH for 2 minutes.
2. Put the potatoes in the upper compartment of the steamer and add salt. Put the steamer into the oven, cover and microwave on HIGH for 17 minutes.
3. Put the crabmeat in a bowl and pour the lemon juice over. Season with salt and pepper. Add the sour cream (crème fraîche) and stir well. Heat for 1 minute on HIGH.
4. Drain the potatoes and transfer to a vegetable dish. Add pepper. Pour the crab sauce over and stir carefully. Sprinkle with chopped dill and serve hot.

Potatoes with crabmeat

Pommes de terre aux poireaux

Potatoes and Leeks with Roquefort Cheese

	00.10	00.20
	Serves 6 as side dish	

American	Ingredients	Metric/Imperial
7 oz	chopped onions	200 g/7 oz
10½ oz	leeks, white part only, cut into strips	300 g/10½ oz
1 lb	firm waxy potatoes	450 g/1 lb
2 tbsp	butter	1 tbsp
2 oz	Roquefort cheese	50 g/2 oz
3 tbsp	sour cream (crème fraîche)	2 tbsp
	salt	
	pepper	

1. Put the onions in a colander and rinse carefully, then leave to drain.
2. Put the onions and leeks in a casserole with 2-3 tablespoons of water. Cover and microwave on HIGH for 7 minutes.
3. Slice the potatoes as for French fries (chips).
4. Add the potatoes to the casserole with the butter, cut into small pieces. Cover and microwave on HIGH for 3 minutes.
5. Crumble the Roquefort over the potatoes and add the sour cream (crème fraîche). Season with salt and pepper and stir well. Cover and microwave on HIGH for 10 minutes.
6. Serve in the casserole.

Pommes de terre à la forestière

Potatoes with Wild Mushrooms

	00.08	00.18
	Serves 4-5 as side dish	

American	Ingredients	Metric/Imperial
3½ oz	smoked bacon, cut into small pieces	100 g/3½ oz
3	finely chopped shallots	3
1 lb	coarsely chopped wild or field mushrooms	450 g/1 lb
1¾ lb	finely diced potatoes	700 g/1¾ lb
2 tbsp	butter	1 tbsp
	salt	
	pepper	

1. Put the bacon and shallots into a casserole. Cover and microwave on HIGH for 3 minutes.
2. Add the mushrooms to the bacon and shallots. Cover and microwave on HIGH for 5 minutes, stirring midway through the cooking time.
3. Put the potatoes in another casserole with 2-3 tablespoons of water and the butter cut into small pieces. Cover and microwave on HIGH for 9 minutes.
4. Combine the contents of the two casseroles. Season with salt and pepper. Cover and microwave on HIGH for 1 minute. Transfer to a heated dish and serve.

Potatoes and leeks with Roquefort cheese

Couronne Parmentier

Ring Mold (Mould) of Puréed Potatoes

	00.10	00.27
	Serves 6 as side dish	

American	Ingredients	Metric/Imperial
2 lb	frozen potato purée	1 kg/2 lb
1 cup	grated Gruyère cheese	100 g/3½ oz
2 tbsp	butter	1½ tbsp
2	eggs	2
	salt	
	pepper	
½ tsp	grated nutmeg	½ tsp
2 tbsp	breadcrumbs	1 tbsp

1. Put the frozen potato purée in a casserole. Cover and microwave on HIGH for 10 minutes, stirring midway through the cooking time.
2. Add the grated cheese and two-thirds of butter to the purée and stir. Break the eggs and separate the yolks from the whites. Add the yolks to the purée. Add salt and pepper to taste and the grated nutmeg. Stir well.
3. Generously butter a small Pyrex ring mold (mould) 9 inches (22 cm) in diameter. Sprinkle with the breadcrumbs.
4. Add 1 pinch salt to the egg whites and whisk to firm peaks. Fold carefully into the purée.
5. Spoon the mixture carefully into the mold (mould) and smooth the surface. Cover and microwave on HIGH for 12 minutes.
6. Leave to stand for 5 minutes, then turn out on to a serving dish. This purée may be served on its own as an accompaniment to meat or with a cream of mushroom sauce or Madeira sauce.

Sweet potatoes in milk and honey

Patates douces à la cassonade

Sweet Potatoes in Brown Sugar

	00.10	00.15
	Serves 5-6 as side dish	

American	Ingredients	Metric/Imperial
¼ cup	butter	50 g/2 oz
¼ cup	soft dark brown sugar	2 tbsp
	Tabasco sauce	
	salt	
	pepper	
2 lb	sweet potatoes, sliced into rounds	1 kg/2 lb

1. Put the butter in a bowl and melt in the microwave oven for 1 minute on HIGH.
2. Add the brown sugar, a few dashes of Tabasco sauce and some salt and pepper to the melted butter.
3. Pour one-third of the seasoned butter into a deep round dish about 10 inches (25 cm) in diameter. Arrange a layer of sweet potatoes on top, pour some butter over, then another layer of sweet potatoes, then more butter until the ingredients are used up. Cover and microwave on HIGH for 10 minutes.
4. Baste the sweet potatoes with the liquid in the base of the dish. Microwave, uncovered, on HIGH for a further 3-4 minutes until all the sweet potatoes are tender.
5. Serve in the same dish. This vegetable is a fine accompaniment to roast pork or lamb.

Patates douces au lait

Sweet Potatoes in Milk and Honey

	00.10	00.13
	Serves 4-6 as side dish	

American	Ingredients	Metric/Imperial
1¾ lb	sweet potatoes	700 g/1¾ lb
⅔ cup	milk	150 ml/¼ pint
2 tbsp	honey	1 tbsp
½ tsp	ground ginger	½ tsp
½ tsp	grated nutmeg	½ tsp
	salt	
	pepper	
1 tbsp	butter	½ tbsp
1	egg	1

1. Peel the sweet potatoes and slice into ¼ inch (6 mm) rounds.
2. Mix together the milk and honey in a bowl and add the ginger, nutmeg, and salt and pepper to taste. Heat in the oven on HIGH for 1½ minutes.
3. Sprinkle salt and pepper in the base of a round dish 9 inches (22 cm) in diameter and arrange the sweet potato slices in it. Sprinkle with salt and pepper. Stir the contents of the bowl and pour over the vegetables. Dot with butter. Cover and microwave on HIGH for 10 minutes.
4. Whisk the egg with a fork and pour into the dish, stirring carefully. Cook on HIGH for 1 minute. Serve in the same dish.

Turban orange

Ring Mold (Mould) of Carrots and Onions

00.15 00.31

Serves 4

American	Ingredients	Metric/Imperial
3½ oz	finely sliced onions	100 g/3½ oz
3½ oz	lean streaky bacon, de-rinded, cut into strips	100 g/3½ oz
1 lb	grated carrots	450 g/1 lb
¼ cup	vinegar	3 tbsp
1 tsp	sugar	1 tsp
4	large eggs	4
	salt	
	pepper	
1 tsp	garlic powder	1 tsp
½ tsp	grated nutmeg	½ tsp
¼ cup	slivered almonds	50 g/2 oz
1 tsp	butter	1 tsp

1. Put the onions and bacon into a dish. Cover and microwave on HIGH for 3 minutes.
2. Add the carrots and vinegar and sprinkle with sugar. Stir well. Cover and microwave on HIGH for 13 minutes.
3. Purée in a food processor.
4. Break the eggs into a bowl and whisk with a fork. Add the carrot purée and stir thoroughly, seasoning with salt and pepper to taste. Add the garlic powder, grated nutmeg and almonds.
5. Butter the base of a small Pyrex ring mold (mould) and pour in the mixture. Cover and microwave on HIGH for 10 minutes.
6. Leave to stand for 5 minutes, pass the blade of a knife around the edge of the mold (mould) and turn out on to a serving dish. This dish can either be served hot on its own or as the vegetable accompaniment to a veal roast.

Carottes à la forestière

Carrots with Mushrooms

00.07 00.21

Serves 4 as side dish

American	Ingredients	Metric/Imperial
3	finely chopped shallots	3
3 tbsp	butter	1½ tbsp
1 lb	sliced white button mushrooms	450 g/1 lb
1 lb	very finely sliced carrots	450 g/1 lb
⅓ cup	white wine	4½ tbsp
½	chicken bouillon (stock) cube	½
1 tsp	superfine (caster) sugar	1 tsp
½ tsp	grated nutmeg	½ tsp
3 tbsp	sour cream (crème fraîche)	2 tbsp
	salt	
	pepper	
1 tbsp	chopped fresh chervil	1 tbsp

1. Put the shallots in a casserole with one-third of the butter. Cover and microwave on HIGH for 3 minutes.
2. Add the mushrooms to the shallots in the casserole. Cover and microwave on HIGH for 5 minutes, stirring midway through the cooking time.
3. Put the carrots in another casserole with the white wine. Crumble the ½ bouillon (stock) cube into the casserole and dot with the remaining butter. Sprinkle with the sugar and grated nutmeg. Cover and microwave on HIGH for 10 minutes.
4. Mix the contents of the two casseroles. Add the sour cream (crème fraîche), taste and adjust seasoning. Cover and microwave on HIGH for 3 minutes.
5. Sprinkle the chopped chervil over the vegetables and serve hot.

Ring mold (mould) of carrots and onions

Carrots with fresh sage

Carottes à la sauge

Carrots with Fresh Sage

◖▷ 00.10 00.20 〰

Serves 4 as side dish

American	Ingredients	Metric/Imperial
12	scallions (spring onions)	12
1¾ lb	finely sliced carrots	750 g/1¾ lb
6	crumbled fresh sage leaves	6
2 tbsp	olive oil	1 tbsp
2 tbsp	sugar	1 tbsp
¼ cup	white wine	4 tbsp
	salt	
	pepper	
	sprig of sage	

1. Peel the scallions (spring onions) and remove most but not all of the green stalk. Put in a casserole with 4 tablespoons (2 tablespoons) of water. Cover and microwave on HIGH for 3 minutes.
2. Add the carrots to the scallions (spring onions) with the crumbled sage leaves. Add the olive oil, sugar, white wine and salt and pepper to taste. Stir well. Cover and microwave on HIGH for 12 minutes.
3. Leave to stand for 5 minutes before serving. Garnish with a sprig of sage.

Carottes aux oignons

Carrots with Onions

◖▷ 00.10 00.18 〰

Serves 4 as side dish

American	Ingredients	Metric/Imperial
10½ oz	finely sliced onions	300 g/10½ oz
10½ oz	very finely sliced carrots	300 g/10½ oz
2 tbsp	sugar	1 tbsp
3 tbsp	wine vinegar	2 tbsp
2 tbsp	butter	1½ tbsp
10½ oz	granny smith apples	300 g/10½ oz
	salt	
	pepper	

1. Put the onions in a casserole with ⅓ cup (4½ tablespoons) of water. Cover and microwave on HIGH for 5 minutes.
2. Drain the onions, return to the casserole and add the carrots. Sprinkle with sugar and add the vinegar. Dot with the butter. Cover and microwave on HIGH for 10 minutes.
3. Peel, core, quarter and slice the apples. Add to the casserole. Cover and microwave on HIGH for 3 minutes.
4. Season with salt and pepper, stir carefully and serve hot.

Carrots with onions

Couronne de carottes au jambon

Carrot and Ham Ring Mold (Mould)

◣▷   00.15   00.36   〰
Serves 4 as side dish

American	Ingredients	Metric/Imperial
1	chopped garlic clove	1
5 oz	chopped onions	150 g/5 oz
1 lb	very finely sliced carrots	450 g/1 lb
¼ lb	cooked ham	125 g/4 oz
3 tbsp	port wine	2 tbsp
3	large eggs	3
½ tsp	grated nutmeg	½ tsp
	pepper	
	salt	
1 oz	butter	25 g/1 oz
2 tbsp	all-purpose (plain) flour	1 tbsp
1 cup	milk	250 ml/8 fl oz
3 tbsp	sour cream (crème fraîche)	2 tbsp
2 tbsp	chopped fresh chervil	2 tbsp

1. Put the garlic and onions in a casserole. Cover and microwave on HIGH for 5 minutes.
2. Add the carrots and ¼ cup (3 tablespoons) of water to the casserole. Cover and microwave on HIGH for 12 minutes.
3. Chop the ham and purée in the food processor. Add the port. Leave the ham purée in the food processor bowl.
4. When the carrots are cooked, drain and add to the ham purée.
5. Break one egg and separate the yolk from the white. Add the yolk and the 2 whole eggs to the ham and carrot mixture.
6. Add the grated nutmeg and pepper. Taste before adding salt. Stir well and pour the mixture into a bowl.
7. Whisk the egg white to firm peaks and fold into the mixture.
8. Butter the base and sides of a Pyrex ring mold (mould) 9 inches (22 cm) in diameter. Pour in the mixture. Cover and microwave on HIGH for 10 minutes.
9. Leave the mixture to stand for 5 minutes and prepare the sauce.
10. Melt the butter in a bowl for 1 minute on HIGH.
11. Stir in the flour, then add the milk. Cook for 3 minutes on HIGH, whisking after every minute.
12. Add the sour cream (crème fraîche) and chopped chervil. Taste and adjust seasoning.
13. Turn out the ring mold (mould) on to a round platter, coat with the sauce and serve.

Microwave hint: To cook carrots, slice neatly and place in a suitable dish. Spoon over ¼ cup (4 tablespoons) of orange juice and add a pinch of ground mace. Cover and cook on HIGH for 4 minutes, stir and test for tenderness. Cover again and cook for a further 2 minutes, test again and add salt to taste. Leave to stand for 2 minutes before serving.

Petits légumes à la crème

Carrots and Leeks in Cream Sauce

◣▷   00.10   00.13   〰
Serves 4 as side dish

American	Ingredients	Metric/Imperial
7 oz	grated carrots	200 g/7 oz
10½ oz	leeks, white part only, cut into strips	300 g/10½ oz
1	stick celery, cut into strips	1
1	large egg	1
¼ cup	sour cream (crème fraîche)	3 tbsp
¼ cup	fresh lemon juice	3 tbsp
½ tsp	curry powder	½ tsp
	salt	
	pepper	
1 tbsp	chopped fresh parsley	1 tbsp

1. Put the carrots, leeks and celery in a small casserole and add ¼ cup (3 tablespoons) of water. Cover and microwave on HIGH for 12 minutes.
2. Mix together the egg, sour cream (crème fraîche), lemon juice and curry powder. Pour over the vegetables. Season with salt and pepper. Cover and microwave on HIGH for 1 minute.
3. Sprinkle with chopped parsley and serve. This dish is a good accompaniment to fish or poultry.

Carottes au lard 🧑‍🍳

Carrots with Bacon

◣▷   00.10   00.19   〰
Serves 3-4

American	Ingredients	Metric/Imperial
3½ oz	smoked streaky bacon, cut into strips	100 g/3½ oz
5 oz	thinly sliced onions	150 g/5 oz
1 lb	thickly sliced carrots	450 g/1 lb
	salt	
	pepper	
1 tsp	garlic powder	1 tsp
⅓ cup	white wine	4 tbsp

1. Put the bacon and onions in a dish. Microwave, uncovered, on HIGH for 3 minutes.
2. Add the carrots, salt and pepper, the garlic powder and white wine. Cover and microwave on HIGH for 8 minutes.
3. Stir well and cook for a further 5 minutes on HIGH.
4. Leave to stand for 3 minutes before serving.

Gâteau de céleri à la banane

Céleriac and Banana Cake

00.10 00.27
Serves 6 as side dish

American	Ingredients	Metric/Imperial
3½ oz	very finely sliced potatoes	100 g/3½ oz
7 oz	finely sliced onions	200 g/7 oz
1½ lb	peeled, sliced céleriac	700 g/1½ lb
1	banana	1
	salt	
	pepper	
4	eggs	4
3 tbsp	sour cream (crème fraîche)	2 tbsp
1 tsp	butter	1 tsp

1. Put the potatoes, onions and céleriac in a casserole with ¼ cup (3 tablespoons) of water. Cover and microwave on HIGH for 12 minutes.
2. When the vegetables are cooked, drain and purée in the food processor until smooth. Add the banana and salt and pepper to taste. Continue liquidizing, adding the eggs one at a time, then add the sour cream (crème fraîche). Taste and adjust seasoning.
3. Butter the base of a soufflé mold (mould) 7 inches (18 cm) in diameter. Pour in the mixture and cook on HIGH for 10 minutes.
4. Leave the cake to stand for 5 minutes, then turn out on to a serving dish. Serve this gâteau with pork or venison. If you prefer, simply double the proportion of potatoes and omit the banana.

Purée de céleri-rave

Céleriac and Onion Purée

00.10 00.17
Serves 4 as side dish

American	Ingredients	Metric/Imperial
1 lb	cubed céleriac	450 g/1 lb
7 oz	finely sliced onions	200 g/7 oz
1	egg	1
1 cup	grated Gruyère cheese	50 g/2 oz
½ tsp	allspice	½ tsp
	pepper	
	salt	

1. Put the céleriac and onions in a casserole with 2-3 tablespoons of water. Cover and microwave on HIGH for 12 minutes. Leave to stand for 5 minutes.
2. Drain the céleriac and onions, and purée in a food processor, adding the egg, grated Gruyère and allspice while continuing to purée. Season lightly with pepper. Taste before adding salt.
3. Pour the purée into a vegetable dish and serve.

Purée de céleri-rave

Céleriac Purée

00.10 00.13
Serves 4 as side dish

American	Ingredients	Metric/Imperial
1 lb	finely sliced céleriac	450 g/1 lb
½ lb	finely sliced onions	225 g/8 oz
	salt	
	pepper	
2 tsp	strong mustard	2 tsp

1. Put the céleriac and onions in a dish and season with salt and pepper. Add 2-3 tablespoons of water. Cover and microwave on HIGH for 5 minutes.
2. Stir, cover again and cook for a further 5 minutes on HIGH.
3. Remove the dish from the oven and leave to stand for 3 minutes.
4. Purée the mixture in a food processor, adding the mustard. Taste and adjust seasoning. Serve hot. This purée is the perfect accompaniment to any kind of game, particularly venison.

Gâteau-mousse de céleri-rave

Céleriac Mousse

00.15 00.39
Serves 5-6

American	Ingredients	Metric/Imperial
1	large baking potato	1
7 oz	finely sliced onions	200 g/7 oz
1¾ lb	peeled, sliced céleriac	700 g/1¾ lb
	salt	
	pepper	
½ tsp	allspice	½ tsp
4	eggs	4
2 tsp	butter	1 tsp

1. Scrub and wash the potato and prick the skin in several places with a fork. Put the potato on a piece of kitchen paper on a plate and microwave on HIGH for 4 minutes. Turn and cook for another 3 minutes on HIGH.
2. Mix together the onions and céleriac in a dish. Add 2-3 tablespoons of water and cover.
3. Remove the potato from the oven and cover with a clean cloth. Put the céleriac and onions in the oven and microwave on HIGH for 12 minutes. Leave to stand for 5 minutes.
4. Peel the potato and cut into small pieces and purée in a food processor. Drain the onions and céleriac and add to the potato purée. Purée again, adding salt and pepper, the allspice and then the eggs one at a time.
5. Butter the base of a 7 inch (18 cm) soufflé mold (mould) and pour in the mixture. Cover and microwave on HIGH for 10 minutes.
6. Leave to stand for 5 minutes, then turn out on to a serving dish. This mousse can be served on its own or as an accompaniment to fish or white meat. If served as a main dish, it could be accompanied by a cream sauce or tomato sauce.

Salsifis crémeux
Creamed Salsify

■▷ 00.05   00.22   **〰**
Serves 4 as side dish

American	Ingredients	Metric/Imperial
½	chicken bouillon (stock) cube	½
1¼ lb	frozen salsify	500 g/1¼ lb
1 oz	butter	25 g/1 oz
4 tbsp	all-purpose (plain) flour	2 tbsp
4 tbsp	sour cream (crème fraîche)	2 tbsp
1 oz	grated Cheddar or other hard cheese	25 g/1 oz
2 tbsp	fresh lemon juice	1 tbsp
	salt	
	pepper	
2 tbsp	chopped chervil	2 tbsp

1. Pour ¾ cup (200 ml/7 fl oz) of water into a bowl and heat in the microwave oven on HIGH for 2 minutes. Crumble over the ½ bouillon (stock) cube and mix well.
2. Put the salsify in a casserole and pour over the bouillon (stock). Cover and microwave on HIGH for 12 minutes. Leave to stand for 5 minutes.
3. Put the butter in a bowl and melt for 1 minute on HIGH. Stir in the flour.
4. Drain the salsify and put on a serving dish. Keep hot. Pour the cooking liquid into the bowl and whisk. Microwave for 1 minute on HIGH. Whisk again.
5. Add the sour cream (crème fraîche), cheese and lemon juice to the bowl and stir well. Heat for 30 seconds on HIGH. Taste and adjust the seasoning.
6. Pour the sauce over the salsify, sprinkle with chervil and serve.

Salsifis aux petits pois
Salsify with Petits Pois

■▷ 00.20   00.21   **〰**
Serves 6 as side dish

American	Ingredients	Metric/Imperial
2 lb	salsify	1 kg/2 lb
½ glass	vinegar	½ glass
¼ cup	fresh lemon juice	3 tbsp
2 tbsp	butter	1 tbsp
2 tbsp	all-purpose (plain) flour	1 tbsp
1 cup	milk	250 ml/8 fl oz
	salt	
	pepper	
1	can extra small petits pois	1
1	egg yolk	1
1 tbsp	chopped fresh chervil	1 tbsp

1. Clean the salsify under running water. Pour the vinegar into a bowl of cold water. Peel the salsify with a sharp paring knife, remove each end and cut into ¼ inch (6 mm) pieces, putting them immediately into the vinegared water.
2. Drain the salsify and put in a casserole with the lemon juice and ⅔ cup (150 ml/¼ pint) of water. Cover and microwave on HIGH for 15 minutes.

3. Put the butter in a bowl and melt in the microwave oven for 1 minute on HIGH. Stir in the flour and add the milk, whisking constantly. Microwave on HIGH for 3 minutes, whisking after every minute. Season with salt and pepper.
4. Season the salsify with salt and pepper. Stir. Drain the petits pois and add them to the salsify along with the egg yolk and the sauce. Add the chopped chervil and stir well. Cover and microwave on HIGH for 2 minutes. Serve hot.

Salsifis à la normande
Normandy-Style Salsify

■▷ 00.15   00.20   **〰**
Serves 4 as side dish

American	Ingredients	Metric/Imperial
3 tbsp	vinegar	2 tbsp
1 lb	peeled, sliced salsify	450 g/1 lb
	salt	
	pepper	
⅔ cup	cider	150 ml/¼ pint
1	finely sliced onion	1
2 tbsp	butter	1 tbsp
2 tbsp	all-purpose (plain) flour	1 tbsp
1	egg yolk	1
2 tbsp	sour cream (crème fraîche)	1 tbsp
1 tbsp	chopped fresh parsley	1 tbsp

1. Pour the vinegar into a bowl of cold water. Put the salsify into the bowl, making sure all the slices are covered by the vinegar and water.
2. Drain the salsify and put it in a dish. Season with salt and pepper and pour the cider over. Cover and microwave on HIGH for 12-14 minutes, depending on the thickness of the salsify.
3. Put the onion in a bowl and microwave, uncovered, for 3 minutes on HIGH.
4. Drain the salsify, setting aside the cooking liquid. Mix together the butter, flour and onion. Stir in the salsify liquid and microwave for 2½ minutes on HIGH.
5. Whisk the mixture vigorously. Add the egg yolk and sour cream (crème fraîche), whisking. Taste and adjust seasoning.
6. Put the salsify in a dish, pour the sauce over, sprinkle with parsley and serve hot.

Normandy-style salsify

Microwave hint: To save time cooking root vegetables to be used as part of a composite recipe, grate or chop very finely. This will reduce cooking time by about half. Fine chopping, if appropriate, reduces time for green vegetables too.

Navets à la moutarde

Baby Turnips in Mustard Sauce

	00.05	00.14

Serves 3-4 as side dish

American	Ingredients	Metric/Imperial
1 lb	peeled, quartered baby turnips	450 g/1 lb
3 tbsp	white wine	2 tbsp
2 tbsp	sugar	1 tbsp
	salt	
	pepper	
½ tsp	cornstarch (cornflour)	½ tsp
2 tsp	mustard	2 tsp
2 tbsp	sour cream (crème fraîche)	1 tbsp
2 tbsp	chopped fresh parsley	2 tbsp

1. Put the turnips in a dish with the white wine. Sprinkle with the sugar, salt and pepper. Cover and microwave on HIGH for 10 minutes. Leave to stand for 3 minutes.
2. Transfer the turnips to a heated serving dish and put the cooking liquid in a bowl. Add the cornstarch (cornflour) and mustard and mix to a smooth paste, then put the bowl in the microwave oven for 30 seconds on HIGH.
3. Whisk the sauce vigorously and add the sour cream (crème fraîche). Pour over the turnips, sprinkle with chopped parsley and serve at once.

Navets confits

Spiced Baby Turnips

	00.10	00.18

Serves 4-5 as side dish

American	Ingredients	Metric/Imperial
1 lb	baby turnips	450 g/1 lb
¼ cup	butter	1 tbsp
	salt	
	pepper	
3 tbsp	honey vinegar	2 tbsp
¾ cup	sugar	75 g/3 oz
2 tsp	cornstarch (cornflour)	2 tsp
3 tbsp	white port wine	2 tbsp

1. Peel and rinse the turnips, slice into ¼ inch (6 mm) slices and each slice into four.
2. Put the turnips in a casserole and add ⅓ cup (4½ tablespoons) of water, the butter, and salt and pepper to taste. Cover and microwave on HIGH for 5 minutes.
3. Add the vinegar and sugar and stir well. Microwave, uncovered, on HIGH for 12 minutes, stirring once or twice during cooking.
4. Mix the cornstarch (cornflour) to a smooth paste with the port wine. Add to the turnips, stir and cook for 1 further minute. Stir again and serve at once. These turnips are excellent with meat that has a heavy fat content: duck, goose, pork, etc.

Navets sauce poulette

Baby Turnips in Cream of Chicken Sauce

	00.15	00.21

Serves 6-7 as side dish

American	Ingredients	Metric/Imperial
2 lb	very finely sliced baby turnips	1 kg/2 lb
	salt	
	pepper	
2 tbsp	sugar	1 tbsp
2 tbsp	butter	1 tbsp
3 tbsp	all-purpose (plain) flour	2 tbsp
½ tsp	grated nutmeg	½ tsp
1	chicken bouillon (stock) cube	1
2	egg yolks	2
2 tbsp	fresh lemon juice	1 tbsp

1. Arrange the turnip slices in layers in a deep dish, seasoning each layer lightly with salt and pepper and a little sugar. Add ½ cup (5 tablespoons) of water. Cover and microwave on HIGH for 13 minutes.
2. Put the butter in a large bowl and melt in the microwave oven on HIGH for 30 seconds.
3. Add the flour and grated nutmeg and stir well. Crumble the bouillon (stock) cube into the mixture.
4. Carefully remove about 1¼ cups (300 ml/½ pint) of the cooking liquid from the turnips, leaving the dish covered. Stir the cooking liquid into the flour and butter mixture, and cook for 2 minutes on HIGH.
5. Stir the sauce well, then cook for a further 2 minutes.
6. Whisk the egg yolks with the lemon juice. Gradually pour the sauce over, whisking vigorously the whole time. Pour over the turnips. Cover and microwave on HIGH for 3 minutes. Serve at once.

Radis à la crème

Radishes in Cream

	00.10	00.08

Serves 4 as side dish

American	Ingredients	Metric/Imperial
2	bunches radishes	2
1 tbsp	chopped fresh chives	1 tbsp
3 tbsp	sour cream (crème fraîche)	2 tbsp
	salt	
	pepper	

1. Remove the roots and leaves of the radishes and peel. Rinse thoroughly to remove any grit.
2. Pour 1 cup (250 ml/8 fl oz) of water into the lower compartment of a microwave steamer. Cover and microwave on HIGH for 3 minutes.
3. Slice the radishes thinly and put in the perforated compartment of the steamer, then put it on top of the lower section. Cover and microwave on HIGH for 5 minutes.
4. Put the chopped chives in a serving dish with the sour cream (crème fraîche). Add salt and pepper to taste.
5. When the radishes are cooked, add to the dish, stir well and serve at once.

Beetroot purée

Betteraves à la crème
Creamed Beetroot

⏱ 00.05 00.10

Serves 4 as side dish

American	Ingredients	Metric/Imperial
5 oz	finely chopped onions	150 g/5 oz
2 tbsp	butter	1 tbsp
1¼ lb	cooked beetroot, peeled and sliced into strips	600 g/1¼ lb
⅓ cup	honey vinegar	4 tbsp
	salt	
	pepper	
⅓ cup	sour cream (crème fraîche)	5 tbsp

Creamed beetroot

1. Put the onions in a casserole with the butter. Cover and microwave on HIGH for 5 minutes.
2. Add the beetroots to the onions in the casserole. Pour the vinegar over. Season with salt and pepper and stir. Cover and microwave on HIGH for 5 minutes.
3. Pour the sour cream (crème fraîche) over the hot beetroot, stir well and serve at once.

Purée rose
Beetroot Purée

⏱ 00.15 00.14

Serves 4 as side dish

American	Ingredients	Metric/Imperial
1	chopped shallot	1
14 oz	céleriac, peeled and sliced	400 g/14 oz
10½ oz	floury potatoes, grated	300 g/10½ oz
½ lb	cooked beetroot, peeled and coarsely chopped	225 g/8 oz
2 tbsp	Dijon mustard	1 tbsp
3 tbsp	sour cream (crème fraîche)	3 tbsp
2 tbsp	butter	1½ tbsp
	salt	
	pepper	

1. Put the shallot, céleriac and potatoes in a casserole with ½ cup (5 tablespoon) of water. Cover and microwave on HIGH for 12 minutes, stirring midway through the cooking time.
2. When the vegetables are cooked, drain and purée with the beetroot until smooth.
3. Add the mustard, sour cream (crème fraîche) and butter. Taste and adjust seasoning. Reheat for 1-2 minutes on HIGH, if necessary, and serve very hot.

Onions in cream sauce

Stuffed onions

Crème d'oignons
Onions in Cream Sauce

00.10   00.12

Serves 4 as side dish

American	Ingredients	Metric/Imperial
1¾ lb	finely sliced onions	700 g/1¾ lb
½ cup	white wine	5 tbsp
1½ tbsp	butter	1 tbsp
2 tbsp	instant potato flakes	1 tbsp
¼ cup	sour cream (crème fraîche)	3 tbsp
	salt	
	pepper	
½ tsp	allspice	½ tsp

1. Put the onions in a dish with the white wine and butter. Cover and microwave on HIGH for 10 minutes.
2. When the onions are tender, drain, setting aside the cooking liquid. Purée the onions in a food processor. Pour the purée into a dish.
3. Reheat the cooking liquid for 1 minute on HIGH. Stir in the instant potato flakes.
4. Stir the mixture into the onion purée. Add the sour cream (crème fraîche), salt, pepper and allspice. Stir thoroughly, re-heat for 1 minute and serve at once.

Oignons farcis
Stuffed Onions

00.10   00.14

Serves 2-4 as a side dish

American	Ingredients	Metric/Imperial
4	large onions	4
3 tbsp	cream cheese	2 tbsp
1	egg	1
1 tsp	grated horseradish	1 tsp
	salt	
	pepper	
1 tbsp	chopped mixed fresh herbs	1 tbsp

1. Peel the onions and cut the tops off. Take a little off the bases as well, if they do not stand firmly. Arrange in a circle in a small dish. Add ⅓ cup (4½ tablespoons) of water. Cover and microwave on HIGH for 10 minutes.
2. Leave the onions to cool, then drain and scoop out the insides with a small spoon, being sure to leave at least two layers of skin so that they retain their shape.
3. Purée the scooped-out pulp in a food processor, adding the cream cheese, egg, grated horseradish, salt and pepper.
4. Put the onion shells back in the dish (it does not matter if the bases now have holes in). Fill with the purée, put the dish in the microwave oven and cook for 4 minutes on HIGH.
5. Sprinkle the onions with the chopped herbs and serve hot.

Snow-peas (Mange-tout) in Lemon Sauce

00.05   **00.07**
Serves 4

American	Ingredients	Metric/Imperial
1 lb	snow-peas (mange-tout)	450 g/1 lb
2 tsp	oil	2 tsp
⅔ cup	whipping cream	150 ml/¼ pint
3 tbsp	plain yogurt	2 tbsp
	zest of lemon, finely grated	
	salt	
	pepper	
¼ tsp	sugar	¼ tsp
2 tbsp	chopped mint	2 tbsp

1. Top and tail the snow-peas (mange-tout) and put in a dish with ½ cup (125 ml/4 fl oz) of water. Cook on HIGH for 5 minutes. Drain.
2. Stir the oil into the snow-peas (mange-tout).
3. Mix together the cream, yogurt, lemon zest, salt and pepper to taste and sugar. Microwave on MEDIUM for 1½ minutes.
4. Pour the sauce over the peas and sprinkle with the mint.

French Beans with Hollandaise Sauce

00.08   **00.21**
Serves 4

American	Ingredients	Metric/Imperial
1¾ lb	French beans	700 g/1¾ lb
⅓ cup	butter	75 g/3 oz
5	egg yolks	5
	salt	
	pepper	
	grated zest (peel) and juice of a lemon	
	Tabasco sauce	
½ tsp	dried basil	½ tsp

1. Top and tail the beans and put in a dish with ½ cup (125 ml/4 fl oz) of water. Cover and microwave on HIGH for 8 minutes. Leave to stand for 5 minutes.
2. Melt the butter in a bowl in the microwave for 2 minutes on HIGH.
3. Whisk together the egg yolks, salt and pepper, a few drops of lemon juice and 1 teaspoon of water in a Pyrex bowl. Gradually whisk in a little of the foaming butter. Heat on HIGH for 1 minute, remove and whisk again, gradually adding the remaining butter. Return to the microwave for 1 minute on HIGH. Whisk again.
4. Add the remaining lemon juice and zest (peel) and a drop of Tabasco sauce. Whisk well, and if the sauce has not thickened enough, return the bowl to the microwave for 30 seconds, whisking constantly.

5. Drain the beans, sprinkle with basil and return to the microwave. Cook on HIGH for 3 minutes. Stir and serve with the sauce poured over.

Microwave hint: To cook green beans, trim the ends, cut long beans in half and put in a a suitable dish. Sprinkle with salt to taste and add ¼ cup (3-4 tablespoons) of water. Cover and cook on HIGH for 3 minutes. Test for tenderness, re-cover and cook for a further 2-3 minutes. Leave to stand, covered for a further 2 minutes before serving, sprinkled with chopped savory.

Venetian Green Beans

00.06   **00.16**
Serves 4-6

American	Ingredients	Metric/Imperial
1	finely sliced onion	1
1	crushed garlic clove	1
2 tbsp	butter	1 tbsp
1 lb	green beans	450 g/1 lb
14 oz	can tomatoes, drained and chopped	400 g/14 oz
¼ tsp	dried marjoram	¼ tsp
	salt	
	pepper	

1. Put the onion, garlic and butter in a medium casserole and cook on HIGH for 3 minutes.
2. Add the beans, tomatoes and marjoram. Cover and heat on HIGH for 8 minutes. Leave to stand for 5 minutes.
3. Season lightly with salt and pepper.

Flan de chou
Cabbage Flan

00.10   **00.36**
Serves 4 as side dish

American	Ingredients	Metric/Imperial
1¼ lb	shredded white or green cabbage	600 g/1¼ lb
3	eggs	3
½ lb	cream cheese	225 g/8 oz
2 tbsp	Dijon mustard	1 tbsp
1 cup	grated Gruyère cheese	50 g/2 oz
	salt	
	pepper	
1 tsp	butter	1 tsp

1. Rinse the cabbage very thoroughly and put it in a dish with ⅓ cup (4½ tablespoons) of water. Cover and microwave on HIGH for 12 minutes. Leave to stand for 5 minutes.
2. Break the eggs into a bowl and whisk with a fork. Add the cream cheese, mustard, Gruyère, salt and pepper, whisking continuously.
3. Add the cabbage and stir thoroughly. Butter the base of a Pyrex cake mold (mould) and pour in the mixture. Smooth the surface. Cover and microwave on HIGH for 14 minutes.
4. Leave to stand for 5 minutes, then turn out on to a platter and serve hot.

Paupiettes de chou

Stuffed Cabbage Leaves

◄▷ 00.15   00.17
Serves 4

American	Ingredients	Metric/Imperial
8	Savoy cabbage leaves	8
3½ oz	onions	100 g/3½ oz
½ lb	veal, cut into small pieces	225 g/8 oz
2 tbsp	golden raisins (sultanas)	1 tbsp
1	egg	1
3 tbsp	breadcrumbs	2 tbsp
3 tbsp	pine kernels	2 tbsp
	salt	
	pepper	
⅓ cup	white wine	4½ tbsp
⅓ cup	sour cream (crème fraîche)	4½ tbsp
1 tsp	mustard	1 tsp

1. Pour 1 cup (250 ml/8 fl oz) hot water into the lower compartment of a microwave steamer. Put the cabbage leaves into the upper compartment. Cover and microwave on HIGH for 6 minutes.
2. Run the cabbage leaves under cold water and then spread out on a clean cloth.
3. Purée the onions coarsely in a food processor. Add the veal and purée again. Transfer the mixture to a bowl.
4. Rinse the golden raisins (sultanas).
5. Break the egg into a bowl and whisk with a fork.
6. Add the egg, golden raisins (sultanas), breadcrumbs and pine kernels to the veal and onion mixture. Season with salt and pepper and knead, as for pastry or dough.
7. Divide the stuffing between the 8 cabbage leaves. Roll up into small parcels, making sure the stuffing is well enclosed.
8. Put the parcels in a circle in a round dish. Add the white wine. Cover and microwave on HIGH for 10 minutes.
9. When the cabbage parcels are cooked, remove with a slotted spatula and arrange in a heated serving dish.
10. Pour the cooking liquid into a bowl and stir in the sour cream (crème fraîche) and mustard. Cook for 1 minute on HIGH, pour over the stuffed cabbage and serve at once.

Chou chinois au raifort

Chinese Cabbage with Horseradish Cream

◄▷ 00.05   00.08
Serves 3-4 as side dish

American	Ingredients	Metric/Imperial
14 oz	shredded Chinese cabbage	400 g/14 oz
1	egg	1
1 tsp	mustard	1 tsp
2 tsp	horseradish sauce	2 tsp
2 tbsp	sour cream (crème fraîche)	1 tbsp

1. Rinse and drain the Chinese cabbage, and put in a dish with 2-3 tablespoons of water. Cover and microwave on HIGH for 6 minutes.
2. Mix together the egg, mustard, horseradish sauce and sour cream (crème fraîche). Stir the mixture into the cabbage, re-cover and cook for 2 minutes on HIGH. Serve hot.

Pain au chou chinois

Chinese Cabbage and Meat Loaf

◄▷ 00.15   00.34
Serves 4

American	Ingredients	Metric/Imperial
1 lb	Chinese cabbage	450 g/1 lb
2 oz	smoked streaky bacon, cut into strips	50 g/2 oz
2	quartered garlic cloves	2
7 oz	finely sliced onions	200 g/7 oz
1	bunch fresh parsley	1
10½ oz	ground (minced) beef	300 g/10½ oz
2	eggs	2
¼ cup	sour cream (crème fraîche)	3 tbsp
3 tbsp	juniper brandy	2 tbsp
½ tsp	cumin powder	½ tsp
¼ tsp	allspice	¼ tsp
	salt	
	pepper	
½ tsp	butter	½ tsp

1. Pour 1 cup (250 ml/8 fl oz) water into the lower compartment of a microwave steamer. Cover and microwave on HIGH for 3 minutes.
2. Remove the hard stem and outer leaves of the cabbage. Cut into strips and put in the upper compartment of the steamer, on top of the lower compartment. Cover and microwave on HIGH for 10 minutes.
3. Put the bacon and garlic in a small casserole and microwave, uncovered, for 1 minute on HIGH.
4. Add the onions. Cover and microwave on HIGH for 5 minutes.
5. Drain the cabbage in a colander. Rinse the parsley and pat dry on kitchen paper. Discard the stalks.
6. Put the ground (minced) beef, eggs, sour cream (crème fraîche), juniper brandy, cumin powder and allspice in a large bowl. Season with salt and pepper and stir thoroughly.
7. Purée the cabbage in a food processor. Add the parsley, bacon, garlic and onions. Purée until smooth and add to the other ingredients in the bowl. Stir thoroughly, taste and adjust seasoning.
8. Butter the base of a Pyrex cake mold (mould) very lightly. Pour in the mixture and smooth the surface. Cover and microwave on HIGH for 15 minutes. Serve hot or, if preferred, cold with a tomato sauce.

Microwave hint: To cook cabbage, shred and put in a suitable bowl with ¼ cup (4-5 tablespoons) of apple juice, ¼ teaspoon of caraway seeds and a little black pepper. Stir the ingredients, cover the bowl and cook on HIGH for 3 minutes. Stir again, test for tenderness and add salt to taste. Cover and cook for a further 2-3 minutes on HIGH. Leave to stand for 2 minutes before serving.

Chou rouge aux marrons

Red Cabbage with Chestnuts

00.05 **00.17**

Serves 4 as side dish

American	Ingredients	Metric/Imperial
1 lb	shredded red cabbage	450 g/1 lb
½	chicken bouillon (stock) cube	½
3 tbsp	vinegar	2 tbsp
¼ cup	butter	2 tbsp
½ lb	canned chestnuts	225 g/8 oz
	salt	
	pepper	

1. Put the cabbage in a casserole.

2. Crumble the ½ bouillon (stock) cube into ⅓ cup (4½ tablespoons) of hot water and pour over the cabbage. Add the vinegar and dot with half the butter. Cover and microwave on HIGH for 12 minutes.

3. Drain the chestnuts. Season the cabbage lightly with salt and pepper and add the chestnuts. Cover and microwave on HIGH for 5 minutes.

4. Stir in the rest of the butter, pour into a vegetable dish and serve.

Red cabbage with chestnuts

Savoy cabbage with cheese and bacon

Chou à la tomme basque

Savoy Cabbage with Cheese and Bacon

	00.10	00.19	
	Serves 3-4 as side dish		

American	Ingredients	Metric/Imperial
1 lb	Savoy cabbage	450 g/1 lb
3½ oz	smoked streaky bacon, cut into tiny strips	100 g/3½ oz
2 oz	chopped shallots	50 g/2 oz
1 cup	Cheshire or Cheddar cheese	50 g/2 oz
3 tbsp	olive oil	2 tbsp
2 tbsp	honey vinegar	1 tbsp
2 tbsp	mild mustard	1 tbsp
	salt	
	pepper	

1. Pour 1 cup (250 ml/8 fl oz) of water into the lower compartment of a microwave steamer. Cover and heat on HIGH for 3 minutes.

2. Remove any damaged outer leaves from the cabbage and shred with a kitchen cleaver. Rinse and put the cabbage in the perforated compartment of the steamer. Place this on top of the lower compartment. Cover and microwave on HIGH for 6 minutes.

3. Put the bacon and shallots in a casserole. Cover and microwave on HIGH for 5 minutes.

4. Drain the cabbage, add to the bacon and shallots and stir well. Cover and microwave on HIGH for 5 minutes.

5. Cut the cheese into tiny dice. Make a vinaigrette sauce with the olive oil, vinegar and mustard. Add salt and pepper to taste.

6. When the cabbage is cooked, pour the vinaigrette sauce over and add the cheese. Stir thoroughly, put into a dish and serve.

Pâté au chou vert

Green Cabbage and Bacon Terrine

00.15　　　00.50
Serves 4-6

American	Ingredients	Metric/Imperial
1¼ lb	green cabbage	600 g/1¼ lb
3 tbsp	white wine	2 tbsp
10½ oz	sausage meat (veal and pork)	300 g/10½ oz
3	eggs	3
1 cup	grated Gruyère cheese	50 g/2 oz
½ tsp	cumin powder	½ tsp
½ tsp	garlic powder	½ tsp
	salt	
	pepper	
3	strips (rashers) streaky bacon	3

1. Bring a large pan of water to boil on a conventional cooker. Remove the thick stem and any tough outer leaves and shred the cabbage. Plunge it into the boiling water and cook for 5 minutes after the water has returned to the boil. Put in a colander and leave to drain.
2. Put the cabbage in a dish with the white wine. Cover and microwave on HIGH for 10 minutes. Leave to stand for 5 minutes.
3. Carefully mix together the sausage meat, eggs, Gruyère, cumin and garlic powder. Season with salt and pepper.
4. Stir the cabbage into the mixture, stir thoroughly. Stretch the bacon strips (rashers) as much as possible and line a Pyrex cake mold (mould) with them. Pour the cabbage mixture into the terrine. Smooth the surface.
5. Cover and microwave on HIGH for 20 minutes.
6. Leave to stand for 10 minutes, then turn out on to a platter. Serve hot or cold.

Green cabbage and bacon terrine

Épinards aux fines herbes

Spinach with Herbs

00.03　　　00.07
Serves 2-3 as side dish

American	Ingredients	Metric/Imperial
10½ oz	frozen chopped spinach	300 g/10½ oz
2 tbsp	frozen chives	1 tbsp
2 tbsp	frozen tarragon	1 tbsp
2 tbsp	mustard	1 tbsp
1	egg yolk	1
2 tbsp	chopped fresh parsley	1 tbsp
	salt	
	pepper	

1. Put the frozen spinach in a casserole. Microwave, uncovered, on HIGH for 5 minutes.
2. Stir the spinach and add the chives and tarragon. Microwave, uncovered, on HIGH for a further 2 minutes.
3. Mix together the mustard and egg yolk and add to the spinach. Stir well. Add the chopped parsley. Season with salt and pepper to taste and serve.

Spinach and Potato Grill

00.10　　　00.30
Serves 4

American	Ingredients	Metric/Imperial
1¾ lb	sliced potatoes	700 g/1¾ lb
5 oz	chopped streaky bacon	150 g/5 oz
1¼ cups	grated Cheddar cheese	150 g/5 oz
	salt	
	pepper	
1¼ cups	milk	300 ml/½ pint
1¾ lb	spinach	700 g/1¾ lb
1	chopped onion	1
1	crushed garlic clove	1
1 tbsp	butter	½ tbsp

1. Arrange a layer of potatoes, overlapping in a round dish, leaving an empty ring around the edge.
2. Arrange a layer of bacon on top of the potatoes. Sprinkle some of the cheese on top of the bacon. Sprinkle with salt and pepper. Add another layer of potatoes, one of bacon, more cheese, salt and pepper, and so on – until the ingredients are used up.
3. Pour the milk into a bowl and heat in the microwave for 5 minutes on HIGH. Pour over the potatoes, cover and cook on HIGH for 15 minutes.
4. Rinse the spinach, drain and cook in the microwave for 5 minutes on HIGH. Drain again.
5. Mix the onion and garlic with the spinach. Arrange the spinach in the empty space round the potatoes and dot with butter. Microwave on HIGH for 5 minutes. Serve hot.

Couronne d'épinards à la crème

Spinach Ring Mold (Mould) with Cream Sauce

◣▷ 00.05   00.27 Ⓜ
Serves 4

American	Ingredients	Metric/Imperial
1¼ lb	chopped frozen spinach	500 g/1¼ lb
3½ oz	frozen sorrel	100 g/3½ oz
1 tsp	sugar	1 tsp
4 tbsp	chopped tarragon	2 tbsp
	salt	
	pepper	
2 tbsp	butter	1 tbsp
4 tbsp	all-purpose (plain) flour	2 tbsp
1 cup	milk	250 ml/8 fl oz
3	egg yolks	3
¼ cup	sour cream (crème fraîche)	3 tbsp
2 tbsp	chopped chervil	2 tbsp

1. Put the frozen spinach and sorrel in a casserole. Microwave, uncovered, on HIGH for 7 minutes.
2. Add the sugar and tarragon. Season with salt and pepper and mix well.
3. Melt the butter in a bowl for 30 seconds on HIGH. Add the flour and mix well. Pour in the milk, whisking constantly. Microwave on HIGH for 1½ minutes. Whisk and cook for a further 2 minutes. Whisk again.
4. Season the sauce with salt and pepper. Divide into 2 equal portions. Add the egg yolks to one of the portions, mix well and add to the spinach mixture. Pour into a small 9 inch (22 cm) ring mold (mould). Cover and microwave on HIGH for 12 minutes. Leave to stand for 3 minutes.
5. Add the sour cream (crème fraîche) to the remaining of sauce. Reheat for 1 minute on HIGH. Add the chervil.
6. Turn out the spinach mold (mould) on to a plate, pour the sauce over and serve at once.

Chou-fleur aux olives

Cauliflower with Stuffed Olives

◣▷ 00.10   00.20 Ⓜ
Serves 4-5 as side dish

American	Ingredients	Metric/Imperial
3 tbsp	vinegar	2 tbsp
2 lb	cauliflower florets	1 kg/2 lb
12	pimento-stuffed olives	12
⅓ cup	sour cream (crème fraîche)	4½ tbsp
	salt	
	pepper	
1 tbsp	chopped fresh chives	1 tbsp
½ cup	pine kernels	50 g/2 oz
3 tbsp	grated Parmesan cheese	2 tbsp

1. Pour the vinegar into a bowl of water and rinse the cauliflower florets in it.

2. Pour 1 cup (250 ml/8 fl oz) of hot water into the lower compartment of a microwave steamer. Put the cauliflower florets into the upper compartment. Cover and microwave on HIGH for 15 minutes.
3. Slice the olives. Season the sour cream (crème fraîche) with salt and pepper.
4. Drain the cauliflower and put in a deep dish. Season with salt and pepper. Add the olives, chopped chives and pine kernels. Stir carefully. Pour the cream over and heat for 5 minutes on HIGH.
5. Sprinkle with grated Parmesan and serve hot.

Chou-fleur sauce aurore

Cauliflower in Tomato Sauce

◣▷ 00.05   00.14 Ⓜ
Serves 3 as side dish

American	Ingredients	Metric/Imperial
1¼ lb	cauliflower florets	500 g/1¼ lb
¾ cup	milk	200 ml/7 fl oz
	salt	
	pepper	
1 oz	butter	25 g/1 oz
2 tbsp	all-purpose (plain) flour	1 tbsp
2 tbsp	concentrated tomato juice	1 tbsp

1. Put the cauliflower florets in a casserole and pour over the milk. Season lightly with salt and pepper. Cover and microwave on HIGH for 12 minutes.
2. Put most of the butter in a bowl and melt in the microwave oven for 1 minute on HIGH. Add the flour and stir well. Drain the cauliflower and pour its cooking liquid over the flour and butter mixture. Whisk vigorously. Heat in the oven for 1 minute on HIGH. Whisk again. Add the concentrated tomato juice and the remaining butter. Stir well. Taste and adjust the seasoning.
3. Transfer the cauliflower to a serving dish, pour the sauce over and serve.

Norwegian Cauliflower

◣▷ 00.06   00.13 Ⓜ
Serves 4

American	Ingredients	Metric/Imperial
1	medium size cauliflower	1
1½ oz	butter	2 tbsp
1 cup	soft white breadcrumbs	100 g/3½ oz
1¼ cups	milk	300 ml/½ pint
	salt	
	pepper	
3½ oz	shelled shrimp (prawns)	100 g/3½ oz
1 tsp	sugar	1 tsp
2 tbsp	brandy	1 tbsp
4 tbsp	light (single) cream	3 tbsp
	sprigs parsley	

1. Remove any leaves from the cauliflower and trim the stalk. Put the cauliflower in a straight-sided soufflé dish with ¼ cup (4 tablespoons) of water. Cover with saran wrap (cling film), pierce and cook on HIGH for 6-8 minutes.
2. Put the butter in a bowl and melt in the microwave for 1 minute on HIGH.
3. Add the breadcrumbs, milk and salt and pepper to taste. Heat on HIGH for 2 minutes.
4. Set aside a few shrimp (prawns) to garnish. Add the remaining shrimp (prawns) to the sauce and stir in the sugar and brandy. Heat on HIGH for 2 minutes.
5. Stir in the cream.
6. Drain the cauliflower and transfer to a warmed serving dish. Pour the sauce over and serve hot garnished with the reserved shrimp (prawns) and parsley.

Microwave hint: One stage methods are easy when cooking vegetables by microwave. For instance, chop up a cucumber, roughly. Put in a suitable dish and pour over enough cream to cover. Sprinkle with salt and pepper and cook uncovered on HIGH for 10 minutes. Sprinkle with chopped mixed herbs and serve at once.

Chou-fleur à la crème

Cream of Cauliflower

◄ 00.10   00.19

Serves 4 as side dish

American	Ingredients	Metric/Imperial
1¾ lb	cauliflower florets	700 g/1¾ lb
1¼ cups	milk	300 ml/½ pint
	salt	
	pepper	
3 tbsp	butter	1½ tbsp
3 tbsp	all-purpose (plain) flour	2 tbsp
½ tsp	grated nutmeg	½ tsp
¼ cup	sour cream (crème fraîche)	3 tbsp

1. Rinse and drain the cauliflower florets and put in a large casserole with the milk. Season lightly with salt and pepper. Cover and microwave on HIGH for 15 minutes, stirring once, midway through the cooking time.
2. Put the butter in a large bowl and melt in the oven for 1 minute on HIGH.
3. Stir in the flour.
4. Drain the cauliflower and pour the cooking liquid into the flour and butter mixture, whisking constantly. Microwave for 2 minutes on HIGH, whisking once, midway through the cooking time.
5. Add the grated nutmeg and sour cream (crème fraîche). Stir and microwave for 1 further minute on HIGH. Whisk. Taste and adjust seasoning.
6. Put the cauliflower into a vegetable dish, pour the sauce over and serve.

Cream of cauliflower

Mousse de brocolis
Broccoli Mousse

▬◸	00.10	00.12	〰
	Serves 4 as side dish		

American	Ingredients	Metric/Imperial
1¼ lb	broccoli florets	600 g/1¼ lb
3 tbsp	vinegar	2 tbsp
2 tbsp	butter	1 tbsp
1	egg	1
½ tsp	cumin powder	½ tsp
	salt	
	pepper	

1. Put the broccoli in a dish and add the vinegar. Dot with the butter.
2. Cover and microwave on HIGH for 10 minutes. Leave to stand for 2 minutes.
3. Transfer to a food processor and purée. Continue to liquidize while adding the egg, cumin and salt and pepper to taste.
4. Arrange the mousse on a serving dish.

Choux de Bruxelles aux foies de volaille
Brussels Sprouts with Chicken Livers

▬◸	00.10	00.14	〰
	Serves 3-4		

American	Ingredients	Metric/Imperial
1 lb	frozen Brussels sprouts	450 g/1 lb
2	finely chopped shallots	2
3½ oz	coarsely chopped chicken livers	100 g/3½ oz
2	finely sliced garlic cloves	2
	salt	
	pepper	
3 tbsp	wine vinegar	2 tbsp
2 tbsp	butter	1½ tbsp

1. Put the Brussels sprouts, still frozen, in a casserole with ¼ cup (4 tablespoons) of water. Cover and microwave on HIGH for 10 minutes.
2. Put the shallots in a small casserole. Cover and microwave on HIGH for 2 minutes.
3. Add the chicken livers and garlic to the shallots. Cover and microwave on HIGH for 1½ minutes.
4. Season with salt and pepper. Pour the vinegar over and stir well.
5. Drain the Brussels sprouts and season with salt and pepper. Add the butter in small quantities and stir until melted.
6. Transfer the sprouts to a serving dish, add the contents of the casserole, stir and serve.

Choux de Bruxelles aux amandes
Brussels Sprouts with Almonds

▬◸	00.05	00.16	〰
	Serves 3-4 as side dish		

American	Ingredients	Metric/Imperial
1 lb	frozen Brussels sprouts	450 g/1 lb
3 tbsp	slivered almonds	2 tbsp
¼ cup	butter	50 g/2 oz
2 tbsp	fresh lemon juice	1 tbsp
	salt	
	pepper	

1. Put the frozen sprouts in a casserole with ¼ cup (4 tablespoons) of water. Cover and microwave on HIGH for 10 minutes.
2. Spread the slivered almonds out on a plate and microwave for 3-4 minutes on HIGH, turning once or twice during cooking, until golden brown.
3. Put the butter in a bowl and melt in the microwave oven for 1½ minutes on HIGH. Add the lemon juice. Season with salt and pepper. Stir well.
4. Drain the sprouts. Put into a vegetable dish and pour the lemon butter over, stir well.
5. Sprinkle with slivered almonds and serve hot.

Microwave hint: To add variety to Brussels sprouts, add a teaspoon of lemon juice, ½ teaspoon of grated lemon zest (peel) a pinch of allspice and generous seasoning to the cooking water. This produces a lemon flavored sauce. Orange can be substituted.

Courgettes au parmesan
Zucchini (Courgettes) with Parmesan Cheese

▬◸	00.05	00.11	〰
	Serves 4 as side dish		

American	Ingredients	Metric/Imperial
1¾ lb	very thinly sliced zucchini, (courgettes)	700 g/1¾ lb
1	lemon, squeezed for juice	1
3 tbsp	roast chicken cooking liquid	2 tbsp
1½ tbsp	garlic powder	1 tbsp
	salt	
	pepper	
2 tbsp	butter	1 tbsp
¼ cup	grated Parmesan cheese	2 tbsp

1. Put the zucchini (courgettes) in a dish and pour the lemon juice and the chicken cooking liquid over. Sprinkle with garlic powder and season with salt and pepper. Cover and microwave on HIGH for 8 minutes. Leave to stand for 3 minutes.
2. Transfer the zucchini (courgettes) to a serving dish. Add the butter and Parmesan. Stir and serve hot. This dish obviously goes well with roast chicken, and the cooking liquid can be used for this recipe, but the juices from any roast meat will serve.

Brussels sprouts with chicken livers

Courgettes farcies
Stuffed Zucchini (Courgettes)

◼▷ 00.10   00.12 ▨
Serves 4 as side dish

American	Ingredients	Metric/Imperial
4	zucchini (courgettes)	4
1 tsp	butter	1 tsp
2	garlic cloves	2
1	shallot	1
10	fresh parsley sprigs	10
½ cup	breadcrumbs	2 tbsp
½ cup	pine kernels	2 tbsp
1	egg	1
½ cup	grated Parmesan cheese	2 tbsp
	salt	
	pepper	

1. Rinse the zucchini (courgettes), top-and-tail and halve lengthwise. Remove the flesh with a small spoon, leaving enough for the shells to retain their shape.
2. Butter the base of an oval dish and arrange the zucchini (courgette) shells on it side by side, skin-side down. Microwave, uncovered, on HIGH for 6 minutes.
3. Peel the garlic and shallot.
4. Rinse the parsley and discard the stalks.
5. Put the zucchini (courgette) pulp, garlic, shallot, parsley, breadcrumbs, pine kernels, egg and grated Parmesan in the food processor. Season with salt and pepper and purée until smooth.
6. Fill the zucchini (courgette) shells with the mixture, return the dish to the oven and cook for a further 6 minutes on HIGH. Serve hot.

Courgettes aux herbes
Zucchini (Courgettes) in Herb and Parmesan Sauce

◼▷ 00.15   00.16 ▨
Serves 4-5 as side dish

American	Ingredients	Metric/Imperial
1¾ lb	finely sliced zucchini (courgettes)	700 g/1¾ lb
2 oz	frozen sorrel	50 g/2 oz
1	bunch fresh chives	1
3	fresh parsley sprigs	3
2 tbsp	sour cream (crème fraîche)	1 tbsp
2	eggs	2
	salt	
	pepper	
¼ cup	grated Parmesan cheese	4 tbsp

1. Put the zucchini (courgettes) in a casserole with ¼ cup (3 tablespoons) of water. Cover and microwave on HIGH for 10 minutes, stirring once midway through cooking.
2. Drain the zucchini (courgettes) in a colander. Put the sorrel in a bowl and defrost in the microwave oven on HIGH for 1½ minutes.
3. Rinse the chives and parsley and chop finely. Add the sour cream (crème fraîche) to the sorrel. Break the eggs into a bowl and whisk them with a fork. Add the sorrel, chives and parsley to the eggs. Season generously with salt and pepper.
4. Put the zucchini (courgettes) in a round dish 9 inches (22 cm) in diameter. Smooth the surface. Pour the egg and herb mixture over, carefully mixing with a fork. Microwave, uncovered, on HIGH for 4 minutes. Sprinkle with the Parmesan and serve hot.

Zucchini (courgettes) in herb and Parmesan sauce

Stuffed zucchini (courgettes)

Courgettes au gruyère

Zucchini (Courgettes) with Gruyère Cheese

◪▷   00.10   00.15   ▦
Serves 4 as side dish

American	Ingredients	Metric/Imperial
1¾ lb	zucchini (courgettes), cut into strips	700 g/1¾ lb
1 tbsp	butter	½ tbsp
	salt	
	pepper	
½ tsp	garlic powder	½ tsp
1 tsp	cornstarch (cornflour)	1 tsp
¼ cup	fresh lemon juice	3 tbsp
1	egg	1
1 cup	grated Gruyère cheese	50 g/2 oz

1. Put the zucchini (courgettes) in a casserole with the butter and 2-3 tablespoons of water. Season with salt and pepper, add the garlic powder and stir well. Cover and microwave on HIGH for 14 minutes.
2. Put the cornstarch (cornflour) in a small bowl and mix to a smooth paste with the lemon juice. Add the egg and whisk until foamy.
3. Drain the zucchini (courgettes), reserving the cooking liquid. Pour the liquid into the bowl containing the cornstarch (cornflour) and egg mixture. Microwave, uncovered, on HIGH for 1 minute. Whisk. Taste and adjust seasoning.
4. Put the zucchini (courgettes) in a warmed serving dish. Add the Gruyère, stirring carefully. Pour the sauce over, stir again and serve.

Chips de courgettes à la provençale

Provençale Style Zucchini (Courgettes)

◪▷   00.10   00.15   ▦
Serves 4 as side dish

American	Ingredients	Metric/Imperial
¼ lb	chopped shallots	125 g/4 oz
3 tbsp	olive oil	2 tbsp
1¾ lb	finely grated zucchini (courgettes)	700 g/1¾ lb
¼ cup	concentrated tomato juice	3 tbsp
50	fresh basil leaves	50
¼ cup	ground almonds	1 tbsp
	salt	
	pepper	
¼ cup	grated Parmesan cheese	1 tbsp

1. Put the shallots in a large casserole. Pour half the olive oil over. Cover and microwave on HIGH for 3 minutes.
2. Add the zucchini (courgettes) to the casserole with the tomato juice. Cover and microwave on HIGH for 12 minutes.
3. Rinse the basil leaves and pat dry on kitchen paper. Put in the food processor with the remaining oil and the ground almonds. Purée until smooth.
4. Season the zucchini (courgettes) with salt and pepper and add the basil purée and the grated Parmesan. Stir carefully, transfer to a vegetable dish and serve. This makes an equally good accompaniment for fish or meat.

Provençale-style zucchini (courgettes)

Petits pâtés de courgette
Zucchini (Courgette) Ramekins

	00.10	00.17	

Serves 4 as side dish

American	Ingredients	Metric/Imperial
1 lb	finely diced zucchini (courgettes)	450 g/1 lb
	salt	
1 tbsp	butter	½ tbsp
1	large egg	1
3 tbsp	sour cream (crème fraîche)	2 tbsp
	pepper	
1 cup	grated Parmesan cheese	50 g/2 oz
1 tbsp	chopped fresh chives	1 tbsp
1 tbsp	chopped fresh chervil	1 tbsp

1. Put 1 cup (250 ml/8 fl oz) of water in the lower compartment of a microwave steamer, cover and heat for 3 minutes on HIGH.
2. Put the zucchini (courgettes) in the upper compartment of the steamer. Add salt, cover and microwave on HIGH for 8 minutes.
3. Carefully drain the zucchini (courgettes) in a colander.
4. Butter 4 ramekin dishes. Whisk the egg with the sour cream (crème fraîche). Add pepper, the grated Parmesan, chopped chives and chopped chervil. Carefully add the zucchini (courgettes) and divide the mixture between the 4 ramekins.
5. Put the ramekin dishes in a circle in the microwave oven, leaving the center empty. Cook for 4 minutes on HIGH.
6. Slide a knife-blade around the edge of the ramekins and turn out on to a plate. Leave to stand for 1-2 minutes. Arrange on a platter and serve.
These ramekins make a good accompaniment for roast meat or chicken.

Courgettes à la dijonnaise
Zucchini (Courgettes) in Mustard Sauce

	00.05	00.07	

Serves 4 as side dish

American	Ingredients	Metric/Imperial
1¾ lb	zucchini (courgettes)	700 g/1¾ lb
2	crushed garlic cloves	2
	salt	
	pepper	
2 tbsp	mustard	1 tbsp
2 tbsp	yogurt	1 tbsp
1	egg	1
3 tbsp	fresh lemon juice	2 tbsp
1 tbsp	chopped fresh parsley	1 tbsp

1. Rinse and top-and-tail the zucchini (courgettes). Quarter lengthwise and cut into strips.
2. Mix together the garlic and zucchini (courgettes) in a dish and season with salt and pepper. Add 2-3 tablespoons of water. Cover and microwave on HIGH for 6 minutes.

Zucchini (courgette) ramekins

3. Mix together the mustard, yogurt, egg and lemon juice and pour over the zucchini (courgettes). Stir well. Cover and microwave on MEDIUM-HIGH for 1 minute. Sprinkle with chopped parsley and serve hot.

Flan de courgettes
Zucchini (Courgette) Flan

	00.15	00.29	

Serves 4

American	Ingredients	Metric/Imperial
7 oz	grated onions	200 g/7 oz
1 lb	grated zucchini (courgettes)	450 g/1 lb
¼ cup	butter	25 g/1 oz
6	eggs	6
1 tsp	garlic powder	1 tsp
1½ tsp	mild curry powder	1½ tsp
1 tsp	sugar	1 tsp
½ tsp	mixed herbs	½ tsp
	salt	
	pepper	
1 cup	grated Gruyère cheese	50 g/2 oz

1. Put the onions in a large dish with 1-2 tablespoons of water. Microwave, uncovered, on HIGH for 4 minutes.
2. Add the zucchini (courgettes) and half the butter to the onions. Cover and microwave on HIGH for 6 minutes. Leave to cool.
3. Break the eggs into a bowl and whisk with a fork. Add the garlic powder, curry powder, sugar and mixed herbs. Season generously with salt and pepper (remember that the vegetables have not been seasoned).
4. Pour the zucchini (courgettes) and onions over the eggs and stir thoroughly.
5. Butter the base of a small ring mold (mould) and pour in the mixture. Cover and microwave on MEDIUM for 10 minutes, then on HIGH for a further 2 minutes. Leave to stand for 5 minutes.
6. Turn out the mold (mould) on to a serving dish. Sprinkle with the Gruyère and put the flan back into the oven for 1½ minutes on MEDIUM-HIGH or until the cheese has melted. Serve immediately.

Cucumber with chives and dill

Concombre aux fines herbes

Cucumber with Chives and Dill

00.05   **00.10**

Serves 3-4 as side dish

American	Ingredients	Metric/Imperial
1	large cucumber, peeled and cubed	1
2 tbsp	sugar	1 tbsp
	salt	
	pepper	
2 tbsp	butter	1 tbsp
3 tbsp	fresh lemon juice	2 tbsp
1 tbsp	chopped fresh dill	1 tbsp
1 tbsp	chopped fresh chives	1 tbsp

1. Put the cucumber in a small casserole and sprinkle with sugar, salt and pepper. Cover and microwave on HIGH for 10 minutes.
2. Drain the cucumber in a colander. Put in a serving dish, dot with the butter, pour the lemon juice over, sprinkle with dill and chives, stir thoroughly and serve hot.

Concombre à la cassonade

Cucumber in Brown Sugar

00.05   **00.10**

Serves 4-5 as side dish

American	Ingredients	Metric/Imperial
2 oz	smoked streaky bacon, cut into strips	50 g/2 oz
2	chopped shallots	2
1¾ lb	peeled, cubed cucumber	700 g/1¾ lb
¼ cup	butter	25 g/1 oz
	salt	
	pepper	
1 tsp	cornstarch (cornflour)	1 tsp
2 tbsp	Dijon mustard	1 tbsp
2 tbsp	soft dark brown sugar	1 tbsp
1 tsp	dark soy sauce	1 tsp
2 tbsp	white port wine	1 tbsp

1. Put the bacon and shallots in a casserole. Microwave, uncovered, on HIGH for 2 minutes.

Cucumber in brown sugar

Concombre au jambonneau

Cucumber with Country Ham

	00.05		00.10	
	Serves 4			

American	Ingredients	Metric/Imperial
1	peeled and diced cucumber	1
8	peeled scallions (spring onions)	8
1 tbsp	butter	½ tbsp
3 tbsp	white wine or lemon juice	2 tbsp
	salt	
	pepper	
7 oz	Virginia (country) ham	200 g/7 oz
3 tbsp	sour cream (crème fraîche)	2 tbsp
1 tbsp	chopped fresh parsley	1 tbsp
	Cayenne pepper	
½ cup	grated Gruyère cheese	25 g/1 oz

2. Add the cucumber to the casserole with the butter. Season lightly with salt and pepper. Cover and microwave on HIGH for 7 minutes.
3. Mix the cornstarch (cornflour) to a smooth paste in a small bowl with the mustard, brown sugar, soy sauce and port.
4. Drain the cucumber and put in a vegetable dish. Add the cooking liquid from the cucumber to the mustard and brown sugar mixture and stir. Microwave for 1 minute on HIGH, then whisk vigorously and pour over the cucumber. Serve at once. This dish is an excellent accompaniment to roast pork.

1. Put the cucumber and scallions (spring onions) in a dish with the butter and the lemon juice or white wine. Season with salt and pepper. Cover and microwave on HIGH for 8 minutes.
2. Cut the Virginia (country) ham into large cubes. Mix together the sour cream (crème fraîche), chopped parsley and a pinch of Cayenne pepper.
3. Add the ham and the sour cream (crème fraîche) mixture to the cucumber, stir well and sprinkle with the Gruyère cheese. Cover and microwave on HIGH for 1½ minutes. Serve hot. If liked, slide the dish under a conventional broiler (grill) for a few minutes to brown the top.

Cucumber with country ham

Concombre aux crevettes

Cucumber with Shrimp (Prawns)

00.08   00.15

Serves 4-5 as side dish

American	Ingredients	Metric/Imperial
10½ oz	red bell peppers, coarsely chopped	300 g/10½ oz
3	coarsely chopped shallots	3
1¾ lb	seeded and diced cucumber	700 g/1¾ lb
½ tsp	sugar	½ tsp
2 tbsp	olive oil	1 tbsp
2 tbsp	sherry vinegar	1 tbsp
	salt	
½ tsp	garlic powder	½ tsp
	pepper	
3½ oz	shelled shrimp (prawns)	100 g/3½ oz

1. Put the bell peppers and shallots in a casserole with 2-3 tablespoons of water. Cover and microwave on HIGH for 6 minutes.
2. Put the cucumber in a casserole. Cover and microwave on HIGH for 7 minutes.
3. Drain the bell peppers and purée in a food processor, adding the sugar, oil and vinegar. Add salt to taste.
4. When the cucumbers are cooked, drain carefully in a colander and return to the casserole. Add the garlic powder, salt and pepper to taste, the shrimp (prawns) and the purée of bell peppers. Stir well and reheat for 2 minutes on HIGH.
5. Transfer to a heated dish and serve as an accompaniment to salmon steaks or other broiled (grilled) fish.

Microwave hint: Green vegetables with a high water content, such as cucumber, cook more quickly by microwave than denser, drier vegetables like cabbage.

Concombre aux herbes

Herbed Cucumber with Shrimp (Prawns)

00.10   00.10

Serves 4

American	Ingredients	Metric/Imperial
1	peeled, cubed cucumber	1
	salt	
1	large red bell pepper, cubed	1
1 tbsp	butter	½ tbsp
1 tbsp	honey	½ tbsp
3 tbsp	fresh lime juice	2 tbsp
2 tbsp	white rum	1 tbsp
2 oz	shrimp (prawns) in shells	50 g/2 oz
	Cayenne pepper	
	pepper	
2	fresh mint sprigs	2
4	fresh chive stalks	4
6	fresh chervil sprigs	6

1. Put 1 cup (250 ml/8 fl oz) of water in the lower compartment of a microwave steamer and heat in the oven for 2 minutes on HIGH.
2. Put the cucumber in the upper compartment of the steamer. Season with salt. Add the bell pepper. Cover the steamer and microwave on HIGH for 6 minutes.
3. Put the butter, honey, lime juice and rum in a casserole.
4. Add the shrimp (prawns), a pinch of Cayenne pepper, the cucumber and bell pepper. Stir well. Taste and adjust seasoning. Cover and microwave on HIGH for 2 minutes.
5. Rinse the mint, chives and chervil, pat dry on kitchen paper and chop finely. Stir the herbs into the casserole. Transfer the mixture to a serving dish and serve.

Cucumber with shrimp (prawns)

Herbed cucumber with shrimp (prawns)

Pumpkin ring mold (mould)

Potiron en couronne
Pumpkin Ring Mold (Mould)

◤▭▷ 00.10 00.19 〰
Serves 4-6 as side dish

American	Ingredients	Metric/Imperial
1¼ lb	cubed pumpkin	600 g/1¼ lb
3 tbsp	instant mashed potato flakes	2 tbsp
1 tsp	butter	1 tsp
¼ cup	sour cream (crème fraîche)	3 tbsp
4	small eggs	4
½ tsp	grated nutmeg	½ tsp
	salt	
	pepper	

1. Put the pumpkin cubes in a small casserole with ¼ cup (3 tablespoons) of water. Cover and microwave on HIGH for 10 minutes.
2. Drain the pumpkin in a colander, then put in a food processor and purée until smooth. Add the instant mashed potato flakes, stir, and leave the purée in the food processor bowl. Leave to stand for 1 minute.
3. Butter the base of a Pyrex ring mold (mould) 9 inches (22 cm) in diameter.
4. Add the sour cream (crème fraîche), eggs, grated nutmeg, salt and pepper to the pumpkin purée. Purée once more.
5. Pour the mixture into the ring mold (mould). Microwave, uncovered, on HIGH for 6 minutes.
6. Leave to stand for 2 minutes, then turn out the mold (mould) on to a serving dish. This purée makes an excellent accompaniment for roast duck or guinea fowl.

Purée de potiron au cantal
Cheese and Pumpkin Purée

◤▭▷ 00.10 00.12 〰
Serves 4 as side dish

American	Ingredients	Metric/Imperial
1¾ lb	pumpkin (1 large slice), coarsely chopped	700 g/1¾ lb
7 oz	floury potatoes, diced	200 g/7 oz
1	quartered garlic clove	1
3 tbsp	sour cream (crème fraîche)	2 tbsp
	pepper	
3½ oz	mild Cheshire or Cheddar cheese	100 g/3½ oz
	salt	

1. Put the pumpkin, potatoes and garlic in a casserole with ¼ cup (3 tablespoons) of water. Cover and microwave on HIGH for 12 minutes, stirring midway through the cooking time.
2. When the vegetables are cooked, drain in a colander and purée in a food processor until smooth. Pour the purée into a terrine, add the sour cream (crème fraîche) and season generously with pepper.
3. Grate the cheese and add to the purée, mixing until it has completely melted. Taste and add salt if necessary. Pour into a dish and serve.

Potimarron au naturel
Summer Squash with Parmesan Cheese

◤▭▷ 00.10 00.14 〰
Serves 4 as side dish

American	Ingredients	Metric/Imperial
2	chopped shallots	2
1¾ lb	summer squash, skinned, seeded and cubed	700 g/1¾ lb
3 tbsp	butter	1½ tbsp
	salt	
	pepper	
3 tbsp	grated Parmesan cheese	2 tbsp

1. Put the shallots in a casserole. Cover and microwave on HIGH for 3 minutes.
2. Add the squash and ¼ cup (3 tablespoons) of water. Cover and microwave on HIGH for 10 minutes.
3. Put the butter in a bowl and melt for 1 minute on HIGH. Sprinkle with salt and pepper and pour over the squash. Add the Parmesan and stir well. Transfer to a vegetable dish and serve.

Microwave hint: To cook lentils by microwave, wash well, then put in a suitable container and cover with boiling water. Put a plate over the container and cook on HIGH for 10 minutes. Leave to stand for 5 minutes, then cook for a further 10 minutes, or until the pulses are tender but not breaking up.

Summer squash with Parmesan cheese

Ratatouille Nicoise

Ratatouille 1

00.15   00.22

Serves 4 as side dish

American	Ingredients	Metric/Imperial
¾ lb	eggplant (aubergines), finely sliced	350 g/12 oz
	salt	
1	orange	1
½ lb	finely sliced onions	225 g/8 oz
3½ oz	de-rinded smoked streaky bacon, cut into thin strips	100 g/3½ oz
½ lb	red bell peppers, coarsely chopped	225 g/8 oz
½ lb	zucchini (courgettes), sliced into rounds	225 g/8 oz
10½ oz	sliced tomatoes	300 g/10½ oz
2	crushed garlic cloves	2
1	bayleaf	1
2	crushed fresh thyme sprigs	2
	pepper	
3 tbsp	olive oil	2 tbsp
3½ oz	pitted (stoned) black olives	100 g/3½ oz

1. Put the eggplant (aubergines) in a strainer, add salt and leave to drain. Rinse the orange extremely carefully under plenty of cold running water and remove the zest (peel) with a small sharp knife or vegetable peeler, taking care not to bring any of the bitter white pith with it. Cut the zest (peel) into matchstick (julienne) strips.

2. Put the onion, bacon and bell peppers in a large casserole. Cover and microwave on HIGH for 5 minutes.

3. Add the eggplant (aubergines), zucchini (courgettes), tomatoes, garlic, orange zest (rind), bayleaf and crushed thyme. Season with salt and pepper and stir carefully. Pour the olive oil over. Cover and microwave on HIGH for 10 minutes.

4. Stir in the olives, cover and microwave on HIGH for a further 2 minutes. Leave to stand for 5 minutes.

5. Remove the bayleaf, pour the ratatouille into a warmed dish and serve at once.

Ratatouille

Ratatouille 11

	00.15	00.25	
	Serves 4-5		

American	Ingredients	Metric/Imperial
14 oz	eggplant (aubergines), sliced into thin rounds	400 g/14 oz
	salt	
7 oz	finely sliced onions	200 g/7 oz
3	crushed garlic cloves	3
3½ oz	smoked streaky bacon, de-rinded, cut into thin strips	100 g/3½ oz
2	red bell peppers, seeded, coarsely chopped	2
3	sticks celery, cut into matchstick (julienne) strips	3
½ lb	finely sliced zucchini (courgettes)	225 g/8 oz
	pepper	
½ tsp	mixed herbs	½ tsp
¼ cup	olive oil	3 tbsp
7 oz	tomatoes	200 g/7 oz

1. Put the eggplant (aubergines) in a colander, sprinkle with salt and leave to drain.
2. Put the onions, garlic and bacon in a large casserole. Cover and microwave on HIGH for 5 minutes.
3. Add the bell peppers and the celery to the casserole. Cover and microwave on HIGH for 5 minutes.
4. Remove the eggplant (aubergines) from the colander and pat dry with kitchen paper. Add the zucchini (courgettes) and eggplant (aubergines) to the casserole and season with salt and pepper. Sprinkle with mixed herbs and add the olive oil. Stir well. Cover and microwave on HIGH for 10 minutes.
5. Rinse the tomatoes and remove the stalks. Cut them in half and squeeze slightly, to get rid of the seeds and liquid. Slice and add to the casserole, stirring well. Microwave, uncovered, on HIGH for 5 minutes. Adjust seasoning and serve hot.

Ratatouille aux pieds-de-mouton

Ratatouille with Wild Mushrooms

	00.10	00.16	
	Serves 4		

American	Ingredients	Metric/Imperial
7 oz	diced red bell peppers	200 g/7 oz
7 oz	chopped onions	200 g/7 oz
2 oz	smoked streaky bacon, cut into strips	50 g/2 oz
¾ lb	cubed eggplant (aubergines)	350 g/12 oz
2	crushed large garlic cloves	2
½ tsp	crumbled fresh thyme	½ tsp
3 tbsp	olive oil	2 tbsp
	salt	
	pepper	
1	bayleaf	1
10½ oz	wild or field mushrooms, coarsely chopped	300 g/10½ oz

1. Put the peppers, onions and bacon in a casserole. Cover and microwave on HIGH for 5 minutes.
2. Add the eggplant (aubergines) and garlic to the casserole. Sprinkle with the thyme, add the olive oil and season with salt and pepper to taste. Add the bayleaf. Cover and microwave on HIGH for 6 minutes.
3. After 6 minutes of cooking, add the mushrooms to the casserole. Cover and microwave on HIGH for a further 3 minutes. Stir, do not replace the lid, then cook for a further 2 minutes on HIGH. Remove the bayleaf and serve hot.

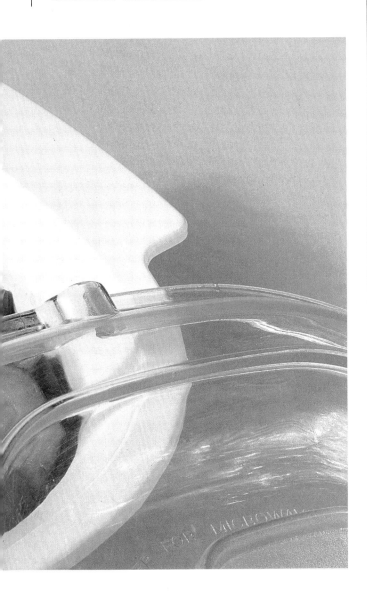

Ratatouille

Tomato casserole

Gratin de tomates

Tomato Casserole

00.10　　**00.13**

Serves 4 as side dish

American	Ingredients	Metric/Imperial
1¾ lb	thickly sliced tomatoes	750 g/1¾ lb
	salt	
7 oz	coarsely chopped onions	200 g/7 oz
2	crushed garlic cloves	2
3½ oz	smoked streaky bacon, cut into strips	100 g/3½ oz
4 tbsp	olive oil	2 tbsp
1	bunch fresh parsley	1
8 tbsp	couscous semolina	4 tbsp
1 tsp	turmeric	1 tsp
½ tsp	dried thyme	½ tsp
1½ oz	grated Parmesan cheese	40 g/1½ oz
	pepper	
1	finely sliced scallion (spring onion)	1

1. Put the tomato slices in a strainer, sprinkle with salt and leave to drain.
2. Purée the onions and garlic in a food processor. Put the onions, garlic and bacon in a small casserole with half of the olive oil. Cover and microwave on HIGH for 3 minutes.
3. Rinse the parsley under plenty of cold running water. Pat dry on kitchen paper. Chop finely. Mix together the parsley, bacon, onions, couscous, turmeric, thyme and grated Parmesan.
4. Sprinkle the tomatoes with pepper. Place half of the tomatoes in a large Pyrex dish and cover with one-third of the couscous-vegetable mixture. Top with the rest of the tomatoes and another third of the vegetable mixture. Cover and microwave on HIGH for 8 minutes.
5. Add the final third of the couscous-vegetable mixture and the scallion (spring onion) slices to the dish. Pour over the remaining olive oil. Microwave, uncovered, on HIGH for 2 minutes. Serve very hot in the same dish.

Tomates au parmesan

Tomatoes with Parmesan Cheese

00.10　　**00.13**

Serves 4 as side dish

American	Ingredients	Metric/Imperial
1¾ lb	thickly sliced tomatoes	750 g/1¾ lb
	salt	
7 oz	peeled onions	200 g/7 oz
2	peeled garlic cloves	2
2 tbsp	olive oil	1 tbsp
1 tbsp	chopped fresh parsley	1 tbsp
3 tbsp	breadcrumbs	2 tbsp
½ tsp	oregano	½ tsp
¾ cup	grated Parmesan cheese	75 g/3 oz
	pepper	
¼ cup	sour cream (crème fraîche)	3 tbsp

1. Put the tomatoes in a colander, sprinkle with salt and leave to drain.
2. Purée the onions and garlic in a food processor. Put the purée in a small casserole with the olive oil. Cover and microwave on HIGH for 3 minutes.
3. Mix together the chopped parsley, onion purée, breadcrumbs, oregano and Parmesan cheese.
4. Pepper the tomatoes. Put half in a round dish 7 inches (18 cm) in diameter. Cover with half the parsley-onion-Parmesan mixture, then the remaining tomatoes, and finish with the second half of the cheese mixture. Cover and microwave on HIGH for 8 minutes.
5. After 8 minutes, pour the sour cream (crème fraîche) over the contents of the dish and heat for a further 2 minutes, uncovered. Serve very hot in the same dish.

Tomatoes with Parmesan cheese

Purée d'aubergines
Eggplant (Aubergine) Purée

▬◁	00.10	00.12	〰
	Serves 2-3 as side dish		

American	Ingredients	Metric/Imperial
1¼ lb	sliced eggplant (aubergines)	500 g/1¼ lb
7 oz	coarsely chopped tomatoes	200 g/7 oz
2	halved garlic cloves	2
1 tsp	vinegar	1 tsp
4 tbsp	sour cream (crème fraîche)	2 tbsp
½ tsp	curry powder	½ tsp
	salt	
	pepper	

1. Put the eggplant (aubergines), tomatoes, garlic and 4 table-spoons (2 tablespoons) of water in a casserole. Cover and microwave on HIGH for 10 minutes. Leave to stand for 2 minutes.
2. Drain the contents of the casserole and discard the cooking liquid. Purée the vegetables in a food processor, adding the vinegar, sour cream (crème fraîche) and curry powder. Add salt and purée once more. Taste before adding pepper.
3. Pour the purée into a dish and serve hot.

Aubergines à la crème
Eggplant (Aubergines) in Cream Sauce

▬◁	00.10	00.13	〰
	Serves 4 as side dish		

American	Ingredients	Metric/Imperial
1	crushed garlic clove	1
1	large onion, finely sliced	1
3½ oz	smoked streaky bacon, de-rinded and finely chopped	100 g/3½ oz
1¼ lb	small eggplant (aubergines), finely chopped	600 g/1¼ lb
½ tsp	dried thyme	½ tsp
3 tbsp	dry white wine	2 tbsp
	salt	
	pepper	
3 tbsp	sour cream (crème fraîche)	2 tbsp
½ cup	grated Parmesan cheese	2 tbsp

1. Put the garlic, onion and bacon in a casserole. Cover and microwave on HIGH for 3 minutes.
2. Add the eggplant (aubergines) to the casserole.
3. Add the thyme, white wine and salt and pepper to taste. Stir well. Cover and microwave on HIGH for 10 minutes.
4. When the eggplant (aubergines) are tender, add the sour cream (crème fraîche) and Parmesan cheese. Stir carefully and serve at once.

Mousseline d'aubergines
Eggplant (Aubergine) Mousse in Ramekins

▬◁	00.10	00.24	〰
	Serves 4		

American	Ingredients	Metric/Imperial
3½ oz	finely sliced onions	100 g/3½ oz
1¼ lb	eggplant (aubergines), peeled, sliced in rounds	500 g/1¼ lb
¼ cup	olive oil	4 tbsp
3 tbsp	dry white wine	2 tbsp
	salt	
	pepper	
½ tsp	garlic powder	½ tsp
½ tsp	dried thyme	½ tsp
2	eggs	2
3 tbsp	sour cream (crème fraîche)	2 tbsp
1 tbsp	butter	½ tbsp
¼ cup	concentrated tomato juice	3 tbsp
2 tbsp	vinegar	1 tbsp
1	shallot	1

1. Put the onions in a dish and microwave, uncovered, on HIGH for 2 minutes.
2. Add the eggplant (aubergine) slices. Pour the oil and white wine over. Season with salt and pepper and sprinkle with garlic powder and thyme. Cover and microwave on HIGH for 10 minutes. Leave to stand for 5 minutes.
3. Purée in a food processor, adding the eggs and half the sour cream (crème fraîche). When the purée is smooth, taste and adjust seasoning.
4. Butter 4 ramekin dishes and divide the mixture between them. Place in the microwave in a circle, leaving the center of the oven empty. Microwave, uncovered, for 5 minutes on HIGH.
5. Serve in the ramekin dishes or unmold (unmould) them on to individual plates. These ramekins can be served as an accompaniment to chicken or on their own. If serving as a dish by themselves, accompany with the following sauce.
6. Mix together the concentrated tomato juice with the vinegar, the remaining sour cream (crème fraîche) and 1 shallot peeled and crushed in a garlic press. Heat the sauce in the microwave oven for 2 minutes on HIGH.

Eggplant (aubergines) mousse in ramekins

Gratin d'aubergines

Eggplant (Aubergines) with Tomatoes

00.15 00.23

Serves 4-5 as side dish

American	Ingredients	Metric/Imperial
5 oz	*finely sliced onions*	*150 g/5 oz*
¼ lb	*smoked streaky bacon, de-rinded, cut into small strips*	*125 g/4 oz*
1 lb	*sliced eggplant (aubergines)*	*450 g/1 lb*
	salt	
	pepper	
3	*fresh thyme sprigs*	*3*
¼ cup	*grated Parmesan cheese*	*2 tbsp*
2	*large crushed garlic cloves*	*2*
2	*large tomatoes, finely sliced*	*2*
¼ cup	*breadcrumbs*	*2 tbsp*
3 tbsp	*olive oil*	*2 tbsp*

1. Put the onions and bacon in a bowl. Microwave, uncovered, on HIGH for 5 minutes.
2. Arrange half the eggplant (aubergines) in a round Pyrex dish 10 inches (25 cm) in diameter. Season with salt and pepper and crumble 1 thyme sprig over. Sprinkle with 1 tablespoon of grated Parmesan and cover with the onion and bacon mixture. Arrange the remaining eggplant (aubergines) on top, season with salt and pepper, crumble the second thyme sprig over and sprinkle with half the crushed garlic. Cover and microwave on HIGH for 10 minutes.
3. Put the tomatoes in a colander, sprinkle with salt and leave to drain.
4. Mix the remaining garlic with the breadcrumbs.
5. After the eggplant (aubergines) have cooked for 10 minutes, sprinkle with the remaining grated Parmesan and cover with the tomato slices. Crumble the third thyme sprig over, season with pepper and sprinkle with the breadcrumb and garlic mixture. Pour the olive oil over and microwave, uncovered, for 5 minutes on HIGH.
6. Leave to stand for 3 minutes and serve in the same dish.

Aubergines au vinaigre de miel

Eggplant (Aubergines) in Honey Vinegar

00.05 00.08

Serves 4 as side dish

American	Ingredients	Metric/Imperial
1 lb	*cubed eggplant (aubergines)*	*450 g/1 lb*
½ tsp	*garlic powder*	*½ tsp*
½ tsp	*powdered dried thyme*	*½ tsp*
	salt	
	pepper	
¼ cup	*concentrated tomato juice*	*3 tbsp*
3 tbsp	*honey vinegar*	*2 tbsp*
3 tbsp	*sour cream (crème fraîche)*	*2 tbsp*

1. Put the eggplant (aubergines) in a casserole, sprinkle with garlic powder and thyme and season with salt and pepper. Mix the tomato juice with the vinegar, pour over the eggplant (aubergines) and mix thoroughly. Cover and microwave on HIGH for 8 minutes.
2. When the eggplant (aubergines) are cooked, add the sour cream (crème fraîche), stir well and serve.

Eggplant (aubergine) in honey vinegar

Poivrons farcis
Stuffed Peppers

00.10 **00.16**
Serves 2-4

American	Ingredients	Metric/Imperial
¼ lb	small white button mushrooms, finely sliced	125 g/4 oz
3 tbsp	fresh lemon juice	2 tbsp
1	finely sliced large onion	1
½	red bell pepper, diced	½
2	large green bell peppers	2
¼ cup	golden raisins (sultanas)	3 tbsp
¼ cup	couscous semolina	4 tbsp
½ tsp	curry powder	½ tsp
2 tbsp	olive oil	1 tbsp
1	egg yolk	1
2 tbsp	sour cream (crème fraîche)	1 tbsp
	salt	
	pepper	

1. Put the mushrooms, half the lemon juice, the onion and red bell pepper in a casserole. Cover and microwave on HIGH for 4 minutes.
2. Rinse and seed the green bell peppers, remove the pith and cut them in half lengthwise. Place side by side, in a large round dish with 2-3 tablespoons of water. Cover and microwave on HIGH for 3 minutes.
3. Drain the vegetables from the casserole and put in a bowl.
4. Add the golden raisins (sultanas), couscous, curry powder, oil, egg yolk, sour cream (crème fraîche) and remaining lemon juice. Season with salt and pepper and stir well.
5. Drain the green bell peppers and discard the cooking liquid. Fill the green peppers with the vegetable stuffing. Cover and microwave on HIGH for 6 minutes. Leave to stand 3 minutes before serving.

Champignons et courgettes à la crème
Mushrooms and Zucchini (Courgettes) in Cream Sauce

00.10 **00.16**
Serves 3-4 as a side dish

American	Ingredients	Metric/Imperial
2 tbsp	butter	1 tbsp
2 tbsp	oil	1 tbsp
¼ lb	zucchini (courgettes), finely sliced	125 g/4 oz
14 oz	finely sliced mushrooms	400 g/14 oz
⅔ cup	sour cream (crème fraîche)	150 ml/¼ pint
	salt	
	pepper	
	paprika	

1. Heat a browning dish in the microwave oven for 6-8 minutes, following the manufacturer's instructions.

2. Put the butter and oil in the hot browning dish and add the zucchini (courgettes) and mushrooms. Stir well. Cover and microwave on HIGH for 3 minutes.
3. Add the sour cream (crème fraîche) to the vegetables. Season with salt and pepper, stir well and cook uncovered for a further 5 minutes on MEDIUM HIGH.
4. Sprinkle with paprika and serve hot.

Moravian Mushrooms

00.05 **00.08**
Serves 6

American	Ingredients	Metric/Imperial
1 lb	quartered button mushrooms	450 g/1 lb
3 tbsp	butter	2 tbsp
½ tsp	salt	½ tsp
1 tsp	cumin seeds	1 tsp
1 tbsp	finely chopped parsley	1 tbsp
2 tbsp	all-purpose (plain) flour	1 tbsp
1 tsp	lemon juice	1 tsp
⅔ cup	milk	150 ml/¼ pint
3 tbsp	heavy (double) cream	2 tbsp

1. Put the mushrooms in a dish with the butter, salt, cumin seeds and parsley. Microwave on HIGH for 5 minutes.
2. Stir in the flour and gradually add the lemon juice and milk. Cook on HIGH for 2 minutes.
3. Stir in the cream and heat for 1 minute.
4. Serve hot with toast.

Champignons à la paysanne
Peasant Style Mushrooms

00.10 **00.12**
Serves 4 as side dish

American	Ingredients	Metric/Imperial
4	finely chopped shallots	4
5 oz	smoked streaky bacon, cut into strips	150 g/5 oz
2 tbsp	butter	1 tbsp
1¾ lb	white button mushrooms, coarsely sliced	700 g/1¾ lb
2 tbsp	fresh lemon juice	1 tbsp
2	crushed garlic cloves	2
2 tbsp	all-purpose (plain) flour	1 tbsp
	salt	
	pepper	
2 tbsp	chopped fresh parsley	2 tbsp

1. Put the shallots, bacon and butter in a casserole. Cover and microwave on HIGH for 3 minutes.
2. Pour the lemon juice over the mushrooms.
3. Add the mushrooms and garlic to the casserole. Cover and microwave on HIGH for 6 minutes.
4. Sprinkle the mushrooms with flour. Season with salt and pepper and stir well. Cover and microwave on HIGH for a further 3 minutes.
5. Put the mushrooms in a vegetable dish, sprinkle the parsley over and serve.

Champignons farcis

Mushrooms Stuffed with Crab

	00.05	00.09
	Serves 4 as side dish	

American	Ingredients	Metric/Imperial
4	large mushrooms	4
1 tbsp	butter	½ tbsp
3 tbsp	fresh lemon juice	2 tbsp
	salt	
	pepper	
4	crab sticks	4
2 tbsp	chopped fresh parsley	2 tbsp
¼ cup	sour cream (crème fraîche)	3 tbsp
1 tsp	cornstarch (cornflour)	1 tsp
3 tbsp	Madeira	2 tbsp

1. Separate the mushroom stalks from the caps, Rinse and chop in a food processor. Put the chopped stalks in a bowl with the butter and lemon juice. Microwave, uncovered, on HIGH for 2 minutes.
2. Wipe the mushroom caps with a damp cloth or kitchen paper and put face down in a circle in a small casserole. Season with salt and pepper. Cover and microwave on HIGH for 3 minutes.
3. Cut the crab sticks into pieces with kitchen scissors. Mix with the chopped parsley, half the sour cream (crème fraîche), the chopped mushroom mixture, and salt and pepper to taste. Fill the mushroom caps with the mixture. Cover and microwave on HIGH for 3 minutes.
4. Transfer the mushrooms to a serving dish with a slotted spatula.
5. Mix the cornstarch (cornflour) to a smooth paste with the Madeira and add the remaining sour cream (crème fraîche) and the mushroom cooking liquid. Stir well and cook for 1 minute on HIGH. Stir again. Coat the mushrooms with the sauce and serve. These stuffed mushrooms go well as an accompaniment to fish.

Champignons au beurre d'escargots

Mushrooms with Garlic Butter

	00.05	00.11
	Serves 4 as side dish	

American	Ingredients	Metric/Imperial
8	large button mushrooms	8
4	crushed garlic cloves	4
3 tbsp	fresh lemon juice	2 tbsp
	salt	
	pepper	
1 tbsp	chopped fresh parsley	1 tbsp
3 tbsp	butter	2 tbsp
1	egg yolk	1

1. Separate the stalks from the caps of the mushrooms, rinse and grind (mince) the stalks in a food processor. Put into a bowl with the garlic and lemon juice. Microwave, uncovered, on HIGH for 3 minutes.

2. Wipe the mushroom caps with a damp cloth or kitchen paper. Arrange in a circle, face downwards on a plate, leaving the center of the plate empty. Season with salt and pepper. Cover and microwave on HIGH for 5 minutes.
3. Add the chopped parsley and butter to the puréed mushroom stalks. Season with salt and pepper. Fill the mushroom caps with the mixture. Cover and microwave on HIGH for 2 minutes.
4. Transfer the mushroom caps to a serving dish with a slotted spatula.
5. Whisk the egg yolk in a bowl and add the cooking liquid from the mushrooms. Microwave for 1 minute on HIGH, stir, pour over the mushrooms and serve hot.

Pieds-de-mouton au parmesan

Wild Mushrooms in Parmesan Sauce

	00.10	00.17
	Serves 3-4 as side dish	

American	Ingredients	Metric/Imperial
2 oz	smoked streaky bacon, cut into strips	50 g/2 oz
2	chopped large shallots	2
1¼ lb	wild or field mushrooms, sliced	600 g/1¼ lb
½ tsp	garlic powder	½ tsp
2 tbsp	olive oil	1 tbsp
	salt	
	pepper	
1½ tsp	cornstarch (cornflour)	1½ tsp
3 tbsp	Madeira	2 tbsp
1 tsp	fresh lemon juice	1 tsp
1 cup	grated Parmesan cheese	3 tbsp
2 tbsp	sour cream (crème fraîche)	1 tbsp
1 tbsp	chopped fresh parsley	1 tbsp

1. Put the bacon and shallots in a casserole. Microwave, uncovered, on HIGH for 3 minutes.
2. Add the mushrooms to the casserole, with the garlic powder, olive oil and salt and pepper to taste. Stir well. Cover and microwave on HIGH for 10 minutes.
3. After 10 minutes of cooking, mix the cornstarch (cornflour) to a smooth paste in a bowl with the Madeira and add to the mushrooms. Microwave, uncovered, on HIGH for 2 minutes.
4. Add the lemon juice, grated Parmesan, sour cream (crème fraîche) and chopped parsley to the casserole. Stir, leave to stand for 2 minutes and serve.

Endives au lait

Belgian Endive (Chicory) in Cream Sauce

■▷   00.10   00.15   ☲

Serves 4 as side dish

American	Ingredients	Metric/Imperial
1 lb	Belgian endive (chicory)	450 g/1 lb
1 tbsp	butter	½ tbsp
½ tsp	sugar	½ tsp
¾ cup	milk	200 ml/7 fl oz
	salt	
	pepper	
1 tsp	cornstarch (cornflour)	1 tsp
2 tbsp	fresh lemon juice	1 tbsp
1 tsp	Madeira	1 tsp
1	egg yolk	1
2 tsp	mild mustard	2 tsp
½ tsp	grated nutmeg	½ tsp
	bunch chives	

1. Remove any damaged leaves from the Belgian endive (chicory) and cut out the hard core using a small pointed knife. Arrange in a casserole and add the butter, sugar, milk, and salt and pepper to taste. Cover and microwave on HIGH for 12 minutes.
2. When the vegetables are cooked, remove with a slotted spatula and arrange in a deep serving dish.
3. Mix together the cornstarch (cornflour), lemon juice and Madeira to a smooth paste in a small bowl. Add the egg yolk and mustard and whisk, then add the cooking liquid from the Belgian endive (chicory). Whisk vigorously. Add the grated nutmeg, still whisking. Taste and adjust seasoning.
4. Rinse the chives and pat dry on kitchen paper. Snip finely with kitchen scissors. Add to the sauce and pour over the vegetables. Reheat in the microwave oven for 3 minutes on HIGH and serve at once. This dish makes a delicious accompaniment to roast pheasant.

Endives au curry

Belgian Endive (Chicory) with Curry Sauce

■▷   00.05   00.11   ☲

Serves 3 as side dish

American	Ingredients	Metric/Imperial
1¼ lb	Belgian endive (chicory)	500 g/1¼ lb
4 tbsp	fresh lemon juice	2 tbsp
1 tsp	sugar	1 tsp
	salt	
	pepper	
4 tbsp	sour cream (crème fraîche)	2 tbsp
1	egg yolk	1
½ tsp	curry powder	½ tsp

1. Remove the base and outer leaves of the Belgian endive (chicory). Cut out the hard core using a small pointed knife, then cut in half and in slices widthwise. Put in a casserole with the lemon juice, sugar and salt and pepper to taste. Stir well. Cover and microwave on HIGH for 10 minutes.
2. Mix together the sour cream (crème fraîche), egg yolk and curry powder and pour over the vegetables. Stir well. Cook for 1 minute on HIGH. Stir again and serve.

Belgian endive (chicory) in cream sauce

Fennel with tomatoes

Artichauts aux carottes

Globe Artichokes with Carrots

	00.10	00.20	
	Serves 4 as side dish		

American	Ingredients	Metric/Imperial
2	globe artichokes	2
14 oz	carrots, cut into strips	400 g/14 oz
⅓ cup	white wine	4½ tbsp
1 tbsp	butter	½ tbsp
¼ tsp	sugar	¼ tsp
	salt	
	pepper	
1 tsp	cornstarch (cornflour)	1 tsp
3 tbsp	Madeira	2 tbsp
1	egg	1
1 tbsp	chopped fresh parsley	1 tbsp

1. Remove the stalks from the artichokes, rinse and stand them upright in a casserole with ¼ cup (3 tablespoons) of water. Cover and microwave on HIGH for 8 minutes. Check whether the artichokes are cooked by pulling out a leaf: it should come away easily. Put the artichokes in a colander upside-down to drain.
2. Put the carrots in a casserole with the white wine, butter and sugar. Add salt and pepper to taste. Stir well. Cover and microwave on HIGH for 10 minutes, stirring once midway through the cooking time.

3. When the artichokes have cooled, remove the leaves and scrape the flesh off the base of each leaf with a small spoon. Remove the choke and cut the base into strips.
4. Mix the cornstarch (cornflour) to a smooth paste in a bowl with the Madeira. Pour over the carrots, stir and cook for 1 minute on HIGH.
5. Add the artichoke bases and the flesh from the base of the leaves. Stir very carefully and reheat for 1 minute on HIGH.
6. Beat the egg with a fork and add to the vegetables.
7. Sprinkle with the chopped parsley and serve.

Fenouil à la tomate

Fennel with Tomatoes

	00.10	00.16	
	Serves 4		

American	Ingredients	Metric/Imperial
2 tbsp	oil	1 tbsp
2 oz	smoked streaky bacon, cut into strips	50 g/2 oz
3½ oz	finely sliced onions	100 g/3½ oz
1 lb	fennel	450 g/1 lb
2	large tomatoes, skinned and coarsely chopped	2
3 tbsp	fresh lemon juice	2 tbsp
½ cup	grated Parmesan cheese	2 tbsp
	salt	
	pepper	
1 tbsp	chopped fresh parsley	1 tbsp

1. Pour the oil into a dish large enough to cook the fennel in. Add the bacon and onions. Cover and microwave on HIGH for 3 minutes.

2. Remove the stalks and tough base of the fennel. Slice finely, rinse and drain.

3. Add the fennel and tomatoes to the onions and pour the lemon juice over. Cover and microwave on HIGH for 10 minutes.

4. Add the grated Parmesan and season with salt and pepper. Stir well. Cover and microwave on HIGH for 1 further minute. Leave to stand for 2 minutes, then sprinkle with chopped parsley and serve.

Fenouil au parmesan

Fennel with Parmesan Cheese

	00.08	00.09	
	Serves 3-4 as side dish		

American	Ingredients	Metric/Imperial
14 oz	finely sliced fennel	400 g/14 oz
2 tbsp	fresh lemon juice	1 tbsp
	salt	
	pepper	
6	fresh chervil sprigs	6
¼ cup	grated Parmesan cheese	1 tbsp
1 tbsp	butter	2 tsp

1. Put the fennel slices in a dish and add the lemon juice, salt and pepper. Cover and microwave on HIGH for 7 minutes. Leave to stand for 2 minutes.

2. Rinse the chervil and pat dry carefully on kitchen paper.

3. Sprinkle the fennel with the Parmesan. Add the butter in small pieces and the chopped chervil. Stir, transfer to a warmed dish and serve as an accompaniment to any meat.

Purée de fenouil

Fennel Purée

	00.05	00.14	
	Serves 4 as side dish		

American	Ingredients	Metric/Imperial
1¾ lb	fennel	750 g/1¾ lb
¼ cup	white wine	3 tbsp
2 tbsp	horseradish mustard	1 tbsp
	salt	
	pepper	
3 tbsp	instant potato flakes	2 tbsp
2 tbsp	butter	1 tbsp

1. Remove the tough base and the stalks from the fennel. Set aside the green fronds. Rinse and slice the bulbs. Put in a dish with the white wine. Cover and microwave on HIGH for 14 minutes.

2. Purée the fennel in a food processor, adding the mustard and salt and pepper to taste. Purée until smooth.

3. Pour the purée into a deep dish. Add the instant potato flakes and stir well,

4. Add the butter and stir again. Sprinkle with the fennel fronds and serve hot.

Céleri à la crème de mascarpone

Celery in Blue Cheese Sauce

	00.10	00.15	
	Serves 4 as side dish		

American	Ingredients	Metric/Imperial
1	bunch young celery	1
3 oz	Mascarpone	75 g/3 oz
3 tbsp	sour cream (crème fraîche)	2 tbsp
	Tabasco sauce	
2 tbsp	dry champagne	1 tbsp
1 tbsp	chopped fresh chervil	1 tbsp

1. Discard the celery leaves, rinse the stalks and cut into strips, removing any tough fibres.

2. Put the celery in a casserole with ¼ cup (4 tablespoons) of water. Cover and microwave on HIGH for 10 minutes. Leave to stand, covered, for 3 minutes.

3. Put the Mascarpone in a bowl with the sour cream (crème fraîche) and heat in the microwave oven on HIGH for 1½ minutes until the cheese has melted. Add several dashes of Tabasco sauce and the champagne. Stir thoroughly.

4. Drain the celery, put in a vegetable dish, pour the sauce over, sprinkle with the chopped chervil and serve.

Mascarpone is a type of Gorgonzola with a very high cream content. If it is not available, try for Cambozola, or failing that use equal quantities of Gorgonzola and cream cheese.

Celery in Yogurt Sauce

	00.08	00.26	
	Serves 4		

American	Ingredients	Metric/Imperial
1	finely sliced onion	1
4 tbsp	butter	2 tbsp
1 lb	roughly chopped celery	450 g/1 lb
1¼ cups	chicken bouillon (stock)	300 ml/½ pint
2 tbsp	all-purpose (plain) flour	1 tbsp
⅔ cup	natural yogurt	150 ml/¼ pint
⅔ cup	sour cream	150 ml/¼ pint
¼ tsp	grated nutmeg	¼ tsp
	salt	
	pepper	

1. Put the onion in the base of a shallow dish with half the butter. Microwave on HIGH for 3 minutes.

2. Arrange the celery on top, pour over the bouillon (stock) and cover with saran wrap (cling film) and pierce. Cook on HIGH for 12 minutes. Leave to stand for 5 minutes.

3. To make the sauce, melt the remaining butter in a bowl for 30 seconds on HIGH. Stir in the flour.

4. Measure ⅔ cup (150 ml/¼ pint) of cooking liquid from the celery and stir into the butter and flour. Microwave on HIGH for 3 minutes, stirring twice.

5. Add the yogurt, sour cream, nutmeg and salt and pepper to taste and stir until smooth. Microwave on HIGH for 2 minutes, pour over the celery and serve hot.

Purée tricolore

Tricolor Vegetable Purée

⏱ 00.15   00.19

Serves 4-5 as side dish

American	Ingredients	Metric/Imperial
¾ lb	frozen carrot purée	350 g/12 oz
¾ lb	frozen céleriac purée	350 g/12 oz
	salt	
	pepper	
¾ cup	instant mashed potato flakes	6 tbsp
¾ lb	frozen broccoli purée	350 g/12 oz
1 tbsp	butter	½ tbsp

1. Put the frozen carrot purée in a small casserole. Microwave, uncovered, on HIGH for 4 minutes, and pour into a colander.
2. Rinse the casserole and put in the céleriac purée. Microwave, uncovered, on HIGH for 4 minutes.
3. Pour the carrot purée into a small bowl and season with salt and pepper to taste. Add a quarter of the instant mashed potato and stir well.
4. Pour the céleriac purée into the colander. Rinse the casserole and put the broccoli purée into it. Microwave, uncovered, on HIGH for 4 minutes.
5. Transfer the céleriac purée to a second bowl and season with salt and pepper. Add 3 tablespoons (2 tablespoons) of instant mashed potato flakes and stir well.
6. Pour the broccoli purée into the colander and leave to drain for 1 minute. Pour into a third bowl, season with salt and pepper and add the remaining instant mashed potato.
7. Butter the base of a 1 quart (1 litre/1¾ pints) terrine dish. Place a piece of buttered non-stick parchment (greaseproof paper) on the base and spread the carrot purée over in a smooth layer. Cover with a layer of céleriac purée and finish with the broccoli purée. Microwave, uncovered, on HIGH for 6 minutes.
8. Just before serving, pass a knife-blade around the edge of the terrine and turn out the contents on to a serving dish. Remove the non-stick parchment (greaseproof paper). This purée may be served on its own with a white cream sauce, or as an accompaniment to broiled (grilled) meat.

Purée aux quatre légumes

Four-Vegetable Purée

⏱ 00.10   00.24

Serves 6 as side dish

American	Ingredients	Metric/Imperial
10½ oz	finely sliced onions	300 g/10½ oz
3	halved garlic cloves	3
10½ oz	red bell peppers	300 g/10½ oz
10½ oz	zucchini (courgettes)	300 g/10½ oz
2 lb	eggplant (aubergines)	1 kg/2 lb
½ tsp	dried thyme	½ tsp
	salt	
	pepper	
3 tbsp	olive oil	2 tbsp

1. Put the onions and garlic in a dish and add 2 (1) tablespoons of water. Microwave, uncovered, on HIGH for 4 minutes.
2. Rinse and seed the bell peppers, remove the pith and chop the flesh coarsely. Top-and-tail the zucchini (courgettes), peel and slice in rounds.
3. Put the cooked onions in a colander and leave to drain. Put the bell peppers in the dish the onions were cooked in. Microwave, uncovered, on HIGH for 3 minutes, then add the zucchini (courgettes) and 2-3 tablespoons of water. Cover and microwave on HIGH for 6 minutes.
4. Peel the eggplant (aubergines), halve lengthwise and cut into strips. Put in a large casserole and add ⅓ cup (5 tablespoons) of water. Cover.
5. Purée the onions in a food processor. Leave in the food processor bowl.
6. Drain the bell peppers and zucchini (courgettes) in the colander. Microwave the eggplant (aubergines) for 9 minutes on HIGH.
7. Add the bell peppers and zucchini (courgettes) to the onions in the food processor and purée.
8. When the eggplant (aubergines) are cooked, drain in the colander then add gradually to the food processor, puréeing at the same time. Add the thyme, salt and pepper and olive oil, still puréeing. Taste and adjust seasoning.
9. Reheat the purée for 2 minutes on HIGH in the microwave oven and serve.

Tricolor vegetable purée

Semolina ring mold (mould) with fresh vegetables

Couronne de semoule aux légumes frais

Semolina Ring Mold (Mould) with Fresh Vegetables

00.10 00.24
Serves 6

American	Ingredients	Metric/Imperial
¼ cup	butter	50 g/2 oz
¾ cup	semolina	150 g/5 oz
1	chicken bouillon (stock) cube	1
	salt	
	pepper	
2	eggs	2
1	red bell pepper, seeded and diced	1
1	peeled cucumber, scooped into balls	1
3 tbsp	fresh lemon juice	2 tbsp
½ tsp	sugar	½ tsp
2 tbsp	all-purpose (plain) flour	1 tbsp
1¼ cups	milk	300 ml/½ pint
½ tsp	curry powder	½ tsp
2 tbsp	chopped fresh chervil	2 tbsp

1. Put half the butter in a casserole and melt in the microwave oven for 1 minute on HIGH.
2. Add the semolina, stir, return to the oven and microwave for a further 2 minutes on HIGH.
3. Pour 2¼ cups (500 ml/¾ pint) of water into a bowl and heat in the oven for 3 minutes.
4. Crumble the chicken bouillon (stock) cube over the semolina and pour the hot water over. Season with salt and pepper and stir until all the water is absorbed, then microwave for 5 minutes on HIGH.
5. Whisk the eggs with a fork and add to the semolina.
6. Butter the base of a small Pyrex ring mold (mould), 9 inches (22 cm) in diameter. Spoon in the mixture, press well down and smooth the surface. Microwave, uncovered, on HIGH for 3 minutes.
7. Place the bell pepper and cucumber in a small casserole and pour the lemon juice over. Season with salt and pepper and add the sugar. Cover and microwave on HIGH for 6 minutes.
8. Put the remaining butter in a bowl and melt in the oven for 1 minute on HIGH. Sprinkle with the flour and stir well. Add the milk, stirring constantly. Microwave on HIGH for 3 minutes, whisking after every minute.
9. Add the curry powder.
10. Drain the vegetables and set aside the cooking liquid. Season the sauce with salt and pepper if needed and add the cooking liquid and half the chopped chervil.
11. Turn out the semolina mold (mould) on to a serving plate. Put the vegetables in the center and sprinkle with the remaining chervil. Pour the sauce into a sauceboat and serve hot.

Couronne de légumes
Vegetable Ring Mold (Mould) with Mushrooms in Sauce

⏱ 00.15   00.37   Serves 6

American	Ingredients	Metric/Imperial
¾ lb	frozen carrot purée	350 g/12 oz
1 lb	frozen céleriac purée	450 g/1 lb
	salt	
	pepper	
1 lb	frozen chopped spinach	450 g/1 lb
¼ cup	butter	4 tbsp
1 tsp	grated nutmeg	1 tsp
3	egg yolks	3
1 tsp	oil	1 tsp
¾ lb	white button mushrooms	350 g/12 oz
4	chopped shallots	4
1	crushed garlic clove	1
3 tbsp	green peppercorns in brine	1½ tbsp
⅓ cup	white wine	4½ tbsp
1 tbsp	all-purpose (plain) flour	½ tbsp
¾ cup	milk	200 ml/7 fl oz
3 tbsp	sour cream (crème fraîche)	2 tbsp

1. Put the carrot purée in a casserole. Microwave, uncovered, on HIGH for 4 minutes. Pour the purée into a colander.
2. Rinse the casserole and put the céleriac purée into it. Microwave, uncovered, on HIGH for 5 minutes.
3. Pour the carrot purée into a small bowl and season with salt and pepper.
4. Put the céleriac purée in the colander to drain. Rinse the casserole and put the frozen spinach into it. Microwave, uncovered, on HIGH for 6 minutes.
5. Put the céleriac purée into a second bowl and season with salt and pepper.
6. Put the spinach into the colander and press with the back of a wooden spoon to squeeze out as much liquid as possible. Put it in a third bowl and season with salt and pepper. Add half the butter and ½ teaspoon of grated nutmeg. Stir well.
7. Add 1 egg yolk to each purée.
8. Oil the base and sides of a Pyrex ring mold (mould) 9 inches (22 cm) in diameter. Cover the base of the mold (mould) with the carrot purée. Spread the céleriac purée in an even layer on top of it, then repeat with the spinach. Microwave, uncovered, on HIGH for 7 minutes.
9. Wipe the mushrooms with a damp cloth or kitchen paper. Slice thinly.
10. Put half the shallots and the garlic in a casserole with the remaining butter. Microwave, uncovered, on HIGH for 3 minutes.
11. Add the mushrooms and season with salt and pepper. Cover and microwave on HIGH for 5 minutes.
12. To make the sauce, put the remaining shallots in a bowl with the drained green peppercorns and white wine. Microwave on HIGH for 3 minutes.
13. Put the remaining butter in a bowl and melt in the oven for 1 minute on HIGH.
14. Add the flour and stir well, then add the milk, whisking constantly. Microwave for 3 minutes on HIGH, whisking after every minute.

15. Add the white wine and peppercorns and the sour cream (crème fraîche). Add salt and pepper to taste and add ½ teaspoon of grated nutmeg.
16. Turn out the ring mold (mould) on to a large round dish. Add half the sauce to the mushrooms and put in the center of the mold (mould). Pour the remaining sauce into a sauceboat and serve alongside.

Purée de papayes créole
Creole Style Paw-paw (Papaya)

⏱ 00.15   00.15   Serves 6

American	Ingredients	Metric/Imperial
2 lb	paw-paw (papaya)	1 kg/2 lb
7 oz	coarsely chopped onions	200 g/7 oz
5	fresh parsley sprigs	5
2	large eggs	2
2 tbsp	fresh lime juice	1 tbsp
2 tbsp	concentrated tomato juice	1 tbsp
½ tsp	chili paste	½ tsp
½ cup	Gruyère cheese	50 g/2 oz
1 tbsp	butter	½ tbsp
1 tbsp	all-purpose (plain) flour	½ tbsp
⅔ cup	milk	150 ml/¼ pint
	salt	
	pepper	

1. Cut the paw-paws (papayas) in half, remove the seeds with a small spoon, peel, and chop the flesh coarsely. Purée in a food processor.
2. Rinse the parsley and discard the stalks. Pat dry on kitchen paper. Add to the food processor together with the eggs, lime juice, tomato juice, chili paste and Gruyère. Purée until smooth. Pour into a soufflé dish 6 inches (15 cm) in diameter.
3. Melt the butter in a small bowl on HIGH for 1 minute. Stir in the flour and add the milk, stirring constantly. Microwave on HIGH for 1 minute. Whisk, cook for a further 30 seconds, whisk again and cook for a final 30 seconds.
4. Season the sauce with salt and pepper to taste and add to the contents of the soufflé dish. Cover and microwave on HIGH for 12 minutes. Serve hot in the soufflé dish.

Vegetable ring mold (mould) with mushrooms in sauce

Couscous with fruit and nuts

Couscous aux fruits secs

Couscous with Fruit and Nuts

00.03 00.09

Serves 6 as side dish

American	Ingredients	Metric/Imperial
2 cups	*couscous semolina*	*300 g/10½ oz*
2 tbsp	*butter*	*1 tbsp*
	pepper	
2 tbsp	*mixed spice*	*1 tbsp*
	salt	
3½ oz	*golden raisins (sultanas)*	*100 g/3½ oz*
3 tbsp	*fresh lemon juice*	*2 tbsp*
¼ cup	*shelled unsalted pistachios*	*50 g/2 oz*
¼ cup	*slivered almonds*	*50 g/2 oz*

1. Pour 1¼ cups (300 ml/½ pint) of water into a bowl and heat in the microwave oven for 3 minutes on HIGH.
2. Put the couscous in a casserole and add the butter, pepper and mixed spice. Stir well.
3. Salt the boiling water and pour it over the couscous. Cover and microwave on HIGH for 4 minutes.
4. Rinse the golden raisins (sultanas) and put in a bowl with water to cover. Leave to swell in the oven for 2 minutes on HIGH.
5. Turn the couscous with a fork to aerate it and separate the grains, then pour the lemon juice over. Drain the golden raisins (sultanas) and add to the couscous, with the pistachios and almonds. Transfer to a bowl and serve.

Couronne de légumes

Vegetable Ring Mold (Mould)

00.15 00.26

Serves 4

American	Ingredients	Metric/Imperial
14 oz	*finely sliced leeks, white part only*	*400 g/14 oz*
	salt	
½ lb	*grated carrots*	*225 g/8 oz*
2	*fresh mint sprigs*	*2*
3	*eggs*	*3*
½ lb	*cream cheese*	*225 g/8 oz*
	pepper	
1 tsp	*butter*	*1 tsp*

1. Put the leeks in a dish, add salt, stir and add 2-3 tablespoons of water. Cover and microwave on HIGH for 10 minutes.
2. Put the carrots in a dish with 1-2 tablespoons of water. Cover and microwave on HIGH for 3 minutes.
3. Drain the leeks in a colander then purée in a food processor.
4. Rinse the mint and chop the leaves from 1 sprig.
5. Whisk the eggs with a fork. Add the cream cheese. Season with salt and pepper and stir well. Add the leeks, carrots and chopped mint.
6. Butter the base of a Pyrex ring mold (mould) and pour in the mixture. Cover and microwave on HIGH for 10 minutes.
7. Leave to stand for 3 minutes, then turn out on to a serving dish and garnish with the remaining mint sprigs.

Vegetable ring mould (mould)

Vegetables with eggs and cream

Légumes à la crème d'oeufs

Vegetables with Eggs and Cream

00.10   00.19

Serves 5-6 as side dish

American	Ingredients	Metric/Imperial
7 oz	carrots, cut into matchstick (julienne) strips	200 g/7 oz
1 oz	fennel, cut into matchstick (julienne) strips	25 g/1 oz
½ lb	zucchini (courgettes), cut into matchstick (julienne) strips	225 g/8 oz
1	peeled cucumber, cut into matchstick (julienne) strips	1
3	egg yolks	3
	salt	
	pepper	
¼ cup	sour cream (crème fraîche)	3 tbsp

1. Pour 1 cup (250 ml/8 fl oz) of water into the lower compartment of a microwave steamer. Cover and microwave on HIGH for 2 minutes.
2. Put the carrots and fennel into the upper compartment of the steamer. Put this on top of the lower compartment. Cover and microwave on HIGH for 5 minutes.
3. Add the zucchini (courgettes) and the cucumber to the steamer. Cover and microwave on HIGH for 5 minutes. Leave to stand for 5 minutes.
4. Whisk the egg yolks in a bowl. Add salt and pepper. Pour the sour cream (crème fraîche) into a cup and heat in the microwave oven for 1 minute on HIGH. Pour over the egg yolks, whisking vigorously. Reheat for 30 seconds on HIGH, then whisk again.
5. Put all the vegetables in a serving dish and coat with the sauce. Stir thoroughly and serve hot.

Petits légumes au madère
Vegetables in Madeira

00.10 **00.13**
Serves 2 as side dish

American	Ingredients	Metric/Imperial
2	finely sliced large carrots	2
2	sliced leeks, white part only	2
	salt	
	pepper	
1 tsp	tomato paste (purée)	1 tsp
3 tbsp	Madeira	2 tbsp
1 tbsp	butter	½ tbsp
2 tbsp	sour cream (crème fraîche)	1 tbsp

1. Put the carrots in a dish with 2-3 tablespoons of water. Cover and microwave on HIGH for 5 minutes.
2. Add the leeks to the carrots and season with salt and pepper. Mix the tomato paste (purée) with the Madeira and pour over the vegetables. Add the butter. Cover and microwave on HIGH for 5 minutes.
3. Leave the vegetables to stand for 3 minutes, then transfer to a heated serving dish and add the sour cream (crème fraîche). Serve.

Légumes à la vietnamienne
Vietnamese Style Vegetables

00.10 **00.16**
Serves 4 as side dish

American	Ingredients	Metric/Imperial
2	leeks, white part only	2
1	red bell pepper, seeded and coarsely chopped	1
2	small carrots, finely sliced	2
2 tbsp	oil	1 tbsp
½	Granny Smith apple, peeled, cored and cut into thin strips	½
1 tsp	cornstarch (cornflour)	1 tsp
2 tbsp	wine vinegar	1 tbsp
2 tbsp	sherry	1 tbsp
2 tbsp	nuoc nâm (Vietnam fish sauce)	1 tbsp
1 tsp	sugar	1 tsp

1. Remove the roots and outer leaves of the leeks, cut in two and then into slices across. Wash thoroughly to remove any grit.
2. Put the leeks and bell pepper in a casserole with ¼ cup (3 tablespoons) of water. Cover and microwave on HIGH for 5 minutes.
3. Add the carrots, oil and 2-3 tablespoons of water to the casserole and stir well. Cover and microwave on HIGH for 7 minutes.
4. Add the apple and cook for 3 minutes, covered, on HIGH.
5. When the vegetables are cooked, mix the cornstarch (cornflour) to a smooth paste in a small bowl with the vinegar, sherry and nuoc nâm (Vietnamese fish sauce). Add the sugar and stir. Microwave for 30 seconds on HIGH and stir again.

6. Pour the sauce over the vegetables and toss them in it thoroughly. Transfer to a vegetable dish and serve.

Flan aux marrons
Chestnut Flan

00.10 **00.25**
Serves 4-5 as side dish

American	Ingredients	Metric/Imperial
9 oz	frozen chestnuts	250 g/9 oz
⅔ cup	milk	150 ml/¼ pint
2	chopped small celery sticks	2
3½ oz	diced smoked streaky bacon	100 g/3½ oz
3	finely chopped shallots	3
¾ cup	sour cream (crème fraîche)	200 ml/7 fl oz
3	large eggs	3
	salt	
	pepper	
½ tsp	allspice	½ tsp

1. Put the frozen chestnuts in a deep casserole and pour over the milk. Cover and microwave on HIGH for 10 minutes.
2. Put the celery, bacon and shallots in a small casserole and cover.
3. Leave the chestnuts to stand for 5 minutes and microwave the bacon, celery and shallots on HIGH for 4 minutes.
4. Purée the chestnuts in a food processor. Add the sour cream (crème fraîche), eggs, salt and pepper and allspice. Purée again.
5. Pour the purée into a bowl. Add the bacon, shallots and celery. Stir well. Put the mixture in an oval dish. Cover and microwave on HIGH for 6 minutes. Serve hot, in the same dish.

Chestnut flan

Desserts

Cold Desserts

Gâteau Milly
Chocolate Crunch with Strawberries

American	Ingredients	Metric/Imperial
5 oz	bitter chocolate	150 g/5 oz
7 oz	butter	200 g/7 oz
3 oz	golden raisins (sultanas)	75 g/3 oz
⅓ cup	cognac	4½ tbsp
2	eggs, separated	2
1	egg yolk	1
½ cup	confectioners' (icing) sugar	6 tbsp
15	graham crackers (digestive biscuits)	15
2 tbsp	oil	1 tbsp
1¼ lb	strawberries	500 g/1¼ lb

1. Break the chocolate in pieces and melt in a bowl with the butter on HIGH for 1½ minutes.
2. Beat until the chocolate is completely melted.
3. Rinse the raisins (sultanas) under plenty of cold running water. Pat dry on kitchen paper and put in a bowl with the cognac. Microwave on HIGH for 1 minute and leave to cool.
4. Add the 3 egg yolks to the chocolate mixture one at a time, beating after each addition. Add the confectioners' (icing) sugar and stir extremely carefully.
5. Crumble the graham crackers (digestive biscuits) over the mixture and mix with a wooden spoon to mash the biscuits completely. Add the raisins (sultanas) and cognac and mix.
6. Oil the base of a small soufflé mold (mould) and line with a circle of oiled non-stick parchment (greaseproof paper).
7. Whisk the egg whites to firm peaks and fold carefully into the mixture. Pour into the mold (mould), smooth the surface and refrigerate for at least 4 hours.
8. Rinse the strawberries under plenty of cold running water. Pat dry on kitchen paper and remove the stalks.
9. Put the blade of a knife between the mold (mould) and the edge of the cake and turn out on to a platter. Remove the non-stick parchment (greaseproof paper). Decorate the top of the cake with 6 of the largest strawberries and arrange the rest around the base.

Rhubarbe en gelée aux fruits rouges
Rhubarb Jello (Jelly) with Strawberries and Raspberries

American	Ingredients	Metric/Imperial
7 oz	frozen raspberries	200 g/7 oz
7 oz	frozen strawberries	200 g/7 oz
14 oz	frozen rhubarb	400 g/14 oz
3½ oz	superfine (caster) sugar	100 g/3½ oz
½ cup	crème de cassis	5 tbsp
¼ cup	fresh lemon juice	4 tbsp
3 tbsp	unflavored gelatin	2 tbsp

1. Leave the raspberries and strawberries to defrost at room temperature.
2. Put the frozen rhubarb in a casserole with the sugar, crème de cassis and 3 (2) tablespoons of water. Cover and microwave on HIGH for 8 minutes.
3. Put the lemon juice in a bowl and sprinkle over the unflavored gelatin. Let the gelatin swell. Put the bowl in the microwave oven for 1 minute on MEDIUM-LOW. Stir. If the gelatin is not completely dissolved, return to the oven for 1 minute on MEDIUM-LOW.
4. Purée the rhubarb and its cooking liquid in a food processor. Stir the lemon juice and gelatin mixture and add to the rhubarb purée while still hot. Purée again.
5. Pour the rhubarb mixture into a large bowl. Add the strawberries and raspberries. Mix carefully. Leave to cool.
6. Refrigerate the mixture for at least 6 hours.
7. Just before serving, plunge the bowl into hot water for a few seconds, place a serving dish upside-down on top and invert the bowl to remove the jello (jelly). Serve well chilled.

Oeufs à la neige aux fruits
Floating Islands with Fruit and Custard

American	Ingredients	Metric/Imperial
1	rhubarb stick	1
¼ lb	sugar	125 g/4 oz
2¼ cups	milk	500 ml/18 fl oz
4	eggs, separated	4
¼ lb	raspberries	125 g/4 oz
9 oz	strawberries	250 g/9 oz

1. Remove and discard the leaves, trim the root end and remove the thin membrane that covers the rhubarb. Wash the stick and cut in ½ inch (1.25 cm) pieces. Put in a dish with 1 oz (25 g/1 oz) of sugar and 2 (1) tablespoons of water. Cover and microwave on HIGH for 2 minutes. Leave to cool.
2. Heat the milk in a large bowl in the microwave oven for 5 minutes on HIGH. Whisk the egg yolks in a bowl with 2 oz (50 g/2 oz) of sugar.
3. Pour the boiling milk over the egg yolks, whisking vigorously. Pour the mixture back into the milk bowl and microwave on HIGH for 2 minutes. Whisk again. If the custard has not 'taken', return to the oven for 1 minute. Pour into a deep serving dish and leave to cool.
4. Whisk the egg whites to soft peaks, then gradually add the remaining sugar, still whisking. Put in large spoonfuls on to 2 plates.
5. Rinse the raspberries under plenty of cold running water. Pat dry on kitchen paper. Push the raspberries into the egg whites with the tip of your finger.
6. Put one of the plates into the oven and microwave for 1 minute on HIGH. Repeat the process with the second plate. Arrange the egg whites on the custard and chill for 2 hours.
7. Just before serving, rinse the strawberries under plenty of cold running water. Pat dry on kitchen paper and top-and-tail. Cut in half. Arrange with the rhubarb on top of the custard in between the 'floating islands' of meringue.

Floating islands with fruit and custard

Red berry mousse

Crème aux fruits rouges

Red Berry Mousse

00.10 plus chilling time   **00.21**

American	Ingredients	Metric/Imperial
¼ lb	pitted (seeded) frozen redcurrants	125 g/4 oz
9 oz	pitted (seeded) frozen blackcurrants	250 g/9 oz
¼ lb	superfine (caster) sugar	125 g/4 oz
1 cup	milk	250 ml/8 fl oz
4	eggs	4
3 tbsp	cornstarch (cornflour)	2 tbsp
⅓ cup	sour cream (crème fraîche)	4½ tbsp
3 tbsp	raspberry liqueur	2 tbsp

1. Put the frozen redcurrants and blackcurrants in a bowl with half of the sugar and defrost in the microwave oven for 5 minutes on MEDIUM. Stir.

2. Heat the milk in a cup on HIGH for 2½ minutes.

3. Whisk the eggs with the remaining sugar in a bowl. Add the cornstarch (cornflour). Pour in the hot milk in a thin stream, whisking vigorously. Stir in the sour cream (crème fraîche) and microwave, uncovered, for 5 minutes on HIGH, whisking after every minute.

4. Add the fruit and the raspberry liqueur. Microwave, uncovered, on HIGH for 8 minutes, stirring twice during cooking time.

5. Stir the mousse again, then refrigerate, stirring from time to time to prevent a skin from forming.

6. Divide the mousse into 5 or 6 individual serving glasses and refrigerate until ready to serve.

Compote de poires épicée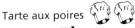

Spiced Pear Compote

▬▷ 00.05   00.04 〰
plus cooling and chilling time

American	Ingredients	Metric/Imperial
4	ripe juicy pears	4
3 tbsp	fresh lemon juice	2 tbsp
¼ tsp	ginger	¼ tsp
¼ tsp	cinnamon	¼ tsp
¼ tsp	pepper	¼ tsp
2 tbsp	superfine (caster) sugar	1 tbsp
¼ cup	raspberry liqueur	3 tbsp

1. Peel and core the pears and slice thinly.
2. Put in a bowl and add the lemon juice, ginger, cinnamon, pepper and sugar. Pour over the raspberry liqueur and stir carefully.
3. Cover and microwave on HIGH for 4 minutes.
4. Leave to cool. Refrigerate until ready to serve.

Tarte aux poires

Pear Flan

▬▷ 00.15   00.11 〰
plus cooling and chilling time

American	Ingredients	Metric/Imperial
7 oz	all-purpose (plain) flour	200 g/7 oz
3½ oz	softened butter	100 g/3½ oz
2 oz	superfine (caster) sugar	50 g/2 oz
	salt	
2 oz	ground almonds	50 g/2 oz
1¼ lb	ripe juicy pears	500 g/1¼ lb
1	egg	1
½ cup	sour cream (crème fraîche)	6 tbsp
¼ tsp	ground vanilla	¼ tsp

1. To make the pastry, mix the flour, butter, 2 (1) tablespoons of sugar and a pinch of salt, adding 2-3 (1-2) tablespoons of water. Roll the dough into a ball and refrigerate for at least 30 minutes.
2. When the pastry is ready for use, roll out on a board and use to line a 10 inch (25 cm) flan case. Prick all over with a fork. Microwave, uncovered, on HIGH for 6 minutes. Leave to cool.

3. When the pastry case is cold, put in the ground almonds. Peel and core the pears and slice thinly. Arrange in rows on top of the ground almonds so that they overlap each other slightly. Microwave, uncovered, on HIGH for 3 minutes.
4. Whisk the whole egg with the sour cream (crème fraîche), vanilla and the remaining sugar. Pour this mixture over the pears, tilting the flan case in all directions to cover evenly. Microwave, uncovered, on HIGH for 2 further minutes. Serve cold with whipped cream.

Pears in Chocolate Sauce

▬▷ 00.05   00.15 〰
Serves 6

American	Ingredients	Metric/Imperial
6	firm pears	6
1¼ cups	water	300 ml/½ pint
2 tbsp	lemon juice	1 tbsp
2 oz	sugar	50 g/2 oz
1	vanilla pod	1
¼ lb	semisweet (plain) chocolate	125 g/4 oz
1 oz	butter	25 g/1 oz
	vanilla ice cream	

1. Peel the pears and remove the stalks. Stand the pears in a casserole dish.
2. In a jug, mix together the water, lemon juice and sugar and heat on HIGH for 2 minutes. Pour over the pears. Put the vanilla pod in the base of the dish and cover the dish with saran wrap (cling film). Pierce and cook on MEDIUM for 10 minutes. Leave to cool.
3. Break the chocolate into pieces. Put in a jug and add ¼ cup (4 tablespoons) of liquid from the pears. Heat on HIGH for 3 minutes, stirring every minute. Beat in the butter until the sauce is smooth.
4. Drain the pears and arrange on a flat dish or plate. Pour over the sauce. Serve with scoops of vanilla ice cream.

Pear flan

Charlotte aux poires et au chocolat

Pear and Chocolate Charlotte

◀▭▷ 　00.25　　00.11　〰
plus cooling and chilling time

American	Ingredients	Metric/Imperial
5 oz	semisweet (plain) chocolate	150 g/5 oz
1½ cups	milk	375 ml/13 fl oz
1	egg	1
2	egg yolks	2
5 oz	superfine (caster) sugar	150 g/5 oz
1½ oz	cornstarch (cornflour)	40 g/1½ oz
¼ cup	pear brandy	4 tbsp
1	large crisp pear	1
30	ladyfingers (sponge fingers)	30
2 tbsp	sour cream (crème fraîche)	1 tbsp
2 tbsp	instant caramel syrup	1 tbsp
¼ cup	whipped cream	4 tbsp

1. Break 3½ oz (100 g/3½ oz) of chocolate into pieces and melt in a bowl in the microwave oven for 1 minute on HIGH. Stir.
2. Heat the milk in a bowl for 4 minutes on HIGH.
3. Put the whole egg, 2 egg yolks and 3½ oz (100 g/3½ oz) of sugar in a large bowl and whisk, gradually adding the cornstarch (cornflour).
4. Pour the hot milk over the melted chocolate and stir well. Pour this mixture in a thin stream over the eggs, whisking constantly. Microwave, uncovered, on HIGH for 3 minutes, whisking vigorously after each minute. Remove from the oven and stir in half of the pear brandy. Whisk again, then refrigerate, stirring from time to time.
5. To make the syrup, put the remaining sugar in a bowl with ⅓ cup (4½ tablespoons) of water and heat in the microwave oven for 2 minutes on HIGH. Mix until the sugar is completely dissolved, add the remaining pear brandy, stir and pour into a flat dish.
6. Peel and core the pear, set aside 1 or 2 slices for decoration and cut the rest into small cubes. Fold carefully into the chocolate cream mixture.
7. Dip the ladyfingers (sponge fingers) one by one into the syrup, flat side only. As you do so, line the base and sides of a 1¾ quart (1.75 litre/3 pint) charlotte mold (mould), curved side to the mold (mould). Trim if taller than the sides of the mold (mould).
8. Pour half of the chocolate cream mixture into the mold (mould), cover with a layer of ladyfingers (sponge fingers) dipped in syrup, then the rest of the chocolate cream. Finish with a layer of ladyfingers (sponge fingers), flat side upward. Fill any little gaps with the trimmings. Put a weighted board on top of the charlotte and refrigerate for at least 3 hours.
9. Just before serving, break the remaining chocolate into pieces and put in a bowl with 1 teaspoon of water. Melt in the microwave oven for 1 minute on HIGH. Stir in the sour cream (crème fraîche) and beat thoroughly.
10. Invert the charlotte on to a plate. Pour over the caramel syrup, then the melted chocolate and sour cream (crème fraîche) mixture. Cut the slices of pear into decorative shapes and arrange on top of the charlotte. Finish with rosettes of whipped cream.

Pear and chocolate charlotte

Gâteau Parmentier

Chocolate Cake with Pears in Custard

◀▭▷ 　00.15　　00.22　〰
plus cooling time

American	Ingredients	Metric/Imperial
1	large floury potato	1
3½ oz	semisweet (plain) chocolate	100 g/3½ oz
2 oz	butter	50 g/2 oz
3	eggs	3
3 oz	superfine (caster) sugar	75 g/3 oz
¾ cup	sour cream (crème fraîche)	200 ml/7 fl oz
2 tbsp	coffee extract (essence)	1 tbsp
2 tbsp	caramel syrup	1 tbsp
1 tsp	active dry yeast	1 tsp
1 tsp	oil	1 tsp
4-6	pear halves in syrup	4-6
1	piece candied orange zest (peel)	1
2 tbsp	pear liqueur	1 tbsp
¾ cup	custard sauce	200 ml/7 fl oz

1. Scrub the potato under running water. Pat dry on kitchen paper. Prick in several places with a fork. Put in the center of the microwave oven on kitchen paper and microwave for 6 minutes on HIGH.
2. Cover the potato with a cloth and leave to stand for 5 minutes.
3. Break the chocolate and melt in a bowl with the butter for 1 minute on HIGH. Stir well.
4. Whisk the eggs in a bowl.
5. Peel the potato and mash with a fork. Add to the melted chocolate and butter mixture along with the beaten eggs, sugar, sour cream (crème fraîche), coffee extract (essence) and caramel syrup. Beat thoroughly.
6. Sift the yeast over the mixture and stir again.
7. Oil the base of a 9 inch (23 cm) soufflé mold (mould) and line with a circle of oiled non-stick parchment (greaseproof paper). Spoon the mixture into the mold (mould) and microwave for 10 minutes on HIGH.
8. Leave the cake to cool in the container. Turn out on to a platter and remove the non-stick parchment (greaseproof paper). Surround with the pear halves in syrup. Cut the candied orange zest (peel) into 4-6 diamonds and put one on each pear half.
9. Add the pear liqueur to the custard and pour into a jug. Serve with the cake.

Microwave hint: To avoid overnight soaking for dried pear halves, peach halves and prunes, place in a bowl, cover with boiling water and microwave on HIGH for 1 minute. Leave to stand for 5 minutes, then drain before using.

Pommes rouges
Apples in Red Berry Sauce

00.05 plus cooling time   **00.06**

American	Ingredients	Metric/Imperial
2	large apples	2
2 oz	frozen blackcurrants	50 g/2 oz
¼ cup	redcurrant syrup	3 tbsp
3 tbsp	raspberry liqueur	2 tbsp

1. Core the apples with an apple-corer and peel. Put in a small oval dish and surround with the frozen blackcurrants. Pour over the redcurrant syrup.
2. Microwave, uncovered, on HIGH for 6 minutes.
3. When the apples are tender but still retain their shape, pour over the raspberry liqueur and leave to cool.
4. To serve, place each apple on an individual serving dish and pour over the blackcurrants and syrup.

Apples in red berry sauce

Pommes en surprise
Apple Surprise

00.15 plus cooling and chilling time   **00.16**

American	Ingredients	Metric/Imperial
2	large Granny Smith apples	2
1 tbsp	butter	½ tbsp
1¼ cups	milk	300 ml/½ pint
2	egg yolks	2
1	egg, separated	1
½ cup	superfine (caster) sugar	6 tbsp
3 tbsp	cornstarch (cornflour)	2 tbsp
2 tbsp	Calvados (apple brandy)	1 tbsp

1. Peel the apples, halve horizontally and remove the cores with an apple corer. Cut the butter in 4 pieces and put 1 piece in the hollow of each apple. Put the apple halves in a circle in a deep round dish, cut side down. Microwave, uncovered, for 5 minutes on HIGH.
2. Heat the milk for 3 minutes on HIGH.
3. Put the 3 egg yolks in a bowl and add all but 2 tablespoons (1 tablespoon) of sugar. Beat well. Stir in the cornstarch (cornflour).
4. Pour the boiling milk into the bowl, whisking constantly. Microwave, uncovered, on HIGH for 3 minutes, whisking after every minute. Add the Calvados (apple brandy).
5. Whisk the egg white to firm peaks and add the remaining sugar, still whisking. Fold carefully into the custard cream and pour over the apple halves.
6. Microwave, uncovered, on HIGH for 5 minutes.
7. Leave to cool, then refrigerate. Serve chilled.

Compote de pommes exotique
Exotic Apple Compote

00.15 plus chilling time   **00.10**

American	Ingredients	Metric/Imperial
2	Golden Delicious apples	2
1	Granny Smith apple	1
1 (2 lb)	pineapple	1 (1 kg/2 lb)
3 tbsp	superfine (caster) sugar	2 tbsp
¼ tsp	cinnamon	¼ tsp
¼ cup	lime juice	3 tbsp
2 oz	golden raisins (sultanas)	50 g/2 oz
1	large mango	1
3 tbsp	Kirsch	2 tbsp

1. Peel and core the apples, quarter and slice the quarters thinly.
2. Cut off the 2 ends of the pineapple. Put on a board and peel from top to base with a large knife. Cut into 8 lengthwise and remove the core. Chop into cubes.
3. Put the apples and pineapple in a casserole and sprinkle with the sugar and cinnamon. Pour over the lime juice and stir well. Cover and microwave on HIGH for 5 minutes.
4. Rinse the raisins (sultanas) under plenty of cold running water. Pat dry on kitchen paper. Peel the mango, remove the pit (stone) and cut the flesh into cubes.
5. Add the raisins (sultanas) and mango to the casserole and stir. Cover and microwave on HIGH for a further 5 minutes.
6. Pour the Kirsch over the compote and refrigerate. Serve well chilled.

Exotic apple compote

Entremets à la compote de pommes

Caramel Apple Dessert

00.20   00.23

plus cooling and chilling time

American	Ingredients	Metric/Imperial
2 lb	Golden Delicious apples	1 kg/2 lb
1 oz	butter	25 g/1 oz
5 oz	superfine (caster) sugar	150 g/5 oz
1½ oz	ground almonds	40 g/1½ oz
½ tsp	ground vanilla	½ tsp
3	large eggs	3

1. Peel and core the apples, quarter and cut each quarter in half. Put in a casserole. Cover and microwave on HIGH for 5 minutes, stirring midway through. Cooking time will depend on the size and ripeness of the apples.

2. When the apples are tender, mash with a fork and add the butter and ¼ lb (100 g/4 oz) of sugar. Stir well and leave to cool.

3. To make the caramel, put the remaining sugar in a 6 inch (15 cm) Pyrex soufflé mold (mould) and add 3 (2) tablespoons of water. Microwave on HIGH for 5½ minutes.

4. When the caramel is a deep golden brown, remove from the oven, protecting yourself with oven gloves. Tilt the container in all directions to distribute the caramel as far up the sides as possible. Leave to cool.

5. Add the ground almonds and vanilla to the apple purée. Whisk the eggs in a bowl and fold carefully into the apple purée with a wooden spoon.

6. Spoon the mixture into the mold (mould). Microwave, uncovered, on HIGH for 12 minutes. The soufflé should shrink away from the edge but be firm in the middle.

7. Leave to stand for a few minutes, then refrigerate.

8. Just before serving, pass a knife-blade round the edge of the soufflé and turn out on to a plate.

The only difficult part of this recipe is the making of the caramel, but the microwave oven makes this vastly simpler than conventional methods. Do not forget that the sugar will continue to cook for several minutes after being removed from the oven and that this will deepen the brown color.

Caramel apple dessert

Apple charlotte

Pommes charlotte

Apple Charlotte

00.20 00.15
plus cooling and chilling time

American	Ingredients	Metric/Imperial
2 lb	Granny Smith apples	1 kg/2 lb
¼ cup	soft dark brown sugar	4 tbsp
1 tsp	cinnamon	1 tsp
3 tbsp	Calvados (apple brandy)	2 tbsp
1 tbsp	unflavored gelatin	1 tbsp
¼ cup	apricot preserve	4 tbsp

1. Core the apples with an apple corer, peel and cut in thin slices. Cut the slices in half widthwise.
2. Put all but 2 tablespoons (1 tablespoon) of brown sugar in a 9 inch (23 cm) Pyrex mold (mould). Add 3 (2) tablespoons of water. Microwave, uncovered, on HIGH for 3 minutes.
3. Tilt the mold (mould) in all directions to coat with the caramel half-way up the inside.
4. Mix the remaining brown sugar with the cinnamon. Arrange the apple slices in the mold (mould), sprinkling each layer of apple with the brown sugar and cinnamon mixture. Microwave, uncovered, on HIGH for 10 minutes.
5. Put the Calvados in a cup and sprinkle over the gelatin. Purée the apricot preserve in a food processor. Put in a small bowl and melt in the microwave oven for 1½ minutes on HIGH.
6. Pour the gelatin mixture into the hot preserve and stir until dissolved. Pour over the apples and tilt the container so that the preserve sinks through the layers. Leave to cool.
7. Refrigerate for at least 3 hours before serving.

Coupe panachée

Apple and Custard Cup

| | 00.20 | 00.21 |
plus cooling and chilling time

American	Ingredients	Metric/Imperial
2 cups	milk	450 ml/¾ pint
3	egg yolks	3
¼ lb	superfine (caster) sugar	125 g/4 oz
3 tbsp	cornstarch (cornflour)	2 tbsp
1 tsp	cinnamon	1 tsp
3 tbsp	sour cream (crème fraîche)	2 tbsp
3 tbsp	Calvados (apple brandy)	2 tbsp
2 lb	Golden Delicious apples	1 kg/2 lb
3 tbsp	fresh lemon juice	2 tbsp
5 oz	chopped assorted glacé fruit	150 g/5 oz
4	meringues	4

1. To make the custard cream, pour the milk into a bowl and heat in the microwave oven for 3 minutes on HIGH.
2. Whisk the egg yolks in a large bowl. Add 3 oz (75 g/3 oz) of sugar, the cornstarch (cornflour) and cinnamon. Pour over the hot milk, whisking constantly. Microwave, uncovered, on HIGH for 1½ minutes. Whisk again and microwave for a further 1½ minutes. Whisk again. Add the sour cream (crème fraîche) and Calvados. Stir well, cover with a plate and leave to cool.
3. Peel and core the apples and slice thinly. Put in a casserole, add the remaining sugar and pour over the lemon juice. Cover and microwave on HIGH for 10 minutes.
4. Leave the apples to rest for 5 minutes, then mash with a fork. Refrigerate.
5. Add half of the glacé fruit to the custard cream.
6. Pour half the apple purée into a glass serving bowl. Cover with half the cream custard, then the remaining apple purée and finally the remaining custard. Refrigerate for 2 hours.
7. Just before serving, add the remaining glacé fruit and serve with the meringues.

Apple and custard cup

Apricot charlotte

Charlotte aux abricots

Apricot Charlotte

◀▭▷ 00.20 (plus chilling time) **00.30** 〰

American	Ingredients	Metric/Imperial
9 oz	dried apricots	250 g/9 oz
2 tbsp	oil	1 tbsp
24	ladyfingers (sponge fingers)	24
1 oz	crumbled small almond macaroons	25 g/1 oz
2	eggs	2
7 oz	superfine (caster) sugar	200 g/7 oz
¼ tsp	ground vanilla	¼ tsp
1 cup	milk	250 ml/8 fl oz
3 tbsp	coarsely crushed slivered almonds	2 tbsp
½ tbsp	butter	¼ tbsp

1. Put the apricots in a bowl with 2¼ cups (500 ml/18 fl oz) of hot water. Cover and microwave on HIGH for 15 minutes.
2. Oil a 1¾ quart (1.75 litre/3 pint) soufflé mold (mould) and line the base and sides with ladyfingers (sponge fingers), curved side to the mold (mould). Trim if taller than the mold (mould).

3. Drain the apricots and put in the goblet of a food processor. Add the crumbled macaroons, purée and pour into a large bowl.
4. Whisk the eggs in a second bowl and add half of the sugar and the ground vanilla. Pour in the milk, still whisking. Microwave, uncovered, on HIGH for 3 minutes until the custard begins to boil. Remove from the oven and whisk vigorously until the mixture is smooth and creamy.
5. Pour the custard gradually into the apricot purée and stir carefully. Pour into the mold (mould) and cover the top with the remaining ladyfingers (sponge fingers), filling in any holes with the trimmings. Cover and microwave on HIGH for 6 minutes.
6. Remove the cover and leave to cool. Refrigerate for at least 12 hours.
7. Just before serving, loosen the charlotte by running a knife-blade around the edge and unmold (unmould) on to a plate.
8. Put the remaining sugar in a bowl with ¼ cup (3 tablespoons) of water and microwave for 5 minutes on HIGH until the caramel is golden brown. Add 3 (2) tablespoons of cold water, taking care to avoid splashing. Add the crushed almonds and the butter. Return to the oven for 1 minute on HIGH, stir and pour over the charlotte.

Pêches aux abricots

Peach and Apricot Delight

00.20	00.10
plus chilling time	

American	Ingredients	Metric/Imperial
1	orange	1
½ cup	superfine (caster) sugar	5 tbsp
9 oz	ripe apricots	250 g/9 oz
1	lime	1
6	large white peaches	6
2 tbsp	crumbled small almond macaroons	1 tbsp
3 tbsp	maraschino liqueur	2 tbsp

1. Squeeze the orange and pour the juice into a bowl. Add the sugar and heat in the microwave oven for 2 minutes on HIGH. Stir until the sugar has melted.
2. Rinse the apricots under plenty of cold running water. Pat dry on kitchen paper. Cut in half and remove the pits (stones). Put in a round dish, pour over the orange syrup and microwave on HIGH for 2 minutes.
3. Remove the apricots from the dish with a slotted spoon and put in the goblet of a food processor. Leave the syrup in the dish.
4. Wash the lime very carefully and pat dry on kitchen paper. Slice one half extremely thinly and squeeze the juice from the other half.
5. Blanch the peaches, cut in half, remove the pits (stones) and peel. Put 6 half-peaches in the dish the apricots were cooked in, pour over 2 (1) tablespoons of lime juice and microwave on HIGH for 2½ minutes.
6. Remove the peaches with a slotted spoon and put in a deep dish. Repeat the process with the other 6 half-peaches.
7. Return the dish to the oven and reduce the liquid for 3 minutes on HIGH.
8. Add the crumbled macaroons to the apricots in the food processor goblet. Purée, adding the maraschino liqueur and cooking syrup from the fruit.
9. Coat the peaches with the apricot purée. Decorate with the lime slices and refrigerate for at least 2 hours before serving.

Pêches abricotines

Peaches in Apricot Syrup

00.05	00.14
plus chilling and cooling time	

American	Ingredients	Metric/Imperial
6	large ripe peaches	6
¼ cup	apricot preserve	3 tbsp
3 tbsp	Kirsch	2 tbsp
3 tbsp	slivered almonds	2 tbsp

1. Make a cross in the skin of each peach and put one at a time in the microwave oven for 1 minute each on HIGH. Peel.
2. Put the apricot preserve in a bowl and microwave on HIGH for 1 minute. Mix well, then add ¼ cup (3 tablespoons) of water and the Kirsch and mix again.
3. Cut the peaches in half and remove the pits (stones). Place the half-peaches in a dish, round side upward. Pour over the apricot syrup. Microwave, uncovered, on HIGH for 3 minutes.
4. Leave the peaches to cool. Refrigerate for at least 2 hours.
5. Spread the slivered almonds on a plate and microwave for 3-4 minutes on HIGH until golden. When the peaches are completely cold, sprinkle with slivered almonds and serve.

Pêches à l'orange

Peaches in Orange Syrup

00.10	00.08
Serves 4	

American	Ingredients	Metric/Imperial
4	large ripe peaches	4
2 tbsp	fresh lemon juice	1 tbsp
1	orange	1
2 oz	sugar	50 g/2 oz
3	egg yolks	3
2 tbsp	Cointreau	1 tbsp

1. Halve the peaches, remove the pits (stones) and peel. Put in a round dish, sprinkle with lemon juice and microwave, uncovered, for 3 minutes on HIGH. Place 2 half-peaches on each of 4 plates.
2. Squeeze the orange to obtain ⅓ cup (4½ tablespoons) of juice. Add the sugar and heat for 1 minute on HIGH. Stir until the sugar is dissolved.
3. Put the egg yolks in a bowl with the Cointreau and whisk until foamy. Gradually add the orange syrup, whisking constantly. Microwave, uncovered, for 4 minutes on MEDIUM, whisking after every minute.
4. When the sauce has thickened, pour over the peaches and serve immediately.

Peach and apricot delight

Peaches in apricot syrup

Entremets à l'ananas et à la noix de coco

Pineapple and Coconut Dessert

	00.10	00.15	
		plus cooling and chilling time	

American	Ingredients	Metric/Imperial
5 oz	superfine (caster) sugar	150 g/5 oz
1	large can pineapple chunks	1
2 oz	dried shredded (desiccated) coconut	50 g/2 oz
5	eggs	5

1. Put 2 oz (50 g/2 oz) of sugar in a fluted 1½ quart (1.5 litre/2¾ pint) Pyrex mold (mould). Add 3 (2) tablespoons of water and microwave for 5 minutes on HIGH until the caramel is a light golden color. Remove from the oven using protective gloves and tilt in all directions to coat the sides of the container.
2. Drain the pineapple chunks and purée in a food processor. Add the coconut, remaining sugar and the eggs and purée once more.
3. Pour the mixture on top of the caramel and microwave on HIGH for 10 minutes.
4. When the center of the soufflé is firm and the sides have shrunk a little, remove from the oven and leave to cool.
5. Refrigerate for at least 3 hours.
6. Just before serving, loosen the soufflé by passing a knife-blade round the edge. Turn out on to a plate and serve well chilled.
Cooking time of the caramel will depend very much on the type of container and amount of water; pay careful attention after 4 minutes, and remember that the caramel will continue to cook for several minutes after being removed from the oven.

Salade d'ananas au caramel

Pineapple in Caramel Syrup

	00.10	00.07	
		plus chilling time	

American	Ingredients	Metric/Imperial
1	large ripe pineapple	1
1 tsp	ground vanilla	1 tsp
5 oz	superfine (caster) sugar	150 g/5 oz
2 tbsp	fresh lemon juice	1 tbsp
¼ cup	Kirsch	3 tbsp

1. Cut off the ends of the pineapple. Put the pineapple on a board and peel from top to base with a large knife. Cut out the eyes with a small pointed knife. Slice the pineapple crosswise and cut out the core. Cut each slice into 6-8 pieces.
2. Put the fruit in a serving dish and sprinkle with the ground vanilla.
3. Put the sugar in a bowl and add ¼ cup (4 tablespoons) of water. Microwave, uncovered, on HIGH for 6-7 minutes, depending on the size of the bowl.
4. As soon as the sugar turns pale gold, remove from the oven with oven gloves: it should not brown too deeply. Add 3 (2) tablespoons of hot water, taking care to avoid splashing. Wait several seconds until it stops boiling, then add the lemon juice and Kirsch. Stir well and pour gradually over the pineapple chunks. Refrigerate for at least 2 hours. Serve well chilled.

Pineapple in caramel syrup

Microwave hint: To soften sugar that has gone hard in the carton or packet, place in the cooker together with a jug containing ⅔ cup (150 ml/¼ pint) of hot water. Cook on HIGH for 2-3 minutes, according to the size of the pack of sugar. Break up the lumps with a fork. Repeat the process if necessary.

Flan à la banane
Banana Flan

	00.05	00.06	
	plus cooling and chilling time		

American	Ingredients	Metric/Imperial
2	sliced large bananas	2
3 tbsp	fresh lemon juice	2 tbsp
3	large eggs	3
3 oz	superfine (caster) sugar	75 g/3 oz
2 tbsp	cognac or rum	1 tbsp
2 oz	dried shredded (desiccated) coconut	50 g/2 oz

1. Put the banana slices in a 6 inch (15 cm) soufflé mold (mould). Pour over the lemon juice.
2. Whisk the eggs in a bowl. Add the sugar and cognac or rum, still whisking. Stir in the coconut and whisk again. Pour over the bananas.
3. Microwave for 6 minutes on MEDIUM-HIGH, until the flan shrinks away from the edges of the mold (mould).
4. Leave to cool, then refrigerate. Serve well chilled.

Entremets à la banane
Banana Soufflé

	00.10	00.10	
	plus cooling and chilling time		

American	Ingredients	Metric/Imperial
4	bananas	4
¼ cup	fresh lemon juice	3 tbsp
3	eggs	3
3½ oz	superfine (caster) sugar	100 g/3½ oz
2 oz	dried shredded (desiccated) coconut	50 g/2 oz
3 tbsp	cocoa powder	2 tbsp
	butter, for greasing	
3 tbsp	grated milk chocolate	2 tbsp

1. Peel and slice 3 of the bananas. Purée in a food processor. Add the lemon juice, eggs, sugar, dried shredded (desiccated) coconut and cocoa. Purée again, until the mixture is smooth and runny.
2. Grease the base of a soufflé mold (mould) 6 inches (15 cm) in diameter and pour in the mixture. Microwave, uncovered, on MEDIUM-HIGH for 10 minutes.
3. Leave to cool. Transfer to a serving dish. Garnish with the remaining banana, sliced, and sprinkle with the grated chocolate. Refrigerate and serve very cold.

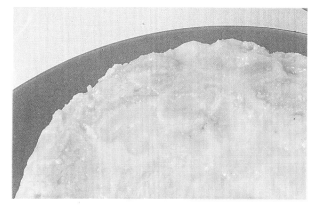

Banana flan

Crème renversée au citron
Lemon Crème Brulée

	00.10	00.22	
	plus cooling and chilling time		

American	Ingredients	Metric/Imperial
9 oz	superfine (caster) sugar	250 g/9 oz
2	lemons	2
2½ cups	milk	600 ml/1 pint
¾ cup	sour cream (crème fraîche)	200 ml/7 fl oz
6	eggs	6

1. Sprinkle the base of an oval dish with 3 oz (75 g/3 oz) of sugar. Add 3 (2) tablespoons of water, making sure that all the sugar is covered. Microwave, uncovered, on HIGH for 7 minutes. Remove the dish from the oven and tilt to make sure that the caramel covers the entire base.
2. Wash the lemons thoroughly and dry on kitchen paper. Remove the zest (peel) with a small sharp knife. Put the zest (peel) in a large bowl with the milk and sour cream (crème fraîche). Heat in the microwave oven for 6 minutes on HIGH.
3. Whisk the eggs in a bowl, gradually adding the remaining sugar.
4. Gradually pour the hot milk and cream over the eggs and sugar, whisking constantly. Pour this mixture over the caramel, straining through a fine sieve. Microwave for 9 minutes on MEDIUM-HIGH.
5. Leave the mousse to cool. Refrigerate for at least 3 hours.
6. To serve, run the blade of a knife around the top of the mousse and invert on to a platter. Serve well chilled.

Microwave hint: Sugar dissolves more quickly if it is warmed before adding to the liquid. Place the sugar in a shallow dish and cook on HIGH for about 3 minutes, stirring halfway through. Don't overheat as the sugar may discolor or burn if it gets too hot.

Amandine aux fruits

Fruit and Almond Tart

00.25   **00.12**
plus cooling and chilling time

American	Ingredients	Metric/Imperial
2	eggs, separated	2
7 oz	confectioners' (icing) sugar	200 g/7 oz
3½ oz	ground almonds	100 g/3½ oz
3 tbsp	cognac	2 tbsp
2 tbsp	oil	1 tbsp
1 cup	milk	250 ml/8 fl oz
3 oz	superfine (caster) sugar	75 g/3 oz
3 tbsp	cornstarch (cornflour)	1½ tbsp
2 oz	butter	50 g/2 oz
2	ripe nectarines	2
12	strawberries	12

1. To make the pastry, put 1 egg white into a bowl, and gradually add the confectioners' (icing) sugar, ground almonds and half of the cognac, mixing well with a wooden spatula.
2. Line the base and sides of a 9 inch (23 cm) Pyrex mold (mould) with non-stick parchment (greaseproof paper), allowing at least ½ inch (1.25 cm) to overlap the top. Brush with oil. Put the almond dough into the mold (mould). Dip a tablespoon into iced water and spread the dough smoothly with the back of the spoon. If the dough starts to stick to the spoon, dip in the water again.
3. Microwave, uncovered, for 7 minutes on MEDIUM, then for 1 minute on HIGH. Dip a clean cloth in cold water, fold into 4 and put on a work surface.
4. When the dough is cooked (it will still be soft, but hardens as it cools), remove from the mold (mould) using the non-stick parchment (greaseproof paper) as support and set gently on the wet cloth to cool.
5. To make the filling, heat the milk in a bowl for 2 minutes on HIGH. Whisk the 2 egg yolks with the sugar. Add the cornstarch (cornflour), whisking constantly. Gradually pour in the hot milk in a thin stream, whisking vigorously. Microwave for 2 minutes on HIGH. Whisk again for 1 minute. Add the remaining cognac and the butter in small pieces and stir until the butter has melted. Leave to cool.
6. Remove the non-stick parchment (greaseproof paper) and put the tart base on a platter. Put a flan case round it or make a circle out of strong paper and cover with aluminum (aluminium) foil. Whisk the second egg white and fold into the cooled custard cream. Pour on to the tart base. Smooth the surface.
7. Rinse the nectarines under plenty of cold running water. Pat dry on kitchen paper. Slice finely and arrange in a circle on the custard cream. Refrigerate until completely cold.
8. When ready to serve, rinse the strawberries under plenty of cold running water. Pat dry on kitchen paper and remove the stalks. Use to decorate the tart.

Microwave hint: Citrus fruits will yield more juice if put whole in the microwave cooker. Heat on HIGH for 1-3 minutes (depending on the quantity) before squeezing the juice.

Crème renversée aux nectarines

Nectarine Custard Cream

00.05   **00.13**
plus cooling and chilling time

American	Ingredients	Metric/Imperial
2¼ cups	milk	500 ml/18 fl oz
3	eggs	3
4	egg yolks	4
3½ oz	superfine (caster) sugar	100 g/3½ oz
	butter, for greasing	
9 oz	ripe nectarines	250 g/9 oz
	fresh fruit salad	

1. Heat the milk in the microwave oven for 4 minutes on HIGH.
2. Put the whole eggs, egg yolks and sugar in a bowl and whisk. Add the hot milk in a thin stream, still whisking vigorously.
3. Grease a 10 inch (25 cm) ring mold (mould) and pour in the egg custard.
4. Rinse the nectarines under plenty of cold running water. Pat dry on kitchen paper. Cut in half and remove the pits (stones). Slice thinly and stir into the custard mixture.
5. Microwave, uncovered, on HIGH for 9 minutes, until the custard is firm to the touch. Leave to cool, then refrigerate for at least 12 hours.
6. Just before serving, invert the custard cream on to a dish and fill the center with fresh fruit salad.

Couronne aux fruits exotiques

Ring Mold (Mould) with Exotic Fruits

00.20   **00.20**
plus cooling time

American	Ingredients	Metric/Imperial
3½ oz	butter	100 g/3½ oz
¼ cup	liquid honey	3 tbsp
¼ cup	cane sugar syrup	3 tbsp
⅔ cup	milk	150 ml/¼ pint
1	egg	1
1 tsp	vanilla extract (essence)	1 tsp
1 oz	soft dark brown sugar	25 g/1 oz
7 oz	self-rising (self-raising) flour	200 g/7 oz
	butter, for greasing	
½ cup	apricot preserve	6 tbsp
5 oz	raspberries	150 g/5 oz
1	mango	1
1	paw-paw (papaya)	1
4	passionfruit	4
3 tbsp	lime juice	2 tbsp
2 tbsp	Cointreau	1 tbsp
2 tbsp	raspberry liqueur	1 tbsp
2 tbsp	superfine (caster) sugar	1 tbsp

1. To make the dough, melt the butter and the honey in a bowl for 2 minutes on HIGH. Add the cane sugar syrup and milk and stir well. Add the egg, whisking vigorously, then the vanilla extract (essence) and brown sugar, still whisking.

2. Sift the flour into a second bowl. Pour in the mixture in a thin stream, beating constantly until the dough is smooth and runny.

3. Grease the base and sides of a 10 inch (25 cm) Pyrex ring mold (mould). Pour in the dough. Microwave, uncovered, on HIGH for 7 minutes, until the cake begins to shrink from the sides of the container. Leave to stand for 10 minutes. Turn out on to a wire rack to cool.

4. Put the cake on a platter. Purée the apricot preserve and put in a bowl. Melt for 1 minute on HIGH. Leave to cool, then use to brush the top and sides of the cake.

5. Rinse the raspberries under plenty of cold running water. Pat dry on kitchen paper. Put 12 raspberries on top of the cake at regular intervals.

6. Peel the mango and chop the flesh. Cut the paw-paw (papaya) in half, remove the pits (seeds) and peel and chop the flesh. Cut the passionfruit in half and scoop out the pulp with a small spoon. Add to the mango and paw-paw (papaya). Pour over the lime juice, Cointreau and raspberry liqueur, sprinkle with sugar, stir carefully and refrigerate.

7. Just before serving, add the remaining raspberries to the other fruit. Stir well and pour into the center of the cake.

Ring mold (mould) with exotic fruits

Couronne aux fruits confits

Ring Mold (Mould) with Glacé Fruit

00.20
Serves 6-8

00.16

American	Ingredients	Metric/Imperial
2 oz	golden raisins (sultanas)	50 g/2 oz
½ cup	Grand Marnier	5 tbsp
3 oz	butter	75 g/3 oz
2	eggs	2
1	pot natural flavor yogurt	1
¼ cup	milk	3 tbsp
½ cup	cane sugar syrup	125 ml/6 tbsp
1½ tsp	active dry yeast	1½ tsp
5 oz	all-purpose (plain) flour	150 g/5 oz
7 oz	mixed glacé fruit	200 g/7 oz
	butter, for greasing	
6 oz	confectioners' (icing) sugar	175 g/6 oz
½ cup	fresh orange juice	6 tbsp

1. Rinse the raisins (sultanas) under plenty of cold running water. Pat dry on kitchen paper. Add half of the Grand Marnier. Coarsely chop 6 oz (175 g/6 oz) of the glacé fruit.

2. Melt the butter in a bowl for 1 minute on HIGH.

3. Whisk the eggs in a bowl and add the yogurt, milk, cane sugar syrup and melted butter. Sift the yeast and flour over the mixture and stir well. Add the raisins (sultanas) and chopped glacé fruit.

4. Grease the base and sides of a 10 inch (25 cm) ring mold (mould) and pour in the mixture. Smooth the surface.

5. Microwave, uncovered, on HIGH for 10 minutes.

6. When the cake begins to shrink from the sides of the mold (mould), remove from the oven and leave to stand for 5 minutes.

7. Mix 2 oz (50 g/2 oz) of confectioners' (icing) sugar with ¼ cup (4 tablespoons) of the orange juice and 2 (1) tablespoons of Grand Marnier. Pour over the cake and leave to cool.

8. When the cake has cooled completely, turn out on to a platter. Mix the remaining confectioners' (icing) sugar with the remaining Grand Marnier and orange juice into a thick runny paste. Pour over the ring mold (mould) and spread equally over top and sides with a metal spatula.

9. Cut the remaining glacé fruits into decorative shapes and place on the frosting (icing) before it hardens.

Ring mold (mould) with glacé fruit

Semolina and almond ring mold (mould)

Gâteau à la semoule et aux amandes

Semolina and Almond Ring Mold (Mould)

	00.15	00.09	
	plus chilling time		

American	Ingredients	Metric/Imperial
2½ oz	butter	65 g/2½ oz
2	eggs	2
⅔ cup	cane sugar syrup	150 ml/¼ pint
¾ cup	orange liqueur	200 ml/7 fl oz
¼ tsp	almond extract (essence)	¼ tsp
3½ oz	semolina	100 g/3½ oz
½ tsp	active dry yeast	½ tsp
2 oz	ground almonds	50 g/2 oz
	butter, for greasing	

1. Put the butter in a bowl and melt in the microwave oven on HIGH for 30 seconds.
2. Whisk the eggs in a bowl. Add ¼ cup (3 tablespoons) of cane sugar syrup, 3 (2) tablespoons of orange liqueur, the almond extract (essence), melted butter, semolina, yeast and ground almonds. Whisk vigorously after each addition.

3. Grease the base of a small Pyrex ring mold (mould). Pour in the mixture and smooth the surface. Microwave, uncovered, on HIGH for 8 minutes.
4. To make the syrup, mix the remaining cane sugar syrup and orange liqueur and ½ cup (6 tablespoons) of water in a bowl. Pour this mixture over the cake while it is still hot. Leave to cool in the container.
5. Invert the cake on to a serving dish. Refrigerate until cold. Serve a mixed fruit salad with this dish. Put the fruit in the center of the ring.

Microwave hint: Frozen orange juice or other fruit juices may be thawed in their container. Remove the metal lid and place the open container in the microwave cooker. Heat on HIGH for 30 seconds. Check and repeat the process if necessary.

Savarin

Savarin

Savarin

	00.20	00.31	
	plus cooling time		

American	Ingredients	Metric/Imperial
1 tsp	active dry yeast	1 tsp
5 oz	all-purpose (plain) flour	150 g/5 oz
¼ tsp	salt	¼ tsp
2 oz	butter	50 g/2 oz
	butter, for greasing	
2	eggs	2
3 tbsp	cane sugar syrup	2 tbsp
2	oranges	2
¼ lb	superfine (caster) sugar	125 g/4 oz
¼ cup	Cointreau	4 tbsp
¼ cup	apricot preserve	4 tbsp
	fresh fruit salad	
	whipped cream	

1. Put ¼ cup (4 tablespoons) of water in a glass and microwave for 20 seconds on HIGH. It should reach a temperature of between 40°C-50°C. Add the yeast and leave to stand for 15 minutes.

2. Sift the flour and salt into a bowl. Melt the butter in a bowl in the oven for 1 minute on HIGH. Grease a 9 inch (23 cm) Pyrex ring mold (mould). Whisk the eggs in a bowl with a fork.
3. When the yeast is dissolved and swollen, add to the flour along with the cane sugar syrup and beaten eggs. Beat for 5 minutes with a wooden spoon until the dough is smooth and elastic. Stir in the melted butter and beat for a few more seconds.
4. Pour the dough into the mold (mould). At this stage it should not fill more than ⅓ of the container. Cover and microwave on HIGH for 20 seconds. Leave in the oven for 5 minutes, then heat again for 20 seconds on HIGH. Repeat this process until the dough rises to the top of the mold (mould). At no time remove from the oven or open the oven door.
5. When the dough has risen, microwave, uncovered, for 4½ minutes on HIGH. Remove from the oven and leave the savarin to cool in the container.
6. Turn the savarin out on to a dish, flat base down, and prepare the syrup. Squeeze the oranges to obtain 1 cup (250 ml/8 fl oz) of juice. Add the sugar, stir, and microwave for 3 minutes on HIGH. Stir again, and spoon over the savarin. Scoop up any juice not absorbed first time around and pour over again.
7. Just before serving, pour the Cointreau over the savarin. Purée the apricot preserve. Put in a cup with 2 tablespoons (1 tablespoon) of water and heat on HIGH for 1 minute. Leave to cool slightly, then brush over the savarin. Fill the center of the cake with fresh fruit salad and serve with whipped cream.

Charlotte surprise aux cerises

Cherry and Chocolate Charlotte

00.25 **00.13**
plus chilling and cooling time

American	Ingredients	Metric/Imperial
¼ lb	butter	125 g/4 oz
1	egg	1
¼ cup	cane sugar syrup	3 tbsp
2 oz	all-purpose (plain) flour	50 g/2 oz
	butter, for greasing	
7 oz	semisweet (plain) chocolate	200 g/7 oz
¼ cup	Kirsch	3 tbsp
3	eggs, separated	3
1	can pitted (stoned) red cherries	1
22-24	langues de chat	22-24
½ cup	whipped cream	6 tbsp

1. First make the base: put 2 oz (50 g/2 oz) of butter in a bowl and melt in the microwave oven for 30 seconds on HIGH.

2. Whisk the egg with a fork. Add the cane sugar syrup, flour and melted butter. Beat thoroughly.

3. Grease the base of a Pyrex mold (mould) 9 inches (23 cm) in diameter. Spoon in the cake mixture and microwave on MEDIUM-HIGH for 5 minutes. Leave to stand for 5 minutes. Invert on to a rack and leave to cool.

4. When the base is completely cool, prepare the filling. Break the chocolate in pieces, put in a bowl with the remaining butter and melt on HIGH for 2 minutes.

5. Add the Kirsch and the 3 egg yolks to the melted chocolate and mix. Whisk the egg whites to firm peaks, then fold carefully into the chocolate mixture.

6. Transfer the cake base to a serving platter. Drain the cherries and pour ¼ cup (3 tablespoons) of their syrup over the sponge. Place a flan ring around the sponge and arrange the langues de chat around the cake but inside the flan case, flat side inward. Spoon the chocolate mousse on top of the base. Smooth the surface. Refrigerate for at least 2 hours.

7. To serve, arrange the drained cherries carefully on top of the mousse. Remove the flan ring. Decorate with the whipped cream.

The only difficult part of this recipe is arranging the langues de chat. Do not try to put all on at once; after putting about a dozen in place, spoon some of the chocolate mousse against them so that they stand upright, then proceed patiently in stages. If you do not have a flan ring, use a strip of non-stick parchment (greaseproof paper) and secure with Scotch tape.

Cherry and chocolate charlotte

Upside-down chocolate custard

Crème renversée au chocolat

Upside-down Chocolate Custard

	00.05	00.15	
		plus cooling and chilling time	

American	Ingredients	Metric/Imperial
2¼ cups	milk	500 ml/18 fl oz
3	eggs	3
4	egg yolks	4
3½ oz	superfine (caster) sugar	100 g/3½ oz
3½ oz	semisweet (plain) chocolate	100 g/3½ oz
	butter, for greasing	
	fresh fruit salad	

1. Heat the milk in a cup in the microwave oven for 5 minutes on HIGH.
2. Put the 3 whole eggs and 4 egg yolks in a bowl with the sugar and whisk until pale and foamy. Add the milk in a thin stream, still whisking vigorously.
3. Break the chocolate in pieces and melt in a bowl in the microwave oven for 1 minute on HIGH. Mix until smooth, then add to the egg mixture.
4. Grease a 10 inch (25 cm) ring mold (mould) and pour in the mixture.
5. Microwave, uncovered, on HIGH for 9 minutes until the soufflé is firm to the touch. Leave to cool. Refrigerate for at least 12 hours.
6. Turn out on to a serving dish and serve with the fresh fruit salad.

Galette croquante au chocolat

Chocolate Soufflé

	00.05	00.09	
		plus cooling time	

American	Ingredients	Metric/Imperial
3½ oz	semisweet (plain) chocolate	100 g/3½ oz
3½ oz	butter	100 g/3½ oz
2	eggs, separated	2
3 oz	superfine (caster) sugar	75 g/3 oz
	butter, for greasing	

1. Break the chocolate into pieces and put in a bowl with the butter. Melt in the microwave oven on HIGH for 1½ minutes.
2. Add the egg yolks to the chocolate and butter mixture.
3. Whisk the egg whites to firm peaks, then gradually add the sugar, whisking continuously. Gently fold this meringue into the chocolate mixture.
4. Grease the base of a mold (mould) 7 inches (18 cm) in diameter and pour in the mixture. Cover and microwave on HIGH for 7 minutes.
5. Remove the mold (mould) from the oven, uncover and leave the soufflé to cool completely. Turn out on to a platter and serve.

Fondant au chocolat

Chocolate Sponge Cake with Caramel Sauce

	00.15	00.18	
		plus cooling and chilling time	

American	Ingredients	Metric/Imperial
5 oz	semisweet (plain) chocolate	150 g/5 oz
5 oz	butter	150 g/5 oz
2	eggs	2
1 oz	all-purpose (plain) flour	25 g/1 oz
¼ cup	cane sugar syrup	4 tbsp
2 tbsp	coffee extract (essence)	1 tbsp
1 tsp	oil	1 tsp
¼ lb	superfine (caster) sugar	125 g/4 oz
¾ cup	sour cream (crème fraîche)	200 ml/7 fl oz
3 tbsp	cognac	2 tbsp
2 tbsp	cocoa powder	1 tbsp

1. Break the chocolate into pieces and put in a bowl with the butter. Melt in the microwave oven for 2 minutes on HIGH.
2. Whisk the melted chocolate and butter and add the eggs, flour, cane sugar syrup and coffee extract (essence), still whisking.
3. Oil the base of a 6 inch (15 cm) soufflé mold (mould) and line with a circle of oiled non-stick parchment (greaseproof paper). Spoon the dough into the mold (mould) and smooth the surface. Microwave, uncovered, for 7 minutes on MEDIUM-HIGH. Leave the cake to cool in the container.
4. To make the sauce, put the sugar in a bowl, add ¼ cup (3 tablespoons) of water and microwave for 7 minutes on HIGH until a deep golden color. Add ¼ cup (4 tablespoons) of hot water to the caramel, taking care to avoid splashing.
5. Pour the sour cream (crème fraîche) into a bowl and heat in the oven for 1½ minutes on HIGH.
6. Pour the hot cream over the caramel and mix with a spatula. Stir in the cognac. Leave to cool, then refrigerate.
7. Turn the cake out on to a platter and remove the non-stick parchment (greaseproof paper). Sift the cocoa over the top. Pour the sauce into a sauceboat and serve with the cake.

Microwave hint: To soften hard ice-cream ready for serving, microwave on MEDIUM for 15 seconds. Test the consistency with a fork and repeat the process if necessary. Do not extend the heating time without testing as the ice-cream could melt and lose its fluffy texture.

Chocolate praline mousse

Crème au chocolat amer
Chocolate Cream Pots

◄▭▷ 00.15   00.06   〽
plus chilling time

American	Ingredients	Metric/Imperial
3 oz	bitter chocolate	75 g/3 oz
1¼ cups	milk	300 ml/½ pint
1	egg	1
2	egg yolks	2
¼ cup	superfine (caster) sugar	3 tbsp
	salt	
2 tbsp	Cointreau	1 tbsp
3 tbsp	golden raisins (sultanas)	2 tbsp

1. Break the chocolate in pieces and heat in a bowl with the milk for 3 minutes on HIGH.
2. Put the whole egg and 2 egg yolks in a large bowl with the sugar and a pinch of salt and whisk until foamy.
3. Stir the chocolate and milk mixture and pour in a thin stream into the eggs, whisking constantly. Microwave, uncovered, on HIGH for 1½ minutes.
4. Remove the bowl from the oven and beat the mixture until smooth. Add the Cointreau, beat again and divide the mousse between 4 ramekins.
5. Rinse the raisins (sultanas) under plenty of cold running water. Put in a bowl. Cover with water and heat in the oven for 1 minute on HIGH. Drain on kitchen paper and add to the ramekins. Leave to cool, then refrigerate for at least 3 hours. Serve well chilled.

Mousse au chocolat praliné
Chocolate Praline Mousse

◄▭▷ 00.05   00.01   〽
plus chilling time

American	Ingredients	Metric/Imperial
5 oz	chocolate praline	150 g/5 oz
1 oz	butter	25 g/1 oz
1	orange	1
3	eggs, separated	3
3 tsp	chocolate vermicelli	3 tsp

1. Break the chocolate in pieces and melt with the butter in a bowl for 1 minute on HIGH.
2. Stir carefully until smooth. Rinse the orange under plenty of cold running water. Pat dry on kitchen paper and grate the zest (peel) over the bowl.
3. Add the egg yolks one at a time, beating after each addition.
4. Whisk the egg whites to firm peaks and fold carefully into the mixture. Divide the mousse into 4 serving glasses and refrigerate for at least 2 hours.
5. Just before serving, sprinkle the mousse with chocolate vermicelli.

Chocolate Mousse

◄▭▷ 00.10   00.02   〽
plus chilling time

American	Ingredients	Metric/Imperial
6 oz	semisweet (plain) chocolate	175 g/6 oz
¼ cup	strong black coffee	3 tbsp
2 tbsp	orange juice	1 tbsp
2 tbsp	rum or brandy	1 tbsp
4	eggs	4

1. Break the chocolate into pieces. Put in a bowl with the coffee and orange juice and heat on HIGH for 2 minutes, stirring once. The chocolate should have melted; if not, heat for a further 1 minute. Stir until smooth. Stir in the rum or brandy.
2. Separate the eggs and add the yolks to the chocolate, beating well. Leave the mixture to cool.
3. In a clean bowl, whisk the egg whites until stiff peaks form. Fold 2-3 (1-2) tablespoons of the egg white into the chocolate. Gently fold in the remaining egg white with a metal spoon or spatula, taking care not to let the mixture become flat and heavy.
4. Pour into a serving bowl and chill for 3 hours before serving.

Tarte aux amandes
Almond Tart

American	Ingredients	Metric/Imperial
5 oz	plain white flour	150 g/5 oz
5 oz	wholewheat (wholemeal) flour	150 g/5 oz
5 oz	soft dark brown sugar	150 g/5 oz
	salt	
1	egg	1
6 oz	softened butter	175 g/6 oz
	butter, for greasing	
1	jar apricot preserve	1
3	egg yolks	3
¼ lb	ground almonds	125 g/4 oz
3	seedless clementines	3
3 tbsp	sour cream (crème fraîche)	2 tbsp

1. To make the pastry, mix the two flours, 2 oz (50 g/2 oz) of the brown sugar and a pinch of salt in a bowl. Add the whole egg and 3½ oz (100 g/3½ oz) of butter in small pieces. Rub in gently and quickly with the fingertips. As soon as the ingredients are smoothly blended and the dough is supple but still has a breadcrumb texture, roll into a ball, flatten slightly and refrigerate for at least 1 hour.

2. Roll out the dough on a board. Grease a 9 inch (24 cm) flan case with a removable base and line with the pastry dough. Prick all over with a fork. Microwave on HIGH for 7 minutes. Leave to cool.

3. Transfer the tart carefully to a serving platter.

4. To make the filling, purée the apricot preserve in a food processor. Spread the base of the tart with half of the preserve. Put the remaining butter in a bowl and melt on HIGH for 1 minute.

5. Mix the remaining brown sugar with the egg yolks. Add the melted butter and ground almonds. Mix well. Spread the mixture on top of the apricot preserve in the tart. Microwave on MEDIUM for 10 minutes.

6. Put the remaining preserve in the oven and melt for 30 seconds on HIGH. Pour carefully over the tart, covering completely. Refrigerate for 2 hours.

7. Peel the clementines and remove all white pith and membranes. Arrange the clementine segments side by side around the edge of the tart and put the sour cream (crème fraîche) in the middle. Serve well chilled.

Figues farcies
Stuffed Figs in Chocolate Sauce

American	Ingredients	Metric/Imperial
1	egg	1
3½ oz	ground almonds	100 g/3½ oz
3½ oz	superfine (caster) sugar	100 g/3½ oz
1 tsp	fresh lemon juice	1 tsp
12	ripe fresh figs	12
3½ oz	milk chocolate	100 g/3½ oz
2 tbsp	cane sugar syrup	1 tbsp
¼ cup	unsweetened condensed milk	4 tbsp
2 tbsp	raspberry liqueur	1 tbsp

1. Whisk the egg in a cup. Mix the ground almonds and sugar in a bowl. Stir in the lemon juice and the beaten egg, mixing with a fork. Work the mixture to a smooth paste with the fingers.

2. Rinse the figs under plenty of cold running water. Pat dry on kitchen paper. Cut in quarters without separating the quarters from the base. Stuff with the almond paste and close up as much as possible. Put on a wire rack.

3. Break the chocolate into pieces and put in a bowl with the cane sugar syrup and condensed milk. Heat on HIGH in the microwave oven for 2 minutes, watching to make sure that the mixture does not boil over.

4. Remove from the oven and stir until smooth. Add the raspberry liqueur and stir again. Leave to cool.

5. Coat the stuffed figs with the chocolate sauce, taking care to cover completely. Leave to cool. Arrange on a serving dish.

Almond tart

Gâteau aux figues
Figgy Pudding

| | 00.10 plus cooling time | 00.17 | |

American	Ingredients	Metric/Imperial
5 oz	semisweet (plain) chocolate	150 g/5 oz
3½ oz	butter	100 g/3½ oz
¼ cup	liquid honey	4 tbsp
9 oz	dried figs	250 g/9 oz
⅓ cup	port wine	4½ tbsp
5	eggs	5
6 oz	ground almonds	175 g/6 oz
1 tsp	active dry yeast	1 tsp
3 oz	chopped candied orange zest (peel)	75 g/3 oz
1 tsp	oil	1 tsp

1. Break the chocolate into pieces and melt in a bowl with the butter for 2 minutes on HIGH. Stir until the chocolate is melted.

2. Set several figs aside for decoration and chop the rest with kitchen scissors. Put the pieces in a bowl, pour over the port and microwave on HIGH for 5 minutes.

3. Whisk the eggs in a large bowl.

4. Add the ground almonds and yeast to the chocolate and butter mixture. Stir well. Add the beaten eggs, chopped figs and candied orange zest (peel). Mix well together.

5. Oil a 7 inch (18 cm) soufflé mold (mould) and line with a circle of oiled non-stick parchment (greaseproof paper). Spoon the mixture into the mold (mould) and microwave on MEDIUM-HIGH for 10 minutes.

6. Leave the gâteau to cool in the container. Turn out on to a plate and remove the non-stick parchment (greaseproof paper).

This pudding should not be refrigerated.

Figgy pudding

Date pudding

Pudding aux dattes
Date Pudding

	00.10	00.05	
	plus cooling and chilling time		

American	Ingredients	Metric/Imperial
1 tsp	oil	1 tsp
¼ lb	fresh dates	125 g/4 oz
1	egg, separated	1
1	egg	1
3 oz	ground almonds	75 g/3 oz
2 tbsp	self-rising (self-raising) flour	1 tbsp
½ tsp	active dry yeast	½ tsp
¼ cup	cane sugar syrup	4 tbsp
2 tbsp	sour cream (crème fraîche)	1 tbsp
2 tbsp	cognac	1 tbsp
3 tbsp	confectioners' (icing) sugar	2 tbsp

1. Oil the base of a 6 inch (15 cm) soufflé mold (mould). Line with oiled non-stick parchment (greaseproof paper). Remove the pits (stones) from the dates, set aside 4 for decoration and chop the rest coarsely with kitchen scissors.
2. Put the egg yolk and whole egg into a bowl and add the ground almonds, flour, yeast, cane sugar syrup, sour cream (crème fraîche) and cognac, beating well after each addition. Stir in the chopped dates.
3. Whisk the egg white to firm peaks and fold carefully into the mixture with a wooden spoon.
4. Pour the mixture into the mold (mould) and smooth the surface. Microwave, uncovered, on HIGH for 5 minutes.
5. Leave to cool in the container. Turn out on to a plate and remove the non-stick parchment (greaseproof paper). Refrigerate until ready to serve.
6. Cut the reserved dates in half. Sprinkle the pudding with the confectioners' (icing) sugar and decorate with the date halves. Serve well chilled.

Winter fruit salad

Compote d'hiver

Winter Fruit Salad

| | 00.05 plus cooling time | 00.22 | |

American	Ingredients	Metric/Imperial
12	pitted (stoned) prunes	12
6	dried figs	6
7 oz	dried apricots	200 g/7 oz
1 oz	golden raisins (sultanas)	25 g/1 oz
¼ lb	superfine (caster) sugar	125 g/4 oz
¼ cup	fresh lemon juice	3 tbsp
2	apples	2
½ tsp	cinnamon	½ tsp
1 oz	slivered almonds	25 g/1 oz

1. Rinse the dried fruits under plenty of cold running water. Pat dry on kitchen paper. Put in a casserole. Add 2¼ cups (500 ml/18 fl oz) of water, 3 oz (75 g/3 oz) of sugar and 3 (2) tablespoons of lemon juice. Cover and microwave on HIGH for 14 minutes.

2. Peel and core the apples, and cut in thick slices. Put in a dish with the remaining sugar and lemon juice and the cinnamon. Cover and microwave on HIGH for 3 minutes.

3. Drain the dried fruit, reserving the cooking liquid, and put in a salad bowl. Add the apples.

4. Pour the cooking liquid from the dried fruit and the apples into a bowl and reduce by half in the microwave oven for about 5 minutes on HIGH. Pour over the fruit and leave to cool.

5. Add the almonds and serve.

Sherry Trifle

| | 00.10 plus chilling time | 00.05 | |

American	Ingredients	Metric/Imperial
¼ cup	custard powder	3 tbsp
3 tbsp	sugar	2 tbsp
2 cups	milk	450 ml/¾ pint
6	slices sponge cake	6
3 tbsp	raspberry preserve	2 tbsp
1¾ lb	can sliced peaches	750 g/1¾ lb
½ cup	sherry	6 tbsp
⅔ cup	heavy (double) cream	150 ml/¼ pint
2 oz	toasted split almonds	50 g/2 oz

1. In a large heatproof jug, blend the custard powder, sugar and a little milk to a paste. Stir in the remaining cold milk. Heat on HIGH for 2 minutes, stir and heat for a further 2-3 minutes until thick. Cover the surface with damp non-stick parchment (greaseproof paper) and set aside to cool.

2. Cut the sponge into small pieces and spread with preserve. Arrange around the base and sides of a serving dish. Drain the peaches. Mix ¼ cup (3 tablespoons) of the juices from the can with the sherry and sprinkle over the sponge. Reserve a few peaches for decoration and arrange the rest on top of the sponge.

3. Uncover the cool custard and beat well. Pour over the peaches and chill for at least 1 hour.

4. Whip the cream until stiff, then pipe on to the trifle. Decorate with the reserved peaches and sprinkle with the almonds.

Pudding de pain perdu
Bread Pudding

◧▷ 00.10   00.38   〰
plus cooling time

American	Ingredients	Metric/Imperial
3½ oz	golden raisins (sultanas)	100 g/3½ oz
3 tbsp	rum	2 tbsp
1 quart	milk	1 litre/1¾ pints
1 oz	butter	25 g/1 oz
4	eggs	4
1	egg yolk	1
3½ oz	superfine (caster) sugar	100 g/3½ oz
	butter, for greasing	
½	loaf stale crusty bread, cut into small cubes	½
1 tsp	vanilla extract (essence)	1 tsp

1. Rinse the raisins (sultanas) under plenty of cold running water. Pat dry on kitchen paper. Put in a bowl and pour over the rum. Put the milk and butter in a bowl and microwave, uncovered, for 7-8 minutes on HIGH until the mixture comes to the boil. Take care not to boil over.
2. Whisk the eggs and egg yolk in a large bowl with the sugar. Grease the base of a 7 inch (18 cm) soufflé mold (mould).
3. Gently pour the milk over the eggs, whisking constantly. Add the bread, raisins and rum, and vanilla extract (essence). Stir with a wooden spoon and leave to stand for 5 minutes.
4. Pour the mixture into the buttered mold (mould). Microwave, uncovered, for 25 minutes on MEDIUM-HIGH. The pudding is ready when a knife blade inserted into the center comes out clean. Remove from the oven and leave to cool at room temperature.

Pain perdu aux pommes
Bread Pudding with Apples

◧▷ 00.10   00.10   〰
plus cooling time

American	Ingredients	Metric/Imperial
	butter, for greasing	
2	apples	2
4	eggs	4
3 oz	superfine (caster) sugar	75 g/3 oz
3 tbsp	cognac	2 tbsp
6	slices raisin brioche	6

1. Grease the base of a small mold (mould). Peel and core the apples, quarter and cut the quarters in 3 or 4 thick slices.
2. Whisk the eggs in a bowl and add the sugar and cognac, still whisking.
3. Spread a layer of apples on the base of the mold (mould). Dip 2 slices of brioche in the beaten egg and arrange on top of the apples. Repeat with another layer of apples, another layer of brioche dipped in egg, another layer of apples, a layer of brioche dipped in egg and finish with the remaining apple slices. Pour over the remaining beaten egg.
4. Cover and microwave on HIGH for 10 minutes.
5. Leave to stand in the mold (mould). When cool, invert on to a platter and serve.
If brioche is not available, use regular raisin bread.

Bread pudding with apples

Pudding à la poire

Bread Pudding with Pears

00.20 plus cooling time   **00.30**

American	Ingredients	Metric/Imperial
6	pears	6
2 tbsp	fresh lemon juice	1 tbsp
3 oz	golden raisins (sultanas)	75 g/3 oz
	butter, for greasing	
¾ lb	quince preserve	350 g/12 oz
10	slices brioche or raisin bread	10
2¼ cups	milk	500 ml/18 fl oz
4	eggs	4
½ tsp	cinnamon	½ tsp
3½ oz	superfine (caster) sugar	100 g/3½ oz
3½ oz	chopped mixed glacé fruit	100 g/3½ oz

1. Peel and core the pears, quarter and cut each quarter in half. Put in a casserole and sprinkle with the lemon juice. Cover and microwave on HIGH for 5 minutes.

2. Rinse the raisins (sultanas) under plenty of cold running water. Leave to drain.

3. Grease the base of a 7 inch (18 cm) soufflé mold (mould) and line with a circle of buttered non-stick parchment (grease-proof paper). Spread the preserve on the brioche and cut each slice in 4 pieces.

4. Heat the milk in a cup on HIGH for 5 minutes. Whisk the eggs in a bowl and add the cinnamon and sugar, still whisking. Pour the boiling milk over the mixture in a thin stream, whisking constantly.

5. Line the base of the soufflé mold (mould) with half of the brioche, overlapping the pieces. Arrange the pears in a layer on top and sprinkle with the raisins (sultanas) and chopped glacé fruit. Cover with the remaining brioche. Pour carefully over the egg and milk mixture.

6. Microwave, uncovered, on MEDIUM-HIGH for 20 minutes.

7. Leave the pudding to cool completely. Turn out on to a serving dish.

Bread pudding with pears

Couscous with fresh fruit

Couscous aux fruits frais

Couscous with Fresh Fruit

00.10
plus cooling time

00.05

American	Ingredients	Metric/Imperial
7 oz	medium grain couscous	200 g/7 oz
¼ cup	superfine (caster) sugar	3 tbsp
1 cup	milk	250 ml/8 fl oz
1	squeezed orange	1
6	apricots	6
6	nectarines	6
2 tbsp	fresh lemon juice	1 tbsp
1	diced pear	1
2	kiwi fruits	2

1. Put the couscous in a casserole. Sprinkle over the sugar and pour in the milk. Stir well. Cover and microwave on HIGH for 2 minutes.

2. Lift the couscous grains with a fork to aerate them. Cover and microwave on HIGH for a further 3 minutes. Separate the grains again with a fork. Cover and leave to stand.

3. Pour ⅓ cup (4½ tablespoons) of orange juice over the couscous. Stir well. Leave to cool completely.

4. Rinse the apricots and nectarines under plenty of cold running water. Pat dry on kitchen paper. Cut in half and remove the pits (stones), then slice. Pour over half of the lemon juice. Pour the remaining lemon juice over the pear cubes. Peel and slice the kiwi fruits.

5. Put the couscous in a serving dish. Arrange the fruits on top and serve cold.

Charlotte diplomate
Royal Charlotte

00.20 plus chilling time   **00.10**

American	Ingredients	Metric/Imperial
¼ cup	cognac	4 tbsp
1 tbsp	unflavored gelatin	1 tbsp
1¼ cups	milk	300 ml/½ pint
2	egg yolks	2
¼ lb	superfine (caster) sugar	125 g/4 oz
½ tsp	vanilla extract (essence)	½ tsp
1 tsp	cornstarch (cornflour)	1 tsp
2 oz	golden raisins (sultanas)	50 g/2 oz
5 oz	chopped mixed glacé fruit	150 g/5 oz
20	ladyfingers (sponge fingers)	20
⅔ cup	sour cream (crème fraîche)	150 ml/¼ pint
¼ cup	apricot preserve	4 tbsp

1. Put 3 (2) tablespoons of cognac in a cup, sprinkle the gelatin on top and leave to swell.
2. Pour the milk into a bowl and heat on HIGH for 2 minutes.
3. Whisk the egg yolks and 2 oz (50 g/2 oz) of sugar in a bowl until pale and foamy. Add the vanilla and cornstarch (cornflour), still whisking.
4. Add the hot milk in a thin stream, whisking continuously. Microwave on HIGH for 1½ minutes. Whisk again. Add the gelatin mixture, stirring until completely dissolved. Plunge the bowl into a basin of iced water to cool.
5. Put the raisins (sultanas) in a cup, cover with water and heat in the microwave oven for 2 minutes on HIGH. Drain and pat dry on kitchen paper. Add, with the glacé fruit, to the gelatin mixture.
6. To prepare the syrup, put the remaining sugar and ½ cup (5 tablespoons) of water in a small dish. Heat on HIGH for 2½ minutes. Mix until the sugar is completely dissolved. Stir in the remaining cognac.

Royal charlotte

7. Take the ladyfingers (sponge fingers) one by one and dip the flat side into the syrup. Use at once to line the base and sides of a charlotte mold (mould), sugared side outward. Set 4 or 5 biscuits aside to arrange on top of the charlotte. Crush any remaining biscuits and fold into the fruit mixture.
8. Add 3 (2) tablespoons of iced water to the sour cream (crème fraîche) and whip until firm. Fold carefully into the fruit mixture. Pour into the charlotte mold (mould). Dip the remainder of the biscuits in the syrup and use to cover the top of the charlotte, flat side upward. Put a weighted board on top and refrigerate for at least 4 hours.
9. Just before serving, turn the charlotte out on to a platter. Melt the apricot preserve for 2 minutes on HIGH, pour over the charlotte and serve.

Entremets au vin blanc
White Wine Soufflé

00.05 plus cooling and chilling time   **00.13**

American	Ingredients	Metric/Imperial
1¾ cups	good dry white wine	400 ml/14 fl oz
5 oz	superfine (caster) sugar	150 g/5 oz
¼ lb	ground almonds	125 g/4 oz
2 tbsp	cognac	1 tbsp
5	egg yolks	5

1. Mix together the white wine and sugar in a bowl and heat in the microwave oven for 6 minutes on HIGH: the wine should boil for at least 1 minute.
2. Stir until the sugar is completely dissolved. Stir in the ground almonds and cognac.
3. Whisk the egg yolks in a second bowl and gradually add the wine and ground almond mixture, whisking constantly.
4. Divide the mixture into 4 individual serving glasses and put in a circle in the microwave oven, leaving the center empty. Microwave, uncovered, on MEDIUM-HIGH for 7 minutes until the soufflé is firm.
5. Leave to cool at room temperature, then refrigerate. Serve very cold.

Crème mousseuse pralinée
Caramel Cream Mousse

00.15 plus cooling and chilling time   **00.08**

American	Ingredients	Metric/Imperial
2¼ cups	milk	500 ml/18 fl oz
2	eggs, separated	2
1	egg yolk	1
3½ oz	superfine (caster) sugar	100 g/3½ oz
3 tbsp	cornstarch (cornflour)	2 tbsp
2 oz	ground praline	50 g/2 oz
2 tbsp	Grand Marnier	1 tbsp
3 oz	butter	75 g/3 oz

1. Heat the milk in a bowl for 5 minutes on HIGH.
2. Put the 3 egg yolks in a bowl. Add the sugar and whisk until pale and foamy. Stir in the cornstarch (cornflour).

Caramel cream with wine

3. Pour the milk in a thin stream over the mixture, whisking continuously. Transfer to a casserole. Microwave, uncovered, on HIGH for 2 minutes, whisk, then microwave for 1 further minute.

4. Add the ground praline and Grand Marnier to the boiling custard and stir thoroughly. Cut the butter into small pieces and add piece by piece. Stir again, leave to cool, and refrigerate until just before serving.

5. When ready to serve, whisk the egg whites to firm peaks and fold carefully into the custard cream. Serve well chilled.

Crème bordelaise

Caramel Cream with Wine

	00.10	00.21	
	plus chilling time		

American	Ingredients	Metric/Imperial
3½ oz	superfine (caster) sugar	100 g/3½ oz
1¼ cups	sweet white dessert wine	300 ml/½ pint
1	lemon	1
6	eggs	6
¼ tsp	cinnamon	¼ tsp
⅔ cup	cane sugar syrup	150 ml/¼ pint

1. Put the sugar in a flat Pyrex dish 9 inches (23 cm) in diameter and add ¼ cup (4 tablespoons) of water. Microwave, uncovered, on HIGH for 6 minutes, taking care that the caramel does not get too brown, because it will continue to cook for several seconds after being removed from the oven. Make sure the caramel is spread evenly over the base of the dish.

2. Pour the wine into a bowl and heat in the microwave oven for 3 minutes on HIGH.

3. Wash the lemon thoroughly. Pat dry on kitchen paper. Remove the zest (peel) with a small sharp knife, taking care not to bring away any of the bitter white pith. Whisk the eggs in a bowl. Add the cinnamon, lemon zest (peel) and cane sugar syrup.

4. Carefully pour the hot wine into the egg mixture, whisking vigorously the whole time. Pour the mixture into the dish containing the caramel and microwave for 12 minutes on HIGH.

5. Leave the caramel cream to cool a little. Remove from the mold (mould) and refrigerate. Serve well chilled.

This dish could be accompanied by a mixed fruit salad (grapes, strawberries, pineapple) macerated in ⅓ cup (4½ tablespoons) of the same dessert wine used for the caramel cream.

Entremets charentais

Caramel Cheesecake

	00.15	00.09	
	plus cooling time		

American	Ingredients	Metric/Imperial
5 oz	cream cheese	150 g/5 oz
¼ lb	apricot preserve	125 g/4 oz
2	eggs	2
2	eggs, separated	2
3 tbsp	cornstarch (cornflour)	2 tbsp
3 tbsp	cognac	2 tbsp
2 oz	chopped candied angelica	50 g/2 oz
1 tsp	oil	1 tsp
3 tbsp	caramel sauce	2 tbsp

1. Put the cream cheese in a strainer to drain off any liquid.
2. Purée the apricot preserve in a food processor. Put the 2 whole eggs and 2 yolks into a bowl.
3. Whisk the eggs, adding the cream cheese, preserve, cornstarch (cornflour) and cognac. Beat thoroughly.
4. Stir in the chopped angelica.
5. Whisk the 2 egg whites to firm peaks and fold carefully into the mixture.
6. Oil the base of a 6 inch (15 cm) soufflé mold (mould) and line with a circle of oiled non-stick parchment (greaseproof paper).
7. Spoon the mixture into the mold (mould) and microwave, uncovered, for 9 minutes on MEDIUM-HIGH.
8. Leave to cool. Turn the cheesecake out on to a platter and remove the non-stick parchment (greaseproof paper).
9. Just before serving, coat with the caramel sauce.

Chocolate truffles

Ramequins au fromage blanc

Cream Cheese Ramekins

	00.45	00.08	
	plus cooling and chilling time		

American	Ingredients	Metric/Imperial
7 oz	cream cheese	200 g/7 oz
¼ cup	apricot preserve	3 tbsp
2	eggs	2
2	eggs, separated	2
3 tbsp	cornstarch (cornflour)	2 tbsp
2 oz	chopped assorted glacé fruit	50 g/2 oz
½ tsp	vanilla extract (essence)	½ tsp
3 tbsp	superfine (caster) sugar	2 tbsp

1. Drain the cream cheese in a strainer for at least 30 minutes.
2. Purée the apricot preserve in a food processor. Put the 2 whole eggs and 2 yolks into a bowl.
3. Whisk the eggs until pale. Add the cream cheese, apricot preserve, cornstarch (cornflour), glacé fruit and vanilla and mix thoroughly.
4. Whisk the 2 egg whites to very firm peaks. Add the sugar all at once, still whisking, then fold into the mixture.
5. Wrap a double thickness of non-stick parchment (greaseproof paper) around each of 4 ramekin dishes and secure with an elastic band.
6. Divide the mixture between the 4 ramekins and place in a circle in the microwave oven, leaving the center empty. Microwave, uncovered, on MEDIUM-HIGH for 8 minutes.
7. Leave to cool. Remove the non-stick parchment (greaseproof paper). Serve chilled.

Truffes au chocolat

Chocolate Truffles

	00.10	00.03	
	plus chilling time		

American	Ingredients	Metric/Imperial
9 oz	semisweet (plain) chocolate	250 g/9 oz
3 tbsp	cognac	2 tbsp
3½ oz	butter	100 g/3½ oz
⅓ cup	sour cream (crème fraîche)	4½ tbsp
	chocolate vermicelli	
	cocoa powder	

1. Break the chocolate into pieces and melt in a bowl with the cognac for 2 minutes on HIGH. Beat well.
2. Put the butter and sour cream (crème fraîche) in a bowl and heat for 1 minute on HIGH.
3. Add the butter and sour cream (crème fraîche) to the melted chocolate and stir carefully. Refrigerate for 30 minutes to harden.
4. When the mixture is sufficiently firm to work with, take in small spoonfuls and form into balls with the palms of the hands. Place the truffles on non-stick parchment (greaseproof paper) as they are made.
5. Spread the chocolate vermicelli on one plate and the cocoa on another. Roll the truffles either in the vermicelli or in the cocoa. Place on a board and refrigerate. Do not put in a bowl until ready to eat as they soften very quickly.

Galettes antillaises

Coconut Dreams

	00.10 plus resting time	00.04	

American	Ingredients	Metric/Imperial
3½ oz	confectioners' (icing) sugar	100 g/3½ oz
3½ oz	dried shredded (desiccated) coconut	100 g/3½ oz
1	egg white	1
¼ tsp	oil	¼ tsp
2 oz	semisweet (plain) chocolate	50 g/2 oz
1 tbsp	butter	½ tbsp

1. Mix the confectioners' (icing) sugar and coconut in a bowl and add the egg white. Mix with a fork, then work with the fingers to a firm dough.
2. Cut a circle of non-stick parchment (greaseproof paper) the size of the microwave turntable (about 11 inches (28 cm) in diameter). Oil the edge of the paper but not the center.
3. Scoop up portions of the coconut mixture the size of walnuts and form into balls. Arrange on the oiled area of the non-stick parchment (greaseproof paper), spaced equally apart.
4. Microwave, uncovered, on HIGH for 3 minutes; the dough will spread a little.
5. Remove from the oven and leave to harden at room temperature. When cold and firm, lift off with a spatula and arrange on a plate.
6. Break the chocolate in pieces and melt with the butter for 1 minute on HIGH. Stir thoroughly. Coat each coconut ball with chocolate. Leave to harden.
These coconut dreams will keep very well for several days in a tightly sealed cake tin.

Coconut dreams

Hot Desserts

Tarte Tatin
Upside-down Apple Tart

00.20 plus chilling time   **00.27**

American	Ingredients	Metric/Imperial
7 oz	all-purpose (plain) flour	200 g/7 oz
1 tsp	cinnamon	1 tsp
2 oz	soft dark brown sugar	50 g/2 oz
	salt	
5 oz	butter	150 g/5 oz
1	egg	1
3½ oz	superfine (caster) sugar	100 g/3½ oz
4	large Granny Smith apples	4
2 tbsp	fresh lemon juice	1 tbsp

1. To make the pastry, mix the flour, cinnamon, brown sugar and salt in a large bowl. Add 3½ oz (100 g/3½ oz) of butter in small pieces, and the egg. Work quickly with the fingers to make the dough, adding 1 or 2 tablespoons of iced water if necessary. Roll into a ball and leave to chill in the refrigerator for at least 30 minutes.
2. Put 2 oz (50 g/2 oz) of the sugar in a 10 inch (25 cm) mold (mould). Add ¼ cup (3 tablespoons) of water and microwave for 6 minutes on HIGH until the caramel is a deep golden brown. Wearing a protective oven glove, tilt the mold (mould) in all directions to distribute the caramel up the sides. Add 2 tablespoons (1 tablespoon) of butter and leave to melt, still tilting the container from side to side.
3. Peel the apples, quarter and remove the core. Sprinkle with the lemon juice. Arrange the apple quarters on top of the caramel and microwave, uncovered, for 5 minutes on HIGH.
4. Roll out the pastry into a circle 11 inches (28 cm) in diameter. Push the apples slightly away from the sides of the mold (mould) and sprinkle with the remaining sugar and the remaining butter cut into little pieces. Put the pastry circle over the apples and press the edges down between the apples and the sides of the container. Microwave, uncovered, on HIGH for 6 minutes.
5. Check whether the pastry is cooked: it should be still supple but dry. Leave to stand for 10 minutes before turning out on to a serving dish. Serve warm.

Gratin de pommes
Windsor Apple Pie

00.10   **00.08**
Serves 4

American	Ingredients	Metric/Imperial
1¼ lb	Golden Delicious apples	500 g/1¼ lb
3 tbsp	golden raisins (sultanas)	2 tbsp
5 oz	ground almonds	150 g/5 oz
3½ oz	softened butter	100 g/3½ oz
3 oz	soft dark brown sugar	75 g/3 oz
1	egg yolk	1
½ cup	sour cream (crème fraîche)	4 tbsp

1. Peel, quarter and core the apples. Cut the quarters in half.
2. Arrange the apple pieces in a 9 inch (23 cm) dish and sprinkle with raisins (sultanas). Microwave, uncovered, on HIGH for 4 minutes.
3. Mix together the ground almonds, butter, brown sugar and egg yolk. Cover the apples with this mixture and microwave, uncovered, for 4 minutes on HIGH.
4. Serve warm with sour cream (crème fraîche).

Stuffed Baked Apple Pudding

00.15   **00.28**
Serves 4

American	Ingredients	Metric/Imperial
6	small dessert apples	6
3 tbsp	white wine	2 tbsp
¼ cup	superfine (caster) sugar	4 tbsp
	redcurrant jello (jelly)	
1	egg	1
2 tbsp	cornstarch (cornflour)	1 tbsp
1¼ cups	milk	300 ml/½ pint
½	vanilla pod	½

1. Peel and core the apples and put in a deep dish. Brush with the wine and sprinkle with 2 (1) tablespoons of the sugar. Cover and cook on HIGH for 10 minutes.
2. Fill the centers of the apples with redcurrant jello (jelly). Heat on HIGH for 5 minutes.
3. Separate the egg and mix the yolk with the cornstarch (cornflour), 2 (1) tablespoons of the remaining sugar and 3 (2) tablespoons of the milk.
4. Put the remaining milk and vanilla pod in a bowl and heat on HIGH for 5 minutes. Pour some of the milk into the egg mixture, then return all the mixture to the bowl. Mix well. Heat on HIGH for 3 minutes. Stir, then cook for a further 2 minutes. Remove the vanilla pod and pour the sauce over the apples. Heat on HIGH for 3 minutes.
5. Whisk the egg white in a clean bowl until stiff. Whisk in the remaining sugar. Spoon over the vanilla cream and put under a hot broiler (grill) until the top turns golden brown.

Upside-down apple tart

Sussex Pond Pudding

▰▷   00.15   00.07   ▩
       Serves 6-8

American	Ingredients	Metric/Imperial
½ lb	self-rising (self-raising) flour	225 g/8 oz
2 oz	shredded suet	50 g/2 oz
⅔ cup	water	150 ml/¼ pint
	butter, for greasing	
3½ oz	butter	100 g/3½ oz
¼ lb	brown sugar	125 g/4 oz
3½ oz	golden raisins (sultanas)	100 g/3½ oz
1	large thin-skinned lemon	1

1. Mix the flour and suet in a bowl. Add the water a little at a time to form a soft but not sticky dough. Knead the dough lightly.
2. Grease a 1½ quart (1.5 litre/2¾ pint) pudding basin. Roll out three-quarters of the dough and line the basin.
3. Cream together the butter and sugar until light and fluffy. Stir in the raisins (sultanas). Put half of the mixture into the base of the pudding. Prick the lemon all over and press into the butter. Top with the remaining butter mixture.
4. Roll out the remaining dough and cover the filling, sealing well at the edges. Cook on HIGH for 6-7 minutes. Unmould and serve immediately with custard.

Cherry Pudding with Preserve Sauce

▰▷   00.10   00.12   ▩
       Serves 4-6

American	Ingredients	Metric/Imperial
¼ lb	butter	125 g/4 oz
¼ lb	sugar	125 g/4 oz
2	eggs	2
6 oz	sifted self-rising (self-raising) flour	175 g/6 oz
3 oz	glacé cherries	75 g/3 oz
⅔ cup	milk	8 tbsp
½ tsp	almond extract (essence)	½ tsp
	butter, for greasing	
2 oz	raspberry preserve	50 g/2 oz
⅔ cup	water	8 tbsp
1 tsp	arrowroot	1 tsp
2 tbsp	lemon juice	1 tbsp

1. Cream together the butter and sugar until light and fluffy. Gradually beat in the eggs one at a time. Fold in the sifted flour and cherries. Add the milk and almond extract (essence) to form a soft dropping consistency.
2. Lightly grease a pudding basin. Spoon in the mixture and cook on HIGH for 5-6 minutes. Leave to stand.

3. Put the preserve and water in a jug and heat on HIGH for 3 minutes. Mix together the arrowroot and lemon juice. Stir into the preserve. Heat on HIGH for 3 minutes. Stir well.
4. Unmould the pudding on to a plate and pour over a little of the sauce. Serve the remaining sauce in a sauceboat.

Tarte renversée aux abricots

Apricot Upside-down Flan

▰▷   00.15   00.26   ▩
       plus chilling and cooling time

American	Ingredients	Metric/Imperial
7 oz	all-purpose (plain) flour	200 g/7 oz
1 tsp	cinnamon	1 tsp
2 oz	soft dark brown sugar	50 g/2 oz
6 oz	softened butter	175 g/6 oz
1	egg	1
2 lb	apricots	1 kg/2 lb
3½ oz	superfine (caster) sugar	100 g/3½ oz
3 tbsp	Kirsch	2 tbsp
	whipped cream	

1. To make the pastry, mix the flour, cinnamon and brown sugar in a bowl. Add half of the butter in small pieces, and the egg. Rub in gently and quickly with the fingertips. As soon as the ingredients are blended and the dough is supple but still has a breadcrumb texture, roll into a ball, flatten slightly, wrap in a plastic bag and refrigerate for at least 1 hour.
2. Rinse the apricots under plenty of cold running water. Pat dry on kitchen paper. Cut in half to remove the pit (stone), then close up again.
3. Put half of the remaining butter in a flan case 9 inches (23 cm) in diameter and add half of the sugar and the Kirsch. Microwave on HIGH for 6 minutes until golden.
4. Arrange the apricots side by side, so close together that they almost overlap, in the base of the flan case. Sprinkle with the remaining sugar and dot with the remaining butter. Microwave, uncovered, on HIGH for 5 minutes. Leave to cool.
5. Roll out the dough into a circle about 11 inches (28 cm) in diameter. Cut the remaining dough into strips.
6. Gently push the apricots toward the center of the flan case to leave a small space all round. Cover with the pastry circle, folding it over between the apricots and the sides of the flan case. Arrange the pastry strips on top in the form of a cross. Microwave on HIGH for 10 minutes.
7. Leave to stand for 5 minutes. Invert the tart on to a platter and serve with whipped cream.

Apricot upside-down flan

Riz au lait
Rice Pudding

	00.05	00.50	
	Serves 4		

American	Ingredients	Metric/Imperial
3 oz	rice	75 g/3 oz
1½ oz	superfine (caster) sugar	40 g/1½ oz
½ tsp	vanilla extract (essence)	½ tsp
3¼ cups	milk	750 ml/1¼ pints
3 oz	golden raisins (sultanas)	75 g/3 oz

1. Put the rice in a large casserole. Add the sugar, vanilla and milk. Stir well. Cover and microwave on HIGH for 10 minutes.
2. Rinse the raisins (sultanas) under plenty of cold running water. Pat dry on kitchen paper.
3. When the milk comes to the boil, add the raisins (sultanas) and stir well. Cover and microwave on MEDIUM for 30 minutes.
4. Mix the rice and leave to stand for at least 10 minutes.
It is very important to use a large casserole to avoid the danger of the pudding boiling over in the oven. Not much time is gained by cooking rice in this way, but it has the advantages of the rice pudding turning out very creamy and the cooking receptacle being easy to clean.

Bananes au caramel
Caramel Bananas

	00.05	00.06	
	Serves 4		

American	Ingredients	Metric/Imperial
4	bananas	4
¼ cup	superfine (caster) sugar	4 tbsp
1½ oz	slivered almonds	40 g/1½ oz

1. Cut 4 squares of non-stick parchment (greaseproof paper). Peel the bananas, put 1 banana on each square of paper and form into an envelope.
2. Put the envelopes in a circle on a plate and microwave on HIGH for 2 minutes.
3. Put the sugar in a bowl with 3 (2) tablespoons of water. Microwave, uncovered, on HIGH for 3 minutes. Add the almonds, stir, cover to avoid splashing and microwave on HIGH for 1 minute.
4. Remove the bananas from the envelopes and set on individual dessert plates. Coat with the caramel and serve at once.

Rice pudding

Stuffed pears in chocolate sauce

Poires farcies
Stuffed Pears in Chocolate Sauce

	00.15	00.10	
	plus cooling time		

American	Ingredients	Metric/Imperial
3 oz	ground almonds	75 g/3 oz
3 oz	sugar	75 g/3 oz
1	egg	1
1 tbsp	butter	½ tbsp
3 tbsp	fresh lemon juice	2 tbsp
6	large crisp pears	6
7 oz	semisweet (plain) chocolate	200 g/7 oz
¼ cup	sour cream (crème fraîche)	3 tbsp
2 tbsp	pear liqueur	1 tbsp

1. Mix together the ground almonds, sugar, egg and butter. Beat until smooth.
2. Add the lemon juice to a bowl of iced water. Peel and core the pears, halve and put immediately in the water and lemon juice.
3. Remove the pears and pat dry on kitchen paper. Stuff the centers with the ground almond mixture. Put in a round dish, leaving the center empty. Microwave, uncovered, on HIGH for 8 minutes.
4. When the pears are tender, leave to cool. Transfer to a serving dish.
5. Just before serving, break the chocolate into pieces and put in a bowl with the sour cream (crème fraîche). Microwave on HIGH for 2 minutes. Beat until the mixture is creamy. Stir in the pear liqueur.
6. Coat the stuffed pears with the hot chocolate sauce and serve at once.

Cakes

Amandier aux fraises

Strawberry Marzipan Cake

00.30   00.16

plus cooling time

American	Ingredients	Metric/Imperial
¼ lb	butter	125 g/4 oz
½ lb	ground almonds	225 g/8 oz
½ cup	cane sugar syrup	6 tbsp
3	eggs, separated	3
¼ cup	cornstarch (cornflour)	3 tbsp
¼ cup	cocoa powder	3 tbsp
1 tsp	oil	1 tsp
¼ lb	confectioners' (icing) sugar	125 g/4 oz
½ tsp	fresh lemon juice	½ tsp
1	egg yolk	1
¼ tsp	green food coloring	¼ tsp
2 oz	superfine (caster) sugar	50 g/2 oz
¼ cup	Kirsch	4 tbsp
1¼ lb	strawberries	500 g/1¼ lb
3 tbsp	redcurrant jello (jelly)	2 tbsp
¼ cup	sour cream (crème fraîche)	3 tbsp

1. Soften the butter in a bowl in the microwave oven for 1 minute on HIGH.
2. Add half of the ground almonds and the cane sugar syrup to the butter and beat with a wooden spoon. Add the 3 egg yolks one at a time, beating after each addition. Sift the cornstarch (cornflour) and cocoa powder over the mixture and fold in carefully.
3. Whisk the 3 egg whites to firm peaks and fold carefully into the mixture.
4. Oil the base of a 7 inch (18 cm) soufflé mold (mould) and line with a circle of oiled non-stick parchment (greaseproof paper). Pour the mixture into the mold (mould) and micro-wave, uncovered, on MEDIUM-HIGH for 8 minutes; the cake should shrink from the edges of the mold (mould) when cooked.
5. Leave to stand for 5 minutes. Turn out on to a wire rack and leave to cool completely.
6. Meanwhile, prepare the marzipan by mixing the remaining ground almonds with 3½ oz (100 g/3½ oz) of confectioners' (icing) sugar, the lemon juice and remaining egg yolk. Stir in the green food coloring.
7. Mix the superfine (caster) sugar with ¼ cup (4 tablespoons) of water and heat for 1 minute on HIGH. Stir in the Kirsch. Slice the cake into 2 equal layers and pour over the Kirsch syrup.
8. Rinse the strawberries under plenty of cold running water. Top-and-tail and pat dry on kitchen paper. Melt the red-currant jello (jelly) in a cup in the microwave oven for 50 seconds on HIGH.
9. Mix the remaining confectioners' (icing) sugar with the sour cream (crème fraîche) to form a thick paste. Spread over the lower layer of the cake. Start cutting the strawberries in half and arrange on the cream as you go. Put the second cake layer carefully on top of the strawberries and cream. Brush with melted redcurrant jello (jelly).
10. Roll out the marzipan and cut a circle the same size as the cake. Put this circle on top of the cake and decorate with the remaining strawberries.

Gâteau aux fraises

Strawberry Gâteau

00.20   00.12

plus cooling and chilling time

American	Ingredients	Metric/Imperial
2 oz	butter	50 g/2 oz
2	eggs	2
3½ oz	all-purpose (plain) flour	100 g/3½ oz
½ cup	cane sugar syrup	5 tbsp
½ cup	milk	5 tbsp
1½ tsp	active dry yeast	1½ tsp
	butter, for greasing	
3 tbsp	superfine (caster) sugar	2 tbsp
¼ cup	fresh orange juice	3 tbsp
2 tbsp	Cointreau	1 tbsp
1½ lb	strawberries	600 g/1½ lb
¼ cup	confectioners' (icing) sugar	3 tbsp
¼ cup	sour cream (crème fraîche)	3 tbsp
2 tbsp	raspberry preserve	2 tbsp

1. Put the butter in a dish and melt in the microwave oven for 40 seconds on HIGH.
2. Break the eggs into a bowl and whisk with a fork.

Strawberry marzipan cake

3. Add the flour to the melted butter, beating with a wooden spoon. Add the eggs, cane sugar syrup and milk, beating after every addition. Sift the yeast over the mixture and mix in carefully.

4. Lightly grease the base of a small Pyrex cake dish and pour in the mixture. Microwave, uncovered, for 9 minutes on MEDIUM-HIGH.

5. To prepare the syrup, put the superfine (caster) sugar into a bowl with 3 (2) tablespoons of water. Microwave for 1½ minutes. Stir well. Add the orange juice and Cointreau.

6. Pour the syrup over the gâteau while it is still hot. Leave to cool.

7. For the filling, rinse the strawberries under plenty of cold running water. Top-and-tail and pat dry on kitchen paper. Mix the confectioners' (icing) sugar with the sour cream (crème fraîche).

8. When the gâteau is completely cool, remove from the mold (mould) with the aid of a metal spatula. Carefully cut into 2 equal layers. Place the lower layer on a cake dish and spread with the cream frosting (icing). Start slicing the strawberries in rounds and arrange on the cream as you go. Make only one layer of strawberries.

9. Put the second half of the cake very carefully on top of the strawberries. Put the raspberry preserve in a cup and melt for 30 seconds on HIGH. Coat the top and sides of the gâteau. Decorate with the remaining whole strawberries and refrigerate until ready to serve.

Fraisier au chocolat

Chocolate Gâteau with Cream and Strawberries

00.15 00.10
plus standing and cooling time

American	Ingredients	Metric/Imperial
5 oz	semisweet (plain) chocolate	150 g/5 oz
5 oz	butter	150 g/5 oz
4	eggs	4
3 tbsp	cornstarch (cornflour)	2 tbsp
1½ tbsp	active dry yeast	1 tbsp
½ cup	cane sugar syrup	8 tbsp
	butter, for greasing	
10½ oz	strawberries	300 g/10½ oz
¼ cup	sour cream (crème fraîche)	4 tbsp
¼ cup	whipped cream	4 tbsp

1. Break the chocolate into pieces and put in a bowl with the butter. Melt in the microwave oven for 1½ minutes on HIGH. Remove the bowl from the oven and beat the mixture with a wooden spoon until smooth and shiny.

2. Break the eggs into a bowl and whisk with a fork for 2 minutes.

3. Add the cornstarch (cornflour), yeast and cane sugar syrup to the melted chocolate and mix thoroughly. Fold in the beaten eggs.

4. Grease the base of a cake mold (mould) 9 inches (23 cm) in diameter. Pour in half the chocolate mixture. Microwave, uncovered, for 4 minutes on HIGH. When ready, the mixture will shrink away from the edge of the cake mold (mould) but should still be moist.

5. Leave the first cake to stand for 10 minutes. Turn out on to a wire rack and leave to cool.

Chocolate gâteau with cream and strawberries

6. Wash the mold (mould) and grease the base. Pour in the remaining chocolate mixture. Microwave, uncovered, on HIGH for 4 minutes. Leave to stand for 10 minutes. Turn out on to a wire rack and leave to cool.

7. Rinse the strawberries under plenty of cold running water. Pat dry on kitchen paper and remove the stalks. Save the six largest for decoration, and cut the others in half.

8. Spread the sour cream (crème fraîche) on one of the chocolate cakes. Cover the cream with the halved strawberries. Place the second cake on top, taking care not to press down too hard. Decorate the top of the cake with whipped cream and the whole strawberries. Serve cold.

Génoise aux fraises

Genoese Sponge Cake with Strawberries and Cream

	00.20	00.18	
	plus cooling and chilling time		

American	Ingredients	Metric/Imperial
2 oz	butter	50 g/2 oz
4	eggs	4
3½ oz	superfine (caster) sugar	100 g/3½ oz
¼ tsp	salt	¼ tsp
3½ oz	all-purpose (plain) flour	100 g/3½ oz
	butter, for greasing	
9 oz	strawberries	250 g/9 oz
2	oranges	2
¼ cup	strawberry liqueur	3 tbsp
⅓ cup	sour cream (crème fraîche)	4½ tbsp
¼ cup	confectioners' (icing) sugar	3 tbsp

1. Melt the butter in a bowl in the microwave oven for 1 minute on HIGH.
2. Whisk the eggs in a bowl. Add the sugar and whisk with an electric beater for 5 minutes. Sift the salt and flour together over the bowl and mix in carefully with a wooden spoon. Add the melted butter and mix carefully.
3. Grease the base of a 7 inch (18 cm) soufflé mold (mould). Pour in the mixture through a sieve. Microwave, uncovered, on HIGH for 6 minutes.
4. Leave the cake to stand for 10 minutes. Turn out on to a wire rack and leave to cool completely.

5. Cut the cake in 2 equal layers. Put the lower layer on a serving dish. Top-and-tail the strawberries. Rinse under plenty of cold running water. Pat dry on kitchen paper. Cut in half.
6. Squeeze the oranges to obtain ½ cup (150 ml/¼ pint) of juice. Stir in the strawberry liqueur and heat in the microwave oven for 1 minute on HIGH. Pour over the 2 cake layers.
7. Mix the sour cream (crème fraîche) with the confectioners' (icing) sugar and spread over each layer. Cover the lower layer with half of the strawberries. Put the upper layer carefully on top and arrange the remaining strawberries, cut side down, over the surface. Serve chilled.

Poiré au chocolat

Pear and Chocolate Cake

	00.10	00.10	
	plus cooling time		

American	Ingredients	Metric/Imperial
3½ oz	semisweet (plain) chocolate	100 g/3½ oz
2 oz	butter	50 g/2 oz
3 tbsp	liquid honey	2 tbsp
3 tbsp	cornstarch (cornflour)	2 tbsp
2	eggs, separated	2
1 tsp	oil	1 tsp
1	ripe juicy pear	1
3 tbsp	apricot preserve	2 tbsp
3 tbsp	cocoa powder	2 tbsp

1. Break the chocolate into pieces and melt in a bowl with the butter for 1 minute on HIGH.
2. Whisk the melted butter and chocolate and stir in the honey and cornstarch (cornflour).

Sponge cake with fresh fruit

3. Add the egg yolks to the mixture, beating well. Whisk the whites to firm peaks and fold in carefully.

4. Oil a 6 inch (15 cm) Pyrex soufflé mold (mould) and line the base with oiled non-stick parchment (greaseproof paper). Spoon in the mixture.

5. Peel and core the pear and slice thinly. Arrange the pear slices on the surface of the cake. Microwave, uncovered, on HIGH for 8 minutes.

6. Leave the cake to cool in the container.

7. Purée the apricot preserve in a food processor and heat for 1 minute on HIGH. Leave to cool.

8. Remove the cake from the mold (mould), remove the non-stick parchment (greaseproof paper) and transfer the cake to a serving dish. Brush the pear slices with the apricot preserve.

9. When ready to serve, sift the cocoa over the surface of the cake.

Galette aux fruits

Sponge Cake with Fresh Fruit

� 00.10   00.22
plus macerating and chilling time

American	Ingredients	Metric/Imperial
¼ lb	all-purpose (plain) flour	125 g/4 oz
3½ oz	ground almonds	100 g/3½ oz
3 oz	soft dark brown sugar	75 g/3 oz
1	egg	1
5 oz	butter, cut into pieces	150 g/5 oz
9 oz	plums	250 g/9 oz
¼ lb	strawberries	125 g/4 oz
¼ lb	large purple (black) grapes	125 g/4 oz
1	orange	1
3 tbsp	confectioners' (icing) sugar	2 tbsp
½ tsp	vanilla extract (essence)	½ tsp
2 tbsp	fresh lemon juice	1 tbsp
2 tbsp	Kirsch	1 tbsp
	butter, for greasing	
3 tbsp	apricot preserve	2 tbsp

1. First make the cake base: sift the flour into a bowl, add the ground almonds and, soft dark brown sugar. Mix until blended. Make a well in the center and break in the egg. Add the butter. Rub in with the fingertips of one hand, pushing in the flour, ground almond and sugar mixture from the sides of the well with the other hand. Work until a smooth paste is formed. Do not add water. Roll the mixture into a ball and put in the refrigerator to rest for at least 1 hour.

2. Prepare the fruit: rinse the plums, strawberries and grapes under plenty of cold running water. Pat dry on kitchen paper. Remove the pits (stones) from the plums, top-and-tail the strawberries and remove the pits (seeds) from the grapes. Peel the orange carefully, removing all white pith, and cut into small pieces. Put all the fruit into a bowl, sprinkle with confectioner's (icing) sugar and vanilla, add the lemon juice and Kirsch and leave to macerate for at least 1 hour.

3. Cut a double thickness of non-stick parchment (greaseproof paper) into a square roughly 12 inches (30 cm) across. Grease the surface. Put the ball of cake mixture in the center and roll out carefully with a pastry roller (rolling pin) to form a disc about 10 inches (25 cm) in diameter. Use a flan case as a guide.

4. Using the non-stick parchment (greaseproof paper) as support, transfer the cake mixture to the microwave oven and cook on MEDIUM for 12 minutes. The cake will still be moist; if you prefer it firmer, microwave for 8 minutes on HIGH instead.

5. Leave the cake to stand for 10 minutes. Turn out on to a rack, remove the non-stick parchment (greaseproof paper) and leave to cool.

6. Just before serving, drain the fruit and add the juice to the apricot preserve. Mix well. Transfer the cake to a serving platter, spread with the apricot preserve and carefully arrange the fruit on top.

You can use sour cream (crème fraîche) instead of the preserve, but it should be firm enough to hold the fruit in place.

Gâteau aux pommes

Apple Cake with Almonds

▬▷ 00.20   00.22
plus cooling time

American	Ingredients	Metric/Imperial
3½ oz	butter	100 g/3½ oz
3½ oz	superfine (caster) sugar	100 g/3½ oz
3½ oz	ground almonds	100 g/3½ oz
3 tbsp	cornstarch (cornflour)	2 tbsp
1 tsp	active dry yeast	1 tsp
½ tsp	cinnamon	½ tsp
2	eggs	2
2½	Granny Smith apples	2½
2 oz	golden raisins (sultanas)	50 g/2 oz
	butter, for greasing	
3 tbsp	slivered almonds	2 tbsp
¼ cup	apricot preserve	3 tbsp

1. Put the butter in a bowl and melt in the microwave oven for 1½ minutes on HIGH.

2. Add the sugar, ground almonds, cornstarch (cornflour), yeast and cinnamon to the melted butter. Whisk the eggs with a fork and add to the mixture. Mix well.

3. Peel and core the 2 whole apples, cut into quarters and remove the pits (seeds). Slice extremely finely in a food processor.

4. Add the apples and raisins to the mixture. Grease a soufflé mold (mould) 7 inches (18 cm) in diameter and pour in the mixture. Microwave, uncovered, on HIGH for 13 minutes.

5. Leave to cool in the container.

6. Prepare the decoration. Peel, core and remove the pits (seeds) from the remaining half-apple and cut in slices. Put in a small dish and microwave on HIGH for 2 minutes. Spread the slivered almonds on a plate and microwave for 5 minutes on HIGH until golden brown.

7. Force the apricot preserve through a strainer into a bowl. Melt in the microwave oven for 30 seconds on HIGH.

8. Invert the apple cake on to a platter. Brush the top and sides with some of the melted apricot preserve and sprinkle with the slivered almonds. Arrange the apple slices on top of the cake and coat with apricot preserve.

Gâteau aux abricots

Apricot Gâteau

	00.45	00.34	
	plus resting and cooling time		

American	Ingredients	Metric/Imperial
½ cup	white wine	125 ml/6 tbsp
9 oz	butter	250 g/9 oz
	salt	
13 oz	all-purpose (plain) flour	375 g/13 oz
2 (2 lb)	cans apricots in syrup	2 (500 g/2 lb)
5	egg yolks	5
2 oz	small macaroons	50 g/2 oz
⅓ cup	sour cream (crème fraîche)	4½ tbsp
3 tbsp	superfine (caster) sugar	2 tbsp

1. Heat the white wine in a bowl in the microwave oven for 1 minute on HIGH.
2. Cut the butter in small pieces and add bit by bit to the wine, beating with a whisk. Add a pinch of salt and the flour and mix well. Leave to rest in the refrigerator for 2 hours.
3. When the pastry is firm enough to work with, divide into 3 equal portions. Line the base of a 10 inch (25 cm) flan case with the first portion, flattening with the palm of the hand. Prick all over with a fork and microwave, uncovered, for 6-6½ minutes on HIGH.
4. Leave to stand for 2 minutes. Turn out on to a wire rack.

5. Leave the flan case to cool. Repeat the process with the other 2 portions of pastry.
6. To make the filling, drain 1 can of apricots and reserve 1¾ cups (400 ml/14 fl oz) of syrup. Purée the apricots in a food processor. Whisk the syrup and egg yolks together until foamy. Stir in the apricot purée. Microwave, uncovered, on HIGH for 6 minutes, whisking after every 2 minutes.
7. Pulverize the macaroons in a food processor and add to the apricot purée. Leave to cool.
8. Not longer than 2 hours before serving, put the various parts of the gâteau together: drain the second can of apricots. Place 1 pastry circle on a serving platter, spread with one-third of the apricot purée and top with a layer of apricots, round side upward. Repeat with the second circle of pastry, the second third of the apricot purée and a layer of apricots. Cover with the third pastry circle and spread with the remaining apricot purée and a final layer of apricots.
9. Whip the sour cream (crème fraîche) until firm. Add the sugar and whip until the sugar is incorporated. Decorate the top of the cake with the whipped cream and serve as soon as possible.

Gâteau aux abricots frais

Fresh Apricot Gâteau

	00.15	00.16	
	plus standing and cooling time		

American	Ingredients	Metric/Imperial
6 oz	butter	175 g/6 oz
⅓ cup	cane sugar syrup	4½ tbsp
1	egg, separated	1
2	whole eggs	2
5 oz	self-rising (self-raising) flour	150 g/5 oz
½ tsp	active dry yeast	½ tsp
1 tsp	vanilla extract (essence)	1 tsp
1¼ lb	fresh apricots	500 g/1¼ lb
	butter, for greasing	
2 oz	superfine (caster) sugar	50 g/2 oz

1. Melt the butter in a large bowl in the microwave oven for 1 minute on HIGH. Add the cane sugar syrup and stir well.
2. Whisk the egg yolk and 2 whole eggs and add to the butter and sugar mixture. Stir well. Add the flour, yeast and vanilla and beat to a smooth paste.
3. Rinse the apricots under plenty of cold running water. Pat dry on kitchen paper. Halve and remove the pits (stones).
4. Grease the base of a 7 inch (18 cm) soufflé mold (mould) and line with a circle of buttered non-stick parchment (grease-proof paper).
5. Whisk the egg white to firm peaks and fold carefully into the mixture with a wooden spoon. Pour the mixture into the mold (mould). Set aside 6 apricot halves and arrange the rest on top of the mixture side by side, pushing in slightly.
6. Microwave, uncovered, on HIGH for 10 minutes. Leave to stand in the container for 30 minutes. Turn out on to a plate and leave to cool completely.

Apricot gâteau

Orange sponge cake

7. Put the superfine (caster) sugar in a dish with ⅓ cup (4½ tablespoons) of water and heat on HIGH for 3 minutes. Stir until the sugar is completely dissolved. Slice 5 of the 6 apricot halves thinly and add to the sugar syrup along with the remaining apricot half. Microwave, uncovered, on HIGH for 1½ minutes. Leave to cool.

8. Drain the apricot slices and arrange on top of the gâteau, with the half-apricot in the center. Serve well chilled.

Fondant à l'orange

Orange Sponge Cake

	00.20	00.12
	plus standing and chilling time	

American	Ingredients	Metric/Imperial
7 oz	butter	200 g/7 oz
2	eggs, separated	2
1	egg	1
⅓ cup	cane sugar syrup	4½ tbsp
5 oz	all-purpose (plain) flour	150 g/5 oz
2 tsp	active dry yeast	2 tsp
2 oz	chopped preserved orange zest (peel)	50 g/2 oz
⅓ cup	fresh orange juice	4½ tbsp
3 tbsp	confectioners' (icing) sugar	2 tbsp
3 tbsp	curaçao liqueur	2 tbsp
2	oranges	2
½ cup	apricot preserve	8 tbsp

1. Cut the butter into 4 pieces and put in a long dish. Microwave on HIGH for 40 seconds to soften.

2. Put the 2 egg yolks and whole egg into a bowl, add the cane sugar syrup and whisk. Add the flour and yeast, still whisking, then the softened butter. Continue to whisk until the mixture is smooth and shiny. Add the preserved orange zest (peel).

3. Whisk the egg whites to firm peaks and fold carefully into the mixture.

4. Pour the mixture into the long dish in which the butter was softened. Smooth the surface. Microwave on MEDIUM-HIGH for 10 minutes.

5. Remove the dish from the oven and leave to stand for 30 minutes.

6. Pass a metal spatula under the cake and transfer to a serving dish. Mix together the orange juice, confectioners' (icing) sugar and curaçao liqueur and use to frost (ice) the cake. Refrigerate for 2 hours.

7. Peel the oranges, removing all white pith and membranes, and slice finely in rounds, then cut each round in half. Arrange decoratively along the top of the cake.

8. Melt the apricot preserve in a small bowl for 1 minute on HIGH.

9. Pour the melted preserve over the cake through a strainer (sieve), pressing down with the back of a wooden spoon.

Sicilienne

Sicilian Orange Cake

00.15   00.11
plus cooling and chilling time

American	Ingredients	Metric/Imperial
2	oranges	2
2	eggs, separated	2
1	egg yolk	1
¼ lb	ground almonds	125 g/4 oz
½ cup	cane sugar syrup	125 ml/6 tbsp
2 oz	chopped candied orange zest (peel)	50 g/2 oz
1 tsp	oil	1 tsp
3 tbsp	Cointreau	2 tbsp
5 oz	confectioners' (icing) sugar	150 g/5 oz
1 tsp	cognac	1 tsp

1. Cut the oranges in half and squeeze the juice.
2. Whisk the 3 egg yolks in a bowl. Add the ground almonds, all but 2 (1) tablespoons of the cane sugar syrup, ¼ cup (3 tablespoons) of orange juice and the chopped candied zest (peel). Beat thoroughly.
3. Whisk the egg whites to firm peaks and fold carefully into the mixture.
4. Oil a 6 inch (15 cm) soufflé mold (mould) and cover the base with a circle of oiled non-stick parchment (greaseproof paper). Spoon the dough into the mold (mould). Microwave, uncovered, for 6 minutes on MEDIUM-HIGH.
5. Leave the gâteau to stand for 5 minutes. Turn out on to a plate. Remove the non-stick parchment (greaseproof paper). Mix ⅓ cup (4½ tablespoons) of orange juice with the remaining cane sugar syrup and the Cointreau. Pour over the cake while still hot. Leave to cool completely.
6. Mix the confectioners' (icing) sugar to a thick paste with 3 (2) tablespoons of hot water and the cognac. Spread over the cake and chill until set.

Gâteau aux cerises

Cherry Cake with Cream

00.10   00.22
plus cooling time

American	Ingredients	Metric/Imperial
2 oz	semisweet (plain) chocolate	50 g/2 oz
2 oz	butter	50 g/2 oz
2 oz	cornstarch (cornflour)	50 g/2 oz
½ tsp	active dry yeast	½ tsp
2 oz	superfine (caster) sugar	50 g/2 oz
1	egg, separated	1
	butter, for greasing	
1¾ lb	pitted (stoned) cherries	750 g/1¾ lb
⅓ cup	sour cream (crème fraîche)	4½ tbsp
¼ tsp	ground vanilla	¼ tsp
2 tbsp	confectioners' (icing) sugar	1 tbsp

1. Break the chocolate in pieces and melt in a bowl with the butter for 1 minute on HIGH.
2. Sift the cornstarch (cornflour) and yeast over the bowl and add the sugar and egg yolk, beating well.

Cherry cake with cream

3. Grease the base of a 6 inch (15 cm) soufflé mold (mould) and line with buttered non-stick parchment (greaseproof paper).
4. Add 5 oz (150 g/5 oz) of cherries to the mixture. Whisk the egg white to firm peaks and fold in carefully. Pour into the mold (mould) and microwave, uncovered, for 6 minutes on HIGH.
5. Leave to stand in the container for 15 minutes. Turn out on to a wire rack and remove the non-stick parchment (greaseproof paper). Leave to cool completely.
6. Whisk the sour cream (crème fraîche) until firm. Stir in the vanilla and confectioners' (icing) sugar and whisk a little longer.
7. When the cake is cold, transfer to a serving dish and spread the whipped sour cream (crème fraîche) over the top and sides. Serve with the remaining cherries.

Entremets aux griottes

Cherry Refrigerator Cake

00.05   00.15
plus macerating and chilling time

American	Ingredients	Metric/Imperial
1	can pitted (stoned) black cherries	1
7 oz	superfine (caster) sugar	200 g/7 oz
¼ cup	Kirsch	4 tbsp
5 oz	ladyfingers (sponge fingers)	150 g/5 oz
3	egg yolks	3
1	whole egg	1
2¼ cups	milk	500 ml/18 fl oz
	butter, for greasing	

1. Drain the cherries and put in a dish. Add the sugar and Kirsch and macerate for 2 hours.

2. Break up the ladyfingers (sponge fingers) and pulverize in a food processor.

3. Mix the egg yolks and the whole egg in a bowl, add the milk, stir in the ladyfinger (sponge finger) crumbs and add the cherries with their macerating liquid. Mix thoroughly.

4. Butter the base of a 7 inch (18 cm) soufflé mold (mould) and pour in the mixture. Microwave, uncovered, on HIGH for 15 minutes.

5. Leave to cool. Turn out on to a serving dish and refrigerate for at least 30 minutes. Serve cold.

Gâteau renversé à l'ananas

Pineapple Upside-down Cake

◢ 00.10   00.26
Serves 4-6

American	Ingredients	Metric/Imperial
¼ lb	butter	125 g/4 oz
5 oz	soft dark brown sugar	150 g/5 oz
1	can pineapple slices	1
5	maraschino cherries	5
2	eggs	2
5 oz	all-purpose (plain) flour	150 g/5 oz
1 tsp	active dry yeast	1 tsp
	whipped cream	

1. Put 1 oz (25 g/1 oz) of butter in a 7 inch (8 cm) soufflé mold (mould) and melt in the microwave oven on HIGH for 1 minute. Sprinkle 2 oz (50 g/2 oz) of the brown sugar over the melted butter.

2. Drain the pineapple slices, reserving the syrup. Put 4 slices in the base of the mold (mould). Put a maraschino cherry in the center of each slice and put 1 cherry in the middle.

3. Break the eggs into a bowl and whisk. Chop the remaining pineapple. Put the remaining brown sugar and the pineapple syrup in a bowl and microwave on HIGH for 2 minutes to melt the brown sugar. Add the remaining butter in tiny pieces and mix well. Add the eggs, flour, yeast and chopped pineapple.

4. Spoon the mixture carefully into the mold (mould) so as not to displace the pineapple slices. Microwave, uncovered, on HIGH for 8 minutes.

5. Leave to stand for 15 minutes. Invert the cake on to a platter. Serve cold, with whipped cream.

Gâteau à la patate douce

Sweet Potato Gâteau I

◢ 00.15   00.24
plus cooling and chilling time

American	Ingredients	Metric/Imperial
1¼ lb	sweet potatoes	500 g/1¼ lb
1	sliced banana	1
2 oz	butter	50 g/2 oz
2 oz	dried shredded (desiccated) coconut	50 g/2 oz
7 oz	superfine (caster) sugar	200 g/7 oz
¼ cup	white rum	3 tbsp
3 tbsp	milk	2 tbsp
2	eggs	2
½ tsp	ground vanilla	½ tsp
½ tsp	cinnamon	½ tsp
1 tsp	oil	1 tsp
¼ cup	sour cream (crème fraîche)	3 tbsp
12	walnuts	12

1. Peel the sweet potatoes and slice thinly. Put in a small casserole with ¼ cup (3 tablespoons) of water. Cover and microwave on HIGH for 10 minutes.

2. When tender, drain and purée in a food processor. Add the sliced banana to the food processor goblet along with the butter, coconut, half of the sugar, 3 (2) tablespoons of rum, milk, eggs, vanilla and cinnamon. Purée until smooth.

3. Oil the bottom of a 7 inch (18 cm) soufflé mold (mould) and line the base with a circle of oiled non-stick parchment (greaseproof paper). Pour the purée into the mold (mould). Microwave, uncovered, on HIGH for 8 minutes.

4. Leave the gâteau to cool in the container. Refrigerate.

5. To make the sauce, put the remaining sugar in a bowl with ¼ cup (3 tablespoons) of water. Microwave, uncovered, on HIGH for 5 minutes until the caramel is golden brown. Immediately add ¼ cup (3 tablespoons) of cold water, taking care to avoid splashing. Wait until the caramel stops boiling, then return to the microwave oven for 40 seconds on HIGH. Stir well, add the remaining rum, and leave to cool. Stir in the sour cream (crème fraîche) and refrigerate.

6. Just before serving, turn the gâteau out on to a plate and remove the non-stick parchment (greaseproof paper). Decorate with the walnuts. Pour the sauce into a sauceboat and serve very cold.

Sweet potato gâteau

Fondant à la patate douce

Sweet Potato Gâteau II

00.15 00.24
plus cooling and chilling time

American	Ingredients	Metric/Imperial
1¾ lb	*sweet potatoes*	*750 g/1¾ lb*
3 tbsp	*cocoa powder*	*2 tbsp*
5 oz	*soft dark brown sugar*	*150 g/5 oz*
¼ cup	*sour cream (crème fraîche)*	*3 tbsp*
2	*eggs*	*2*
1	*egg yolk*	*1*
3 tbsp	*dark rum*	*2 tbsp*
1 tsp	*ground vanilla*	*1 tsp*
1 tsp	*oil*	*1 tsp*
3 oz	*semisweet (plain) chocolate*	*75 g/3 oz*
1 oz	*butter*	*25 g/1 oz*
3 tbsp	*confectioners' (icing) sugar*	*2 tbsp*
3 tbsp	*chocolate vermicelli*	*2 tbsp*

1. Peel the sweet potatoes and cut in slices. Put in a casserole with ¼ cup (3 tablespoons) of water. Cover and microwave on HIGH for 12 minutes.
2. When the sweet potatoes are tender, drain and put in the goblet of a food processor. Add the cocoa powder, brown sugar, sour cream (crème fraîche), whole eggs and egg yolk, rum and vanilla. Purée to a smooth paste.
3. Oil the base of a 7 inch (18 cm) soufflé mold (mould) and line with a circle of oiled non-stick parchment (greaseproof paper). Pour the mixture into the mold (mould) and smooth the surface. Microwave, uncovered, on HIGH for 10 minutes.
4. Leave the gâteau to cool. Refrigerate for at least 2 hours until firm.
5. Turn out on to a serving dish and remove the non-stick parchment (greaseproof paper).
6. To make the frosting (icing), break the chocolate into pieces and melt in a bowl with the butter for 1½ minutes on HIGH.
7. Mix the confectioners' (icing) sugar to a smooth paste with ½ teaspoon of water and add to the chocolate mixture. Stir thoroughly. Pour the frosting (icing) on top of the cake and spread with a metal spatula over the top and sides. Sprinkle with chocolate vermicelli and refrigerate to allow the frosting (icing) to harden. Serve well chilled.

Fondant aux deux chocolats

Two-Chocolate Cake

00.20 00.18
plus cooling and chilling time

American	Ingredients	Metric/Imperial
5 oz	*semisweet (plain) chocolate*	*150 g/5 oz*
5 oz	*butter*	*150 g/5 oz*
3	*eggs, separated*	*3*
¼ cup	*cane sugar syrup*	*3 tbsp*
½ cup	*ground almonds*	*5 tbsp*
	butter, for greasing	
3 tbsp	*golden raisins (sultanas)*	*2 tbsp*
3½ oz	*milk chocolate*	*100 g/3½ oz*

1. Break the semisweet (plain) chocolate into pieces and melt in a bowl with the butter for 2 minutes on HIGH. Stir until creamy.
2. Add the egg yolks one at a time to the chocolate and butter mixture, then the cane sugar syrup and ground almonds, beating well after each addition.
3. Lightly grease the base of a 7 inch (18 cm) soufflé mold (mould) and cover the base with a circle of buttered non-stick parchment (greaseproof paper).
4. Whisk the egg whites to firm peaks and fold carefully into the mixture. Pour into the mold (mould). Microwave, uncovered, on HIGH for 8 minutes.
5. Leave the cake to cool in the container.
6. Turn the cake out on to a wire rack and prepare the frosting (icing): put the raisins (sultanas) in a bowl, cover with water and microwave on HIGH for 2 minutes. Drain and pat dry on kitchen paper. Leave to cool.
7. Break the milk chocolate into pieces and melt in a bowl in the microwave oven for 1 minute on HIGH. Stir with a wooden spoon until smooth and creamy. Leave to cool for 5 minutes.
8. Pour the chocolate over the cake and spread over the top and sides with a metal spatula. Sprinkle with the raisins (sultanas) and leave to harden.
9. Transfer the cake to a plate and serve.

Gâteau au yaourt au cacao

Chocolate Yogurt Cake

00.10 00.09
plus standing time

American	Ingredients	Metric/Imperial
½ cup	*natural flavor yogurt*	*6 tbsp*
½ cup	*oil*	*6 tbsp*
3 tbsp	*cane sugar syrup*	*2 tbsp*
¼ cup	*superfine (caster) sugar*	*3 tbsp*
3	*eggs*	*3*
¼ cup	*cocoa powder*	*3 tbsp*
1 cup	*self-rising (self-raising) flour*	*250 g/8 oz*
¼ tsp	*salt*	*¼ tsp*
½ tsp	*active dry yeast*	*½ tsp*
	butter, for greasing	

1. Mix together the yogurt, oil, cane sugar syrup, sugar and eggs. Sift the cocoa powder, flour, salt and yeast into the mixture, beating well after each addition.
2. Grease a 7 inch (18 cm) soufflé mold (mould) and line with a circle of buttered non-stick parchment (greaseproof paper).
3. Spoon the mixture into the mold (mould) and smooth the surface. Microwave, uncovered, on HIGH for 9 minutes.
4. Leave the gâteau to stand for 20 minutes. Turn out on to a wire rack and remove the non-stick parchment (greaseproof paper).
5. Serve warm or cold.

Chocolate yogurt cake

Craquelin au chocolat

Crunchy Chocolate Refrigerator Cake

	00.15	00.07	
	plus chilling time		

American	Ingredients	Metric/Imperial
7 oz	dark bitter chocolate	200 g/7 oz
7 oz	butter	200 g/7 oz
5 oz	superfine (caster) sugar	150 g/5 oz
3 oz	golden raisins (sultanas)	75 g/3 oz
¼ cup	cognac	4 tbsp
3 tbsp	cane sugar syrup	2 tbsp
2	egg yolks	2
1 tsp	oil	1 tsp
30	ladyfingers (sponge fingers)	30
⅓ cup	sour cream (crème fraîche)	4½ tbsp

1. Break the chocolate into pieces and melt with the butter in a bowl for 2 minutes on HIGH. Add ¼ lb (125 g/4 oz) of sugar, stir thoroughly and leave to cool.
2. Rinse the raisins (sultanas) under plenty of cold running water. Pat dry on kitchen paper and put in a bowl with ¼ cup (3 tablespoons) of cognac and the cane sugar syrup. Heat in the microwave oven for 3 minutes on HIGH.

3. To make the syrup, put the remaining sugar and cognac and ¼ cup (3 tablespoons) of water in another bowl and microwave for 2 minutes on HIGH. Stir well and pour into a deep bowl.
4. Add the egg yolks and the raisins (sultanas) in their cooking liquid to the chocolate and butter mixture. Beat thoroughly.
5. Lightly oil the base of a charlotte mold (mould) and line with a circle of oiled non-stick parchment (greaseproof paper).
6. Set aside a few of the ladyfingers (sponge fingers). Pour a thin layer of the chocolate mixture into the base of the mold (mould) and put a layer of ladyfingers (sponge fingers) on top. Cover with another layer of chocolate, then a layer of lady-fingers (sponge fingers), until all the ingredients are used up, ending with a layer of chocolate. Dip the reserved ladyfingers (sponge fingers) into the cognac syrup and arrange on top of the charlotte, flat side upward. Fill any spaces with pieces of ladyfinger (sponge finger). Put a weighted board on top of the charlotte and refrigerate for at least 12 hours.
7. Just before serving, run a knife-blade round the edge of the charlotte and turn out on to a plate. Remove the non-stick parchment (greaseproof paper). Whip the sour cream (crème fraîche) and decorate the top of the cake with whorls of cream forced through a piping tube.

Crunchy chocolate refrigerator cake

Chocolate gâteau with cointreau

Gâteau Plaka

Chocolate Gâteau with Cointreau

| | 00.30 plus cooling time | 00.20 | |

American	Ingredients	Metric/Imperial
9 oz	butter	250 g/9 oz
2	eggs, separated	2
4	egg yolks	4
6 oz	ground almonds	175 g/6 oz
2 oz	cornstarch (cornflour)	50 g/2 oz
¼ cup	cocoa powder	3 tbsp
1 cup	cane sugar syrup	250 ml/8 fl oz
1 tsp	oil	1 tsp
½ cup	Cointreau	6 tbsp
2 oz	superfine (caster) sugar	50 g/2 oz
2 tbsp	raspberry jello (jelly)	1 tbsp
3½ oz	bitter chocolate	100 g/3½ oz

1. Melt 5 oz (150 g/5 oz) of the butter in a bowl in the microwave oven on HIGH for 1 minute.
2. Mix 5 of the egg yolks with ¼ lb (125 g/4 oz) of the ground almonds. Sift the cornstarch (cornflour) and cocoa powder over the mixture, stir, add the cane sugar syrup and mix well.

3. Whisk the 2 egg whites to firm peaks and fold into the mixture.
4. Oil the base of a 7 inch (18 cm) soufflé mold (mould) and line with a circle of oiled non-stick parchment (greaseproof paper). Pour the cake mixture into the mold (mould) and microwave for 11 minutes on MEDIUM-HIGH.
5. Leave the cake to stand for 5 minutes. Pour over ¼ cup (3 tablespoons) of Cointreau. Leave to cool completely.
6. Turn the cake out on to a wire rack and remove the non-stick parchment (greaseproof paper). Cut the cake into 2 equal layers.
7. To make the filling, melt 3 oz (75 g/3 oz) of butter for 30 seconds on HIGH. Add the sugar, remaining egg yolk, remaining ground almonds and 3 (2) tablespoons of Cointreau. Beat for 1 minute with a wooden spatula. Spread over the lower layer of the cake. Put the second layer gently on top.
8. To make the frosting (icing), melt the raspberry jello (jelly) in a bowl for 30 seconds on HIGH. Brush the top and sides of the cake. Leave to cool.
9. Break the chocolate in pieces and melt in a bowl with the remaining butter and Cointreau for 2 minutes on HIGH. Leave to cool.
10. Pour the chocolate on the middle of the cake and spread over the top and sides with a metal spatula. Leave to harden.
11. Slide the gâteau on to a platter and serve.

Gâteau au chocolat fourré
Chocolate Marzipan Cake

◼▷ 00.15   00.08 〰
plus cooling time

American	Ingredients	Metric/Imperial
3½ oz	semisweet (plain) chocolate	100 g/3½ oz
3 oz	butter	75 g/3 oz
1 oz	cornstarch (cornflour)	25 g/1 oz
½ tsp	active dry yeast	½ tsp
¼ cup	cane sugar syrup	4 tbsp
2	eggs	2
	butter, for greasing	
2 oz	ground almonds	50 g/2 oz
2 oz	superfine (caster) sugar	50 g/2 oz
1	egg yolk	1
1 tsp	Cointreau	1 tsp
¼ tsp	almond extract (essence)	¼ tsp
2 tbsp	confectioners' (icing) sugar	1 tbsp

1. Break the chocolate and melt in a bowl with the butter for 1½ minutes on HIGH.

2. Sift the cornstarch (cornflour) and yeast over the bowl and whisk. Add the cane sugar syrup and the 2 whole eggs, still whisking.

3. Grease the base of a 6 inch (15 cm) soufflé mold (mould) and spoon in the mixture. Microwave, uncovered, on HIGH for 6 minutes.

4. When the cake begins to shrink from the sides of the container, remove from the oven and leave to cool at room temperature.

5. Turn the cake out on to a wire rack and leave to cool completely.

6. To make the marzipan, mix together the ground almonds and sugar. Add the egg yolk, Cointreau and almond extract (essence). Stir thoroughly.

7. Cut the cake in 2 equal layers and spread the lower layer with marzipan. Put the second layer on top. Sift the confectioners' (icing) sugar over the top of the cake.

Sachertorte
Viennese Chocolate Cake

◼▷ 00.20   00.30 〰
plus cooling time

American	Ingredients	Metric/Imperial
¾ lb	semisweet (plain) chocolate	350 g/12 oz
3½ oz	butter	100 g/3½ oz
¼ cup	cane sugar syrup	3 tbsp
4	eggs, separated	4
4 tbsp	cornstarch (cornflour)	3 tbsp
	butter, for greasing	
½ cup	apricot preserve	6 tbsp
⅓ cup	sour cream (crème fraîche)	4½ tbsp

1. Break 7 oz (200 g/7 oz) of the chocolate into pieces and put in a bowl with the butter. Melt in the microwave oven for 2 minutes on HIGH.

2. Mix well. Add the cane sugar syrup. Add the egg yolks one by one to the melted chocolate, beating vigorously with a wooden spoon after each addition. Beat in the cornstarch (cornflour).

3. Whisk the egg whites to firm peaks and fold carefully into the mixture. Put a circle of non-stick parchment (greaseproof paper) in the base of a soufflé mold (mould) 7 inches (18 cm) in diameter. Grease the paper, spoon the chocolate mixture into the mold (mould) and microwave on HIGH for 10 minutes.

4. Leave the cake to stand for 15 minutes. Turn out on to a rack and leave to cool completely.

5. When the cake is cold, cut horizontally into 2 equal layers. Spread the bottom layer with two-thirds of the apricot preserve and cover with the second layer.

6. Force the rest of the preserve through a strainer (sieve). Microwave the purée for 30 seconds. Coat the top and sides of the cake.

7. To make the frosting (icing), break the remaining chocolate into pieces and melt with 2 (1) tablespoons of water in the oven for 2 minutes on HIGH. Mix, add the sour cream (crème fraîche) and mix again. Pour the frosting (icing) over the cake and spread smoothly with a metal spatula. Leave to harden before serving.

Sachertorte

◼▷ 00.20   00.13 〰
Serves 8-10

American	Ingredients	Metric/Imperial
¼ lb	butter	125 g/4 oz
¼ lb	sugar	125 g/4 oz
2	eggs	2
¼ lb	self-rising (self-raising) flour	125 g/4 oz
¼ cup	cocoa powder	4 tbsp
2 oz	ground almonds	50 g/2 oz
⅔ cup	milk	150 ml/¼ pint
¼ cup	maple (golden) syrup	4 tbsp
1¼ cups	heavy (double) cream	300 ml/½ pint
6 oz	semisweet (plain) chocolate	175 g/6 oz
3 oz	butter	75 g/3 oz
	hazelnuts	

1. Cream together the butter and sugar until light and fluffy. Beat in the eggs, one at a time. Sift in the flour and cocoa powder. Fold in the ground almonds. Stir in the milk and syrup and beat until light and soft.

2. Line the base of an 8 inch (20 cm) soufflé dish with non-stick parchment (greaseproof paper). Spoon in the mixture and cook on HIGH for 4½-5½ minutes. Cool for 5 minutes in the dish before turning out on to a wire rack to cool completely.

3. Whip the cream. Cut the cake in half and sandwich together with half of the cream.

4. Break the chocolate into pieces. In a jug, heat together the chocolate and butter on HIGH for 1-2 minutes until melted. Stir until smooth. Leave to cool until of coating consistency, then spread over the top and sides of the cake.

5. Pipe large swirls of the remaining cream around the edge of the cake. Decorate each swirl with a hazelnut.

Millefeuille praliné-chocolat

Caramel Chocolate Napoleon Gâteau

00.30 plus chilling time | 00.15

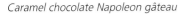

American	Ingredients	Metric/Imperial
14 oz	puff pastry	400 g/14 oz
3 tbsp	all-purpose (plain) flour	2 tbsp
¾ cup	milk	200 ml/7 fl oz
2	egg yolks	2
2 oz	superfine (caster) sugar	50 g/2 oz
2 tbsp	cornstarch (cornflour)	1 tbsp
1 oz	ground praline	25 g/1 oz
2 tbsp	Kirsch	1 tbsp
3 oz	semisweet (plain) chocolate	75 g/3 oz
6	sugar violets or roses	6

1. Divide the puff pastry into 3 equal portions. Flour a pastry board and roll out one of the portions as thinly as possible. Using a plate as a guide, cut a circle 9 inches (23 cm) in diameter. Prick all over with a fork and put in the refrigerator to rest for 30 minutes. Repeat the process with the other 2 portions of pastry.

2. Make the custard cream. Heat the milk in a bowl in the microwave oven for 2 minutes on HIGH. Whisk the egg yolks in a bowl, add the sugar and whisk until pale and foamy. Add the cornstarch (cornflour) and whisk once more. Pour over the hot milk in a thin stream, whisking constantly.

3. Microwave, uncovered, on HIGH for 3 minutes, whisking after every minute.

4. Remove from the oven and whisk again, adding the ground praline and Kirsch. Refrigerate, stirring from time to time.

5. Place one of the puff pastry circles on a double sheet of kitchen paper and microwave on HIGH for 3 minutes. Transfer to a wire rack and repeat the process with the other 2 circles.

6. When the pastry has cooled, assemble the gâteau: put 1 circle of pastry on a plate and spread with half of the caramel cream. Gently put the second circle of pastry on top and spread with the remaining caramel cream. Set the third circle gently on top.

7. Break the chocolate in pieces and melt in a bowl with 2 (1) tablespoons of water for 1 minute on HIGH. Stir until the chocolate is smooth. Pour over the top layer of pastry and spread evenly with a metal spatula. Decorate with the sugar flowers and refrigerate until ready to serve.

Caramel chocolate Napoleon gâteau

Gâteau Marie-Thérèse
Gâteau Marie-Thérèse

� 00.20   00.14   〰

plus cooling time

American	Ingredients	Metric/Imperial
7 oz	semisweet (plain) chocolate	200 g/7 oz
6 oz	softened butter	175 g/6 oz
¼ cup	cane sugar syrup	3 tbsp
3	eggs, separated	3
¼ cup	ground almonds	4 tbsp
1 tsp	oil	1 tsp
	salt	
1	egg white	1
3 oz	superfine (caster) sugar	75 g/3 oz
½ tsp	coffee extract (essence)	½ tsp
3 tbsp	chocolate vermicelli	2 tbsp

1. Break the chocolate into pieces and melt in a bowl with ¼ lb (125 g/4 oz) of softened butter for 2 minutes on HIGH. Stir to obtain a smooth cream. Stir in the cane sugar syrup, egg yolks and ground almonds, beating well after each addition.
2. Stir to obtain a smooth cream. Stir in the cane sugar syrup, egg yolks and ground almonds, beating well after each addition.
3. Oil the base of a 7 inch (18 cm) mold (mould) and line with a circle of oiled non-stick parchment (greaseproof paper).
4. Add a pinch of salt to the egg whites and whisk to firm peaks. Fold carefully into the mixture.
5. Spoon the mixture into the mold (mould) and microwave, uncovered, on HIGH for 10 minutes. Leave to cool completely in the container.
6. Turn the gâteau out on to a wire rack on top of a plate. Slice very carefully into 2 equal layers.
7. To make the filling, put the egg white in a bowl, add the sugar and beat with a wooden spoon. Heat in the microwave oven for 1 minute on MEDIUM. Whisk with an electric beater for 2 minutes. Return to the oven for 1 minute on MEDIUM and whisk again until the meringue is thick and cold. This process should take at least 10 minutes. Add the coffee extract (essence) and the remaining softened butter in small pieces, continuing to whisk constantly.
8. Spread some of the buttercream frosting (icing) on the lower layer of the cake, then cover with the second layer and spread with the remaining buttercream. Sprinkle with chocolate vermicelli. Keep cool but do not refrigerate.

Gâteau marbré
Marble Cake I

▬▭ 00.10   00.23   〰

plus cooling time

American	Ingredients	Metric/Imperial
¼ lb	butter	125 g/4 oz
3	eggs	3
2 oz	all-purpose (plain) flour	50 g/2 oz
2 oz	cornstarch (cornflour)	50 g/2 oz
1 tsp	active dry yeast	1 tsp
⅓ cup	cane sugar syrup	4½ tbsp
½ tsp	almond extract (essence)	½ tsp
¼ lb	semisweet (plain) chocolate	125 g/4 oz
3 tbsp	cognac	2 tbsp
	butter, for greasing	

1. Melt the butter in a bowl for 2 minutes on HIGH.
2. Whisk the eggs in a bowl with a fork.
3. Sift the flour, cornstarch (cornflour) and yeast into the melted butter, beating constantly. Stir in the cane sugar syrup, almond extract (essence) and beaten eggs. Mix thoroughly.
4. Break the chocolate into pieces and melt in a bowl with the cognac for 1½ minutes on HIGH.
5. Stir the melted chocolate with a spatula and fold in half of the cake mixture.
6. Lightly grease the base of a Pyrex cake mold (mould) and spoon in the 2 doughs, alternating them. The mixture will rise considerably during cooking. Microwave, uncovered, on HIGH for 9 minutes.
7. Leave the cake to cool for 10 minutes. Turn out on to a wire rack to cool completely.

Gâteau marbré
Marble Cake II

▬▭ 00.10   00.19   〰

plus cooling time

American	Ingredients	Metric/Imperial
3½ oz	butter	100 g/3½ oz
3½ oz	self-rising (self-raising) flour	100 g/3½ oz
½ tsp	active dry yeast	½ tsp
½ cup	cane sugar syrup	6 tbsp
½ tsp	almond extract (essence)	½ tsp
3 tbsp	cognac	2 tbsp
2	eggs	2
1	egg yolk	1
2 tbsp	cocoa powder	1 tbsp
1 tsp	oil	1 tsp

1. Melt the butter in a bowl in the microwave oven for 1 minute on HIGH.
2. Sift the flour and yeast over the melted butter and stir well. Add the cane sugar syrup, almond extract (essence), cognac, whole eggs and egg yolk, stirring thoroughly after each addition.
3. Put half of the mixture into another bowl, sift the cocoa powder over and stir well.
4. Oil the base of a 1½ quart (1.5 litre/2¾ pint) Pyrex cake mold (mould) and line with a circle of oiled non-stick parchment (greaseproof paper).
5. Pour the 2 mixtures into the mold (mould) in alternating spoonfuls. The level of the mixture will seem very low, but the cake rises considerably during cooking. Microwave, uncovered, on HIGH for 8 minutes.
6. Leave to stand for 10 minutes. Turn out on to a wire rack and remove the non-stick parchment (greaseproof paper). Leave to cool.

Marble cake

Gâteau aux noisettes

Hazelnut Gâteau

00.10 00.07
plus cooling time

American	Ingredients	Metric/Imperial
3½ oz	butter	100 g/3½ oz
¼ cup	cocoa powder	3 tbsp
3½ oz	ground hazelnuts	100 g/3½ oz
1	egg, separated	1
1	egg yolk	1
3 tbsp	breadcrumbs	2 tbsp
¼ cup	maple syrup	3 tbsp
3 tbsp	cane sugar syrup	2 tbsp
1 tsp	oil	1 tsp
3 tbsp	caramel syrup	2 tbsp
12	whole hazelnuts	12

1. Melt the butter in a bowl for 1 minute on HIGH.
2. Sift the cocoa over the butter, add the ground hazelnuts and mix. Add the 2 egg yolks, the breadcrumbs, maple syrup and cane sugar syrup.
3. Oil the base of a 6 inch (15 cm) diameter soufflé mold (mould) and line with a circle of oiled non-stick parchment (greaseproof paper).
4. Whisk the egg white to firm peaks and fold carefully into the mixture. Pour into the mold (mould) and microwave, un-covered, for 6 minutes on HIGH.
5. Leave the gâteau to cool in the container. Turn out on to a platter. Coat with the caramel syrup and decorate with whole hazelnuts.

Hazelnut gâteau

Gâteau chocolat-noisette

Hazelnut and Chocolate Gâteau

00.10 plus cooling time   00.24

American	Ingredients	Metric/Imperial
3½ oz	milk chocolate	100 g/3½ oz
¼ cup	apricot preserve	3 tbsp
3	eggs	3
3 oz	ground hazelnuts	75 g/3 oz
1 oz	cornstarch (cornflour)	25 g/1 oz
⅓ cup	sour cream (crème fraîche)	4½ tbsp
	butter, for greasing	
3½ oz	semisweet (plain) chocolate	100 g/3½ oz
3 tbsp	crème de cacao liqueur	2 tbsp

1. Break the milk chocolate into pieces and put in a small bowl with 2 (1) tablespoons of water. Melt in the microwave oven for 1 minute on HIGH.
2. Put the apricot preserve, eggs, ground hazelnuts and cornstarch (cornflour) into the goblet of a food processor. Purée until the mixture is smooth.
3. Pour over the melted chocolate, add the sour cream (crème fraîche) and mix thoroughly. Grease a soufflé mold (mould) 7 inches (18 cm) in diameter and pour in the mixture. Microwave, uncovered, on HIGH for 12 minutes.
4. Leave the gâteau to stand for 10 minutes. Turn out on to a wire rack and leave to cool.
5. Prepare the frosting (icing). Break the semisweet (plain) chocolate into pieces and put in a small bowl with the crème de cacao. Melt in the microwave oven for 1 minute on HIGH. Mix, pour the chocolate over the gâteau and smooth with a metal spatula. Allow the frosting (icing) to harden slightly before serving.

Hazelnut and Honey Cake

00.10 plus cooling time   00.14

American	Ingredients	Metric/Imperial
6 oz	butter	175 g/6 oz
5 oz	soft dark brown sugar	150 g/5 oz
2 oz	clear honey	50 g/2 oz
3	eggs	3
½ lb	wholewheat (wholemeal) self-rising (self-raising) flour	225 g/8 oz
¼ tsp	salt	¼ tsp
¼ lb	chopped toasted hazelnuts	125 g/4 oz
⅔ cup	milk	8 tbsp

1. Cream the butter with the sugar and honey. Beat in the eggs, one at a time. Fold in the flour, salt and chopped hazelnuts alternately with the milk.
2. Line the base of an 8 inch (20 cm) soufflé dish with non-stick parchment (greaseproof paper). Spoon in the mixture and cook on HIGH for 8-9 minutes. Cool for 5 minutes, then turn out on to a rack to cool completely.

Gâteau amandier

Almond Gâteau I

00.20 plus cooling time   00.16

American	Ingredients	Metric/Imperial
¼ lb	butter	125 g/4 oz
3½ oz	ground almonds	100 g/3½ oz
1 cup	cane sugar syrup	250 ml/8 fl oz
4	egg yolks	4
2 oz	cornstarch (cornflour)	50 g/2 oz
3 tbsp	cocoa	2 tbsp
1 tsp	oil	1 tsp
3 tbsp	Grand Marnier	2 tbsp
2 oz	semisweet (plain) chocolate	50 g/2 oz
¼ lb	confectioners' (icing) sugar	125 g/4 oz
1	egg white	1
3	drops almond extract (essence)	3

1. Put the butter in a bowl and soften for 1 minute in the microwave oven on HIGH.
2. Add the ground almonds and cane sugar syrup to the softened butter. Mix well. Add the egg yolks one at a time, the cornstarch (cornflour) and cocoa, beating well after each addition.
3. Oil the base of a 7 inch (18 cm) soufflé mold (mould). Line the base with a circle of oiled non-stick parchment (greaseproof paper). Pour the mixture into the mold (mould). Microwave on MEDIUM-HIGH for 8 minutes or until the edges of the cake begin to shrink away from the sides of the container.
4. Leave the gâteau to stand for 5 minutes. Pour over the Grand Marnier and leave to cool completely.
5. When the gâteau is cold, turn out on to a cake rack and remove the non-stick parchment (greaseproof paper).
6. To prepare the frosting (icing), break the chocolate into pieces in a small bowl and melt for 2 minutes on HIGH.
7. Mix the confectioners' (icing) sugar and the egg white with a wooden spoon. Stir in the almond extract (essence) and melted chocolate. Mix carefully. Pour this frosting (icing) on to the center of the gâteau and spread carefully over the top and sides with a metal spatula. Transfer the gâteau to a cake platter and allow the frosting (icing) to harden at room temperature.

Almond Gâteau II

00.20 plus cooling time   **00.16**

American	Ingredients	Metric/Imperial
5 oz	butter	150 g/5 oz
¼ lb	ground almonds	125 g/4 oz
½ cup	cane sugar syrup	6 tbsp
3	eggs	3
⅓ cup	cognac	4½ tbsp
¼ cup	cornstarch (cornflour)	3 tbsp
1 tsp	oil	1 tsp
3½ oz	finely chopped candied orange zest (peel)	100 g/3½ oz
2 tbsp	redcurrant jello (jelly)	1 tbsp
7 oz	confectioners' (icing) sugar	200 g/7 oz
1	egg white	1
¼ tsp	fresh lemon juice	¼ tsp
½ tsp	coffee extract (essence)	½ tsp
3	halved candied apricots	3
½ cup	whipped cream	6 tbsp

1. Soften the butter in a bowl for 1 minute on HIGH.

2. Add the ground almonds, cane sugar syrup, eggs, ¼ cup (4 tablespoons) of cognac and cornstarch (cornflour), beating well after each addition.

3. Oil the base and sides of a 6 inch (15 cm) soufflé mold (mould) and line the base with a circle of oiled non-stick parchment (greaseproof paper).

4. Pour the mixture into the mold (mould), smooth the surface and sprinkle with the chopped orange zest (peel). Microwave, uncovered, on MEDIUM for 14 minutes.

5. When the cake begins to shrink away from the sides of the container, remove from the oven and leave to cool completely.

6. Turn the cake out on to a wire rack and remove the non-stick parchment (greaseproof paper).

7. Melt the redcurrant jello (jelly) in a small bowl for 30 seconds on HIGH. Use to brush the top and sides of the cake.

8. Pour the confectioners' (icing) sugar into a bowl and add the egg white and lemon juice. Mix with a wooden spoon to a smooth paste. Add the remaining cognac and coffee extract (essence). If the paste is too runny, add a little more confectioners' (icing) sugar. Pour the frosting (icing) on to the cake and spread over the top and sides with a metal spatula.

9. Arrange the candied apricot halves around the top of the cake. Leave the frosting (icing) to harden at room temperature.

10. Just before serving, decorate the cake with whipped cream forced through a piping tube.

Almond gâteau 11

Almond and Carrot Cake

00.15 plus cooling time   **00.26**

American	Ingredients	Metric/Imperial
3½ oz	butter	100 g/3½ oz
6 oz	finely grated carrots	175 g/6 oz
3	eggs	3
¼ cup	liquid honey	4 tbsp
¼ cup	orange liqueur	3 tbsp
¼ cup	soft dark brown sugar	3 tbsp
3½ oz	ground almonds	100 g/3½ oz
2 tbsp	cornstarch (cornflour)	1 tbsp
1 tsp	active dry yeast	1 tsp
5 tbsp	slivered almonds	3 tbsp
	butter, for greasing	
9 oz	confectioners' (icing) sugar	250 g/9 oz
1	egg white	1
¼ cup	fresh orange juice	3 tbsp

1. Put the butter in a bowl and melt in the microwave oven for 1 minute on HIGH.

2. Put the grated carrots in a dish. Cover and microwave on HIGH for 2 minutes.

3. Break the eggs into a bowl. Add the honey, orange liqueur and brown sugar and whisk vigorously. Add the ground almonds, cornstarch (cornflour) and yeast, and the melted butter. Beat well until the mixture is smooth. Add the carrots and slivered almonds.

4. Grease the base and sides of a 9 inch (23 cm) Pyrex ring mold (mould) and pour in the mixture. Microwave, uncovered, on HIGH for 13 minutes.

5. Leave to stand for 10 minutes. Turn out on to a wire rack to cool.

6. For the frosting (icing), mix together the confectioners' (icing) sugar, the egg white and the orange juice. Frost (ice) the cake, working fast so that it does not harden before you are finished.

Chocolate and almond gâteau

6. To make the syrup, put the superfine (caster) sugar and ½ cup (5 tablespoons) of water in a bowl and heat in the microwave oven for 3 minutes on HIGH. Stir until the sugar is dissolved. Stir in the remaining cognac.

7. When the cake has cooled completely, turn out on to a rack and cut into 2 equal layers. Pour over the cognac syrup and put the lower layer on a cake plate. Spread with a thick layer of filling. Put the second layer of cake on top and spread the remaining filling over the top and sides. Press the chocolate vermicelli on the top and sides of the cake with the palms of your hands. Decorate with the sugar violets.

Chocolate and Almond Gâteau

American	Ingredients	Metric/Imperial
	00.20 plus resting time	**00.12**
6 oz	butter	175 g/6 oz
5 oz	ground almonds	150 g/5 oz
2	eggs	2
2	egg yolks	2
2 oz	self-rising (self-raising) flour	50 g/2 oz
2 oz	cornstarch (cornflour)	50 g/2 oz
3 tbsp	cocoa powder	2 tbsp
1 tsp	active dry yeast	1 tsp
2 tsp	coffee extract (essence)	2 tsp
1 tsp	vanilla extract (essence)	1 tsp
⅔ cup	cane sugar syrup	150 ml/¼ pint
	butter, for greasing	
3 tbsp	cognac	2 tbsp
3 tbsp	confectioners' (icing) sugar	2 tbsp
½ cup	superfine (caster) sugar	5 tbsp
¼ cup	chocolate vermicelli	4 tbsp
3	sugar violets	3

1. Melt half of the butter in a large bowl in the microwave oven for 1 minute on HIGH.

2. Add 3 oz (75 g/3 oz) of ground almonds, the 2 whole eggs, 1 egg yolk, flour, cornstarch (cornflour), cocoa powder, yeast, coffee extract (essence), vanilla extract (essence) and cane sugar syrup to the melted butter. Mix thoroughly.

3. Grease the base of a 7 inch (18 cm) soufflé mold (mould) and line the base with buttered non-stick parchment (greaseproof paper). Spoon the cake mixture into the mold (mould) and microwave, uncovered, for 8 minutes on HIGH.

4. Remove the mold (mould) from the oven and leave to stand at room temperature.

5. To make the filling, mix together the remaining butter with the remaining ground almonds, 3 (2) tablespoons of cognac, the remaining egg yolk and the confectioners' (icing) sugar to form a smooth almond paste. Leave to rest at room temperature.

Walnut Gâteau

American	Ingredients	Metric/Imperial
	00.25 plus cooling and chilling time	**00.09**
5 oz	walnuts	150 g/5 oz
5 oz	softened butter	150 g/5 oz
½ cup	liquid honey	6 tbsp
2	eggs	2
3 tbsp	self-rising (self-raising) flour	2 tbsp
1 tsp	oil	1 tsp
2	egg whites	2
6 oz	confectioners' (icing) sugar	175 g/6 oz
2 tbsp	cognac	1 tbsp
¼ tsp	fresh lemon juice	¼ tsp
¼ tsp	coffee extract (essence)	¼ tsp

1. Set aside 8 walnuts for decoration and pulverize the rest in a food processor.

2. Melt 3½ oz (100 g/3½ oz) of the butter in a large bowl in the microwave oven for 1 minute on HIGH. Stir until the butter has just melted. Add the honey and whole eggs. Add the walnut powder and flour and stir thoroughly.

3. Oil the base of a 7 inch (18 cm) soufflé mold (mould) and line with oiled non-stick parchment (greaseproof paper).

4. Whisk 1 egg white to firm peaks and fold into the mixture. Spoon the mixture into the mold (mould) and smooth the surface. Microwave, uncovered, on HIGH for 8 minutes. Leave to cool completely in the container.

5. Turn the gâteau out on to a rack and remove the non-stick parchment (greaseproof paper). Put the wire rack on top of a plate. Slice the cake carefully into 2 equal layers.

6. To make the filling, beat the remaining butter with 2 oz (50g/2 oz) of confectioners' (icing) sugar and cognac to form a smooth paste. Spread over the lower layer of the cake and top with the upper layer, pressing gently.

7. To make the frosting (icing), put the remaining confectioners' (icing) sugar in a bowl and add the lemon juice. Pour in the remaining egg white, stirring constantly, until the paste is smooth but not runny. You may not need the entire egg white. Stir in the coffee extract (essence) to obtain a light caramel color.

8. Pour the frosting (icing) over the cake and spread on the top and sides with a metal spatula. Arrange the reserved walnuts at regular intervals around the top of the cake. Refrigerate until the frosting (icing) hardens. Serve cold.

Walnut gâteau

Two-Nut Gâteau

	00.15	00.10	
	plus cooling time		

American	Ingredients	Metric/Imperial
¼ lb	walnuts	125 g/4 oz
¼ lb	ground hazelnuts	125 g/4 oz
½ tsp	active dry yeast	½ tsp
2 tbsp	instant coffee	1 tbsp
4	eggs, separated	4
2 oz	superfine (caster) sugar	50 g/2 oz
¼ cup	cognac	3 tbsp
¼ cup	cane sugar syrup	4 tbsp
1 tsp	oil	1 tsp
	salt	
½ tbsp	superfine (caster) sugar	½ tbsp
7 oz	praline chocolate	200 g/7 oz
¼ tsp	coffee extract (essence)	¼ tsp

1. Set aside 6 walnuts and pulverize the rest in a food processor. Stir in the ground hazelnuts and yeast. Mix the instant coffee with 2 (1) tablespoons of water.
2. Whisk the egg yolks in a bowl with the sugar. Stir in 3 (2) tablespoons of cognac, the instant coffee mixture and cane sugar syrup. Add the nut and yeast mixture. Stir until smooth.
3. Oil a 7 inch (18 cm) soufflé mold (mould) and line with a circle of oiled non-stick parchment (greaseproof paper).
4. Add a pinch of salt to the egg whites. Whisk to firm peaks, then add the ½ tablespoon of sugar, still whisking. Fold carefully into the cake mixture.
5. Pour the mixture into the mold (mould) and smooth the surface. Microwave, uncovered, on HIGH for 8 minutes.
6. Leave the cake to cool completely in the container.
7. Turn the cake out on to a plate and remove the non-stick parchment (greaseproof paper). Cut into 2 equal layers.
8. To make the frosting (icing), break the chocolate into pieces and melt in the microwave oven on HIGH for 2 minutes. Stir in the coffee extract (essence) and remaining cognac and beat until smooth. Spread some of the frosting (icing) on the lower layer of the cake and set the upper layer carefully on top. Spread the rest of the frosting (icing) over the top and sides using a metal spatula.
9. Arrange the reserved walnuts on top of the cake and leave to stand until ready to serve.

Two-nut gâteau

Pistachio and Coconut Gâteau

	00.30	00.33	
	plus resting and cooling time		

American	Ingredients	Metric/Imperial
⅓ cup	milk	4½ tbsp
1 tsp	superfine (caster) sugar	1 tsp
1½ tsp	active dry yeast	1½ tsp
6 oz	all-purpose (plain) flour	175 g/6 oz
	salt	
¼ lb	butter	125 g/4 oz
3	eggs	3
	butter, for greasing	
3 tbsp	confectioners' (icing) sugar	2 tbsp
1 oz	dried shredded (desiccated) coconut	25 g/1 oz
3 tbsp	sour cream (crème fraîche)	2 tbsp
⅓ cup	frozen passionfruit juice	4½ tbsp
3 tbsp	cognac	2 tbsp
1 oz	shelled unsalted pistachios	25 g/1 oz

1. Put the milk in a bowl and warm in the microwave oven for 30 seconds on HIGH Power. Add the sugar and yeast and mix with a fork.
2. Sift the flour and a pinch of salt over a bowl. Warm in the microwave oven for 20 seconds on HIGH. Make a well in the center of the flour, pour in the milk and yeast mixture, push some of the flour over, cover with a cloth and set in a warm place for 40 minutes until the mixture begins to froth.
3. Put the butter in a saucer and soften in the microwave oven for 20 seconds on HIGH, without melting. Break the eggs into a bowl and whisk with a fork. Add the beaten eggs and the butter in tiny pieces to the flour and milk. Beat for 5 minutes by hand until the mixture is smooth.
4. Grease the base of a soufflé mold (mould) 7 inches (18 cm) in diameter and pour in the mixture. Cover with saran wrap (cling film) and microwave for 15 minutes on MEDIUM-LOW.
5. Pierce the film and microwave for a further 4 minutes on HIGH. Remove the film completely and cook for 1 minute on HIGH.
6. Leave the cake to stand for 10 minutes. Invert on to a rack and allow to cool.
7. Prepare the filling. Mix the confectioners' (icing) sugar with the dried (desiccated) coconut and the sour cream (crème fraîche). Put the passionfruit juice into another bowl and defrost for 30 seconds on HIGH. Whisk the fruit juice with a fork and add the cognac.
8. Bring a small saucepan of water to the boil. Put in the pistachios and boil for 1 minute. Drain and remove their skins. Purée coarsely in a food processor and add to the coconut and sour cream (crème fraîche) mixture.
9. Slice the cake carefully into 2 layers. Prick each layer with a fork. Pour over the fruit juice. Spread the lower layer with the coconut filling and place the second layer on top.

Fruit Loaf

	00.15	00.22	
	plus cooling and chilling time		

American	Ingredients	Metric/Imperial
3 oz	dates	75 g/3 oz
3½ oz	prunes	100 g/3½ oz
2	squeezed oranges	2
3½ oz	golden raisins (sultanas)	100 g/3½ oz
1	coarsely chopped large apple	1
2	sliced large bananas	2
1 tsp	active dry yeast	1 tsp
3 tbsp	cornstarch (cornflour)	2 tbsp
3½ oz	superfine (caster) sugar	100 g/3½ oz
2	eggs	2
	butter, for greasing	

1. Remove the pits (stones) from the dates and prunes. Measure out ⅔ cup (150 ml/¼ pint) of orange juice and pour into a large bowl. Add the dates and prunes. Microwave, uncovered, on HIGH for 5 minutes, stirring half-way through.

2. Rinse the raisins (sultanas) under plenty of cold running water. Pat dry on kitchen paper. Put the apple and banana into the goblet of a food processor and add the yeast, cornstarch (cornflour), sugar and eggs. Purée until the mixture is smooth.

3. Leave the cooked fruit to stand for 5 minutes. Add the raisins (sultanas) and the banana and apple mixture.

4. Grease the base of an 11 inch (28 cm) long 1½ quart (1.5 litre/2¾ pint) Pyrex mold (mould). Pour in the mixture, distributing the fruit as evenly as possible. Microwave, uncovered, on HIGH for 12 minutes.

5. Leave the fruit loaf to cool in the container. Refrigerate for at least 2 hours.

6. Turn out on to a long dish and serve chilled.

Fruit Cake

	00.20	00.25	
	plus cooling time		

American	Ingredients	Metric/Imperial
7 oz	orange marmalade	200 g/7 oz
3 oz	honey	75 g/3 oz
3 oz	soft dark brown sugar	75 g/3 oz
2 oz	butter	50 g/2 oz
5 oz	all-purpose (plain) flour	150 g/5 oz
3 tbsp	active dry yeast	2 tbsp
1	egg	1
½ tsp	grated nutmeg	½ tsp
½ tsp	cinnamon	½ tsp
¼ tsp	salt	¼ tsp
3½ oz	golden raisins (sultanas)	100 g/3½ oz
2 oz	slivered almonds	50 g/2 oz
1 tsp	oil	1 tsp
5 oz	superfine (caster) sugar	150 g/5 oz
1	egg, separated	1
1	egg yolk	1
1¼ cups	milk	300 ml/½ pint

Fruit loaf

1. Put the marmalade, honey, brown sugar and butter in a bowl. Melt in the microwave oven for 3 minutes on HIGH.

2. Stir well. Sift the flour and yeast over the bowl, beating constantly. Add 1 whole egg and ⅓ cup (4½ tablespoons) of water, still beating. Add the grated nutmeg, cinnamon and salt. Work the dough until smooth. Add the raisins (sultanas) and almonds.

3. Oil a Pyrex cake mold (mould) and cover the base with a piece of oiled non-stick parchment (greaseproof paper).

4. Spoon the dough into the mold (mould) and microwave for 12 minutes on MEDIUM-HIGH.

5. Leave the cake to cool in the container.

6. To prepare the sauce, put 3½ oz (100 g/3½ oz) of superfine (caster) sugar and ¼ cup (3 tablespoons) of water in a bowl and microwave, uncovered, for 5½ minutes on HIGH.

7. Whisk the 2 egg yolks together, beating in the remaining sugar.

8. When the caramel is a deep golden color, remove from the oven and add ¼ cup (4 tablespoons) of hot water, taking care to avoid splashing. Dissolve the caramel by shaking the bowl. Pour in the milk and stir. Heat for 2 minutes on HIGH. Pour the caramel mixture over the egg yolks and sugar, whisking constantly. Microwave, uncovered, for a further 2 minutes on HIGH. Whisk again and leave to cool.

9. Just before serving, turn the cake out on to a platter and remove the non-stick parchment (greaseproof paper). Whisk the egg white to soft peaks and fold carefully into the caramel sauce. Pour into a sauceboat and serve with the cake.

Moist Date and Ginger Cake

⬛▷ 00.15   00.15   ▨
plus cooling time

American	Ingredients	Metric/Imperial
½ lb	pitted (stoned) dates	225 g/8 oz
1 tsp	baking soda	1 tsp
⅔ cup	boiling water	150 ml/¼ pint
¼ lb	butter	125 g/4 oz
¼ lb	dark brown sugar	125 g/4 oz
3 tbsp	molasses (black treacle)	2 tbsp
2 tbsp	maple (golden) syrup	1 tbsp
2	eggs	2
½ lb	self-rising (self-raising) flour	225 g/8 oz
2 tsp	ground ginger	2 tsp
2 tbsp	sifted confectioners' (icing) sugar	1 tbsp

1. Chop the dates and put in a small bowl. Sprinkle with baking soda, then pour on the boiling water. Leave to cool.
2. Cream the butter with the sugar until light and fluffy. Beat in the molasses (treacle) and syrup. Add the eggs one at a time, beating well. Sift in the flour and ginger and add the dates and soaking liquid. Stir well until blended.
3. Line the base of a 9 inch (23 cm) round dish with non-stick parchment (greaseproof paper) and pour in the mixture. Cook on HIGH for 8½-9½ minutes. Cool in the dish for 5 minutes before turning on to a wire rack to cool completely.
4. Sprinkle with confectioners' (icing) sugar and serve.

Princess Cake

⬛▷ 00.10   00.19   ▨
plus standing and cooling time

American	Ingredients	Metric/Imperial
9 oz	dried apricots	250 g/9 oz
3½ oz	butter	100 g/3½ oz
½ cup	cane sugar syrup	6 tbsp
¼ tsp	almond extract (essence)	¼ tsp
2	eggs	2
3½ oz	self-rising (self-raising) flour	100 g/3½ oz
2 oz	ground almonds	50 g/2 oz
½ tsp	active dry yeast	½ tsp
⅓ cup	sour cream (crème fraîche)	4½ tbsp
	butter, for greasing	
¼ lb	confectioners' (icing) sugar	125 g/4 oz
3 tbsp	Kirsch	2 tbsp

1. Put the apricots in a bowl and cover with 2¼ cups (500 ml/18 fl oz) of hot water. Microwave, uncovered, on HIGH for 8 minutes, until swollen and juicy. Leave to stand.
2. Melt the butter in a large bowl for 1 minute on HIGH. Beat in the cane sugar syrup, almond extract (essence) and the eggs one at a time. Whisk in the flour, ground almonds, yeast and sour cream (crème fraîche), until smooth.

3. Drain the apricots.
4. Grease the base of a 7 inch (18 cm) soufflé mold (mould) and line the base with a circle of buttered non-stick parchment (greaseproof paper).
5. Pour the dough into the mold (mould) and arrange the apricots on top as neatly as possible. Microwave, uncovered, on HIGH for 10 minutes.
6. Leave to stand for 30 minutes. Turn out on to a wire rack and remove the non-stick parchment (greaseproof paper). Leave to cool completely.
7. To make the frosting (icing), put the confectioners' (icing) sugar in a bowl and add the Kirsch little by little, stirring constantly with a wooden spoon until the mixture is just liquid enough to pour. Pour over the cake and spread evenly over the top and sides with a metal spatula. Leave to harden. Slide the gâteau on to a plate and serve.

Caramel Ring Cake

⬛▷ 00.15   00.12   ▨
Serves 12

American	Ingredients	Metric/Imperial
¼ lb	butter	125 g/4 oz
¼ lb	brown sugar	125 g/4 oz
2	eggs	2
2 tbsp	maple (golden) syrup	1 tbsp
6 oz	self-rising (self-raising) flour	175 g/6 oz
1 tsp	ground cinnamon	1 tsp
¼ tsp	salt	¼ tsp
¼ tsp	baking soda	¼ tsp
⅔ cup	milk	8 tbsp
	vanilla extract (essence)	
	butter, for greasing	
1½ oz	butter	40 g/1½ oz
3 tbsp	maple (golden) syrup	2 tbsp
2 tbsp	milk	1 tbsp
1 tsp	vanilla extract (essence)	1 tsp
½ lb	sifted confectioners' (icing) sugar	225 g/8 oz
1 tsp	ground cinnamon	1 tsp
	flaked almonds	

1. Cream the butter with the sugar and beat in the eggs and maple (golden) syrup. Sift in the flour, cinnamon and salt and beat well. Mix the baking soda with the milk, add the vanilla extract (essence) and stir into the mixture.
2. Lightly grease a 10 inch (25 cm) ring mold (mould). Spoon in the mixture and bake on HIGH for 5-6 minutes. Cool for 5 minutes in the dish before turning out on to a wire rack.
3. To make the frosting (icing), put the butter and the syrup in a jug and heat on HIGH for 1 minute. Stir in the milk and vanilla. Stir in half of the sifted confectioners' (icing) sugar and the cinnamon and beat well. Stir in the remaining sugar.
4. Pour the frosting (icing) over the cake and smooth with a spatula dipped in hot water. Sprinkle with flaked almonds.

Coffee Ring Cake

00.20 00.10
Serves 16

American	Ingredients	Metric/Imperial
6 oz	butter	175 g/6 oz
6 oz	sugar	175 g/6 oz
¼ tsp	salt	¼ tsp
2	eggs	2
1	orange	1
2 tbsp	instant coffee powder	1 tbsp
6 oz	self-rising (self-raising) flour	175 g/6 oz
¼ tsp	ground cinnamon	¼ tsp
2 oz	grated semisweet (plain) chocolate	50 g/2 oz
	butter, for greasing	
6 oz	confectioners' (icing) sugar	175 g/6 oz
2 tsp	instant coffee powder	2 tsp
1 tsp	cocoa	1 tsp
3 tbsp	hot water	2 tbsp
	vanilla extract (essence)	

1. Cream the butter, sugar and salt until light and fluffy. Gradually add the eggs and beat well. Grate the orange rind and add to the mixture.
2. Squeeze the juice from the orange and mix with the coffee. Sift the flour and cinnamon and add alternately with the coffee mixture. Stir in the grated chocolate. Add more orange juice or water to form a soft dropping consistency.
3. Lightly grease an 8 inch (20 cm) ring mold (mould). Spoon in the mixture and cook on HIGH for 4-5 minutes. Leave to cool for 5 minutes. Turn out on to a wire rack to cool completely.
4. To make the frosting (icing), sift the confectioners' (icing) sugar into a bowl. Dissolve the 2 teaspoons of coffee and the cocoa in the hot water. Stir into the icing sugar with a few drops of vanilla extract (essence). Mix well until smooth. Pour over the cake and smooth the surface with a knife. Leave to set before cutting.

Spice Bread

00.10 00.14
plus cooling time

American	Ingredients	Metric/Imperial
10½ oz	honey	300 g/10½ oz
3 oz	butter	75 g/3 oz
3½ oz	wholewheat (wholemeal) flour	100 g/3½ oz
3 oz	rye flour	75 g/3 oz
1	egg	1
½ cup	milk	6 tbsp
2 tsp	active dry yeast	2 tsp
1 tsp	grated nutmeg	1 tsp
1 tsp	cinnamon	1 tsp
¼ tsp	ginger	¼ tsp
¼ tsp	powdered cloves	¼ tsp
	pepper	
	salt	
1 tsp	oil	1 tsp

1. Melt the honey and butter in the microwave oven for 2 minutes on HIGH. Stir.
2. Add the 2 flours, and the egg and milk, whisking continuously. Sift the yeast over the mixture. Add the grated nutmeg, cinnamon, ginger, powdered cloves, 3 grinds of the peppermill and a pinch of salt. Whisk vigorously for 1 minute.
3. Oil the base of a Pyrex cake mold (mould) and line with a circle of oiled non-stick parchment (greaseproof paper). Spoon the dough into the mold (mould) and microwave, uncovered, for 12 minutes on MEDIUM-HIGH.
4. Leave the spice bread to cool in the container. Turn out on to a rack and remove the non-stick parchment (greaseproof paper). Keep in a tightly closed tin until ready to serve.

Chestnut Gâteau

00.15 00.14
plus cooling time

American	Ingredients	Metric/Imperial
3½ oz	golden raisins (sultanas)	100 g/3½ oz
3 tbsp	cognac	2 tbsp
3 oz	semisweet (plain) chocolate	75 g/3 oz
3 oz	softened butter	75 g/3 oz
3 tbsp	sour cream (crème fraîche)	2 tbsp
1	egg, separated	1
9 oz	sweetened chestnut purée	250 g/9 oz
	butter, for greasing	
2 oz	confectioners' (icing) sugar	50 g/2 oz
¼ tsp	coffee extract (essence)	¼ tsp

1. Rinse the raisins (sultanas) under plenty of cold running water. Pat dry on kitchen paper. Put 2 oz (50 g/2 oz) in a bowl with the cognac. Set the rest aside. Heat in the microwave oven for 1 minute on HIGH.
2. Break the chocolate into pieces and melt in a bowl with 1 oz (25 g/1 oz) of butter for 2 minutes on HIGH.
3. Stir until smooth and creamy. Add the sour cream (crème fraîche), egg yolk and chestnut purée. Beat until smooth. Stir in the raisins (sultanas) and cognac.
4. Grease the base of a 6 inch (15 cm) soufflé mold (mould) and line with a circle of buttered non-stick parchment (greaseproof paper).
5. Whisk the egg white to firm peaks and add to the mixture. Pour into the mold (mould). Microwave, uncovered, on HIGH for 9 minutes. Allow to cool in the container.
6. When cold, invert on to a plate and remove the non-stick parchment (greaseproof paper).
7. To make the frosting (icing), put the remaining raisins (sultanas) in a bowl and cover with hot water. Heat in the microwave oven for 2 minutes on HIGH. Drain.
8. Beat the remaining butter with a wooden spoon. Stir in the confectioners' (icing) sugar little by little. Beat until completely smooth. Stir in the coffee extract (essence) and beat once more. Use to frost (ice) the cake, smoothing with a metal spatula. Sprinkle with the raisins (sultanas) and leave to harden.

Chestnut gâteau

Chocolate Chestnut Gâteau

	00.10 plus cooling time	00.20

American	Ingredients	Metric/Imperial
¼ lb	semisweet (plain) chocolate	125 g/4 oz
2 oz	butter	50 g/2 oz
2	eggs, separated	2
⅓ cup	sour cream (crème fraîche)	4½ tbsp
¼ cup	cognac	3 tbsp
¼ cup	cane sugar syrup	3 tbsp
1 lb	creamed chestnut purée	450 g/1 lb
	butter, for greasing	
10	maraschino cherries	10
	whipped cream	

1. Break the chocolate into pieces, put in a bowl and melt with the butter in the microwave oven for 2 minutes on HIGH.
2. Add the egg yolks, sour cream (crème fraîche), cognac and cane sugar syrup to the chestnut purée, beating with a wooden spoon. Add the melted chocolate and butter.
3. Whisk the egg whites to firm peaks and fold carefully into the mixture.
4. Grease the base of a 7 inch (18 cm) soufflé mold (mould) and line with buttered non-stick parchment (greaseproof paper).
5. Pour the mixture into the mold (mould) and smooth the surface. Microwave, uncovered, on HIGH for 13 minutes.
6. Leave the cake to stand for 5 minutes. Invert on to a rack, remove the non-stick parchment (greaseproof paper) and leave to cool completely. Decorate with maraschino cherries and whipped cream.

Chestnut Cream Gâteau

	00.10 plus cooling time	00.09

American	Ingredients	Metric/Imperial
1¼ lb	sweetened chestnut purée	500 g/1¼ lb
⅓ cup	sour cream (crème fraîche)	4½ tbsp
½ tsp	ground vanilla	½ tsp
3	eggs, separated	3
1 tsp	oil	1 tsp
	salt	
3 tbsp	superfine (caster) sugar	2 tbsp
2 oz	semisweet (plain) chocolate	50 g/2 oz
1 oz	butter	25 g/1 oz
3 tbsp	cognac	2 tbsp

1. Put the chestnut purée in a bowl, add the sour cream (crème fraîche) and vanilla and mix well.
2. Add the egg yolks and mix thoroughly.
3. Oil the base of a 7 inch (18 cm) soufflé mold (mould) and line with a circle of oiled non-stick parchment (greaseproof paper).
4. Add a pinch of salt to the egg whites and whisk to firm peaks. Add the sugar, whisking constantly.
5. Fold the meringue mixture into the chestnut purée and spoon into the mold (mould). Microwave, uncovered, on HIGH for 8 minutes.
6. Leave the gâteau to cool. Turn out on to a plate and remove the non-stick parchment (greaseproof paper).
7. To make the frosting (icing), break the chocolate into pieces and melt in a bowl with the butter and cognac for 1 minute on HIGH. Beat until the mixture is smooth and shiny. Pour over the gâteau and spread with a metal spatula over the top and sides. Allow to harden.
Do not refrigerate as the chocolate will lose its luster.

Chocolate chestnut gâteau

Chestnut cream cake

Chestnut Cream Cake

00.10 plus cooling time **00.13**

American	Ingredients	Metric/Imperial
3 oz	butter	75 g/3 oz
1¼ lb	canned sweetened chestnut purée	500 g/1¼ lb
5 oz	ground almonds	150 g/5 oz
2	eggs, separated	2
2	egg yolks	2
3 tbsp	cocoa powder	2 tbsp
1 tsp	active dry yeast	1 tsp
3½ oz	coarsely chopped candied orange zest (peel)	100 g/3½ oz
	butter, for greasing	
6	marrons glacés	6

1. Melt the butter in a large bowl for 1 minute on HIGH.
2. Add the chestnut purée, ground almonds and 4 egg yolks to the melted butter. Sift the cocoa powder and yeast into the mixture. Add the chopped orange zest (peel) and mix thoroughly.
3. Grease the base of a 7 inch (18 cm) soufflé mold (mould) and line with buttered non-stick parchment (greaseproof paper).
4. Whisk the egg whites to firm peaks and add to the mixture. Pour into the mold (mould). Microwave, uncovered, on HIGH for 12 minutes.
5. Leave the gâteau to cool in the container. Turn out on to a platter. Decorate with the marrons glacés. Serve at room temperature.

Coconut Cake

	00.15	00.26	
	Serves 4		

American	Ingredients	Metric/Imperial
2 oz	golden raisins (sultanas)	50 g/2 oz
2	Golden Delicious apples	2
¼ cup	superfine (caster) sugar	4 tbsp
2 tbsp	butter	1 tbsp
2	eggs	2
2 tbsp	dark rum	1 tbsp
3 oz	dried shredded (desiccated) coconut	75 g/3 oz
3 tbsp	cornstarch (cornflour)	2 tbsp
	butter, for greasing	
¼ cup	apricot preserve	3 tbsp
¼ cup	chopped mixed glacé fruit	3 tbsp

1. Put the raisins (sultanas) in a bowl and cover with warm water.
2. Quarter the apples, peel and core and cut each quarter in half. Put in a dish, sprinkle with the sugar and add the butter, cut into small pieces. Cover and microwave on HIGH for 3 minutes.
3. Whisk the eggs with a fork and add the rum, coconut and cornstarch (cornflour). Grease the base of a deep mold (mould) 6 inches (15 cm) in diameter.
4. Mash the cooked apples to a coarse purée with a fork and add to the egg mixture. Mix well. Pour into the mold (mould). Cover and microwave on HIGH for 7 minutes.
5. Leave the cake to stand for 15 minutes. Invert on to a cake rack and leave to cool.
6. Purée the apricot preserve in a food processor, put in a bowl and melt for 30 seconds on HIGH.
7. Brush the top of the cake with the melted preserve. Drain the raisins (sultanas). Decorate the top of the cake with raisins (sultanas) and the glacé fruits. Serve cold.

Tipsy Cake

	00.10	00.20	
	plus cooling time		

American	Ingredients	Metric/Imperial
¼ lb	butter	125 g/4 oz
1	whole egg	1
3	egg yolks	3
¼ lb	superfine (caster) sugar	125 g/4 oz
3 oz	cornstarch (cornflour)	75 g/3 oz
1 tsp	active dry yeast	1 tsp
1 tsp	almond extract (essence)	1 tsp
⅓ cup	peach liqueur	4½ tbsp
2 tbsp	dried shredded (desiccated) coconut	1 tbsp

1. Put the butter in a soufflé mold (mould) 6 inches (15 cm) in diameter and melt on HIGH for 1 minute.
2. Put the whole egg and the 3 yolks into a bowl. Add the sugar and whisk until the mixture is pale and foamy. Add the cornstarch (cornflour) and the yeast, the melted butter and finally the almond extract (essence). Mix thoroughly after each addition.
3. Pour the mixture back into the mold (mould). Cover and microwave on HIGH for 9 minutes.
4. Leave the cake to stand for 10 minutes. Turn out on to a wire rack to cool.
5. Transfer the cake to a serving platter. Carefully pour over the peach liqueur. Sprinkle with dried shredded (desiccated) coconut.

Semolina Gâteau

	00.20	00.24	
	plus cooling time		

American	Ingredients	Metric/Imperial
2¼ cups	milk	500 ml/18 fl oz
¼ lb	semolina flour	125 g/4 oz
3 oz	sugar	75 g/3 oz
½ tsp	vanilla extract (essence)	½ tsp
3 oz	golden raisins (sultanas)	75 g/3 oz
3 oz	butter	75 g/3 oz
	butter, for greasing	
2	eggs	2
3½ oz	ground almonds	100 g/3½ oz
1¼ lb	drained apricots in syrup	500 g/1¼ lb
2 oz	confectioners' (icing) sugar	25 g/2 oz
1 tsp	cognac	1 tsp

1. Bring the milk to the boil in a bowl in the microwave oven for 4-5 minutes on HIGH, depending on the thickness of the receptacle and the coldness of the milk. Take care that it does not boil over.
2. Put the semolina flour, sugar and vanilla in a casserole. Add the boiling milk, stirring with a wooden spoon. Microwave, uncovered, on HIGH for 5 minutes, stirring half-way through.
3. Rinse the raisins (sultanas) under plenty of cold running water. Put in a bowl and cover with water. Heat for 3 minutes on HIGH. Drain.
4. Put the butter in a bowl and melt in the oven for 1 minute on HIGH.
5. Grease the base of a 6 inch (15 cm) soufflé mold (mould).
6. Whisk the eggs in a bowl and add to the semolina mixture along with the ground almonds, raisins and melted butter. Mix carefully.
7. Pour the mixture into the mold (mould) and smooth the surface. Cover and microwave on HIGH for 10 minutes.
8. Leave the gâteau to cool in the container. Turn out on to a plate.
9. Purée the apricots in a food processor along with the confectioners' (icing) sugar and cognac.
10. Just before serving, coat the gâteau with some of the apricot purée and serve the rest separately in a sauceboat. Do not put this cake in the refrigerator as it will harden.

Coconut cake

Basic Recipes

Chicken Bouillon (Stock)

00.05   00.35
Makes 3½ cups (900 ml/1½ pints)

American	Ingredients	Metric/Imperial
1	uncooked chicken carcass, chopped, giblets cleaned	1
1	large onion, quartered	1
1	large, sliced carrot	1
2	sliced sticks celery	2
1	bayleaf	1
2	fresh thyme sprigs	2
1	small dried chili	1
½ tsp	black peppercorns	½ tsp
2	cloves	2
½ tsp	coarse salt	½ tsp

1. Put the chicken pieces in a casserole. Add the onion, carrot, celery, bayleaf, thyme, chili, peppercorns, cloves and salt. Pour 1 quart (1 litre/1¾ pints) of water over. Cover and microwave on HIGH for 15 minutes.
2. After 15 minutes reduce the power to MEDIUM and cook for a further 20 minutes.
3. Filter the bouillon (stock). Discard the solid ingredients and degrease the liquid.
This bouillon (stock) may be kept for 3 or 4 days in the refrigerator in a closed container. Use it in place of instant bouillon (stock) cubes.

Fish Bouillon (Stock)

00.15   00.18
Makes 2½ cups (600 ml/1 pint)

American	Ingredients	Metric/Imperial
1 lb	fish trimmings (heads and bones), coarsely chopped	450 g/1 lb
1	sliced carrot	1
1	sliced onion	1
1	chopped stick celery	1
½ tsp	black peppercorns	½ tsp
1	fresh thyme sprig	1
1	bayleaf	1
¾ cup	white wine	200 ml/7 fl oz
1	clove	1

1. Put all the above ingredients in a casserole and add 2¼ cups (500 ml/18 fl oz) of hot water. Cover and microwave on HIGH for 8 minutes until it reaches the boil.
2. Reduce the power to MEDIUM and microwave for a further 10 minutes.
3. Filter the (bouillon) stock through a strainer lined with muslin and keep in a closed container in the refrigerator for not more than 48 hours.

Tomato Sauce

00.05   00.12
Serves 4

American	Ingredients	Metric/Imperial
2	chopped sticks celery	2
2	sliced shallots	2
1	quartered garlic clove	1
2 tbsp	olive oil	1 tbsp
1 lb	ripe tomatoes	450 g/1 lb
¼ tsp	dried thyme	¼ tsp
1	bayleaf	1
	salt	
	pepper	

1. Put the celery, shallots and garlic in a small casserole. Pour the oil over. Cover and microwave on HIGH for 2 minutes.
2. Skin the tomatoes (first plunging them into boiling water for 10 seconds), remove the seeds and chop into large pieces. Add to the casserole with the thyme and bayleaf. Add salt and pepper to taste. Stir well. Cover and microwave on HIGH for 10 minutes.
3. Remove the bayleaf, then purée the other ingredients in a food processor. Taste and adjust seasoning.

Béchamel Sauce

00.02   00.04
Makes 1¼ cups (300 ml/½ pint)

American	Ingredients	Metric/Imperial
¼ cup	butter	50 g/2 oz
2 tbsp	flour	1½ tbsp
1¼ cups	milk	300 ml/½ pint
	salt	
	pepper	

1. Melt the butter in a bowl in the microwave for 1 minute on HIGH.
2. Stir the flour into the melted butter. Pour the milk over, stir again and microwave on HIGH for 3 minutes, whisking after every minute.
3. When the sauce is cooked (it should boil for several seconds) whisk until smooth and season with salt and pepper to taste.
If the sauce is too thick, dilute it with a little sour cream (crème fraîche) or increase the amount of milk. In the latter case, cooking time will be a little longer.

Custard Sauce

	00.02	00.09	

Makes 2¼ cups (500 ml/18 fl oz)

American	Ingredients	Metric/Imperial
2¼ cups	milk	500 ml/18 fl oz
4	egg yolks	4
5 oz	sugar	100 g/5 oz

1. Heat the milk in a large bowl, in the microwave for 5 minutes on HIGH.
2. Put the egg yolks in a bowl, add the sugar and whisk until pale and foamy. Pour the boiling milk over in a thin stream, whisking constantly.
3. Filter the custard over a bowl and microwave for 3-4 minutes on HIGH, whisking every minute: it should not actually boil, but thicken lightly.

Pastry Cream

	00.02	00.04	

Makes 1¼ cups (300 ml/½ pint)

American	Ingredients	Metric/Imperial
1 cup	milk	250 ml/8 fl oz
2	egg yolks	2
¼ cup	sugar	75 g/3 oz
3 tbsp	cornstarch (cornflour)	2 tbsp

1. Heat the milk in a cup in the microwave on HIGH for 2 minutes.
2. Whisk the egg yolks with the sugar in a bowl. Add the cornstarch (cornflour), still whisking.
3. Pour the boiling milk over in a thin stream, whisking constantly. Microwave on HIGH for 1 minute. Whisk. Microwave on HIGH for 1 further minute. Whisk again.
Add any flavorings (liqueur, almond, coffee, vanilla) after cooking. To obtain a fluffy cream, add 2 egg whites beaten to firm peaks.

Chocolate Sauce

	00.03	00.02	

Makes 1¼ cups (300 ml/½ pint)

American	Ingredients	Metric/Imperial
7 oz	semisweet (plain) chocolate	200 g/7 oz
3 tbsp	cane sugar syrup	2 tbsp
¼ cup	butter	50 g/2 oz

1. Break the chocolate into pieces and put in a bowl with the cane sugar syrup and ¼ cup (4 tablespoons) of water. Microwave on HIGH for 2 minutes.
2. Stir the contents of the bowl and add the butter in small quantities, stirring until melted. Beat until smooth and shiny. You can make this sauce ahead of time and heat on HIGH for 1 minute when needed.

Caramel

	00.02	00.08	

American	Ingredients	Metric/Imperial
¼ cup	sugar	75 g/3 oz

1. Put the sugar in a bowl and add 3-4 tablespoons of water. Microwave on HIGH for 7 minutes until the caramel is a deep golden color (remember that it will continue to cook for a few minutes once it is removed from the oven).
2. Add 3 (2) tablespoons of hot water, taking care to avoid splashing. Microwave on HIGH for 1 further minute until smooth.

RECIPE INDEX

Soups

Hors d'oeuvres

Fish

Beef

Lamb

Vegetables

Cakes

Cold Desserts

Hot Desserts

Basic Recipes